THE GENERALS

THE
GENERALS

Ulysses S. Grant and Robert E. Lee

NANCY SCOTT ANDERSON
DWIGHT ANDERSON

VINTAGE BOOKS

A DIVISION OF RANDOM HOUSE | NEW YORK

First Vintage Books Edition, February 1989
Copyright © 1987 by Nancy Scott Anderson and Dwight Anderson
All rights reserved under International and Pan-American Copyright
Conventions. Published in the United States by Random House, Inc.,
New York, and simultaneously in Canada by Random House of Canada
Limited, Toronto. Originally published, in hardcover,
by Alfred A. Knopf, Inc., in 1987.

Library of Congress Cataloging-in-Publication Data
Anderson, Nancy Scott.
The generals—Ulysses S. Grant and Robert E. Lee.
(Vintage Civil War library)
Reprint. Originally published: New York: Knopf:
Distributed by Random House, 1988, c1987.
Bibliography: p.
Includes index.
1. United States—History—Civil War, 1861–1865—Biography.
2. Generals—United States—Biography.
3. United States. Army—Biography.
4. Grant, Ulysses S. (Ulysses Simpson), 1822–1885.
5. Lee, Robert E. (Robert Edward), 1807–1870.
6. United States—History—Civil War, 1861–1865—Campaigns.
7. United States—History, Military—To 1900.
I. Title II. Series.
[E467.A53 1989]   973.7′092′2 [B]   88-40037
ISBN 0-394-75985-0 (pbk.)

Manufactured in the United States of America
10 9 8 7 6 5 4 3 2 1

TO

William Thomas Scott III

and

Theodore Scott Anderson
Frederick Grant Anderson

How could we help
Falling on our knees,
All of us together, and praying
God
To pity and forgive us all!

—Brigadier General Joshua Chamberlain,
20th Maine, on the stacking of
arms at Appomattox Court House,
April 12, 1865

ACKNOWLEDGMENTS

Gratitude is due and happily extended to the incomparable staff at the Virginia Historical Society library in Richmond, Virginia. Howson W. Cole, Waverly Winfree, the late James A. Fleming, and their assistants tirelessly proved that Virginia hospitality was not lost with the Cause. Special thanks go to Dr. Oliver Orr, Civil War archivist, and manuscripts division staff member Ruth Nicholson at the Library of Congress in Washington, D.C.; also to Richard Shrader, archivist of the Southern Historical Collection in Wilson Library at the University of North Carolina in Chapel Hill; the splendid staff at Duke University's Perkins Library in Durham, North Carolina; and Julia Strong, at the Georgia Historical Society in Savannah. Thanks are also due to Gordon Cotton and Blanche Terry at the Vicksburg Historical Society in Vicksburg, Mississippi; R. C. Peniston and the library staff at Washington and Lee University, Lexington, Virginia; staff members in the manuscript division of Alderman Library at the University of Virginia in Charlottesville; and the manuscripts division staff at Richmond's Virginia State Library. Mary Custis Lee deButts, of Upperville, Virginia, was helpful and supportive. Betty Gore at the Lee Boyhood Home in Alexandria, Virginia, and Evelyn Ferrell at the Siege Museum in Petersburg, Virginia, were very helpful, and Ed Harris, of Richmond, Virginia, provided period housing on Church Hill. Karen Hogarth and the staff at San

Diego State University's Inter-Library loan department supplied a constant stream of rare and sometimes obscure material.

Very special thanks to Margaret McBride, who made the book possible; to Teresa Morris, whose intelligent and constant assistance was crucial; and to Ashbel Green, for patience exceeding an editor's duty. Thanks also for material aid and support to Cyrus and Malinda Gray, Beverly and Gary Burke, Karen Kessler, Jim and Valerie Alvord, and Neil Morgan.

N.S.A.

THE GENERALS

CHAPTER

1

ULYSSES GRANT sat on the porch of Mr. McLean's red brick farmhouse, deep in quiet thought. The house fronted the single dirt lane which cut through the village of half a dozen dwellings. To its right, a thousand feet away, was Appomattox Court House. It was raining, and Grant warmed his chin in the collar of his blue military coat, which was splashed and dampened with red Virginia clay. He had just returned from an hour's ride with Robert E. Lee across the gentle slopes of green fields which separated the Union Army of the Potomac from the Confederate Army of Northern Virginia. The day before, Grant had accepted Lee's surrender of his army, and when the two men met for the second time, they talked about the future, about peace and union and Jefferson Davis and Abraham Lincoln.

Here Grant was alone, smoking a cigar and waiting for his few headquarters belongings to be packed. He was bound for the Federal supply dump at City Point on the James River, then on to Washington and a visit with Lincoln. To the surprise and disgust of his staff, he had no desire to savor the capture of the army he could see camped on the hills to his right, behind the courthouse. Earlier in the war, at Vicksburg, Mississippi, a subordinate called Grant a "plain businessman of the Republic." Now he had to tend to business as commander of the United States Army. The war was costing the Federal government $4 million a day. But he also wanted to spare the old man he had just left the gratuitous humiliation of an all-out Union celebration of the final victory. Grant had not always felt that way. A year earlier, when he came east to take the field with the Army of the Potomac, he was mounting an internal campaign against Robert E. Lee. Even earlier, he had vowed to punish Virginia for seceding from the Union. But on April 10, 1865, the war itself, and fate, had punished both Lee and Virginia far beyond Grant's power to exact retribution.

As he sat staring into the rain around him, he could see some disheveled riders approach. They dismounted and climbed the steep wooden steps. Grant jumped to his feet, gave a short whoop, and threw his arms around the shoulders of Confederate general James Longstreet, commander of the Army of Northern Virginia's First Corps. Called "my old war horse" by Lee and "Pete" by everyone else, Longstreet had been a witness at Grant's 1849 wedding to Julia Dent in St. Louis. The last time he had seen his friend, Grant had been drinking heavily, and delivering firewood cut from St. Louis land given him by his father-in-law. "Pete!" Grant exclaimed, pummeling Longstreet's back, "let's return to the happy old days by playing a game of brag!" Only the night before, Longstreet had tearfully approached some none-too-friendly Federals to beg rations for his hungry men. Grant's warmth undid him, and he turned away, while Grant tactfully talked instead to General Cadmus Wilcox, a groomsman in that same St. Louis wedding and one of Grant's best friends. By now the porch was crowded with Confederates—Henry Heth, Grant's fellow junior officer in Mexico; George Pickett, the man who lost a division on the way to Cemetery Ridge at Gettysburg; and John Gordon, his handsome cheeks marred by wounds he had taken at Antietam Creek in Maryland. Handshakes went all around and talk and laughter rose through the rain.

Grant was disappointed when his orderly came to announce that headquarters was packed and ready to go. Reluctantly, he said goodbye to the men who had been enemies and now were friends again, motioned to his staff to join him, and swung aboard his big roan, Cincinnati. On the way out of town, he met Elihu Washburne, congressman from Galena, Illinois, close friend of Abraham Lincoln, and a Republican who had carefully guided Grant's stars through the House of Representatives. Washburne managed to be on hand for most of Grant's more dramatic successes, but he had missed this one—ironically held up by roads deep in Virginia mud and the detritus of the vanquished Confederate army which spelled the very victory he hadn't seen. After a hail-and-farewell to Washburne, Grant followed those same roads, headed for Burkeville. The day was raw, and rain still fell, and the sights along the way were sobering to the euphoric cavalcade—mules and horses, barely alive, collapsed in their traces and still hitched to burned-out shells of wagons; thousands of useless muskets, knapsacks, frying pans, and little Dutch ovens scattered through the woods; corpses leaning against trees, the rain washing away the last remnants of their tattered gray clothes; smoldering fences, bridges, houses, and caissons; artillery pieces jammed into the wet clay because gunners had been too weak to spike them.

Near dusk, Grant stopped, and his staff pulled down fences to make a bonfire. Spirits cheered and the men began to talk. The last campaign was mentioned. So was going home. John Rawlins, black-haired and deep-eyed, a stump lawyer from Galena, Illinois, who had run Grant's headquarters with zealous fanaticism about everything from demon rum to Robert Lee, celebrated, between his tubercular coughs, his chief's great success. He had been with Grant from the first, but other staffers were closer now that peacetime promised great things for Grant—stewardship of the Army, certainly; the presidency of the United States, perhaps.[1]

At Burkeville, Grant boarded a train for Petersburg and experienced firsthand a major southern shortcoming. Creaking and jerking on a hastily repaired roadbed, his cars derailed three times and barely managed five miles an hour. Dawn was brightening the broad James River when he finally rushed down the wharf at City Point to the steamer hawsered at the quay, shouting to his wife.

Julia Dent Grant had been one of the first to know Lee had surrendered to her husband, whom she called "Ulyss," or "Victor"—after King Victor Emmanuel of Italy—or "Dudy," depending on his mood. She had spent most of the war with Grant at various command posts, and had moved to City Point just after New Year's. Ever since Grant had left her for his final race against Lee's Confederates, she had been worried that the Rebels might run the opposite way and make her go home. When Richmond fell on April 3, her anxiety turned to depression. Julia went to Richmond the same day Lincoln, who had been visiting Grant, strolled through the fallen capital. She ordered a carriage and bumped along a few streets, but then told her driver to go back to the boat. There, she sobbed aloud for hours, and wondered to herself if she grieved so because of her plantation home in Missouri where she had grown up cared for by slaves. In 1865, though her girth pushed against the whalebone stays of ever-larger corsets and gray streaked her brown hair, Mrs. General Grant was still a belle to her husband, and as he charged through the headquarters boat his staff left them alone. He found her asleep, still dressed in the hoops and rumpled silk she'd worn the night before. She and Mrs. Rawlins had planned a gala dinner, but at three—exhausted from celebrating and somewhat petulant from waiting—Julia curled up and slept.

When the Grants emerged from their cabin, the belated dinner was consumed by chief and staff and fifty generals. There was much cork-popping and laughter, but no plans for a victory trip to Richmond. Grant refused, saying he would not add to the distress of Virginians. That afternoon, he ushered the merry-makers out of his office and sat down to business. But after a few minutes, he looked up from his papers, and stared out into space as a small smile softened the corners of his thin, set mouth. "More of Grant's luck!" he explained triumphantly to no one in particular. Finishing a dispatch to Sherman, he pushed back his chair and rose. *"Now for Mexico."*[2]

Grant left Julia at Willard's Hotel in Washington on April 14, and went to Lincoln's Cabinet meeting, where the normally staid statesmen vied to congratulate the general and hear firsthand of the surrender. He kept quiet while the secretaries argued about reconstruction, but he interrupted when Lincoln described a dream he'd had the night before about some strange vessel approaching a distant shore. The President thought it meant that William Tecumseh Sherman would soon send news of the capitulation of the last large Confederate field force—Joe Johnston's army in North Carolina. Grant wasn't sure. After the meeting, he and Julia were invited to join the Lincolns at the theater that night. Julia declined. She had been snubbed and embarrassed by Mary Lincoln during the President's visit to City Point and had no desire to submit to such treatment again.[3]

At dusk the Grants were on their way to catch a train for Philadelphia and then Burlington, New Jersey, where their four children lived with Grant's sister. The ride to the station was through streets full of celebrants and lit by hundreds of illuminated signs proclaiming peace. Julia started when a horseman pulled up and kept pace with the carriage. It was the same man, she told Grant, who had loitered near her table at Willard's that afternoon. Probably just a hero-worshipper. But it frightened her.

The Grants didn't register at Bloodgood's Philadelphia hotel until after midnight, and Julia, exhausted, sank down on the couch and was taking off her hat when there was a knock on the door. It was a courier, who handed Grant a telegram. The general stood over a table on which a light supper had been spread and read the message. Impassively, he handed the telegram to Julia, who read it quickly:

"The President was assassinated at Ford's Theater at 10:30 tonight and cannot live. The wound is a pistol shot through the head. Secretary Seward and his son Frederick were also assassinated at their residence and are in a dangerous condition. The Secretary of War desires that you return to Washington immediately. Please answer on receipt of this."[4]

ON THE MORNING of April 12 at Appomattox Court House, Robert E. Lee pulled his U.S. Army overcoat over his Confederate uniform. He sat at a small wooden table inside his tent, put on his spectacles, and, shuffling through a pile of final reports submitted to him by his field commanders, started a letter to Jefferson Davis:

"Mr. President," he wrote. "It is with pain that I announce to Your Excellency the surrender of the Army of Northern Virginia." He briefly told the story of his seven-day westward race with Grant for a vantage point from which he could move south and join Joe Johnston, then ended by trying to reason with Davis. "The enemy was more than five times our numbers. If we could have forced our way one day longer it would have been at a great sacrifice of life; at its end, I did not see how a surrender could have been avoided."

As he wrote, Lee could hear the rhythmic roll of Federal drums summoning his army for the formal stacking of arms. His army— 150 tarnished and fouled artillery pieces, a three-mile line of wagons and caissons with trembling, bony horses still hitched to them in the drizzling mist, and 13,000 men, stronger now from Federal rations, who shuffled into final formation. Lee kept to his tent. Though he wanted the men to know he was there, he would not lead them today. Grant was gone. It would not do for Lee to appear before a lesser Union officer. At noon, an aide arrived and quietly told him the ceremonies were over.

Lee ordered his tent struck and went to Union headquarters, where he signed his parole: "We, the undersigned Prisoners of War, belonging to the Army of Northern Virginia, having been this day surrendered by General Robert E. Lee, C.S.A., Commanding said Army, to Lieut Genl U.S. Grant, Commanding Armies of the United States, do hereby give our solemn parole of honor that we will not hereafter serve in the armies of the Confederate States, or in any military capacity whatever, against the United States of America, or render aid to the enemies of the latter, until properly exchanged, in such manner as shall be mutually approved by the respective authorities."[5]

That done, and after declining the offer of an honor escort of Federal cavalry, Lee left Appomattox Court House. Two aides were with him. What gear was left followed in a battered ambulance covered with a rotting quilt. During the last hours of retreat, while he struggled against his own desire to fight on and die, Lee had soothed a young aide by saying the question of capitulation was not a military or historical decision, but a moral one: "If it is right," he said, "then I will take all the responsibility." If Lee needed any support for the decision to surrender his Army, he got it on that ride through the grim scenes that had quieted Grant two days earlier. Usually erect, he slumped over his gray horse's head, and bent his ashen face away from the rain. Clusters of civilians and barefoot soldiers on their way home lined the road. They removed their hats as Lee rode by. He was, as southern editors had begun to say in 1865, the only Cause left to the South.[6]

The first night out, Lee camped with Pete Longstreet, still cheerful from his meeting with Grant, and in the morning said goodbye forever to his "old war horse," who was heading back to Petersburg to collect his wife and infant son, Robert Lee Longstreet. The future would find a reconstructed Pete bitterly denouncing Lee for what he called ineptitude at Gettysburg, but on April 13 the men parted as close and loving friends. The following day, Good Friday, Lee rode into the yard of his brother's home in Powhatan County. Carter was the eldest Lee, a lawyer, a Harvard graduate, a man too old to fight. He had sent a teenage son to his brother's army. Robert Lee was offered lodging from neighbors, but he declined. He had lived outdoors during the whole war—an aide insisted that he preferred to be uncomfortable—and saw no reason to change simply because he was at his brother's home. His sagging, faded tent was unloaded and pitched in the yard. That night, the fourth anniversary of the fall of Fort Sumter, he slept under canvas for the last time in his life. He had no way of knowing that Abraham Lincoln lay dying in Washington.

In the morning Lee was joined by his son Rooney, a cavalry officer, twice wounded, once captured, widowed, with both children dead of wartime disease, and his land in Virginia's Peninsula swept clean by Federal troops, who used it as a supply base. Father and son arrived at Manchester at midday. The wait to cross the James was long. Bridges had been blown the night of April 2 by the rear guard of fleeing troops, and returning citizens had either to use the pontoons laid by Federal soldiers or to take ferry boats manned by ragged Rebels already earning greenbacks. Lee found Richmond in shambles. Retreating soldiers had fired munitions dumps, and exploding shells and burning timbers had ignited other buildings. By the time the Federals rode into town on April 3, nearly a third of central Richmond would ever after be known as "the burnt district." Scorched brick skeletons towered crazily over rubble-filled streets. Garbage, sodden with whiskey dumped into gutters by police, littered sidewalks. Household furnishings, rescued by frightened inhabitants from burning homes, were stacked on curbs. Papers of the Confederate States of America blew into useless heaps around the feet of rigidly proud women attended by black servants, lined up for Federal rations to keep their families from starvation. Wooden blinds that covered windows in the better houses were drawn against scenes of black freedmen collecting on street corners and lounging under the statue of George Washington on Capitol Square.

A silent crowd collected around Lee when he turned into Franklin Street and reined to a stop before a red brick Federal row house. Out of old habit, women drew handkerchiefs to wave at their general, but stopped and began to weep. Men started to cheer him as usual, but fell quiet before the hollow-eyed old man who bared a thinning white head to them, then slowly climbed the steps to the house. Inside, his wife was waiting. Crippled now for almost two years by the arthritis which had begun thirty years earlier, Mary Custis Lee had met the hysteria of Richmond's fall with stony calm. Urged by friends and daughters to leave the house before it burned, she answered that Richmond was not the Confederacy and kept her seat. Later, when she heard her husband had surrendered to Grant, she said there were other armies to fight for southern independence.

Mary was the great-granddaughter of Martha Washington, and had grown up an only child in Arlington, a plantation maintained by her father as a shrine to George Washington. She had married the handsome but impoverished young Robert Lee because he shared her anti-slavery sentiments and had a Revolutionary lineage as impeccable as her own. Mary was, if anything, more opposed to secession than her husband, but once the war came, her proprietary pride in the Union hardened into fury against it. Turned out of Arlington soon after the first shot, she joined the caravan of the patrician southern homeless and spent her time knitting socks and gloves for Lee's army. Arlington was a Federal cemetery in 1865, lost to her and mourned forever, along with one child, her only grandchildren, her 11,000 acres of Virginia land, and her hope that her husband would head a new republic founded on virtue and love.[7]

Mary had seen in Robert Lee a new George Washington. She was not alone. When he was received by Virginia's secession convention in 1861 as leader of their troops, Lee was told that, like Washington, he would soon become "first in war, first in peace, and first in the hearts of his countrymen." The expression had a hidden irony. He had spent a lifetime emulating Washington and refuting the example of the man who had authored those words about Washington's place in American history—Henry Lee, his father.

CHAPTER

2

WHEN HENRY LEE brought his bride, Ann Hill Carter, from her James River plantation home to Richmond in 1793, he was a disappointed man. A widower with an unsavory reputation for improvident financial ventures, Lee at thirty-seven was much changed from the dashing young soldier who had fired the imaginations of his compatriots. His prospects had once been brilliant. His family, among the first in the state since the seventeenth century, had sent two men to Philadelphia to sign the Declaration of Independence, and one, Henry, to fight the war it required.

Born in 1756 in Leesylvania, Henry Lee graduated from Princeton in 1773 and three years later joined the Continental Army, with such success that a fellow officer said Lee seemed "to have come out of his mother's womb a soldier." George Washington, who was rumored to have proposed to Henry's mother, offered him a post on his staff and later asked Congress to give him a separate command. Lee, now known as "Light-Horse Harry," had a predilection for plumed hats and showy clothes, and he disciplined his men more stringently than he controlled himself. When he sent to Washington's headquarters the head, with the rope still around the neck, of a soldier he had hanged for desertion, his act was understood—with difficulty—as overzealous compliance with Washington's desire to frighten deserters. But his 1781 torture of a North Carolinian loyal to England could not be explained away, nor could Lee's involvement in a one-sided blood-bath that came to be known as "Pyle's Hacking Match." Amidst friends' allusions to his "distress," "anxiety," and "melancholy," Lee left the army before the end of the war.[1]

When he married his nineteen-year-old cousin, Matilda Lee, shortly after resigning his commission, he gained control of Stratford, a thriving Westmoreland County fiefdom. But instead of settling into the pastoral routine he said he wanted, Lee set out with Matilda's money to make a fortune in the real estate that had suddenly become American. Beginning with a series of speculations in North Carolina and Georgia, and culminating in a new town on the Potomac River named "Matildaville" out of love or guilt, Harry launched himself into a round of investing that eventually left his family destitute. His wife, once known as the "Queen of Stratford," with legal advice from Lee's younger brother, on her deathbed placed the diminished and half-ruined plantation in trust to her eldest son, who would receive it outright when he was twenty-one.

Despite his improvidence, Lee was elected in 1785 to the Virginia house of delegates, where he was named a representative to the Continental Congress. He supported ratification of the Constitution in the 1788 debates, and in 1789 was reelected. He began three one-year terms as governor of the state in 1791, but the same year he tried to abandon the floor for the field when Congress created an army to quell a disturbance in Pennsylvania. Washington, however, counseled wariness about a man who "lacks economy," and Lee was not given the command. Perceived disloyalty to Washington and not his own shortcomings, he thought, had cost him the coveted position. Once again, he sought solace in domesticated romance.[2]

Ann Hill Carter was born in 1773 into a family reputed to be the wealthiest on the American continent. Carters—by blood or marriage—built vast plantations, were often loyal to England, and, later, opposed Virginia's ratification of the Constitution, fearing that the southern states might become "mere appendages" of the North. Such anxieties were common among the landed descendants of wealthy Virginia planters, and they were nourished by the collapse of the tobacco market after the Revolution. But Charles Carter switched to wheat, and raised his daughter Ann in an easy atmosphere of security and affluence, cared for by what was considered to be the largest body of slaves in Virginia.

Charles Carter's "immense wealth flowed like silent streams" from "his mansion of hospitality," it was said, and he housed the clergy, forgave the debtor, fed the hungry, and kept the doors of his plantation, Shirley, always open. Unlike Stratford, which faced northward across the Potomac, Shirley looked south over the slow-moving James River. Built in the early part of the eighteenth century, Shirley's square, mansard-roofed house had a brick forecourt that enclosed a laundry and kitchen. Storehouses, a root cellar, an icehouse, a dovecote, a smokehouse, stables, and barns were close by. Lines of kinship linked the plantation to its neighbors, and visits, parties, and weddings enlivened a domestic scene which already burgeoned with the activities of Charles Carter's twenty-one children.[3]

Governor Light-Horse Harry Lee would have been warmly received at Shirley in the early 1790s, but the welcome surely cooled when Charles Carter discovered his designs of matrimony on his favorite daughter. Traditionally, Lee marriages augmented family fortunes. So did Carters'. Though there was something a Lee might gain by marrying a Carter, in Ann's father's eyes there was little for a Carter to gain by marrying a Lee, especially this Lee. Even worse, Harry was toying with the idea of joining France's revolutionary army. "Bred to arms," Lee explained in a letter to Washington, since the death of his first wife he had "wished for a return to my profession, as the best resort for my mind in its affliction." Washington urged Lee to refuse the commission and apparently was heard, for Lee soon wrote Alexander Hamilton that instead of going to France, he now meant to "become a farmer & get a wife as soon as possible." In May 1793, Charles Carter, with some reluctance, agreed to supply the wife. "Mrs. Carter and I are perfectly satisfied that our dear girl will make you a dutiful and loving wife," he wrote, "and we flatter ourselves that you will be to her a most affectionate and tender husband. . . ." The anxious father had added "and tender" as an afterthought.[4]

The wedding was held in June in Shirley's great hall. The bride, with soft dark hair and deep black eyes, wore around her neck a miniature of George Washington inscribed ". . . to his dear Ann." Washington offered congratulations to the groom, wishing Harry happiness and success now that he had "exchanged the rugged and dangerous field of Mars for the soft and pleasurable bed of Venus."

Ann soon discovered that she had exchanged the soft and pleasurable life of a daughter of Charles Carter for the rugged and dangerous bed of Light-Horse Harry Lee. A friend later wrote that "in the short space of a fortnight" the new Mrs. Lee found "her affections were trampled on by a heartless & depraved profligate. I am right as to time. One fortnight was her dream of happiness from which she awoke to a life of misery. Her fortune was soon thrown away upon his debts contracted previous to marriage. She was despised and neglected. . . ." How neglected became the subject of lasting gossip among friends and family who were soon calling the former Miss Carter "poor Ann."

The new Mrs. Lee set up housekeeping in Richmond but often was at Shirley, and soon settled at Stratford, where she assumed the role of mistress of her husband's first wife's ancestral home. Such accommodations were not unusual in eighteenth-century Virginia, but the mausoleum for Matilda which Henry was building at the time may have given her pause. So too might have the manor house itself. One of the bedchambers on the ground floor was kept as a museum to the "Divine Matilda," with her gowns, slippers, and jewelry still in their places. On the main floor, reached by a narrow interior winding staircase, the man's study stood unused, the dining room remained neglected, and in the great hall, with double doors which opened on one side to the Potomac and the other to a magnificent grove of tulip poplars, was Matilda's closed harpsichord and shrouded harp. Ann was left to cope with Matilda's son, Henry, and daughter, Lucy—who detested her stepmother—while Lee busied himself again with real estate, this time with Ann's money.[5]

Harry bought shares in 200,000 acres of the vast Fairfax estate on the Potomac River, assumed George Washington's interest in the Great Dismal Swamp area of North Carolina for $20,000, involved himself with Robert Morris and others in the purchase of one million acres of "cheap back lands," and invested in ore fields, coal mines, currency transactions, and interest-bearing loans. Despite his continued misrepresentations to creditors and prospective investors, most of Lee's associates accepted his protestations of integrity until 1798, when he passed a bad banknote off on the Father of His Country. "It is a mode of dealing to which I am not accustomed," Washington chastised Lee. "I pray you not to deceive me."

Luckily, Harry was given a chance to redeem himself for history. He was asked to deliver the funeral oration for Washington in 1799. "First in war, first in peace, and first in the hearts of his countrymen," said Lee of the dead President, and his characterization became an enduring description of Washington's mythic role. Later, arguing in favor of a contested appropriation for Washington's mausoleum, Lee declared that the country's father was great because he was good. Moral purity, sound character, and virtue had been the foundations of all Washington's worldly success. Introduced at a time when even Washington himself had questioned Lee's goodness, this analysis of greatness became the only important legacy that Lee as a father passed on to his own sons.[6]

By 1801, Henry Lee's taxable land in Westmoreland County stood at 236 acres, a tenth of what had once adjoined Stratford Hall. Half a dozen creditors were seeking satisfaction. In reaction to Ann's already having signed over to Harry her land in Spotsylvania County and Richmond, her father changed his will. The property he was leaving Ann on Malvern Hill, just north of Shirley, was to be cared for by four executors, "in such a way that she solely during her natural life may enjoy the rents, issues, profits, emoluments, interests and advantages of the said property . . . free from the claim, demand, let, hindrance or molestation of her husband, General Lee."

As Harry's fortunes declined, Ann's health deteriorated. By

the time she was thirty, she was describing herself as a "chronic invalid," mentioning only dropsy as a cause. Though early in her marriage she had somewhat defensively insisted that she was "cheerful and happy" away from the social bustle of Shirley, her family home was the emotional center in a life increasingly devoted to making do in the face of disaster. In the summer of 1806, accompanied by her three small children and pregnant with a fourth, she traveled across Virginia's Peninsula in Harry Lee's last carriage, one not fit to sell. When she turned into the familiar road laid between Shirley's fields of corn and wheat, and entered the cool, tree-shaded forecourt of the old house, Ann discovered that Charles Carter had died suddenly. Instead of welcome, she wrote her husband, she found that "the arms which had ever received me in so much delight were folded in death! . . . We all feel that our best hopes are buried in the grave of our blessed and dearly beloved friend." She had perhaps more reason than other family members to grieve for lost hope, and she closed her letter to Harry on a desperate note. "Oh, my dearest Mr. Lee, remember that your poor, afflicted Fatherless wife can now only look to you, to smooth her rugged path through life, and soften her bed of death!"[7]

Harry couldn't even smooth her path to Stratford. Repeated requests to him for transportation went unanswered, and it was not until December that he finally sent an old open carriage for the trip to the Potomac. Ill and eight months pregnant, Ann arrived at a ruined home. There were weeds in the fallow gardens, and the fields lay unworked. Barns were empty and one of the dependencies had collapsed. The overseer had left. Harry had sold the massive exterior staircase which ascended to the great hall, and had chained the doors against surprise from bill collectors. Most of the furnishings were gone, and rooms were sealed off against the cold. In a rare display of bitterness, Ann wrote her sister-in-law, who was also expecting the birth of another Lee, "You have my best wishes for your success, my dear, and *truest assurances* that I do not envy your prospects nor wish to *share* in them."

Such prospects could not be wished away, however, and on January 19, 1807, in the mother's chamber at Stratford, Ann deliv-

ered a large black-eyed boy. She named him after her two brothers—Robert Edward Lee—and was given up for dead.

Few celebrated the birth. It was only the occasional family
member or creditor whose carriage came up the rutted lane of
Stratford that winter. Grieving for her father, her favorite
brother, and Mildred Carter, "the darling sister of my heart" who
died in March, Ann kept to the Mother's room next to the
nursery. The following year, Harry Lee tried to leave the country. The year after that, he went to jail as a debtor.[8]

Ann Lee, not Harry, was now head of the household, and she
decided to move her family to Alexandria as soon as Harry was
released. The Potomac River town was home to two of his brothers and one sister. Veterans of Lee's Legion of Revolutionary
fame lived there, and the old part of town exuded the spirit of
George Washington, whose plantation, Mount Vernon, was close
by. Ann may have hoped the area would recall her husband to his
duties. Certainly she could fulfill hers better there. In the spring
of 1811, the old carriage waited under Stratford's porte cochere
while Ann Kinloch Lee went to look for her little brother inside
Stratford Hall. Robert climbed into the carriage with his mother
and his brothers, Carter and Smith. A cart piled with trunks,
Light-Horse Harry's manuscripts and books, Robert's swinging
cradle, and Ann's four slaves followed.

If she had serious hopes for a more settled life, Ann was
disappointed. Harry took part in a Baltimore melee over the War
of 1812 and was seriously injured. When he finally returned,
heavily bandaged, to Alexandria, he complained of "deranged"
health, and for months wore a dramatic black cloth to cover his
facial wounds. Ignoring the protestations of his brother Edmund,
whose finances would be devastated by his forfeiting his bank-
ruptcy bail, Harry left for the West Indies in 1813. He said he
would return to the United States in a few months, but it took
five years. His family never saw him again.[9]

Harry left behind a wife and five minor children. Mildred, the
youngest, was born in 1811 in Alexandria. Robert was six; Smith,
eleven; Ann, thirteen; and Carter, fifteen. Ann Lee's income was

not great, but she managed to provide a comfortable home for her family. The Lees had moved twice after first settling on Cameron Street across from George Washington's town house, and in 1811 Ann had written to a relative asking for help in getting a large home at 607 Oronoco Street, which was owned by William Fitzhugh. Though the red brick house was built during the Federal period, the style, like that of most established Alexandria dwellings, was conservatively Georgian. Outside was a fenced garden, green even in winter with splendid boxwoods, and brightened in summer by snowball bushes that were Robert's favorites.

The house was not far from the Potomac River, and children could watch sailing vessels landing at the Alexandria wharves with their cargoes from Europe. Across the river the new buildings of the Federal capital could be seen through the fringe of trees that bordered its northern shore. Ann Lee bought a carriage the year her husband left and made visits to the Fitzhugh plantation Ravensworth, and to Chatham, to Shirley, and to Eastern View, the place in nearby Fauquier County where the Carters kept a school for their boys. She even traveled with Robert to Philadelphia, an unheard-of adventure for a woman alone. Her health was poor, and she often was too weak to walk, but she managed her household as she did herself, with determination. A family member described Ann as "intense, loving and sweet. Although she was gentle, she was firm, resolute, and strong." She insisted that her children follow her example and "practise self-denial and self-control, as well as the strictest economy in all financial concerns." She sent Carter to Harvard, but was disappointed in what she saw as his irresponsible behavior. *"To you, I had looked, for the restoration of that happiness, in part,* which my widowed lot had deprived me of," she wrote during his freshman year. "I had hoped that you would be a highly educated, discreet, judicious man. That you would have been an example for your Brothers imitation—a dignified protector of your Sisters, and the pride & solace of your Mother's declining years." He never was. That duty fell to her youngest boy, the child she hadn't wanted.[10]

Ann kept up a spotty correspondence with Henry Lee until his death, and received letters from him which were curious combinations of self-pity, guilt, and inconsequential practicality. Harry's correspondence with Carter, however, provided moral parenting in absentia which Light-Horse Harry was unable to supply in person. He warned against debt, "the sink of mental power and the subversion of independence, which draws into debasement even virtue, in appearance certainly, if not in reality." Fame was meaningless "unless bottomed on virtue." Above all else, complete self-command was essential. "It is the pivot upon which the character, fame and independence of us mortals hang." If the elder Lee's message was "Do as I say, not as I have done," he was hardly unique in such paternal disjunctions.

Alexandria tradition had it that Robert was playing in the yard that sided the house when word came that Light-Horse Harry Lee was dead. He had made good on one promise—to return to the country. He had secured passage on March 1, 1818, from Nassau to Georgia. Too ill to continue his trip, he sought a sickroom in Dungeness, the Cumberland Island home in which his old Revolutionary War commander Nathanael Greene had meant to retire. Lee died there March 24, and was buried in the Greene family cemetery.

His death could have had little practical effect on eleven-year-old Robert. If anything, with debts finally canceled, it may have made it easier to accept the near-greatness of the man who was not very good.[11]

In 1820 Ann took Robert out of the school at Eastern View and enrolled him in Mr. Leary's Academy in Alexandria. There he read "all the minor classics in addition to Homer & Longinus, Tacitus & Cicero." He did well in mathematics, and earned commendations for his "gentlemanly deportment." That same year, scandal once again broke over the family. Robert's half-brother, Henry, the new master of Stratford, had followed Lee tradition by marrying a young heiress. With Anne McCarty's money, Henry set about restoring his plantation to its former splendor. But the Lees had used up all their luck in Westmoreland County. Henry's two-year-old daughter darted through the huge doors of the second-story great hall at Stratford and fell to her death. His wife sought comfort from morphine. Henry's solace was the bed of his sister-in-law, who became pregnant. A lawsuit was filed against him, for he was also the girl's legal guardian, and evidence surfaced that he had misused her money. His young ward cut off her hair after her baby was born, dead, and went into public mourning. His wife left him, and Henry Lee the younger, now called Black-Horse Harry Lee, left Virginia after first selling Stratford for $25,000.

Only Robert and his younger sister were at home when this latest difficulty surfaced. It seemed the children of Light-Horse Harry—the unstable Lucy, the sexually and financially undisciplined Henry, and the perhaps profligate Carter—had inherited their father's weak character. Smith seemed sound enough—handsome and charming, a young man who enjoyed the company of Virginia belles and didn't cause any trouble. But Robert was more than sound. Light-Horse Harry had observed that it was his youngest son's "nature" to be good, and relatives said that when Robert first arrived in Alexandria at age three, he impressed them with his "exemplary behavior."

Though he read his Catechism for Bishop Meade at Alexandria's Christ Church, Lee was not confirmed as a youngster, and evidenced no particular piety. Perhaps he was naturally "good," but the native desire to please, if it existed, was carefully cultivated by his mother. Ann Carter made no secret of her wish that her children compensate her for the disappointments suffered at their father's hands. Relatives and friends never forgot Robert's tender solicitude for his ailing mother. "At the hour when the other school-boys went to play," a neighbor recalled, "he hurried home to order his mother's drive, and would then be seen carrying her in his arms to the carriage, and arranging her cushions with the gentleness of an experienced nurse." During the daily rides Robert prodded his mother into cheerfulness and clowned to elicit her laughs. By the time he was thirteen, it was he who looked after the house, taking care of horses and carriage, marketing and managing the servants. He "carried the keys," an honor usually assigned to the eldest daughter, and a necessity in an era when valuables such as silver, linens, and even tea were commonly locked away from possible depredations of slaves.

With his leisure devoted to caring for Ann, he had little time for boyish pursuits. Most reminiscences about young Lee center on his relationship with his mother. There were apparently no romances, and Robert had few friends except his cousins Cassius and Edmund Lee, who went with him to Alexandria's markets and visited the municipal stables. He honed his social skills by accompanying his mother on calls—short social engagements—or on visits—long stays in the plantation houses of relatives, and he developed the physical prowess necessary for a Virginian of station. He was an excellent swimmer, skater, and dancer, had a good seat on a horse, and ran a decent footrace. He was also an excellent student at the boys' school which Benjamin Hallowell opened in the house adjoining the Lees'.

Years later Hallowell remembered the young Lee as being an "exemplary pupil in every respect. He was never behind in time at his studies; never failed in a single recitation; was perfectly observant of the rules and regulations of the Institution; was gentlemanly, unobtrusive and respectful in all his deportment to teachers and his fellow-students." Hallowell said Lee's "specialty was *finishing up*. He imparted a finish and a neatness as he proceeded, to everything he undertook. One of the branches of mathematics he studied with me was Conic Sections, in which some of the diagrams are very complicated. He drew the diagrams on a slate; and although he well knew that the one he was drawing would have to be removed to make room for another, he drew each one with as much accuracy and finish, lettering and all, as if it were to be engraved and printed."[12]

Lee's schoolwork reflected a need to reach an abstract mark of perfection which he had himself set. Such displays of self-discipline were remarkable, especially in the South, where there were ample diversions for a young man. But in Alexandria folklore, they were not unique. The town's first citizen had lived out his life on just such a basis.

By the early 1820s, through the agency of such mythmakers as Parson Weems, George Washington for most of America was a shadowy presence who watched over the growing country from godly heights. In Alexandria and northern Virginia, Washington was only slightly less exalted, but very much more human. His infatuations with various belles—including Robert Lee's grandmother—were well known, as was his fondness for fine food, drink, and furnishings. Alexandria tradesmen had been proud of serving "the General," and most of the town's best people were guests at Washington's last birthday party, held at City Tavern. Ann Lee and her children attended Christ Church, which still maintained Washington's pew, and heard Scripture read from Washington's Bible. They were regulars at Arch Hall, the Alexandria home of Washington's foster daughter, Nelly Parke Custis Lewis, and were often invited to Arlington, the nearby plantation of Washington's adopted son, George Washington Parke Custis.

The Lees were guests at an Arlington reception, held under Washington's campaign tent, for the Marquis de Lafayette, who included Alexandria in a triumphal tour of America in 1824. A band, marshaled by a handsomely uniformed Robert Lee, led the procession through an arch inscribed with a message from one of Lafayette's speeches—"For a Nation to be Free, It is Sufficient That She Wills It." After the Alexandria parade, Lafayette paid a series of ceremonial calls, including one on Ann Lee. The visit made the Revolution seem all that much closer to a young man who already knew that republican virtue was not ensconced in godlike myths or relegated to books of history. Especially if the young man had committed himself to the restoration of his mother's happiness—happiness destroyed by one Revolutionary's singular lack of virtue—he might himself find pride and solace in following the classical ideal.[13]

That same year, when Robert was seventeen, the family had to decide upon educating him for a career. Because the value of Ann Lee's bank stock had declined, college was out of the question. Smith had joined the Navy, so perhaps the Army would do for Robert. Robert Edward Lee's 1824 application to West Point was formidable. He was introduced to Tennessee senator Andrew Jackson and Secretary of War John C. Calhoun. He had a letter of introduction from the family patron, William Fitzhugh, that reminded Calhoun of Light-Horse Harry's military services and described Lee's mother as "one of the finest women, the State of Virginia has ever produced."

There were letters of recommendation—one signed by five senators and three members of the House—that referred to his being the son of a Revolutionary War hero, but his half-brother's was the most eloquent. Black-Horse Harry Lee had fled from Virginia to Tennessee, where he worked as secretary to Andrew Jackson—who with his Rachel was no stranger to scandal. When Jackson took office, Black-Horse Harry returned to Virginia and the modicum of respectability reserved for friends of the powerful. Harry wrote Calhoun a rather peremptory request. "To a person of your enlarged sentiments, and accurate knowledge of our national history it would be unnecessary to enumerate the exertions of my father in the cause of this country, or to trace the grand and beautiful process of morality, by which the orphans of publick benefactors, become the children of the State." Calhoun may have been reluctant to adopt Robert Lee in the name of the state, but he did admit him to the United States Military Academy.

With his new gear packed into a regulation Army leather trunk, Robert Lee left Virginia for West Point in June 1825. His mother came to see him off. The parting was perhaps the most difficult trial in the lives of both, but they were resolute and dignified people. Only after Robert had gone did Ann turn to her sister-in-law with a sob. "You know what I have lost. He is son, daughter, and every thing to me!"[14]

CHAPTER

3

W H E N   L E E   L E F T Virginia for West Point in the summer
of 1825, Ulysses Grant was three years old. "Lyss" was the eldest
son of Jesse Root Grant, a frontier businessman who had moved
his family to Georgetown, Ohio, in 1823, built a brick house, and
established the only tanyard in Brown County. Jesse Grant meant
to get rich quick.

The Grant family was an old and prosperous one which had
set down American roots in Connecticut in 1630. But Ulysses
Grant's grandfather, Noah, had squandered his inheritance. Noah
told people he had fought in the Revolutionary War, and his
family believed it was this that "spoilt" the old man "for all
financial business" and weakened him for drink. He lied. He
apparently wasn't interested in the Revolution or business or
much of anything else. When his second wife, Rachel, died in
Portage County, Ohio, in 1805, Noah abandoned seven of his
children—the eldest only twelve—and went to Kentucky to be
cared for by a grown son.

"My father," Jesse Grant remembered, "was born rich and was
a man of education; but he died poor. His children were born poor,
but all acquired a comfortable competency." At eleven, Jesse
went to work on the few odd jobs available to a boy alone in the
woods. Eventually, he attracted the sympathetic attention of
Judge Tod, who took Jesse to his Youngstown home to raise as

one of his own. There Jesse saw his first set of china and silver-ware and got his only formal schooling—five months in all—then moved to Kentucky to serve as apprentice in his half-brother's tannery. Five years later, in 1816, he was back in Ohio, working as tanner for a God-fearing Western Reserve farmer named Orvil Brown. Brown kept a way station on the Underground Railroad and reared his children on Scripture and the rod. One of those children, Orvil's oldest boy, impressed Jesse with his "purity of character," but neighbors later said they always knew there was something odd about John Brown. Jesse soon went into a partner-ship in Ravenna, Ohio, where his industry and thrift earned him $1,500 in savings and the title of the richest man in town. But Jesse fell victim to "ague"—a malarial fever—and was ill almost a year. When he got out of his sickbed, he had to start again.

By the time Jesse made his second beginning, the population of Ohio was twelve times what it had been when his family floated in from Pennsylvania. Fortune seemed to point westward, and the road west was the Ohio River. From the wharf at Maysville, Kentucky, where Jesse convalesced, he could watch boats laden with wheat, pork, cloth, and wood set off for New Orleans and return with cotton for New England's mills. Steamers, piled with household furnishings and crowded with farm animals, headed for the Mississippi with the current, carrying their cargoes of hopeful farmers out to cheap new lands. Action, growth, and the feel of money to be made rose from the river's very waters, and Jesse wanted to be a part of it. Point Pleasant, Ohio, sat on steep, dun-colored rocky banks, a sturdy red brick port and last stop before Cincinnati. Jesse found a man there who would take him on as a partner, and, even better, who knew a family with a marriageable daughter.[1]

When Jesse Grant began calling, he found the Simpsons "peo-ple of veracity and integrity; but not of any particular ambition beyond that of living as independent farmers." They were just the opposite of Jesse, who bristled to get ahead and was willing to bend the truth a little if it helped, but he overlooked the differen-ces. The Simpsons had lived on a farm outside of Philadelphia until 1817, when "Ohio Fever," a land-greed contagion that swept through the East in the early 1800s, hit their peaceful homestead. They traveled 500 miles overland in a Conestoga wagon to Wheeling, Virginia, then transferred to a flatboat for Point Pleasant. By paying cash for their 600-acre farm, they established a reputation as upper-class, a notion enhanced by Mrs. Simpson's penchant for books. Jesse was not impressed. The object of his visits, Hannah, was no beauty and, at twenty-three, already an old maid by the standards of the time. Jesse thought Hannah "a plain unpretending country girl, handsome but not vain," steady, firm, and strong of character. Hannah's stepmother, Rebecca, remembered that when she met the seven-year-old girl she "had as much the deportment of a woman as most girls at twenty," an assessment shared, in slightly altered forms, by other Simpson relatives. She was unduly "strict" about doing one's duty, it was said, and "thought nothing you could do would entitle you to praise . . . you ought to praise the Lord for giving you an opportunity to do it." Hannah had been a Philadelphia Presbyterian before moving to Ohio, then became a "devoted and consistent member" of the Methodist Church. Her one passion was the belief that man was totally depraved and entirely at the mercy of a God who had predestined the future. Apparently assuming that God had sent Jesse Grant to be her husband, she accepted his proposal.[2]

"A few of the neighbors expressed their surprise that one of Mr. Simpson's daughters should marry a young man hardly yet established in business," Jesse wrote. "But this did me no harm; and as soon as it was seen how I was getting along, I heard nothing more of it."

Jesse and Hannah were married on June 24, 1821, and went to live in a white frame house on a hill overlooking the river at Point Pleasant. Ten months later, on April 27, 1822, Hannah bore their first child, a boy, who went nameless for six weeks while the family argued over what to call him. The baby's grandmother, who "had an enthusiastic admiration for the ancient commander," urged the name Ulysses. That was acceptable to Jesse, who christened his son—"a most beautiful child"—Hiram Ulysses Grant.

By the summer of 1823, Jesse Grant knew it was time to leave Point Pleasant. The picturesque little town wasn't growing as fast as his fortunes. By saving $1,100, he had proven himself not only an "excellent manager" but also a shrewd trader who bought cheap and sold dear and kept an eye out for helping chance along. Georgetown, ten miles back from the river, had recently been named the seat of Brown County, and promised to thrive. Jesse chose Georgetown and in August paid fifty dollars for a lot.[3]

All Ohio, along with Indiana, Illinois, Michigan, Wisconsin, and Minnesota, had once been part of Virginia, a lavish example of royal generosity called Boutetort County, which the state ceded to the Continental Congress in 1784, retaining a piece of land between the Little Miami and Scioto rivers as a reserve for veterans. Brown County, part of the Virginia Military Lands, was slow to fill—a 1799 petition to have the anti-slavery clause of the Northwest Ordinance set aside failed. A sodden old soldier named Brown managed to win or steal deeds to 40,000 acres, which he dispensed, free, along with corn whiskey, to friends. By the early 1820s some of those cohorts had settled the county, named it Brown for their benefactor, and built twenty-four distilleries. Brown County became famous for its drunks.

Along with camp-meeting revivals, drink was one of the few recreations available to settlers. Life was brutalizing in the great hardwood forests of southern Ohio. Working from first light to sundown, a farmer might, if he was lucky and strong, be able to clear as much as an acre of land a month. If he had a team of horses, he could girdle the biggest trees—usually more than 100 feet high—and leave them eight or nine years to die, then pull out the stumps. The land was disappointingly poor, and tobacco planted by southern farmers and wine grapes nurtured by Pennsylvania Germans failed to thrive. Cabins of unhewn logs, replaced after three or four years by plaster-chinked, broadax-smoothed log houses, sat isolated amidst the damp dirt of tiny clearings which light penetrated only a few hours each day. Laws were crude—the penalty for horse theft was cropping of the ears—and religion itself, one visiting cleric noted, had become a bestial outgrowth of the Kentucky revivals.[4]

But the wilderness was being tamed by educators, Old Light

ministers, lawyers, merchants, and men like Jesse Grant. As soon as he had bought his lot in Georgetown, Jesse started his tannery. There were no more than half a dozen finished houses in the town, and only one hostelry, the American Hotel, which put on a series of vinous "feeds" in support of political candidates. When Jesse acquired another lot two weeks later and began to construct a solid and unimaginative brick house, he became one of the biggest landholders in town. He employed local boys to work the hides, and struck up friendships with the handful of George-town's literate men. The Grants' neat house had thirty books—a massive library for the area—and Jesse sent Ulysses to school when he was only five or six.

Still, though the domestic life of the Grants was a cut above the norm, it was not accorded the respect of the town. Perhaps it was Jesse's business, and the stink that wouldn't wash out of even the nicest clothes, but the old boys who sat on their stoops passing around gossip and jugs of good corn found the fast-talk-ing, nervous little tanner absurd. They taught their children to make fun of Jesse's much-vaunted son, the one with the preten-tious name that they pronounced "Useless."

Like all western children, Ulysses assumed a share of hard labor when he was very young, and received a spotty education. But he was small and thin, daintily dressed in clothes which were by far the fanciest in town, and had a fastidious distaste for the more common vulgarities of boyhood. Moreover, he was seem-ingly ignored by his mother. The women of Georgetown never got over their shock at Ulysses's mother allowing him to crawl between the feet of horses tethered outside the tannery. Nothing to worry about, she said, horses seemed to understand her baby. They also remembered that Hannah never nursed her eldest when he fell ill. She dosed him with castor oil, then "put him to bed and went calmly about her work, trusting in the Lord and the boy's constitution." Ulysses said later that he had never once seen his mother cry, and no one remembered her ever laughing. She was a well-groomed, smallish woman with an open face and smooth dark hair. She seldom smiled and spoke only when she had to. No one played cards in Hannah Grant's house, and no one danced or played music there either. Her excessive reticence led some observers to guess that she harbored some great secret. More likely, she was simply keeping the strict Calvinist faith of her fathers. Salvation was a gift of God in this cosmic view, not a reward for good works, and nothing anyone could do would alter that. A baby might be allowed to play among the feet of horses or lie unwatched when he was ill. If God meant to call him, He would.

Jesse Grant boasted of Ulysses's exploits, and he was never above endangering the health and emotional welfare of the boy if it would enhance his own social standing. An early recollection of Jesse's eldest child was of a neighbor testing Ulysses's mettle. The boy's fingers were wrapped around the trigger of a gun. One of the adults squeezed. The blast rocked the neighborhood, and Jesse proudly said the boy never even winked. This initiation into firearms seems not to have engendered any fondness for guns in Ulysses, however. He never hunted with the other boys, and when a few years after the incident a doctor prescribed "powders" for an illness, the child became unaccountably hysterical, sobbing, "No, no, no! I can't take powder; it will blow me up." The story of his terror passed for humor in Georgetown, and became a staple in the Grant family. So did the tale of Ulysses's horse bargaining.[5]

Ulysses was known to be scrupulously truthful. But this character trait did not stand particularly high in the estimation of a businessman like Jesse, who had slyly noted that the "veracity" of his in-laws accompanied their lack of ambition. Honesty was often taken for stupidity in a society which admired pulling a fast one on the gullible. Such was his family's and neighbors' attitude toward Ulysses, and it bothered him all his life. In his *Memoirs,* he repeated a story which was often told in his hometown. It had to do with a colt Jesse was going to buy from a Mr. Ralston, and Ulysses was to do the dealing. "When I got to Mr. Ralston's house, I said to him: 'Papa says I may offer you twenty dollars for the colt, but if you won't take that, I am to offer twenty-two and a half, and if you won't take that, I am to give you twenty-five,' " Grant wrote. At the time, he went on, he "could not have been over eight years old. . . . This transaction caused me great heart-burning. The story got out among the boys of the village, and it was a long time before I heard the last of it. Boys enjoy the misery of their companions, at least village boys in that day did, and in later life I have found that all adults are not free from the peculiarity." It was probably Jesse who spread the tale. For one thing, he had been right about the value of the colt. "I kept the horse until he was four years old, and he went blind," wrote Grant, "and I sold him for twenty dollars."[6]

Luckily, Ulysses was better at riding horses than buying them. Beginning with an infant whirl on a carnival pony, the boy never failed to win approval for his horsemanship. Townsfolk learned not to be startled by his tearing through the courthouse square on half-wild horses or dashing to the creek at top speed, balancing himself on one foot aboard their bare backs. By the time he was eight he was working as a regular driver for the tannery and was good enough to transport travelers around southern Ohio. His specialty was breaking colts, a skill that gave Jesse opportunities to brag about his son's "self-possession" and to say that he "never appeared to have any distrust of himself or any misgiving about his ability to do anything which could be expected of a boy his size and age." That was not quite true.

Ulysses had learned from his mother that it was safest to be quiet. When he was given a job, he thought about it long enough to figure out how to do it. Brown County problems were physical ones, and Grant, even as a small boy, had the ability to envision the physical world as a mathematically ordered, three-dimensional stage. He tried out solutions in his mind until he hit on one that worked. His reinvention of the lever and fulcrum, for example, not only allowed him to load cords of wood by himself, it made his prowess the talk of the town. Why didn't Ulysses stall his wagon on the hills of Brown County like everyone else did, he was asked. "Because I never get stalled myself," was the reply. He was too sensitive to risk humiliation, so he never attempted anything he knew he couldn't do. He could learn how to tame a horse, ford a swollen river, or travel alone to Louisville on business. People, especially those his own age, were more difficult. He tried to avoid them.[7]

A few stories survive concerning Ulysses's prankishness, but many more portray him as a "sober, thoughtful boy, who preferred the society of men to that of younger companions . . ." Classmates remembered that he was too well behaved to get whippings at school, and that at recess, rather than joining in games, he usually sat alone on a stump, watching. He drove the sleigh on winter rides, turning his back to the jollity on board. He "went about everything in such a peculiarly businesslike way," a schoolmate recalled. "I don't remember that I ever saw him excited." Years later, Georgetown neighbors could recall only two or three times when Ulysses even fought.

He had plenty of spending money, and shared the candy he bought, but it seems not to have made him popular. His closest friend was the son of his neighbors, the Baileys. He used to challenge the boy to horse races—which he always won—and tease him about the outcome. One day Ulysses taunted young Bailey into spurring his horse so hard the animal panicked, reared, and fell. The boy was killed. Townsfolk observed that Ulysses grew even quieter after that, and as he entered his teens, "was more like a grown person than a boy," one woman remembered.

That maturity didn't help him scholastically. Though he was competent in elementary mathematics, he demonstrated no interest in literature, and had a horror of public speaking. An assignment to deliver Washington's "Farewell Address" was disastrous. "He made fearful work of it and after school said he would 'never speak there again, no matter what happened,' " said his teacher. He apparently never did, and in a short time he left Georgetown schools for the richer academic fields of Maysville, Kentucky.[8]

When Jesse asked him what he wanted to do with his life, Ulysses said he'd like to be a farmer or a "down-the-river trader," or else get an education. He didn't mention joining Jesse in the tannery. He "detested the trade," he said later, "preferring almost any other labor." It was nasty work. Fresh or dried beef hides were soaked in vats of lime, then dragged to the "beam house," where they were stretched and scraped clean of hair, fat, and flesh. After another soaking in sulfuric acid, the hides were cured for months in oak-bark liquor, then rinsed, scrubbed, and rubbed with tallow and fish oil. In order to make certain of a constant supply of fresh hides, Jesse had added a slaughterhouse to the works. The yard swarmed with flies, reeked of acid and manure, rotting blood and flesh, and was filled with the moans of dying cattle. Grant developed a lifelong aversion to fleshly food, and sickened if a piece of meat was too rare. Always obedient, Ulysses had told Jesse he would work in the tannery until he was twenty-one, but after that would never set foot in the yard.

Since Jesse owned only a small amount of land, he couldn't set Ulysses up as a farmer. He also didn't think much of the boy shipping South and joining the motley caravan of traders on the Ohio and Mississippi. Despite Ulysses's poor showing in Georgetown schools, an education might be the answer, especially one that didn't cost much money. Grant relatives later said that Jesse "had determined to use all the influence he could bear when his son was old enough, to get him into West Point." In 1836 Ulysses was enrolled in Richeson and Rand's Maysville academy. Though he responded to his father's prodding and joined a debating society at school, Ulysses remembered his year there as less than successful. The term was spent "going over the same old arithmetic which I knew every word of before, and repeating: 'a noun is the name of a thing,' which I had also heard my Georgetown teachers repeat, until I had come to believe it." Jesse didn't send him back. "I was not studious in habit, and probably did not make progress enough to compensate for the outlay for board and tuition."[9]

Though the family income was enhanced in 1837 by Hannah's share of Simpson property rents after her father died, the increase didn't cover losses resulting from the financial panic that swept the nation that spring. By that time, there were five Grant children to support: Samuel Simpson, born in 1825; Clara Rachel, born in 1828; Virginia Paine, born in 1832; Orvil Lynch, born in 1835 (probably named after John Brown's father); and Ulysses. Jesse's eldest would stay in Georgetown and return to the inexpensive subscription school. But he didn't stay long. Something more than economics was on Jesse's mind that year.

In the 1830s the Democratic Party, which represented the majority of Georgetown citizens, was nationally committed to a states' rights and pro-slavery position. The Republicans would not exist for two more decades, but there was free-soil or abolitionist support among the Whigs, the political party which also backed a strong Federal government. Jesse Grant said he joined the Whig Party because he thought Democrat Andrew Jackson was trifling with the country's finances. He also said he was never an "Abolitionist." But he admired John Brown his whole life, and contributed to the *Castigator,* an anti-slavery newspaper published in Georgetown—making certain, however, to avoid mention of the "peculiar institution." The publisher of the *Castigator* sold the paper to a group of Whigs in 1837, the year Ulysses returned from Kentucky and the same year Jesse Grant was elected mayor of Georgetown on the Whig ticket. It may have been coincidence, but shortly after the *Castigator* opened new offices in Ripley, the strongly anti-slavery river town ten miles from Georgetown, Jesse enrolled Ulysses in Ripley's Presbyterian Academy.

The academy's president, a man Jesse more than a decade earlier had invited to address the Georgetown Masons, was the Reverend John Rankin, an outspoken organizer for the American Anti-Slavery Society. Rankin was involved in the Lane Seminary abolitionist circles in which the Reverend and Mrs. Calvin Stowe moved, and Harriet Beecher Stowe later used Rankin's Ripley home as Eliza's goal over the frozen Ohio River. In 1838, when Ulysses attended the Presbyterian Academy, there was a trial in Ripley of a Rankin associate indicted in Kentucky for allegedly stealing a slave, whom he then hid in his Brown County temperance "tavern." The governor of Ohio had allowed extradition, and a onetime friend of Jesse Grant, Tom Hamer, had refused to defend the Ripley minister.[10]

If Jesse hoped that such surroundings might sway his son into joining the anti-slavery "apostles" filling Ohio, he was disappointed. Ulysses found his new school no better than the institution in Maysville. He followed his inclinations, avoided the central passions of the town, and whiled his time away on the

Ripley wharves. That Christmas, Jesse told him his Ohio education was over. He had applied for an appointment for Ulysses to
West Point. "But I won't go," Ulysses responded. His father, he
said, "thought I would, *and I thought so too, if he did.*"

Following normal routine, Jesse would have applied to Representative Tom Hamer for Ulysses's appointment to the Military
Academy, but instead he asked another Georgetown native, Senator Thomas Morris, who was sound on abolition, and defended
the same Rankin associate whom Hamer had earlier turned away.
Years later, when Jesse Grant said he "was never what was
technically known as an Abolitionist," he was not denying that
he had associated himself with the American Anti-Slavery Society, and it was likely he was relying on political connections when
he wrote to Morris. In this he was disappointed. Morris told Jesse
there was a vacancy for the Brown County district at West Point,
but that Representative Hamer was the only man who could fill
it. Never one to sacrifice practicality to pride, Jesse wrote Hamer
in Washington. Hamer made the appointment in the name of
"U.S. Grant," apparently thinking the boy's middle name was
Simpson.[11]

Georgetown was shocked by the news. "So Hamer has made
Ulysses a cadet," wondered a townsman to Jesse. "I am astonished that he did not appoint someone with intellect enough to do
credit to the district." The neighbor was no more surprised than
the appointee himself. "I really had no objection to going to West
Point," remembered Grant, "except that I had a very exalted idea
of the acquirements necessary to get through. I did not believe I
possessed them, and could not bear the idea of failing." He drove
to Cincinnati to buy an algebra book, but was not reassured. He
tried to understand it, he said, "but having no teacher it was Greek
to me."

Soon it was time to go. Ulysses had saved $100, which would pay
for his $75 passage and his uniforms. The $60 deposit demanded
by the academy and spending money came from Jesse. His uncle
Samuel Simpson and his cousin thought they might monogram his
hard leather trunk with his initials—H.U.G.—but, fearing his

classmates would call him "Hug," he rearranged the brass tacks to U.H.G. As Ulysses Hiram Grant, he said goodbye to his family on May 15. Next door, Mrs. Bailey wished him a tearful farewell. "Why, you must be sorry I am going," said young Ulysses. "They didn't cry at our house."

Freighted with the refurbished trunk, a fear of failure, and the fragile sensibilities of the often scorned, Grant embarked at Ripley for the East. The steamer to Pittsburgh made good time, and in only three days he left behind the river of his youth. "From Pittsburgh I chose passage by the canal to Harrisburg, rather than by the more expeditious stage. This gave a better opportunity of enjoying the fine scenery of Western Pennsylvania, and I had rather a dread of reaching my destination at all." He thought the train he took from Harrisburg to Philadelphia "perfection of rapid transit." Traveling eighteen miles an hour, it "seemed like annihilating space." He stayed five days in Philadelphia with a friend of Hannah's who found the five-one, 117-pound youngster "a rather awkward country lad, wearing plain clothes and large, coarse shoes as broad at the toes as at the widest part of the soles." The unprepossessing young man continued his trip via New York City, where he saw more sights, and then turned toward the Hudson and West Point. "When these places were visited I would have been glad to have had a steamboat or railroad collision, or any other accident happen, by which I might have received a temporary injury sufficient to make me ineligible, for a time, to enter the Academy. Nothing of the kind occurred, and I had to face the music."[12]

CHAPTER

4

THE DAY GRANT arrived at West Point, Robert Lee stood on the wharf at Guyandotte, Virginia, looking over the Ohio River in the direction Grant had gone. Lee was waiting for a steamer to take him to Cincinnati, where he would transfer to a paddleboat headed for St. Louis. Dressed in the uniform of a captain of engineers, the dark-eyed, handsome Virginian seemed out of place. The boys and men around him tended to look awkward and coarse, like Ulysses Grant. Lee's trip was not his first venture west. He had been working in St. Louis constructing dams and breakwaters on the Mississippi River for three years. But he still found his crude traveling companions amusing, and said he felt alone and "solitary" in that "strange crowd" of rough-hewn Westerners. Lee always responded to such feelings of isolation with extreme examples of the "gentlemanly deportment" praised by his boyhood teachers. Strangers often found him aloof. At West Point, fellow cadets who were excluded from his small social circle dubbed him the "Marble Model." There was much about his West Point career to warrant the title.[1]

THE UNITED STATES Military Academy had been open only twenty-three years when Robert Lee arrived by boat in June 1825. Though a house in which George Washington had headquartered during the Revolution was almost on the grounds, there was nothing about the place to suggest much history or grandeur. West Point commanded little but a noteworthy view of the Hudson River. Built on a bluff, the academy had a drill field, two dormitories, a mess hall, and a two-story schoolhouse. The architectural variety of the buildings was imperfectly disguised by a layer of stucco applied to create a uniformity that reflected the requirements of the school.

Once Lee had passed the easy entrance test, he bought the few items allowed by Army code: a broom and scrubbing brush, a tin pail, basin, washstand, and pitcher, and a mirror. He also purchased the regulation gray uniform, a dress uniform, and several caps—including a plumed leather-brimmed one reserved for special occasions and designed to excite the sensibilities of any teenage boy. All items were charged against his $16 monthly pay or $11 subsistence allowance. There were no classes in July and August, only four hours each day learning the rudiments of marching to command. In September the cadets moved indoors, and Lee and his seventy classmates took their oaths and registered. Oddly, he gave Westmoreland County, Virginia, as his place of residence, and said his half-brother, Harry Lee, was his guardian. It is possible that out of nervousness he mistook place of residence for place of birth. But more likely the young cadet was laying a prideful claim on the Revolutionary heritage of the Lees of Westmoreland, the same county which produced George Washington.

The school day began at sunrise with room inspection, followed by an unnourishing and often cold breakfast, three hours of mathematics, two of study, lunch, two hours of French, and drill. Lights were out at ten. The routine of Lee's first few months at the academy was broken briefly by a short visit from Lafayette, and by an equally interesting court-martial in which Cadet Jefferson Davis was found guilty for being off premises and using alcohol. As was usual in such cases, Davis was not dismissed. Regulations were so rigid that academy commanders expected occasional rebellion. Minor infractions, such as imperfectly groomed hair or a slightly disordered room, earned demerits. More egregious failings, such as drinking or fighting, were referred to the military court. Cadets were not allowed to smoke, play cards or other games, or perform in plays or on musical instruments. Visitors were discouraged, and, except for illness or a death in the family, students could not leave West Point until the end of their second year.

Lee actually enjoyed the routine, and did well academically. He stood fourth in mathematics and fifth in French after the June examinations. He'd earned no demerits, and was good enough on the drill yard to win an appointment as cadet sergeant for the following year—an honor usually reserved for older students. The demerit system was something to pit himself against, and he did so with such success that his tally was still zero at the end of his second year. He had improved at math and was asked to teach the subject during his third year.

Some West Point cadets found Lee intimidating, others described a young Adonis who bounded along the parade field "as if he spurned the ground on which he trod." Those closer saw a different and more complex Robert Lee. Cadet Joe Johnston, a Virginian whose father had served in the Revolution with Light-Horse Harry, said Lee "was full of sympathy and kindness, genial and fond of gay conversation, and even of fun." At the same time, "his correctness of demeanor and attention to all duties, personal and official, and a dignity as much a part of himself as the elegance of his person, gave him a superiority that every one acknowledged in his heart. He was the only one of all the men I have known that could laugh at the faults and follies of his friends in such a manner as to make them ashamed without touching their affection for him. . . ." It required a heightened sense of personal balance to be correct, dignified, and dependable on the one hand, and warm, genial, and fun-loving on the other, all the while denying familiarity through an ability to make men ashamed. This was the eighteenth-century ideal of the public man, and within this model it was unthinkable to behave in one's official capacity as one behaved with intimates. Lee's intimates were very few, and his official duties were many.[2]

At the end of his third year he was selected adjutant of the corps, an appointment that made him the most prestigious cadet

at the academy and enabled him to experience both the praise of
his associates and the grumblings of malcontents who felt the
position had been awarded along sectional lines. Southerners, it
was said, did well at West Point because they had the "habit of
command," learned ordering slaves around the plantation. Lee
had had no experience with plantation slaves, but he had spent
years commanding himself and had developed a studied attitude
about leadership. Student command at West Point "will make
you more liberal, more just," he later wrote. The cadet officer
must do his "duty, *honestly,* & *faithfully.* Without *favour* &
without *partiality.* Do not seek to report, but let it be seen that
though it gives you *pain,* still you *must* do your duty. That this
duty is *equal.* Never more or less rigid, but always the *same* &
your duty. The same as regards your dearest friend or worst
enemy. You will, thus gain esteem and affection & not dislike or
hatred. The *just* are always loved and never hated." Lee was right
on one count: The just are esteemed. They are seldom loved,
however, and often hated. His confusion was the melancholy
mistake of a lonely boy awarded with affection for an admirable
perfection.[3]

Lee visited Virginia in the summer of 1827, and returned to a
political world increasingly threatened by decay from within and
assault from without. The entire nation, but especially that part
of Virginia which claimed for itself an almost natural right to the
legacy of the American Revolution, was embroiled in the upcom-
ing presidential election, which was sure to be won by Andrew
Jackson. That would mark the end of the political hegemony of
Virginia's Golden Age. Riven with financial depression which
saw the planter economy nearly collapse in the first quarter of the
century, tidewater Virginia was losing control of the country. To
many Virginians, the American future seemed proof that the
Revolutionary ideal of refounding a Roman republic—where men
of property and education were willing to serve the common
good—had failed. What they saw as leather-apron democracy—in
which men of limited ability wanted to serve themselves—appeared to be emerging on a wave of mudsill votes. Few Americans

had been more clever in their defense of elite national republican-
ism than Alexander Hamilton. And Robert Lee in 1828 seemed
bent on learning all he could about Hamilton's thought. He
checked out of the West Point library Volume II of the 1810
edition of Hamilton's works, which included the essays he contributed to the *Federalist* in elegant defense of the Constitution. It
would have been unlike Lee to skim over any subject he wished
to pursue seriously, and it is plain from his having withdrawn the
book nine times that he found some difficulty in grasping Hamilton's subtleties.[4]

When Lee left West Point, he took with him a clear understanding of the politics of Hamilton, along with an excellent
record. Though he failed to graduate first in his class, his second
place allowed him to choose the branch of service he wanted. He
had no interest in his father's passion, the cavalry, and was commissioned a second lieutenant of engineers, the most prestigious
branch of the Army. He also got back $103 of his spending-money
account, and received perfect marks in deportment—not one demerit in four years. At the end of June, he boarded the Hudson
River steamer for New York and headed south, toward home, and
his mother.

Ann Carter Lee had given up the Alexandria house and moved
across the river to live with Carter, in Georgetown, where she
settled into a routine of discontent with her eldest son. "Alas,
alas," she wrote, "I wish I had my little boys Smith and Robert
living with me again." She invoked her "disease," which she called
"unconquerable," and sank into a final decline. She was moved to
the Fitzhugh plantation, Ravensworth, where she kept herself
alive until Robert returned.

A Lee relative remembered that during Ann's last days her
youngest son "mixed every dose of medicine she took, and he
nursed her day and night. If R[obert] left the room she kept her
eyes on the door until he returned. He never left her but for a
short time." She died on July 10.[5] Lee carried with him his whole
life the image of Ann on her deathbed. And years later he exhorted a similarly bereaved young man to think of the "efforts of
your heroic mother. Think what she accomplished. Think what

she did for you. . . . I know that your Mothers heart turned hopefully & trustfully to you in her last moments. Do not disappoint her. Endeavour to perform all your duties truly & faithfully. They become easier to you each day & every difficulty will yield to a firm determination to Conquer . . . No one Can help you & you must rely upon your own exertions." But that summer of 1829 Lee sought the kind of comfort in the company of a distant cousin—Mary Anna Randolph Custis—that he later distrusted.[6]

Mary was born October 1, 1808, at Annefield, a plantation set in Virginia's Clarke County. Her parents, Mary Lee Fitzhugh and George Washington Parke Custis, had been married for six years, and it was becoming clear that they were not particularly compatible. It had been an odd match from the beginning. Mary Fitzhugh's father, William, had nearly beggared his family with the lavish hospitality he dispensed from his elegant Georgian mansion on the Rappahannock, and may have found Custis's 15,000 acres of land and hundreds of slaves attractive. Little else about the young man qualified. Tiny, with small weak eyes, thin hair, and a narrow nose which hooked over his recessed chin, he was often abstracted and given to histrionics. Still, his father, John Parke Custis, was heir to an old and rich legacy in land and slaves, and his mother was a Maryland Calvert, granddaughter of Lord Baltimore. His grandmother Custis had married twice and done well each time. With her first she gained a fortune, with her second, George Washington. When Custis's father died at Yorktown, Martha Washington took him and his sister Nelly to be raised at Mount Vernon.[7]

In time, Washington adopted Custis, but proved less successful at fathering the boy than he did at fathering a country. He urged on his charge the qualities he valued and nourished in himself, but to no avail. In 1797 he admitted to Custis's teacher that from the boy's infancy "I have discovered an almost unconquerable disposition to indolence in every thing that did not tend to his amusement:—and have exhorted him in the most parental and friendly manner, often, to devote his time to more useful pursuits." After Washington's death in 1799, Custis lived on at Mount Vernon with his grandmother, who died in 1802. Since Mount Vernon reverted to Augustine Washington's descendants at the time of Martha Washington's death, Custis was homeless at twenty-two. He turned to 1,100 acres on the Potomac left him by his father, named it Arlington after the first Custis plantation on Virginia's Eastern Shore, and started to build a house. It was then that associates in northern Virginia began to know that Washington's assessment of his ward had been correct. Custis was an incorrigible dabbler. He modeled his new home after the temple of Theseus in Athens, and drew grand plans for a columned, two-story central portion flanked by two wings. But construction bogged down in a flood of financial insolvency caused by Custis's willful inattention to financial affairs. For years, nothing but the wings was completed, and little Mary Custis had to toddle from the dining room to her bedroom across an open field. Even when the main pavilion was erected in 1817, it remained an unpainted shell. It was in this central portion that Custis stored memorabilia from Mount Vernon.

George Washington may have suffered some anxiety over the idea of Custis as caretaker of the legacy of virtue, but Martha made certain her grandson was well endowed with worldly goods. When Custis moved out of Mount Vernon, he took with him the Washington china, the Washington silver, the Washington crystal, the Washington military gear, the Washington deathbed, even the Washington clothes. Such "relics," as they were styled, were less interesting to Custis than were the boxes of letters, notebooks, ledgers, and books he hauled out of Mount Vernon. On days when he was not attending the theater or making social visits in Washington City, Custis would mull over the neat script of his "father," scribbling notes, or turn to his easel, where he limned dreadful crayon representations of the founder. He rented out much of Arlington's land, and dedicated the remainder to a park where tourists from the capital were welcomed with lemonade and speeches. Northern visitors recorded their surprise over the dishabille of the proprietor and the impoverished quality of the plantation, but they were not as familiar with the nature of great houses in the South as were family friends.[8]

Southern plantations were first and foremost working farms.

Though manor houses incorporated varying degrees of luxury, and grounds were usually planted with carefully positioned trees and flower gardens, yards were often beaten bare by horses and wagons which were parked adjacent to the houses. Wash kettles, kilns, ovens, and woodpiles were scattered among dependent wooden shacks. Nearby, often in plain view, was housing for "the people"—as Virginians preferred to call their slaves—which might be neat whitewashed stucco cabins or a woeful conglomeration of wooden shanties. The provisional quality of Arlington, with its half-finished house, incomplete fences, patchy paint, and rutted driveway, was not unique. Plantation revenues often just covered the costs of feeding, clothing, and sheltering slaves. Rich families like the Custises were land-poor, which often meant slave-poor, only more nicely put.[9]

Years after Robert Lee first came visiting Mary Custis at Arlington, the wife of a South Carolina planter swore she had never met a southern woman who approved of slavery. Certainly, the Custis women did not. The later critic was outraged by the half-white slaves on her father-in-law's plantation, though it was not unusual for planters' sons to get their introduction to sex in the slave quarters. There are hints that Parke Custis indulged himself in such ways. Washington often wrote him warnings against "indolence," "vice," and "dissipation." The language could have been Enlightenment semantics, but Mount Vernon was home to many slaves, and Custis inordinately admired slightly unseemly women his entire life. But the most damning evidence was an 1859 newspaper account of an Arlington slave escape. The story was embroidered with a fictional drama aimed at embarrassing Robert Lee, but it named Custis, who was dead, not Lee, as father to fifteen half-white Arlington slaves.[10]

If Custis dallied in the "quarters," his wife would have seen it as one more example of the great moral wrong of slavery. Mary Fitzhugh was a deeply religious woman who governed her actions by strict Christian principles and even immersed herself in the intellectual rigors of ecclesiastical disputation. Her fundamentalist faith was very much like Hannah Grant's. Though good works could not remove the onus of sin, ignoring perceived evil was denying one's duty to God. Slavery, she thought, was evil. She introduced William Meade, Episcopal bishop of Virginia, to membership in Virginia's Colonization Society, which supported freeing slaves and sending them to Africa. Bishop Meade wrote to Mrs. Custis that he regarded liberation "as first in importance to our unhappy and I must say guilty land.—We make the sins of our Fathers our own, we clash our chains, we entail misery & vice upon our children by not adopting the most effectual me[thod] of removing an evil which grows with our growth & strengthens with our strength, and will soon outgrow us & bear us to the ground.—" Like most women in her position, Mary Custis assumed personal responsibility for Arlington's "people," providing for their food, clothing, and shelter, nursing them when they were ill or sending them to the Custis family physician, caring for their spiritual needs, and conducting a school for their children. In all this, she was helped by her daughter, Mary.[11]

When Robert Lee turned his attention to Mary Custis, she was twenty-one. She had her father's nose and chin, and the grim set of her mouth added austerity to her plainness. But her eyes— direct, clear, penetrating, and light brown—reflected intelligence and self-possession. Among her contemporaries she was thought to be a "young lady of sound and vigorous intellect" who had "the real artist temperament." She painted, like her father, but unlike Parke Custis, demonstrated some talent. She had a profound but uncritical attachment to literature and was accused by those who didn't share it of wasting all her time reading. Family intimates recalled that she "had received a fine classical education," which meant lessons in Latin and Greek, needlework and piano, mathematics and French. Mary never immersed herself in the social effervescence around her; even as a teenager, she watched from the sidelines, usually making wry observations on the passing scene. Her great passion was Arlington. She loved the beauty of the estate and often rode her mare Kate through the woods around her home in search of scenery and peace. She gardened, and could often be found up to her elbows in mud, digging and weeding. She liked to be alone, cared little for social conventions, was untidy, and had the habit of "losing everything that could be lost." She was gentle, sympathetic, and loving—the Arlington "people" were devoted to her—found great pleasure in the company of animals and children, and was said to have a heart "as unworldly and artless as a child's." She was also otherworldly and shared her mother's religiosity with such fervor that Robert Lee thought her piety "afflicted the sweet girl with a little of that over-righteousness which the bluelights brought into Virginia." Indeed, her tendency to be opinionated and outspoken—characteristics not admired in a culture where women were meant to charm—may well have offset the 30,000 acres which suitors knew would be hers. She apparently had few beaux.[12]

This complex and interesting young woman had been reared as the only child of George Washington's only adopted son. The Mount Vernon "relics" were in daily use, and Mary's father, who preferred to be called the "Child of Mount Vernon," devoted his life to tending the flame of Washington's memory. Mary dutifully sat through years of Custis's speeches on Washington's life and character. She was hostess when her father pitched Washington's campaign tent in Arlington's yard and invited international dignitaries to drink punch from Washington's bowl. Though neighbors found Custis ridiculous, and privately called him "old man eloquent," they never disputed his claim to the Washington legacy. Mary knew that that legacy, with all its perquisites and responsibilities, would one day be hers. So did Robert Lee.

Friends of Mary Custis said she fell in love with Lee during his second-year West Point furlough. She was not alone. Accounts of his "manly beauty and attractiveness of manner" followed his two-month 1827 tour through Virginia plantations, and a relative of Mary's wrote that "everyone was filled with admiration for his fine appearance and lovely manners." Lee was unusually handsome. Five feet ten inches tall and filling out to his mature weight of 180 pounds, he was broad-shouldered and erect. His hair was dark brown, almost black. A long, straight nose and a strong jaw lent character to the sensual mouth and languid black Carter eyes.

Lee followed Mary to Chatham, her Fitzhugh grandfather's estate, in the late summer of 1829. He sat beside the modestly dressed young woman with the smooth dark hair on the rolling Stafford Heights grounds across the Rappahannock from Fredericksburg. They talked about the future. Lee could not have been unaware that marrying Mary, as a friend said, "in the eyes of the world" would make him "the representative of the founder of American liberty." He certainly knew that the founder, like himself, had been an unlanded soldier with no money until he married the Custis fortune. If Parke Custis saw any similarities between Washington and Lee, he chose to ignore them—the child of Arlington could do better than an impoverished Lee. But Mary, like Ann Carter, insisted on having a Lee, and Mary's mother thought the young officer splendid. Mrs. Custis saw in Lee not only a faultless character but also a warm heart. "I have no fear of an excess of love when guided by wisdom; it seeks the best interest of its object." Outnumbered, Parke Custis agreed to the wedding.

Lee had followed family tradition by catching an heiress, but this particular woman would have appealed to him at any rate. He had known her since he was a child, was related to her, attended the same church, and visited the same friends. Mary's mother was sister to the Lees' landlord and mentor, William Henry Fitzhugh, and Mary's aunt, Nelly Lewis, had taken Lee to Washington to meet Secretary of War Calhoun. Ann Lee had died and was buried at Ravensworth, the home of Mary's uncle. Even Mary's father was close to the Lees as one of Light-Horse Harry's few supporters, thinking him merely unfortunate in his business dealings—sharing the same attitude about finance—and writing an impassioned defense of the elder Lee's anti-war Baltimore involvement. Lee was comfortable in the familiar company of the young woman who was almost like another sister to him. And though he admired enormously the charms of the Virginia belles, he admired even more Mary's unpretentious pride. Though she was far from beautiful, there was much about Mary Custis to remind Robert Lee of his mother.[13]

Two years elapsed before Mary and Robert were married. When Lee's post-graduation leave—extended because of his mother's death—was over in the autumn of 1829, he was ordered to Georgia, to prepare a fort site on Cockspur Island, a drop of land in the mouth of the Savannah River. The duty was unpleasant—much of Cockspur was below sea level—but there were compensatory pleasures. A classmate, Jack Mackay, invited Lee to meet his Savannah family, which included four beautiful sisters. Lee was captivated. He saw no harm in indulging in a little southern flirting, which caused Mackay family members to insist for generations that he had fallen in love with one of the girls. He admitted to "love dearly" Jack's witty eldest sister, Margaret, and he also admired the "sparkling black eyes" of Eliza, to whom he wrote playfully seductive letters for years. In Savannah, away from the constraints of West Point and the responsibilities of Alexandria, he found a place devoted to little more than having fun. In the spring of 1830, Lee needed to have fun.

That March, the scandal of Black-Horse Harry was resurrected, and this time the tale was not whispered about Virginia drawing rooms but resounded in the chambers of the United States Senate. Shortly after being inaugurated, President Jackson had named Harry Lee consul to Morocco. Jackson opponents used the confirmation process to air the story of Henry's Stratford and embarrass the President. The dreary affair had become current when Stratford's buyer defaulted and Black-Horse Harry sold the plantation again—this time to the husband of the sister-in-law who had borne his dead child. The confirmation went down in a wave of outrage. Black-Horse Harry fled to Paris, but Robert Lee had only the comforts of the Mackay house for refuge from the affair, which "blackened with his disgrace everyone that bore his name." Had Lee needed any reminders that misplaced affections were potentially disastrous, his half-brother's ruin served the purpose well. Within the year Lee was transferred to Virginia, and he had Mary set their wedding date.[14]

Hundreds of candles lit the interior of Arlington house, which got a rare polishing for the wedding on June 30, 1831. Mrs. Fitzhugh emptied Ravensworth's cupboards to augment the scanty linen supply and sent over well-trained dining-room slaves to help serve the "feast." Nelly Custis Lewis played the piano as

Mary, tall and slender, the gown designed by Washington's most chic couturier billowing from her twenty-inch waist, on the arm of her father descended the staircase. The ceremony was conducted in the unfinished great hall disguised for the occasion with a huge flowered bell and garlands of spring blossoms. Lee wrote Andrew Talcott, his commanding officer, that there was "nothing strange" at his wedding. "The Parson had few words to say, though he dwelt upon them as if he had been reading my Death warrant, and there was a tremulousness in the hand I held that made me anxious for him to end. I am told I looked 'pale and interesting,' which might have been the fact. But I felt as 'bold as a sheep' & was surprised at my want of courage (?) in so great a degree as not to feel more excitement than that at the Black Board at West Point."[15]

Nineteenth-century Virginia wedding parties lasted for days, and the Lees' was no exception. Second-day festivities began at dawn, and that evening Mary wore a hugely plaided silk dress of blue, cerise, and dark green, which made her brown eyes look even darker. After a week of dancing, punch-drinking from the Washington bowl, and storytelling at Arlington, guests repaired to the home of General John Mason for another week of festivities. When the company finally broke up, the newlyweds and Mary's mother began a series of family visits to Woodlawn and Ravensworth, where Lee wrote Talcott that his bride and mother-in-law had been sick. "Their health has been re-established though not their looks," he admitted. Playing nursemaid on his honeymoon seems not to have bothered him overmuch. He was excited about setting up housekeeping at Fortress Monroe, his new assignment, and left with Mary in August.

Washed by Chesapeake Bay, which emptied into the Atlantic Ocean below Virginia's Eastern Shore on the East, and by Hampton Roads on the south and west, Fortress Monroe was built on the site of the fashionable resort, Old Point Comfort. The fort was part of a series of coastal defenses Congress hoped would put an end to embarrassments such as the English fleet sailing unmolested up the James to Richmond during the Revolution. Lee was to help build a moat around the outer works and shore up the seawall escarpments. Subtly deferential to superiors, he was also able to exert the mildest sort of coercion on his crew of enlisted men and hired slaves. He ran a smooth operation which progressed on schedule, and on budget. But he was not as successful on his new domestic front.[16]

Mary was twenty-three when she married, but her only ventures away from home had been visits to relatives. She had never liked parties, and was unaccustomed to fitting herself into a schedule based on something other than whim. Nothing was quite right for Robert Lee's bride at Old Point. The Lees lived in two rooms in a yellow brick barracks, and Mary kept to herself. She wrote her mother that there was only one "actively pious" family on the base, and she hadn't even met them. She disapproved of the careless way Old Pointers handled their slaves and devoted herself to Bible-reading. But she worried that her faith was weak, and confessed to her mother that she often found herself listlessly perusing "what ought to be my highest pleasures." A newly married woman might be forgiven a certain laxness in the pursuit of religion, but Mary's depression seemed general. She wanted to take a trip, "but we have not fixed any time yet," and she longed for "one stroll on the hills at Arlington this bright day. The only objection I have to this place is it is so public that you can never go out alone except sometimes to bathe, but I must add that I have a husband always ready to go with me when his duties will permit. I must give him a little just commendation sometimes."[17]

Mrs. Custis was as unhappy as her daughter over their first separation, and started to agitate for the couple's return. She told Mary a friend "thinks as your Father is so literary a character that he would find it greatly to his advantage to withdraw Robert from his present profession and yield to him the management of affairs" at Arlington. Lee would hardly have welcomed such patronization and he had no desire to live with Mary in what he said was the lack of privacy at her home. But he did agree to a holiday visit there, and took time from the round of Christmas parties to write a letter of congratulation to Eliza Mackay, whose recent marriage, he said, had kept him "in tears ever since at the thought of losing you." He commiserated with her wedding-day nerves, standing before the "Parson with all eyes bent on you (except one pair) he mournful and solemn as if he were reading your funeral service. A man feels of so much, and I am sure, he could not add to the stillness of the scene though he were dead." Mary added a sour little postscript which was no more heartening than Lee's metaphor of the funereal wedding. She hoped Eliza's "pathway in life may be as bright as our beneficent Creator and Father sees best for you," she said. "I am now a wanderer on the face of the earth and know not where we are going next and hope it will be East. I suppose you remain in Savannah near your Mother? What happiness! I am with mine now—the past and the future disregarded."[18]

After Christmas, Mary opted for a more pleasant future and let Lee return to Fortress Monroe alone. What may have been planned as a lengthy holiday visit became a six-month stay, for Mary was pregnant. Lee kept busy with work on the fort and with the social life of Old Point—which he thoroughly enjoyed—but he pressured Mary throughout the spring of 1832 to return to him. He moved into more spacious private rooms, and used permanent housekeeping as an attraction to his wife, but Mary wanted to furnish their new apartment with Arlington goods. Lee balked. "I know your dear Mother will be for giving you everything she has, but you must recollect *one* thing & that is, that they have been accustomed to comforts all their life, which now they could not dispense with and that we in the commencement ought to contract our wishes to their smallest compass & enlarge them as opportunity offers." Mary gave in on that score, but refused to make other plans. Six weeks later Lee complained that she had "but few purchases made."

Domesticity failing, Lee took up another weapon. In April, he wrote that he had been escorting ladies about the post. "Think of that Mrs. Lee! and hasten down, if you do not want to see me turned out a Beaux again. How I did strut along with one hand on my whiskers & the other elevating my coat tail! And my whole face thrown into the biggest grin I could muster. Surely it was a sight for the Old Pointers to see, and I only wish you could have been of the numbers. How you would have triumphed in my happiness." No response. Mary Lee seemed incapable of even rudimentary jealousy. So Lee changed his tack again. Apparently at his father-in-law's request, he made a visit to Smith Island, a piece of Custis land in Chesapeake Bay, and took the opportunity to look at farms on Virginia's Eastern Shore. He was impressed by what he saw. "The land is fertile & productive & strange to tell (for the South) the people are sober and *industrious.*" The farms were small, he said—"two, three, four hundred acres"—but choice, and he implied an interest in buying one. "I saw a very pretty little farm on the Atlantic side with some improvements on it, House etc., that sold for $10 per acre." Lee's inheritance from his mother would just pay for the farm, which might satisfy Mary's objections to life at the post. But not any farm would do. Lee gave up the idea and deposited money in a savings account.[19]

Only when Mrs. Custis agreed to bring her to Fortress Monroe did Mary return, with the help of "providence," said Lee, "in whom I know you have confidence." She spent the summer working on her little house and garden, walking on "this beautiful beach," and doing needlework at night "while Robert reads to me." Their child, a boy, was born September 16 and was named George Washington Custis Lee. Mary was ecstatic. Her letters reported every prattle, drool, and smile made by "Boo," "Bunny," "Bun," "Bouse," or "Dunket"—the pet names varied. Lee referred to the baby as Mary's "limb," but admitted to Jack Mackay that Custis was beautiful. The new family, not unexpectedly, went to Arlington for Christmas. Equally predictably, Mary and the baby stayed on while Lee rode overland back to Fortress Monroe—"up to my ears in mud and alone."[20]

The next few years were relatively happy ones for the Lees despite the strains of mutual accommodation to their strong dissimilarities. Mary continued to make long visits to Arlington, and when she was at Fortress Monroe, preferred a quiet evening at home reading Fénelon, the Bible, or Latin verse. Lee, on the other hand, immersed himself in the social life of the post, which he chronicled in clever reports to absent friends. He began judiciously to indulge his taste for excellent clothing.

Joe Johnston, who said Lee could make people feel ashamed without feeling angry, accompanied him to bachelor parties, but where Johnston played the participant, Lee was an amused on-looker. Guests were amazed that Lee was a social lion even though he "never uttered a word among his most intimate associates that might not have been spoken in the presence of the most refined woman." And refined women were Lee's favorite companions. He wrote to Jack Mackay during one of Mary's absences that he was "consoling" the wives of men ordered off to the Seminole War. Old Point's "daughters of Eve," he said, were "framed in the very poetry of nature & would make your lips *water* & fingers *tingle.*" He went on to instruct his old classmate to tell the Mackay women—including Eliza—that he was "famishing for the sight of them. The idea alone thrills through my heart like the neigh of my blooded stallion." He declared himself as happy as a "clam at high water" when Mary and her mother left, but insisted he "would not be unmarried for all you could offer me. Hope never again to interfere in the remotest way with the prerogatives of you Bachelors. A Bad life *(for me)* to lead, Flat, stale & unprofitable."[21]

His marriage was none too profitable in the fall of 1833. Lee and Mary were arguing. "I don't know that I shall ever overcome my propensity for order & method," Lee wrote to her. "But I will try. And as I have lately learned such good reasons against it, I hope they will weaken my idea of their necessity, which will tend much to diminish my predilection." It was inevitable that the styles of the fastidious son of Ann Lee and the careless daughter of Parke Custis would clash, but Lee was thoroughly miserable. "My Sweet little Boy what would I give to see him! The house is a perfect desert without him & his Mother. I am waking all night to hear his sweet little voice & if in the morning I could only feel his little arms around my neck & his dear little heart fluttering against my breast, I should be too happy. The want of so much that I have been accustomed to drives me from my bed sometimes before day." Lee's anguish centered on Boo. His marriage, it seemed, had settled into a routine which Mary shared.

"I often long for a little rural scenery," she wrote during an

1834 stay at Fortress Monroe, "but ought not to complain of what I have not when I have so many comforts & especially that of a tender & affectionate husband who spends his evenings at home instead of frequenting the card parties which attract so many . . ." It was faint praise which did little to offset a major criticism. She swore her mother to secrecy before sharing the disappointing news. "I cannot but feel that he still wants the one thing needful without which all the rest may prove valueless; Oh that I could pray for this with the faith which can remove mountains—We read the Bishop's pastoral letter which he pronounced very excellent but made no further comment." To a woman of Mary's religious training, humankind was divided into two categories, and only two: the saved and the damned. God determined who would be saved, but it was necessary to acknowledge His presence, and to allow the redemption of Christ to infuse the body and soul. If her husband denied this saving grace, then his goodness, his affection and his tenderness were in truth "valueless" to her.[22]

Lee, however, had the upper moral hand in child-rearing. During Mary's Christmas visit to Arlington, he told her not to let the infant Custis "be spoiled, direct him in *every* thing & leave *nothing* to the Guidance of his Nurse." She was open to such admonitions. "If his energies can only be well directed," she wrote about the baby, "they may be the means of much usefulness. But I already shrink from the responsibility. It requires so much firmness & consistency to train up a child in the right way & I know that I am so remiss in the government of my servants & so often neglect to correct them when they do wrong. I must endeavor with God's assistance to be more faithful."

Lee had seen his half-brother and half-sister grow up bad without Ann Lee's consistent rigors, and his brother Carter had softened into self-indulgence. Leisure, money, the availability of easy sex in the slave quarters, a code of behavior that rewarded displays of temperament and violence, and a social system lubricated by alcohol were dangers which lured the unwary Virginian. Like George Washington, Lee could avoid such pitfalls not only because of self-restraint but also because of a youth spent in relative poverty. The anxious warnings Washington had sent young

Parke Custis were to be repeated by Lee to Parke Custis's grand-children. And Mary had very early come to doubt that she could set a proper example for her children. It was a difficult situation, one which Lee often used against her.[23]

By 1835, Lee had almost lost the Arlington battle. When he was ordered to Washington to serve as assistant to the chief of engi-neers, he predictably failed to find suitable housing in the city. The Lees settled in Mary's home, and she began to prepare for the birth of their second child.

Washington was a bucolic backwater where farm animals ran loose across the grounds of government buildings and goats grazed on the Capitol lawn. Walks were board and roads were mud. Public accommodations were primitive. But a handful of good houses sprinkled the area, and the town hummed with activ-ity when Congress was sitting. Lee hated office duty, but he liked the social life of the capital, and he went to an officer's "mess" frequented by old Fortress Monroe acquaintances when the weather was bad and he couldn't get back to Arlington. He was having fun. "Your humble servant," he wrote his former com-mander, "has returned to a state of rejuvenescency . . . and has attended some weddings and parties in a manner that is uncom-mon. My brother Smith was married on the 5th inst. and the Bride I think looked more beautiful than usual. We kept agoing till Sunday and . . . my spirits were so buoyant last night, when relieved from the eyes of my Dame, that my sister Nanie was trying to pass me off as her spouse, but I was not going to have my sport spoiled that way, undeceived the young ladies and told them I was her younger brother. Sweet innocent things, they concluded I was single and I have not had such soft looks and tender pressure of the hand for many years." "Washington is filled to overflowing," he wrote Jack Mackay, "Bank, Bank, Deposites speeches, Memorials, wrangling & quarelling & dou-bling of fists—very gay. Two or Three parties every night. The Ladies by their mild & winning ways at night endeavoring to calm the storms that rage by day. . . . Went to Baltimore, saw all the pretty girls, but I believe you know none of them. Saw John

Magruder, poor fellow ordered to Beaufort, N.C. . . . J. E. Johnston waiting in the *Alabama* for orders, nothing to do & never has been. Intended to amuse themselves by giving large party, but the Ladies got *drunk* & could not come."[24]

Lee honored his "rejuvenescency" by gently teasing Washington conventions—observers remembered for fifty years his inviting a friend to share a horse and giving a tandem bow to the Secretary of the Treasury as they passed the White House—and by hosting several small dinner parties which thoughtfully included sleeping accommodations for guests who might indulge too freely in his hospitality. But the expense of keeping up socially worried him, and when Congress voted a pay cut for Army officers, he requested a transfer.

In the spring of 1835 he joined Andrew Talcott as assistant astronomer in a trek to the Northwest to settle the dispute between Ohio and Michigan over their common state line. He expected to return within a month, but the work was slow—storms over Lake Erie and sluggish politicians complicated matters—and Lee was still in Michigan when a girl her mother named Mary Custis was born. The delivery was apparently difficult, and Mary went "riding out" too soon. Enflamed lymph nodes in the groin and thrombophlebitis were treated by cupping—the application of leeches to the abscess—which caused her "exquisite pain," but amazingly didn't kill her. She was very ill, and apparently frightened, and wrote her husband on August 13 to come home.[25]

Lee's response to Mary was a full expression of the character she had once admired. There was no hint of the young cavalier in the letter:

> But why do you urge my *immediate* return, & tempt one in the *strongest* manner, to endeavour to get excused from the performance of a duty, imposed on me by my Profession, for the pure gratification of my private feelings? Do you not think that those feelings are enough of themselves to contend with, without other aggravation; and that I rather require to be strengthened & encour-

aged to the *full* performance of what I am called on to execute, rather than excited to a dereliction, which even our affection could not palliate, or our judgement excuse? It is this first part Mary that I had expected from you; and the last is so contrary to your good sense, patient disposition & the conduct you have hitherto pursued, that it must be caused by an indisposition, greater I fear than you acknowledge to me. Yet in your calmer moments, I am sure you would not have me to succeed, & an attempt without success would be more mortifying, in what would prove me less worthy of your love than I would hope to be, & plainly shew to the Dept.: that I am one of those fair Weather Gentlemen whose duty & pleasure must go together; or that if I should be called on to sacrifice the latter, I cannot be trusted to execute the former . . . You see therefore dear Mary, that however strongly I may be tempted by my own feelings, backed by your request, I cannot in conscience do what you ask. And that however harassing will be to me the idea, that your recovery may be retarded by a delay of my return, I must not consent to do aught that would lower me in your eyes, my own & that of others. . . .

Lee can be forgiven his assumption that he had no duty to Mary—their life together had convinced him that her greatest support was her childhood home. But he was unwilling to assume the obligations of his choice. By assigning to his family the status of "pleasure," he was able to remove any claims domestic responsibilities might have on him. Moreover, it was Mary's responsibility to see that the pleasure was unalloyed: "And now that you see my situation in its proper light, will you not cheerfully consent to a few more weeks absence, and not let an over anxiousness on your part, deprive me of the pleasure of seeing my wife & children *well & happy* on my return; it will be a poor return for the sacrifice I have already made to duty, to find that it has cost me so dear. . . ." Mary was to ensure his reward, and Lee went on to urge her to "cheer up & pack up" and go on a visit to the up-country. He was considerably heartened by his own advice, and waxed lyrical about his return to "dear Arlington—How happy shall we all be once more. And you will be well & hearty too

Molly, & its Pa'a will see his *little daughter* & his *Boo,* who will be a *very* good Boy, & our dear Mothers face will smile so kindly and serenely happy on her children."[26]

Lee's insisting could not make it so. When he returned to Virginia in mid-October he found Mary in "constant and corroding pain," "dreadfully reduced" at Ravensworth, the house in which his mother had died. He immediately moved her to Arlington and summoned doctors she apparently was too modest to call. She never fully recovered. She was bedridden more than four months, and could not walk until the spring of 1836. When she finally had strength enough to sit in bed, she hacked off the mat of hair tangled by her immobility, then wrote to Mrs. Talcott inquiring about the cost of a silver comb Lee had brought her from Michigan. "I have lost all my fine suit of hair, I may as well dispose of it," she said. "I scolded Robert for getting it. . . ."[27]

A relative said she had never seen "a man so changed and saddened" as Lee. He reentered the Corps of Engineers office in Washington, but was careful, now, always to return to Arlington exactly at three. He gave up entertaining and fell back into his boyhood nursing habits. But the routine, brightened by Boo and the new baby, called "Daughter"—Arlington's "brightest flower," said her father—began to grate, and he toyed with the idea of looking for a civilian job. As an Army engineer, he wrote Talcott, "you are expected to work to the extent of your abilities *always* to receive no advantages . . . but to reap all the abuse that every petty-fogger and political demagogue can find time to heap upon you." He advised Jack Mackay's brother not to enter the cavalry because of "abstract regret" over "any friend of mine incurring the indiscriminate and unmerited abuse, which is now so lavishly heaped upon all members of the Regular Army."[28]

American politicians did abuse the Army. When state militias proved inadequate, legislators gave up their opposition to a standing army and a military academy, but kept both small and weak. At the outbreak of the Civil War, there were fewer than 16,000 soldiers in the Army. In the mid-1830s, there were fewer still, and they were increasingly attacked by the Democratic Party, which saw a national army as one more threat to the political supremacy of the states. The rate of promotion—Lee waited seven years for a first lieutenancy—and the pay scale—he was earning only several hundred dollars a year—served to keep politicians happy and guarantee a steady supply of West Point–educated employees to private business.

In the late winter of 1837 Lee told Talcott he had few prospects in the Corps. "There is one thing certain, I must get away from here. . . . I should have made a desperate effort last spring, but Mary's health was so bad I could not have left her, and she could not have gone with me." Still, he procrastinated, he said, and behaved as if the opportunity to leave Washington was "to drop in my lap like a ripe pear."

Two months later he got not a pear, but a plum—Joseph Totten, the chief engineer, assigned him to superintend the re-channeling of the Mississippi River at St. Louis. Lee was delighted. He stayed with Mary until she delivered William Henry Fitzhugh Lee in early June, then went overland to Pittsburgh, where he caught a steamer for Louisville. Lee often stood on deck, making mental gibes at western passengers, chatting with "a handsome young widow," and looking at the scenery. The second day out he passed Maysville, Kentucky, which Ulysses Grant had just left because of not making "progress enough" at his school.

Lee thought the *domestic* filth" of St. Louis "revolting," and housing "hard to get, badly arranged," and expensive. "The lower class are a swaggering, noisy set," he said, "careless of getting work except occasionally for which they get high wages and which goes at the Theater & etc., but a well disposed people in the main too and somewhat amusing." Though he found the better sort of people "very kind and friendly," he subtly criticized their uncultured Yankee proclivities for being "engrossed in business in which too it Seems their pleasures all Consist." The land around St. Louis was "rich and fertile," he said, "but little improved, and having been originally prairie is *growing* up in *shrubby trees.*"

Despite its squalor and violence, St. Louis in the 1830s was one of America's most cosmopolitan areas. Every day when the river wasn't frozen, boatloads of Easterners arrived to be outfitted for wagon-train treks to free land in the territories. French-speaking Creoles from Louisiana threaded through crowds of French-speaking trappers on leave from the Missouri Breaks. Bawdy houses flourished amid homes of German burghers on the way to becoming merchant princes. The city was a boom town, and Lee looked for property to buy.

When Lee, his assistant Montgomery Meigs, and a draftsman went upriver in the summer of 1837 to study the rapids, he wrote excited, touristy letters describing thriving little communities—he singled out Galena—miles of prairies, and Chippewa Indians "sick with whiskey," who always wanted *"Eat."* Despite his obvious good mood, he told Mary he was anxious for news from his family because "there alone I can expect pleasure or happiness." The letter that finally arrived from Arlington made him distinctly unhappy.[29]

"Our dear little Boo Seems to have among his friends a *reputation* of being hard to manage, a distinction not at all desirable, as it indicates a Self will and obstinacy. Perhaps these are qualities which he really possesses and he may have a better *right* to them than I may be willing to acknowledge. But it is our duty if possible to counteract them and assist him to bring them under his control." He went on to enumerate his methods of fathering, carefully explaining the reasons for each, and ended by confessing that he had "altogether failed" as a parent. Lee sometimes called his family his pleasure. In this letter he alluded to the duty of parenting. In his view, it was permissible only to do one's duty, not to seek one's pleasure. It was imperative, therefore, to divine which was which, and in the autumn of 1837 he turned, for the first time, to God's arbitration. "I pray God," he wrote Mary, "to watch over and direct our effort in guarding our dear son, that we may bring him up 'in the way he should go.' "[30]

Mary may have felt that her own prayers had been answered with her husband's turning to God. The following spring she rewarded Lee with the unlikely decision to return with him to St. Louis after his winter holiday at Arlington. They set out with little Custis and the baby, nicknamed "Rooney," at the end of March, stayed several days in Baltimore, and went on to Philadelphia, where they took up the same route Ulysses Grant traveled a year later, and Mary had her first train ride—the one Grant would describe as "perfection of rapid transit"—followed by a trip on a steamboat boarded at Pittsburgh. From Blennerhasset Island, where Light-Horse Harry Lee's friend Aaron Burr planned liberty or treason, to Cincinnati, she could stand on deck and watch the watery no-man's-land of the anti-slavery movement. At Ripley, the roof of John Rankin's Academy was just visible from the wharf where the Lees put up.[31]

The Custis family involvement in the Virginia Colonization Society would not have prepared Mary for Missouri in 1838. A year earlier, anti-slavery publisher Elijah Lovejoy had fled from St. Louis to Alton, Illinois, just across the river, where he set up a new printing press. The Revolutionary-era tradition of cranking out rebellious broadsides had been resumed in the early 1830s, and augmented with steam. Hundreds of thousands of abolitionist tracts could be broadcast nationwide. Anti-abolitionists fought back with attacks on presses which were also aimed at frightening freed blacks. Lovejoy's Illinois office was stormed, and he was killed. Two hundred miles north of Alton, in Springfield, a young lawyer used the incident to decry the "mobocratic spirit" which he thought was threatening the work of the Founders. Abraham Lincoln had made his first important speech.[32]

In St. Louis, supporters of slavery defended the Alton mob from the abolitionists, who claimed Lovejoy as the first martyr in their holy war against the South. As Southerners who did not support slavery, the Lees found themselves in an ironic predicament, one that mirrored their reaction to an earlier incident which was indirectly responsible for the St. Louis response to Elijah Lovejoy's death.

Shortly after the newlywed Lees arrived at Fortress Monroe, Virginia, in 1831, the commander of the post called out his troops to suppress a long-feared slave revolt in South Hampton, forty miles up the James. Lee wrote his mother-in-law a detailed description of what came to be called the Nat Turner Rebellion, citing instances of slaves "defending their masters," and describing one slave who was "shot dead" by twenty blacks. "I am glad that no further mischief was done," he concluded, "& hope it is all at an end." The insurrection, in which more than sixty slaves had been involved in the murder of almost sixty whites, *was* at an end, and with it went Virginia's flirtation with emancipation.

Immediately after the uprising, a convention met in Richmond to decide the status of slavery in Virginia. Of the 132 delegates assembled, 58 were committed to emancipation and 60 backed slavery, but the 14 uncommitted delegates eventually went to the pro-slavery side, convinced that freeing the slaves not only would disrupt the balance of political power within the state—where a slave was counted as three-fifths of a person—but would also create havoc with the already precarious relations between the races.

Mary's mother was distressed. Some of the people she talked to, she wrote, "think that as the Liberator is edited in Boston and the authorities of the United States do not prevent it, *therefore* the whole New England states are arrayed against us, and that the final remedy must be *now* and *separation*. A conclusion about as logical as many others that are made under the influence of passion or prejudice." Lee remembered that everyone "fully expected" emancipation to carry "at the next convention." But there was no next emancipation convention. A change had occurred in Virginia while Robert Lee worked to keep the Atlantic Ocean out of Fortress Monroe, and its effects were apparent in St. Louis in 1838 when the Lees settled there.[33]

By June the Lees were living in a pleasant apartment which overlooked the Mississippi River. Mary read Coleridge, Shelley, Wordsworth, and Goldsmith, looked to the care of Custis and Rooney, occasionally paid calls on a few locals, and wrote her mother for a portrait of "Daughter," who was considered too dainty for the western wilds and was kept at Arlington. She was pregnant again, and said she found looking after Rooney—"such an unsettled brat"—tiresome. Lee's work was generally going well and St. Louis inhabitants were delighted with the restoration of their river, but Lee wrote Mackay that he wished *"all* were done and I was back in Virginia." He also responded to congratulations over his promotion to captain by saying that if he had the money, he would retire "to some quiet corner among the hills of Virginia where I can indulge my natural propensities without interruption." He didn't say what those propensities were, but he admitted that "the more comfortably I am fixed in the Army, the less likely I shall be to leave it." He dabbled in family genealogy, read, and wrote letters to his mother-in-law in which he tried to assert his greater claim on his wife and children than the one by the Custises.

Mary's mother had stepped up pressure on her daughter to come home and on Lee to leave the Army. Lee now patronizingly called his father-in-law "the Major," and his responses to Mrs. Custis ranged from the humorous—"Suppose you and the Major break up and campaign with us!"—to the self-pitying—"you know Mother a man ought not to be separated from his children." He even gave Mrs. Custis a painstaking explanation for what she obviously thought was his stealing her family. It was his "duty," he said, "to make a sacrifice, and even a great one, to try and advance myself in my profession, and be thereby enabled to give our dear children such an education and standing in life as we could wish."[34]

He also told Mrs. Custis he had been "provoked" into replying to her charge that Mary's living in St. Louis was an "impropriety." On the contrary, he said, "it has appeared to me highly *proper* to be as much as possible with my wife and children." In a rare display of sarcasm, Lee turned his mother-in-law's own religious doctrines against her. "If we could and you would permit it," he said, "we would locate ourselves at Arlington and I would have $20,000 a *year* to put everything in Apple-pie order and make us all comfortable. Then Mother we could all live together, enjoy the daily expansion of our little children and witness their improvement in knowledge & goodness and beauty—But as Such a life would be too happy for us and prevent us from thinking of a better—So it has been *determined* that it cannot be and we must try and be Satisfied with that which has been allotted to us."

Lee lost. It was he who had to try and be satisfied. He took Mary and the children back to Arlington in the spring of 1839. When he returned to St. Louis that summer, he was alone. He continued working on the Mississippi for two more years, but Mary and the children never came back.[35]

CHAPTER

5

WHEN GRANT arrived at West Point in the summer of 1839, no one seemed to know who he was. He tried to register as Ulysses Hiram Grant and was told there was no such person on the roster. Could he be U.S. Grant? Grant assumed the error could be corrected. No, he had to enter as named. Stretching the truth to save face, Grant stiffly told the adjutant his name made "no particular difference" to him, and signed in.

The name already had caused some hilarity among Grant's new schoolmates. When the list of incoming plebes was posted on the academy bulletin board, fourth-year man William Tecumseh Sherman suggested the initials stood for "United States" or "Uncle Sam" and joined the laughter when "U.S." turned out to be, not a tall and lanky Yankee, but a small, rosy-cheeked Ohioan. "A more unpromising boy never entered the Military Academy," Sherman said of the plebe, and promptly dubbed him "Sam."[1]

Grant, for his part, didn't think much of the academy. He was embarrassed by his reception from his classmates, hated the regimentation, and discovered that, try as he might, he could not march in time. Worst of all was the demerit system. He wrote a cousin that the authorities "give a man one of these 'black marks' for almost nothing, and if he gets two hundred a year they dismiss him." He had recently seen an astonishing example of such unreasonableness. "To show how easy one can get these, a man got eight of the 'marks' for not going to church. He was also put under arrest so he cannot leave his room perhaps for a month and all this for not going to church. We are not only obliged to go to church, but must march there by companies." Grant had grown up believing that he was "compensated" for hard work and exact obedience to his parents by never receiving any "scolding or punishing." His outrage over what he considered the excessive rigidity at West Point thinly concealed his anxiety. He always wanted to do what was expected of him, to be good, but when a boy could be arrested for not going to church, how was it possible to be good enough?

Grant tried. He couldn't bear the idea of failing, and his father was keeping nervous tabs on his progress through the office of Colonel Joseph Totten, Robert Lee's commander and executor of the academy. Such vigilance couldn't have heartened the boy, and his first year at West Point was one of precipitous mood swings. Though he later remembered thumbing through newspapers to see if Congress was really going to disband the academy, as he hoped, he just as eagerly indulged himself in the romance of "this prettiest of places West Point." He wrote an Ohio relative that from his window he could see "the Hudson; that far famed, that beautiful river with its bosom studded with hundreds of snow sails. Again if I look another way I can see Fort Putnam frowning far above; a stern monument of a sterner age which seems placed there on purpose to tell us of the glorious deeds of our fathers and to bid us remember *their* sufferings—to follow their examples. In short this is the best of all places—the *place* of all *places* for an institution like this. I have not told you *half* its attractions. Here is the house Washington used to live in . . . Over the river we are shown the duelling house of Arnold, that *base* and *heartless* traiter *to* his country and his God. I do love the *place*. It seems as though I could live here forever if my friends would only come too."

It was the *place* he loved, not the people, and he even invented a pack of Georgetown buddies to miss. Still, he could see that Jesse had been right in sending him to West Point. "I would not go away on any account," he said, "if a man graduates here, he is safe fer life, let him go where he will." The pursuit of safety was a restrictive quest for an eighteen-year-old, but this was Jesse Grant's son, just beginning to grapple with the wilderness outside the Ohio woods.[2]

Grant did well enough the first year. He accumulated only fifty-nine "black marks"—all for general scruffiness rather than disobedience—and finished twenty-seventh out of sixty cadets. Rufus Ingalls, a classmate, described Grant as "careless and lazy." Instead of studying a lesson, he "would merely read it over once or twice; but he was so quick in his perceptions that he usually made very fair recitations. . . . His memory was not at all good in an attempt to learn anything by heart." Grant admitted that he "did not take hold of studies with avidity," and looked for other ways to fill up his time. The restriction on extracurricular reading had been lifted and Grant used the library often. "Much of the time, I am sorry to say, was devoted to novels, but not those of a trashy sort." The books offered adventure and escape and gave him, at least vicariously, the companionship he craved and apparently wasn't getting. He read, he said, because he "could not sit in my room doing nothing."

Years later, dozens of men who had shared Grant's days at the academy claimed intimate friendship with him. But in fact he was largely ignored. "He was not particularly tidy about his dress," said a fellow student, "and he even had a certain slouchy air about him that many of the class thought unsoldierly, but he never did anything positively offensive, and, as he was always quiet and attended to his own affairs, we liked him well enough, but only in a negative way." Grant joined no clubs his first year, attended no dances or receptions, and kept clear of the roistering fellowship at Benny Haven's tavern. Sam Grant, it was remembered, "exhibited but little enthusiasm for anything."

His clearest memory of that first year was a visit from Winfield Scott, head of the United States Army. Grant was thrilled with the general. "With his commanding figure, his quite colossal size and showy uniform, I thought him the finest specimen of manhood my eyes had ever beheld, and the most to be envied." What was most remarkable, though, was the rush of ambition stimulated in the unsoldierly little cadet from Ohio by this military giant. "I did have a presentiment for a moment," Grant confessed later, "that some day I should occupy his place." Such a presentiment, which was more like an aspiration, had to be kept secret. He dared not share his excitement, he said, because the ridicule of that infamous Georgetown horse trade of his was still "too fresh" in his mind.[3]

But just as horsemanship had once before saved his reputation from complete ruin, so it did at West Point. Cavalry training had been added to the curriculum, and Grant, during his second year, had a chance to show his stuff. Pete Longstreet, a huge bear of a young man, recalled Grant as too "girlish" and "delicate" to participate in contact sports, but also as "the most daring horseman in the academy." This show of talent was completely unexpected. "He was a tiny-looking little fellow, with an independent air," said a fellow West Pointer, "and a good deal of determination. . . . I can still see Grant, with his overalls strapped down on his boots, . . . going to the riding hall, with his spurs clanging on the ground, and his great cavalry sword dangling by his side." Grant always chose the largest and most fractious horses, and soon outshone even the riding instructors. "It was as good as any circus to see Grant ride," said a cadet. "The whole class would stand around admiring his wonderful command."

Such successes stirred Grant's pride, and as his second-year furlough approached, he ordered a new uniform to be delivered that June. His clothes were certain to attract attention in Ohio, especially as the uniform featured pants which buttoned up the front rather than closing at the side, a shocking innovation introduced at West Point the previous fall. Thus outfitted, he started for home in June to begin what he later remembered as the most pleasant ten weeks of his life.

The Grant family now lived in Bethel, twelve miles west of Georgetown, where Jesse was operating an even bigger tannery, with a retail branch in the thriving upper Mississippi Valley. Grant had not seen his family's new house, or his new sister, Mary Frances, born after he'd gone to school. He docked at Ripley, took the stage as far as it went into Clermont County, and hitched a ride into Bethel. The neighbor who drove him said he expected to see "a warm greeting" at Grant's homecoming, because the boy had been gone so long. But it "was simply 'How are you, my son?' and 'How are you, brother?' Ulysses was entirely cool and without emotion." Hannah Grant eyed her son, who was on his way to adding more than six inches to his stature, and laconically observed that he had "grown much straighter." Yes, Ulysses replied, "that was the first thing they taught me."

"They" were far away that summer of 1841. It may have been the new uniform, or the new horse Jesse had bought him, but neighbors remarked how much Ulysses had changed. He seemed more confident socially, and even called on girls. But the furlough, which Grant said went faster than one week at West Point, was over by August 28. When he arrived back at West Point, he discovered, to his surprise, that he had been made cadet sergeant for his junior year.[4]

It was commonly assumed in the Army that Southerners received preferential treatment at West Point, but only eight of the thirty-three men who taught at the academy were southern, and though half the cadets came from the South, they didn't do as well academically as their northern classmates. Richard Ewell, a testy Virginian whose subsequent military career would demonstrate some remarkably bad thinking, said that Yankees outstripped Southerners because they entered West Point better prepared intellectually. Most of Grant's fellow cadets were middling types: Bill Sherman and big, steady George H. Thomas—both seniors when Grant entered; or William Rosecrans, Earl Van Dorn, Daniel Hill, and John Pope—sophomores; or Pete Longstreet and Lafayette McLaws—juniors. There were exceptions. The cadet adjutant during Grant's junior year was Irvin McDowell, a wealthy Ohio-born nephew of the powerful Northwest senator Lewis Cass, who possessed all the earmarks of a gentleman and displayed a requisite breadth of cultural knowledge. Another was George McClellan, who had been admitted though he was underage—only fifteen—because of impeccable social credentials and prodigious talent.

An occasional cadet might be impossible to classify. Thomas

J. Jackson arrived from Virginia in homespun and mountain clogs, carrying a sweat-stained pair of saddlebags slung over one shoulder. Dabney Maury smiled and turned toward his friend Ambrose P. Hill and condescendingly noted, "That fellow looks as if he had come to stay." Stay he did, though he stumbled over classmates in drill, wobbled precariously in the saddle, and was considered unsafe with a sword in his hand. His ignorance was so profound he required round-the-clock tutoring to pass his first-year exams. Even then he attracted the attention of the entire academy with his "painful" performance, standing pale and drenched with sweat, shaking with fear at the blackboard.[5]

Grant's unexpected appointment to sergeant was an honor, and he should have been pleased. But looking back on his West Point years, he decided the "promotion was too much" for him. According to Robert Lee's definition of the duties of a cadet officer, of paramount importance was scrupulous attention to reporting the infractions of subordinates. The honor system imposed this requirement on all cadets—Grant had already been forced embarrassedly to testify that one student had called another "a d——d shit ass"—but as an officer, he was expected to preserve an even higher regard for those detested "black marks." It was difficult to enforce standards which he himself didn't think appropriate. But it was even harder for him to be singled out as an authority figure. There was no "habit of command" for Grant to fall back on at West Point, no desire for preeminence to compensate for the loss of fellowship, nothing to be gained in some abstract pursuit of excellence or virtue.[6]

He started his senior year demoted to private, a rank in which he was more comfortable. His roommate, Frederick Dent, had become a friend, and knew Grant as a "pure minded and even-tempered" fellow who was very quiet. It came as something of a surprise when Dent found himself challenged to a fight by Grant. Accounts vary on the particulars, but the subject was slavery. Dent came from a farm south of St. Louis which his slaveholding father had pointedly named White Haven. Apparently Grant took exception to something Dent said regarding the status of blacks in America, and the two cadets decided to fight it out. But before blows were exchanged, Grant stood back and began to laugh. It was absurd, he thought, to strike a friend over something so inconsequential as an idea.

Grant was elected president of the dialectic society during his senior year, and joined with eleven others in the secret brotherhood of TIO, "Twelve in One." He also was secure in his unchallengeable horsemanship. "That horse will kill you some day," a cadet warned Grant during his last year. "Well, I can't die but once," Grant answered as he swung aboard. The jumping record he set—"Grant on York"—stood for more than twenty-five years. It was natural that he would pick the cavalry as his first choice for military service. But grades, not expert horsemanship, determined placement, and Grant didn't make it. Infantry, the bottom of the barrel and a sure thing, was his second, and successful, choice.

Grant maintained during his cadetship and later that he wanted to serve out his enlistment on the faculty of West Point, then return to Ohio and "retire on a competency." This meant, he said, teaching in some small college. But that was Jesse Grant's dream for his son. What Grant really wanted for himself was to remain in the Army and become a Winfield Scott—leader of men, dashing hero. Even President John Tyler, who visited West Point during Grant's sophomore year, did not inspire feelings of awe the way Scott did. "In fact," Grant said, "I regarded General Scott and Captain C. F. Smith, the Commandant of Cadets, as the two men most to be envied in the nation."[7]

Bearing this inarticulate desire, and a class standing of twenty-first out of thirty-nine—in the middle, just where he was comfortable—Grant boarded the steamer for home. He had a new name. For four years he had stubbornly signed his official correspondence "U. H. Grant" or "Ulysses H. Grant." But West Point had graduated "U. S. Grant," and just as adamantly refused to comply with the new officer's last effort to force his preference on the Army. Grant resigned himself, and for the rest of his life he used "Ulysses S. Grant," but always said the "S" stood for nothing.

His two-month leave was not the pastoral idyll his earlier furlough had been, even though his father had another new saddle horse and a horse and buggy for him. He worried that he might have tuberculosis, a fear grounded in a six-month cough and being "very much reduced" to a lank 117 pounds. There was also the incident of the uniform. When Grant was finally notified at the end of July that he would be entering the 4th Infantry, he ordered the appropriate clothes from the West Point tailor. "I was impatient to get on my uniform and see how it looked," he said, "and probably wanted my old school-mates, particularly the girls, to see me in it." Indeed, he'd written his cousin that he wanted to "astonish you *natives*" with his military glory, a forgivable impulse in a young man who had been laughed out of town as an incompetent appointee. Even so, he hoped "you won't take me for a Babboon."

"Soon after the arrival of the suit, I donned it," said Grant, "and put off for Cincinnati on horseback. While I was riding along a street of that city, imagining that every one was looking at me, with a feeling akin to mine when I first saw General Scott, a little urchin . . . turned to me and cried: 'Soldier! will you work? No sir-ee; I'll sell my shirt first!!' " Grant was apparently still quite fragile on the subject of dress, because the child's jeer, he said, knocked the conceit out of him. Worse waited in Bethel.

When he returned from Cincinnati, still uniformed, he found a crowd of neighbors laughing over the antics of a sodden stable hand dressed "in a pair of sky-blue nankeen pantaloons—just the color of my uniform trousers—with a strip of white cotton sheeting sewed down the outside seams in imitation of mine. The joke was a huge one in the mind of many people, and was much enjoyed by them; but I did not appreciate it so highly." The incidents, he said, recalled the "horse trade and its dire consequences" and gave him "a distaste for military uniforms" that lasted the rest of his life. He spent the remainder of his visit out of uniform, quietly visiting relatives.[8]

At the end of September he caught a steamer for St. Louis and reported to Jefferson Barracks, the largest and most lavish military installation in the country. The limestone and brick fort, set on 1,700 wooded acres overlooking the Mississippi, housed sixteen companies, and was a launching point for western campaigning. Six weeks after he arrived at Jefferson, Grant tried to transfer to the cavalry, but was turned down again. Disappointed, he bowed to pressure from home and inquired about a berth on the West Point faculty. He began to study mathematics and history, but his commitment wavered and he veered off into novel-reading. He also started to call on Fred Dent's family.[9]

White Haven was located south of Jefferson Barracks, twelve miles from St. Louis on Gravois Creek. There were more than 1,000 acres of land at White Haven, but Fred Dent's father didn't farm. He had bought the place as a retreat and stocked it with assorted domesticated animals which he bred as a hobby. The white frame house had two stories. The yard was planted in locust trees, and the veranda—or piazza, as the Dents called it—was covered with jasmine.

White Haven was as close to a southern plantation as Missouri weather allowed, and even had "quarters" for the family's eighteen slaves. Frederick Dent, Sr., "Colonel Dent," told his children that vast estates in Maryland had been home to the early Dents, and that still earlier their forebears had been English nobility. But in truth, Colonel Dent's father was an up-country Marylander—not a tidewater grandee—who migrated to Pittsburgh to make a living. Dent grew up there, started a business, and married Ellen Wrenshall, the daughter of a riverboat shipper. One child, John, was born in Pittsburgh, then Dent succumbed to western fever, and sometime before 1820 floated his family down the Ohio on flatboats. His children believed that in St. Louis Colonel Dent became a partner of a Mr. Lindell, who "left a vast fortune at his death." They attributed their father's relative impecuniousness to his too nice sense of values, which kept him from spending all his energy laying up stores. But Dent was in business with George Rearwisk, and then only long enough to save up money to buy a piece of land. One of his children said the colonel found life at White Haven "so delightful that he gradually gave up all occupation." Opinionated, belligerent, and

vindictive, Dent filed endless frivolous lawsuits. A Missouri Ben-
tonite and Jackson Democrat, he was thought "grim" by his
neighbors.[10]

Ellen Wrenshall Dent hated farm country, and White Haven
especially. It was not what she had had in mind when she sacri-
ficed society and friendship in Pennsylvania. She bore eight children, and by the time Grant came calling at White Haven was
considered too fragile to run the house. A semblance of social life
was maintained—primarily with the soldiers from Jefferson Barracks—and Mrs. Dent set a beautiful table, but children, servants,
animals, and weeds seemed to be growing wild. The four Dent
boys—John, George, Fred, and Lewis—were earning bad reputa-
tions, and the older girls, Julia and Nell, exercised the kind of
freedom real southern young women would have found shocking.

The first time Grant visited White Haven, six-year-old Emmy
Dent thought the young lieutenant "pretty as a doll," quite the
"handsomest person" she had ever seen. Despite the smooth pink
cheeks, Grant's face was well modeled and strong. The chin was
squared, and the jaw was straight. His nose was narrow, not
overlong, and his forehead broad and high. The hair was light
brown, thick, and in 1843 worn long and parted well down the
side. His eyes, light blue, were somewhat hesitant, but his mouth
had a determined set, and like his mother's, was thin and rigid.
He had regained some of his lost weight, and though he was still
slender, Emmy described him as "well-formed." He was five feet
seven inches tall, and impressed the Dents with the way he rode.
Mrs. Dent was fond of him. Emmy remembered Grant sitting on
the piazza with her father and mother talking about President
Tyler and Texas. "That young man explains politics so clearly
I can understand the situation perfectly," Mrs. Dent told her
daughter. The children thought it was Grant's "quiet, even tones,
free from gestures and without affectation," which their mother
liked. Grant knew how to talk with excitable, dogmatic men like
Colonel Dent—he'd grown up with one.[11]

Grant paid weekly visits to White Haven, until February,
when Julia, the Dents' eighteen-year-old daughter, who had been
visiting in St. Louis, came home. Emmy had already filled Grant

in on Julia—that she was the first girl born in the family and was her father's favorite, that she had her very own slave named Black Julia and a horse that was always kept ready for her. Emmy said Julia was "as dainty a little creature as one would care to see, plump, neither tall nor short, with beautifully rounded arms, brown hair and brown eyes, and a blonde and rosy complexion." But there was the trouble with one of her eyes. In the Dent family it was assumed that the condition had started when a careless nurse took the infant Julia into a cold room after her bath. Whatever the reason, she had a malfunctioning muscle which caused her right eye to quiver spasmodically and focus upward. But Grant immediately became Julia's constant companion and two months later asked her to marry him.

When Julia Dent Grant was an old woman she wrote a whimsical reminiscence of her life, charming in its naïveté and revealing in its pretense. The most telling aspect of her book was its evocation of a mythical plantation wonderland. In Julia's narrative, she was the adored princess of an enchanted world, wending her way daily through bowers of sweet-smelling verdure followed by a "dusky train" of little slaves. Her mother was "beautiful, kind, and gentle." Her home was "the showplace of the county, having very fine orchards of peaches, apples, apricots, nectarines, plums, cherries, grapes, and all of the then rare and small fruits." White Haven's flowers were "the admiration of the county." Its forests a "wealth" of game. The Dent china was the "daintiest," the silver "solid," the linen "the finest." White Haven's eighteen slaves multiplied in Julia's mind, and she recalled hundreds of happy retainers gathered round campfires chanting "wild, plaintive" songs. Drivers, mammies, old black uncles who presented to "Miss Julia" the "first ripe strawberries, the reddest apples," and "all the prettiest birds' eggs," rallied round Colonel Dent's dispensations of copious quantities of fish, molasses, tobacco, and "some whiskey (on cold raw days)."

Had Julia really been the belle she described, she would have frightened the shy lieutenant away. Luckily, she was very much like him, with just enough difference to strike the attraction. She was sturdily healthy, loved to ride and fish, and was more comfort-

able in the woods than in the drawing room. She did attend a
private school in St. Louis, but her early education had occurred
in a one-room log cabin near the farm. Like Grant, she was an
indifferent student, and preferred reading romances and novels.
She alluded to gay social seasons in St. Louis, but admitted that
even at eighteen she'd never had a beau, because she was "the
shyest of little girls," and the parties and balls were always for
someone else. The young mistress from White Haven went to
other girls' debuts, she didn't have one herself. Though Frederick
Dent put on airs, Jesse Grant was richer—he just didn't spend his
money. The Dents and the Grants were similar characters in
different plays. Julia as the "belle of White Haven," however,
was a role as important to Grant as it was to her. A girl who could
go eighteen years without worrying about her father's pretensions
was just right for a fearful, self-conscious would-be Winfield
Scott.[12]

Julia was flattered at Grant's unflagging devotion to her—his
hewing a tiny coffin for a deceased canary was especially important—but she was unprepared when Grant tried to press his class
ring on her. "Oh, no," she responded, "Mamma would not approve of my accepting a gift from a gentleman." She soon regret-
ted her demure hesitation. While Grant was on a short visit to
Ohio, his regiment was ordered to Louisiana. When Julia found
out about the new assignment, she assumed that Grant would go
straight down the Mississippi and she would never see him again.
This made her "restless," she said. She rode over to Jefferson
Barracks alone, "and waited and listened, but he did not come.
The beating of my own heart was all the sound I heard. So I rode
slowly and sadly home."

Grant, however, had no intention of allowing Julia to pine. He
knew his regiment had been ordered south—a friend wrote him
at Bethel—but he decided to honor the letter of his leave, and
reported back at Jefferson Barracks. Once in St. Louis he asked
post commander Richard Ewell for an extension of his leave and
went to White Haven. It had been raining heavily; Gravois Creek
was overflowing, and the current was strong and fast. "One of my
superstitions had always been when I started to go any where or

do anything, not to turn back, or stop until the thing intended was accomplished," Grant said. "So I struck into the stream, and in an instant the horse was swimming and I being carried down by the current. I headed the horse towards the other bank and soon reached it, wet through." Grant stopped at John Dent's house to borrow some dry clothes, then set off for Julia.[13]

"I was about to retire for an afternoon siesta," Julia remembered, "when my colored maid came and, looking up towards the front gate said: 'Law, Miss Julia, if there isn't Mars John and, I declare, Mr. Grant, and he has on citizens clothes and how odd he looks in them too.' " Obviously weakened, Julia was amenable to Grant's second offer of his ring. She said he told her "that without me life would be insupportable . . . When he spoke of marriage, I simply told him I thought it would be charming to be engaged, but to be married—no! I would rather be engaged. I do not think he liked this arrangement, but as he was going away and could not have taken me with him, even if I had thought it as pleasant to be married as engaged, he let the matter rest."

Indeed, the matter was a deep secret. Julia told Ulysses he must not mention the engagement lest Colonel Dent find out. Ulysses agreed. He was too shy to broach the subject with his prospective father-in-law anyway, and a confrontation would have spoiled the visit. At the end of May, Julia waved him off to Louisiana.[14]

GRANT WROTE TO Julia from Camp Salubrity, near Natchitoches, Louisiana, close to the Sabine River and Texas. His trip to New Orleans had been pleasant, he said, though "Musquetoes" had left his face and hands covered with bites. He spent a day going over the town "just fast enough to see nothing as I went, stopped long enough at a time to find out nothing at all and at the end found myself perfectly tired out." He liked New Orleans, but not as well as St. Louis. He was "not disposed to give up a known good for an untried one," he said. From New Orleans he'd traveled northwest, up the Red River, which was "like a little deep and winding canal finding its way through a forest so thickly set, and of such heavy foliage that the eye cannot penetrate. The country is low and flat and overgrown to the first limbs of the trees. Alligators and other revolting looking things occupy the swamps in thousands." Though the camp was on high ground, "with about the best spring water in Louisiana running near," the pine woods surrounding it were "infested in an inormaus degree with Ticks, Red bugs, and a little creeping thing looking like a Lizard, that I dont know the name of. This last vermin is singularly partial to society. . . ."

Grant was happy in Louisiana. He enjoyed the rigors of camp life, played cards with his cronies, learned the game of "Brag," bet on horse races, and paid social calls on Red River planters. When his company was sent out on road-building detail, he lived off the same fare as the enlisted men and rolled himself into a wet blanket on the "still damper ground." His appetite was "extravigant" despite food "cooked in the woods by servants that know no more about culinary matters than I do myself."

Only one sour note sounded through his months at Salubrity. He had arrived at camp a newly engaged man, but couldn't receive congratulations on his enhanced status. Even to his old Georgetown neighbor Mrs. Bailey, he only alluded to a "secret," which he would tell her about later, which was *laughable, curious, important, surprising* &c. &c." Julia was the only one who could acknowledge the vastly important change in his emotional fortunes, and Julia wouldn't write.[15]

Grant concluded his first letter to her with a series of blank lines which were meant to "express more than words" the depth of his feeling. Two months passed with only a bland verbal message from his intended. But that was enough to prompt a long answer despite a case of the *"Blues,"* occasioned by not hearing from her. "Be as punctual in writing to me Julia and then I will be compensated in a slight degree,—nothing could fully compensate—for your absence.—In my mind I am constantly turning over plans to get back to Missouri. . . . Does Mrs. Dent know of the engagement between us?" He signed the letter twice, once as "Yours most Constantly," and again: "be shure and write soon and relieve from suspense your most *Devoted* and *Constant* I ——."[16]

In August he thanked her for writing two letters, complaining, though, that he had to wait "so long for an answer to my three letters (I have written you *three* times Julia . . .)." The news from Missouri was not good. Mrs. Dent refused to take seriously the engagement of her daughter to the absent soldier, one of the girls in the neighborhood was teasing Julia that Grant liked her better, and worst of all, Julia was having bad premonitions. "You say Julia that you often dream of me! do tell me some of your good ones; dont tell me any more of the bad ones; but it is an old saying that dreams go by contraries so I shall hope you will never find me in the condition you drempt I was in—And to think too that wile I am writing this the ring I used to wear is on your hand . . . Most Truly and Devotedly Your Lover Ulysses."[17]

Julia had asked Grant to write her parents requesting their permission for the correspondence. He answered her the first week of September, enclosing a note to the senior Dents. "You can scarsely concieve the embarrassment I felt in writing such a letter, even in commencing the first line. You must not laugh at it Julia." Nevertheless, she was to respond right away, laughing or not. "It has only been a few days since I received your letters. I answered them immediately, wont you be as punctual in answering mine in the future? You dont know Julia with how much anxiety and suspense I await there arrival."

The Dents never answered his nervous and perhaps comic request—they may have been horrified at his spelling—and Julia wrote only one letter during the winter of 1844–45. Grant was hurt and, at last, irritated. "The fact is I thought I must hear from you again—The more than ordinary attachment that I formed for *yourself* and family during my stay at Jeff. Bks. cannot be changed to forgetfulness by a few months absence. But why should I use to you here the language of flattery Julia when we have spoken so much more plainly of our feeling for each other? Indeed I have not changed since and shall hope that you have not, nor will not, at least untill I have seen all of you once more. I intend to apply for a leave in the spring again and will go to St. Louis." Which he did.[18]

Julia remembered that a group of friends was crowding the

White Haven piazza on a Sunday afternoon "when who should dash up to the front gate, mounted on a superb dapple gray, but Lieutenant Grant! He walked hurriedly up to the house. I was sitting near the steps and arose to greet him, as did all the others, but he scarcely touched my hand." It was understood in the Dent family that Grant tended to be somewhat indecisive. Once having made up his mind, however, he was extremely forthright, and on this occasion he meant to confront Colonel Dent. As ill luck would have it, Julia's father was setting off on a trip to the East Coast and had no time for Grant. Not to be outdone, Grant followed Dent to St. Louis and forced him to hear about the engagement.

"Papa," Julia wrote, "said he did not think the roving life I would have to lead as a soldier's wife would suit me at all, when Mr. Grant immediately said he had been offered a professorship in a college in Ohio, so if that was the only objection, he would resign." Dent told Grant that was unwise, and to prove his good fellowship, suggested that the soldier marry Nellie, Julia's younger sister. Julia was flattered by her father's "Laban-like suggestion" and relieved that the two men had parted with an understanding that Julia and Ulysses were to wait a year or two. If they still wished to marry at the end of the proscription, they were free to do so.

A Dent sister acidly suggested the whole drama of permission-getting was just one more charade in Julia and Ulysses's court-ship. "But after all it was all nonsense for father to be pretending that he had anything to say about it. Julia, having once said Yes, had made his decision for him. When Julia wanted a thing from my father, she always got what she wanted." Julia needed Ulysses to play the gallant and wrest her from her father. Just as her sister suspected, the showdown was all a sham. Months earlier, soon after Grant wrote the letter to the Dents, Julia had approached her father about her marriage. Dent said no. "You are too young and the boy is too poor. He hasn't anything to give you." Julia retorted with a withering blow to her father's most vulnerable point. I am poor too, she said, and haven't "anything to give him."

Once that bit of honesty straightened things out, it was safe for Julia to resume her status as a belle.

Grant left for Louisiana and promised to be back as soon as possible. But it was not one or two years before he saw her again, it was three.[19]

The men and officers at Camp Salubrity knew their mission included keeping an eye on Texas. The Army of Observation, as it was styled, had already built roads to the Sabine River, Texas's eastern border, and was daily expecting orders to march. Time would clarify the issues involved in the Texas question, and some of the men, including Grant, would come to see the whole story as a sorry tale of American imperialism. But in 1845 the camp was anxious to be off on an adventure that might win them advances or glory. A lot of land was involved, and some very big words— manifest destiny, slavery, liberty, and cotton.

In 1820, Spanish-owned Texas was bounded on the east by the Sabine River—separating it from Louisiana—on the north by the Red River—separating it from American Indian Territory (now Oklahoma)—and on the south by the Nueces River, which emptied into the Gulf of Mexico at Corpus Christi. Spain was encouraging American settlement, and offered to Moses Austin 66,000 acres of land for colonists. When the area became part of Mexico in 1824, it fell under a constitution that outlawed slavery. This created a problem for Austin and his son Stephen. Cotton grew in Texas and planters thought they couldn't raise cotton without slaves. The Austins would have no colony without planters. Stephen Austin worked out a pro-slavery arrangement with local Mexican authorities, which remained effective until 1835. That year, Santa Anna, Mexico's new president, redrew the national constitution and prohibited states' rights, thus wiping out Austin's agreement. Americans in Texas declared themselves independent from Mexico and went to war, garrisoning in the Alamo. They then redressed that highly publicized disaster by routing Santa Anna's troops and capturing the president. A provision of his release required the signing of a treaty setting the southern limits of Texas on the Rio Grande, more than one hundred miles south of the Nueces. Texas then constituted itself an independent nation, elected military leader Sam Houston president, legalized slavery, and in 1836 offered itself to the United States. After explosive arguments, the United States declined.

The issue came to a head again during the 1844 presidential campaign. Whigs, outraged that Tyler backed the annexation of Texas, coalesced behind Henry Clay. But Democrat James Polk was able to rely on the backing of slaveholders while attracting support from the Northwest. The Democratic press, denouncing Whigs and other Americans who thwarted expansion, hit on an electric phrase. It was the "manifest destiny" of America, it was said, "to overspread the continent allotted by Providence for the free development of our yearly multiplying millions." Texas was the obvious place to start. The last act of the Tyler administration was formalizing the annexation.[20]

SHORTLY AFTER Grant returned to Louisiana, Polk ordered troops there to advance to Corpus Christi, on the Nueces. At the same time, he had San Francisco taken and sent John Frémont overland into southern California. Since Mexico denied the validity of Santa Anna's treaty setting the Texas boundary at the Rio Grande, it was expected to defend the land lying south of the Nueces. When Mexican troops crossed the Rio Grande, the United States could seize California, claiming it as a bounty for Mexican aggression, and, at the same time, scoop up half of Texas and what would become New Mexico and Arizona.

Around the first of July, Grant's regiment was sent to New Orleans, then on to Corpus Christi, where the Americans under Brigadier General Zachary Taylor made themselves at home. Sutlers, or merchants, sold their wares from shacks dotting the periphery of the neatly ordered camps. Further back, the tents of the whores were placed with the canvas gambling halls. To offset the effects of easy but expensive vice, chaplains erected small places of worship where virtue might be maintained for free.

Wives who followed their husbands to Corpus Christi shared tents and helped meet expenses by taking in laundry. Southern officers were accompanied by slaves, Northerners by hired help. Grant had hired a young black boy in New Orleans who spoke French and Spanish and promised more service than he supplied. Regular Army enlisted men were often foreign-born mercenaries from East Coast cities. Many were Irish, some were German, and most were Catholic. All delighted in joining the young Mexican women who bathed nude in the rivers.

Commanders tried to control the motley crowd by establishing a theater in Corpus Christi, and tapped Robert Lee's Fortress Monroe regular, John Magruder—called "Prince John" for his predilection for silk-lined capes and silver campaign accouterments—to supply the stage. The first production was *Othello*, and Grant, called "Little Beauty" by his cohorts, was given the role of Desdemona, but lost it because it was thought his performance lacked "proper sentiment." He was no better on the hunting forays planned by the officers, preferring to stand and marvel at flocks of wild turkeys rather than kill them.[21]

In February, Polk ordered Taylor to move his army to the Rio Grande, opposite Matamoros on the Gulf coast. Grant bought a five-dollar Mexican pony, and rode south on an unbroken horse along with the 3,000-man Army of Occupation. They reached the Rio Grande about the middle of March and went into camp. Soon Taylor was able to tell Washington that several hostile Mexican soldiers had crossed the Rio Grande and captured a small group of American dragoons. Polk finally had his pretext for war.[22]

CHAPTER

6

THREE DAYS AFTER Congress formally declared war on Mexico—May 9, 1846—Robert Lee settled himself at the writing desk in his Fort Hamilton, New York, study, adjusted his eyeglasses, and began a letter to his wife. Mary was at Arlington recovering from the difficult birth of her seventh child, Mildred. Except for his dog Spec, who nervously paced through the empty rooms before settling at his master's feet, Lee was alone.

My Dear Mary
. . . You of course have heard the news from Texas, & that war has commenced in earnest. No one can tell where it will end. There ought surely to be no hesitation any longer on our part, & I fear the Country is already disgraced for its puerile conduct. I never could see the advantage to be gained by Sending Gen. Taylor with 2,000 men into the heart of *Mexico,* as it has been heretofore considered, unless it was to *invite* the Mexicans to attack [him] on account of the feebleness of his force, & thus bring on the War we had not the frankness or manliness at once to declare. . . . The result is not in our own hands & we must take the chance of War, in which victory is not always to the Strong. I wish I was better Satisfied as to the justice of our Cause, but that is not my province to consider, & Should my Services be wanting I Shall promptly furnish them.[1]

In fact, he was eager to go.

Five years earlier, he had welcomed his assignment at Fort Hamilton, located on the Brooklyn side of the Narrows of New York Harbor and connected by steamer to Governors Island, a popular garrison for soldiers of the line, and to Manhattan's Battery, where Hamilton's officers debarked for theatergoing and sightseeing. Lee expected his work in New York to be as energetic as its surroundings. The job was an honor, a reward for his St. Louis excellence, but it turned out to consist of making improvements on rotting defense works. By 1846, he was bored. He was also restive with his domestic routine. When he wrote that letter to Mary about the Mexican War, he was the father of seven children, thirty-nine years old, still a captain, still worried about doing his duty, and not quite resigned to a life without pleasure.[2]

LEE WORKED FOR two seasons in St. Louis after he had settled Mary and the children at Arlington in 1838. He amused himself by writing letters, visiting acquaintances, and renewing old friendships on the upper Mississippi—which included a memorable Galena, Illinois, reunion with Dick Tilghman, an old Fortress Monroe regular and groomsman at his wedding, whom Lee found "well practised in pork-eating and promiscuous sleeping. . . ."[3]

His schedule dragged, and he was lonely. When winter closed in, he was sent south to gather information about the Arkansas and Red rivers, which would be helpful later, then he made good what he called "his escape from the West." The novelty of Indians, tobacco-juiced travelers, and raw frontier vitality had worn off. Back in Virginia, he wrote a cousin that he did not dislike Missouri; "on the contrary I think it is a great country and will one day be a grand one, all is life, animation and prosperity, but . . . it is far more pleasant for *me* to be here than there."[4]

Lee invoked Virginia whenever he was not content. He wondered "to what country" Tennessee belonged, dismissed Florida as "a land to which no man would emigrate from Purgatory," and offered sympathy to colleagues sent to the Carolinas. He cast off the entire West as a land of spittoons, inflated politics—he was still "on the lookout for that stream of gold that was to ascend the Mississippi, tied up in silk-net purses!"—and vulgarity, home to the contemptible *volunteer* Heroes of Florida and the *Mormon* Wars!" The North was the frozen ground of the flinty Yankee. Only Virginia was heart's home—"surely Robt. Lee," he said of himself, "you have fallen upon evil times or evil times upon you. And that is because you have left Virginia!" But Lee had grown up in Alexandria, which had more of the District of Columbia than the Old Dominion about it, and he had never owned any Virginia land except for a few acres left him by his mother. From 1825 when he left for West Point, to 1840, he had been stationed in the state only two years. But the Lees were Virginians, and had been for two hundred years. So were the Carters, Custises, and Washingtons. The notion of that past was home to Lee in ways no physical place could ever be.[5]

Lee stayed only a few weeks in Mary's house during the winter of 1841. After a tour inspecting forts in the Carolinas, in April he went north to Fort Hamilton and sank into anxious depression. With two new daughters, money was an especially bothersome problem. Shortly after his arrival at Fort Hamilton, he confessed to his brother Carter, who had asked him for a loan, that he had never been "poorer" in his life. For the first time he had not been able to pay his debts. "Last year my pay was cut down $300 and the year before $500." Despite protestations of poverty, Lee complied with Carter's request, but not without giving his eldest brother some financial advice. "I can be content to be poor with the knowledge of being able to pay my debts & that no one has a just claim upon me that I cannot meet. But I cannot bear to enter into engagements without the certainty of being able to fulfil them. My wants I can always restrict within my means & the step I now take is peculiarly disagreeable to me. I only do it out of regard for you (for myself I would not do it) & to enable you to make the arrangement you think so desirous."[6]

Lee was making a pointed reference to Light-Horse Harry's failures, a subject he was much engaged with at the time. Lee's half-brother, Black-Horse Harry, had died in Paris in the winter of 1839, and his widow, Anne, was penniless. When Lee was approached for financial aid for the woman, he agreed to send her $100 a year for as long as ten years, saying, however, that it would work a hardship on him and suggesting she return to the United States. His sole recompense was Black-Horse Harry's gold watch, and for that he had to pay $50. Even more troublesome was his role in the settling of the estate of Bernard Carter, Lee's uncle (and half brother-in-law—Ann Carter Lee's brother married Light-Horse Harry's unstable daughter, Lucy). Bernard had been executor of Ann Carter Lee's estate and, in turn, had named Robert Lee to serve him. Lee refused, on the grounds his military duty took too much time. But it gave him "great pain," he said, "not to comply with the wishes of Uncle B." The struggle over familial duty was decided, finally, by the nature of the family. Lee mentioned a "want of harmony" among the heirs—the grandchildren of Light-Horse Harry Lee—and he knew that his co-trustee, Charles Carter, was involved in madcap speculations. It all seemed like a sorry reenactment of a troublesome Lee family trait.[7]

Lee was actually less than candid with Carter about his financial state. It may have been true that he had "never been poorer" in his life, but the bonds he allowed Carter to use as collateral were paid up. It was quite true that he couldn't bear financial insecurity. The horrors of Stratford would always remain in his mind. His military and personal bookkeeping were so excessively scrupulous that he almost seemed to believe his associates expected a Lee to cheat. A couple of Army record-keeping errors stimulated months of nervous letters from Lee to his bank, his commander, his assistant, and his mother-in-law. When he mistakenly cashed an incorrect paycheck, he offered to reimburse the government twice over, saying he'd rather forfeit a whole year's salary than have his honesty impugned. Lee believed a flawless reputation was more important by far than money, and money was important to him. His investments in bank stocks and canal, railway, and state bonds by 1846 amounted to $38,000, a good sum in those days. Ten years later, he was worth almost $70,000. The dividends from his investments augmented his salary, which was less than $2,000 a year, as did the interest on Mary's money, which he never touched, but insisted be used for household expenses. Lee was not rich like his father had occasionally been—but neither was he poor. Though he was always generous to needy kin, he managed his money with a parsimony more Yankee than cavalier.[8]

He could not have chosen a woman whose abstemious financial habits more perfectly matched his own than Mary Custis Lee. Though she shared with him a taste for fine appointments, Mary never spent the money she had on a scale her background suggested. She worried about the cost of blankets, bargained for fabric remnants, and insisted the children's clothing be mended and handed down. She outfitted the Fort Hamilton house handsomely, augmenting the cache of items stored from her stay at Fortress Monroe with new furniture made for her in Alexandria and items from Arlington. She bought books and silver somewhat too easily for her husband's peace of mind, but balked at spending money on herself. A shopping trip to Manhattan might yield a stylish bonnet for a Virginia cousin or a pair of trousers for a child, but seldom anything for herself. She wrote her mother from Fort Hamilton that she'd been to New York "looking out for some kind of covering for myself but have not decided what to get. There are so many things worn which are all too dashing for me."[9]

Never beautiful, always ill groomed, Mary by the mid-1840s was becoming old, though she was only in her early thirties. By all odds, she should have died in 1834, or at least been maimed or sterile. But she had produced seven healthy children, all of whom lived—an extraordinary achievement in that dark age of obstetrics. She had been pregnant or recovering from childbirth the entire fifteen years of her married life, and the intermittent bouts of fever which she shared with other lowland Southerners had made her more susceptible to the arthritis that was now beginning to bother her. Mary and Robert both joined the health hegira which annually had thousands of pilgrims visiting various mountain spas. But the effects were mainly social, and she found little relief. When she was well enough to do anything at all at Fort Hamilton, she tutored her children, saw to the needs of a constant stream of Virginia houseguests, found former Arlington slaves to care for, and looked—vainly she thought—for enough quiet to "think or read."[10] She maintained her interest in colonization, which she said was "never mentioned in this part of the world," and took a daily drive in the carriage Lee had bought so she could have the kinds of outings his mother had enjoyed. Other than that, she was not often out of the house.[11]

Lee did not live so confining a life. Young subordinates thought him "strikingly handsome," a "perfect type of *gentleman*," quiet and dignified, yet cheerful and "pleasant and considerate." Women found him charming, and Fort Hamilton hostesses soon were accustomed to his arriving at parties alone. Lee wrote Henry Kayser, the civilian engineer who had assisted him in St. Louis, that Kayser was "right in my interest in the pretty women, & it is strange that I do not lose it with age. But I perceive no diminution." Though he said he felt "like a patriarch of old when I get my flock around me," Lee was not withering into biblical antiquity.[12] When Mary was old, she said that the society of beautiful women had constituted the "greatest recreation" in her husband's "toilsome life"—a painfully accurate assessment, given with Mary's usual dispassionate honesty. In the company of women—flirting, teasing, joking—Lee experienced none of the pull between duty and pleasure that marked his other associations. The precedent was of long standing. Ann Carter Lee had claimed Lee's filial duty in ways that had been as rewarding for him as they were for his mother. He never gave up the habit of attending to the ladies, and most of the ladies responded. One in particular entered Lee's life in the early 1840s and kept on responding for twenty-five years.[13]

Martha Custis Williams was eighteen in 1844, the year she paid an extended visit to the Lees at Fort Hamilton. She was the daughter of one of the two children of John Parke Custis, whom her grandmother Martha Washington did not take to Mount Vernon to raise. Martha, or "Markie" as she was called, lived in Tudor Place, a large Georgetown mansion. With her younger brother, Orton, she often visited her Custis relatives, and soon became a favorite of Mary's parents. She was handsome and, unlike her cousin Mary Lee, enjoyed society, clothes, and gossip. She reciprocated Lee's admiration of her and wrote him long, newsy letters which contained hints of the romantic morbidity so fascinating to mid-nineteenth-century America. Perhaps it was the combination of her girlish frivolities and her wan depressions which so attracted Lee to Markie. Her complexities seemed to match his own. With the blessing of Mary, the correspondence between the two lasted a quarter of a century. It was not until after Lee's death that the beautiful, talented, and depressed Markie Williams married.[14]

"Oh Markie, Markie, when will you ripen?" Lee wondered in a letter to her from Fort Hamilton. He sharpened his social wit for her and subtly enhanced his own masculinity with sly barbs about Markie's would-be suitors. Markie made the forty-year-old "patriarch" feel that his maturity was a sophisticated asset, and her interest in him relieved an increasingly burdensome routine at Fort Hamilton.[15]

Lee traveled back and forth between New York and Washington many times during those five years, and he spent several winters at Arlington, but superintending the reconstruction of the two forts assigned to him was largely clerical work, which he detested. In the summer of 1843 he had a short break when he was ordered to West Point to design a new dormitory for the cadets. Arriving just days after the newly graduated Grant had left for Ohio, he took measurements and surveyed sites. It was his first visit to the academy since his 1829 graduation, though he had had an offer to teach engineering there when Grant was a cadet. In 1844, he was ordered to sit on the West Point examination board, headed by Winfield Scott. The Secretary of War and his family were at West Point when Lee arrived in June. The class of 1844, Lee said, acquitted itself admirably. He grilled several he would hear from later—Simon Bolivar Buckner, a friend of Grant's, who would surrender troops at Fort Donelson; Alfred Pleasonton, who stood against Lee at Antietam, Fredericksburg, and Chancellorsville; and a big, talkative Pennsylvania namesake of Scott, Winfield Scott Hancock, who went on to command in every Union force Lee faced: on the Peninsula, at Second Manassas, Antietam, Fredericksburg, Chancellorsville, and Gettysburg, where he was blown apart and taped back together enough to get through the Wilderness to Petersburg.[16]

Another war occupied the imaginations of the cadets and examiners in the summer of 1844. The 3rd Infantry and Grant's 4th Infantry were already in Louisiana, waiting to hear from Scott. In the evening, when the day's examinations were over, the superintendent of the academy hosted formal dinners for the visitors. After the ladies had been excused and brandy and cigars were passed around, talk turned to Texas. Erasmus Keyes, a Massachusetts man who did well as a Union officer during the Civil War, was surprised at discovering the "candor and fairness altogether unusual with his fellow Southerners" with which Lee discussed "the topics of the day, and all subjects relating to the Union and the dangers that threatened it."

Keyes approved of Lee because the two men agreed with each other. Lee was no pro-slaver, but he was angry about abolitionists denouncing the Church and calling "the founders of the Constitution & the fathers of the Revolution *swindlers.*" These kinds of charges had been common when he was in St. Louis, but he could overlook them because they seemed limited to the fringes of political life. In 1844, however, major New York dailies were exciting "apprehensions for the peace and prosperity of the country," he said. Abolitionists were tying Texas to slavery, and the Army was tied to Texas. Lee's connection to the Army was noncombatant—the Corps of Engineers never took the field—so it was unlikely he would serve. There seemed to be no relief from his depressing New York duties.[17]

His health was intermittently bad at Fort Hamilton, and not only did his work give him no pleasure, his children had become puzzling difficulties. When they were absent, he complained of longing for them, but felt harassed and often irritated when they were with him. Rooney, who seemed especially willful to his father, had cut the ends off two of his fingers while playing in a forbidden stable, and wrote his brother: "I hope neither of us will disobey our parents for the future & that a similar accident may never happen to you." Lee added his own admonitions to Rooney's letter: "If children could know the misery, the desolating Sorrow, with which their acts Sometimes overwhelm their parents they could not have the heart thus cruelly to afflict them." Custis, who had been urged to study hard in order to "compensate" his father for the "pain" of their separation, could not have missed understanding that the miscreant children were torturing their father.[18]

It had been years since Lee had talked of quitting the Army, but he desperately wanted a change. To do that, he was even willing to give up his prestigious appointment in the Corps of Engineers. The previous summer he had requested "active service in the field" in the "event of War with any foreign government." It seemed certain that "any foreign government" would be Mexico. By May 1846, when he wrote Mary that he didn't approve of the cause, war with Mexico had been declared, and he wanted to be part of the action.[19]

ZACHARY TAYLOR crossed the Rio Grande, marched eighteen miles, and met the enemy in an artillery battle. "Although the balls were whizzing thick and fast about me," Grant wrote Julia, "I did not feel a sensation of fear until nearly the close of the firing a ball struck close by me killing one man instantly, it nocked Capt. Page's under Jaw entirely off and broke in the roof of his mouth . . . Now that the war has commenced with such vengence I am in hopes Dear Julia that we will soon be able to end it."[20]

Robert Lee was afraid the war would end too soon. He'd been to Washington on the chance of being sent to the front, but instead had been ordered to secure Fort Hamilton against English intervention on the side of Mexico. When that scare passed, Lee disappointedly wrote a friend that he would have nothing more to do than his "ordinary Business." Winfield Scott, who apparently had promised Lee a place with him, was out of favor with the Polk administration, and Lee could do nothing but cheer on Taylor's troops in a war he now saw as "a glorious thing for West Point and a complete refutation of the calumnies of its enemies." His relief was obvious when he finally received orders to ship to Texas and report to General John Wool. To outfit himself for campaigning—his first chance to fight in a seventeen-year Army career—he went to Arlington, where old man Custis donated George Washington's field cutlery and neighbors provided brandy.[21]

By August, Lee was on his way to Charleston, where he picked up $60,000 in Army silver to carry to San Antonio. From the steamer he wrote Mary that leaving her always made him think "that it would be better to be fixed permanently in some humble home than to be living this roaming life in the world we do. But then the desire to educate those dear Children—& bring them up as they may think they are entitled to, keeps me as I am, as my pay is enough for our Support, & my private income can be devoted to them." He needed to tell Mary that it was his duty to his children to leave, and he slyly mentioned a "humble home"—something Mary would hate—as a reminder of his real alternatives.[22]

The end of Mexican negotiations which set Lee free from Fort Hamilton put an end to Taylor's army's living it up in Matamoros. "The time," Grant said of the encampment on the Rio Grande, "was whiled away pleasantly enough." Pleasant for a great many American soldiers meant indulging themselves in the charms of the border-town natives. Recruiting agents in the New York slums reportedly promised new enlistments "roast beef, two dollars a day, plenty of whiskey, golden Jesuses and pretty Mexican gals." Apparently the Army made good on all but the first two. Taylor's men recorded triumphant assignations with dark-eyed women of loose morals, and journalists reported scenes of naked girls "chasing each other . . . diving into the depths of the stream or swimming along its surface with their long, loose, raven tresses flowing behind them."[23] It's unlikely the excesses of Matamoros did more than strengthen Grant's already passionate attachment to Julia. He took heated exception to her calling the town an "Earthly paradise," and reminded her that he was there on nasty, dangerous business. Introducing what became a habit of defining wishes as reality, Grant told Julia that the Army would soon be out of Mexico, "and then dearest Julia, if I am not one of the unfortunate who fall, nothing will keep me from seeing you again."

What bothered Grant about Americans in Matamoros was the mayhem. He had heard of many murders and found it "strange there seems to be but very week means made use of to prevent frequent repetitions." Most upsetting was "how much they seem to enjoy acts of violence too!" Other members of Taylor's army noted gringo brutality in Matamoros, and, like Grant, singled out the Texans as the worst offenders—the "wildest and most dissipated set of men" in the Army, said one. Philadelphian George Gordon Meade, who was serving as lieutenant under Taylor, complained that the volunteers were "always drunk . . . and killed for their own amusement." He was disgusted with Taylor's poor discipline. But life on the Rio Grande was deadly for Americans too. Though many feigned disease as a way of going home, many more sickened and died. Farm boys caught mumps, measles, and smallpox. Everyone had diarrhea from contaminated drinking water in the filthy camps. Antisepsis was unknown. Latrines, when they were built at all, were just as likely to be put upstream as down. "The Dead March was played so often on the Rio Grande that the very birds knew it," wrote one officer.

The end of the armistice signaled a move south. New action was in the offing, Grant wrote Julia, but the Americans were sure to beat the Mexicans "no matter how large their numbers. But then, wherever there are battles a great many must suffer, and for the sake of the little glory gained I do not care to see it."[24]

James Polk was helping glory along. He had slipped General Santa Anna through the American blockade at Veracruz because the Mexican had promised the President he could successfully bribe his government. But Polk was rightly accused of orchestrating a full-blown war, and he was also playing sleight of hand with the military. He feared Scott's presidential potential and had given command to Taylor, a Whig. Taylor, however, was becoming a hero to the pro-war Democrats. When he mounted the May attacks on the Rio Grande, he was actually taking the first step overland to Mexico City. From the border town of Matamoros, he planned a march south to Monterrey. From there, he was to keep going south.

Grant had been appointed acting regimental quartermaster, a job he tried to quit. He had to bundle up camp gear and load it, and said years later that he'd never sworn in his life, but would "excuse those who may have done so, if they were in charge of a train of Mexican pack mules at the time." He moved against Monterrey the way he had moved through the woods of Ohio—covered with dirt and coping with the vagaries of beasts. He was understandably irritable. "If these Mexicans were any kind of people they would have given us a chance to whip them enough some time ago and now the difficulty would be over," he wrote Julia. There was not even a chance for the little glory he did not want. "Julia aint you getting tired of hearing war, war, war? I am truly tired of it. Here it is now five months that we have been at war and as yet but two battles. I do wish this would close. If we have to fight I would like to do it all at once and then make friends."[25]

Polk had no intention of providing friends. By September 19, Taylor had pulled his army of 6,500 up to the outskirts of Monterrey, and the next day attacked. Grant, as quartermaster and commissary, had been ordered to stay behind while the 4th Regiment stormed the town, but he said that "curiosity got the better" of his judgment, and he "charged with the regiment." He stayed with the advance and two days later volunteered to get reinforcements. Dodging bullets by hanging off the side of his saddle, he "got out safely without a scratch." He stopped only once, at a house guarded by a sentry, where he found Taylor's chief engineer—Markie Williams's father, as it turned out—dying of head injuries. Grant said he'd send help and rode on. The promise couldn't be kept; the Americans were forced to fall back. That night, as Grant lay on the ground waiting with the army for enough light to resume the attack, he wrote a letter to White Haven, sending his "assurance that in the midst of grape and musket shots, Dearest Julia, and my love for her, are ever in my mind. . . . I am getting very tired of this war, and particularly impatient of being separated from one I love so much." He made no mention of his dramatic contribution to the day.

Zachary Taylor sent notice that the Americans would begin shelling the city at dawn, and that women and children could not be removed. This threat, which Taylor meant to carry out, brought Monterrey to its knees, and as conqueror, he demonstrated exemplary generosity. His terms for surrender included full military honors for the defeated. Officers could keep their side arms and horses. Grant watched as the Mexicans marched out, and later he remembered feeling sorry for them.[26]

Lee reported to General Wool, who had expected to participate in the conquest of Monterrey and was bitterly disappointed when news came of the surrender of the city. He refused to sit out the second armistice Taylor had extracted from the Mexicans, and with Lee attached to his headquarters, crossed the Rio Grande on pontoon bridges and set off southward in search of Taylor.

It was then Lee learned about Markie's father. After Grant had left the house in which he found Williams, the area was retaken by the Mexicans. Williams died during the night. "You can imagine my regret at the death of Capt. Williams," Lee wrote Mary. "His end was a glorious one for a Soldier, on the field of battle with the cry of victory in his ear." Glory was one of the reasons Lee was roaming around northern Mexico, and visiting the house in which his friend had died "affected" him, he said, with "a sad but not unholy pleasure." But by mid-November, his spirits had flagged.[27]

"Since I wrote to you from this place we have been lying here awaiting the expiration of the Armistice. The delay has been rather irksome to me than refreshing, for I am one of those Silly persons when I have anything to do I can't rest Satisfied till it has been accomplished." The cavalry had been reconnoitering in the area, he said, and reported that "the Commanches were in the Mountains. One night they encamped within 4 miles of them . . . but saw nothing of them. They are supposed to be on one of their predatory excursions against the poor defenceless hamlets & towns in this Section. I wish we could fall in with them." Being generally sour, he found the Mexicans "an amiable but weak people. Primitive in their habits and tastes." The border towns were "uninteresting in appearance, Situated in some valley watered by a small stream, & the rest of the Country through which we have passed, a barren Wilderness." He did admit some small compensations. Several weeks later he announced that at last he had found some pretty girls. "Fine teeth and eyes. Small feet & hands & in their Simple dress of a chemise & petticoat looked quite interesting."

Lee became a headquarters favorite, and enjoyed dining in the homes of Mexican sympathizers as well as entertaining in camp. Christmas, which Grant spent in Monterrey on commissary duty, was for Lee a gala celebration. "By the time the egg-nog was prepared and the table ornamented with the evergreen pine, dinner was announced & the guests assembled." Turkeys, chickens, and "an ample supply" of Mexican wine for the "many patriotic toasts" drunk by the celebrants passed the evening "very pleasantly." Lee shared the George Washington silver, which was "passed around the table with much veneration & excited universal admiration."[28]

Grant opened a bakery in Monterrey, leasing ovens from townsfolk and turning the soldiers' flour rations into bread loaves that he sold for a profit for the regimental fund. Though he swore he would get out of Mexico to see Julia—"even if I have to resign"—he was making friends and enjoying himself. Cadmus Marcellus Wilcox said the quartermaster displayed little talent, had "no pretension to genius," but was a "quiet, plain and unobtrusive" man with "good common sense" who was "much esteemed among his immediate associates. . . ." Tom Hamer, the Ohio representative who had appointed Grant to the academy, found Grant more impressive. Hamer had come to Monterrey as brigadier general of volunteers, and like most political officers, hadn't a notion about conducting war.

"I have found in Lieutenant Grant a most remarkable and valuable soldier," Hamer wrote home. "I anticipate for him a brilliant future, if he should have an opportunity to display his powers when they mature. Young as he is, he has been of great value and service to me." Hamer singled out the clarity of Grant's military lessons, but he was to have little use for them. Like many volunteers, he got dysentery. "He died as a soldier died," Grant wrote the congressman's widow, "without fear and without a murmur. His regret was that, if death must come, it should not come to him on the field of battle . . . He was buried with the 'honors of war,' and with the flag of his beloved country about him."

Perhaps Grant was not as immune to the pull of glory as he said. He set Julia straight about his being "safe" while acting as quartermaster and bleakly noted "that luck is a fortune. It is but necessary to get a start in the papers and there will soon be deed enough of ones performances related."[29]

By February, an opportunity for greater glory opened to the Army. Polk, alarmed at Taylor's success and popularity, finally ordered Winfield Scott to Veracruz, 250 miles east of the capital. Then he sent Scott half of Taylor's army, including Grant and Lee. Grant was sick on the march to the Rio Grande, where his brigade would ship to the coast—ill enough, he told Julia, to qualify for leave—but he watched with interest the anxious "restlessness" of his commander, William Worth. He had never seen Zachary Taylor, whom he admired enormously, use men as badly. Nothing at West Point but his own proclivities had prepared Grant for Taylor. Easy on rules and heedless of dress, Taylor liked to hunker down with his men and trade stories. Dressed in blue jeans and a linen duster, with a straw planter's hat shading his eyes, "Old Rough-and-Ready," as he came to be known in Mexico, would sit sidesaddle impassively chewing tobacco during battles. He ambled through Grant's camp aboard a large mule to say goodbye to Worth's brigade. His orderly, dressed to the nines and smartly mounted, got "six salutes to Taylor's one," Grant remembered. And he never forgot what Taylor showed him—that a man could command like Winfield Scott and behave like Ulysses Grant.

Scott and Taylor were opposites in everything but military skill. Scott, the formal disciplinarian who insisted on polish and precision, was outraged at Taylor's volunteers when they finally straggled into the embarkation point at the mouth of the Rio Grande. He wrote the Secretary of War that if "a tenth of what is said be true," the American volunteers "have committed atrocities—horrors—in Mexico sufficient to make Heaven weep, & every American of Christian morals *blush* for his country." Scott rounded up his army the first week of February and began to whip it into shape. Grant's 4th Infantry got a new commander, Francis Lee—a distant cousin of Robert's. Robert Lee joined Scott's headquarters staff and was assigned a cabin with Joe Johnston on the flagship. Grant had been posted aboard the *North Carolina*—the old ship of Robert's brother, Smith Lee, who was also in the convoy—and sailed on February 13. Scott's flagship, the *Massachusetts,* left two days later.

Bad weather kept the troopships anchored for more than a week at Lobos Island, 170 miles north of Veracruz. Both Lee and Grant were miserable. Grant yearned for Julia and found soldiering "insupportable." "I begin to believe like some author has said,—that there are just two places in this world—One is where a person's intended is, and the other is where she is not," he wrote.[30] Lee, a few yards away, urged his sons to grow "in goodness & knowledge as well as stature," despite his lachrymose assertion that the children "would derive little benefit from my presence, & they are with those better able to advise & direct."[31]

Both men were better when Scott's flotilla arrived off Veracruz the first week in March, ran the batteries of the fortress guarding the harbor, and began putting ashore. Lee stood on deck and watched as Grant's 4th Infantry, the first off, was transferred to whaling boats for the landing. A final push through the low Gulf of Mexico surf brought the Americans ashore, with no response from the Mexicans. As daylight faded, more men, holding their bayoneted muskets above their heads, waded onto the beach and settled in under the city's twenty-foot-high walls. Scott chose to lay a siege rather than launch a direct assault on the coastal fortification, and he called on Lee to design the batteries. Once a semicircle of guns was in place, shelling would begin.

Quartermaster Grant made certain that the 4th Regiment was supplied with provisions, then turned his attention to the work of the engineers. George B. McClellan was there, along with Gustavus Smith and a dapper New Orleans Creole, Pierre Gustave Toutant Beauregard. Colonel Totten, to whom Grant had obediently directed his father's nervous West Point queries, was acting head of the engineer group, but Robert Lee was doing most of the work. Speed was essential. It was the season of yellow fever, called the *vómito* by the Mexicans. If the siege failed, or took more than a few days, the Americans would be trapped on the beach by the disease.

On March 23, after eight days of work under a scorching sun, with Mexican mortars whining overhead, the batteries were finished. With the guns manned by sailors in place, Scott demanded capitulation. He was refused. The Americans opened fire, and were awed by what they wrought. West Pointers had studied siege artillery, and the men who had been with Taylor had seen a little of it at Matamoros, but no one expected the horror of Veracruz. Naval lieutenant Raphael Semmes remembered the "hoarse and plaintive" sea crying in the background as the mortar shells, "chasing each other like playful meteors," traced "beautiful parabolas" in the sky. Screams of women echoed the dull, jarring roar as the shells hit, wiping out, Semmes feared, "some family circle." Lee directed the battery commanded by his brother Smith, anxiously watching to see that Smith was all right. He too thought the mortar skills beautiful, but winced at their effect. "My [heart] bled for the inhabitants. The soldiers I did not [care] for, but the women & children was terrible to think of. . . ."

Grant had no tales of risk or sorrow to tell dearest Julia, only "that during the siege I had but little to do except to see to having the Pork and Beans rolled about." He added, somewhat balefully, that she would "no doubt read flaming accounts of the taking of this City . . ."[32]

The formal surrender occurred on March 29, under terms that allowed the officers to keep their side arms and horses, and paroled the entire force of 4,000 Mexicans—with the exception of forty officers whom Scott freed outright to take to the countryside as emissaries of American goodwill. Several days later, Scott issued "To the Good People of Mexico" his first official proclamation. The Americans, he said, were "not your enemies, but the enemies, for a time, of the men who, a year ago, misgoverned you and brought about this unnatural war between two great republics."

Scott's message undoubtedly pleased the people in Washington more than it did the "friends" left in Veracruz. But his military discipline quieted Mexican fears about the rapacious army of the Rio Grande. Scott was adamant that property, especially church property, be protected. Anti-Catholic sentiment was a particularly chronic tenet of Americans' faith in themselves, and in Mexico many officers and men got their first look at a Catholic country. They were not surprised by what they saw as the lavishness of the Church in a destitute culture. Nor did the Mexican clergy's decrying an "unholy" war waged by American Catholics against Mexican Catholics bother them. The priestly charges had already set off widespread desertion, especially at Matamoros, where enough Irish crossed the Rio Grande to form the San Patricio Battalion of the Mexican Army. Scott insisted on paying official homage to the Church. In Veracruz, accompanied by his highly polished "little cabinet," he solemnly bumbled through a candlelit High Mass of welcome during which Lee's straight-faced sotto voce humor kept the staff in barely contained hilarity. "Popery" appeased, the Army got ready to leave.[33]

CHAPTER

7

AMID GRATITUDE from Veracruz's merchants, disappointment from American sutlers and prostitutes, and relief from soldiers who feared yellow fever, Scott moved out of the city on April 12. Like Cortez before him, whose road to Mexico City he used, the invading general began his march westward confident of success. Grant was still acting quartermaster of Worth's division, an onerous job on the trek through the withering heat of Mexico's Terra Caliente. The first day out, unbroken mustangs struggled loose from their traces and mules balked as wagons sank axle-deep under loads of men who toppled into the scalding sand and had to be carried. Six died that day in the 4th Regiment alone, and Grant cared for their corpses. Lee, with General David Twiggs's advance, found the march poetic, and wrote Mary that no one "at their comfortable homes, can realize the exertions, pains & hardships of an Army in the field, under a scorching sun & in an enervating atmosphere. Still we must press on. The crack of the whip & prick of the speer stimulates the animals, & mans untiring ardour drives on the whole. . . ."[1]

Grant brought up the rear of Worth's division, the last to leave Veracruz, so he could only watch a battle occurring ahead at Cerro Gordo, a pass through the coastal range fortified by Mexican artillery. He called the American assault "brave and brilliant" and described the difficulties surrounding it as "almost equal to Bonapartes Crossing the Alps."

The brilliance emanated from the untiring ardor of Robert Lee. Twiggs was stopped by Santa Anna's defenses, and sent word to Scott that further progress was impossible. But Lee assured Scott that the Americans could pass around the rear of the Mexicans. Ferrying artillery pieces by ropes and pulleys, he led a small group up the mountainside which Santa Anna had assumed was unscalable. Lee was awarded a brevet for his work, an honorary advance in rank which carried with it no promotion but the title and the promise of future rewards. But Scott in his report said Lee, "greatly distinguished at the siege of Vera Cruz, was again indefatigable, during these operations, in reconnaissances as daring as laborious, and of the utmost value." Twiggs was even more effusive, and brigade commander Riley said he could not "refrain from bearing testimony to the intrepid coolness and gallantry exhibited by Captain Lee . . ."[2]

The night after Cerro Gordo, Lee wrote Mary that he was safe and grateful "to that merciful God, that, extended his hand over me." Though he prayed to return to her in time, "if my life & strength are spared, I must See this Contest at an end, & endeavor to perform what little Service I can to my country." He didn't mention his glory on the heights, but he was obviously feeling very good about himself. All of the engineers under his command, including McClellan, were sick, several officers had already gone back to Veracruz, and "others are going whose strength & energies have failed. . . . The labour of the whole Corps was very arduous in the trenches & too much for anyone. I am too thankful that I have so far stood it."

The army moved out the next day for Jalapa, which fell at once. Grant wrote an Ohio friend that the area was beautiful, blessed with fruit and "vegitables the year round" and home to a "great many handsome ladies and well dressed men." He told Julia if she were with him he'd like to make Jalapa "home for life." He didn't mention the handsome ladies.[3]

Lee too was charmed by the highland town and told Mary it

would compare with any place he had ever seen, including, apparently, incomparable Virginia. "I wish it was in the U.S. & I was located with you & the children around me in one of its rich bright valleys."

Forty miles west of Jalapa, the army ground to a halt. "The delay has been occasioned by the unwillingness of the Old Volunteers to proceed further into the country," Lee wrote. "It is a beautiful commentary upon the System if our rulers & politicians would read it aright. . . . I do not blame the men. They came for *pleasure* & their officers for political capital. They all found it hard work. In a word they have Seen the Elephant & wish to return home & glorify themselves." The volunteers did leave, but two weeks later Scott pushed on and Worth's division with Lee in the advance walked into Puebla on May 14.[4]

Grant's brigade, commanded by Colonel John Garland, sauntered through the plaza of the town, stacked their arms, and curled up for naps. Grant needed the rest. He'd been sick with chills and fever for two weeks, and was riven with loneliness. Though Julia played little games of romance with Grant, such as coyly suggesting that she was his prisoner, she also tormented him with tales of her parents' cooling on the engagement. Grant's father, by now a full-blown Whig and apparently toeing the anti–Mexican War party line, repeatedly urged Grant to resign. Pressures from home exacerbated his depression, and in Puebla, his tenuous emotional hold on his Army career seemed to be weakening.

My Dearest Julia if this war is to continue for years yet as it may possibly do (but I do not think it will) can I stay here and be separated from you (whom I love so much) all the time? I have no intention of anything of the kind. In the course of a few months more I will see you again if it costs me my commission which by the way I value very low for I have been a very long time ballancing in my mind whether I would resign or not. At one time about two years ago or near then, I was offered a proffessorship in a College in a very pretty town in Ohio and now I regret that I did not go there. I often think how pleasantly I would have been settled now had I gone. No doubt you would have been with me dearest and I have always been happy when I was near you. My Dearest Julia before now I would have applied for a leave of absence and insisted upon getting it had your father and mother given their consent to our engagement. I do not doubt but they will give it, but when I go to Mo. I would like you to become mine forever my dearest, and if I am to stay in the army I would come back myself and see the war out.

With none of the clearly articulated notions of duty or honor or tradition which helped sustain Lee, Grant was victimized by his desires. Only a commitment to decency and a confused wish to do the right thing supported the dissatisfied quartermaster on his weary trek toward Mexico City. "Warring in a foreign country does very well for a while but a person who has attachments at home will get tired of it in much less time than I have been at it," Grant wrote. The observation couldn't have much surprised his fiancée.[5]

Most of the invading army was tired of warring under the circumstances imposed by American politicians. No sooner had Scott's forces encamped at Puebla than he was notified that secret peace negotiations were again occurring between Santa Anna and Polk's agent Nicholas Trist, who had instructions to offer the Mexicans $15 million and a boundary at the Rio Grande. Through Scott, British nationals living in Mexico City notified Trist that Santa Anna could be bought and had again promised delivery of the Mexican legislature. With Scott acting as intermediary, Trist sent Santa Anna a $10,000 down payment—an amount apparently insufficient to sway Mexican opinion, but adequate to help Santa Anna maintain his exalted standard of living.

While this high-level melodrama was occurring, the American army settled down for a three-month stay in Puebla. Lee and other headquarters regulars maintained a vigorous schedule of dinner parties and visitations to clergy and important Pueblans. Messmates remembered Grant at this time as being "careless about his dress, wearing hair and whiskers long and ragged." He "chewed tobacco," they said, "but never drank to excess nor indulged in

the other profligacy so common in that country of loose morals."
He contracted for shoes and clothing with Puebla craftsmen, and
replenished the division's supply of horses and mules from the
countryside. Accompanied by an escort of 1,000 men, he commanded a two-day foraging expedition on which he saw nothing
of the fearsome "Santa Anna and his myriads." Though Grant
had his share of fraternization—including one unpleasant brush
with a rebellious brother of two young ladies favored by the 4th
Regiment's officers—he spent most of his free time doing what he
liked best—sitting and watching. He often saw Lee ride by.[6]

In August, Scott learned that Santa Anna had absconded with
the graft seed money. Since he had received some long-awaited
reinforcements—Franklin Pierce arrived with 2,500 men—he decided to attempt taking Mexico City. On August 7, the advance,
led again by General Twiggs, assembled in Puebla's plaza and
responded with a roar to a demand for "a regular Cerro Gordo
shout." An aide, noting that the Jalapa garrison was in ranks as
the division rattled out of town, solemnly thought the choices
ahead were only "victory or a soldier's grave." Scott had cut his
lines of communication and the American force of 10,000 was
alone. "We had to throw away the scabbard," Scott exulted
afterward, "and to advance with the naked blade in hand." Picking their way up through the passes in the 11,000-foot range surrounding the capital, Twiggs's advance, which included Lee,
caught glimpses of what seemed to be "an immense inland sea"
below. As the road turned down, the view cleared and the men
could see before them "a great garden, dotted with bright lakes,
fields of emerald and the white domes and glittering spires of the
villages that environ the capital." Scott was transfixed. Mexico
City, backed by the towering "White Maiden," the mountain of
Popocatepetl, was in reach. "That splendid city soon shall be
ours," trumpeted "Old Fuss and Feathers."

There was a way to go to get it. Rain dampened the enthusiasm
and speed of the descent, making roads hazardous for artillery and
wagons, but worse waited below. Save for a swamp and a rock-
strewn lava bed which he thought was impassable, Santa Anna
had ringed his capital with defense works. Scott halted at San

Agustín, twelve miles from the city, and called for Lee. A member of Scott's staff noted that Lee by that time was "invaluable"—not only for his "judgment, tact, and discretion" but for his skill on reconnaissance. Scott assembled his staff to hear Lee's plan for crossing the lava bed, known as the *pedregal*. He'd done it that day, he told Scott, and he was certain he could do it again, leading a detachment. He did. After directing the placement of batteries, he spent the rain-soaked night crisscrossing the cindery field three times with information for headquarters. Scott, calling him "gallant and indefatigable," said Lee's work was "the greatest feat of physical and moral courage performed by any individual, in my knowledge, pending the campaign." The following day, after a spirited fight, the Americans took Contreras.[7]

Grant later said that the battle, which he watched from his position far down the road, was like that of Cerro Gordo, "an engagement in which the officers of the engineer corps won special distinction." He commended "the skill of the engineers," but, unlike his commander, did not single out Robert Lee. There were many heroes that day. Pete Longstreet distinguished himself, and so did the theatric "Prince" John Magruder. Fitz-John Porter recovered an American cannon claimed from Taylor at Buena Vista. Tom Jackson proved to be as intractable with his gun as he had been with his West Point studies. But there was grief among the glory. In Contreras, Lee discovered Joe Johnston, who was just recovering from taking a bullet in the leg at Cerro Gordo, huddled in a corner, "his frame shrunk and shivered with agony" over the death of his nephew Preston, who had lost his life manning a gun in Lee's battery. Arms outstretched, Lee rushed to comfort his old friend and "burst into tears," Johnston remembered.

Furious at the prospect of not being the first American general officer into Mexico City, Worth on August 20 lashed his men into what was little more than a footrace with Twiggs's division, took to the main road, and got them cut to pieces. "We rushed our heads against Churubusco," Grant's former Jefferson Barracks commander Dick Ewell said, "and a bloody field it was." After a heavy day of unnecessary fighting, American flags were finally planted on the works of the little town. Among the booty were the survivors of the San Patricio Battalion, who were imprisoned to protect them from the vengeance of their former brothers-in-arms. The following day, Scott sent word that he was honoring another armistice proposed by Trist for further talks with Santa Anna.

The delay gave the Americans time to count their losses—more than 1,000 in two days' fighting. Scores of brevets were handed out for Contreras and Churubusco—Don Carlos Buell, Earl Van Dorn, George McClellan, D. H. Hill, Pete Longstreet, Tom Jackson, Simon Bolivar Buckner, and Fred Dent all got them. Francis Lee, commanding Grant's 4th Regiment, praised each of his officers in his official report, and ended by referring to "Lieutenant Grant, regimental quartermaster, who was usefully employed in his appropriate duties." Thirty-four members of Grant's graduating class were still in the Army, and only nine—Grant among them—were still second lieutenants. It must have seemed to the useful quartermaster that his soldier's life was not altogether different from what "Useless" Grant's had been in Ohio.[8]

For two weeks Scott and his headquarters staff rested near the archbishop's palace at Tacubaya, a stream-fed garden of the Mexico City rich, built with expansive villas and redolent with jasmine. But by September 7, Scott knew the wily Santa Anna had again outwitted the Americans and had used the "armistice" for preparations against the final assault on Mexico City. Scott immediately decided to attack the city gate at Chapultepec. One day's shelling disabled a dozen Mexican guns. One more day brought Chapultepec into American hands.

While Lee watched Longstreet and George Pickett scale the walls of the outpost, Grant was on the road into the city with Garland's brigade. No longer able to support his "appropriate duties," quartermaster Grant took a handful of men and under fire sneaked his way to the final barricade on the southwest side of Mexico City. There he saw a route around the Mexican battery and returned to the brigade for volunteers. At the same time, Garland sent forward the 2nd Artillery Regiment to accomplish exactly what Grant had intended. Everyone knew the game was almost over. "The moment was a very exciting one," said one of the participants involved in the race for glory, who later claimed no memory of which officer had first gained the barrier. Obeying orders to fall back, Grant's men regrouped. After an hour's wait, Grant took off again, accompanied by a small detachment carrying a dismantled howitzer. This time he got as far as a church just outside the city walls which had been used by the Mexicans for defense of the gate.

Grant dragged his gun into the church belfry, aimed it downward, and scattered Mexican defenders. "The effect of this gun upon the troops about the gate of the city was so marked that General Worth saw it from his position. He was so pleased that he sent a staff officer, Lieutenant [John C.] Pemberton—later Lieutenant-General commanding the defences of Vicksburg—to bring me to him. He expressed gratification at the services the howitzer in the church steeple was doing, saying that every shot was effective. . . ."[9]

From his aerie Grant could see the plain from which the division had rushed into the city. There, the San Patricio Battalion waited, with an American officer at attention. Nooses looped around their necks, their cheeks branded with the deserter's "D," they sat silent on extra cavalry horses. A cheer from the city trained the officer's field glasses on the wall where Pickett and Longstreet went over, and in a moment he saw the Stars and Stripes hoisted against the blue sky. Turning, he nodded toward his assistants. The horses were slapped away. The deserters hung in place for days, but they were welcomed into the arms of Holy Mother Church by padres who crept out after dark to say the last rites.

That night, after releasing convicts from the city's jails, Santa Anna fled. At eight o'clock the next morning, General Scott and his staff moved through crowds of Mexicans to the stairs of the capitol building, dismounted amidst the cheers of the soldiers, and occupied the city.[10]

In September, Grant wrote to Julia for the first time in more than two months:

> Since my last letter to you four of the hardest fought battles that the world ever witnessed have taken place, and the most astonishing victories have crowned the American arms. . . . It is to be hoped that such fights it will not be our misfortune to witness again during the war, and how can it be? The whole Mexican army is destroyed or disbursed, they have lost nearly all their artillery and other munitions of war; we are occupying the rich and populace valley from which the great part of their revenues are collected and all their sea ports are cut off from them. Every thing looks as if peace should be established soon; but perhaps my anxiety to get back to see again my Dearest Julia makes me argue thus. The idea of staying longer in this country is to me insupportable. Just think of the three long years that have passed since we met. My health has always been good, but exposure to weather and a Tropicle Sun had added ten years to my apparent age. At this rate I will soon be old.

He was already turning bitter. "No doubt before this the papers are teaming with accounts of the different battles and the courage and science shown by individuals. Even here one hears of individual exploits (which were never performed) sufficient to account for the taking of Mexico throwing out about for fifths of the army to do nothing. One bit of credit need not be given to accounts that are given except those taken from the reports of the different commanders." Years later he somewhat caustically—and inaccurately—noted that he had gone into the battle of Palo Alto in May 1846 a second lieutenant and had entered Mexico City sixteen months later with the same rank, "after having been in all the engagements possible for any one man."[11]

Lee's letter to Jack Mackay took a lighter view of publicity. "We are our own trumpeters, & it is so much more easy to make heroes on paper than in the field. For one of the latter you meet with 20 of the former, but not till the fight is done. The fine fellows are too precious of persons so dear to their countrymen to expose them to the view of the enemy, but when the battle is *won,* they accomplish with the tongue all that they would have done with the sword. . . ."[12]

Just as Scott's forces seized Mexico City, members were being elected to the Thirtieth Congress, which assembled in Washington in December 1847. It was an illustrious group, filled with venerable names—John C. Calhoun, Daniel Webster, Thomas Hart Benton, and John Quincy Adams—and ones destined for greatness—Jefferson Davis, Stephen A. Douglas, and Abraham Lincoln.

Supporters of the war favored the "rescue" of a large part of Mexico or the annexation of the entire country. James Buchanan spoke about fulfilling destiny, and Polk advisers talked about the rich new market for manufacture and agriculture. Even some anti-slavery men joined their expansionist brothers in seeing Mexico as fertile ground, but only because it might strip Virginia and other border states of all slaves.

Whig representative Alexander Stephens said the "principle of waging war against a neighboring people to compel them to sell their country is not only dishonorable, but disgraceful and infamous." His friend Abraham Lincoln worked for days on what would be his first speech as a representative from Illinois. Lincoln demanded clarity and honesty from Polk. "Let him remember he sits where Washington sat, and so remembering, let him answer, as Washington would answer." If the President could not adequately explain aggression against Mexico, then, said Lincoln, "I shall be fully convinced . . . that he feels the blood of this war, like the blood of Abel, is crying to Heaven against him."

By calling on Cain and Abel, Lincoln evoked the mystical urgency of arguments over the Mexican War. Political brothers were fighting over the legacy of their revolutionary and constitutional founding fathers. As the new generation cast lots for the 850,000 square miles of land acquired in the war, arguments centered on the correct interpretation of the Constitution of the

United States. Did the document allow Texas, New Mexico, Arizona, California, and Oregon to become free or slave territories? The issue was ambiguous. The Constitution's tacit sanction of slavery gave it silent legal support. But like the uncertain and qualified approval of Federal supremacy, slavery's initial acceptance served to conceal and postpone conflict rather than resolve it. Congressmen in 1848 who wanted to prohibit slavery in land acquired from Mexico knew they were tampering with the fragile precedent of the 1820 Missouri Compromise, a measure which set the northern boundary of slavery at a geographic point—36°30′ latitude. But legislators easily settled into sectional roles provided by Missouri Compromise debates and just as easily came to a similar deadlock. Pro-slavery men insisted on extending the 36°30′ limitation to the Pacific Ocean. Anti-slavery men would not allow virtually all land gained by the Mexican War to be open to slavery.[13]

While congressmen fought about Mexican territory, the victorious army of occupation was mounting an internecine battle in Mexico City. It was not enough that Americans had won the war. Scott's division commanders fell into squabbles over who had done what, and found their only source of agreement lay in castigating Scott. Always testy over slights, Scott put Generals Worth and Gideon Pillow under arrest. When Pillow demanded a court of inquiry, which was duly seated at Puebla, Lee wrote a sputtering defense of Scott to a friend in Washington—a letter which eventually found its way into print, causing a highly embarrassed Lee to be censured.

Complaints and dissatisfactions were not reserved to the highest level. Grant, stationed with his brigade outside Mexico City, believed—erroneously, it turned out—that his work at the San Cosme gate during the last day's fighting had been overlooked in official reports. "Didn't you see me go first into that work the other day?" he demanded of a messmate, Henry Hunt. When Hunt demurred, a disgruntled Grant insisted that he *"was* in first," but that since no one had seen him, he had lost his last chance for military distinction.[14]

Grant, however, did not join the grab for glory which followed the taking of Mexico City. Polk soothed influential egos by awarding brevets to men slighted by their commanders in the field, thereby angering many of the best soldiers, Lee among them. He wrote his father-in-law that he hoped his "friends will give themselves no annoyance on my account, or any concern about the distribution of favors. I know how these things are awarded at Washington & how the President will be besieged by clamorous claimants. I do not wish to be numbered among them." He also disclaimed the honors he had already won, but, like Grant, was keeping count. "I cannot consider myself very highly complimented by the brevet of 2 grades," he wrote. "They were bestowed on two officers at Palo Alto for one single effort on the part of each . . . if I performed any Services at Vera Cruz, or at the battles around the Capital, they will go for nought."[15]

He was no happier about the political debates on Mexico in Washington: "It is true we bullied her. Of that I am ashamed, as She was the weaker party, But we have since by way of Set-off drubbed her handsomely, & in a manner that women might be ashamed of. They begin to be aware how entirely they are beaten & are willing to acknowledge it. It would be curious now if we Should refuse to accept the territory we have forced her to relinquish & fight her three years more to compel her to take it back. It would be marvellously like us."[16]

Lee took a six-month lease on a Mexico City house, hired a cook who had a "pretty sister," and busied himself with sightseeing in the surrounding mountains and with socializing in the homes of American sympathizers. He had found numerous "handsome" women to enjoy and wrote Mackay that Mexican ladies thought stockings such a harbor for fleas "they have discarded them altogether & wear their polished ankles instead. I admire the change amazingly." He did not, however, admire his brother officers' responses to such delights. He wrote his son that he prayed the boy would always preserve his "innocence & rectitude. Such horrid forms of vice meet one at nearly every Step that I am sickened by its Contemplation, & would prefer a thousand deaths than to

See the l[e]ast, practiced by any of my children. It is distressing to See the depravity to which human nature falls by indulging their Selfish passions & which can only be avoided by guarding well our conduct & governing our thoughts & wishes." This remonstrance against human nature run amok was a stern rebuttal of the graceful humor with which he had accepted colleagues' activities in his youth. Since Custis was sixteen—an age when planters' sons conventionally became interested in the slave cabins—Lee's urging the boy to preserve innocence was understandable. But the opportunities for "vice" in Mexico—that country of "loose morals"—may well have made it difficult for Lee to successfully govern his own thoughts and wishes. "Feeble in will & shallow in heart, what hope is there of my overcoming my natural depravity?" he asked Mary. The question may well have alarmed his wife, no stranger to the racy gossip coming from Mexico.[17]

He seemed to be weakening all around. He told his father-in-law that many officers were resigning in sympathy with General Scott, and that he was tempted. "I wish I was not of the Army myself," he said, "but my desire is rather to allay the excitement than to foment it by my example." But exemplary behavior was not easy. "I have constantly resisted all invitations & opportunities for returning & expressed my willingness to do duty as long as I was able & my Services needed. But I confess there is a change in my feelings now & I should be very happy if I could leave the Country tomorrow without dishonor. Judging from the feelings of my acquaintances, there would be a Slim army left, if the Army could get away. But I must [not] indulge in Such feelings."[18]

Grant's feelings then, as on his first day on the Rio Grande, were confused. Until the Army got to Mexico City, where Scott prohibited all officers, even those who resigned, from leaving, he could simply have turned in his commission and gone home. Others did. He complained about the good health which prevented his sick leave and about being overlooked for recruitment duty in the United States, and often threatened to resign. Just as often, he considered Mexico a happy alternative to life near an Ohio tannery. Though he never articulated any pull between duty

and pleasure, Grant wanted to do the right thing. More important, he wanted to be happy. He wrote Julia that he hoped "if the
Mexicans dont make peace soon that our Government will decide
upon occupying this whole country then the married officers
would bring their families here and with the society we would
then have I would not want a better station, except I would never
be satisfied unless you were here too, my Dearest Julia. Would
you come to Mexico? I look forward to the time for my going back
to Missouri with a great anxiety and dont you think it too bad that
I have never got leave to go!" He was twenty-six years old in the
spring of 1848. He had taken the frustrations and desires of his
Mexican experience and dropped them into a category he called
"Julia."[19]

By the end of April news arrived that the treaty of Guadalupe
Hidalgo, which had been ratified by Congress earlier that month,
had passed the vote in Mexico. Exultant, Lee wrote Markie
Williams that he was on his way to Virginia. At Veracruz, with
the Irish servant he'd brought from Arlington—Jim Connally—a
mare he had acquired in New Orleans before the war—Grace
Darling—and a little white pony named Santa Anna that he
purchased for his youngest son, he boarded the steamer *Portland*
for New Orleans. "Fighting is the easiest part of a Soldiers duty,"
he wrote later. "It is the watching, waiting, labouring, starving,
freezing, willing exposure & privation that is so wearing to the
body & trying to the mind. It is in this state that discipline tells,
& attention night & day on the part of the OffS so necessary. His
eye & thoughts must be continually on his men." Lee had been
privy to the most important military decisions about the war. He'd
seen Scott cut his supply lines more than once, and had learned
the value of audacity and boldness in the face of a much larger
enemy. He had also learned the proper political limitations of the
military. Irritation with the foolishness of legislators had to be
suppressed on the field if Lee were not to abandon his notion of
public virtue. He succeeded in this, just as he succeeded in fulfilling his expectations of himself. He had never faltered in the
execution of his orders, and he had exceeded his commanding

officer's expectations. He never was crippled by fear, and he endured physical hardships. "There are few men more healthy or more able to bear exposure & fatigue," he wrote Mary, "nor do I know any of my personal associates that have undergone as much of either in this campaign." He was proud of himself. From the first "not unholy pleasure" he had experienced contemplating the soldier's grave of Markie's father to the last dramatic forty-eight hours he'd spent in the saddle before riding with Scott into Mexico City, Lee had exercised talents he may not have known he had. He had proved himself to be the "very best soldier in the field" that Winfield Scott ever saw. It seemed, like Light-Horse Harry before him, that "Captain Lee" had "come out of his mother's womb a soldier."[20]

Grant was not long in following Lee to Veracruz, then to New Orleans. On July 16 he headed north to dearest Julia. A handsome gray mare accompanied Grant, as did a small representative of the peonage he said he hated—Grigorio, a little body servant he'd been given in Mexico City. Despite limited opportunities for heroism, Grant had done a good job in Mexico on an assignment he detested. Quartermastering had taught him the valuable lesson that strategy and tactics were meaningless unless men were provisioned with arms, ammunition, food, and clothing. He would agree with Lee that fighting was the easiest part of a soldier's life—certainly it was the most fun. And he was then intensely aware that during his two years in Mexico he'd been actively engaged only twice. He had made enough friends to compensate for Georgetown loneliness and had overcome the horse trade by going into business twice, setting up bakeries in Monterrey and Mexico City. He was proud of this achievement—as it turned out, the sole commercial success of his whole life—and wrote in his *Memoirs* that in two months he "made more money for the fund than my pay amounted to during the entire war." But his most valuable Mexican lessons had to do with the men he'd seen.

Years later, Grant said the "war brought nearly all the officers of the regular army together so as to make them personally acquainted. . . . Lee, J. E. Johnston, A. S. Johnston, Holmes, Hebert, and a number of others on the Confederate side; McCall,

Mansfield, Phil Kearney, and others on the National side. The acquaintance thus formed was of immense service to me in the war of the rebellion. . . . The natural disposition of most people is to clothe a commander of a large army whom they do not know, with almost superhuman abilities. A large part of the National army, for instance, and most of the press of the country, clothed General Lee with just such qualities, but I had known him personally, and knew that he was mortal; and it was just as well that I felt this."[21]

CHAPTER

8

GRANT PRESENTED HIMSELF to his "enchanted" fiancée in July. He was right, the sun had aged him, he was tanned and trim and seemed more self-confident. Julia, on the other hand, was still suffering from the harder financial times into which Colonel Dent had fallen. Since there could be no monetary settlement on her marriage, she offered to release Grant from the engagement. Her "Captain," of course, refused. Julia had moved with her mother and sister into an "unpretending" townhouse in St. Louis, and there was no hope for a gala White Haven wedding. She made the best of things, though, and set the date for August 22. After a few rapturous days filled with "gay company" and quiet planning, Grant left her for Ohio with the promise that he would be back by August 20.

As his stagecoach reached Bethel, Grant had reason to hope his 1848 homecoming would make up for the disappointments he had suffered four years earlier. No one in America then, not even opponents of the war, was making fun of the Army. In St. Louis, Missouri, girls vied for the attention of returning veterans, and Grant had been lionized by friends of the Dents. A good reputation had preceded him to Ohio too. Though Jesse had made a pest of himself crowing about Ulysses's Mexican exploits, the letter Tom Hamer had written home before he died had people thinking they might have been wrong about "Useless." When Grant arrived, they knew they had been wrong. He had shaved off his ragged red whiskers before seeing Julia, but enough of the sunburnt unkempt remained to hint of battlefields in Mexico. And he had with him a Spanish-speaking body servant who not only rode like the wind but was a wizard with the lariat. Apparently foreign duty had diminished Grant's reticence, for he told exciting tales about life at the front. He also knew the Whig candidate for President, Zachary Taylor, and could describe just how the hero of Monterrey sat a horse sideways and smoked cigars in the thick of flying bullets.

Only one thing cast a pall over his visit: his family refused to go to St. Louis for his wedding. Bethel had less of the South in it than Georgetown, and Jesse, who had been to Columbus to help write the platform for the Whig Party, had been elected mayor of the town when it incorporated. His business was prospering—a relative thought he was worth $150,000 at the time—in a political climate which was becoming decidedly anti-slavery. All his life Jesse Grant would call Julia's family "that tribe of Dents," and he could hardly be expected to sully his carefully cultivated reputation by attending a social event presided over by lazy slaveholders. No, Ulysses was told, we won't go, but you bring her home as soon as you like.[1]

Julia put the wedding together in a week. There was no vulgar—and costly—display, just a table "set at the end of the back parlor upon which were served ices, fruits, and all that Papa's hospitality and good taste could suggest for the occasion." Wearing a borrowed dress and "enveloped" in the "fleecy folds" of a white tulle veil fastened with Cape jasmine, Julia said her vows in the front parlor of the little brick house at Fourth and Cerre streets. Grant was attended by Cadmus Wilcox, Bernard Pratte, and Pete Longstreet—who all went South when the time came. After the ceremony, the few witnesses crowded into the back parlor for a slice of the wedding cake. A bridesmaid or two attempted a waltz, then the Grants said good night to their guests. They were off early in the morning for Ohio.

Julia was excited about leaving St. Louis for the first time in her life, especially by steamboat. "How I marveled at this great creature, as I felt it to be, gliding so swiftly along and obeying the slightest motion of the hand in the pilothouse. It seemed to me almost human in its breathing, panting, and obedience to man's will. I was really greatly impressed with the power of man." Sitting alone on the deck with Ulysses, holding hands, was "very, very pleasant," she remembered. "He asked me to sing to him, something low and sweet, and I did as he requested. I do not remember any of the passengers on that trip. It was like a dream to me."[2]

Julia and Ulysses were met in Cincinnati by Grant's younger brother Orvil, who went along on the stage to Bethel. Julia was "nervous, or rather anxious," about meeting "this truly interesting family," but she said she got a cordial welcome from both Jesse—whom she found "much taller than his son"—and Hannah—whom she declared to be the "most self-sacrificing, the sweetest, kindest woman I ever met, except my own dear mother." It is unlikely that the stern mother-in-law met the belle of White Haven with much sweetness, but Julia had the habit of prettifying things. In a smart new buggy drawn by a "fleet little steed," the newlyweds drove around Brown and Clermont counties visiting relatives and family friends. Julia loved the "great forest-clad hills" and "cool and shadowy valleys," and she thought Grant kin "charmingly hospitable," but dismissed their Ohio houses as "humble."

By October, it was time for Grant to report to his regiment in Detroit. Declining invitations to stay with the Grants while Ulys went back to the Army, Julia once again boarded the steamboat and returned with her husband to say goodbye to the Dents. But once Ulysses and Julia arrived in St. Louis, the young Mrs. Grant flagged. The idea of leaving "my dear home" to "make one among strangers" proved too much. Julia spent the better part of a week in "a flood of tears." Grant's confidence as a husband was eroding, and he finally demanded a hearing. He told Julia that for four years he had been "anticipating how pleasant it would be for us to spend our days together, and here at the end of two months I was relenting." Papa Dent interrupted the woeful scene with a solution: Julia should stay at home, and Grant could visit her once or twice a year. Ulys slipped his arm around Julia and bent his head to whisper, "Would you like this, Julia? Would you like to remain with your father and let me go alone?!"

"No, no, no, Ulys. I could not, would not, think of that for a moment," she burst out.

"Then," he said, "dry your tears and do not weep again. It makes me unhappy." Julia obediently left the home that was "so bright, so kind, always, always." Hard times lay ahead of them at Detroit and beyond, but the young couple held hands. They laughed. She sang. They would make a new dream together.[3]

Reality imposed itself as soon as the Grants arrived in Michigan. Grant had been supplanted as regimental quartermaster and was ordered on to Sackets Harbor, New York, on the eastern shore of Lake Ontario. He filed an official protest, then he and Julia started the unexpected final leg of their trip. With Grigorio and Grant's sister Clara, they made the difficult and "expensive" trip in two weeks—an unusually long time.

Married life began in a bleak frame house at Madison Barracks. In later years, Julia remembered herself as an addlepated spend-thrift indulged by a fond husband. But she settled down to the hardships of garrison life in the frozen winter of 1848 and drew upon her midwestern farm girl hardihood to make a home for her husband. She hung curtains—"dark, rich crimson of some soft woolen material and *very* pretty over ivory tinted embroidered muslin"—on the windows, and covered bare floors with "beauti-ful, soft and warm" carpets she and Grant selected on shopping trips in a sleigh to nearby Watertown. Bachelor officers often stopped by for a card game and he and Julia entertained using her wedding silver and flowered china. Julia's table, she said, "was simply delightful." Dudy stood by in rapt admiration of her social skills and made up the deficits in her housekeeping accounts. But the idyll ended in the spring of 1849, when Grant was ordered back to Detroit.[4]

When he returned to Michigan, he reluctantly resumed a cor-respondence with "Dearest Julia," who went to St. Louis for a visit. "This you know is my Birth day," he wrote on April 27, "and I doubt if you will think of it once." Grant's successful petition to be restored to his place at regimental headquarters seemed not to have produced professional contentment. He confessed that he had "nothing atal to do" since he had no company to command or commissary busywork. What may have been worse, he learned that the two brevets he'd received in Mexico were snarled in military red tape. The dates advancing him from second to first lieutenant were confused with the brevet that made him a captain. He was forced formally to return the honors, but stubbornly insisted on signing himself "U. S. Grant, 1st Lt." even though it took two more years to untangle the orders. But most troublesome was the money he owed the government. Sometime during the 4th Regiment's march from Mexico City to Jalapa, $1,000 from the quartermaster funds—money for which Grant was responsible—had disappeared. Grant asked for a board of inquiry and swore that he had placed the money in Captain Gore's trunk and that the trunk had been stolen on the night of June 16. Though Grant was exonerated of wrongdoing, he still had to pay the $1,000 debt, which could be removed only by act of Congress.[5]

It was Julia's job to compensate him for such soldierly vexations, and Grant braved a cholera epidemic in St. Louis which claimed 4,500 lives to bring her to their new home in Detroit. The house on East Fort Street was not quite the retreat he had described to her in letters. Located in the worst part of town, the flimsy frame dwelling was little more than a kitchen with a bedroom and "double parlour" tacked on. The "garden filled with the best kind of fruit" was actually sparse and dreary, and a rickety grape arbor failed to rescue the place from meanness. Grant had put a soldier to work to make the house more comfortable, and had arranged the furniture, including a sturdy bedstead with cornhusk mattress, as best he could. Julia pronounced his product "snug and convenient," and soon was pregnant. Forced to do without her "dusky train" of slaves, she was aided in her housekeeping efforts by the cook and maid Grant hired to supplement the labors of Grigorio, who served as valet and attended "the table and door." Such arrangements were hard to support on a salary of less than $1,000 a year, but the Grants managed to keep everyone but their unpaid help. It did not take Detroit abolitionists long to discover that Grant's houseboy was virtually a slave. Julia said "some meddlesome person" convinced Grigorio "that he could do better for himself," which caused the "nice cheerful boy" to become "sullen." Grant told him "he was at liberty to go."[6]

Slavery and freedom were issues much discussed in 1850 as Congress argued the merits of a compromise introduced by Henry Clay to solve the ideological puzzle created by the Mexican War. Dissolution of the Union and civil war were cited as threats or rewards as the often violent debates moved toward a conclusion that left no one happy. When the crazy-quilt compromise finally passed, slavery would be legal in all territory acquired from Mexico except California; the slave trade was outlawed in the District of Columbia; and the fugitive slave provision of the Constitution, which prohibited "a person held to service" from escaping to freedom in another state, was codified. Only the increasingly intractable positions of opposing forces emerged from the 1850 compromise debates with any clarity or force. Clay, Calhoun, and Daniel Webster spoke for the last time on the compromise, and voices of the future—including Jefferson Davis and William Seward—drowned them out. Seward, especially, with a speech naming a "higher law" than the Constitution, created an edge on which New England intellectuals were as happy as southern slave owners to sever the Union.

Even during the great debates of 1850, slavery was a forbidden subject at the Detroit sutler's store where soldiers gathered to kill time. Mud in spring and summer, ice in winter, and "nothing atal to do" made for a dreary post which the presence of wives and children could not brighten. Mexican veterans found it hard to settle down, and they tried to re-create the thrills of Monterrey or Churubusco in Detroit's rutted streets. Grant shared the wildness which had ministers warning their flocks to stay away from the soldiers. He didn't read much, smoked incessantly, played cards constantly, "and was regarded as a restless, energetic man who must have occupation, and plenty of it, for his own good."

What few official duties he had, he did poorly, attracting superiors' attention only for desultory bookkeeping and carelessness. He filled up his life with Julia and with friends. When Julia left for St. Louis in the spring of 1850 for the delivery of their first baby, Grant had only his friends.

He moved into a house rented by Major John Gore and lived so quietly that Gore's landlord thought he was a boy hired to help with chores. But townsfolk along Jefferson Avenue saw a different Grant. Horseflesh was a passion of the area, and Grant fit right in, barreling through town on the back of one of the French ponies bred on Michigan's plains. But pacers were the premium horses in Detroit, so Grant raffled off his pony and bought a little mare for $250. He harnessed her to a buggy and racked up a string of wins. Once he bet $50 that his horse could pull him down Jefferson Avenue in less than three minutes. Streaking along a corridor of cheering takers, he crossed the finish line in something over two minutes, pocketed the $50, gave the horse a rubdown, and led his friends to a tavern to share the wealth. "No man was permitted to leave the party before refreshing himself at least a dozen times," a celebrant remembered. Grant couldn't stand to lose races or games and would keep competing until he finally won something. Each victory was celebrated at "Mother" Weaver's or "Coon" Ten Eyck's, where Grant's cronies noticed how he took his whiskey. Hand on edge on the bar, he'd have a glass filled to the index finger.[7]

The May 30 birth of his son, Frederick Dent Grant, kept him home more often. The Grants continued to live with the Gores, an "arrangement" which Julia said was "much more economical as there was but one house and one set of servants to be kept instead of two." Though Julia was often seen on Detroit's imperfectly boarded walks with a "great lump of baby in her arms," she needed people to know she was a woman of quality. She made herself memorable by hosting a costume ball which threatened— with justification, it turned out—to be such a bash that it was denounced from Detroit pulpits. The Grants attended every party on the barracks calendar, but Ulysses tended to "hold down a seat all evening" while Julia danced with a seemingly endless supply of her husband's fellow officers. One regular remembered Grant "standing rather aloof from the company and uncommunicative with his hands behind his back, impassive. He always gave me the impression of a school-boy who had not learned his lesson, but he was always very devoted and tender to his wife. She, as I think, was his salvation." But he was remembered as always willing to slip outside for a drink when the occasion arose.[8]

When Julia left Detroit for a month in Bethel with her in-laws and a lengthy stay at White Haven, Grant initially seemed not to mind her absence and wrote lively letters filled with gossip and questions about the progress of their son. But as the weeks went on and Julia once again proved an inadequate correspondent, Grant began to complain. In his anxiety, he invented illness or even death for the baby, who he feared had forgotten him anyway. His spirits rose somewhat with a transfer back to Sackets Harbor, but fell again when Julia ignored his instructions to return. As if to remind her of her failures, he launched into decorating their new rooms by himself, then took a vacation at West Point, where he decided he "should really like very much to be stationed. . . ."[9]

Julia returned that fall and found that the "Captain had our quarters all prettily fitted up." The "Captain" himself may not have been so well turned out. Within weeks, Grant joined the Sackets Harbor division of the Sons of Temperance and pledged not to "make, buy, sell, or use, as a beverage, any Spiritous or Malt Liquors, Wine or Cider." Townsfolk remembered him wearing the red, white, and blue Temperance ribbon in his lapel, and holding a succession of offices in the lodge, which was said to have been "kept in a flourishing condition" through his efforts. Grant's decision to join more than 150,000 teetotalers in a movement that was designed to stem American alcoholism would not have been made without Julia's approval and even urging. Perhaps the trouble began in Detroit, and contributed to her overlong absence. But more likely, her overlong absence added to the trouble. Though Julia played helpless for Grant's sake, it was he who couldn't stand being alone. The whiskey barrel was a convivial way of blurring isolation. Drinking out of need was a different thing from drinking with his buddies, and apparently both Grant and Julia recognized the change. She never again took a vacation without him.[10]

With the spring thaw new orders arrived. The regiment was going to California. The men at Sackets Harbor were to rendez-vous at Governors Island, and board steamships for the Isthmus of Panama, which they would cross, then pick up boats in the Pacific. Grant had to dispose of government property on Lake Ontario and transport three companies of the 4th Regiment to New York City. But he also had to deal with Julia, who was six months pregnant and insisting on going along. After a predictably tearful encounter, Julia said Grant told her that "he thought it would be running a great risk, both of my life and that of our boy, but that he could not insist on my remaining at home if I still continued opposed to it. So I slept well and did conclude that it would be a great deal better to remain with our friends until this, the greatest of women's ordeals, was over, but I expected, hoped, to yet accompany my dear husband to California."[11]

Grant sent Julia to Bethel to stay with his family, and left for Governors Island, where he found that Benjamin Bonneville had been made commander of the expedition. Bonneville didn't like Grant. Some of the officers said the trouble had something to do with an incident in Mexico, but others thought his antipathy toward Grant was self-indulgent whimsy. Bonneville was a vain-glorious prima donna whose service as a western explorer in the 1830s was idealized in reports written by Washington Irving. Political connections seemed responsible for his subsequent Army advancement. Now, with no demonstrated ability to lead large groups of men, he was in charge of transporting an entire regiment around the continent to California. He demanded another quar-termaster, failed to get one, and reluctantly accepted Grant, who set to work finding accommodations for the eight companies as-signed to the sidewheeler *Ohio*—already overbooked with civil-ians when the War Department chartered it.

A delay gave Grant a chance to go to Washington and look into the $1,000 he owed the government. But his timing was poor.

When he arrived, he discovered all government offices closed in honor of Henry Clay, who had died on June 29. The committee he wished to address did not sit until his leave had expired. He had to make do with a lukewarm promise of help from an Ohio congressman and spent the remainder of his time sightseeing. Even that proved disappointing. He stopped in Philadelphia on his way back to New York and arrived at Governors Island to find that the regiment was to sail the next day.[12]

"I never knew how much it was to part from you and Fred. until it come to the time for leaving," he wrote Julia. "You must be a dear good girl and learn Fred. to be a good boy. I will rite to you from evry place we put in shore. You must write to me soon and direct as I have told father. It distresses me dearest to think that this news has to be broken to you just at this time. But bear it with fortitude."[13]

Crowded with the 700 soldiers who swung in hammocks tacked up on deck, the *Ohio* paddled southward through seas so choppy that everyone on board—including Grant—became violently seasick. Colonel Bonneville, who was dismissed by most of the party as a "very stupid man mentally," responded to the stress with a "testy temper" and began issuing a series of "hasty and uncertain" orders. Grant, who cared for the troops during the seven-day trip to Panama, was called upon to arbitrate disagreements that arose between Bonneville and his staff, and won praise for his "particular good sense." Torn with loneliness for Julia and anxiety over the birth of his second child, he mused alone on deck when he was off duty. He had lost weight, was "quiet and reticent," and paced back and forth, head bent into a cloud of pipe smoke, lost in "deep thought."

The boat docked in Panama on July 16 at Aspinwall, a new town thrown up three years earlier to skim money from Americans traveling toward the California goldfields. It was the height of the cholera season and Aspinwall was eight inches deep in water. Grant directed Indian and black porters to carry baggage across the rickety boardwalks to the head of the railroad spur, which extended twenty miles into the jungle. Speed was essential. The regimental surgeon was already on record with his view that it was "murder" to transport soldiers across the Isthmus. Within twenty-four hours, Grant had most of the regiment to the end of the railway, where they were to meet dugout canoes for transportation to Cruces. Frightening tales of "drunken barbarians" poling boatloads of thirty to forty unarmed soldiers and their families up the river filtered back to Grant, and it was said cholera was raging in the tiny town twenty-five miles from Panama City.

When Grant got to Cruces, he found the rumors were true. Men, women, and children were sickening and dying. The War Department had previously contracted for mules to transport the regiment to Panama City, but the local agent had absconded with the money and there were no mules. Grant immediately started the men marching overland, and stayed behind to find enough mules to carry baggage. Junior officers noted that he remained calm and dealt confidently with the hysteria at Cruces. Colonel Bonneville did not. He raced ahead to Panama City, where he ordered the sick and dying onto the steamer waiting to take the regiment to California. When Grant and the surgeon got to Panama City, they discovered that Bonneville had quarantined the Army transport, but had also packed it with still healthy soldiers and their families.

Grant leased an old hulk of a boat lying at anchor a mile away from the *Golden Gate* Army transport, moved the ill soldiers and civilians onto this new hospital ship, and volunteered himself for nursing duty when the enlisted men on board deserted. "He was like a ministering angel to us all," one officer wrote, adding that Grant's endurance was amazing. He seldom slept, "and then only two or three hours at a time." At no time did he reveal his strength more dramatically than when Major Gore, his closest friend and messmate from Sackets Harbor, collapsed with the shout: "My God, I've got the cholera." Grant arranged for his friend's burial in one of the cannonball-weighted canvas sacks he had made for the dead, and saw to getting Mrs. Gore and the children back home.[14]

By the time the regiment was finally under way, more than 100 people had died. On August 9 Grant wrote his first letter to Julia in a month. It was a spare account of death and tragedy which made no mention of his part in the rescue of the regiment. Only a clenched comment hinted at the degree of his rage. "I will say however that there is a great accountability somewhere for the loss which we have sustained." He was too exhausted to ask her to write.[15]

WHILE GRANT WAS struggling to get the 4th Regiment across the Isthmus of Panama, Lee was wrestling with an offer to become superintendent of West Point—an offer he eventually accepted. Though he would be steering the academy toward the strengthened position demanded after the Mexican War, he felt he had "never undertaken any duty with such reluctance as I enter upon this." He would "endeavor to meet the views of the Dept. & deserve its approbation," he wrote Colonel Totten, but would be "ready at all times to relinquish a command which I know under the most favourable circumstances must be onerous," especially "when it is thought any other can better administer it." His sourness was mistaken as further evidence of his modesty, but he was quite sincere. He had experienced the brotherhood and glory of the Mexican War, and he had liked it. West Point offered no such opportunities. It seemed, if anything, worse than his duties during the four years which separated his letter to Totten and his return from Mexico—as frustrating and unrewarding a period as any in his life.[16]

"Here I am again, my dear Smith," Lee wrote his brother about his homecoming from Mexico, "perfectly surrounded by Mary and her precious children, who seem to devote themselves to staring at the furrows in my face and the white hairs in my head. It is not surprising that I am hardly recognizable to some of the young ones around me and perfectly unknown to the youngest."

Word had reached Arlington on June 29, 1848, that Lee had arrived in Washington. A carriage was dispatched, and family members gathered in the parlor. Lee's namesake, called Rob, insisted that his nurse outfit him in a favorite blue cotton dress, and his golden curls were smoothed for the return of this exotic and slightly fearsome father. The approach of a horseman riding up Arlington's lane went unnoticed until the Lee dog, Spec, dashed down the steps to greet the newcomer, who had dismounted and was striding up the walk. The homecoming was a shock for everyone. Little Rob later said he was "humiliated" when Lee embraced a visitor as his own child. Even the older children were reserved at his return, Lee told Smith, apparently unable to "reconcile what they see and what was pictured in their imaginations."[17]

The father had as much trouble as the children. He was permanently assigned to duty repairing Fort Carroll, at the mouth of the Patapsco River in Baltimore, and was sent first to New England and then to the Gulf of Mexico on a series of investigations of coastal defenses. He stopped at Cumberland Island on his way south, but did not call on the Greene family, who still lived in the house where Light-Horse Harry died. Nor did he visit his father's grave. Lee dined with the Mackays in Savannah, but Eliza, long married and soon to be a grandmother, was living in Vienna. And Jack, the only close friend he ever had, was dead; tuberculosis had claimed him the week Lee sailed from Veracruz.[18]

Lee moved alone to Baltimore in the spring of 1849 after having spent only one day visiting "Mary and her children" at Arlington. In May, he wrote an angry reply to a note from her: "Yet when you have every reason to believe that I am well and busy, wishing to be with you, yet cannot come, why are you disapp*d?* Pray do not be expecting letters, or imagining all conceivable things painful to you & very distressing to me. . . . The real distresses of life I think are sufficient for us. These are imposed by a kind Providence & ought to be borne without complaint. But we are not authorized to persecute ourselves and others with imaginary evils. This embitters life. Is poor return for the real happiness bestowed upon us. Carries with it no compensation."

The "evils" Mary was imagining may have emerged from the gossip about the excesses of Mexico. Even the Lees were not immune to rumor. Everyone in the Army knew they often lived apart, and there were whispers that they had separated. There was that anguished letter she had received from Mexico City in which Lee addressed his depravity and vice. And despite his assertion that he wanted to be with her, his departure had been precipitous enough to prove he was anxious to get away. His 1849 letter recalled his 1835 retort from Michigan when Mary was ill, but it ended with a vague threat which announced a new theme. "You have borne with my faults so long," he reminded his wife, "bear with them for the little remaining space to which perhaps my life is doomed."[19]

Two months later he was less irritable, but no more hopeful. He had just come from church, he wrote Mary, where he had heard the minister deliver a sermon which demonstrated that only by conforming to God's commandments can man escape "evil & calamity. No one can be more Sensible of these facts than I am," Lee said. "But it is so difficult to regulate your conduct by them. Mans nature is So Selfish So weak. Every feeling every passion urging him to folly, excess & sin that I am disgusted with myself & Sometimes with all the world. My efforts to improve are too feeble to Succeed, & I fear I Shall never be better."

The confessional did not restore harmony in the marriage. When Lee several weeks later developed a malarial fever, he went to Ravensworth, not Arlington, to recuperate. After regaining strength, he paid a short visit to his family, then went back to Baltimore. Still ill when he received orders to inspect defenses at Newport and getting no relief from the laudanum he was using as a balm, he wrote Mary that he could not accompany her to the Virginia mountain spas and suggested that she come along to Rhode Island. She declined. When he finally wrote her from Newport in August, it was with some pleasure that he recounted a collapse in Philadelphia and another, worse one in New York, where he was forced to rely on the attentions of strangers. He closed on a chilly note. He had attended a wedding, he said, and thought the bride had made an imprudent marriage. However, when a "thing *is done* we ought always make the best of it. Death will soon come to cure all our ills in this life." Hope for deliverance by death was not a very merry view of the conjugal state, but Lee was feeling trapped. He had been home for a year and had come up with no relief from the restlessness that shook the Army in the wake of the Mexican War. When he got back to Baltimore in September, he toyed with an uncharacteristic plan of escape.[20]

Agents for a junta preparing a revolutionary takeover of Spanish-held Cuba were trying to hire Mexican War veterans in New York. The group intended to offer command to General Worth, but he died that spring. Jefferson Davis, honored for his display at Buena Vista and in 1849 chairman of the Senate's military appropriations committee, declined the offer—and the $200,000 salary—but suggested the agents contact Robert Lee. Lee met with the Cubans in Baltimore, and was so tempted that he made a trip to Washington to discuss it with Davis. Davis apparently weighed the expedition's chances for success. But Lee was most interested in the moral aspects of an American-trained soldier leading foreign troops in a foreign military conflict. What Davis failed to make clear in his later observations was the piratical nature of the Cuban adventure. American expansionists, particularly southern slaveholders, still saw the United States growing southward into a huge empire. The head of the Cuban mission, Narcisco López, was in reality hoping for the American annexation of his country, a hope shared by many wealthy Cuban sugar planters. When the expedition finally made an unsuccessful foray against the Spaniards in Cuba and had to flee for safety to Key West, the U.S. government arrested the participants and prosecuted them for violating neutrality laws. Davis apparently then, as later, favored the Cuban mission. Nothing in Lee's life except, perhaps, the fact of his father, had prepared him for heading a filibustering attempt against Cuba, and his final refusal was to be expected. But that he should involve himself in such an unsavory—and illegal—enterprise at all is an indication of his emotional desperation at that time. Perhaps his desire to flee all domestic duties for the excitement of a foreign war was what he meant by his "folly, excess & Sin." That route closed, there was nothing more to do than accommodate himself to the peacetime routine at Fort Carroll and the questionable pleasures of family life.[21]

When the three-story brick Federal townhouse Lee had rented from his uncle Williams Carter was finished in January 1850, Mary, some of the children, and all the pets came to Madison Street. Though Lee, who slept alone, had a bedroom "hardly big enough to swing a cat in," the house was an interesting change for the youngest children. Rob, who had never lived with his father, discovered that Lee "was a great favorite in Baltimore, as he was everywhere, especially with ladies and children." Certainly he continued to be a favorite of Markie Williams. Her father's death in Mexico had made her a regular at Arlington, and she was a constant visitor in the Lees' Baltimore house. When Lee wrote to her, he often referred to his heart—which "always returns warmth & softness when touched with the thought of you." He thought of her constantly, he said. "I have followed you in your pleasures, & in your duties, in the house & in the streets, & accompanied you in your walks to Arlington, & in your search after flowers. Did you not feel your cheeks *pale* when I was so near you?" Markie was one of the few bright spots in Lee's life, though he kept up socializing and was as charming to strangers as ever. Rob Lee later recalled overhearing a visitor exclaim that everyone, "and everything—his family, his friends, his horse, his dog—loves Colonel Lee." The boy never forgot the excitement of watching his father in full uniform, dressed for parties, "waiting for my mother, who was generally late. He would chide her gently, in a playful way, and with a bright smile. He would then bid us good-bye, and I would go to sleep with this beautiful picture in my mind, the golden epaulets and all—chiefly the epaulets."[22]

Always bookish, opinionated, and ill groomed, Mary made no effort to hide her contempt for the Maryland *beau monde.* Her time, she complained to her aunt, was "frittered away [by] company & matters of little moment," and she shared her mother's dismissal of wealthy townsfolk who seemed to live for "no purpose but to show fine furniture and fine dress." Burdened by the ever-encroaching debilitation of her body and dissatisfied with arranging her life around Lee's career, Mary centered her pleasures on her God, her children, and her home. Baltimore, like Fort Hamilton and St. Louis, was not home. "It seems a pity that in this short life we should be so much separated from those we love," she wrote her mother, "yet all is meant to teach us that this earth is not our home, that only in heaven are we to look for perfect bliss. There parting and sorrow are alike unknown." Bliss, for the forty-year-old wife of Robert Lee, remained what it had been when she was a bride envying Eliza Mackay's closeness with her mother in Savannah. But twenty years had made a difference in Mary's need for Arlington. Her arthritis was a real and constant source of discomfort and she seems to have borne it uncomplainingly. There was no cure for the disease and only opium—which Mary wouldn't take—to relieve its pain. She needed care, not all the time, but enough of the time to strengthen her dependence on her mother. And her mother never stopped wanting Mary home permanently, or complaining about Lee's unwillingness to exchange "soldiering for farming."

It was not as if the soldiering in Baltimore was giving him much pleasure. Looking to the pouring of footings, the hiring of labor, bookkeeping, and struggling to stay within a budget continually constricted by the military appropriations committee kept Lee miserable, and Mary knew it. She also knew why he refused to quit. During his southern tour, he had written her a letter describing an uproarious dinner he'd had with a group of Army colleagues. "You have often heard me say that the cordiality & friendship in the Army, was the gr[ea]test attraction in the Service," he wrote. "It is that I believe that has kept me in it So long, & it is that which makes me now fear to leave it. I do not know where I should meet with so much friendship out of it."[23]

Lee was more honest than Grant in admitting that he feared leaving the Army, but his emotional options were more limited. Grant at least thought he could have everything—friendship, love, and the safety of Julia—within a military career. If he had to choose, he could leave the Army for the safer, friendlier environment of civilian life with his "Dearest." Lee had no such hopes. He was the living legacy of George Washington, and a noble cavalier who could move his friends to laughter with his stories and to praise over his gallant exploits. Out of the Army,

Lee was the son-in-law of George Washington Parke Custis, the husband of a woman who preferred the company of her mother, and the father of children who seemed scarcely to know him.

Most of the children, not just Mary, were reluctant to be away from Arlington. At any given time since they were born, at least one of the seven had made their home with the Custises. Little Mary had stayed in Virginia when her parents went to St. Louis, and Custis and Rooney were schooled near Arlington. Mildred, the youngest, and Rob were cared for by an Arlington nurse, and Annie and Agnes seemed to have permanently settled themselves there. Impelled to participate in their rearing, Lee began a series of exhortive missives to his children which bore all the earmarks of Light-Horse Harry's pathetic letters from the Caribbean.

Despite Lee's adamant opposition, Custis wanted to go to West Point. "The same application, the same self denial, the same endurance in any other profession, will advance him faster & farther," Lee wrote. "Nothing but an unconquerable passion for Military life, would induce me to recommend the Military profession." Nevertheless, Lee spoke with Winfield Scott in Custis's behalf, and wrote a letter to the Adjutant General citing the Revolutionary services of Light-Horse Harry. Custis got the appointment and thus opened himself to years of righteous advice from his father. "I pray you may have *strength, fortitude & Capacity* to accomplish the Course before you with honour to yourself & advantage to your Country. It will require a *firm resolve* on your part; *persevering industry* & a Courageous *heart*. You know my great affection for you, my earnest wishes for your welfare; & my proud ambition for your distinction. You must therefore pardon my anxiety & extreme Sensitiveness to all that Concerns you. You have, like an affectionate Son, nobly responded to my expectations. May God reward you for it & help you to Continue to the end as you have begun."[24]

In what Lee might have assumed was a divine smite for his own pride, within a month Custis was disgraced. Liquor had been found in the boy's academy room and he immediately wrote to his father, explaining his innocence in what apparently was a practical joke. But the threat of even undeserved scandal was humiliating to Lee. Apparently only Mary knew of the affair, and she didn't even tell her mother about it. Custis was cleared of charges and got off with only eight demerits, and Lee wrote him, adopting the playful nickname of Custis's childhood—"Mr. Boo"—saying he was delighted that the *"slanderous* report" had been set aside. "I could not believe it before to the extent of the report, & supposed it must have been greatly exaggerated. I am happy to have my impressions confirmed. I trust there will be no cause for even suspicions in the future." He tempered the stiff congratulations with admiration for his son's refusal to let friends aid him. "I am fond of independence," he wrote. "It is that feeling that prompts me to come up strictly to the requirements of law and regulations. I wish neither to seek nor receive indulgence from anyone. I wish to feel under obligation to no one." Now that the matter was over, Custis could join the corps again. "I was very sad before," Lee wrote, "when I thought of you trailing to meals after the guard, and deprived of the relaxation and enjoyment of your Comrades. It seemed unnatural. I could not realize that such a position was befitting my son." Later, teasing, Lee clarified what Custis's rightful place was. "Press forward" in your work he said. "You must be No. 1. It is a fine number. Easily found and remembered. Simple and unique. Jump to it fellow . . ."[25]

Custis jumped. But he failed to prosper, and Lee had to urge him to shake off "gloomy feelings." "Why man, when I am troubled, harrassed or vexed, I think of you to cheer & Support me. I feel as if I had Somebody to fall back upon. To Stand by me. To take care of my wife & children when I am gone." Lest the young man not be heartened by such cheer, Lee gave him some additional hints. "All is bright if you will think it so. All is happy if you will make it so." At the same time he urged Custis to look "upon things as they are," not as he wished them to be, and to give up dreaming as "too ideal, too imaginary." He closed the letter by saying that all "that is bright must fade, & we ourselves have to die. Keep that in view & live to that end."[26]

Custis, understandably, might have failed to rally under such confusing advice, but the letter was a good reflection of Lee's frame of mind. Earlier he had written his mother-in-law, rhetorically wondering if humankind were "so weak, shortsighted & ignorant . . . that we must be *made* to do what was *right?*" He was more decisive in the copy he kept for himself. "We are so weak, shortsighted & ignorant . . . that we must be *made* to do *right.*"[27]

Lee knew that doing "right" and accepting the "onerous" command of West Point was particularly important in the spring of 1852. There were portents that the military might be called upon to play some role in the ongoing ideological war between the ever stronger abolitionist camp and the ever more strident pro-slavers. Just before he formally accepted the position, the Democrats had chosen Franklin Pierce—a New Hampshire man considered a toady of the "slavocracy"—to run against the Whig Winfield Scott for President. But the Whigs as a party were finished, pushed offstage by a new, tougher team of Free-Soilers. Scott would have been the candidate backed by Arlington, and he undoubtedly put pressure on Lee, who he thought was the "best soldier" in the country, to go to West Point. But as Lee packed his bags for the North and his new duty, he knew that Scott hadn't a chance, and the Union was in peril.

"My good dame as is natural is lingering with her parents," Lee wrote in October from West Point. "Her departure is always a sorrowful event to them & sad to her. She will probably be on by the last of the month." Lee knew Mary would never be like the women he celebrated as true soldiers' wives, but he had no cause to complain about her at West Point. She had well-defined social duties at the academy, and she performed them well. Though Agnes and Annie stayed at Arlington and Rooney was at boarding school in New York City, the rest of the Lee children were with them. Custis was in his third year as a cadet, and Mary, Rob, and little Milly attended day school near the academy. The superintendent's house was large, well suited to entertaining, and had a fine garden, which Mary immediately set about to improve, and a greenhouse with an exotic lemon tree.[28]

Routine was very pleasant, picturesque, far away from the politics on the Potomac. Every weekend the Lees were at home to calls from upperclassmen and their friends, and holidays were kept with gala receptions. New faculty brides entertained by the superintendent and his wife were dazzled by George Washington's "superb candelabra" and wine coolers on tables perfectly set for Lee's "scrutinizing eye." Mary fought against her arthritis and kept up long walks over the surrounding hills. Lee rowed his daughters on the Hudson during fine weather, and oversaw skating lessons for the youngest children in winter. He had brought some of the family horses from Arlington, and every day rode his Mexican War mare, Grace Darling, while Rob bounced along at his side on Santa Anna, the wide white pony Lee had shipped from Veracruz. Lee insisted that the boy make the pony trot, saying playfully that the hammering he got from the dragoon-style seat was good for him. Character-building extended to the children's household duties too. Rob was expected to care for his room as if he were a cadet. Lee would inspect it, "to see if I had performed my duty properly," said Rob, "and I think I enjoyed this until the novelty wore off. However, I was kept at it."

Military standards were imposed on the absent children too. Lee wrote Mrs. Custis that Annie and Agnes were to be tutored in sewing and knitting and taught to "do everything to make them useful and independent. It is the only way to make them happy." In addition to domestic arts, the Lee girls were ordered "to write a good hand, & to be *regular orderly* & *energetic* in the performance of all their duties," and to sing. "I Cannot admit their assertion that 'they can't,' " he wrote. "They *Can* if they *try* & I say in addition they *Must.* " They were also to "hold themselves properly" while they were at their studies, and take "regular exercize in the open air." "I do not know what the Cadets will say if the Superintendent's *children* do not practice what he demands of them," he wrote twelve-year-old Annie. "You and Agnes must not, therefore, bring me into discredit with my young friends."[29]

Lee's notions of rearing had a distinctly Yankee slant. The arts, mathematics, and even French—all essential subjects for southern girls with prospects of planter marriages—were omitted from his syllabus. But his rigorous demands were always sweetened and paternal prods were made nearly irresistible by expressions of his love. "I long to see you through the dilatory nights," he wrote Annie. "At dawn when I rise, and all day, my thoughts revert to you in expressions that you cannot hear or I repeat. I hope you will always appear to me as you are now painted on my heart, and that you will endeavour to improve and so conduct yourself as to make you happy and me joyful all our lives." Lee freely admitted that prospective spouses would have a hard time getting his children away from him—and they did. None of the girls ever married. Neither did Custis. All were taught to be responsible for their father's happiness. He examined the character of his children, especially the boys, for early symptoms of Lee-Custis family weaknesses—and perhaps his own. Perceived failures were actually the fault of their failed father, they were told, and any remorse they might feel was weighted with guilt.[30]

His attitude toward his new charges at West Point was less tortured, but just as diligent. He demonstrated a scrupulous regard for impartiality by recommending the immediate dismissal of his nephew Fitzhugh—Smith Lee's oldest son—for a drinking episode. The Secretary of War rejected this recommendation, thus saving for the Confederacy a brilliant cavalry leader. But the Secretary approved Lee's dismissal on academic grounds of James McNeill Whistler, thus saving for America a brilliant painter. "Had silicon been a gas, I would have been a major general," Whistler, who failed chemistry, was fond of remarking during the Civil War.

Lee received prodigals with special commendations for increased efforts, and outright scoundrels left West Point under the protection of confidentiality, which, on Lee's insistence, extended all the way to the young men's parents. A cadet's word was never challenged during his administration, and unsubstantiated suspicions were ignored. His instinctive thriftiness was responsible for squeezing excess dollars from the academy budget while at the same time providing an enhanced curriculum, more comfortable uniforms, and better housing. Each student became a personal charge to Lee, who treated negligent young men to lengthy interviews about their slow progress. He wrote to disappointed parents explaining that their sons' dismissals on the grounds of Grant's hated "sins" did not arise from conduct that was "disgraceful" or calculated to affect their "moral character or standing." If cadets were failing for academic reasons, Lee urged that their parents allow them to resign before the examinations which would result in their being dropped. "He is a youth of such fine feelings and good character," Lee wrote one father, "that I should not like to subject him to the mortification of failure, to which he might give more value than it deserves. For I consider the character of no man affected by want of success provided he has made an honest effort to succeed."

If such sterling official performance were not enough to endear the superintendent to his charges, his social behavior assured it. Rob Lee, then ten or eleven years old, remembered how painfully shy were most of the cadets who paid formal calls on the Lees during their weekend open houses. As soon as his father "got command, as it were, of the situation," Rob wrote, "one could see how quickly most of them were put at ease. He would address himself to the task of making them feel comfortable and at home, and his genial manner and pleasant ways at once succeeded."

Lee won commendations from the War Department for his West Point work, but the new Secretary, Jefferson Davis, observed that the job was wearing the superintendent out. It was obvious, Davis said after an 1853 visit to the academy, that Lee's "sympathy with young people was rather an impediment than a qualification for the superintendency."[31] Long office hours, hated paperwork, and a massive amount of correspondence added to Lee's woes. In addition, he found himself handling a flood of requests for recommendations from graduates, most of which he denied for lack of firsthand information. Lee's eyesight was bad, his digestion suffered, and he was mildly irritable all the time. The exercise he took—and forced his children to take—did not produce the ruddy stamina he had possessed in Mexico. Surrounded by family, supported by friendly acquaintances, and sustained by official praise, Lee failed to thrive. Whatever good spirits he could muster were completely destroyed in May 1853, when Mary Lee Custis died. He wrote to Markie Williams:

> I have no language to express what I feel, or words to tell what I suffer. The blow was so sudden & crushing, that I yet shudder at the shock & feel as if I had been arrested in the course of life, & had no power to resume my onward March. . . . Do not think me so selfish as to repine, or to wish undone, what has been done in mercy & charity. Nor would I if I could, recall a glorious angel from heaven to resume the ills, the griefs, & infirmities of life. But well as I know the happiness it has brought to her, I feel the anguish it has left to me. But I must bear it, & for her sake would bear more. May God give me the necessary strength, & above all the power so to live, that when I die, my last end may be like hers.

It was his own mother, not his mother-in-law, who had been ill, infirm, and burdened with grief. But when Ann Lee died in 1829, Mary Lee Custis had absorbed some of Lee's inchoate sorrow, and though he struggled with her over his family, he had turned to her for maternal support. "As a son I have always loved her, and as a son I deeply mourn her," Lee wrote Mary at Arlington. "My heart will cherish her affections & remembrance till it too ceases to beat, when I pray & trust I may be privileged to join her."

Until the spring of 1853, Lee had never mentioned joining the dead; after the death of his mother-in-law, it became a leitmotif in his correspondence. Hopes for meeting loved ones in the beyond supplanted his musings on his own depravity. Perhaps to assure these reunions, two months later, during a visit to Virginia, he was confirmed along with two of his daughters at Christ Church in Alexandria. With the exception of a few short years in the 1860s, Lee never again valued life as much as he yearned for death. "May God give you strength to enable you to bear and say, 'His will be done,' " he wrote to Mary. "She has gone from all trouble, care and sorrow to a holy immortality. . . . Let that be our comfort and that our consolation. May our death be like hers, and may we meet in happiness in Heaven."[32]

Life as a purgatory was not lightly borne. In the fall of 1853 he had a visit from his brother-in-law, Edward Childe, and his nephew Vernon, with whom Lee struck up a friendship. "It was very painful to me," Lee wrote Vernon, "to part with you and your father & when I reflect upon the vicissitudes of life & the uncertainty of human affairs my regrets are not diminished. To you life is new & bright, & you can naturally look forward with anticipations of Joy & pleasure. To me looking at the future from the past, it brings feelings of apprehension & resignation."

Markie Williams, who had moved into the Arlington house to help look after Parke Custis, was Lee's only other confidante. He wrote to her with increasing frequency after 1853, and easily discussed the depression they seemed to share. "You who give so much pleasure to others, ought yourself to be happy & joyous at the benefits you bestow," he wrote. "We are all prone I think to undervalue the gifts of a merciful God, & to make our own unhappiness. I am conscious of my faults in this respect & make many resolutions & attempts to do better, but fail. I will continue my efforts & am resolved to improve. You who know my weakness will I fear have little confidence in my success." Even Custis's graduating first in his class failed to cheer the morose superintendent, and commencement festivities only added to his gloom. His surroundings, he said, were "as harsh to me as my duties, & neither brings any pleasure." "Toil & trust, must be our aim," he wrote Markie, "as it is our lot."[33]

Lee's West Point assignment came to an end when Congress, prodded by Jefferson Davis, created two new infantry and cavalry regiments for the Army. The 1st Cavalry Regiment was to be commanded by Colonel E. V. Sumner with Joe Johnston as lieutenant colonel. Albert Sidney Johnston was commander of the 2nd Cavalry Regiment and the lieutenant colonel was Robert E.

Lee. The immediate inspiration for the new units was a "massacre" of a recent West Point graduate and thirty of his men near Fort Laramie by the Sioux Indians. But violence was erupting in Kansas, and the cavalry was the Army's most effective weapon against frontier turmoil. Davis chose Lee, he said, because it was time to see the son of Light-Horse Harry in the saddle.

If Lee was excited about his new appointment, he was careful not to show it. Though he admitted to Markie that the change would be "agreeable to my feelings & serviceable to my health," he said he would not be happy. "You know Markie how painful it will be to part from you. But I shall not anticipate that it will be long, but shall hope that we shall all again be united, here and here after." Short of the eternal union, Lee said his "trust is in the mercy & wisdom of a kind Providence who ordereth all things for our good, & who can guard & protect us whether united or separate. To him I pray that my absence may not be felt by those I so much love, & that he will provide them with all they need." *"Personal* considerations," Lee told Markie, would never have prompted him to accept the new duty, but "in a military point of view I have no other course." From that view, the course was somewhat irregular. Lee was severed from his twenty-five-year connection with the Corps of Engineers and made an officer of the line. Such action would not have been taken without his knowledge and approval.

At West Point he learned how to work directly with the War Department and how to appease politicians. He also got experience commanding occasionally headstrong young men who were little more than children. With several important exceptions— notably Pete Longstreet and Stonewall Jackson—Lee's later attitude toward his field officers was unremittingly paternal. The habit he acquired of hiding his students' failings would show itself later as protecting his subordinates from the consequences of their shortcomings—an affectionate but dangerous method of command.

The rain poured down as Lee gathered up his belongings and shooed Mary, Agnes, Annie, Mildred, Rob, and sundry pets onto the omnibus bound for the West Point wharf. The cadet band played "Carry Me Back to Ole Virginny." Crowds of umbrellas jostled against the family as well-wishers waved handkerchiefs. Lee embraced his associates and wept. The boat turned south. The Lees would never live in the North again.[34]

CHAPTER

9

AT THE TIME Robert Lee arrived at Jefferson Barracks
to assume temporary command of his new cavalry regiment, the
military post near White Haven was being supplied with wood
by a seedy-looking farmer who lived in the neighborhood. Dressed
in a dirty and threadbare Army blouse, old crumpled boots, and
faded pants thinning at the knees, Ulysses S. Grant usually arrived late in the day, driving a Missouri buckboard. He swung
down off the seat and unloaded cords of White Haven wood by
himself, stopping to chat occasionally with cohorts from the Mexican War. Later, after he had driven off southward, the men
wondered how the quartermaster from Ohio had come to such a
sorry end. There were several versions of the story—some said
he'd been dismissed, others believed he had resigned voluntarily—
but everyone knew Grant was out of the Army. Most thought the
reason was his drinking.

Grant had started sliding almost as soon as his regiment arrived
at San Francisco in August 1852. His work in getting the survivors
of the 4th Infantry across the Isthmus of Panama had been near-
heroic. But the experience had left him bitter—as he had told
Julia, somewhere there had to be an accounting. The anger turned
to shock when he found he was being held responsible for loss of
Army property. And if that was not bad enough, some journalists

embellished the tragedy to include cowardice and miscreancy on the part of the officers. One newspaper report even had Grant running away. He was outraged, but he was also anxious. He had always needed people to think him a fine fellow. It was a bad beginning for a tour of duty which became more unpleasant each day.

It was six months before he even got word that Julia was alive—a real concern when nineteenth-century women were bearing children. Lonely—"I am almost crazy sometimes to see Fred"—and fearful that he had been forgotten in the West, Grant nevertheless wrote a string of unanswered letters to Julia in which he recounted attempts to join in the California race for financial glory. He'd been raised on stories of enterprise in the wilderness—look how well Jesse had done—and now had the chance to make good himself. There was no reason, he wrote Julia, "why an active energeti[c] person should not make a fortune evry year. For my part I feel that I could quit the Army to-day and in one year go home with enough to make us comfortable, on Gravois, all our life." Two of Julia's brothers were ferrying prospectors across the Stanislaus River, and Grant wrote descriptions of the ease with which the Dent boys were making "fifty to one hundred dollars daily." But he lacked their vigorous commitment to gain, and he was no Jesse. All his investments—and there were many—came to grief because of a gullibility so profound that Julia would later say the *Vicar of Wakefield*'s Moses was a financier compared with her husband. He was no more shrewd in his business transactions than he had been buying that embarrassing colt in Ohio. He never demanded security for loans he made, nor did he ask for negotiable or signed notes, and he almost willfully failed to protect himself against the vagaries of nature or the marketplace. He failed, in fact, at everything, including soldiering.[1]

Grant was assigned to Fort Vancouver in Oregon, where his lackluster bookkeeping and report-writing became even worse. He was commissary officer of the fort and acting quartermaster, and was responsible for supplying both the military base and government-backed survey expeditions to the interior of the state. His slowness, it was said, was often due to his socializing, and socializing in the tiny, forested outpost near Portland—then a log village of thirty houses—meant drinking. Commander Bonneville had learned to tolerate Grant, but some of the leaders of survey parties had not. George McClellan, the young engineer who had won Robert Lee's praise for his Mexican War work, arrived at Vancouver during a Grant drinking bout. "When the expedition was being fitted out, Grant got on one of his little sprees," a Vancouver regular said. The spree "annoyed and offended McClellan exceedingly, and in my opinion he never forgave Grant for it. . . ."[2]

All Grant's Oregon acquaintances found him melancholy. He seemed to liven up only when old friends asked about little Fred or Julia. "Oftentimes while reading letters from his wife, his eyes would fill with tears," said the wife of an enlisted man, "he would look up with a start and say . . . 'I have the dearest little wife in the world, and I want to resign from the Army and live with my family.'" Subordinates thought the captain was "always sad," and one never forgot the day Grant, trembling and tearful, opened a carefully creased letter to show the imprint of his new baby's hand.[3]

More misery and worse circumstances were waiting at Fort Humboldt, California, when Grant reported there on his first anniversary in the West. He dismissed nearby villages as not producing "enough ladies to get up a small sized Ball," and said he had no idea what the inhabitants "depend upon for support." He himself had nothing. His Vancouver caretakers were gone, and Humboldt was commanded by Robert Buchanan, a martinet who had earlier humiliated Grant for being slow to return to Jefferson Barracks after courting sessions at White Haven. "You do not know how forsaken I feel here!" Grant wrote Julia in February 1854. "I do nothing here but set in my room and read and occationally take a short ride on one of the public horses. There is game here such as ducks, geese &c. which some of the officers amuse themselves by shooting but I have not entered into the sport." A few days later he wrote again, despondent that the mail ship had brought no letter. "The state of suspense that I am in is scarsely bearable. . . . There is but one thing to console; misery loves company and there are a number in just the same fix as myself . . ." The fix was often alcohol.[4]

A careful observer concluded that Grant actually drank "far less than other officers, whose reputation for temperance was unsullied; but with his peculiar organization a little did the fatal work of a great deal." A Fort Vancouver regular insisted that Grant "was not by any means a drunkard"; he merely indulged in "two or three sprees a year . . . was always open to reason, and when spoken to on the subject would own up and promise to stop drinking, which he did." With much of the frontier and virtually all of the Army half pickled in whiskey most of the time, why was Grant singled out as a drunk? The "peculiar organization," of which profound depression was an important part, undoubtedly was at fault. Grant hated to feel alone, and whiskey was his solace. And if that was the reason to drink, then a "little" could do "the fatal work of a great deal."[5]

By late winter, he believed even Julia had abandoned him. She never complained of being lonely, he said, "so I infer that you are quite contented. I dreamed of you and our little boys the other night the first time for a long time. I thought you were at a party when I arrived and before paying any attention to my arrival you said you must go you were engaged for that dance. . . . I am getting to be as great a hand for staying in the house now as I used to be to run about. I have not been a hundred yards from my door but once in the last two weeks. I get so tired and out of patience with the lonliness of this place." The news from Humboldt was minor, he said. A man had accidentally shot himself, another had a tree limb crush him to death, and there had been a disaster at sea. Three weeks later he said he didn't know how much longer he could endure the separation. "But how do I know that you are thinking as much of me as I of you? I do not get letters to tell me so."[6]

On April 11, 1854, Grant wrote a letter to the Adjutant General acknowledging "the receipt of my commission as Captain in the 4th Infantry and my acceptance of the same." Then he wrote another: "I very respectfully tender my resignation of my commission as an officer of the Army, and request that it take effect from the 31st July next."[7]

That was it, he was out. Eleven days shy of his thirty-second birthday, Grant had resigned from the Army. There was much speculation about his finally taking the step he had threatened since the Mexican War. The most dependable accounts came from Grant supporters and agreed in all particulars. Rufus Ingalls, an old West Point friend who lived for a while with him in Oregon, said that "Grant, finding himself in dreary surroundings, without his family, and with but little to occupy his attention, fell into dissipated habits, and was found, one day, too much under the influence of liquor to properly perform his duties. For this offense Colonel Buchanan demanded he should resign, or stand trial. Grant's friends at the time urged him to stand trial, and were confident of his acquittal; but, actuated by a noble spirit, he said he would not for all the world have his wife know that he had been tried on such a charge. He therefore resigned his commission, and returned to civil life."[8]

It was characteristic of Grant to wait to be acted upon rather than to act on his resignation. He was good at doing what he was told to do, as long as his instructions correlated with what he thought was right. Given a choice, he tended to stick with the known, even when that meant severe personal suffering. Family members had described him as indecisive, and he certainly seemed so on the West Coast. During his two-year stint in California and Oregon he had tried, or said he wanted to try, farming, commerce, ice shipping, cattle raising, hog selling, timber cutting, card-house running, and hotel leasing. His failures were almost predictable, just as his drinking was bound to catch up with him professionally sooner or later. Grant meant it when he told Julia he could not endure being separated from her. But neither could he bear leaving the financial and emotional security of the Army. He set his course for self-destruction and waited for superiors to make the move.[9]

Apparently penniless, and actually in debt to an Oregon farmer, Grant swooned boozily into the arms of brother officers, who looked after him in San Francisco, and helped him book passage on a sailing ship bound around the Cape for New York. There were several claimants to the role of Grant's caretaker after he had made a better name for himself in the Civil War, but no one disputes his need at the time. With the airy observation that whoever heard from him in ten years would hear of a rich farmer, Grant went home. This was the same boast he'd given when he left Mexico. In 1854, there was even less reason to believe him.

When Grant arrived in New York he was down, and apparently still out. Simon Bolivar Buckner, a Mexican War acquaintance, guaranteed his hotel bill, and offered to underwrite a trip to Sackets Harbor, where he hoped—bootlessly, it turned out—to collect a debt.[10]

By then, his family knew the worst. He had written a terse letter to Julia before leaving Humboldt: "I have not yet received a letter from you and as I have a 'leave of absence' and will be away from here in a few days do not expect to. After recieving this you may discontinue writing because before I could get a reply I shall be on my way home. You might write directing to the City of New York."

Jesse got the news from Andrew Ellison, who was representing the Georgetown-Bethel district in Congress, and immediately asked him to write to Secretary of War Jefferson Davis to see if Grant's resignation couldn't be stopped. Jesse, who never doubted he knew what was best for Ulysses, also wrote Davis that his boy had done a silly little thing by resigning, and why couldn't the grown-ups just get together and forget the whole thing? But Davis ignored Jesse's letter. The resignation would stand.[11]

When Grant received money in New York to get to Julia, he waited until he heard from her before actually beginning the trip to White Haven. Julia alludes to this in her memoirs, but does not say why it was so. Apparently Grant had convinced himself his wife didn't want him back. She did. The separation had been hard on her too. Grant had been Julia's first—and apparently her only—suitor, and she needed to perceive him still as the handsome and desirable young officer who had courted her. This made her particularly vulnerable to feeling her own kind of abandonment while he was in the West. She had stayed in Ohio with the Grants until her baby, whom she named Ulysses S. Grant, Jr., was several months old, and she apparently hated it. She was not accustomed to Jesse's brand of parsimony, and was unprepared for the seething political climate of the area. By 1852, with the passage of the Fugitive Slave Law, southern Ohio had become a violent arena of anti-slavery action and, as "Uncle Tom" land, the focus of abolitionist sentiment. Julia removed herself first to St. Louis, then to White Haven, and she refused to visit the Grants again.

Living under her parents' roof was not all that pleasant either. She found herself once more subjected to constant invidious comparisons with her mother, whom she treated with barely concealed hostility. Colonel Dent was no longer a reliable support. She had married, and apparently not very well, against his wishes. Her pretty and popular sisters were doing far better at keeping alive the myth of old Maryland aristocracy. What was more, Dent actively disliked having children about—his irascible and infantile temperament was ill suited to the role of grandfather.[12]

But White Haven was not the only source of Julia's unhappiness. There were also disquieting stories filtering eastward from the Pacific coast. Julia's girlhood home was on the direct Army gossip line, and she could not have avoided "friends" or family who wished to inform her about her husband's activities. Grant's drinking had alarmed her at Sackets Harbor, and hearing about a repetition must have been unsettling. Even more disturbing were tales of the wide-open sex life on the coast. Grant had lightheartedly dismissed her worries by telling her that anyone saying he was making love to Spanish girls at Vancouver must be "desperately ignorant of the history of their own country," since there were no Mexicans within hundreds of miles of the place. But she apparently kept nagging, and finally irritated Grant. "You speak of not joining me on this coast in a manner that would indicate that you have been reflecting upon a dream which you say you have had until you really imagine that it is true. Do not write so any more dearest. It is hard enough for us to be separated so far without borrowing imaginary troubles." Julia's imagination created a semi-conjugal living arrangement for Grant in Oregon despite his correctly staying in bachelor's quarters. To make matters worse, the "story of the Indian daughter" and her romance with Grant was being whispered around. The wife of a Fort Vancouver enlisted man later said the tale was "baseless and malicious," but a frightened and lonely young wife might just have believed it.[13]

"How happy I was at having my beloved one near me again, to have him hold my hand in his and feel his warm breath on my cheek," Julia wrote of Grant's return. She was proud to be "nestled by his side," and rebuked "pretended personal acquaintances" of her husband's for asserting "that he was dejected, low-spirited, badly dressed, and even slovenly" on his return from California. "Well," she wrote, "I am quite sure they did not know *my* Captain Grant, for he was always perfection." Soon Julia was pregnant again, and after a suitably lengthy idyll at White Haven, the Grants prepared themselves for facing Jesse and Hannah, who had recently left Bethel for Covington, Kentucky.

Jesse was now semi-retired and had turned the running of his Galena, Illinois, leather-goods store over to his son Simpson. He was angry at Ulysses, humiliated by the scandal of the drinking, and irritated that his son's resignation—which he had been pushing for years—had been accomplished through no agency of his own. "West Point spoiled one of my boys for business," Jesse remarked when he saw Ulysses. "I guess that's about so," was Grant's quiet reply. When Julia and Ulysses talked with Jesse about their future, Jesse offered to set Grant up as a partner in the Galena shop. Grant was relieved. But Jesse had a final word: He would take his son into the business only if Julia and the two children stayed with him in Covington. Having had experience with family members he assumed were besotted veterans, Jesse thought Grant couldn't be trusted. Julia was aghast, and Grant "positively and indignantly refused his father's offer." The young family returned to Missouri and lived in the Dent house in St. Louis for the winter—apparently subsisting on White Haven food. In the spring of 1855 they moved to White Haven. Grant would farm the sixty acres Dent had given Julia as a wedding present.[14]

He was not starting his new life from a position of strength. His reputation, if not his constitution, was shaky, his own father had treated him like a ne'er-do-well, and his father-in-law could hardly be expected to receive the broken-down soldier as a family pillar. Once more depending on the indulgence of friends, Grant bought a team of horses on time and began cutting cordwood to sell at Jefferson Barracks and to Dent acquaintances in St. Louis. Since Julia's slaves—"Black Julia," Eliza, and Dan—were house servants, Grant hired freemen at ten to fifteen cents above the going rate, earning the irritation of other white employers and the scorn of neighbors who thought the arrangements ludicrous. The family also attracted considerable gossip around White Haven. No one could get along with Colonel Dent, and even the mild-tempered Grant was having his problems, it was rumored. The colonel's aristocratic sensibilities were bruised by his daughter's husband's lazing about the house until noon, then engaging himself in manual labor.

Politics had always been a problem between the two men, and it was impossible in Missouri to avoid the topic of slavery. Friends of Grant remembered that the issue was such a tender subject "it got so that it was not very pleasant living under the same roof with Col. Dent." Others thought Grant was unhappy in the "dependent position he occupied in the house of his father in law." By summer, the situation was intolerable, and Julia and Grant moved into Lewis Dent's house on White Haven land. A girl Julia reluctantly named Ellen after her mother was born on the Fourth of July.[15]

Julia settled into keeping chickens, churning butter, and attending sewing bees. By winter, Grant was making plans for farming on a grander scale and for building a house of his own. Julia tried to be game during this period, and succeeded at maintaining her cheer in everything but the house. "I cannot imagine why the Captain ever built it," she wrote, "as we were then occupying

Wish-ton-wish, a beautiful English villa belonging to my brother
. . . and situated in a primeval forest of magnificent oaks." Given
Julia's penchant for the romantic, it is safe to assume that Lewis's
small frame house was at least comfortable. Grant, she said, also
planned a frame house, "but my father most aggravatingly urged
a log house, saying it would be warmer. So the great trees were
felled and lay stripped of their boughs; then came the hewing
which required much time and labor, then came the house-raising
and a great luncheon. . . . It was so crude and so homely I did
not like it at all, but I did not say so. I got out all my pretty covers,
baskets, books, etc., and tried to make it look home-like and
comfortable, but this was hard to do. The little house looked so
unattractive that we facetiously decided to call it Hardscrabble."[16]

Hardscrabble had more the ring of Grant's wry sense of the
absurd than Julia's appreciation of the facetious. But Hardscrabble it was, and a comfortable and attractive house too—despite the
dismissal given it by its mistress. It was a southern-style log house,
with timbers planed square and chinked with plaster, and the
interior was whitewashed. Built on the plan of the old Georgian
farmhouses, it had a center hall with a sitting room and dining
room on either side. Upstairs were three small bedrooms tucked
under dormers. The kitchen was in the rear. Window and door
frames were milled by a local cabinetmaker and gave the place a
jaunty look.[17]

Neighbors thought the house pretentious. Grant was not making a living, and everyone around White Haven knew it. A year
after settling in Missouri, apparently undeterred by the treatment
he'd received earlier from Jesse, Grant wrote his father and asked
for help. "Evry day I like farming better and I do not doubt but
that money is to be made at it. So far I have been laboring under
great disadvantages but now that I am on my place, and shall not
have to build next summer I think I shall be able to do much
better." Grant gave his father a description of his plantings which
included a hint that the hopeful list of potatoes, corn, cabbage, and
melons might not yield everything it promised. "I have in some
twenty five acres of wheat that looks better, or did before the cold

weather, than any in the neighborhood." Once again, something was going wrong, and Grant was not quite sure what it was. He changed his tack at the end of the letter, saying that all the plans would probably come to nothing because he would have to "neglect" the farm "to make a living in the meantime," but he still hoped within a year "to be independent." Now came the crunch. "If I had an opportunity of getting about $500.00 a year at 10 pr. cent I have no doubt but it would be of great advantage to me." Grant's indirect request had something of an adolescent cajole about it, but he was not at all sure his father even wanted to hear from him. "Some three weeks since," he ended his letter, "I went into the Planter's House and saw registered 'J. R. Grant, KY.' on the book. Making enquiry I found that J.R.G. had just taken the Pacific R.R. cars. I made shure it was you and that I should find you when I got home. Was it you?" It probably was. But Jesse had not called. Nor did he respond to Grant's letter. Six weeks later, Grant had to write again.[18]

He began by reiterating his lack of money for seed, then came directly to the point. "To this end I am going to make the last appeal to you. I do this because, when I was in Ky. you voluntarily offered to give me a Thousand dollars, to commence with, and because there is no one els to whom I could, with the same propriety, apply. It is always usual for parents to give their children assistance in begining life (and I am only begining, though thirty five years of age nearly) and what I ask is not much." Emboldened by the idea that Jesse owed him this favor, Grant went on to ask for the $500 at 10 percent, but for two years rather than for one.

"The fact is," Grant wrote, "without means, it is useless for me to go on farming, and I will have to do what Mr. Dent has given me permission to do; sell the farm and invest elsewhere. For two years now I have been compelled to neglect my farm and to go off and make a few dollars to buy any little necessaries, sugar, coffee, &c. or to pay hired men. As proof of this I will state that since the 2d day of April last I have kept a strict account of evry load of wood taken to the City or coal Banks, by my team and it has amounted, up to Jan.y 1st, to a fraction over 48 dollars per month. Now do not understand from this that if I had what I ask for my exertions wood sease; but that they would be directed to a more profitable end . . ." Poor Grant obviously still bore the reputation of a bad businessman with his family. And he knew they thought Julia regal in her spending habits.[19]

No one around White Haven accused Grant of not working hard, but they did remember that he liked to sleep late and he was always a soft touch. Not a little of the $48-a-month earnings went to petitioners with stories of harder luck than his. It was like Grant to give away money which he had to replace by borrowing. This habit, seen as generosity, kept up his morale when he was financially strapped. Though Grant from the time he was a cadet at West Point talked about "competency" and "independence," these were not ends he pursued with any zeal. He never reneged on a debt, and was scrupulously honest in keeping track of what he owed, but he almost always owed somebody something.

Jesse gave his son the money he asked for, and during the summer of 1857, Grant was able to write his sister that his farming venture was a qualified success. But Julia later reported that her husband's "crops yielded well—that is, much better than papa's but not as much as he anticipated from his calculations on paper."[20]

Such was Grant's reputation around White Haven that a neighbor declared "in those days he could not have borrowed a hundred dollars." He seemed, to hard-bitten Missourians, "unpractical, a dreamer, with no turn at all for business." He was also thought to be drinking again. It was said he often "stopped before a certain resort on the Gravois road, watered his team and took a little something stronger himself." The handsome Grant horse team could be seen being driven home by a slave while the master "made a night of it" with a group of buddies. But the cronies were a new set of acquaintances. Grant's old Army friends found him broken and derelict.[21]

Brigadier General William Harney nearly rode down a middle-aged fellow on the streets of St. Louis one day. Finally recognizing the wearer of a worn blue uniform from which all insignia had been stripped, he called out, "Why, Grant, what in blazes are

you doing here?" Grant crossed one muddy boot over the other
and drawled, "Well, General, I'm hauling wood," a response
which sent peals of laughter through Harney's polished retinue.
"Great God, Grant, what are you doing?" was the greeting of an
old Mexican War friend, shocked at his appearance. "I am solv-
ing the problem of poverty," was the answer. At least once, Grant
declined to join a military party bound for the Planter's Hotel in
St. Louis because he wasn't "dressed for company." He happened
into Bill Sherman on a St. Louis street in 1857 and was too proud
to reveal anything of his troubles. Sherman, on his way back to
his in-laws in Ohio after having failed at banking in San Francisco, was calling himself "a dead cock in the Pit" at this period
and could have given Grant some company in his misery. Pete
Longstreet, who saw Grant several months later, was moved by
pity to accept repayment of a fifteen-year-old Grant debt. It was
to save his impoverished friend from further "mortification" that
Pete took the five dollars, even though he knew Grant could ill
afford it. Such meetings were bound to abrade so sensitive an ego
as Grant's, but they did not prevent him from approaching a New
Mexico–bound Army expedition in 1857 and asking for work.
The commander noticed a "horseman in a blue overcoat, a hat
broken and worn, and a stubby, sandy beard" catch up with the
column a few miles west of St. Louis and talk to the commissary,
who reported that the intruder was "old Ulysses S. Grant of the
Fourth Infantry. He wanted to be employed as commissary clerk
to drive beef cattle and issue rations while we were crossing the
plains. I couldn't employ him." Grant reportedly made several
such requests—one of which was to accompany a civilian to the
Colorado silver mines and set up a sutler's post. Nothing came of
any of them.[22]

Through it all, Julia maintained a sturdy regard for her husband's talents, and remembered only one moment of despair. "Is
this my destiny?" she said she cried aloud in her "cabin." "Is this
my destiny? These crude, not to say rough, surroundings; to eat,
to sleep, to wake again and again to the same—oh sad is me!" Her
mood was dispelled, she said, by a visit from reassuring fairies, but
her mother's death provided the means for her leaving Hardscrab-

ble. Ellen Wrenshall Dent died in early 1857, and Colonel Dent agreed to move into St. Louis and let Julia and Ulysses have the White Haven house. Portions of the land had already been sold to keep the Dents going, but Grant would have at least two hundred acres to farm. In addition, he bought a slave from Colonel Dent—William Jones—and was then master of four. But brightened prospects did little to enliven Christmas that year. Grant went to St. Louis and pawned a gold hunting watch and was thus able to buy a few merriments for his children.[23]

The new year brought a rise in spirits, though Grant confessed to his sister Mary that he would "wait until the crops are gathered" before making any grand predictions. As it turned out, he could not have predicted that things would go so badly. Another baby, Jesse Root Grant II, was born on February 6, 1858, and apparently was in good health. But Fred caught typhoid fever later in the year and lingered for weeks between life and death. His parents were ill too. Grant was laid low by another attack of fever—as virulent and long-lasting as the one that had incapacitated him at West Point. In September he wrote his sister saying he was thinking of visiting the family in Kentucky but decided he was not up to it. "Not being able to even attend to my hands, much less work myself, I am getting behind hand so that I shall have to stay here and attend to my business." The letter apparently moved Jesse to come to Missouri with an offer of help. In October, Grant wrote his father that Colonel Dent was selling all the White Haven stock, implements, and forty acres of land. "As I explained to you, this will include my place. I shall plan to go to Covington towards Spring, and would prefer your offer to any one of mere salary that could be offered. I do not want any place for permanent stipulated pay, but want the prospect of one day doing business for myself. There is a pleasure in knowing that one's income depends somewhat upon his own exertions and business capacity." Jesse might be forgiven for doubting any capacity for business in his son. But he wasn't risking much. He would be putting Ulyss on a percentage.[24]

Julia was intractably opposed to the move. She got her way. Grant would not go to Kentucky, but would work as a partner in a real estate business run by a Dent relative in St. Louis. "I cannot imagine how my dear husband ever thought of going into such a business, as he never could collect a penny that was owed to him," Julia wrote. She must have known that she was the reason. "I was joyous," she said, "at the thought of not going to Kentucky, for the Captain's family, with the exception of his mother, did not like me, which may, perhaps have been my own fault; but I always respected them and could have been fond of them, but we were brought up in different schools. They considered me unpardonably extravagant, and I considered them inexcusably the other way and may, unintentionally, have shown my feelings." Julia was only half right. The Grants didn't like her because she was of the "tribe of Dents."[25]

The Grant family in 1858 was actively supporting abolitionist candidates for public office, and the Dents were still slaveholders, as were Julia and Ulysses. When Grant wrote Jesse about coming to Kentucky—a slave state—he asked his father if he could bring along a young slave Colonel Dent had recently given Julia. The reason, he said, was to educate the boy into the farrier's business. No such altruism could accompany the house servants which Julia demanded, and what would happen to the field hand Grant had just bought?

By 1858, Missouri was a virtual war zone because of slavery. Four years earlier, Stephen Douglas, Illinois's Little Giant, had introduced a bill in the Senate allowing slavery in the Kansas-Nebraska area, a bill which would repeal the Missouri Compromise. The fight that ensued reached its climax during an all-night session at the end of May, with senators delivering half-drunk monologues and threatening violence. Dawn ended the debate, and as the exhausted solons stumbled down the steps of the Capitol into a morning that echoed with the cannon shots of victorious supporters, Salmon Chase turned to Charles Sumner. "They celebrate a present victory, but the echoes they awake shall never rest until slavery itself shall die."

"Since there is no escaping your challenge, I accept it in behalf of the cause of freedom," Seward declared when the Kansas-

Nebraska bill became law. The gauntlet thus thrown down was picked up by Missouri's David Atchison. "We are playing for a mighty stake," he exhorted pro-slavery friends, "if we win we carry slavery to the Pacific Ocean, if we fail, we lose Missouri, Arkansas, and Texas and all the territories; the game must be played boldly." The game, soon called "bleeding Kansas," was bold enough. Within weeks of the bill's passage, the New England Emigrant Society was formed to underwrite the expenses of settling anti-slavery families in the area. At the same time, pro-slavery Missourians, occasionally led by Senator Atchison himself, intimidated anti-slavery families and stuffed ballot boxes. Reports of violence filtered east, and some of the northern clergy, led by Harriet Beecher Stowe's brother Lyman Ward Beecher, began drawing on Old Testament precedents for violent revenge. "Beecher's Bibles"—rifled Sharp muskets—were touted as better defenses than prayers.[26]

The game had a political front as the autumn elections of 1854 approached. Stumping for Democratic candidates in Illinois, Douglas kept assuring his audiences that there was little to fear, because the climate in Kansas would prohibit the growth of slavery. Douglas won adherents, but he did not attract the kind of interest that was focusing on Abraham Lincoln. Calling for the repeal of the Kansas-Nebraska law, Lincoln condemned the abolitionists as well as the pro-slavery side. His higher law was not God's, but man's, more specifically Thomas Jefferson's, and he cited the Declaration of Independence and the Revolutionary fathers as his "authority." "Our republican robe is soiled, and trailed in the dust," he said. "Let us repurify it. Let us turn and wash it white, in the spirit, if not the blood of the Revolution. Let us turn slavery from its claims of 'moral right'; back upon its existing legal rights, and its arguments of 'necessity.' Let us return it to the position our fathers gave it; and there let it rest in peace."

Lincoln's assertion that the Declaration of Independence, not the Constitution, was the founding document of the country showed conservatives that it was not necessary to ignore documented legitimacy and plunge into civil disobedience to oppose the Kansas-Nebraska law. His allusion to the blood of the Revolution echoed a common theme. Unable to solve the riddle of the fathers' constitutional secrets, both abolitionists and fire-eating pro-slavers by 1854 were arguing over who had a stronger claim on the fathers' blood. It was an ominous metaphor. The omen seemed prophetic when abolitionist Senator Charles Sumner from Massachusetts was beaten insensate at his desk after delivering a lurid anti-slavery diatribe that pained his supporters as much as it outraged his adversaries.

For the next three and a half years the Senate seat to which the gravely injured Sumner had been reelected stood empty—a mute but telling testimony to the violence of "slavocracy." Conservative Southerners were unhappily quiet about the affair. Many southern newspapers congratulated Preston Brooks, his attacker, for finally giving the much-hated Sumner the kind of thrashing they believed he deserved. The North responded with more mass meetings and more appeals for money to settle Kansas—the issue for which Sumner had been martyred.

Two days after Sumner's caning, seven hundred pro-slavers sacked Lawrence, Kansas, settled by anti-slavery immigrants from New England and the upper Midwest. Two newspaper publishing houses were destroyed, and a hotel was burned, but the most serious damage was the absence of Lawrence's self-avowed defender.[27]

By 1856 Jesse Grant's old friend John Brown had gone through three wives, had produced upwards of fifteen children, and had convinced himself that God had singled him out to fight the sin of slavery. Brown was all spirit as he shouldered the Old Testament role of vengeance. He was being helped by the New England Emigrant Society, and he had formed a working relationship with transcendental abolitionists. But the question that would puzzle future historians was one of who was helping whom. Sending an ignorant ex-tanner to do abolitionist work in Kansas was a relatively inexpensive moral investment for well-housed, well-read, and well-fed New Englanders.

Brown had gathered together a small guerrilla band that included two of his sons and was on his way to Lawrence when he heard that the pro-slavery men had already struck. The news threw him into a "frenzy," and he turned back with vows to "strike terror in the hearts of the pro-slavery people" and to hit again as soon as it was practical. Next day word came to Kansas of Sumner's caning. Brown, said one of his followers, "went crazy—*crazy*. It seemed to be the finishing, decisive touch." Within hours, accompanied by four of his sons and two other men, Brown approached a pro-slavery settlement on Pottawatomie Creek. Bashing in the doors of the cabins, Brown's raiders seized the male inhabitants, and while the women shrieked and the children fled for safety, split the heads of five men with broadswords.

The Pottawatomie "massacre" was a passionate campaign issue in 1856. The Democrats chose James Buchanan, a portly bachelor who had been absent in England for the previous four years. Millard Fillmore would represent the American Party—the last vestige of Whiggery. And John Frémont, the Army explorer who had earned for himself the title "Pathfinder to the West," was picked by a new party, the Republicans.

The Republicans brought to the campaign of 1856 a moral fervor unprecedented in American politics. Democrats said a vote for Buchanan was a vote for the Union. Robert Lee supported Buchanan so that the "Union & Constitution" would be "triumphant." He thought Buchanan would "be able to extinguish fanaticism North & South & Cultivate love for the Country & Union & restore harmony between the different Sections." Ulysses Grant agreed, and voted the same. He had never before participated in a presidential election, and did so in 1856, he told his father, only to prevent Frémont from winning.[28]

The victory of James Buchanan did not bring stability to the country. Two days after he delivered his inaugural address, the United States Supreme Court read its decision in the Dred Scott case, which included the momentous information that the Court had found the Missouri Compromise unconstitutional. Abolitionists and Republicans mourned the decision as another example of what was becoming a reign of evil in the United States. The Chicago *Tribune*, among hundreds of other newspapers, railed at

Chief Justice Roger Taney and called for the defeat of Democrats and pro-slavery politicians at the polls. "Let the next President be Republican, and 1860 will make an era kindred with that of 1776."

Kansas had catapulted sixty years of gentlemanly debate on states' rights versus centralized power into the streets, where it was given a new name—"the irrepressible conflict"—and a new focus—slavery itself. Abraham Lincoln, debating Douglas for the Illinois senatorial seat, said a house divided against itself cannot stand, it must be all one thing or all the other. Though many voters were unwilling in 1858 to accept Lincoln's assertion, thousands took the statement as a truism, and were determined to act upon it.

Soon after Lincoln depicted the country's divided dwelling, he asked a rhetorical question of the southern half of the householders. When you have "succeeded in dehumanizing the negro," he said, "and made it forever impossible for him to be but as the beasts of the field; when you have extinguished his soul, and placed him where the ray of hope is blown out in darkness like that which broods over the spirits of the damned; are you quite sure the demon which you have roused *will not turn and rend you?*" Indeed, most Southerners were quite sure that was exactly what would happen. Lincoln's asking served many slaveholders as yet another example of abolitionist carelessness, but he had touched a sensitive southern nerve. The 1850s were rife with stories of slaves turning on their masters, and though many of them were fabrications by the northern press, such stories were widely circulated and believed by slave owners. This real fear was a powerful rebuttal to the "banjo-picking, heel-flinging, hi-yi-ing happy jack of the levees and the cotton fields" image of slaves exported by Southerners. If they were as childlike and happy as their owners insisted, then what was there to fear?

By 1859, many Southerners had come to describe slavery as a positive good rather than a necessary evil. But the notion that it was an institution designed by God to assist the savage African's ascent to heaven was a thin and hence brittle veneer. To speak aloud against slavery was so strongly tabooed in the South that even natives, like the North Carolinian Hinton Helper, were ostracized for doing so. The state of Georgia officially offered a five-thousand-dollar reward for anyone brave enough to capture William Lloyd Garrison and bring him South to stand trial on charges of inciting a slave insurrection. This was the great fear, the constant fear, and abolitionist harangues or stump debates by Illinois politicians which seemed to support such action were taken as abuse tantamount to war.[29]

CHAPTER

10

THERE WERE STARTLING REPORTS in American newspapers in late October 1859. An armed band of men had attacked the Federal arsenal at Harpers Ferry, Virginia. Lurid accounts of a slave army bent on freeing their brothers and slaughtering whites soon filled southern journals. Governor Henry Wise had ordered out the militia, upland white Virginians had formed a citizens' army at the little town overlooking the confluence of the Shenandoah and Potomac rivers, and President Buchanan had sent in the United States Marines under the command of Colonel Robert E. Lee.

Lee was at Arlington when he received a note from the War Department to report at once. He met with Buchanan and Secretary of War John Floyd, and got a sketchy outline of events. An appealing young cavalry lieutenant who had been a cadet when Lee was superintendent at West Point—James Ewell Brown Stuart, called "Jeb" for short—was to accompany him. The two commandeered a locomotive headed west into the Blue Ridge Mountains, and arrived at Harpers Ferry within hours.

Lee had been on leave for almost two years when Buchanan sent him to Harpers Ferry. Mary's father died in the autumn of 1857 and Lee had come from Texas to take care of the ruin old man Custis left behind. He was miserable at Arlington. But he had also been unhappy in Texas.

He began to fall into one of his black moods as soon as he arrived at Jefferson Barracks to take up duty as lieutenant colonel in the 2nd Cavalry. The swing from hope to despair when he left Arlington was usual for him, but this time he stayed down. The political climate didn't help. He was ordered to sit on a court-martial at Fort Riley, Kansas, and rode through the middle of the territory's most contested land at the time when pro-slavery and anti-slavery men were arming themselves for the "Wakarusa War." The military men who assembled with Lee at Fort Riley all had pledged themselves to defend the Union, but many, like Lee, were southern-born. It was not a comfortable time.

Lee barely tolerated months of court-martial duty, first at Fort Riley, then back at Carlisle Barracks, Pennsylvania, and didn't get to Texas until February 1856. He landed at Lavaca and sloughed overland through thigh-high mud to San Antonio, where he spent "a tedious time" outfitting himself for camp life. He complained that he had to pay outrageous prices for "common white crockery" and furniture which he needed only for entertaining, hired a cook whom he didn't like, and packed his belongings into an ambulance wagon. On March 21 he set out north for Fort Mason, where he was a guest at the regimental headquarters of his colonel, Albert Sidney Johnston. Mrs. Johnston said later that Lee displayed indecision and a mean spirit by refusing to stay at Mason and serve on yet another court-martial, but she didn't know how sorely his patience was tried.[1]

His destination was Camp Cooper, on the Clear Fork of the Brazos River, near what is now Abilene. He was to oversee the peaceful habitation of a small group of the Peneteka Comanches, and to conduct mopping-up exercises against their less tractable brethren. The land around Cooper was green and rolling and burgeoned with wild game and it cheered the new commander. The camp was pitched on a plain with a high rocky hill to the north and the winding, hardwood-cordoned Brazos to the south. Parallel rows of tents housed four companies. Lee's tent stood off to one side. He teased his daughter about the "prepossessing" interior of headquarters, with its iron camp bed, a trunk, a table and chair, and a wooden horse for his saddle and bridle.[2]

Once settled at Cooper, Lee planted a garden, prepared his kitchen for entertaining, and hung his chicken coop from a tree to keep the hens safe from snakes and coyotes, wryly noting they were not immune to weather. "Soldier hens, however must learn not to mind the rain," he wrote to Agnes, but admitted that the chickens spent most of their time inside his tent. He had hoped for a cat, and had seen a likely candidate in San Antonio "dressed up for company," but it was not available. He met another in Lavaca, which he told his daughter he would take "to Camp Cooper, provided Madame can trust her pet into such barbarous country & Indian society." Madame would not trust. His third choice died of apoplexy. "I foretold his end. Coffee & cream for breakfast. Pound cake for lunch. Turtle & oysters for dinner. Buttered toast for tea, & mexican rats, taken raw, for Supper! Cat nature Could not stand so much luxury. He grew enormously & ended in a spasm. His beauty could not save him." Lee finally bought "a noble specimen of the Rio Grande wild cat—spotted all over with large spots like a leopard," but had to abandon the animal two months later. It had "grown as large as a small-sized dog, had to be caged, & would strike anything that came within its reach."

Lee considered the Indians under his care just as untamable. He met Katumse, head of the Peneteka, for a long talk, "very tedious on his part, very sententious on mine," and came away with the fear that the government's efforts to "humanize" the tribe, "will be uphill work." The fact of Katumse's six wives apparently didn't bother him as much as the appearance of the women—"their paint & ornaments rendering them more hideous than nature made them." He archly recounted a visit to a sick Indian which caused an "explosion among the curs, children and women" and poked fun at the tribe's superstitions. "The medicine man," Lee wrote, "rushed at me—made significant signs that I must disrobe before presenting myself before the august patient— I patiently sat on my horse till I ascertained what garment they considered most inimical to the practice of the healing art, which

I learned to be—the cravat. Then alighting, unbuttoning my coat, & slipping off the noxious article—I displayed to their admiring eyes a blue check shirt—& I was greeted by a general approving 'humph'—The charm was fully developed, & I walked boldly in."

In May, he set out to chase a rebellious chief named Sahnaco over what he called "the most barren & least inviting country" he had ever seen. Lee had reveille sounded at two every morning. The company, in Army regulation wool, was on the trail by three for a twelve-hour march into the heart of a Texas summer. When the search for water became as pressing as the search for Comanches, the lieutenant colonel allowed no displays of disappointment if the company pushed through mesquite and grass and found the creek bed dry. Lee even hosted an Independence Day celebration. He might be camped on the plains of hell, but tradition was tradition.[3]

By July 31 he was back at camp, after the punishing 1,200-mile, two-month ordeal. Camp Cooper seared in the summer heat, and the Clear Fork clouded, dropped, and became stagnant. Lee's men fell ill. Gardens, both his and chief Katumse's, withered and died, and life under the suffocating shade of canvas became an exercise in endurance. "It is all right," he wrote, "I like the Wilderness— & the vicissitudes of Camp life are no hardship to me." For company he had his hens and his snake and the junior officers at Cooper—Earl Van Dorn, George Stoneman, Charles Whiting and Theodore O'Hara. Others came and went, including his nephew Fitz Lee, and John Hood and Edmund Kirby-Smith. They took their meals with their commander, and learned that he liked to tease them. It was exasperating, but each of the young men developed strong filial attachments to Lee. John Hood, blond, six feet two inches tall, was one of Lee's favorites. Hood had been at West Point while Lee was superintendent, and Lee liked his spirit. The two often rode together across the prairie around Cooper, talking about the Army and Hood's tour in Oregon, where his regimental quartermaster, U. S. Grant, had ruined his career. Hood thought Lee liked to give him advice, and never forgot an evening's ride when Lee earnestly told him that he should never "marry unless you can do so into a family which will enable your children to feel proud of both sides of the house."[4]

Pride seemed all that was left of Lee's marriage. By the mid-1850s, the arthritis that had bothered Mary for years had settled into crippling pain. Lee knew she was ill, but didn't seem to understand her suffering and often chastised her for complaining. "I wish you would take a happier view of things & not be dissatisfied because things do not accord more nearly to your views and wishes," he wrote. Though Mary did a good job running herd on the six children still dependent on her, and looked after Lee's finances and Arlington as well, Lee continued to criticize her for laxity. He made thinly veiled invidious comparisons between Mary and the officers' wives he knew in Texas, shared with her his pity for the unavoidable heartbreak in store for hopeful newly-weds, and acidly reported the death of a young soldier as leaving the widow happily "undisturbed by real or imaginary disappointments" in the future.

He had urged Mary to put Annie, Agnes, and Rob in school in Virginia and come to Texas with Milly and Mary, but soon withdrew the invitation, saying the hardships would be too great for her. Indeed, they would be, but he was not talking about her health problems. Though he had become more involved with her cure, urging her to visit Virginia's mountain springs and to take the specially prepared opium pills he sent her, he still criticized her for an emotional state which apparently was similar to his own. If she got no relief from various remedies, he wrote, then she must be resigned and "leave the result in the hand of our merciful father in heaven."[5]

Another call for court-martial duty didn't help Lee's spirits, and he fell into deeper depression in November, when the proceedings moved to Brownsville. He rallied briefly there, sending lighthearted letters to his daughters and filling subordinate Shanks Evans in on racy garrison gossip, but he soon flagged. At Christmas, he bought gifts for all the Army children, but found the round of formal call-paying tedious. So sour was his mood that he merely pronounced as a failure the attempt to introduce a camel corps in the American West, an enterprise he normally would have found hilarious.[6]

More distress awaited him when he returned to Camp Cooper in April. He was furious to discover that Rooney had dropped out of school. "It is time," Lee wrote, "he began to think of Something else besides running about amusing himself, & I wish him to do so at once." Lee had seemed to have trouble with Rooney from the time the boy was born. He called the baby Mary's "limb" and once told a friend that the boy was "ugly as ever." He described Rooney as "large and heavy," a "big double-fisted fellow with an appetite that does honor to his big mouth," who required a "tight rein." Like Custis, Rooney desperately wanted to go to West Point and wept bitterly when Lee told him he could not possibly get in, and that even if he did would get "over two hundred demerits the first year," and that would be the end of "all his military aspirations." Rooney did fail to get an appointment to the academy. He enrolled instead at Harvard, and a worse second choice could not have been made. The Lees didn't do well at Harvard.

The Adamses did very well indeed at Harvard, and Henry Adams, great-grandson of John, grandson of John Quincy, and son of Charles Francis, was Rooney's classmate there. That scion of America's most prestigious intellectual family found the off-shoot of the Lees "tall, largely built, handsome, genial, with liberal Virginian openness toward all he liked." For a year he "was the most popular and prominent young man in his class, but then seemed slowly to drop into the background. The habit of command was not enough, and the Virginian had little else. He was simple beyond analysis; so simple that even the simple New England student could not realize him. No one knew enough to know how ignorant he was; how childlike; how helpless before the relative complexity of a school. As an animal, the Southerner seemed to have every advantage, but even as an animal he steadily lost ground. . . . Strictly, the Southerner had no mind; he had temperament. He was not a scholar; he had no intellectual training; he could not analyze an idea, and he could not even conceive of admitting two."[7]

Adams was right about Rooney, but Rooney was game, and pleased his father by giving the school another try. "You must not think me so unreasonable as to expect you to be proficient in *every* branch of literature," Lee wrote, "but I do expect you in graduating to have what you say you will have, 'a good foundation for pursuing the studies of any profession,' & of being also *above* 'the general run of educated men' as regards scholarship, gentlemanly deportment & virtue. Is that asking too much? I cannot believe you *inferior*, & I am Sure you do not wish to prove yourself So." What Lee couldn't understand was the impossibility of Rooney's achieving superior status in his father's estimation without demonstrating himself simple to Henry Adams. Rigorous scholarship, in which intellectual disputation took the form of contests of will, was not at all the Lee ideal of gentlemanly deportment. And Lee's notion of learning as an "ornament" was as out of place at Harvard in the 1850s as was stodgy Washingtonian virtue. The campus attracted the sons of the first New England families—young men who not only delighted in the intellectual challenge of the school but also were passionately involved in the anti-slavery movement. Rooney did what any miserably homesick young Southerner would have done in the abolitionist North—he fell ill with fever, that most southern complaint.

Lee tried a variety of parental pressures to get Rooney to the mark, including reassurance. "I Still feel the glow of your infant cheek as I Carried you in my arms. I yet feel your arms clasping my neck as I swam with you on my back . . . I long to have you near me, with me. To See you, hold you, talk to you. But that Cannot be now, for the duty of each keeps us apart. I Cannot leave mine & you must perform yours."[8] In another vein, Lee soon wrote Mary that he doubted whether Rooney "knows his indebtedness, & if he did, & it was all cancelled, whether he would remain So. He inherits much of the disposition from both branches of his family & does not Seem to Strive to overcome it, or to restrict his wishes to his circumstances."[8]

Lee's advice to Rooney was only his most irritated; all the children—including little Milly, who was told that Mary's illness was God's way of trying the daughterly devotion of the child—got harsh warnings from Texas about reality as trial. His demands contained more than a hint of self-admonition. Eight years earlier, when he had written his son Custis to be done with dreaming, he was trying to force his own professional life back into the bureau-cratic mold of a peacetime army and to accept the sad limits of his own domestic life. In 1857 he turned fifty, and he celebrated that milestone birthday sitting on a hung court-martial in a dreary outpost, earning $1,200 a year. His wife didn't need him, and his children, almost grown, were showing him how useless his father-ing had been. Failing to be sustained by his spiritual quest for duty, he began to blend his suffering with the nation's. "The scourge of God Seems to be necessary in various forms & at as many points to repress the Sin of our people," he wrote Mary. "I acknowledge the justice of his afflictions & tremble to think how much mine have contributed towards them."9

He told Mary that the Texas assignment he had wanted at West Point was "just punishment" for his sins. But God's justice was inscrutable, and perhaps contained mercy. His Texas tour "might also be intended to prepare you & my children for any longer absence. To let each See how much will devolve upon them, & what will be necessary to bear & meet their responsibili-ties, when I shall have passed that journey from which no traveller returns."10

Though he was sensitive to the potential for a new military conflict in the late 1850s, his directions for a familial dress re-hearsal of his demise were too melodramatic for the threat of civil war. Ten years earlier Lee first addressed the possibility of his imminent death when he was on his way to Mexico. He had alluded to his death in Baltimore, and at West Point actively anticipated the event which would reunite him with all he had lost. In the late 1850s, he felt his losses were mounting. Lee began to write Eliza Mackay Stiles again while he was in Texas, and he reminisced with her about youthful days in Savannah. He asked her about her mother. "I confess that when I was with her, I was so taken up with her daughters, that I could make myself agreeable to no one else—They were blessed creatures—Where are they all now . . . ?" The real woman was his correspondent. The blessed creatures, like other happinesses, had vanished. With another of his sons gone off to adulthood, "we can scarce hope to see much of them in this world. Probably they and I will never meet again," he mourned to Mary. "One after one are taken from us, till none are left," Lee wrote to Markie. And to his brother-in-law he observed that as "one by one precedes us, our bonds to earth are loosened, & we are taught by tearful experience that we can only look for happiness & a lasting union beyond the grave." Perhaps the urgent need for the happiness that had eluded him in earthly unions made that "journey from which no traveller returns" desirable. "For myself," Lee wrote, "I only ask that before that day, I may truly repent of the many errors of my life." Dying was not a frightening prospect. Indeed, "the day of my death will be better for me than the day of my birth."

Though he had written Mary that he trusted his death would "bring no loss to you & my dear Children," he told Eliza Stiles—whose letters he carried with him constantly—that he grieved over his earthly separation from his wife and children. In September 1857 he wrote Anna Maria Fitzhugh of Ravensworth that his being so far from all he held dear was "almost intolerable when seasons of sickness or afflictions might make my presence beneficial." Within a month he learned that his presence at Arlington was necessary. George Washington Parke Custis had folded his hands over his chest one morning after breakfast and, silent for once, quietly died. Lee immediately applied for leave.[11]

He arrived in Virginia at the end of October 1857, and found he missed the old man who he said had treated him like a son. But more disturbing was the chaos he left behind. For more than a decade, Custis had done nothing to keep his estate in order. He had retreated into his study and devoted his energies to painting dozens of dreadful pictures of George Washington's battles. Though he still managed the annual convocation of sheep growers under the old Washington campaign tent he pitched near Arlington landing, Custis was retired. The death of Mary's mother, a woman he had largely ignored while she was alive, had taken the spirit out of him. In 1855, he drew up a will that was as whimsical as everything else he produced. Lee, named executor along with three other men—all of whom refused the honor—found himself unhappily coping with Custis's legal vagaries.

According to the provisions of the will, Mary was given a life interest in Arlington and adjacent lands in Alexandria and Fairfax County, but the plantation went to Lee's son Custis. Rooney received the White House, the old Custis plantation of 4,000 acres on the Pamunkey River east of Richmond where George Washington had married Martha Dandridge Custis. Rob's share of the estate was Romancoke, another 4,000-acre farm near the White House. Smith Island, in Chesapeake Bay, was to be sold as partial compensation for the Lee girls, who were given $10,000 each. Lee's bequeathal was a lot in Washington, D.C. The Custis silver would be Mary's during her lifetime, then it was to be divided among her children. This was the wish of her mother, who years earlier had wistfully told her daughter that she had planned to leave Mary the silver, but Custis had withdrawn his permission for her to do so. The most stringent conditions in the document concerned the Washington relics. According to the will, "the Mount Vernon plate, together with every article I possess relating to Washington, that came from Mount Vernon, is to remain with my daughter at Arlington House during said daughter's life, and at her death to go to my eldest grandson, George Washington Custis Lee, he taking my name and arms, and to descend from him entire and unchanged to my latest posterity." All the Custis slaves—nearly two hundred—were to be freed no later than January 1, 1863.[12]

The disposition of Custis's worldly goods seemed simple enough, but the entire estate was in a shambles. Arlington house was a wreck, Romancoke and the White House were unproductive and run-down, the slaves were scattered throughout Virginia, and Custis Lee apparently had to change his name to Custis Custis in order to qualify for his legacy. Lee turned the will over to the Virginia courts for a legal judgment and got to work on the property.

In the early 1850s, a visitor to the plantation noted in his diary that Arlington was "in a most neglected condition, and the house itself, never finished, is hastening to premature decay." The location "overlooking the Potomac and the cities of Washington and Georgetown is superb, but it must be highly malarious. The condition of the roads, buildings, and fences bears witness to a social malaria worse than the natural." Before Lee had left for Texas he had used his own money for repairs on the house, not "from any expectation of enjoying them" himself, he told Mary. "It is not with that view that I do anything, farther than incidentally." There was not even incidental enjoyment involved in Lee's work during 1858.

Lee had to replace the house's timbers and shore up the foundation, work not done earlier, when the unfinished great hall was finally completed. The Mount Vernon paintings so long stacked in storage had been hung on the walls in 1855. White marble mantels ordered by Lee from New York were now installed on the fireplaces. Doors and flooring were stained walnut, and a rare rose Aubusson rug was laid. There were deep cherry curtains on the windows and velvet-covered chairs and settees. The room was plastered and painted white. The former parlor was turned into a dining room and furnished with a mahogany table, Hepplewhite chairs, and matching Sheraton sideboards, which displayed the Mount Vernon silver. The family sitting room, where Lee kept a favorite armchair pulled up close to the fireplace, was painted white and hung with French blue silk drapes. The sheds adjacent to the two wings of the house were repaired, and the floor of the greenhouse was relaid. Stables were rebuilt, fences were mended, and the roadway curving up to the house from Arlington landing was graded. "Papa is very busy with the workmen," Agnes wrote Rooney. "Mending and building all the time." The mill had to be rebuilt and the wheel trued, and fields needed fertilizing with marl, a calciniferous lime discovered by Virginia agronomist Edmund Ruffin.[13]

Lee paid small Custis debts himself, and tried to find a manager for Arlington, "who would be a protection to the establishment & a relief to your mother in my absence," he wrote Custis. "I fear I shall not succeed. The accommodation is so poor on the farm that it deters respectable men with families from engaging. The inability to procure an overseer for Arlington has kept me a close prisoner."

The prison was the focus of an active social life during his confinement. The large house with the distinctive pillars was a landmark for Washington townsfolk, and a trip across the Long Bridge for a day with the Lees was an important social coup. Guests came away with glowing descriptions of "priceless" Washingtonia, gleaming silver, blooming gardens, and magnificent views. Even the most sophisticated callers felt the spirit of the father of the country hovering over Arlington. Lee enjoyed playing host—at least to the ladies who bounced up Arlington's lane. He wakened early and, in season, cut roses for visitors' breakfast plates. He was drawn to his daughters' friends, and relished giving them a quick tease or an entertaining story. Mary kept to her chair and watched. She took her breakfast in her room, and was carried downstairs, where she sat until evening tea was finished. She attended no social functions in Washington. For the first time, Lee followed her example. Parties in the capital in the late 1850s were not very pleasant.[14]

The social tone of Washington, like the city itself, had always been southern. The best families had little to do with the annual crowd which spun in and out of town in conjunction with the sessions of Congress. They were linked by kinship with Maryland and Virginia and with the cotton South. Southern legislators and their wives were naturally singled out for entertainment and became the lions of Pennsylvania Avenue. During the Pierce administration, the Jefferson Davises, the James Chesnuts, the Clement Clays, and the James Wigfalls composed an inner circle into which the most amusing Northerners were admitted with a cool formality. By the time James Buchanan became President, most of the amusing Northerners and all the Republicans had been excluded. Buchanan, a bachelor, depended on his niece Harriet

Lane as hostess. Her skin and violet eyes were admired, and at least one popular song, "Listen to the Mockingbird," was dedicated to her charms. But the belles who continued to dominate society found her chilly, and her entertainments at the White House stiff. Stephen Douglas built a mansion for his new bride, Adele Cutts of Maryland, and glittered with the best until he broke with the administration over Kansas. Society was distressed. The grandniece of Dolley Madison, Adele had been one of the inner circle. During the era of compromise, Washington hostesses, forbidding discussion of politics, put a soothing gloss on feelings ruffled by debate in the House or Senate. But a well-turned witticism or ankle was powerless against the passions stirred by Kansas-Nebraska and Dred Scott. One didn't have one's deadly enemy in to dine. Intense and soberly dressed Northerners sat at one another's tables. Hugely hooped southern women, with garlands of fresh flowers twined in their hair, attended one another's balls.[15]

Lee dismissed the ideology of intransigent pro-slavery men, and would not have felt comfortable attending parties given by their wives. And he would not have found a welcome at those given by Northerners. His social moratorium was broken only by a celebration for his brother's return from sea and by the gala wedding of his son. Rooney had finally failed at Harvard, but did get into the Army with the help of Henry Adams, who wrote his letter of request to Winfield Scott. Without Robert Lee's knowing it, Mary assisted in the transfer which had Rooney marching overland to Utah and then on to California, where he joined Custis at San Francisco's Presidio for work on Fort Point. Lee was a generous loser, and showered enthusiastic praise on Rooney for being a good trooper. But he soured when Rooney immediately resigned from the service in order to get married. Mary reluctantly allowed that it was just as well her lusty son wanted to establish a holy relationship, but Lee was uncertain about Rooney's intended mate. The girl he chose was a cousin, Charlotte Wickham, whose grandfather, Williams Carter, was Lee's uncle. Her parents had both died when she was very young. Lee was enchanted by her beauty and admired enormously her skill in music and art, but he pronounced her sickly and ill suited for the life of an Army officer. Custis's death buried Lee's major objection, for Rooney was now a landed planter and could give up his profession. Besides, Charlotte was rich. The wedding was set for Shirley.

Accompanied by his daughters—Mary was too ill to go—Lee made the trip to his mother's old home on the James, where all the Carter clan had settled in for a weeklong wedding visit. Rooney and Charlotte were married in the room where Light-Horse Harry Lee had claimed Ann sixty years earlier. The same portraits of Carter kin hung in the same places. The stables, the dovecote, the kitchen were all unchanged. Even Light-Horse Harry's ironic presence was near as Lee bore witness to Harry's grandson's carrying off another wealthy Carter girl. Like his father, Lee had always said he yearned for a settled life on a Virginia farm. And like his father, no sooner was he in the plantation traces than he strained to bolt.[16]

Lee had written his commander, Albert Sidney Johnston, that his father-in-law's death meant "I have at last to decide the question I have staved off for twenty years, whether I am to continue in the army all my life, or leave it now." The deciding was not easy. "What am I to do?" he asked Anna Fitzhugh. "I fear Mary will never be well enough to accompany me in my wandering life, & it Seems to be cruel to leave her—Custis I fear could not supplant his grd-father's name & place as he desired. Everything is in ruins & will have to be rebuilt—I feel more familiar with the military operations of a campaign than the details of a farm." He repeated himself anxiously four days later. "My uncertainty as to the best course for me to pursue, under the new duties devolved upon me, arises not from what would be the most agreeable to me, but what would be the best for my children, the most prudent for my wife."

There was little question about the best course for Lee's wife and children. Struggling through the mess of the estate, Lee discovered that Custis had run up debts in excess of $10,000 and had been systematically robbed by a string of worthless overseers. It would take years to turn the plantation into a self-supporting operation, and years more to earn enough from any of the land to accumulate $40,000—the Lee girls' legacies. Mary, who confessed to a friend that she dreaded her husband's return from Texas because she didn't want him to see her "crippled state," was unable even to climb the stairs at Arlington house. She could not run a plantation of 1,100 acres and look after an additional 8,000 acres at the White House and Romancoke. Milly was only twelve years old, Rob was fifteen. Lee knew that it was his duty to stay in Virginia, but he couldn't bring himself to resign from the Army.[17]

Six months after his arrival in Virginia, Lee had written his eldest son saying that if the heir of Arlington "wished to resign & take over the place . . . there would be no necessity for my leaving the Army." But Custis had already signed the plantation's deed over to his father. "I am deeply impressed by your filial feeling of love & Consideration," Lee wrote when he received the notarized title to Arlington, "as well as your tender Solicitude for me, of which however I require no proof, & am equally touched by your gracious disinterestedness. But . . . I Cannot accept your offer." Though Lee gave Mr. Custis's wishes as reason for rejecting Arlington, he very much didn't want to own it.

His need for order, for precision—that special boyhood excellence at finishing up—found no reflection in the lackadaisical schedules of Arlington. He hadn't the money to buff the place into perfection, and though he did much to improve both the appearance and the function of the farm, it still was far from satisfying to him. Lee also found himself playing nursemaid in Virginia not only to Mary but to all the "womankind" at Arlington. His daughter Mildred was the only "hearty woman" in the house. Young Mary had fallen victim to some mysterious ailment, went to live at Ravensworth for a cure, and returned "still feeble in appetite & strength." Little Annie was "by no means strong," and Agnes suffered from an eye complaint. Even Markie, who was a constant visitor while Lee was at Arlington, became "a Martyr to Neuralgia." Lee despaired of Mary's health ever improving, and disapproved of such "fearful" experiments as midwinter cold-water bathing. He thought the miraculous mountain springs offered the only possible cure, and bundled up the family to make the circuit from the "Hot" to the "Warm" to the "White" to the "Alum" and to the "Sweet"—none of which helped. Rooney and his wife were living at Arlington after the marriage, and a pregnant Charlotte soon crumpled in the distressing atmosphere and was added to the sick list. "You see what a suffering set we are," Lee wrote Custis—who labored in San Francisco under attacks of rheumatism.[18]

By the autumn of 1858, Lee amplified the call of duty from the Army. "I have been away a long time from my military duties & though I have not accomplished all I wished, I feel that I ought to return," Lee wrote his nephew Vernon Childe. He said it would be sad to leave his family "to themselves & with the apprehensions that they may want many things I could procure for them, yet there is no help for it & I will trust them to the care of a kind Providence, who has hitherto upheld them & protected them." But there had been help for it. Lee was offered a job as Winfield Scott's military secretary in the summer of 1859, but he turned it down. God would have to fill Lee's role as father-protector. God or Custis Lee.

When Custis signed over the deed to Arlington he did so as much from self-interest as from concern for his father. He was dutiful, but didn't relish the idea of living with his mother and sisters. He was not keen to stay in California, but neither was he anxious to return to Virginia. He hoped for an appointment on the West Point faculty, and having graduated first in his class, stood a decent chance of getting it. But Lee wanted his son at Arlington. He wrote Custis during the summer of 1859 that West Point was not an option. "I doubted whether you would have been advantaged by it" at any rate, Lee said. "If you Could be Stationed in Washington, you would then be near your Mother. Could in fact, live here, unless for a few months in the winter, be a great Comfort to her & your Sisters & Carry on the work of the farm, & thus accomplish much to your individual advantage." Lee said he had pressed the case of Custis's appointment with officials in Washington. He wanted out so badly he had uncharacteristically pulled strings to accomplish an end his son didn't desire.[19]

Just at that time he was burdened by the heaviest responsibility of his father-in-law's estate—the slaves. A year earlier he had written Rooney that there was "some trouble with some of the people. Reuben, Park & Edward in the beginning of the previous week, rebelled against my authority—refused to obey my orders, & Said they were as free as I was. . . . I succeeded in Capturing them however, tied them & lodged them in jail. They resisted till overpowered & Called upon the other people to rescue them." The following month Lee sent three men to Richmond. He planned to create the $10,000 legacies for his daughters by land sales and revenues from the labor of hired-out slaves. When the $40,000 was accumulated and the properties cleared of debt, the slaves were to be freed according to Mr. Custis's will—"the said emancipation to be accomplished in not exceeding five years from the time of my decease." Knowing Mr. Custis as he did, Lee was aware that his father-in-law could well have told some favored house servants that they were to be free when their old master died. He knew he was in for trouble in the "quarters."

Two letters to the editor were published in the New York Tribune in June 1859. "Sir:" began the first, signed "A," "It is known that the venerable George Washington Parke Custis died some two years ago; and the same papers that announced his death announced also the fact that on his deathbed he liberated his slaves. The will, for some reason, was never allowed any publicity, and the slaves themselves were cajoled along with the idea that some slight necessary arrangements were to be made. . . . Finally they were told five years must elapse before they would go." The writer then detailed a list of hardships experienced by the slaves, including near-starvation, old women sewing clothes for field hands "from daylight till dark," and an ancient uncle "turned out as a regular field hand. A year ago, for some trifling offense, three were sent to jail, and a few months later three more, for simply going down to the river to get themselves some fish, when they were literally starved. Some three or four weeks ago, three, more courageous than the rest, thinking their five years would never come to an end, came to the conclusion to leave for the North. They were most valuable servants, but they were never advertised, and there was no effort made to regain them which looks exceedingly as though Mr. Lee, the present proprietor, knew he had no lawful claim to them." The slaves were caught by "some brute in human form," and returned to Lee, who ordered them whipped. When the slave driver refused to beat the female runaway, "Mr. Lee himself administered the thirty and nine lashes to her. They were then sent to Richmond jail, where they are now lodged. Next to Mount Vernon, we associate the Custis place with the 'Father of this free country.' Shall 'Washington's body guard' be thus tampered with, and never a voice raised for such utter helplessness?'"

The second letter, signed "A Citizen," was written by a correspondent who claimed to live "one mile from the plantation of George Washington P. Custis, now Col. Lee's, as Custis willed it to Lee. All the slaves on this estate, as I understand, were set free at the death of Custis, but are now held in bondage by Lee. I have inquired concerning the will, but can get no satisfaction. Custis had fifteen children by his slave women. I see his grandchildren every day; they are of a dark yellow. Last week three of the slaves ran away. . . . Col. Lee ordered them whipped. They were two men and one woman. The officer whipped the two men, and said he would not whip the woman, and Col. Lee stripped her and whipped her himself. These are facts as I learn from near relatives of the men whipped. After being whipped, he sent them to Richmond and hired them out as good farm hands."

Three slaves had run away from Arlington—Lee had written Custis about it. The slaves were also "overpowered." A new overseer had recently been hired for the plantation, and he, like everyone else on the place, fell sick, but he was still working when the incident occurred. If any whipping did take place, the overseer and not Lee would have been the agent of punishment. Though Lee could be riled into flashes of rage, he was never a victim of his temper. Men of his station—particularly military men whose "habit of command" was exercised daily—would not administer physical punishment with their own hands. But it was a good story, and with various changes and embellishments, it made the rounds for more than a decade. "The N.Y. Tribune has attacked me for my treatment of your Grandfather's slaves but I shall not reply," Lee ruefully wrote Custis. "He has left me an unpleasant legacy."[20]

CHAPTER

11

ROBERT LEE'S use of the word "legacy" was technically
correct applied to his father-in-law's will, but the term in 1859 was
a common American metaphor. The "legacy of the Fathers"—by
which was meant the political institutions of the country—had
become the invocation and the prize fought over by the generation
of sons who would either save or destroy the Union. But the
legacy was ambiguous. The political fathers had died, and like
Parke Custis, had left to their sons—or sons-in-law—the problem
of coping with slavery. Though the founders knew the institution
was a moral and social evil, they accepted it as necessary for the
creation of a new country. The Adamses and the Franklins and
the Hamiltons didn't own slaves, but they accepted personal right
in chattels. The Jeffersons and the Madisons and the Washingtons did possess them, but soothed their consciences by freeing
them on their deathbeds. Custis, who struggled to care for the
effects of Washington's beneficence for years, returned the favor
to his son-in-law. Robert Lee, who had supported for thirty years
the liberation of black men and women, found himself responsible
for two hundred slaves and appearing in the newspapers as a
ruthless brute.

Lee had heartily approved a bitter denunciation of abolitionists
and, presumably, the Republican Party, which Franklin Pierce
included in his final State of the Union address. A published

version of the speech prompted Lee to record his views on the "Systematic & progressive efforts of certain people in the North, to interfere with & change the domestic institutions of the South." The abolitionists, Lee wrote, must be aware that freeing the slaves, "for which they are irresponsible & unaccountable," was both "unlawful & entirely foreign to them," and could "only be accomplished by *them* through the agency of a Civil & Servile war."

In this enlightened age, there are few I believe, but what will acknowledge, that Slavery as an institution, is a moral, political evil in any Country. It is useless to expatiate on its disadvantages. I think it however a greater evil to the White than to the black race, & while my feelings are strongly enlisted in behalf of the latter, my Sympathies are more strong for the former. The blacks are immeasurably better off here than in Africa, morally, socially & physically. The painful discipline they are undergoing is necessary for their instruction as a race, & I hope will prepare & lead them to better things. How long their Subjugation may be necessary is known & ordered by a wise & merciful Providence. Their emancipation will Sooner result from the mild & melting influence of Christianity than the storms & tempests of fiery Controversy. This influence, though Slow, is Sure. The doctrines & miracles of our Saviour have required nearly two thousand years to Convert but a Small part of the human race, & even among Christian nations, what gross errors still exist! While we See the Course of the final abolition of human Slavery is onward, & we give it the aid of our prayers & all justifiable means in our power, we must leave the progress as well as the result in his hands who Sees the end; who chooses to work by slow influences, & with whom two thousand years are but as a Single day. Although the Abolitionist must know this; & must See that he had neither the right or power of operating except by moral means & suasion, & if he means well to the slave, he must not create angry feelings in the master; that although he may not approve of the mode by which it pleases Providence to accomplish its purposes, the result will nevertheless be the Same; that the reasons he gives for interference in what he has no concern, holds good for every kind of interference with our neighbors when we disapprove their Conduct; Still I fear he will persevere in his evil Course. Is it not Strange that the descendants of those pilgrim fathers who Crossed the Atlantic to preserve their own freedom of opinion, have always proved themselves intolerant of the Spiritual liberty of others.[1]

It was characteristic of Lee to consign the ultimate liberation of the slaves to God's inscrutable timekeeping. He had placed his own happiness and freedom on the same basis. But his claim that most Americans shared his view that slavery was a moral and political evil was naïve or dissembling. In the Deep South, but also in Virginia, many pro-slavery politicians were stridently insisting that the institution was a positive good. There was little doubt among conservative Southerners that the "positive good" position was a reactive defense against abolitionist attack, but the most candid would admit that the issue in southern minds was very complex. Uncompensated emancipation would be financially ruinous to many planters. Slaves were a cash medium of exchange. When an owner tallied his net worth, he included the value of his chattel, which rose and fell along with the price of other commodities. Though slaves might be expensive to maintain, and in many areas did not produce enough to pay for their keep, they represented an easy form of liquidity in case of economic need. In addition, slaves were a political medium upon which traditional southern domination of Congress in part had rested. Slaves, tallied at three-fifths of all "other persons," provided a considerable boost to a relatively static population count in the South. Emancipation conceivably could augment population by making slaves whole "persons," but given the rigid anti-black bias of the country, it was more likely that freed slaves would become like Indians—no "persons" at all.

Lee's assertion that blacks were better off in America than in Africa, and that freedom was a spiritual essence that did not apply to the actual bondage of men and women, did reflect the feelings of many Americans in the nineteenth century. The personal liberty laws passed in response to the fugitive slave provision of the Compromise of 1850 came out of the upper northern states—New England, upstate New York, Minnesota, Wisconsin, and Michigan. Other "free" states either retained or passed "black laws"—legal exclusion of blacks from voting, serving on juries or in state militias, going to school with whites, or marrying them. Indiana in 1851 adopted a provision forbidding black migration to the state. Illinois and Iowa followed suit. When Oregon joined the Union in 1859, it did so with a constitution which forbade blacks from entering the new state. The position of the earlier Free-Soil Party and much of the Republican Party was both anti-slave and anti-black. David Wilmot admitted he had no "squeamish sensitiveness upon the subject of slavery, nor morbid sympathy for the slave." The author of the anti-slavery proviso asserted that the "negro race already occupy enough of this fair continent." In Wilmot's claim that he was happy to call his measure "the white man's proviso" could be heard the major theme of the antebellum anti-slavery movement.

When Lincoln called for the restoration of the Missouri Compromise in 1854, he said he hated the spread of slavery not only because of the "monstrous injustice of slavery itself" but also because harboring such a practice in America "deprives our republican example of its just influence in the world—enables the enemies of free institutions, with plausibility, to taunt us as hypocrites."[2]

Removing the stain of slavery and perfecting the work of the founders were far sharper prods to most reformers in the 1850s than was concern for the welfare of enslaved men and women. The Illinois housewife might sigh over the fate of Uncle Tom, but she certainly did not want him living next door. Nor did she want to arm him, have him judge her, or educate his children with hers. Neither did the legislators who represented her in the Congress of the United States. If the abstraction of slavery were swept away and an ennobled country could at last claim the unmitigated admiration of the world, what would become of the slave? The Midwest, with the exception of Ohio, which had admitted blacks since 1849, was safe for white democracy. The West was equally secure. Kansas, settled by the New England Emigrant Society, established anti-black provisions. New England, being about the size of Virginia, was not large enough to welcome many ex-slaves.

Even Canada was growing restive as the final stop on the underground railroad. Mary Lee, visiting St. Catherine's Spring, found "a great many runaways here but I have not met with any acquaintances. The White people say that before long they will be obliged to make laws to send them all out of Canada . . . [A]fter enticing them over here the White people will not let their children go to the same schools or treat them as equals in any way so amalgamation is out of the question tho' occasionally a very low Irish woman marries a black man."[3]

Fewer and fewer anti-slavery advocates during the 1850s were addressing the problem of how freed slaves were to live, how they were to be educated, how they would support themselves. Though he admitted it was impractical, Lincoln said his first impulse "would be to free all the slaves, and send them to Liberia—to their own native land." To free them and keep them as "underlings" was little better than slavery, he said. But to free the slaves "and make them politically and socially, our equals? My own feelings will not admit of this; and if mine would, we well know that those of the great mass of white people will not." Gradual emancipation, which seemed the only answer to Lincoln, he dismissed as unfeasible.

Everyone—North and South—seemed to assume that freed slaves would live in the South, and white Southerners could only see that they would be victimized by such an eventuality. That there was no black infrastructure in the South to support a community of more than four and a half million freed slaves—no black doctors, no black teachers, only a handful of black lay preachers, and nearly no land they could buy—did not seem a deterrent to the abolitionist. It was said that many abolitionists tended to think that all slaves were educated, intelligent, and capable of supporting themselves like Frederick Douglass. Many slave owners ignored the examples set by prestigious blacks and generalized their chattel into the hi-yi-yipper or the sullen cutthroat. It was the latter that scared them to death.[4]

Lee's caution about not creating angry feelings in the masters if the orderly progress toward emancipation was to continue was the mildest form of hedge. He spoke more clearly for fellow

Southerners when he said that the object of abolitionists could only be accomplished through civil war or a slave revolt. By the summer of 1859, when the Lees were told some of the Arlington slaves had determined to murder them in their beds, portents of a slave insurrection were seen everywhere in the South. By October 1859, it seemed the reality had come.

Had Lee been more successful in emancipating his father-in-law's slaves, he would have been in Texas when he heard that a revolt was under way at Harpers Ferry. He had applied for a continuation of his leave because the Virginia courts had not yet ruled upon Parke Custis's will, and was still a "close prisoner" at Arlington when Jeb Stuart galloped up the lane with orders to report to Washington. Without taking time to change into a uniform, Lee accepted command of two companies of marines—all that was available—and left immediately for Harpers Ferry. He carried with him a proclamation from President Buchanan that he would read to the citizenry should rumors of five hundred insurgents occupying the arsenal prove true.

It was eleven o'clock at night when Lee and Stuart arrived at the little town. No one had a very clear idea of what was happening. Lee was told that a man named Smith and a band of followers had crossed the Baltimore & Ohio railroad bridge from Maryland about eight o'clock the previous night and had seized bridge guards. The men then moved into town, captured the watchmen at the arsenal and armory, and took possession of Federal property. The leader of the group sent six of his men to a nearby farm belonging to a great-grandnephew of George Washington. Along with four of his slaves, Lewis Washington was captured, and was told to bring with him a ceremonial sword that had belonged to his ancestor. Other hostages were rounded up and also imprisoned in the arsenal. Telegraph wires were cut. By morning, the alarm was spread. The hastily assembled militia joined neighboring farmers armed with squirrel guns and stormed the town.

Lee found the civilians contentedly controlling the situation. Negotiations with the insurgents had been initiated, but the atmosphere was ugly. Rumors that hundreds of armed slaves led by abolitionist commanders were ready to pour out of Maryland or Virginia at any moment and annihilate every citizen within reach were accepted as fact. Tension mounted shortly after midnight when word went through the crowd that the leader of the pack was none other than old Pottawatomie John Brown. Lee notified the War Department that troops from Fortress Monroe would not be necessary, and deployed his marines. He ordered Stuart to approach the arsenal at dawn and demand its surrender. If the occupants came out peacefully, that would end it. If not, Stuart was to signal with a wave of his hat and the marines would attack.

As early light touched the hills, Stuart, tall and straight with auburn hair flowing around a face burnt deep red by duty in Kansas, walked toward the stone building where John Brown waited. Lee watched the door of the arsenal crack open in response to Stuart's knock, and saw a white beard shining in the dark cut. Two minutes passed. Voices came out of the engine house, but one clear shout sounded above the others: "Never mind us, fire!" Lee nodded to himself, pleased at recognizing Mary's cousin, Lewis Washington, and he turned to a bystander. "The old Revolutionary blood does tell," said Lee. Just at that moment, he saw Stuart step back and the door slam shut. Stuart waved his hat. The marines swept forward, bashed at the door with sledgehammers, then seized a ladder to use as a ram. Spectators cheered as they heard the sound of splitting wood. Two marines were shot at the entry. The rest disappeared inside. Three minutes later the dead and wounded—half a dozen—were carted out and laid on the grass. Twelve dirty and frightened hostages stumbled into the daylight. The thirteenth, Lewis Washington, refused to emerge until a pair of clean gloves was fetched from his plantation.

Lee ordered the wounded men taken to a nearby hotel and had Brown carried to the paymaster's office. He asked Brown for the names of his conspirators, then inquired whether he was too tired and weak from his wounds to be interrogated. The answer was no, Brown wanted to talk to Governor Wise and Senator George Mason, who had arrived to question him. After checking the identities of the dead and investigating a few more rumors of violence in the neighborhood, Lee left for Washington with his marines. It had taken him thirty-six hours to dispense with John Brown's uprising at Harpers Ferry. The country Lee served would never be finished with the little town on the Potomac which gave its name to the most important symbolic event of America's progress toward Civil War.[5]

Brown had visited New England in May 1859 and had been given Charles Sumner's blood-stiffened shirt to fondle and more than $4,000. In July, along with two of his sons, he rented a farmhouse in Maryland, five miles from Harpers Ferry, and waited. In time, twenty-one followers assembled, and the "tools"—198 Sharps rifles and 950 pikes—arrived. During interrogation, he said he wanted to launch his attack on Harpers Ferry, gather together slaves who would join him, and keep moving south. Apparently his ultimate aim was the establishment of a free state in the mountainous regions of Virginia, Tennessee, and the Carolinas. During the long night in the Harpers Ferry engine house, before Lee sent in the marines, Brown told one of his hostages he had chosen Harpers Ferry because the guns stored there would be of service to him. If he could conquer Virginia, "the balance of the Southern States would nearly conquer themselves, there being such a large number of slaves in them." When he repeated this expectation during his trial, few listeners could believe that the plan sounded bloodless.[6]

Though he had boasted to an Ohio friend that he could free Kansas and Missouri with less than a hundred followers, then march to Washington and turn the president and cabinet out of office, Brown hinted during his fundraising visit to New England that death might be his reward in Virginia. There was little doubt among Brown's associates that he thought his mission was a holy one. He viewed himself as chosen by God to liberate the black bondsmen from the thrall of American slavery, and his life was no great price to pay. By the time Brown was transferred by Lee to Charles Town for trial, he had tearlessly watched three of his sons die—martyrs to his sacred cause—and was fully prepared to follow them. Many analysts of Brown's work at Harpers Ferry were convinced he wanted to die. The plans were imperfectly laid, none of the access routes into the town were guarded, the surrounding countryside was not studied, and, most telling, Brown had allowed a train to continue on to Washington with the information that it had been stopped on the B&O bridge by armed men. The "insurrection" was doomed from the outset.

Brown's trial began on October 25, and as it progressed even the most truculent abolitionist had to admit the proceedings were fair. Military guards tried to keep order among the circus of journalists, politicians, townsfolk, and counsel. America's attention was riveted on Charles Town, Virginia, and Brown didn't disappoint the country. Still weak from his wounds, he lay wrapped in a blanket on a cot and watched the proceedings. Brown insisted he was of perfectly sound mind, though several depositions attested to his insanity. Jeremiah Brown said he had no doubt his brother "had become insane upon the subject of slavery," and Amos Lawrence, an immensely wealthy anti-slavery New Englander, believed "Brown is a Puritan whose mind has become disordered by hardship and illness."

But Brown's madness had seemed divine to some of the New England intelligentsia. Though there were schemes discussed for rescuing the old man from jail, most of his silent supporters believed his death would be beneficial to abolition. Brown agreed. He often told his followers that "if we lose our lives it will perhaps do more for the cause than our lives would be worth in any other way."

When Brown was found guilty on November 2, the presiding judge asked if he had anything to say. He responded: "I see a book kissed, which I suppose to be the Bible, or at least the New Testament, which teaches me that all things whatsoever that man should do to me, I should even so do to them. . . . I endeavored to act up to that instruction. I say I am yet too young to understand that God is any respecter of persons. I believe that to have interfered as I have done, as I have always freely admitted I have done, in behalf of his despised poor, I did not wrong, but right. Now, if it is deemed necessary that I should forfeit my life for the furtherance of the ends of justice, and mingle my blood further with the blood of my children and with the blood of millions in this slave country whose rights are disregarded by wicked, cruel, and unjust enactments, I say, let it be done."[7]

He was sentenced to hang on December 2.

Southern reaction to Harpers Ferry was on the edge of terror, and Governor Wise of Virginia found he had a wolf by the ears. "From his blood would spring an army of martyrs, all eager to die in the cause of human liberty," wrote a correspondent of Wise's who urged the governor not to hang Brown. "If they hang old Brown, Virginia will be a free State sooner than they expect," an abolitionist observed after the trial. New York's mayor, Fernando Wood, wrote Wise to ask if the governor was bold enough to temper justice with mercy. "Have you nerve enough to send Brown to the State Prison instead of hanging him? Brown is looked upon here as the mere crazy or foolhardy emissary of other men." But Wise was not bold enough. More particularly, he was not enough in control of his passions to be politic.[8]

Henry Wise was an eccentric, learned man, friendly and affable, but apt to spin easily into excess. He had served in various foreign legations in the 1840s and was considered an astute diplomat, though far too outspoken to function properly on the highest levels of government service. By 1859, he was twice a widower, and it was said that slavery killed his second wife, a Philadelphia Meade. Wise was no friend of slavery, but he was spooked on the subject. He saw in John Brown's attack the tip of a conspiracy aimed at annihilating whites. Since 1856, rumors had scudded around the South about huge uprisings mounted variously in Louisiana or Tennessee. Wise had authorized the collection of affidavits from Brown's acquaintances designed to prove the lunacy of the prisoner, but scuttled the plea. John Brown was the logical conclusion of his own fears.[9]

Wise himself seemed slightly deranged during the month-long interim between Brown's trial and execution. He repeatedly asked President Buchanan to send Federal troops to deal with the marauders gathering in the hills of Maryland and Virginia. Buchanan had been convinced by Lee that Brown's raid was "the attempt of a fanatic or madman," but he finally ordered Lee to return to Harpers Ferry. Lee arrived November 30, situated four companies of Fortress Monroe soldiers, and had an interview with John Brown's wife. He listened to her request—to be allowed a visit with her husband—and sent her on to Charles Town with instructions to speak with General Taliaferro of the Virginia militia.[10]

"I am sorry the citizens have been kept out," John Brown told his guard on the morning of December 2. He was seated on a coffin, empty yet and waiting, inside an old wagon which pulled into a forty-acre field on the outskirts of Charles Town. The day was fine and warm. Journalists were gathered at the periphery of the field. Military students and militia formed a hollow square around a gallows in the middle. In their ranks was Edmund Ruffin, a sixty-five-year-old farmer who had asked the commander of the Virginia Military Institute, Thomas J. Jackson, if he could muster in for the day. Ruffin stood at present-arms, his long white hair brushing the crimson VMI blouse, thinking to himself that Brown was admirable in his courage, even though he was the enemy. Jennings Wise, son of the governor and editor of the Richmond *Enquirer,* was there with the Richmond militia. So was a slight, dark-haired young actor named John Wilkes Booth, who later sent his sister the scabbard of General Washington's sword, hot from the hands of the abolitionist.

The black-clad prisoner straightened his long legs, handed a piece of paper to his jailer, and walked quickly forward, outstepping his guards. He was first to mount the platform. A white linen hood was placed over his head. The knot was tied around Brown's neck and his executioner told him to step onto the trap. "You must lead me," Brown said, "I can't see." He was nudged forward. There was a pause as last-minute soldiers jostled into position. Was Brown tired? "No, not tired, but don't keep me waiting longer than is necessary." Nothing more was necessary. The commander nodded at the sheriff. A hatchet was raised into the morning sun. The air was very quiet. The screech of the trap as it sprang split the silence and the old man in black shuddered earthward and jerked to a halt. A clear young voice rang across the field. "So perish all such enemies of Virginia! All such enemies of the Union! All foes of the human race!"

Brown's jailer remembered the note he'd been given. He unfolded the piece of paper and read: "I John Brown, am now quite *certain* that the crimes of this *guilty land:* will never be purged *away;* but with Blood."[11]

" 'Poor fly he done buzz' as the crazy man said," Lee wrote to his cousin Henry Carter Lee. Still in Harpers Ferry four days after Brown's execution, Lee said reports of alarm continued to filter in to his headquarters. Just the night before, he heard that "1,400 men were on their way to meet us. . . . I hardly think they will be here this month, & these young Soldiers will have to return to their oysters at Old Point without their breakfast on the Sympathizers."[12]

Few other Americans felt like dismissing Brown's hanging with such detached irony. Henry Wadsworth Longfellow noted in his diary on December 2: "The date of a new revolution, quite as much needed as the old one." Ralph Waldo Emerson—who would call Brown's statement before being sentenced equal to the Gettysburg Address—welcomed a new saint, and Henry David Thoreau termed him an angel of light. Throughout the North, bells tolled and flags flew at half staff. Black-bordered newspapers described Brown's final moments. "Without the shedding of blood there is no remission of sins"—Brown's favorite biblical adage—was printed and displayed across the nation. Though some anti-slavery men spoke out against Brown, newspaper editors found that Brown's act was lawless but not criminal, and thousands of lithographed portraits of the new saint were sold. A biography, more fable than fact, appeared while Brown was awaiting execution and sold 35,000 copies within weeks.

The South was horrified at northern reaction to Brown, but righted itself on the suspicion that the whole anti-slavery North, and not just a handful of radical abolitionists, had funded Brown's campaign. Old quotes of William Lloyd Garrison and Joshua Giddings, who looked forward to the time when "the torch of the incendiary shall light up the towns and cities of the South, and blot out the last vestiges of slavery," were republished. The notion that the Republican Party not only favored the insurrection at Harpers Ferry but hoped to informally back new ones gained credence. Jefferson Davis spoke for many when he claimed that Brown's raid was an attempt "by extensive combinations among the non-slaveholding States" to wage war against Virginia, and that the Republican Party was "organized on the basis of making war" against the South. David Hunter of Virginia, a moderate, was so moved by the North's apotheosis of Brown that he sought an interview with Senator John Dix of Connecticut. Would the growth of radical abolitionism in the North never stop? Hunter sadly inquired. Was not Seward's irrepressible conflict at hand, and in a terrible form? The elevation of Brown to a heroic status seemed incontrovertible evidence that the North did indeed hate the South, and would not raise a hand to protect fellow countrymen from annihilation at the hands of savage mobs.

Governor Wise daily received letters asking if suspicious strangers in North Carolina, in Louisiana, in Tennessee, were abolitionist agents. Peddlers, booksellers, tourists and tutors were threatened with tarring or worse, and run northward out of southern towns. A correspondent for the New Orleans *Picayune* declared that the time had come "when no Northern man, whatever his business, can safely travel in the Southern states, unless he has a means of showing that his objects are not unfriendly. Many who have business in the South come here to obtain credentials. A proper passport system must be devised and adopted, in order to secure the South from Abolition intruders and spies." The urbane art collector Philip St. George Cooke, whose daughter had recently married Jeb Stuart, wrote his close friend A. J. Davis in New York that the South was prepared to defend itself. "If your Conservative Party at the North does not *put down* and *put out* the accursed and pestiferous abolition faction, they will speedily bring about a dissolution of our hitherto glorious Union! Able men of all parties have come to this conclusion at the South, and as we see no hopes of such a result at the North, we are arming . . ." Cooke ended by telling his friend that he expected soon to turn his own peaceful Virginia lawn into a drill ground. Such dismay was real. Cooke himself, when called upon to demonstrate his loyalty, went against family and served the North as a general officer during the Civil War. But other southern lawns and courthouse squares and village greens were becoming drill grounds. South Carolina and Mississippi appropriated $100,000 each for the maintenance of new militia companies. Wise kept marching his Richmond troops through the city. Plantation owners stepped up surveillance of their blacks. "Never before, since the Declaration of Independence, has the South been more united in sentiment and feeling," a South Carolina newspaper reported, with accuracy. William Lowndes Yancey of Alabama and Barnwell Rhett of South Carolina were elated at the wave of disunionist feeling which swept from the Potomac to the Gulf, carrying with it conservative men such as James Seddon of Virginia, Georgia's Robert Toombs, and Charleston financier Christopher Memminger.[13]

John Brown's hanging set off a tremor which began to split America. Lee once congratulated a political writer on a piece which claimed allegiance to the *"whole country,"* with "no North, no South, no East, no West," but "the broad *Union,* in all its might and strength, present & future. I know no other Country, no other Government, than the *United States* & their *Constitution."* Thousands of his fellow Southerners would have concurred. But that was before Harpers Ferry.[14]

CHAPTER

12

WHEN NEWS OF his father's old friend John Brown
arrived in St. Louis, Grant was out of work and depending on the
kindness of strangers. The business partnership Julia had wanted
for her husband as a way of staying out of Jesse Grant's Kentucky
clutches had failed. The arrangement was doomed from the outset, but there seemed no other choice at the time.

Harry Boggs, a distant cousin of Julia's, was making a mark for
himself in St. Louis real estate, and the Dent family decided
Grant should join him. Why anyone thought the failed Ohio
horse trader could make a go of it in the abrasive atmosphere of
buying and selling property was a mystery that even Julia came
to ponder. Apparently her father had approached Boggs, who had
offices in the law firm of McClellan, Hillyer & Moody in an old
French house on Pine Street in St. Louis, and asked him to take
his son-in-law as a partner. A few days later, with his eyes focused
squarely on his feet, Grant came in and mumbled out his message:
Dent, he said, thought "that my large acquaintance among army
officers would bring enough additional customers to make it support both our families." Boggs was understandably not impressed,
but agreed to accept Grant. By March 1858, Grant had a desk in
the firm, and a pocketful of cards which read: "H. Boggs. U. S.
Grant. Boggs & Grant, General Agents, Collect Rents, Negoti-

ate Loans, Buy and Sell Real Estate, Etc., Etc." He had very little else. For the first few months of his employment, he lived in an unheated storeroom in the house of Boggs and his wife, Louisa. Each Saturday he walked to White Haven, twelve miles away, and each Sunday he walked back. His landlords found that their boarder "seldom smiled," and he "was never heard to laugh aloud." His spirits did not seem to improve when he moved Julia and the four children to town. "We are living now in the lower part of the city, full two miles from my office," Grant wrote Jesse in March. "The house is a comfortable little one just suited to my means."[1]

The house was a cramped, ugly place, but it was cheap. The optimism which Grant usually summoned to help him through new experiences couldn't be mustered in 1858. Julia was alarmed. She said that once the family was "comfortably settled in our very simple little home" she noticed her husband "was not as hopeful as at first"—an admission, for her, that he was severely depressed. Rumors continued to circulate about his drinking, and he suffered recurrences of his bouts with fever. He hated his job, and often arrived at work as late as ten or eleven in the morning. The droop of his shoulders and the shuffle of his walk convinced everyone who saw him in St. Louis that his mood was morbid. "He was like a man thinking on an abstract subject all the time," an acquaintance thought. The only times he seemed to rally were when someone wanted to talk with him about a war. Lawyers Hillyer and McClellan remembered him sitting at his desk, poring over newspaper accounts of the French and Italian war. Grant liked to be asked for a military opinion, and he would discuss battles real or imaginary with a precision and flair his listeners enjoyed. "We considered him more than commonly talkative," Hillyer remembered. "He was entertaining, and I was attracted toward him."[2]

Dent by this time was publicly ridiculing his son-in-law for the kind of inept transactions which once had Grant renting a house to a whore who wanted to set up shop. If Boggs sent the partner out to collect rent from an old soldier, Grant more often than not would spend the afternoon reminiscing and return empty-handed to the office. A St. Louis friend said that Grant was particularly unsuited for collecting debts. "Some unfortunate tenant would appeal to him for time or help, and the time or help would always be given. . . . The real-estate venture naturally did not thrive and many and vigorous were the scoldings given by the older partner to the younger." He was no better at handling family business. He had agreed to sell his brother Simpson's horse, but had to write a letter telling Simpson a prospective buyer had promised $100 and gone to the stables and collected the horse along with its saddle and bridle, "since which I have seen neither man nor horse. From this I presume he must like him."[3]

Julia agreed it was time for Grant to get out of business. "What I shall do will depend entirely upon what I can get," Grant wrote his father. "I do not want to fly from one thing to another, nor would I, but I am compelled to make a living from the start for which I am willing to give all my time and all my energy." Ulyss was not being quite candid with his father. He had plenty of time but no energy at all. In the summer of 1859 a chance to do something emerged from the St. Louis bureaucracy. The position of county engineer was vacant and Grant applied for the job, which would put him in charge of Robert Lee's river works. So anxious was Grant to be hired that he engaged a soothsayer to foretell his chances. She gave him no hope. Despite a hefty list of recommendations, Grant didn't get the job. Waiting on the court-house steps for the verdict, he got the news from a friend: "You're beaten."[4]

Grant always believed the reason for his failure to receive the appointment was political. He wrote Jesse that the two Democrats on the county commission had supported his candidacy while all the Free-Soilers went against him. Aware that this information might raise questions in the mind of his father—who was deeply involved in the Republican Party—Grant nervously insisted that he had "never voted an out and out Democratic ticket" in his life. He went on to explain his practice of selecting "candidates that in my estimation, were the best fitted for the different offices and it never happens that such men are all arrayed on one side." Grant told Jesse he even had Free-Soil friends, and to prove he was no pro-slaver, on March 29 he freed his slave.[5]

Setting William free may have been as practical a move as it was politic. The Grants could scarcely feed themselves. When the family moved from their rented house into an equally modest frame dwelling of their own, they left behind a bill for several months' rent, which they promised to pay as soon as their complicated deeds were cleared. But the man who bought Hardscrabble reneged on his note, and the shaky financial transaction collapsed. Hope came in the form of a clerkship in the St. Louis customs house, but after one month's work, the agent unexpectedly died and the man who succeeded him replaced Grant. With no income at all, either the Grants were living on Dent money—and there wasn't much of that—or Ulyss kept on borrowing. They still managed an occasional outing to the local theater and entertained a few friends, but it was a pinchpenny existence.

In February 1860, Grant reapplied for the county engineer's job. But the rumor that the "Dutchman" who had beaten him out was fired was groundless. He returned home in despair. That night he sat in the parlor alone. The belle of White Haven had taken to her bed. Hours passed. Julia finally broke the silence. She told Ulysses that he had better go see his father. "I do not see that I can very well," Grant replied. "It will cost something, and we have nothing to spare." He meant he had little money, but it was the cost to his self-esteem which made the idea of the trip home so painful.[6]

Grant bought a railroad ticket to Kentucky and arrived at the Covington family home on March 14 "with a headache and feeling bad generally." As he trudged from the railway station he caught sight of his father walking half a block ahead, but was so loath to talk with the old man that he didn't hail him. Hannah and two of his sisters met him with questions about Julia and the children. The news that Jesse would be gone for several days knocked the last bit of drive out of him. He sank into a chair in the empty dining room and sat, his head "nearly bursting with pain," for hours, silent and motionless. He hadn't the energy even to walk through the house.[7]

When Jesse returned, Grant put the question to him—could he have work? Unable to resist launching a barbed reproach at this son who had so disappointed him, Jesse called in Ulyss's younger brother, who was nominally in charge of the Grant leather business. Simpson, wasted and feverish from the tuberculosis which would kill him in less than two years, immediately agreed to have Grant join him at the Galena retail store, and this time Jesse didn't insist upon keeping Julia and the children.

LEE WAS BACK IN Texas in February 1860. Arlington was far behind, safely in the hands of his son. He was acting commander of the entire military department and in that capacity took personal charge of a mission to rid the Rio Grande Valley of the depredations of Juan Cortinas, a border folk hero. Lee looked for Cortinas for two months, then reluctantly called off the search and discontentedly settled into the routine at department headquarters in San Antonio, which included keeping the U.S. Cavalry out of Sam Houston's secret plot for an extralegal attack on the Mexican border.

On the domestic front he began to rationalize his absence by regular allusions to tensions while he was in Virginia. "I do not think my presence would add anything," he wrote his daughter, and "it is better that I am away." Two months later, he was more direct. "You know I was much in the way of everybody, & my tastes & pursuits did not coincide with the rest of the household. Now I hope everybody is happier." "Everybody" meant Mary. Lee had been reluctant but willing at the time of Mr. Custis's death to resume his childhood role of nurse to an ailing woman. But instead of melting into loving dependence like his mother, Mary had hardened into her position as head of a large and undisciplined household. That had made Lee's leaving Arlington easier. But it didn't make him happy. Ironically, his sole pleasure during his final year in Texas came from the miscreant Rooney.[8]

The 4,000-acre White House plantation, where George Washington had married Martha Custis, now belonged to his son, and Lee wanted to help restore it to its golden past. He instructed Rooney on fertilizing, timber-cutting, crop-planting, money-managing, and slave-handling—"I trust you will so gain the affection of your people, that they will not wish to do you any harm." In case that failed, it would be "prudent to have your house & furniture insured." The scenario seemed perfect when Rooney and Charlotte had a son and named him Robert Edward Lee. The new grandfather disclaimed the honor, but he was enormously pleased and offered Chass "my warmest thanks for this promising Scion of my Scattered house, who I hope will resuscitate its name and fame."9

In regular letters throughout 1860 to "my Precious Son" and my "Dear, dear Son," he continued to offer both advice and money. There were no more dour promptings toward virtue and sanctity. Now he urged "happiness in your comfortable home," and told Rooney to "do all in your power to bring joy to your household & let nothing diminish the love you bear them." He hoped that Rooney might live out the life he could not, a life similarly elusive for the melancholy Custis. Custis had been ill again, and Lee thought the reason was emotional. He told his son to "study" his "feelings." "You have been remarkably healthy till the past few years. Some derangement has taken place in your Systems." The analysis was somewhat crude, but Lee was just beginning to understand how costly had been his own quest for virtue. He had been sick again in Texas—rheumatism, he thought—just as he had been sick at Fort Hamilton and in Baltimore. Get a good horse, Lee urged his son, and ride about and see your friends. "You must make friends while you are young, that you may enjoy them when old. You will find when you are old, it will then be too late. I see my own delinquencies now when too late to amend, & point them out to you that you may avoid them." In June he wrote to Anna Fitzhugh that he was "rent by a thousand anxieties" and that his mind as well as his body was "worn and racked to pieces."

A divided heart I have too long had, and a divided life too long led. That may be the cause of the small progress I have made on either hand, my professional and civil career. Success is not always attained by a single undivided effort, it rarely follows a halting vacillating course. My military duties require me here, whereas my affections and urgent domestic claims call me away. And thus I live and am unable to advance either. But while I live I must toil and trust.

Lee was admitting that his "military duties" had claims on his heart equal to those of his family's, a reality his family understood better than he. A Lee daughter once wrote that the Army was "everything" to her father—family, country, home—everything. That was not quite true. His affections were also involved with his wife and children. But he could not, or would not, give up the Army for Arlington and family. He had mentioned brotherhood as a reason for keeping his commission, but there was also a deeper need of Lee's which the Army filled. That was the vision of life as glorious and noble, a vision he never abandoned.[10]

IN APRIL 1860, after having leased Julia's slaves, the Grants boarded the steamer *Itasca* for the trip north and settled themselves on deck in two kitchen chairs they had brought with them. Julia's boundless optimism was a wonder to everyone who knew the Grants. "Wait until Dudy gets to be president" and "we will not always be in this condition" were common rejoinders to acquaintances, who snickered and took her for a fool. There was much folly in Julia, but she was also gritty, determined, and very wise in the ways of keeping her husband afloat. They may have seemed absurd, but the Grants kept going.[11]

Straddling the Galena River, six miles up from the Mississippi, Galena clung to steep limestone bluffs, with tiers of houses stitched together by zigzags of wooden stairways strung along cliffs rising more than two hundred feet above the water. The Grants' new town had passed the zenith Lee anticipated for it in the 1830s and was already on its way down. The De Soto Hotel, a four-story brick rectangle of two hundred rooms, was seldom full anymore. Shops didn't carry as many Paris gowns to tempt lucky gamblers as gifts for their New Orleans fancy women. But 14,000 inhabitants still called Galena home in 1860 and the town reflected a cosmopolitan past and a lively present. A motley crowd of riverboat gamblers, steam pilots, merchants, lawyers, and a few Indian chiefs who watered in the forty taverns repented in the handful of churches. Galena was built on one of the richest lead deposits in the country and it had been a busy port, then shrank when railroads made river traffic obsolete.

J. R. Grant Leather Goods, not dependent on lead, was prospering. There were Grant leather stores in La Crosse and Prairie du Chien, Wisconsin, and Cedar Rapids, Iowa, and pieces of Grant land scattered around in southern Wisconsin, Minnesota, and northern Iowa as well as in Illinois. The firm was respectable, and lent its respectability to Julia and Ulysses and their children.

Everyone in Galena knew the Grant family. Simpson was thought a "pleasant sort," but was known to be sickly. Orvil's outspoken abolitionist views and Yankee business practices earned him a reputation as an "uninhibited sharper, and rather arrogant and conceited as well." Most leather-goods customers knew that Jesse's eldest son was arriving in town, and there was some speculation about how the new partnership would work out. One of Grant's cousins remembered Ulysses as joining his brothers on equal terms. Each received a guaranteed salary of $600 per year. But Grant's withdrawing more than $1,300 from the business to pay off St. Louis debts during his first year apparently was acceptable to Orvil and Simpson. There "was no bossing" of Grant by the younger brothers, "no looking down on Ulysses as a failure. We all looked up to him as an older man and a soldier. He knew much more than we in matters of the world, and we recognized it."

Family pride couldn't quite compensate for the assumptions of the town, though. It was generally understood that Grant "had been a regular army officer, who had become somewhat broken down in health and reduced in fortune; and his misfortunes were quite commonly attributed in some degree to supposed habits of dissipation." Broken-down Army officers were common enough in the West, and Grant was no more than a minor curiosity. Neighbors swore later, when he had become famous, that if he "was to walk up, right now . . . you'd never see him. I'd have to point him out to you. That's the kind of fellow he was." Julia set up housekeeping again in the modest style to which she had unhappily become accustomed. Their house was on High Street, and the narrow, two-story brick dwelling backed onto the local graveyard. She had an Irish girl who helped with the cooking and housework—Julia would remember the servant slavishly kneeling to help her mistress on with her boots—entertained her sister-in-law, and spent much of her time reading paperback romances. Neighborhood children thought Mrs. Grant the loveliest of mothers. She usually offered food, and she never scolded when they turned from boisterous to rowdy. Women who watched Julia market thought she had bad eyes and that explained why her husband's voice could be heard on long summer nights reading aloud. Grant's relationship with his children was unusual, neighbors thought, because he indulged them, and because of the silence. They saw Grant sitting in his yard, smoking his pipe "by the hour" while the children played around him—neither he nor they uttering a word.

Grant was also silent at the leather-goods store—a disadvantage in a place where shopping provided the only socializing many customers got. Jesse, always a well-liked salesman, complained that his eldest son "never would take any pains to extend his acquaintances in Galena." If Grant was not on the road buying hides to ship to Ohio or visiting the other stores, he usually hid in the rear of the shop reading newspapers. "Grant was a very poor businessman, and never liked to wait on customers," one irritable patron remembered. "If a customer called in the absence of the clerks, he would tell him to wait a few minutes till one of the clerks returned." Pressed, Grant "would go behind the counter, very reluctantly, and drag down whatever was wanted; but hardly ever knew the price of it, and in nine cases out of ten, he charged too much or too little."[12]

To be a poor businessman in Illinois in 1860 was to be beneath the contempt of most of the citizenry, and most of Galena summarily dismissed Grant as a "shy and unpractical man." But there were a few who were intrigued by him. Galena's Methodist minister, John Vincent, had seen Grant with Julia and the children at church several times, but paid no attention to him until they met one morning in Dubuque, Iowa. Vincent said Grant stood by the fire in his old blue Army overcoat with his hands clasped behind him and discussed politics with "a knowledge of men and measures, a discrimination, animation and earnestness" that surprised him. After that morning he often watched Grant in Galena, and decided there "was much of the Quaker" in the former Army officer. Vincent joined a handful of people who had sensed something extraordinary in Grant. His mother-in-law called it clarity, a former Georgetown neighbor described it as "soul." Years later, Grant admitted hard times, but said, "I never saw the moment when I was not sure that I would come out ahead in the end." He was not glorying in the nineteenth century's definition of success. He meant it. He might be down, as he was in sodden California, but he had never been really out. "I never get stuck," he'd boasted as a Georgetown boy. He didn't.[13]

Grant was discovered in 1860 by John Aaron Rawlins, a twenty-nine-year-old lawyer who had never been stuck either. Slight, quick, and intense, Rawlins seemed all energy even in bustling Galena. He was middling tall, with thick dark hair framing a face that reflected an odd combination of vulnerability and resolve. The eyes were his most memorable feature—large, somber, and sensitive—they glowed black under heavy dark brows. He'd been born on a farm east of town to Kentucky parents who drifted into Missouri before settling in Illinois. After his father went gold hunting and never came back, John ran the family farm, taught himself to read, and whenever he could get enough money together, he'd go to school. But it only amounted to two years' classes in twelve years' time. He hauled charcoal until 1853, when he walked into the office of Galena's best lawyer and asked to read. A year later he was admitted to the bar. He usually represented clients with good cases and no money and was a Douglas Democrat with an unshakable faith in the progress of young America and a fervent hope that he'd go along for the ride. Politics was his passion and he loved to argue with Orvil and Simpson Grant. But Rawlins's temper was so bad he could never run for office despite his reputation for astute estimates of people's worth.

He was fascinated by Grant before Grant had even arrived in Galena. He had grown up, he said, with "a great idea of a Mexican war soldier," and he knew Grant was a Mexican War veteran. Rawlins was a fanatic teetotaler—he said he had an abiding terror of falling victim to demon rum himself—and the stories of Grant's drinking arrived before Grant did. But Grant didn't drink in Galena, and his conquering whiskey made him even more of a hero to Rawlins. Rawlins was disappointed that the "Captain" seemed to have no "special liking" for him, but he was drawn to "the marks of power" he saw beneath Grant's "simplicity."

No two men seemed more different. Rawlins was a spellbinder, personally magnetic and memorable. Grant was so ordinary, so forgettable, that after he became the second most famous man in the Union, leather-goods customers would gather on the sidewalk and try to figure out which of Jesse's sons had gone to war. A close friend said Rawlins's "controlling sentiment was ambition. . . . He desired fame and dreamed of it and worked for it. . . . He bent all his energies to its achievement." Few people who saw the shabby retired Army captain in Galena could imagine that Grant had much ambition for himself, but Rawlins sensed the secret hopes which came alive during Grant's talk of Veracruz.[14]

The Democratic convention was set for April 1860 in Charleston, South Carolina. Despite the obvious division in party unity— Douglas and his popular sovereignty followers on one side, the Buchanan administration and an odd assortment of disaffected secessionists on the other—there were those who thought it possible to heal breaches, preserve the party which by then was the sole unifying political body in the country, and ride on the wave of

John Brown hysteria to a victory over the Republicans. Realistic men were less optimistic. Unprecedented bitterness and violence in Congress had marked the winter session of 1860, and northern Democrats found themselves reluctantly voting with Republicans to stop radical pro-slavery measures. The trouble started in the House, when the Republicans advanced John Sherman, a moderate from Ohio, for the speakership and ran into a blockade of southern Democrats bent on rule or ruin. The "crack of the revolver" and "the gleam of the brandished blade" were foretold as the floor of the House roiled with insolent speeches punctuated by foot-stamping, hissing, raucous laughter, and applause, while galleries thundered with the responses of hangers-on and neatly bonneted ladies. The only persons in Congress not carrying a revolver, asserted Senator James Hammond, "are those who have two revolvers."[15]

Northern delegates to the convention were irritable even before they arrived in Charleston. The men who came by ship—like those from Massachusetts, who brought along their own brass band—were sickened by a rough passage. Those on trains discovered that southern states laid track by county rights, and a zany conglomeration of narrow, narrower, and narrowest gauges meant numerous changes at out-of-the-way stops. They found that Charleston, like most southern cities, had poor public accommodations. Desirable visitors had always depended upon invitations to private homes; those who needed public lodging were by definition undesirable. Stuffed four and five into the few hotel rooms available or lined up on cots in meeting halls, delegates accustomed to the admiration of their communities smarted under the social censure of Charleston's impeccable aloofness. Only a few Northerners—men like Caleb Cushing, who had consistently demonstrated himself a friend to the South—were welcomed.

The Alabama delegation, headed by Calhoun's protégé, William Lowndes Yancey, had arrived with instructions to bolt should a version of a slave code proposed by Jefferson Davis fail to be included in the platform. No one expected it to pass. Yancey had already extracted promises from six states—Georgia, Florida, Mississippi, Louisiana, Arkansas, and Texas—to join Alabama in quitting the convention. When Yancey demanded that the party adopt Davis's code, northern Democrats responded predictably. "Gentleman of the South, you mistake us—you mistake us! We will not do it!" Indeed, they did not, and most of the Southerners walked out. That night, Yancey collected a huge crowd in the courthouse square which cheered the idea of a separate southern nation. "Perhaps even now," he mused, "the pen of the historian is nibbed to write the story of a new revolution."

No historians were needed to discover which men held the revolutionary quill. Several months earlier, Barnwell Rhett had written Porcher Miles that they must be bold if they were to succeed at breaking up the party and the country, for uprisings had always been fomented by determined minorities. There was no hope, he said, that secessionists would control the convention at Charleston. Therefore it was important to convince the Alabama and Mississippi delegations to walk out on the issue of the slave code. "If they will but do it, the people I am sure will come up to the scratch, and the game will be ours." Southerners from Louisiana to Virginia declared that the game had been thrown from the beginning. Charges of irregularities in selecting delegates and allegations of foul play echoed in southern newspapers for months before, during, and after Charleston. The movement to withdraw was decried in the states represented as "a concerted plan for the dissolution of the Union," but the convention closed in the hall where empty delegates' seats had been filled with flowers by Charleston ladies.[16]

When the Democrats reconvened in Baltimore that June, there were two parties: the southern faction, which nominated John Breckinridge of Kentucky—the incumbent Vice-President—on a slave code platform, and the northern faction, which went with Stephen Douglas. In May, remnants of the old Whigs had gathered and formed themselves into the Constitutional Unionists with a ticket of John Bell of Tennessee and an old Custis friend, Edward Everett of Massachusetts. All three parties were faced with the formidable task of beating out the Republican, Abraham Lincoln of Illinois.

The campaign reflected a country gone mad on politics. Douglas, sick and broke, crisscrossed the nation giving speeches on behalf of the Union and himself. Bell spoke throughout the border states, urging caution and an end to suicidal threats. Breckinridge supporters vowed that the Potomac would run red with their blood before they would submit to the despotism of a Black Republican like Lincoln. In what has been called the most sophisticated politicking ever seen in the country, the Republicans were luring uncommitted but disaffected Democrats into their ranks and trying to quiet fears of radicalism.

Lincoln sequestered himself in Springfield while his managers beat the bushes and his "Wide-Awakes" marched. In August, Wide-Awake brass bands played in Galena as more than 250 soldiers for "Old Abe the Giant Killer" struggled down Main Street carrying huge flags and torches. Galena Wide-Awake chairman Gus Chetlain was given a chair of rails said to have been split by the candidate. Not to be outdone, Rawlins raised a company of "Douglas Guards" and asked Grant to drill it. Grant said no. A leather-goods customer later said Grant did not think it becoming for a man who once held a commission as captain in the United States Army to serve a semi-military citizen's body. But being a sociable man, he dropped in on meetings of both the Wide-Awakes and the Guards to pass the time of night. Circuit Court clerk William Rowley, a hard-line Republican, tried to persuade Grant to find a way around the technical residence restriction and vote in November. Orvil Grant interrupted Rowley with a warning to let Ulysses alone. "If he were to vote he wouldn't vote our ticket." Grant demurred, but admitted that he didn't like the position of either party. He had gone to hear Douglas speak and had come away disappointed.

Rawlins stood with a silent Grant the night of November 8 and watched Galena celebrate the victory of Abraham Lincoln. The riverfront was lit up by victory torches and houses were trimmed with flags and lanterns. Cheering Wide-Awakes dragged a cannon up to the Galena heights, where they set it off with some peril to life and limb. Julia Grant, an avowed Democrat, gathered her children about her and glumly watched the proceedings from her front porch. J. R. Grant Leather Goods was exploding with

Republican merrymakers. Grant helped serve oysters and whiskey, but he was terse and preoccupied. An occasional voice would rise above shouts and laughter, declaring that the "Chivalry" had sure been shown. Grant said he disagreed. The South "will make a strong fight."[17]

Southerners' bombast and braggadocio were "the result of their education," Grant said, but it was froth rolling on a strong base. He had gone to school with Southerners and had seen what effete young men like Pierre Gustave Toutant Beauregard had done in Mexico. He knew they weren't sham. But he was in the minority. Throughout the campaign, Republican speakers had downplayed the danger of southern action—either political or military— should Lincoln be elected. Most, like William Seward, were sincere. But most had not been south since Harpers Ferry. Rumors of slave insurrections—some planted by secessionists who actually hoped for Lincoln's success—increased. From Richmond to New Orleans, newspapers sounded alarms which were taken seriously. When so moderate a man as John Reagan of Texas could tell Congress that a dozen towns and villages in his area had been reduced to ashes by rampaging blacks and that plots of poisonings and mass murders had been uncovered, it was clear that mythical terrors had already thrown the South into an emotional state of war.[18]

The South had feared for years that there was no safety for itself within a Union which seemed to condone slave insurrection and which threatened to grow into a mighty instrument for crushing southern politics and commerce. But deeper than the fear, and informing much antebellum anger against the North, was the idea that the South of 1860 had a proprietary claim on the history and traditions of the country. The region had not changed much since the American Revolution—indeed, it had not changed much since Virginia had been the crown jewel of the American colonies. The population of the United States rose by more than 8,500,000 people between 1850 and 1860, but in Virginia the growth was only 175,000. South Carolina added a mere 35,000.

Some southerners thought that rising population was an indication that the North was home to hordes of non-English-speaking —or worse, Irish—rabble. New England was reluctantly admitted to have some traditions—all bad by 1860—but the rest of the North was dismissible as the home of mudsills and nouveaux. There were new men in the South in 1860, and their desire to etch new names in the history of the region was responsible for much secessionist agitation, but the political and social power structure still rested most securely on colonial or Revolutionary families. As the nineteenth century pressed the slaveholding South ever closer upon itself, Southerners became convinced of the need to retrieve their history from the northern idea of a new, more perfect Union. The original Union of states, founded in many cases by their actual fathers and grandfathers, had served their interests. They wanted nothing different. And they came to see themselves as defenders of the original Union, the Constitution which formed it, and the Revolution which made it possible. Lee's reflexive comment at Harpers Ferry about Lewis Washington's selflessness arising from Revolutionary blood was but one echo of a universal assumption in the region.

Slavery itself had become the dominant issue of constitutional arguments after 1830, but the shrill defenses of it were rooted in the firm conviction that southern men and women were the sons and daughters (or grandnieces and grandnephews) of colonial grandees or Revolutionary patriots. To the Northerners who heard of black butlers pouring tea for Charleston worthies, the slave was the significant symbol in the scene. To the host, though he might splutter and rave about slavery, the importance of the ritual rested, not in the butler, but in the teapot made for his grandfather in London and perhaps borrowed against to outfit his father for rebellion against the Crown. George Washington Parke Custis dismissed his two hundred slaves as insignificant, but codified the Mount Vernon silver "to descend . . . entire and unchanged to my latest posterity." "Entire" and "unchanged" were the important words, and the whole South applied them to the country as well as to teapots.

Southern Unionists who spoke against secession were labeled Cassandras and soon came to be called "croakers." Crowds were told that the economic rape of the region would end with secession, that southern produce—cotton, tobacco, and rice—would continue to find ready world markets without the intervention of northern jobbers who had skimmed major profits from the trade. The dawn of a great new "civilization with orators, poets, philosophers, statesmen and historians equal to those of Greece and Rome" was heralded for the South. The simple act of severing themselves from the northern states could start the process that would lead to glory, and most secessionists said that the cutting would be a bloodless operation. "You may slap a Yankee in the face and he'll go off and sue you but he won't fight," scoffed one. But all the states that threatened to dissolve the Union were drilling militia, and tailors in Charleston and Jackson and Augusta were busy filling orders for uniforms.[19]

President Buchanan was a guest at the lavish December 20 Washington wedding of Louisiana representative J. E. Bouligny to Mary Parker, and he was given the seat of honor and attended by Sarah Pryor, wife of radical states' rights representative Roger Pryor of Virginia. Sarah offered the President her condolences over the wretched treatment he was getting in the press. Only three days earlier the New York *Tribune* had printed what many people were saying privately—that Buchanan had gone mad. The President interrupted the pleasantries when his attention was drawn to shouts and jostlings in the hall. "Madam," he asked Mrs. Pryor, "do you suppose the house is on fire?" Indeed it was, but only in a sense. In the hall Mrs. Pryor found a friend, Lawrence Keitt of South Carolina, leaping in the air, shouting over and over, "Thank God! Oh, thank God! . . . South Carolina has seceded! I feel like a boy let out of school." Sarah walked back into the drawing room and leaned to whisper in Buchanan's ear. "It appears, Mr. President, that South Carolina has seceded from the Union. Mr. Keitt has a telegram." Buchanan turned a blank, stunned face to her and slumped in his chair. A moment later he called for his carriage.[20]

Buchanan rallied with an address which was published and widely circulated. He told his southern friends that the Union was more than a "mere voluntary association of states," and that the founding fathers had not been "guilty of the absurdity of providing for its own dissolution." Secession was "neither more nor less than revolution," and though people did have the right to revolt, the election of a President by constitutional measures did not "justify a revolution to destroy this very Constitution." The Union had "been consecrated by the blood of our fathers, by the glories of the past and the hopes of the future." Secessionists dismissed the speech, and Republicans thought it more Democratic eyewash. Conservatives placed hope in a compromise measure hammered out by the Committee of Thirteen headed by the much-loved Senator John Crittenden of Kentucky. The bill called for the restoration of the Missouri Compromise with the extension of 36°30′ to the Pacific. This line was to be perpetual, and set by an amendment to the Constitution which was unrepealable and unamendable for all time. Crittenden proposed putting the compromise to a public vote—which moderates were certain would have passed—but Republican senators killed it in committee and it was voted down on the floor.[21]

By the first of February, six states had joined South Carolina in seceding—Georgia, Florida, Alabama, Mississippi, Louisiana, and Texas. The Alabama vote, 61–39, was the closest. South Carolina had presented a united front by going out of the Union 169–0.

Washington was a different city. Carriages piled with baggage filled the streets and handsome houses stood empty, their shutters drawn and furnishings shrouded in dustcovers. The Chivalry was leaving. Threats by seceded states to claim Washington and rumors that Abraham Lincoln would not live to see his inauguration day set Winfield Scott, with the aid of Galena representative Elihu Washburne, to work shoring up the capital's defenses. The sole impediment to invasion from the south was a rotting fort opposite Mount Vernon garrisoned by one old Irish pensioner, which Scott said could be taken for a bottle of whiskey. New York police were pressed into service as undercover agents, and the city's four militia companies were purged of doubtful officers and augmented by new enlistments. Scott ordered additional Army troops to Washington, and made a show of drilling on Pennsylvania Avenue. Military activities were curtailed when a Virginia peace commission arrived in Washington. Buchanan feared that too militant a show might discourage the efforts of the assemblage, but no real hope was held out for the group, described in the Republican press as a gathering of political fossils. Led by ex-President Tyler and with hoary names such as David Wilmot on its roster, the conference, as predicted, failed.

On February 4 delegates from the seven seceded states sat in Montgomery, Alabama, and began to create a new government. Though the preamble of the Confederate Constitution announced that the document represented "sovereign and independent states" rather than "we, the people," the work done at Montgomery did not reflect either radicalism or a commitment to states' rights. In their haste, or anxiety, the delegates re-created a strong central government. It would cause problems in the future, but a powerful national structure was best suited for running a war.

Alexander Stephens, Lincoln's old friend, was sworn in as Vice-President of the Confederacy on his birthday, February 11. That same day Lincoln bade an emotional goodbye to his Springfield neighbors, telling them he knew not when, or whether ever, he might return, and swung aboard the eastbound train, holding the hand of his son Tad. Jefferson Davis held his wife, Varina, in his arms at Brierfield, his plantation near Vicksburg, Mississippi, kissed her goodbye, and left for Montgomery, where he would take his oath as President of the Confederate States of America.

In Galena, a customer of J. R. Grant Leather Goods dashed into the store waving a newspaper the second week of February. Grant was standing on the counter, his back to the door, reaching high for an item on the top shelf. "What's that you say?" Grant asked. The customer repeated it. The seceding states had set themselves up as some new government and had made Jeff Davis

President. Grant turned around and eyed the intruder. "Davis and the whole gang of them ought to be hung."[22]

R O B E R T   L E E said goodbye to the officers at Fort Mason, Texas, on February 13, 1861, and climbed into an ambulance wagon for the three-day trip to San Antonio. He had been relieved of command of the 2nd Cavalry on February 4, and was on his way to report to Winfield Scott in Washington. As his driver put the whip to the mules, one of Lee's young officers called out, "Colonel, do you intend to go South or remain North?"

Staff members strained to hear Lee's response. "I shall never bear arms against the Union, but it may be necessary for me to carry a musket in defense of my native state, Virginia, in which case I shall not prove recreant to my duty." The Union, as Lee understood it, would cease to exist if Virginia was not part of it, but his evasive answer reflected his confusion. Lee knew that carrying a Virginia musket might mean bearing arms against the United States, but he refused to admit it, just as he had always refused to admit he was making choices between the Army and Arlington. History was forcing him into the kind of decision he had never in his life been able to make.[23]

Like many other Southerners accused by bolder brethren of wanting neither war nor peace, Lee said he approved both Buchanan's final State of the Union address—which in effect called for Jefferson Davis's slave code—and John Crittenden's proposal, which was Buchanan's antithesis. Anything, it seemed, was better than disunion. His response to Lincoln's election was to say his "little personal troubles sink into insignificance when I contemplate the condition of the country, and I feel as if I could easily lay down my life for its safety." Though he subsequently repudiated this dramatic sentiment—his death "would bring but little good"—a few weeks later he repeated his willingness to die, saying he would make any "personal Sacrifice" to preserve the Union "Save that of honour."

Lee said he felt the "aggressions" of northern states against the South, and resented the North's "denial of the equal rights of our

Citizens to the Common territory of the Common wealth," but he was "not pleased with the Course of the Cotton States as they term themselves. In addition to their Selfish & dictatorial bearing, the threats they throw out against the border States as they call them, if they will not join them, argues little for the benefit or peace of Virginia Should She determine to Coalesce with them." It was clear Lee recognized the possibility of a southern confederacy, and knew that Virginia might join it. Certain "cotton state" demands, such as the renewal of the African slave trade—which he was "opposed to on every ground"—would render his allegiance to either side difficult, though. "While I wish to do what is right, I am unwilling to do what is not, either at the bidding of the South or North."[24]

"How his spirit would be grieved could he see the wreck of his mighty labours," Lee wrote Mary about George Washington. "I will not, however permit myself to believe till all ground for hope is gone that the work of his noble deeds will be destroyed, & that his precious advice & virtuous example will so soon be forgotten by his countrymen. As far as I can judge from the papers we are between a state of anarchy & Civil war. May God avert from us both. It has been evident for years that the country was doomed to run the full length of democracy. To what a fearful pass it has brought us. I fear mankind for years will not be sufficiently Christianized to bear the absence of restraint and force."

Several days later, he wrote his daughter Agnes that he had not yet received her customary letter. "Perhaps the Enemy has Seized it," he postulated. But who the enemy was, he did not say, or had not yet decided. He said what he called the "Sequestering" of Federal property within the seceded states was "unnecessary" except in self-defense. Unnecessary is not the same thing as wrong.[25]

Not surprisingly, Lee was "particularly anxious that Virginia should keep right, & as she was chiefly instrumental in the formation & inauguration of the Constitution, So I would wish that she might be able to maintain it, & to Save the Union." But a letter written to Rooney on the same day reflected little optimism. "As far as I can now judge I have strong apprehensions that Va will secede as it is fashionably termed," he wrote. Such a move would ruin the state financially, he told Rooney, and at the same time render his personal investments of the Custis legacy money difficult. "The last quotations I saw of the Va bonds was 76. They will go down to $50 if she commences revolution. It would not therefore be prudent to purchase now." Still, he was uncertain. "Would Va not secede, or should the political troubles be adjusted, Va stock will rise & I think be as safe as anything I know of." His very security was at stake, and money was only a symbol. "It is the principle I contend for, not individual or private benefit." He did not say what steps for redressing grievances he would consider "proper," but intimated they might be military by saying he "would defend any state if her rights were invaded." He saw "no greater calamity" for the country than a dissolution of the Union, but a Union without "brotherly love & kindness, has no charm for me. I shall mourn for my country & for the welfare & progress of mankind. If the Union is dissolved & the government disrupted, I shall return to my native state & share the miseries of my people & save in her defence will draw my sword no more."[26]

Lee had introduced into his letters of those two months an idea that seldom found words in his correspondence—"honour." His concept of honor had nothing to do with the Hotspur southern dueler's notion of revenging slights to the ego. It was an "unwillingness" to do what was not right, not a refusal to do what was wrong. The difference was subtle, but profound, and he didn't know what was not right in early 1861.

The strain on Lee was visible to Fort Mason colleagues who responded to his "goodbye, God bless you," with waves, and watched his wagon disappear toward San Antonio on February 13. The second day out, Lee stopped for lunch alongside a freshwater spring which provided an oasis of green in the sere landscape. George Blake Cosby, a cavalry captain, was lounging in the shade, and welcomed Lee. The post had been gossiping about Lee's orders to report to Washington. General David Twiggs's comment—"Ah! I know General Scott fully believes that God

Almighty had to spit on his hands to make Bob Lee"—had made the rounds, and post regulars assumed that Scott would offer Lee command of the entire United States Army. Cosby asked Lee what he would do. Lee was afraid that Virginia had already seceded, he said, and that war was certain. His voice broke as he put his fears into words, and his eyes filled with tears. There was an awkward moment as Cosby watched his usually rigid chief turn away to compose himself. When Lee finally spoke again, Cosby had his answer. He could never bare his sword against Virginia, he said. He would "tender his resignation and offer his services to his native State."[27]

The Texas secession convention had passed its ordinance February 1. Lee was aware that all the compromises in Washington had failed and that southern states had gathered in Montgomery. He realized he was traveling toward a decision he didn't want to make as he rode toward San Antonio. The past, with its stately pace of public virtue and private goodness, its rich fields and plantation schoolhouses, and its opportunities for noble glory, held Lee's most urgent affection. He had tried to live for that golden dream.

As Lee's ambulance wagon pulled up to the front of the Read House hotel in midafternoon on February 16, it was surrounded by an excited crowd of men wearing red flannel insignia on their shirts. Lee spied an acquaintance, Caroline Darrow, threading her way through the mob. "Who are those men?" Lee asked.

They were Texas rangers, Mrs. Darrow told him. "General Twiggs surrendered everything to the State this morning, and we are all prisoners of war."

Lee started, and once again began crying. "Has it come so soon as this?" He registered in the Read House, went to his room, and took off his uniform. Dressed in civilian clothes, he walked across the city square to his former headquarters and found that Twiggs had gone home to Louisiana. Members of a committee of public safety were in charge. A committee spokesman demanded that Lee declare himself for the Confederacy, and received for his cheek a rare display of Lee wrath. He was yet a Federal officer and a Virginian, not a Texan. He would make up his mind without pressure or threats. He turned and stalked out of the building. Charles Anderson, a Unionist San Antonian from Kentucky, whose brother Robert was the center of military attention at Fort Sumter, found Lee still furious when he met him later. The committee, Lee told Anderson, had refused to forward his baggage. Would Anderson help? He would. But Anderson had the same important question to ask. What was Lee going to do? Referring to the committee as "those people"—a term for opponents he would use more frequently in the future—Lee said he would not be moved from his sense of duty by their conduct. For the future, however, his loyalty to Virginia must take precedence over his loyalty to the Federal government. "And I shall so report myself at Washington. If Virginia stands by the old Union, so will I. But if she secedes . . . I will still follow my native state with my sword, and if need be with my life. I know you think and feel very differently, but I can't help it. These are my principles, and I must follow them."

Lee didn't sleep that night. He paced slowly back and forth across his room at the Read House.[28]

The next day was Sunday, and he carefully began to keep his February diary up to date:

17. Remained in San Antonio.
18. Obtained from the Commissioners a wagon to convey my baggage to the Coast—& despatched it.
19. Left San Antonio for Indianola in my own conveyance.
22. Arrived at Indianola & made arrangements . . . for the shipment of my baggage on its arrival.
23. Embarked aboard the Steamer Hughes . . . for New Orleans.
25. Reached New Orleans at 4 p.m. at 7 p.m. took passage on the N. O. & Jackson RR for home.

March 1861

1. Arrived in Alex[a] at 2 p.m. took a carriage & reached Arlington to dinner—Found all well.

The rest of the pages were blank.[29]

LINCOLN, ON APRIL 4, after meeting with still another
delegation of Virginia Unionists, sent word to Robert Anderson
that Fort Sumter would be supplied by sea. The decision to push
the point at Charleston went against advice from Winfield Scott
and most of Lincoln's cabinet members. Everyone knew the attempt to send supplies to Sumter would be met by force. It was
certain to start a war.

When word reached Montgomery on April 9 that Sumter
would be supplied, Davis ordered Charleston defense commander
P. G. T. Beauregard to demand its surrender. Robert Toombs,
acting as the Confederate Secretary of State, had warned Davis
not to take this step. If Beauregard fired on Sumter, Toombs said,
echoing the ancient prediction of John Jay, it "will lose us every
friend in the North. You will wantonly strike a hornet's nest.
. . . Legions now quiet will swarm out and sting us to death. It
is unnecessary. It puts us in the wrong. It is fatal."

At Charleston, former U.S. senator James Chesnut carried the
Confederate demand for Sumter's surrender to Anderson, who
refused. The Federal commander did say he would be forced to
leave his island fort by April 15 if he hadn't received supplies by
then. The South Carolinians, not to be inhospitable, had been
sending groceries out to the Sumter garrison, but stopped the
practice when Lincoln launched his plan.

Edmund Ruffin had been in Charleston for weeks, exhorting
crowds and growing giddy at the prospect of a glorious Confederacy. He had received word that an honor greater than bearing
witness to John Brown's hanging had been bestowed on him: He
was to participate in the bombardment of Sumter. Too excited to
sleep, and afraid that his sixty-eight years might overtake him and
cause him to miss reveille, Ruffin lay awake, fully dressed,
throughout the night of April 11–12. He arose at three and was
on the battery at four, stationed by a cannon. As the sky grayed
seaward of South Carolina's offshore islands, Beauregard ordered
the troops to stand ready. Precisely at 4:30 A.M., Ruffin's commander nodded at the silver-haired old man, and a shaky, liver-
spotted hand reached up and yanked the lanyard. A cold iron ball

arced over palmetto trees toward pay dirt inside Sumter. Ruffin got a hit. The American Civil War had begun.

On April 15, with a white Confederate flag flying over Fort Sumter, and a knot of frightened Virginia peace delegates gathered in Washington, Lincoln issued a call for 75,000 American volunteers to put down "combinations" "too powerful to be suppressed by the ordinary course of judicial proceedings." The response was jubilee. From Boston's bay to the delta below New Orleans, American citizens—both Union and Confederate—took to the streets in a martial carnival. Bands played, grown men wept, and the wild rip of sound that came to be called the Rebel yell was heard in the land. Congressmen hurried home, fearful that fellow legislators would claim larger district enlistments, and yard-goods men found their shelves stripped of bunting. Patriots mounted wagons and urged the boys to scratch their names on enlistment rolls. Ninety days, only ninety days, that's all it would take to be a hero, they said in Massachusetts and Illinois. In Alabama and Georgia they thought that ninety days would be more than enough time to rout the Yankees, but were too gentlemanly to set any limits. For years Americans had sensed portents of cataclysm which had only dim connections with constitutional disputes in the 1850s. Writers of the era thought a mystical atmosphere hovered over the country. It was a romantic, superstitious age. Comets held deep meaning. Dreams and facial bones were taken as prophecy. Divines searched their Bibles and discovered America in the Apocalypse. Guilt hung heavy and caused men and women to shudder at God's coming punishment. Slavery or money changing, forgetting blessings bestowed by Providence or tampering with divinely ordained founders' work, were given as reasons. It was a morbid age which sought to explain its disease and death and failed pursuits of happiness as divine pleasure. Stand still and see the work of the Lord, Garrison had cried when Lincoln's election seemed to point to war. To your tents, O Israel, Clement Clay had urged fellow Confederates. The time had come for divine retribution, it seemed. The purging was at hand, and America greeted the onset of its ordeal with a roar of relief.[30]

Sometime on April 16, the venerable power broker Francis Preston Blair left his Silver Spring, Maryland, plantation to seek an interview with Lincoln. Blair's purpose, according to Lincoln's secretary, was to sound out the President about a commander of Union forces. Winfield Scott was far too old to take the field, and though he had stayed right and not returned to his native Virginia, his plans for dealing with the crisis were too bland. Blair proposed Scott's darling, Robert Lee, and Lincoln gave his consent for Blair to "ascertain Lee's intentions and feelings." Next, Blair went to Lincoln's Secretary of War, Simon Cameron, who directed Blair to make a proposition to Lee.

On the afternoon of April 18, Lee crossed the Long Bridge and went up Pennsylvania Avenue to the Blairs' townhouse across the street from Lincoln's new home. Blair made his proposal.

"After listening to his remarks," Lee said, "I declined the offer he made me, to take command of the army that was to be brought into the field; stating as candidly and as courteously as I could, that, though opposed to secession and deprecating war, I could take no part in an invasion of the Southern States. I went directly from the interview with Mr. Blair to the office of General Scott; told him of the proposition that had been made to me, and my decision."

Scott was waiting for Lee and met what he had to say with dismay and irritation. "Lee," the old general sadly said, "you have made the greatest mistake of your life; but I feared it would be so." Scott talked on awhile. An aide later reported Lee as telling his old chief that the "property belonging" to his children, all they possessed, lay in Virginia. "They will be ruined if I do not go with their state. I cannot raise my hand against my children." Finally, there was nothing more for the two to say to each other. Scott gazed at the man he had called "the very best soldier in the field I have ever seen," and gave up. "I suppose you will go with the rest," Scott told Lee. "If you propose to resign, it is proper that you should do so at once; your present attitude is equivocal."

Scott had been right and Lee knew it. His attitude was equivocal. He had recently accepted a new assignment to head the 1st Cavalry, and rumors that Virginia had just passed an ordinance of secession were spreading throughout the state. For the first time in his life Lee felt the sting of a deserved rebuke against his honor. He knew as he crossed the Potomac that he had to decide at last. Only the coward looks back, he had said. Ahead lay the miseries of Virginia. He had said he would share them. This was to be Lee's last crossing of the Potomac as a citizen of the United States. His next trip southward over the river would be at the head of a beaten army. He never expected anything different.[31]

To Winfield Scott
General of the Army

Arlington, Washington City P.O.
April 20, 1861

General:
    Since my interview with you on the 18th instant I have felt that I ought not longer retain my commission in the Army. I therefore tender my resignation, which I request you will recommend for acceptance.
    It would have been presented at once, but for the struggle it has cost me to separate myself from a service to which I have devoted all the best years of my life & all the ability I possessed. . . .

R. E. Lee

To Simon Cameron
Secretary of War

Arlington, Washington City P.O.
April 20, 1861

Sir:
    I have the honour to tender the resignation of my commission as Colonel of the 1st Regt. of Cavalry.

Very resply your obt servt
R. E. Lee/Col. 1st Cavalry[32]

ELIHU WASHBURNE, his mission safeguarding Lincoln's inauguration over, was back in Galena to spur recruitments. A "monster meeting" was called for the night of April 15, and once again the Wide-Awakes were marching through the town, hefting giant American flags and prodding the reluctant. Washburne, who had been rewarded by Lincoln with liberal patronage appointments, was eager to see how Galena's Democrats would respond to the call for troops. The mayor spoke against war and was hissed and booed. Republicans delivered a string of suitable speeches. But before the meeting's close, John Rawlins claimed the floor. He held the crowd riveted for forty-five minutes. "I have been a Democrat all my life," he ended, "but this is no longer a question of politics. It is simply union or disunion, country or no country. I have favored every honorable compromise; but the day for compromise is passed. Only one course is left for us. We will stand by the flag of our country, and appeal to the God of battles." Grant was on his feet with the rest of the men packed into the small room in the courthouse, and was borne homeward on the swells of cheers for Rawlins. Grant never forgot that speech. He said when he was an old man that it was the best he'd ever heard.

That night, he walked slowly alongside his brother. "I think I ought to go into the service," he said. Orvil agreed.[33]

Washburne suggested to Gus Chetlain that Grant be made chairman of the recruitment committee that would sit that night. So named, he dutifully and embarrassedly called the meeting to order and signed up twenty Galena citizens. There would be no trouble getting the necessary number for a company, but Grant wasn't planning on joining. He told Washburne after the meeting that he was going to ask William Dennison, governor of Ohio, for a commission. Washburne counseled Grant to wait, and said he would see what he could do with Governor Yates of Illinois. The next day, Grant wrote a smug letter to his father-in-law, taking up old political arguments from his position of newfound power.

I know it is hard for men to apparently work with the Republican party but now all party distinctions should be lost sight of and evry true patriot be for maintaining the integrity of the glorious old *Stars & Stripes,* the Constitution and the Union. The North is responding to the Presidents call in such a manner that the rebels may truly quaik. I tell you there is no mistaking the feelings of the people. The Government can call into the field not only 75000 troops but ten or twenty times 75000 if it should be necessary and find the means of maintaining them too. It is all a mistake about the Northern pocket being so sensative. In times like the present no people are more ready to give of their own time or of their abundant mea[ns]. No impartial man can conceal from himself the fact that all these troubles the South have been the aggressors and the Administration has stood purely on the defensive, more on the defensive than she would dared to have done but for her conscious-ness of strength and the certainty of right prevailing in the end. The news to-day is that Virginia has gone out of the Union. But for the influance she will have on the other border slave states this is not much to be regreted. Her position, or rather that of Eastern Virginia, has been more reprehensible from the beginning than that of South Carolina. She shoul[d] be made to bear a heavy portion of the burthen of the War for her guilt.—In all this I can see the doom of Slavery. The North do not want, nor will they want, to interfere with the institution. But they will refuse for all time to give it protection unless the South shall return soon to their allegiance. . . .[34]

The authoritative tone was repeated in a letter he wrote his youngest sister. "I am convinced that if the South knew the entire unanimity of the North for the Union and maintenance of Law, and how freely men and money are offered to the cause, they would lay down their arms at once in humble submission." Equally confident was his repetition of the fate deserved by Vir-ginia. "The conduct of eastern Virginia has been so abominable through the whole contest that there would be a great deal of disappointment here if matters should be settled before she is thoroughly punished. This is my feeling, and I believe it univer-sal."

Though Grant was keen to get on with the punishing, he was reluctant to proceed without consulting his father. On April 12 he wrote Jesse saying that he did not want to "act hastily or unadvisadly in the matter." He had agreed to assist in the organi-zation of Galena's volunteer company, and had promised to go with the company to Springfield and see if he could be of service to the governor. "What I ask now is your approval of the course I am taking, or advice on the matter." He apologized for the haste and brevity of his letter, explaining that "though Sunday as it is we are all busy here. In a few minutes I shall be engaged in directing tailors in the style and trim of uniforms for our men."

Grant chose to ignore the irony of his designing the volunteers' uniforms—they featured blue coats and gray trousers striped in blue—but he was busy and excited. As he told his father, he had "been educated for such an emergency" as now faced his country. "Whatever may have been my political opinions before, I have but one sentiment now. That is we have a Government, and laws and a flag and they must all be sustained. There are but two parties now,—Traitors & Patriots and I want hereafter to be ranked with the latter, and I trust, the stronger party."[35]

Grant's new status within the Galena community had stiffened his pride. He had caught the attention of Washburne, the most important man in town. What was more, he had done it on the basis of his own achievements, and not those of his family. Time had caught up with him too, just as it had with Lee. But Grant moved toward a future rich with promise. Ever since he had been an undersized and undistinguished cadet at West Point, he had wanted to do only one thing—soldiering. Despite the dishevelment and failure, Grant, like Lee, "seemed to have come out of his mother's womb a soldier." And he had never given up the dream of being one. Neither had Julia. None of Grant's detractors knew "My Captain Grant," she had said. And she was right. She tended the flame of Grant's hopes for himself and became, through the bad times, "his salvation," as a former associate noted. With the firing on Sumter, the bad times seemed over.

LEE WENT TO Alexandria for services in Christ Church on April 21, and heard the psalm the rector had obviously chosen with care: "What time as they went from one nation to another: from one kingdom to another people; He suffered no man to do them wrong; but reproved even kings for their sakes." Virginia had passed the ordinance of secession on April 17, and Alexandrians were celebrating the event as a second American Revolution. The worshippers at Christ Church were watching Lee, the man the Alexandria *Gazette* on April 20 had called on to command Virginia forces. "His reputation, his acknowledged ability, his chivalric character, his probity, honor, and—may we add, to his eternal praise—his Christian life and conduct—make his very name a 'tower of strength.' " His neighbors were already referring to him as a second Washington. When they saw him accosted by a trio of strangers after services they assumed he was being questioned by emissaries from the governor.

Early Monday morning, alone and dressed in a black suit and black silk hat, Lee left Arlington for the last time in his life. He caught a train at Alexandria, and rode south through little towns and waysides familiar to him and soon to become famous—Manassas Junction, Thoroughfare Gap, Centreville, Orange, and Louisa. He was called out of his car twice to speak to cheering crowds, but declined to offer his well-wishers more than a stiff bow. Lee did not share the mood of jubilation which caught up his fellow Virginians. The war, he thought, might last as long as ten years. He knew there was no safe place in the state, and he anticipated an immediate aggressive move by Federal troops. Arlington, he thought, would quickly be in the hands of the Union Army, and Alexandria would be among the first towns to fall.[36]

But Lee had finally chosen. When he was in Texas, he had written Mary that a man "who has passed his days in retirement & Shone in domestic Scenes, is without the means of directing general interest." Included in this airy dismissal was not only its immediate object, George Washington Parke Custis, but also all the Carters, all the Fitzhughs, all the men and women of his childhood acquaintance—even his mother. Despite a military career devoted to serving the public good, peacetime had shrouded him in obscurity for all but his happy year in Mexico. He was a modest man, never self-serving, but his reticence and probity did not mean he did not yearn for distinction—it was the stuff of his childhood. And he was a Lee. More important, through kinship and kindred spirit, he was a Washington, and was considered by many Americans to be the living representative of the great and good father of the country.

Lee fully believed that he was doing as Washington would have done. The Union which stood as a monument to Washington's noble deeds had been inaugurated, Lee said, by men who were first citizens of states—chiefly by Virginians. That Union was destroyed. It had been wrecked by selfish men—North and South—who could not even perceive the public good. Lee did not travel to Richmond to fight for Virginia soil. He had long ago given that up. But the idea of Virginia—the idea of Washington, and the Lees sacrificing lives and fortunes and honor to join together in brotherly affection and mutual concern for freedom and justice—was a noble thing. It was a glorious cause worthy of Lee's life. He had at last got his call to greatness.

Behind him, at Washington, lay the opportunity to command a great and victorious army in a war he expected to last ten years. He knew that Americans rewarded their successful generals with the presidency of the United States. And behind him, at Arlington, lay the fortunes of his family. Behind him, in a dozen posts scattered throughout the Union, were the brother officers who had provided him with the only real home he ever knew. Ahead of him, at Richmond, arose a specter of misery and loss which he knew in April of 1861 as well as he knew in April of 1865 was the inevitable end of the duty he assumed, an end that reflected his own years of personal despair. To identify with a cause so certain of failure was perhaps a final try at unifying his divided heart. Certainly it offered the possibility of reunion with his southern dead.[37]

Richmonders were in no mood for somber spirits, and were disappointed by the damper Lee placed on their enthusiasm for war. The Virginia Secession Convention had deliberated for almost three months, and until Lincoln issued his call for troops, most Virginians believed that the Old Dominion would stay in the Union. Strong Unionists and conservatives far outnumbered delegates bent on immediately taking her out. But April 14 changed all that. A "Spontaneous People's Convention" sat on April 16 to inform the duly elected body that the "People" had gone South in their hearts. The April 18 news of secession ignited a series of exhortatory speeches from former President Tyler and former governor Henry Wise, and set off the largest torchlight procession in the city's history. The first American Revolution was often evoked, as was Virginia's first "rebel" chieftain— George Washington. Bands played "The Bonny Blue Flag" and "Dixie" while thousands marched around Capitol Square and down Main, Franklin, and Marshall streets. Windows glowing with candles arranged in the Southern Cross illuminated speakers who shouted for attention above the din. "I am neither a prophet nor the son of a prophet," an orator yelled, "yet I will predict that in less than sixty days the flag of the Confederacy will be waving over the White House."

"In less than thirty days," a listener shouted back.[38]

Four days later, Robert Lee walked from his room at the Spotswood Hotel past the equestrian statue of George Washington in Capitol Square. His destination was the second floor of the neoclassic stucco Capitol designed by Thomas Jefferson and new when Light-Horse Harry brought Ann Carter as a bride to Richmond. As he stood in the rotunda waiting to be summoned by the Secession Convention, he looked up at the ivory marble statue of Washington which stood in the flood of skylight. "I hope we have seen the last of secession," he said to the eyeless ghost of the founding father.

Lee was addressed by his new rank—"Major General Lee"— and welcomed to the hall, "in which we may almost yet hear the echo of the voices of the statesmen, the soldiers and sages of by-gone days, who have borne your name, and whose blood now flows in your veins." The convention, Lee was told, had decided that Virginia had to be defended, and in choosing a commander, the state had looked to old Westmoreland County. "We knew how prolific she had been in other days of heroes and statesmen. We knew she had given birth to the Father of his Country; to Richard Henry Lee, to Monroe, and last, though not least, to your own gallant father, and knew well, by your own deeds, that her productive power was not yet exhausted. . . . Sir, we have, by this unanimous vote, expressed our conviction that you are at this day, among the living citizens of Virginia, 'first in war.' We pray God most fervently that you may so conduct the operations committed to your charge, that it will soon be said of you, that you are 'first in peace,' and when that time comes you will have earned the still prouder distinction of being 'first in the hearts of your country-men.' " In summation, Lee was told by the president of the convention that Washington had willed his sword—the same one stolen by John Brown at Harpers Ferry—to his nephew with the understanding it should never be drawn except in defense of the rights and liberties of the country. "Yesterday," Lee was told, "your mother, Virginia, placed her sword in your hand upon the implied condition that we know you will keep to the letter and in spirit, that you will draw it only in her defense, and that you will fall with it in your hand rather than that the object for which it was placed there shall fail."

Lee responded: "Profoundly impressed with the solemnity of the occasion, for which I must say I was not prepared, I accept the position assigned me by your partiality. I would have much preferred had your choice fallen on an abler man. Trusting in Almighty God, an approving conscience, and the aid of my fel-low-citizens, I devote myself to the service of my native State, in whose behalf alone I will ever again draw my sword."

Lee's speech was thought dispirited. Richmonders had hoped for something along the line of Beauregard's impassioned Charles-ton call to arms. A few weeks later, when his solemnity caused active doubts to be voiced about his commitment to the Cause, Lee was visited in his Richmond office by an anxious Virginian who questioned him about the South's chances. "I am not con-cerned with results," Lee answered. "God's will ought to be our aim, and I am quite contented that his designs should be accom-plished and not mine." Virtue was its own reward.[39]

CHAPTER

13

BUTTONED UP in his old blue Army coat and wearing a stained and battered felt hat, Grant left for Springfield at the end of April 1861. Politicians and would-be politicians were flocking to the Illinois capital with the idea of feathering future incumbencies with heroic war records. Burghers who couldn't tell a saber from a saw strutted around town irritating old Regular Army officers. Grant felt like a superior bump on what he called the "log-rolling" process and complained to Julia that he would not accept any position "inferior to that of Col. of a Regt, and will not seek that." He sulked on the sidelines and made do with short-term clerical work Elihu Washburne got for him. Though he said the job was "principally smoking and occasionally giving advice as to how an order should be communicated," it did allow him "to become acquainted with the principle men in the state." This, he admitted, could do him "no harm." Indeed, it did not. Nor did it do him much good in the beginning, when he was eagerly seeking a Regular Army berth. "I feel myself competent to command a regiment," he wrote the Adjutant General. The Army apparently did not share his optimism. Nothing had come of letters Jesse Grant wrote on his son's behalf to Winfield Scott and Attorney General Edward Bates. The Adjutant General's office was equally silent in response to Grant's own request. His confidence began to waver.[1]

Galena's Gus Chetlain found him "depressed" and threatening to go back to the leather-goods store, but instead he went to Kentucky to see Jesse and to Cincinnati to visit the Army head-quarters there commanded by George McClellan, now a major general and still no friend of Grant's. McClellan didn't see Grant, who waited two humiliating hours, ignored. When he returned the following day he was told the "General had just gone out, might be in any moment. Would I wait?" Still no McClel-lan. Next, Grant tried Missouri and Indiana, where friends were organizing volunteers, and was turned down. He made a short stay in Galena, then went back to Springfield.[2]

A Galena friend caught up with him there and asked what he was doing. "Nothing—waiting," was the answer. He understood himself well enough by this time to know the situation was dan-gerous. "I don't know whether I am like other men or not," he said, "but when I have nothing to do I get blue and depressed." He was, he admitted, afraid he would start drinking again. Grant could have gone to Springfield as captain of Galena's volunteers, but he refused, probably because his time in Galena had mended his pride. He'd been a hero to Rawlins and then had acted as military representative of the government putting together the volunteers. He had symbolically restored himself to the ranks of the Regular Army, and he wanted that reality so badly he even offered himself as bread-maker to a regiment. His friends believed he was being overlooked because of his reputation. Stories of his drinking and his St. Louis ruin were common in the tiny Army, and he was considered a "military deadbeat" and a "decayed soldier." His appearance that spring didn't help. His features, it was said, "did not indicate any very high grade of intellectuality," and his clothes were a mess.[3]

But political debts were funding the majority of Army appoint-ments and Elihu Washburne called in a favor from Governor Yates on Grant's behalf. Yates appointed Grant colonel of volun-teers—acceptable now that there seemed no alternative. On June 16, dressed in "an old coat, worn out at the elbows, and a badly dinged plug hat," Grant took a horsecar out to Camp Yates to assume command. "His men," a fellow officer remembered,

"though ragged and barefoot themselves, had formed a high estimate of what a Colonel ought to be, and when Grant walked in
among them they began making fun of him." Grant, the men said,
had the look of someone who couldn't "pound dry sand in a
straight hole." The 21st Illinois Regiment had already redeemed
itself in the eyes of its equally rowdy brothers-in-arms by mutiny-
ing over bad bread and burning down its guardhouse. The men
meant to keep their reputation, and one actually hit Grant on the
back. Grant stopped and picked up the hat which had been
knocked from his head, dusted it off, and put it back on. Without
saying a word, he turned around and stared at the men, who
immediately fell silent. Perhaps, one thought, Grant might "be
like a singed cat, more alive than he looks." All of a sudden the
recruits felt "very much mortified," one of them remembered.
The little deadbeat in the ragged clothes and dinged-up hat
seemed to have some peculiar power in him. "We could not
exactly understand the man," a private said later. "He was very
soon called the 'quiet man' . . . and in a few days reduced matters
in camp to perfect order."[4]

A trip to Galena yielded a $500 loan from Jesse's old business
partner, E. A. Collins, and Grant outfitted himself with a horse,
a saddle, and a new colonel's uniform. He jovially—and reassur-
ingly—wrote to Julia that his staff was so straitlaced he couldn't
even have a game of cards with them, and that "one pint of liquor
will do to the end of a war." By mid-July he was able to boast
to his father that he had "done as much for the improvement and
efficiency of the regiment as was ever done for a command in
the same length of time." Though he still needed Jesse's approval—"I hope you will have only a good account of me and the
command under my charge. I assure you my heart is in the
cause . . ."—he felt independent enough to tell Julia that he
merely shared her "disappointment" about their separation. The
"country calls me elsewhere," he declared, "and I must obey." He
had something to do worth doing, and he could do it alone.[5]

By July, the Confederate States of America consisted of Texas,
Louisiana, Mississippi, Alabama, Florida, Georgia, South Carolina, North Carolina, Virginia, Tennessee, Arkansas, and, nomi-

nally, Kentucky and Missouri, which were also claimed by the Union. Lincoln was adamant about keeping the two states in the Union. Confederate sentiment was strong in Illinois and Indiana, and without Missouri and Kentucky buffering the Ohio River, all of the Mississippi might fall into Rebel hands.

Grant was sensitive to the political and economic issues involved, and on his first foray into Missouri he was careful to assuage the feelings of potential Union supporters. In early August he wrote Jesse that the majority of the Missourians he met were "Secessionists, as we would term them, but deplore the present state of affairs. They would make almost any sacrifice to have the Union restored, but regard it as disolved and nothing is left for them but to choose between two evils. Many too seem to be entirely ignorant of the object of present hostilities. You can't convince them but what the ultimate object is to extinguish, by force, slavery." Grant thought such assumptions were nonsense. A few decisive Union victories would send "the secession army howling," he had said.

All the states will then be loyal for a generation to come, negroes will depreciate so rapidly in value that no body will want to own them. . . . The nigger will never disturb this country again. The worst that is to be apprehended from him is now; he may revolt and cause more destruction than any Northern man, except it be the ultra abolitionist, wants to see. A Northern army may be required in the next ninety days to go south to suppress a negro insurrection. As much as the South have vilified the North they would go on such a mission and with the purest motives.[6]

Though Grant did not change his mind about the ultimate aim of hostilities, he soon came to see that they might go on longer than he originally anticipated. After the embarrassing defeat at Manassas Junction in Virginia, he admitted to his sister Mary that he no longer knew "what to think" about the "continuance of the war &c. That the Rebels will be so badly whipped by April next that they cannot make a stand anywhere I dont doubt. But they are so dogged that there is no telling when they may be subdued."[7]

He had received his first introduction into the actual "war" by then and learned a lesson he never forgot. Hearing that there was an enemy encampment not far from his regiment in Missouri, Grant set out to find the Confederates, who were commanded by a Colonel Harris. He began to feel "anything but easy," he said, as his regiment marched through twenty-five miles of deserted territory. "As we approached the brow of the hill from which it was expected we could see Harris' camp, and possibly find his men ready formed to meet us, my heart kept getting higher and higher until it felt to me as though it was in my throat. I would have given anything then to have been back in Illinois, but I had not the moral courage to halt and consider what to do; I kept right on." When the regiment topped the hill, Grant found the Confederates gone. "It occurred to me at once that Harris had been as much afraid of me as I had been of him. This was a view of the question I had never taken before. . . . The lesson was valuable."[8]

Other military lessons were also coming easily. He had no experience commanding in the field and got a book on tactics with the intention of keeping one chapter ahead of his recruits. But a night's study revealed to him that the much-celebrated new techniques were nothing more than variations of Winfield Scott's old methods. Grant felt comfortable with Scott. He threw away the book. Soon he didn't need to learn more drilling techniques. He'd made brigadier general.

"Mine has been a busy life from the beginning," he admitted to his sister, "and my new friends in Ill. seem to give me great credit. I hope to deserve it and shall spare no pains on my part to do so." He told Julia he felt "very greatful to the people of Ill. for the interest they seem to have taken in me and unasked too," and sent along four gold dollars for the children. He was confident enough during the late summer of 1861 to pay a grudge call on old Harry Boggs. Grant told Julia that his former St. Louis real estate partner "cursed and went on like a Madman. Told me that I would never be welcom in his hous; that the people of Illinois were a poor misserable set of Black Republicans, Abolition paupers that had to invade their state to get something to eat.

Good joke that on something to eat. Harry is such a pittiful insignificant fellow that I could not get mad at him and told him so . . ." Sweeter yet was marching his regiment into Jefferson Barracks before leaving to assume command of an entire brigade at Cairo, Illinois. His last trip to Jefferson Barracks, he'd been hauling wood.[9]

The preeminence which had so frightened Grant when he was young sat on his shoulders with the easy fit of custom-made epaulets. Admiration was his, and friendship too. He wrote Julia that when he left his old command in Missouri, "nearly all the commanders of regiments expressed regret I am told. The fact is my whole career since the beginning of present unhappy difficulties has been complimented in a very flattering manner. All my old friends in the Army and out seem to heartily congratulate me." He sent Julia his new commission and offhandedly told her his command was "third in importance in the country. . . ." He was working hard, he said, but had "never enjoyed better health" in his life.[10]

Julia only dabbled in northern ladies' war work. She was slow to assume the Union "cause," but was eager for Grant to fight for it. She had "no regret about his going," she said, "and even suggested that our eldest son, just then eleven years old, should accompany him." When a battle seemed imminent and Grant wanted to send Fred back to Galena, Julia was outraged. "Do not send him home; Alexander was not older when he accompanied Philip." All those uniforms on White Haven's porticoes during Julia's childhood had dazzled her and she loved having an important part in the drama of war. "You should be cheerful and try to encourage me," Grant wrote to her. "I have a task before me of no trifling moment and want all the encouragement possible. Remember that my success will depend a great deel upon my self and that the safety of the country, to some extent, and my reputation and that of our children greatly depends upon my acts." Her devotion, in short, might save the country.[11]

Grant was not sufficiently puffed up to ignore the source of his success. The brigadier generalship, like the colonelcy, was a political plum, courtesy of Elihu Washburne. In early September,

Grant assured Washburne that "my whole heart is in the cause which we are fighting for and I pledge myself that if equal to the task before me you shall never have cause to regret the part you have taken."[12]

L E E ' S   S T A R was on the decline as Grant's was moving upward. No less anxious than Grant to secure a place and do his duty, he had been buffeted for four months by professional and personal chaos.

On the evening after he had been welcomed by Virginia's Secession Convention, Lee was summoned by Vice-President Alexander Stephens. He walked the several blocks to Richmond's "sporting" district—the major sport being that practiced in high-priced houses of prostitution—where Stephens was staying in the Ballard House, one of the area's few respectable establishments.

Lee was a potential problem for the Confederacy, Stephens said. Virginia would undoubtedly join the Confederate States of America, and the Confederacy as yet had no higher rank than brigadier general, whereas Lee had just been sworn in as a major general of Virginia's militia. Lee's response was that titles were meaningless. The Vice-President, with relief, noted that the Virginian "did not wish anything connected with himself individually, or his official rank or personal position, to interfere in the slightest."[13]

When Lee took office, it was in a tiny room not far from Capitol Square, where he performed the kind of clerical military duty he had hated for thirty years. He had one aide and two or three clerks, and spent more than twelve hours a day curved over a little desk becoming cramped in body and spirit. But even at his worst, Lee was thought wonderful by the young men assigned to him in the spring of 1861. Armistead Long, son-in-law and former aide-de-camp of Federal general Edwin Sumner, enthused over the "ease and grace" of his new chief's bearing, and his "courteous and mild but decided manner." Like other close Lee observers, Long found him physically impressive, and thought the "animated expression of his eyes made him appear much younger" than his fifty-four years. But best of all, said Long, was Lee's republican simplicity. "He exhibited no external signs of his rank, his dress being a plain suit of gray. His office was simply furnished with plain desks and chairs." There were "no handsomely-dressed aides-de-camp or staff officers filling the anteroom. There was not even a sentinel to mark the military headquarters." Long was astonished at Lee's "rapid despatch of business" and found it remarkable "that in the space of two months he was able to equip for the field sixty regiments of infantry and cavalry, besides numerous batteries of artillery, making an aggregate of nearly 50,000 men."

Another aide, Walter Taylor, was a former bank officer and auditor and consequently admired the "conscientious and deliberate way" Lee attended to the business of arming Virginia. Moreover, Taylor said, "he appeared every inch a soldier and a man born to command."

But Lee was not commanding much southern respect in May and June of 1861. Taylor thought the unpopularity of his chief arose from the dim view he took of the military future. Among other things, he wanted recruits sworn in for the duration of the war, not for twelve months. He understood, said Taylor, "the inevitable suffering, sacrifice, and woe, which would attend a determined and bitter conflict between the two sections of the United States." Taylor admitted that he didn't know how widely Lee "endeavored to have his views adopted," but said the general expressed them freely to those who asked his opinion.[14]

Lee did insist upon his idea of warfare, and bluntly stated in his first communication as Virginia's commander that the army "will act on the defensive." No Virginian under his command would make good the "on to Washington" threats. He had to back away slightly when Virginia joined the Confederacy, but Jefferson Davis was, if anything, more strict in his construction of what constituted defense than was Lee. The only difficulty Lee encountered was that Davis seemingly had no intention of using him to defend anything.

"I do not know what my position will be," Lee wrote Mary in June, after he had turned over the command of the military and naval forces of Virginia to the Confederate government. "I should like to retire to private life, if I could be with you & the children, but if I can be of any service to the State or her cause, I must continue." Habits were hard to break. Lee easily summoned up a domestic alternative to military duty, but there was no longer any mention of pleasure. As it turned out, his job with the Confederate States was no different from his labor for Virginia. Managing volunteers took up most of his time.[15]

Confederate troop organization was much like that of the United States, but was even more chaotic. It was not uncommon for wealthy planters to raise, outfit, and arm a company, stick plumes in their hats, and present the whole to the government. Since their proprietorship extended to even the zany costumes they ordered, they were loath to turn the ultimate authority of their companies over to anyone. The drawing-room commanders played havoc with camp life as they huffed about, putting their men through impossible drill paces, flourishing rhetoric about Vandal hordes and Attila flags, and refusing to obey orders from such unworthies as former Regular Army generals.

Men in the ranks were no less fractious. "Our ideas of the life and business of a soldier were drawn chiefly from the adventures of Ivanhoe," wrote one Confederate private. "The men who volunteered went to war of their own accord, and were wholly unaccustomed to acting on any other than their own notion. . . . While actually on drill they obeyed the word of command, not so much by reason of its being proper to obey a command, as because obedience was in that case necessary to the successful issue of a pretty performance in which they were interested. Off drill they did as they pleased, holding themselves gentlemen, and as such bound to consult only their own wills. Their officers were of themselves, chosen by election, and subject, by custom, to enforced resignation upon petition of the men. . . . Officers were no better than men, and so officers and men messed and slept together on terms of entire equality, quarelling and even fighting now and then in a gentlemanly way, but without a thought of allowing differences of military rank to have any influence in the matter." Most young gentlemen arrived in camp with at least one slave, and it was not uncommon to see youths uttering invectives at family retainers sent along to guard the morals of favorite sons, and one South Carolinian was mortified by having to march into camp dogged by a slave bearing a mattress the boy's mother insisted he sleep upon. The wonder was, mused a volunteer, that such light-opera supernumeraries were able to fight at all.[16]

The common people were a good deal more restricted, but no less independent, than the Ivanhoes, and no less committed to an honorable discharge of duty. Sand-hill crackers and upland yeomen arrived at recruitment depots throughout the South and signed on to defend hearth and home. In time the grumble of poor men fighting a rich men's war became ordinary, but from first to last poor white Southerners rubbed shoulders in the lines with their glossier brethren, and took their stand for independence. However, there were some men—even whole companies—who apparently went to war with no purpose other than private mayhem. The Louisiana Tigers, a group of cutthroats who terrorized New Orleans before shipping out to Richmond, laid waste to towns along their route. Others—who came to be known as "plug-uglies" and were already referred to as "trash"—worked alone, robbed their fellow soldiers, murdered sleeping victims, and tried to get hired as military policemen.

Lee attempted to impose military order and found himself hampered by southern ideology. Commitment to states' rights was a thorny problem, and Confederate governors initially insisted that regiments stay at home. But dealing with the touchy tempers of governors was less troublesome than trying to cope with soldiers arriving in Richmond. The Confederate quartermaster's department and commissary were hopelessly boggled from the outset of the war. Even had there been adequate provisions—and there were not—the inept bureaucracy at Richmond would have prevented their being distributed. As it was, when barefoot farm boys loped into town toting squirrel guns, they often as not marched out again hungry and dressed in the same butternut jeans, carrying the same rusty muskets. Few of the men in the ranks ever approximated regulation uniforms of gray jackets and blue pants. Wealthy companies wore gray, dark green, or navy uniforms. Southern Zouaves, like their northern counterparts, favored baggy satin pants, short embroidered jackets, and silk-tasseled fezes. Their scimitars were objects of great envy among the bowie knife crowd.

By early summer Virginia was stripped bare of armaments, and Lee wrote pleading letters to governors asking them not to send any more unarmed men. Some of the men remained without guns—their officers suggested rocks as weapons—until the first set of battles provided equipment from Federal casualties. Though the Confederate ordnance department under Josiah Gorgas became a model of efficiency, during the first few months of recruitment there was not enough ammunition to allow target practice, and visitors to camps were treated to the spectacle of lines of men pointing their muskets at targets and shouting "Bang!" in unison, then collapsing in helpless laughter.

There was much laughter in the early months. Regimental literary and music clubs were founded, drama groups performed for their fellows, and bands gave concerts. Women arrived daily for exciting luncheons under canvas, and more than one officer had the temerity to hold a real ball. The social life of Richmond was stepped up by the arrival of the Confederate government, and it was thought unseemly if hostesses didn't invite young military bloods to dine. Young matrons drifted into drilling camps attended by turbaned blacks bearing linen-covered baskets of dainties for kin. Ladies out for pre-tea strolls crowded sidewalks to wave lace handkerchiefs at companies drilling near Capitol Square.

Less genteel but equally picturesque were the fancy women who offered themselves from windows in Richmond's red-light district. Baptist farmers had read about the whores of Babylon, but they had never seen any in full flesh—much less pressed any to their bosoms. Alas, some wrote home guarded letters about the proliferation of "clap." Gambling houses and grogshops burst with patrons who stumbled out into the disapproval of midsummer mornings which anxious parsons tried to sanctify with daily church services. The Episcopal Church of Virginia held its annual convention in Richmond in May. Lee attended, was moved to tears by Bishop Meade's sermon, but ruefully admitted the ceremonies attracted few communicants.[17]

He worried over the lack of discipline, the lack of provisions, and the lack of order he faced that spring, but when he told Mary he would like to retire to domestic privacy, he knew his public duty had eliminated that alternative. "I know you will blame me," he wrote to his invalid sister, Ann Marshall, "but you must think as kindly as you can, and believe that I have endeavored to do what I thought right." Ann, the girl he had nursed in their mother's Alexandria home, did what she thought was right and sent a son to serve in the Union Army. Markie Williams was gone from Lee's life too—apparently separated from him by her own politics and certainly by the Potomac River.

Markie's brother, Orton Williams, whom Lee urged not to go to West Point, was less decisive than his sister. He served for a time as aide to Winfield Scott, but acted as courier to the Lee family. At the end of April, Williams carried to Scott a letter from Mary Lee which contained a newspaper clipping giving an account of Lee's induction in Richmond. "No honors can reconcile us to this fratricidal war which we would have laid down our lives freely to avert," Mary wrote Scott. "Whatever may happen, I feel that I may expect from your kindness all the protection you can in honor afford. Nothing can ever make me forget your kind appreciation of Mr. Lee. If you knew all you would not think so hardly of me. Were it not that I would not add one feather to his load of care, nothing could induce me to abandon my home. Oh, that you could command peace to our distracted country."[18]

Scott did command Orton Williams to warn Mary that the Yankees were coming. The idea drove her to tell her daughter Milly, "Whatever I have thought & even *now* think of the commencement of this horrible conflict, *now* our duty is *plain,* & to resist unto death."[19]

She had the Mount Vernon paintings removed from their frames, rolled, and sent to Ravensworth. The sterling silver was shipped to Richmond along with boxes of Washington's papers and books. Carpets, drapes, and the Washington bed and other memorabilia were stored in the attic. The state china and the Order of Cincinnati china which Light-Horse Harry Lee had chosen for Washington were put in the cellar. Lee wrote Mary on May 11 saying that the silver had arrived in Richmond and had been sent on to Lexington, to be hidden by a staff member at the Virginia Military Institute. He kept Washington's papers with him.

Mary could hear the drums from Washington echoing across the river, but the air smelled sweet and seemed full of peace. Perhaps nothing would come of all the threats? Nonsense, Lee told her. Finally, Mary sent two of her daughters on to Ravensworth, to her Aunt Maria Fitzhugh, and wrote a third—Milly— the last letter from Arlington. "I must confess I was both hurt & mortified that a *daughter* of *mine,* at a time when her Father's life is in peril, her home in danger of being trampled over by a lawless foe, if not levelled to the ground should allow a disappointment about a *bonnet* to be so *deep* in her mind & the cravings of her appetite." The following morning she kissed the servants goodbye and was helped into her carriage. She had not slept for days. Her arthritis was bad, but it was grief that kept her awake, watching over the house of relics until sunrise. Like friends and neighbors who had already left their homes, she made no attempt to take with her any of the furnishings. There was no way of carrying them, and no place to take them anyway.[20]

Mary carried to her grave a bitter mourning over the loss of Arlington, but she gave it up freely. This sacrifice—the ultimate one she could make—was yet another irony of that confused time. She had finally left her childhood home in order to follow her husband. She left as an old and crippled woman when it was too late to do either of them much good, but she was magnificent in her renunciation of the past. When she was driven down the lane of Arlington she showed all the pluck and toughness of her Revolutionary grandmother. By the first of June, she knew the plantation was in Federal hands. Accompanied by one or another of her children, she ricocheted around Virginia for more than a year. Lee never ordered her to safety. He seldom offered suggestions, and in the spring of 1861 he didn't even offer hospitality.

"You know how pleased I should be to have you & my dear daughters with me," he wrote Mary.

> That I fear cannot be. There is no place that I can expect to be but in the field & there is no rest for me to look to. But I want you to be in a place of safety. To spare me that anxiety. Nor can any one say where safety can be found. . . . Do not go to Berkeley, or the Shenandoah Valley. Those points are much exposed, but you must not talk of what I write. Nor is Richmond perhaps more out of harms way. I take it for granted that our opponents will do us all the harm they can. They feel their power & they seem to have the desire to oppress & distress us. I assume therefore they will do it.[21]

Mary's fellow refugees found her uncomplaining and were touched by her plight. Judith Brockenbrough McGuire, on the run from Alexandria, said all "Virginia has open doors for the family of General Lee; but in her state of health, how dreadful it is to have no certain abiding place. She is very cheerful, and showed me the other day a picture of 'Arlington,' in a number of *Harper's Magazine,* which had mistaken its way and strayed to Dixie." When Mary Lee left Arlington, she joined a great and unusual American folk movement. "Refugees" of the Civil War more often than not were landed gentry who left behind handsome homes. Many were terrified of Yankee depredations, and most adamantly refused to consider taking a loyalty oath—required of civilians who wished to live inside Union lines. From the outset of the war, the most venomous charges leveled against northern invaders had to do with the destruction of southern houses. That Union soldiers failed to understand the significance of their vandalism only added to the contempt in which they were held in the South. Jefferson Davis, speaking in Jackson, Mississippi, following a tour through his own burned-out plantation, Brierfield, sneered at the rootless Yankee invaders who had trampled the myth-enshrouded abode of sectional tradition. Agelessness, immortality even, was symbolized by these houses, and a conservative adherence to changelessness. But change had come.

The political process which had begun with debates over the Mexican War had proven as dangerous as Virginia feared. After the fall of Sumter, families with old and honored ties to Virginia's history were shaken from their equally old and honored houses and took to the road. Carrying with them little more than the clothes they wore, these well-connected refugees washed about the state for four years.[22]

Even within the limits imposed by careful commanders, the needs of encamping troops wreaked havoc on property. The fences Lee had reconstructed at Arlington went for firewood. When they were gone, soldiers cut down the trees. Officers were soon living in the house, the possessions stored in the attic and basement were seized, and interior woodwork was scrapped and burned. The house, indeed, might have been razed as were so many of its neighbors, were it not for its becoming, among all the symbolic homes of the South, the most potent for the Union Army. Mary Lee's garden in time became a Federal graveyard.

"I sympathize deeply in your feelings at leaving your dear home," Lee wrote Mary in May. "I have experienced them myself & they are constantly revived. I fear we have not been grateful enough for the happiness there within our reach, & our heavenly father has found it necessary to deprive us of what He had given us. I acknowledge my ingratitude, my transgressions & my unworthiness, & submit with resignation to what He thinks proper to inflict upon me." Lee had never thought of Arlington as a gift from God, but he honestly sympathized over its loss. And perhaps he was candid when he said he had not sufficiently valued the small pleasures of Mary's home. The alternative—public glory within the Confederacy—was painfully costly, and Mary and the children were paying the greatest portion of the price. Day after day, in his tiny office in Richmond, bent over the task of writing dozens of letters, Lee learned that in a civil war, public and private worlds merged into a chaotic whole. Nervous Virginia commanders were seeking his advice, while Confederate officers were on the one hand threatening to withdraw their defenses— Joe Johnston—and on the other hand threatened with no defenses—John Magruder. Juggling his concern for the safety of his state with his concern for the safety of his family added to Lee's strain, but the major cause of his anxiety was his need to get on with wielding his sword. He wanted to take to the field. Finally, in August, he got his chance. Not as a Washington at the head of his troops, but as Jefferson Davis's military adviser.[23]

CHAPTER

14

CAIRO, ILLINOIS, was a hellhole. Fever, dysentery, a plague of mosquitoes, and hordes of rats made the town at the junction of the Ohio and Mississippi rivers "the most unhealthy post" in the Civil War's western theater. Levees designed to hold back the rivers didn't, and steam-driven pumps worked night and day to keep the town dry. They failed too. The mud was so bad that a slip from the boardwalks meant a waist-high plunge into ooze. The bloated remains of mules and horses were carried by the river current, occasionally snagged on submerged trees, and gave Cairo its distinctive odor.

Grant, who had shed his colonel's uniform when he made brigadier, arrived in Cairo in civilian dress, alone, and went to Headquarters, where he wrote out an order assuming command. The officer in charge was incredulous, and said later he'd had half a mind to have the unkempt fellow with the shaggy beard arrested. But something in Grant stopped him. He begrudgingly gave a salute. Grant was in command.[1]

Shortly after he had been commissioned, Grant wrote to John Rawlins in Galena offering him a job as assistant adjutant general with the rank of captain. Rawlins wanted to accept, but he was leaving for New York, where his dying wife had gone to be with her family. He stayed there until he buried her, then left his three children—the oldest was only five—with their grandparents and came to Cairo. Grant knew Elihu Washburne wanted Rawlins to have the job, but he may not have known why. Rawlins, a Democrat, apparently had convinced Washburne that he could be helpful to the cause beyond fervid speechmaking in Galena. Washburne knew he was taking a chance with Ulysses Grant. Though he had an interest in promoting a local boy for military laurels, he was sensitive to Grant's reputation. Washburne had no desire to champion a deadbeat. Everyone in Galena knew about Rawlins's fanatic teetotaling. Who could be better at keeping an eye on Washburne's protégé?

Rawlins got right to work. He saw the men surrounding Grant and set out to compile dossiers on each with a view to firing them when he had sufficient evidence. Grant's staff in Cairo was described as "roystering, good-hearted, good-natured, hard-drinking fellows, with none of the accomplishments and few of the personal qualities of good soldiers." These men—called "jolly dogs" by a headquarters regular—"did not hesitate, when opportunity offered, to put temptation in the way of those they thought would meet it halfway." Grant was known to be particularly vulnerable "to flattery and to the kind attentions" of his staff. It was a ticklish situation, but Rawlins was "too serious, too stern and unrelenting, to countenance" his chief's cronies.

Grant was delighted with Rawlins, whom he described as the only man he ever knew whom he enjoyed hearing curse. Rawlins stalked around headquarters, throwing baleful glares at interlopers, and decided that his original hopes for a career with Grant had been correct. "Beyond my friendship for Grant," he said several years later, "I felt that I was going to be attached to a man equal to the enlarging situation." Elihu Washburne, apparently wanting to see if Rawlins was right, paid a visit to Cairo headquarters in October. He left satisfied. Washburne, it was said, had "Grant on the brain" from that point on.[2]

Grant not only indulged his ardent, opinionated, and profane adjutant general, he also deferred to him. He acceded to Rawlins's wishes, he was open to Rawlins's suggestions, and he was dependent on Rawlins's personality. A man who knew both men well said Rawlins was "always the complement and counterpart of his taciturn but kind-hearted Chief." Rawlins "appeared to know instinctively a worthless or vicious man, and to abhor his example and influence. But his highest function was in protecting Grant from himself as well as from others, in stimulating his sense of duty and ambition, and in giving direction and purpose to his military training and aptitudes. It was Rawlins, more than any other man, who aroused Grant's sensibilities and gave his actions that prompt, aggressive and unrelenting character which so distinguished them. In fact, it has been frequently said that the two together constituted a military character of great simplicity, force, and singleness of purpose, which has passed into history under the name of Grant." In many ways, Rawlins resembled a perfected version of Jesse Grant. He was outspoken, impetuous, self-satisfied, omniscient, and bombastic. But where Jesse grated at his son's sensibilities, Rawlins soothed them. From the autumn of 1861 until the end of his life, he lived for no purpose other than to serve Ulysses Grant—unless it was to serve John Rawlins through the agency of the Rawlins-Grant creature named "Grant."

Rawlins never rested easy in his position, which also included safeguarding his chief's public reputation. Anytime a disgruntled officer or a civilian disappointed in his claims to preferential treatment wanted to get Grant, all he needed to do was drop a well-placed hint that the general was drinking again. Washburne, concerned that information about bibulous high times at Cairo headquarters might be true, contacted Rawlins for information. Rawlins responded with a candid and telling letter.

He would, he wrote Washburne, "answer your inquiry fully and frankly, but first I would say unequivocally and emphatically that the statement that General Grant is drinking very hard is utterly untrue and could have originated only in malice. When I came to Cairo, General Grant was as he is to-day, a strictly total abstinence man, and I have been informed by those who knew him well, that such has been his habit for the last five or six years." Rawlins went on to detail every drop of wine, beer, or spiritous liquors that he had seen Grant consume during the three months he'd been at Cairo, and assured Washburne that at no time had Grant "drunk liquor enough to in the slightest unfit him for business, or make it manifest in his words or actions." Not only that, Grant had given Rawlins his word that he would not "during the continuance of the war again taste liquor of any kind."

Grant's pledge was the most revealing reflection of the relationship between the two men. And there was no reason to doubt it. Rawlins had many faults, but dishonesty was not one of them. He was scrupulous in the extreme, and that was one of the reasons he was valuable. Washburne would believe Rawlins when he wrote that "if you could look into General Grant's countenance at this moment you would want no other assurance of his sobriety. He is in perfect health, and his eye and intellect are as clear and active as can be. That General Grant has enemies no one could doubt, who knows how much effort he has made to guard against and ferret out frauds in his district, but I do not believe there is a single colonel or brigadier general in his command who does not desire his promotion, or at least to see him the commanding general of a large division of the army, in its advance down the Mississippi when that movement is made. . . . I have one thing more to say, and I have done, this already long letter.

"None can feel a greater interest in General Grant than I do; I regard his interest as my interest, all that concerns his reputation concerns me; I love him as a father; I respect him because I have studied him well, and the more I know him the more I respect and love him."

Only a man like Rawlins, who had bought his father out of the family farm as a teenager, and had acted as family head since he was a boy, would experience his anxious, tutelary guardianship of Grant as filial. But he was quite candid about loving the general. Grant was a likable private person who allowed Rawlins unlimited access to the public power of the American military machine during the Civil War. Rawlins meant to keep Grant safe, and in so doing, make himself safe for life. "Knowing the truth," Rawlins concluded his letter to Washburne, "I am willing to trust my hopes of the future upon his bravery and temperate habits. Have no fears; General Grant by bad habits or conduct will never disgrace himself or you, whom he knows and feels to be his best and warmest friend (whose unexpected kindness toward him he will never forget and hopes sometime to be able to repay). But I say to you frankly, and I pledge you my word for it, that should General Grant at any time become an intemperate man or an habitual drunkard, I will notify you immediately, will ask to be removed from duty on his staff (kind as he has been to me), or resign my commission. For while there are times when I would gladly throw the mantle of charity over the faults of friends, at this time and from a man in his position I would rather tear the mantle off and expose the deformity."[3]

Rawlins's dramatic summation was heartfelt. Like the rest of the letter, it was also politic. He may have been a simple man of the people, but Rawlins knew how to manipulate those people to achieve the right ends. He had not only set Washburne's fears at rest, he had also dropped the idea of Grant's commanding an entire division for a Mississippi River campaign. And he reminded Washburne that Grant was—and would continue to be—beholden to the Galena representative.

An expedition downriver was just what Grant wanted, but supplies were a constant headache. Government contracts for uniforms, arms, and food were let to private companies, and the scramble for the lucrative business tended to prove a favorite homily of the period—"scum rises." Scores of indisputably sound Union supporters rallied to the flag with a stronger mind to line their pockets than to tote a gun. The result was musket caps that wouldn't fire, beef infested with maggots, mules with little left in them, and uniforms made of shoddy—a feltlike material which dissolved with the first raindrop. Theft and graft compounded the quartermastering mess. But these difficulties paled before the problem of Confederate sympathizers.

At no time during the war were suspicions more acute than in 1861. Longtime friends, neighbors, and fellow officers were scrutinized for any hint of southern feeling. Strangers passing in and out of town—and there were thousands in Cairo—might just as easily be spies as the businessmen they claimed to be. Cairo was under martial law—the writ of habeas corpus had been suspended by Lincoln in the first weeks of the war—and that helped Grant keep the local peace. But the mails to and from Kentucky and Missouri went through Cairo, and private letters containing important information were not uncommon. Grant ordered correspondence opened and read, but censorship was imperfect. Passes—often signed by high-ranking government officials—allowing individuals to visit friends or family in "enemy" territory were impossible to contradict when they were presented at Cairo. Requests for passes were easier to control but no less open to error. Cairo had its share of refugees too. Unionists from Missouri and Kentucky fled to Army headquarters and were welcomed as long as they signed a loyalty oath. Grant had a list of known—or suspected—Confederate sympathizers prepared, and forced these families to board or support the refugees. Northern-born sympathizers were more severely treated than their southern-born neighbors. Grant also ordered Secessionist property seized. The measures were somewhat harsher than those dictated by other Union commanders, but they were unambiguous and direct and functioned well enough.[4]

Grant's most sensitive problem was handling runaway slaves. Blacks were "stampeding," he said, and most were running to the Army. Those found to belong to Unionists were returned to their Missouri or Kentucky owners. The others were kept as contraband of war and impressed into Union labor. Grant set his policy on slaves in late 1861: "I do not want the Army used as negro catchers, but still less do I want to see it used as a cloak to cover their escape." He had told his father that he preferred maintaining slavery, but if the "rebellion" could not be whipped in any other way than through a war against slavery, let it come to that legitimately. That was not the kind of thing Jesse wanted to hear. He had backed anti-slavery candidates for years and had worked on abolitionist Salmon Chase's Ohio gubernatorial campaign. Orvil and Simpson Grant were early Republicans and at least one of Ulysses's sisters was strongly abolitionist. Grant's "don't care" stance would have rankled Jesse. But he was following higher authorities than his father. His assertion that journalists pushing for a war on slavery "are as great enemies to their country as if they were open and avowed secessionists" was a direct contradiction of his family's position, but safely reflected the Lincoln administration's policy at that time.[5]

Slavery continued to dominate the political scene long after the South seceded. Radical Republicans wanted a "glorious second American Revolution" to complete the work of the first, which would be "a National Abolition of Slavery." Republican congressman Thaddeus Stevens called for total war: "Free every slave—slay every traitor—burn every Rebel mansion, if these things be necessary to preserve this temple of freedom." Such men were growing restive with what they saw as Lincoln's hedging. Thousands of slaves were coming into Union Army lines wherever the Federals advanced, and their fate depended on the particular commander's ideology. When Lincoln banished John Frémont for emancipating slaves and rescinded abolitionist orders of Ben Butler and David Hunter, he earned the scorn of anti-slavery men. "He has evidently not a drop of anti-slavery blood in his veins," William Lloyd Garrison said of Lincoln. Others called the President halting, prevaricating, irresolute, weak, and—that favorite Civil War epithet—"besotted."

Lincoln's position was delicate. The only way he could wage a successful war for the Union was by keeping what was left of it intact. He could not afford to lose the support of his own party, but he had to appease the Democrats. When Republicans began stirring Congress into one of the most passionate anti-slavery turmoils mounted since the Mexican War, the Democrats turned sour on what they came to see as a radical Republican attempt to overturn all American political institutions. Democratic representatives from the lower Midwest and from large northern cities scorned the "Constitution-breaking, law-defying, negro-loving Phariseeism of New England." So strong were sectional feelings that a number of Midwesterners seriously proposed a confederacy of southern and midwestern states. New England, they argued, had brought on the war, let the rest of us make peace and let New England go. "The Constitution as it is and the Union as it was," became the rallying cry of anxious Democrats. "Copperheads,"

retorted Republicans. Battle lines thus drawn, congressional opponents turned slavery into an ideological no-man's-land. A war
for the Union had all parties in the same trenches. Lincoln was
eager to get on with it.[6]

So was Ulysses Grant. He chafed at the restrictions of the bureaucratic post at Cairo and coveted the rich military pickings in
Kentucky. Both President Lincoln and President Davis insisted
on safeguarding Kentucky's declared neutrality, but on September 3, Confederate general Leonidas Polk—Jefferson Davis's old
West Point classmate—fearing the buildup of Union troops at
Cairo, moved into Kentucky and occupied Columbus, on the
Mississippi River. The Kentucky Unionists invited Federal intervention, and Grant made a show of support by accompanying
troops to Paducah, on the Ohio River. He issued his first—and
only—wartime proclamation, declaring himself and his soldiers to
be friends, not enemies, of the townsfolk. The document had the
ring of John Rawlins—or Winfield Scott—about it, and was not
universally admired. The war was tearing Kentucky families
apart, and the state of divided loyalties seemed to exacerbate the
worst fears of both armies. Union officers—primarily William
Tecumseh Sherman, who commanded at Louisville—multiplied
the number of their Confederate adversaries, while southern "defenders" invented hordes of invading Federal foes. No one knew
much about what anyone was doing, and the spy networks only
added to the problem. Credulously listening to the inflated boasts
of Confederate prowess, northern men wired back information
which was as faithfully believed as it was wrong.[7]

Grant's superiors thought that Polk had a huge force at Columbus, and at the end of October sent Grant a confusing order about
safeguarding Fort Belmont, Missouri, just across the Mississippi
from the small Kentucky town. Rebel troops either had taken the
fort or threatened to do so. Given the hint to proceed, Grant
immediately set off with 2,700 men for Belmont.

The river trip from Cairo was short, the weather was fine, and
troops were in high spirits. They threw away knapsacks and
jaunted along to the strains of regimental bands. Most of the men

had never fired a gun at another human being, but they were soldiers and this was war and they were excited. Every now and again an officer would order his regiment to stop for a speech, and one colonel eyed his boys and told them all Illinois was watching. "If I should show the white feather," he exclaimed, "shoot me dead in my tracks and my family will feel that I died for my country."

Artillery from Confederate batteries across the river jarred the morning, but the aiming was bad and the iron balls rolled harmlessly across the fields. So certain were the Federals that success was theirs that they were surprised when the advance marched right into a line of Confederate defenders. The Southerners were novices too, and most of them took off toward the river and huddled under the bluffs. Union soldiers poured through the Confederate camp, cheering at their speedy rout of the Rebs. Bands struck up "Yankee Doodle." Some officers mounted cannons for more patriotic speeches while others looked for souvenirs. Apparently neither Grant nor anyone else noticed a line of Confederate soldiers quietly collecting between the men and the river. When the Southerners began their advance, the Federals, already scattered in celebration, further scattered in panic. A white-faced officer dashed to Grant's side and said surrender was inevitable. Not so, Grant replied. The Union Army had cut its way in, now it could cut its way out. Grant, on horseback, was the last man out. He left more than 600 wounded and dead behind—almost a quarter of the invading force.

That evening, as the transports steamed back to Cairo, Rawlins and other staffers were ecstatic, but Grant was silent. "We thought he was hard-hearted, cold and indifferent," said one officer, "but it was only the difference between a real soldier and amateur soldiers."[8]

The following day, Grant's troops got another lesson in real soldiering. They returned to Fort Belmont—not to make war, but to make friends. Volunteer officers thought it odd that anyone could raise a flag of truce and call time-out. It made the warring seem a kind of game. Wives of several missing officers went along with Grant, and when the boats arrived at Belmont, the women went ashore to look over the field. While the dead were being collected, Grant and his staff entertained Polk and his staff on board the headquarters boat. Polk was a strange sort for a soldier. Tall, thin, and prepossessing in appearance—despite his lack of teeth—he had resigned his commission shortly after graduating from West Point and entered a seminary. He was ordained, and in 1841 made Episcopal bishop of Louisiana. In June 1861 he changed his miter for a general's hat after searching his soul and confessing his desires to Virginia's pro-war Bishop Meade. He seemed to like being called the "Fighting Bishop of New Orleans." Polk thought Grant looked "like a man who was not at his ease," but said he finally "succeeded in getting a smile out of him, and then got on well enough." One of the subjects of conversation was the exchange of prisoners. Under the rules of war, each side got back equal numbers of their own men, paroled by the enemy. A paroled man was honor-bound not to take up arms again until the terms of his exchange had been satisfied. Both Union and Confederate armies had numbers of soldiers and officers impatiently camped in their rears, watched over by their own superiors, until they could join once again in fighting the opponents who had sent them back.[9]

Belmont was denounced in the press as a meaningless, expensive fight, and Grant's commanding officer, Henry Halleck, was cool on the subject. Though his stated reasons for the attack changed sufficiently to require Rawlins to rewrite the official report three years after it occurred, Grant insisted to the end of his days the battle was a success. At the time, he issued congratulations to the men, saying it had been his "fortune to have been in all the battles fought in Mexico by Generals Scott and Taylor save Buena Vista, and he never saw one more hotly contested or where troops behaved with more gallantry." The truth-stretching order reflected Grant's enthusiasm. He had launched an attack and commanded under fire, had been in more personal danger than he would ever be again—one horse shot out from under him—and he had remained collected.

Belmont, in fact, was something of a mystical experience for Grant. Few men seemed less attuned to the otherworldly, but he

was inordinately sensitive to such things. He took seriously
dreams, forebodings, the writings of seers, the analyses of
phrenologists. The letters he wrote to Julia were peppered with
mystical allusions, and the notion that he was bound to her on
some extraphysical level enhanced their marriage, as it had cemented their courtship. He was not at all surprised when she
arrived at Cairo several days after the "battle of Belmont" with
the news that she had had a vision of him while she was in Galena
packing. "I distinctly saw Ulys a few rods from me. I only saw
his head and shoulders, about as high as if he were on horseback.
He looked as me so earnestly and, I thought, so reproachfully that
I started up and said 'Ulys!' " Grant told her she had her "vision"
just as he was making his final dash away from the battlefield. He
had been thinking of her too, fearing what might happen to her
if he were killed.[10]

Grant's staff soon discovered their "hard-hearted" chief was
not in the least cold or indifferent to his wife. Guards watched
their undemonstrative commander escort his Julia on strolls along
the wharf and approved of the way he held her hand and bent his
head to catch her whispers. These were halcyon days for Julia, and
she lived them to the hilt. Her thickening waist and dulling hair
did not divert the attentions of the handsome young officers who
wanted to curry favor with their chief. The soldiers named a
64-pounder cannon "Lady Grant"—an honor Julia chose to accept, regardless of the implications of her increasing girth—and
the staff deferred to her authority at the dinner table, where they
joined Grant's family for meals. Julia reigned over Grant's office,
which he had moved into his living quarters, upstairs in the bank
building, and was a constant, unobtrusive presence at most military meetings. From November 1861 until April 1865 she was
never far from Grant, and often lived with him at camp. She took
seriously his admonition to "encourage" him, and believed with
him "that the safety of the country" depended on her husband.
Julia was not particularly fond of Rawlins, and in time would
come to hate him, but she did accept him as a necessary safeguard
for her husband.

The soldiers at Cairo had the duty of coping with the four

young Grant children, who managed to be underfoot most of the time. Fred, eleven, a veteran of his father's Springfield camp, was indulged by Grant in high jinks beyond the point where staffers stopped laughing, and Julia indulged Buck, who was nine and only two years out of dresses and curls, in almost everything. Nellie was six, and as the only girl in the family, had a rough go of it with Julia. Grant found her irresistible. No one could resist three-year-old Jesse, who toddled fearlessly around the cannon-balls and cotton bales at Cairo.

Julia's improved social and financial fortunes didn't disturb her domestic commitment. Nor did they change her friendships with the wives of lesser lights. She acquired only a few symbols of worldly success, and those were mainly for Grant. She admired a robe worn by the headquarters surgeon and secretly ordered from Chicago a custom-made red-trimmed dressing gown, which Grant loved, but never wore in public. He was less reluctant about displaying the trappings of his generalship. His new uni-form—corded, sashed, plumed, and burnished—had arrived in Cairo, and Grant sat proudly for a photographer. The old plug hat and the threadbare blue coat were banished forever, and so was his beard. He had worn it very long, almost to mid-chest, but Julia insisted it be trimmed into the neat and natty hedge he wore for the rest of his life.[11]

With Julia and Rawlins manning their respective fronts, Grant had enough free time to feel frustrated. He wrote to his sister, with some degree of smugness, that he controlled "a larger force than General Scott ever commanded prior to our present difficul-ties." But he was impatient. "I do hope it will be my good fortune to retain so important a command for at least one battle." As Grant saw it, the threat to him was coming from department headquarters in St. Louis. John Frémont, the Republican candi-date for President in 1856 and a man of questionable military talent, had reluctantly given Grant the job at Cairo, but little else. When Frémont was fired for unilaterally issuing a proclamation which in effect emancipated slaves from areas occupied by Federal troops, he was replaced by Henry Wager Halleck, a portly, hard-faced West Pointer who had left the Army in California about the same time Grant did, and gone on to make a fortune in San Francisco. Called "Old Brains" for his bookishness, Halleck translated military texts, wrote on strategy, and was a capable administrator. He was also waspish, petulant, and gossipy, and was consumed with the idea of rising to the highest military post in the land. Halleck declared the entire western theater a mess of graft, corruption, trafficking, and profiteering, and set about to put things in order. He seemed to like Grant, but he wasn't impressed with his military capabilities.[12]

Grant was ordered to make a "demonstration" in Kentucky early in January 1862, and he returned disgusted. "This sloshing about in mud, rain, sleet and snow for a week without striking the enemy, only exposing the men to great hardships and suffering in mid-winter is not war." War for Grant was getting on with it, going straight ahead and destroying enemy troops. He had, as one student noted, the "impulse to get to close quarters with his antagonist and slug it out." He knew of a couple of prime prospects for slugfests. There were two key Confederate forts on the Cumberland and Tennessee rivers, which flowed almost parallel to one another into the Ohio. He wanted to attack them, and took his plan to St. Louis in late January 1862. Though Halleck himself had designs on the Tennessee and Cumberland—both direct access routes into the heart of the western Confederacy—he apparently gave Grant's idea of attacking Fort Henry and Fort Donelson short shrift at the time. Grant left St. Louis "very much crestfallen."

Lincoln had been pressuring Halleck to do something to sustain the strong Union feeling of eastern Tennessee, but Halleck's hopes were on Don Carlos Buell, a nasty-tempered martinet who refused to move in midwinter. An exasperated Lincoln wrote to Secretary of War Cameron that the news from Halleck was "exceedingly discouraging. As everywhere else, nothing can be done." Grant felt the same way.[13]

SO DID LEE. Though the Confederate Congress had made him a full general, he was not given a command. It was a widely

held military maxim that engineer's duty unfit a man for belligerence, and Jefferson Davis believed his general could best serve as
an adviser. In the late summer of 1861, Davis sent Lee to the
mountains of western Virginia to make peace between two Confederate officers who were waging war upon one another. Armed
with nothing more than instructions to be diplomatic, Lee, accompanied by two aides, Walter Taylor and Augustine Washington,
grandnephew of George and current owner of Mount Vernon, set
off for "that most impracticable, inhospitable, and dismal country." He wrote Mary as soon as he arrived in the mountains that
his route west from Richmond was the same one he had taken
back to St. Louis in the summer of 1840. "If any one had then told
me that the next time I travelled that road would have been on
my present errand, I should have supposed him insane."[14]

He had reason to believe he was dealing with madmen when
he arrived at the Confederate camp. Former United States Secretary of War John Floyd was commanding the "Army of Ka-
nawha" in the southern end of the Shenandoah Valley. Former
governor Henry Wise was in the same area with a private
"legion" of 3,000 ill-armed but eager patriots. Wise refused to
cooperate with Floyd. Floyd insisted upon exercising authority.
Neither was attending to the work of loosening the Union Army's
stronghold in the northern Shenandoah Valley.

Wise was the hardest nut Lee had to crack that autumn. No
one doubted the sincerity of the former governor's commitment
to the cause of southern independence. But, like many southern
political generals, the excitable, touchy, and easily frightened
Wise raced to the field at the head of a farce. During a disastrous
rout which occurred shortly before Lee's arrival, he had galloped
up to his guns and ordered the battery to fire. When the cannoneer
respectfully declined on the ground that the shot would land
among his own men, Wise brandished his sword and insisted:
"Damn the execution, sir, it's the noise we want."

The only way for Lee to properly handle such misguided
enthusiasm was with firmness. Instead, he wrote Wise a detailed
description of how the chain of command in an army was supposed to work. He ended by apologizing, saying his remarks were

not intended to offend. Several days later, Lee reassured Wise that his legion would not be taken away from him and given to Floyd. "I beg, therefore, for the sake of the cause you have so much at heart, you will permit no division of sentiment or action to disturb its harmony or arrest its efficiency." Finally, when Wise's petulance presented a real threat to the safety of the other troops, Lee was pushed to tell him that the combined "forces are not more than one half of the strength of the enemy. Together they may not be able to withstand his assault. . . . I beg therefore, if not too late, that the troops be united and that we conquer or die together."[15]

Lee's resort to melodrama was a good indication of the tension he felt. But his use of "beg" reflected a different problem. He consistently handled the vagaries of southern egos mildly. He did not suffer fools gladly—Walter Taylor often remarked how sorely his patience was tried—but he did suffer them. Apparently he assumed, or rather insisted, that his compatriots were actuated by the same principles of public virtue which compelled himself. To adopt the high hand would seem to place his colleagues' motives in question. Faced with outright knavery, or, more commonly, ineptitude, Lee resorted to suasion and retreated into the correct gentlemanly deportment which he had mastered so early. He had never exercised force—even the force of his will—over anyone but his own children, and commanded by manipulating subordinates with prods at their honor or ambition. Lee was splendid in his role of first among equals. But those who chose to ignore his sterling example presented him with a discomforting riddle. Henry Wise was just such a problem, and he was only the first of many who would prove intractable.

The condition of the army stretched Lee's already weakened patience to the breaking point. Though the vulnerabilities to attack were "unlimited," he said, officers lazed or pouted in their tents while unarmed, unfed, and unclothed men sat about camp waiting for orders and getting sick. No attempts at supplying or disciplining the men had been made. His old blue Army overcoat dragging in the freezing mud, he sloughed about in thigh-high cavalry boots, shouting orders to novice commanders. The troops could go neither forward nor backward. Roads were impassable and the few wagons or guns that could be moved sank before they could be placed. Cavalry was the most effective force, but it was not enough. Nevertheless, he decided to "advise" the commanders to launch an attack against Federal forces under William Rosecrans. Any battle plan would have been jeopardized by the miserable conditions. Neither the officers and men nor the weather were up to Lee's West Point brilliance. It was a forlorn hope in the first place, and, predictably, failed.[16]

Much of the South was shocked by what they saw as Lee's incompetence. Despite Davis's doubts about his military skills, the public expected much from this son of Light-Horse Harry who was called a second Washington. A disgruntled populace dubbed Lee "Granny," and editors excoriated him in inaccurate newspaper stories. Lee was deeply wounded, but never complained—even privately—about his treatment. It was true, he cautioned Walter Taylor, that the abuse was "very hard to bear," but the only course was "to go steadily on in the discharge of duty to the best of our ability, leaving all else to the calmer judgement of the future and to a kind Providence." Mary got the same advice. Pay no attention to the "vile slanders," he told her. "The papers that published them would not put in a refutation, so what good would be accomplished?" His assertion that history and God were on his side did not, however, preclude his taking a small swipe at the press just before he left western Virginia. "I am sorry, as you say," he wrote Mary in October, "that the movements of the armies cannot keep pace with the expectations of the editors of the papers. I know they can regulate matters satisfactorily to themselves on paper. I wish they could do so in the field. No one wishes them more success than I do & would be happy to see them have full swing. Genl Floyd has the benefit of three editors on his staff. I hope something will be done to please them."[17]

The editors were no better pleased when Lee in November assumed command of the new military district of coastal South Carolina, Georgia, and Florida. The appointment, which put him in charge of building defense works, prompted the caustic hope that Lee would be better at wielding the spade than he had been with the sword. The Union Navy was making forays along the entire coast below Charleston. Port Royal was ready to fall. Federal soldiers occupied many of the sea islands off South Carolina and Georgia, and the network of rivers which fed the Atlantic offered easy access into the states' interiors.

Lee was not happy. The safety of South Carolina—a state he had always disliked—was only marginally connected with defending Virginia. But South Carolina was as eager to have Lee as the Richmond press was anxious to see him go. Light-Horse Harry continued to dominate South Carolina's Revolutionary mythology, and the public was confident that the son would strike the father's mark. Civilians cheered him on his tours of inspection, and though he didn't wear a proper uniform—only a gray suit with no sign of rank—he was recognized wherever he went. A local writer picked him out as "topping the tallest by half a head" in a group at Fort Sumter, and said he was "erect as a poplar, yet lithe and graceful, with broad shoulders, well thrown back, a fine justly-proportioned head posed in unconscious dignity, clear, deep, thoughtful eyes, and the quiet dauntless step of one every inch the gentleman and the soldier."

Lee's aides saw their chief through equally starry eyes, but that didn't help them accept the way he lived. The young Virginians expected displays of magnificence in their commanders, but Lee insisted on a tiny frame house as headquarters and set his table with an unimaginable array of nesting tinware. The "bill of fare corresponded in frugality to the plainness of the furniture," an aide wrote, but the commander "always seasoned the meal with his good humor and pleasant jests, often at the expense of some member of the staff who seemed to miss the luxuries of the table more than himself."[18]

Lee found his sustenance in the idea of American history, and as he worked his way from South Carolina to Georgia to Florida, he also found himself calling upon his own past. And that had the unexpected result of resolving his lifelong separation from the idea of his father. "I went over to Cumberland Island & walked up to Dungeness, the former residence of Genl Green[e]," he wrote Mary, "it was my first visit to the house & I had the gratification at length of visiting my father's grave. He died there you may recollect on his way from the West Indies, & was interred in one corner of the family cemetery. The spot is marked by a plain marble slab, with his name, age, & date of his death." Lee had taken along an aide, Armistead Long, and the two men walked through the abandoned plantation. Neither spoke. When they reached the small, overgrown cemetery, Lee quietly told Long that he was going in to see his father's grave. He walked slowly up to the marble slab and stood over it, silently, for many minutes. Finally, he reached out and picked a flower from a nearby bush, turned, and walked away. He didn't talk to Long about the cemetery but he kept the flower.

Lee was almost fifty-five when he visited Light-Horse Harry's grave. But January 1862 was the first time he was old enough or strong enough or hopeless enough to pay his filial respects to Harry Lee. Acknowledging that bond may have been made easier by Lee's confessing to a lifelong yearning to possess his Virginia house. Annie and Agnes were staying in Westmoreland County and had gone to see the old Lee seat. "I am much pleased at your description of Stratford & your visit," Lee wrote them from Georgia. "It is endeared to me by many recollections & it has always been the great desire of my life to be able to purchase it. Now that we have no other home, & the one we so loved has been so foully polluted, the desire is stronger with me than ever. The horse chestnut you mentioned in the garden was planted by my mother." He wanted Stratford—apparently had always wanted it—and he tried to convince Mary to want it too. He wrote that she must finally give up the idea of Arlington. "With the number of troops incamped around it, the change of officers &c. the want of fuel, shelter, &c., & all the dire necessities of war, it is vain to think of its being in a habitable condition. I fear too books, furniture, & the relics of Mount Vernon will be gone. . . . In the absence of a home, I wish I could purchase Stratford. That is the only other place that I could go to, now accessible to us, that would inspire me with feelings of pleasure & local love. You & the girls could remain there in quiet. It is a poor place, but we could make enough cornbread & bacon for our support, & the girls could weave us clothes. I wonder if it is for sale & at how much. Ask Fitzhugh to try & find out when he gets to Fredericksburg." Now that Arlington was swept away in the rebellion he had joined, he might make good on the boyish dream of reestablishing Revolutionary greatness.[19]

But Lee's zeal was not shared by some of his countrymen. He wrote that his defense work went so slowly he hoped "our enemy will be polite enough to wait for us." Privately he told Secretary of War Judah Benjamin that neither the "sentiment of the people, or the policy" of Georgia "seems to favor the organization of troops for Confederate service." Most southern governors, like Lee himself, believed in a war of strict defense. They wanted their states to be safe and their troops to stay at home. Though the Union Army was the most obvious threat to safety, fears of slave insurrections remained. The offshore presence of Federal soldiers was attracting numbers of lowland slaves. At least one abolitionist commander had taken a plantation house for use as a school for blacks, and several had organized model farms, assuring slaves they would eventually own the land. Some planters feared that such promises would incite their slaves to run off or, worse, riot. Lee had never been bedeviled by phantoms of insurrection. He dismissed such anxieties as yet another example of southern waywardness, and wrote his daughter that his major work was making war on South Carolina's "defenders."[20]

The defenders grumbled enough. Digging coastal fortifications was not what young whites meant by war, and many refused to do it. Lee found such shirking of duty inexcusable. It was plain to him, he said, that "we have not suffered enough, laboured enough, repented enough, to deserve success." Our people, he said, "have thought too much of themselves & their ease, & instead of turning out to a man, have been content to nurse themselves & their dimes, & leave the protection of themselves & families to others. . . . This is not the way to accomplish our independence. I have been doing all I can, with our small means & slow workmen, to defend the cities & coast here. Against ordinary numbers we are pretty strong, but against the hosts our enemies seem able to bring everywhere, there is no calculation.

But if our men will stand to their work, we shall give them trouble & damage them yet."

Merely giving trouble to the enemy did not seem a very hearty projection of the Confederacy's military chances. But Lee was disillusioned with his new countrymen, and he was appalled at his old ones. For almost a year, his attitude toward the Union Army had been objective—even sympathetic. But during his stay in Georgia and South Carolina he changed. On December 20—the anniversary of South Carolina's secession—he wrote Judah Benjamin that he had just gotten word that the Federal Navy had sunk between thirteen and seventeen stone-laden sailing ships in Charleston Harbor. The action destroyed Charleston as a shipping point, for the harbor could never be cleared. "This achievement, so unworthy of any nation, is the abortive expression of the malice & revenge of a people which they wish to perpetuate by rendering more memorable a day hateful in their calendar." A few days later he told Custis the "enemy is quiet and safe in his big boats. He is threatening every avenue. Pillaging, burning & robbing where he can venture with impunity & alarming women & children." No "civilized nation within my knowledge has ever carried on war as the United States government has against us." Lee was aware that the war would be long, bloody, and costly. He knew that the Confederacy had no advantage beyond the spiritual. But he misjudged the temper of the times—an odd oversight for a man who had damned the mendacity of the new American democracy. His notion of a war carried on by "civilized" nations who obeyed the rules and protected women was antiquated, and had little to do with the kind of total effort for which the Union Army was gearing up.[21]

At least Mary and the children shared Lee's assumptions. The boys, from twenty-nine-year-old Custis—who finally left Arlington for a post as aide to Jefferson Davis—to eighteen-year-old Rob—who fled to western Virginia to join an artillery unit as soon as classes were canceled at the University of Virginia—were in the ranks. Rooney, twenty-four, had predictably joined the cavalry. Young Mary, at twenty-six, seemed not to share her family's politics. She often ended up behind enemy lines and seldom wrote. Annie, twenty-two, and Agnes, twenty, were usually with their mother, and occasionally moved in with their sister-in-law, Chass, at the White House. Little Milly, the fifteen-year-old girl chastised by Mary for devotion to bonnets, was kept safely in boarding school despite her protestations. Mary insisted on staying near the military action, she said, to care for her husband and sons should they be injured. She visited for a while at Shirley, then made the trip across Virginia's Peninsula to settle in with Chass and the infant Robert Lee III at the White House. For a woman who in the past had traveled uneasily if at all, she was adapting well to her new circumstances. Despite the Federal Army's nearby camp, she gathered her family together at the White House for Christmas, where Lee wrote to them, sending sweet violets that he gathered "this morning while covered with dense white frost, whose crystals glittered in the bright sun like diamonds."

In early 1862 Lee was called back to Richmond, not to take the field, but to act as President Davis's military secretary. "It will give me great pleasure to do everything I can to relieve him & serve the country," he wrote Mary, "but I do not see either advantage or pleasure in my duties." Though he had just done so, he said he would not complain, since we "must all do what promises the most usefulness."[22]

CHAPTER

15

GRANT WAS GETTING a good chance to be useful
in rewarding ways in February 1862. Winfield Scott had finally
limped away from his post as general of the Army and been
replaced by the "Young Napoleon," George McClellan. Eager to
display aggressiveness, McClellan notified Henry Halleck in St.
Louis that P. G. T. Beauregard was coming from Virginia with
thousands of reinforcements for Albert Sidney Johnston in Tennessee and had to be stopped. Halleck ordered Grant to do the
stopping. When the order arrived in Cairo, Grant's headquarters
reacted "as suddenly as if a one hundred pound bomb had landed
in their midst." Rawlins jumped up yelling, kicked over chairs,
and pounded his fists on the wall. Hats flew into the air, cheers
echoed through the office. The commanding officer leaned against
a doorway, smiling, and finally suggested that everyone get to
work. There was little that needed to be done. Grant had been
prepared for such a move for months. Twenty-three regiments
and a naval force would make the trip eastward along the Ohio
River to the Tennessee, then south on the Tennessee to Fort
Henry. Commodore Henry Foote would go along with four
ironclad gunboats, one of the first technological novelties of the
war. By the end of November they were ready. The Navy was
not. In an era which only reluctantly accepted steam engines on
ships, a boat covered with two-and-one-half-inch overlapping

plates of armor was deemed an oddity fit only for the Army. Grant's soldiers would have to man the boats, but Foote, a clear-eyed teetotaler who personally conducted Sunday services for his sailors, would do the commanding. The commodore liked the gunboats and he liked Grant. The two men worked well together.[1]

The night of February 1, Grant came into the bedroom he shared with Julia at Cairo headquarters. He seemed worried. Julia asked him what was wrong. "Nothing," he said. Then he told her she had better go to Kentucky while he was gone. "If you want to visit me—and I am sure you will want to come, will you not?—you can leave the children with my people and can come to me without anxiety." Julia didn't balk as he feared she would. "Dudy" was no longer a failed businessman or farmer, but General Grant, the leader of legions of soldiers. And the daughter of the tribe of Dents was being honored as the general's lady. Moreover, Grant handed her a roll of several hundred dollars and told her it might be some time before he could send her more. He expected to be "on active duty from this on."

The following morning Grant stood at the bow of the headquarters boat, staring intensely at the wharf where Julia and the children waved and cheered. As the boat swung upriver, and Cairo disappeared, Grant turned to Rawlins, who stood beside him, clapped the surprised subordinate on the shoulder, and said, "Now we seem to be safe, beyond recall. . . . We will succeed, Rawlins, we must succeed."[2]

Fort Henry was an engineering anomaly, built on low land, and in February was almost awash. The greatest peril to Grant's army occurred when the flotilla steamed through a school of Confederate torpedoes torn from their moorings by the flooding Tennessee River. Foote had some of the white spherical drums fished out of the water, and he and Grant joined the group watching a mechanic dismantle one. When the torpedo began to hiss, they sprinted for the ladder to the upper deck. Grant, with "commendable enthusiasm," beat out Foote, who asked him, smiling, "General, why this haste?" A sheepish Grant replied that he didn't want the Navy to get ahead of the Army. But the Navy did win the race for Fort Henry. By the time Grant landed his men and marched the few miles overland, Foote's gunboats had already reduced the fort. Grant telegraphed Halleck in St. Louis: "Fort Henry is ours. . . . I shall take and destroy Fort Donelson on the 8th and return to Fort Henry." When a New York correspondent came to say goodbye, the general told him he "had better wait a day or two" if he didn't want to miss an even bigger story. "I am going over to attack Fort Donelson tomorrow," Grant said.[3]

But on February 9—a day after his projected victory at Donelson—Grant was still at Fort Henry, mired in mud and soaked in rain. His spirits were undampened, though. "You have no conception of the amount of labor I have to perform," he wrote in mock irritation to his sister. "An army of men all helpless looking to the commanding officer for every supply. Your plain brother however has, as yet, had no reason to feel himself unequal to the task and fully believes that he will carry on a successful campaign against our rebel enemy. I do not speak boastfully but utter a presentiment." But he did speak boastfully and could be forgiven. So much of his "busy life" had seemed of late like a stage play that he was caught up in his role. Plain old Useless Grant, the joke of Georgetown, was taking his Tennessee ease at the head of 20,000 men. Not a bad joke that, and Grant was clever enough and sensitive enough to step aside and laugh up his sleeve a little. And he did think he would beat the Confederates in front of him. So did they.[4]

Albert Sidney Johnston, Lee's commander of the 2nd Cavalry in Texas before the war, was in command of the Confederacy's western theater. Johnston did not know until his arrival in Tennessee just how much theater was involved. With a total of 50,000 troops west of the Alleghenies, he was faced with an aggregate Union army of more than 90,000. More bluff than hale, Johnston immediately planted outrageous stories of southern strength in Confederate newspapers. His countrymen believed upwards of 70,000 Rebel defenders were arrayed in the area. Federal fear augmented that number, and it was commonly held in the North that Johnston had more than 100,000. Credence was lent the tally by his habit of stripping troops from one spot and quick-marching them under strict secrecy to endangered points, thus allowing a handful of regiments to be counted not once or twice but three or four times. When Beauregard arrived in January and learned the truth, he wrote a friend that he was taking the helm of a ship already on the shoals. "How it is to be extricated from its present perilous condition, Providence alone can determine." Johnston rushed as much manpower as he could to Donelson while Grant sloughed around at Fort Henry. As commander, he appointed Gideon Pillow, an inept and aged veteran who had made himself unforgettable in the Mexican War by ordering a trench dug on the wrong side of a battery. The following day, February 10, Simon Bolivar Buckner, the man who had supplied both pity and money to Grant in New York in 1856, marched his soldiers into Donelson to join the defense.

If Grant knew about the reinforcements, he didn't care. He wired Henry Halleck that he was on his way. The battle plan would be the same as the one that had worked so well at Fort Henry. February 12 dawned fair—the first fine day since the army left Cairo. Foote's gunboats steamed upriver to get into position for shelling the fort, and Grant landed his men a few miles downstream. But the overland march was through broken scrubland. Hauling two days' rations, forty pounds of ammunition, and all their winter gear on their backs, the men grew tired. They tossed off their coats, threw away their blankets, and left their food by the side of the road. It seemed like spring, and the commissary could always get them something to eat.

Grant rode at the head of two divisions, one commanded by C. F. Smith, the commandant of cadets when Grant was at West Point. Smith had shared Winfield Scott's place as one of the two Americans most envied by Cadet Grant. Now Grant was Smith's superior. His other division commander was John McClernand, a politician who had earned Grant's disgust along with a brigadier-ship from the governor of Illinois. McClernand, like Lincoln, was a Kentucky-born lawyer, and had practiced alongside Lincoln on Illinois's Eighth Circuit. The two remained firm friends, and

McClernand—who had grandiose political ambitions of his own—had a direct line to the White House. He also had no idea of how to conduct himself in battle. McClernand had been one of the speech-givers at Belmont, and he had wired Lincoln after Fort Henry that he had been personally responsible for its fall.

The army slept the night of February 12 a few miles from Donelson and the next morning resumed the march. Despite the assumption Grant shared with his enemy that it was an easy picking, Donelson was no Fort Henry. A frontier log stockade, the post was built on top of a hundred-foot bluff and protected by a battery of well-placed guns. By the time Grant arranged the troops, it was clear the gunboats would not be able to do much more than make noise. Taking Donelson was going to consume some time, but McClernand jumped the gun, launched a hasty assault that afternoon, and got his division cut to pieces. Somewhat taken aback, Grant ordered all firing stopped as darkness covered the field, and the army settled in for the night around the remains of McClernand's men. Rawlins set up headquarters in a farmhouse near the base of the fort, and somehow rustled up a feather bed for his chief. Before tucking in, Grant wrote Halleck: "I feel every confidence of success, and the best feeling prevails among the men."

Grant was feeling a good deal better than his men. A drizzle began to fall at dusk, and the wind shifted around to the north. By midnight, snow was falling. Fires were prohibited—they made easy targets for Confederate sharpshooters—and the Union soldiers, shivering without the coats and blankets they had thrown away, had to keep moving to stay alive. Strange orders echoed through the night: "By companies, in a circle, double-quick, *march!*" and obedient troops trotted around one another in the fight for warmth. First light revealed to the men who had never seen the aftermath of a battle an eerie and misery-filled landscape. Trees and guns and the wounded who froze during the night were covered with ice. Pale blue snow, streaked with red, powdered beards of the still-living maimed crying for water. But Grant ignored the grisly aftermath of McClernand's abortive assault. There was work to do, and that always made him happy. He joked with his aides, teased some of the men who were frightened, and had a good laugh over a pair of wounded boys from Illinois. They looked disfigured, he said, had they been hunting bear? If a bear hunt it was, the bagging got harder and harder. Guns, caissons, and wagons were frozen in the snow. That day's fight did little more than put Foote's gunboats out of commission, and there was no progress on land. Grant knew the Confederates "were digging like beavers," but didn't order his men to build breastworks. Entrenching might save lives, but it slowed the operation. He reluctantly wrote Halleck that perhaps the fort would have to be invested by a siege, but added the optimistic note that he felt "great confidence . . . in ultimately reducing the place." The dispatch had something of the old-time failed-farmer hedge about it, and in truth, Grant's spirits were flagging. He knew Confederate reinforcements had arrived—led by Lee's nemesis from western Virginia, John Floyd. The Confederate troop count was now at 17,000—not impossible odds against his now reinforced 27,000.

On the morning of February 15, Grant spent about an hour on Foote's flagship and was being rowed ashore when he saw one of his aides gesturing frantically on the riverbank. Confederates had attacked, he was told, and McClernand's division was routed. Grant spurred his horse and raced into a chaotic scene. The ground was littered with Union dead and soldiers were running for safety. "This army wants a head," snapped McClernand as Grant arrived.

"It seems so," growled Grant, and then demanded an explanation. The officers had never seen him so angry. His fingers curling into a fist around the sheaf of papers he held, Grant stared at his assembled brigade commanders and very quietly said, "Gentlemen, the position on the right must be retaken." With that, he rode off, leaving the onlookers perplexed at his apparent calm. But Grant was far from unworried. From his headquarters he wrote a message to Foote:

"If all the gunboats that can will immediately make their appearance to the enemy it may secure us a victory. Otherwise all may be defeated. A terrible conflict ensued in my absence, which has demoralized a portion of my command, but I think the enemy is more so. If the gunboats do not show themselves it will reassure the enemy still further to demoralize our troops. I must order a charge to save appearances. I do not expect the gunboats to go into action, but to make an appearance and throw a few shells at long range." Grant's admission that "all may be defeated" was a singular confession that would not be repeated during the rest of the war. But countermanding the anxiety he expressed was the certainty he revealed in his understanding of the emotional stakes of war. His repetition of "appearance" reflected a lifetime of awareness that the appearance of control must precede actual command. He'd faked it as a boy in Ohio. At Donelson he would fake it again.

Part of the game was the race. He turned to an aide and announced: "The enemy will have to be in a hurry if he gets ahead of me." Then he went over to C. F. Smith's headquarters and told his former commandant that he "must take Fort Donelson." Smith got to his feet, brushed his white walrus mustache with his hands, cleared his throat, and answered: "I will do it."

That night, Grant lay resting in his feather bed when a knock came on headquarters' door. It was Smith.

"There's something for you to read, General," said Smith. He handed Grant a note which had come through Confederate lines under a flag of truce, signed by Simon Bolivar Buckner. It asked what terms Grant wanted for the surrender of the fort. Grant turned to Smith and said, "Well, what do you think?"

Smith, who had just taken a slug of brandy, wiped his mouth and said, "I think, no terms with traitors, by damned!"

Grant laughed, sat down at a table lit by a wick burning in a bowl of oil, and replied to his old friend Buckner:

Sir: Yours, of this date proposing Armistice and appointment of Commissioners to settle terms of Capitulation is just received. No terms except unconditional and immediate surrender can be accepted. I propose to move immediately upon your works. I am sir, very respectfully

Your obt. svt.
U. S. Grant
Brig. Gen.

Within an hour, Grant had Buckner's reply. "The distribution of forces under my command incident to an unexpected change of commanders and the overwhelming force under your command compel me, notwithstanding the brilliant success of the Confederate arms yesterday, to accept the ungenerous and unchivalrous terms which you propose."

Certainly unchivalrous and more than ungenerous, Grant's demand for unconditional surrender could hardly be considered "terms." But Buckner was distraught. During the night, Floyd had decided to surrender Donelson, but didn't want to be the man to do it. He turned command over to Pillow, and took two regiments of Virginians out of the fort. Pillow, no keener to be captured, turned command over to Buckner, and followed Floyd south.

Grant and his staff picked their way to Confederate headquarters across a field closely littered with the dead. Their horses shied at carcasses of dead mules, still harnessed to caissons, half sunk in the thawing mud. The weather was warming again and the odor of rotting flesh hung heavy in the morning air. Buckner welcomed his captors into more congenial surroundings, offered them breakfast, and introduced them to "Confederate coffee"—a potion brewed in the absence of coffee beans from barley, wheat, or corn. Grant's people found the drink "vile." Even stranger, they thought, was the ease with which Grant and Buckner, "enemies of an hour before," sat "smoking pacifically," discussing the surrender. Grant allowed the Confederate officers to keep their sidearms and personal baggage—which included their slaves—but insisted that the black work force in the fort and all horses and equipment be forfeited. That out of the way, the two West Pointers could discuss the battle like the students they had been. They joked about General Pillow and complimented one another. When Smith arrived, Buckner rose and told the old man that "charge of yours last night, was a splendid affair." Neither then nor later did Buckner allude to Grant's former life. But before Grant sent Buckner north to prison camp, he offered him money. Buckner refused.[5]

The investment of the fort prompted one observer to write that "our troops, in bright blue, marched in from three points, with streaming banners, gleaming muskets, bands playing, men singing and cheering, and the gun-boats firing a salute." The victors were somewhat taken aback when they saw what they actually had captured. The Confederate army did not look at all like an invincible legion of chivalry. "Some had blankets wrapped around them; others, pieces of carpet, quilts, and buffalo robes." The skinny, dirty, and barefoot Rebels not only had no uniforms, they didn't even have proper weapons—only "single and double barreled shotguns, old Kentucky rifles, and flint-lock muskets." There were almost 14,000 of them, and Grant happily announced in his official commendation that his army had captured more prisoners than had ever been taken in an American war. He seemed to like besting history.

The North went wild over the news. "Chicago reeled mad with joy," reported one newspaper, while another told its readers that any citizen not drunk after nine o'clock in the evening "would be arrested as a secessionist." "The backbone of the rebellion is broken," wrote a Cairo correspondent, and in St. Louis bankers joined arms for a teary rendition of "The Star-Spangled Banner." In Cincinnati, citizens were "shaking hands with everybody else, and bewhiskered men embraced each other as if they were lovers." Governor Yates set off for Tennessee to deliver personal congratulations to the Galena soldier he'd started on the road to glory.

Grant was a hero. "U.S." was said to mean "Unconditional Surrender." "I propose to move immediately upon your works" was the catchphrase of the day, repeated even by Secretary of War Edwin Stanton. The Senate took time out from its deliberations to give cheers for Grant and his army. But Abraham Lincoln gave Grant the best compliment of all. On February 22, Grant wrote Julia the news:

"I see from papers the Administration thinks well enough of me to make me a major general." He said he was "ready for anything." His victory made him think that "Secesh is now about on its last legs in Tennessee. I want to push as rapidly as possible to save hard fighting. Those terrible battles are very good things to read about for persons who loose no friends but I am decidely in favor of having as little of it as possible." But Grant's promotion, which put him second only to Halleck in the West, seemed to stir anxiety in him too. On February 26 he enigmatically wrote Julia that his command might be changed. "Whatever is ordered I will do independently as well as I know how. If a command inferior to my rank is given me it shall make no difference in my zeal. In spite of my enemies, I have so far progressed satisfactorily to myself and the country." Grant may have been making an oblique reference to the possibility of his moving east, but his reference to "enemies" reflected his current emotional state. For the first time in his life, he was bold enough to accept the idea of having some, and the particular adversary he had in mind was very close to home.[6]

Julia had waited in Cairo until news of Donelson arrived, then, disconsolate and weeping, boarded a steamer for Covington and her in-laws' house. Years later, she said that only once again in her whole life—when she left the White House after Grant's presidency—did she experience such a feeling of desolation. Torn from what had been the most prestigious "home" she ever enjoyed, Julia might have been bruised in her vanity. But despite her reassurances to Grant, she dreaded going to his parents'. She blandly wrote in her memoirs that the Grants were "very kind to the children and became very fond of them," but excluded herself from her in-laws' affections. Though she had housed the Grants in Galena the previous September when they came up to bury Simpson, Julia had no special liking for Hannah and Jesse. And Jesse, in 1862, seemed to have no special liking for Ulyss.

When Grant wrote Julia the news of his promotion to major general, he added a bitter question. "Is father afraid yet that I will not be able to sustain myself?" Four days later, he told her he was "anxious to get a letter from Father to see his criticism." Grant was winning the approval of authorities far more powerful than his father. And he was surrounded by a group of aides who protected his vanity and safeguarded his dependence. That gave him strength to meet Jesse on equal terms, and those terms had always been belligerent. Jesse had apparently stepped up his attacks in response to Grant's anti-abolitionist letter, and Grant was in no mood to suffer such assaults patiently. But neither he nor his father was particularly comfortable with the mutual antagonism. Grant still needed to be loved by Jesse, and Jesse was losing control of his boy just at the time Ulyss was giving him more fodder for paternal boasting than he had done since he broke horses in Georgetown.

Julia was right in the middle of the father-son struggle. Part of the money Grant gave her at Cairo went for board in Covington, but apparently it wasn't enough—or Jesse wanted a more major tribute. "Such unmittigated meanness as is shown by the girls makes me ashamed of them. . . . it is too mortifying to me to hear of my sisters complaining about the amount paid for the board of their brother's children." And that was not all. On March 5, Grant wrote Julia that she could lend his father all the money she had except for $100. "Take a note payable to yourself bearing interest. I feel myself worse used by my family than by strangers and although I do not think father, of his own accord, would do me injustice yet I believe he is influanced and always may be, to my prejudice." The most obvious candidate for influencing Jesse against Grant was Hannah. Though Grant's mother apparently paid more than one visit to him in Galena, and also seemed to have welcomed Julia and the children, Grant omitted her name in his correspondence. But the most telling comment Grant made in his March 5 letter to Julia was his feeling worse used by his family "than by strangers." Strangers were using him very poorly on March 5, 1862.[7]

Grant received a telegram that day signed by Henry Halleck: "You will place Maj.-Gen. C. F. Smith in command of expedition, and remain yourself at Fort Henry. Why do you not obey my orders to report strength and positions of your command?"

The order took Grant completely by surprise. "I am not aware of ever having disobeyed any order from Head Quarters, certainly never intended such a thing. I have reported almost daily the condition of my command and reported evry position occupied."

Grant was telling the truth, but his reports either had not been transmitted properly or had been waylaid in St. Louis. But what he didn't know was that Halleck, jealous of his popularity, had been waiting for him to make a mistake—any kind of mistake—so he could be replaced. When the Donelson victory caused such a public splash, taking command away from him became a delicate operation. But by early March, Halleck seemed to have his chance. He telegraphed McClellan on March 3: "It is hard to censure a successful general immediately after a victory, but I think he richly deserves it. I can get no returns, no reports, no information of any kind from him. Satisfied with his victory, he sits down and enjoys it without any regard to the future."

None of Halleck's officers was less likely to sit down and enjoy a victory than Grant. He had gone to Nashville without Halleck's authority, but he did so to gather information for a deeper thrust south. Halleck was close to the truth, however, when he said Grant's army seemed demoralized. Confederate troops, waiting for transportation to Cairo prison camps, lounged around Donelson for weeks, consuming provisions and making friends of the boys in blue. Civilians came into the area on the pretext of caring for the sick and wounded, but stayed long enough to lay their hands on slaves, armaments, and other booty. Friends and family of Union officers made visits—Fred Grant arrived and took home a cache of cannonballs as souvenirs. Grant cared nothing about running a perfectly drilled command, he only wanted to oversee a successful one. Since there was no chance of making an immediate drive south, what harm could there be in letting his men relax a little?

McClellan told Halleck what harm there was. "The future success of our cause demands that proceedings such as Grant's should at once be checked. Generals must observe discipline as well as private soldiers. Do not hesitate to arrest him at once if the good of service requires it, & place CF Smith in command."

The following day, Halleck again wrote McClellan. "A rumor has just reached me that since the taking of Fort Donelson General Grant has resumed his former bad habits. If so, it will account for his neglect of my often-repeated orders."[8]

There it was. Grant on a bender was a reason for negligence that McClellan could easily believe. Since such rumors surrounded Grant's headquarters all the time, they could be aired whenever it was desirable to smack him for too independent a show of spirit. Grant was not at all certain how securely he stood with the War Department, but after Halleck alluded to the "numerous irregularities" in his command attracting "the serious attention of the authorities at Washington," he was ready to fight. Though no one at Grant's headquarters knew of the exchange between Halleck and McClellan, they were aware that whispers about Grant's "dissipations" were current again. Rawlins was ready to take on anyone who dared make direct accusations. Grant was miserable, but was stiffened by Rawlins's resolve. "Every move I made was reported daily to your Chief of Staff, who must have failed to keep you properly posted," Grant wrote Halleck. "My going to Nashville was strictly intended for the good of the service, and not to gratify any desire of my own. Believing sincerely that I must have enemies between you and myself, who are trying to impair my usefulness, I respectfully ask to be relieved from further duty in the Dept."

Acknowledged enemies were a novelty in Grant's life, but during March 1862 he saw them everywhere. So did his staff. The idea that headquarters was besieged by powerful and unnamed adversaries tightened the bond between Grant and Rawlins and strengthened as well the position of Grant's unsavory friends. Shortly after Halleck's first telegram, Grant received a sword inscribed by two men cited in a letter about graft at Donelson and one who was described as not having "gone to bed sober for a week." Grant was reduced to tears when they told him it was an honor to "express our renewed confidence in your ability as a commander" at a time when "jealousy caused by your brilliant success has raised up hidden enemies who are endeavouring to strike you in the dark."

Grant wrote Halleck twice more requesting to be relieved from command. Finally, he made an ominous demand: "There is such a disposition to find fault with me that I again ask to be relieved from further duty until I can be placed right in the estimation of

those higher in authority." He was alluding to a court of inquiry—
a smart move. Halleck had just found out that the War Department wanted just such a hearing. He apparently knew that Grant
would be exonerated and that would embarrass Halleck, perhaps
even ruin his chances for advancement.

"You cannot be relieved from your command," Halleck immediately answered. "There is no good reason for it. I am certain that
all which the authorities at Washington ask is that you enforce
discipline and punish the disorderly. The power is in your hands;
use it, and you will be sustained by all above you." Halleck sent
Washington a hearty and good-natured letter of explanation for
the regrettable misunderstanding. Grant wrote Halleck a weakened and emotional letter of gratitude: "I will again assume command, and give every effort to the success of our cause. . . . Under
the worst of circumstances I would do the same." He thanked
Halleck for his "justness," and promised that Old Brains could
rely upon him. The crisis was over.

Grant had emerged from the set-to a major general in charge
of the entire department of Kentucky and Tennessee and was
given personal field command in an exciting new expedition forming for a thrust at Mississippi and Alabama. Though he didn't
know it at the time, he had also cemented the support of Elihu
Washburne. Grant explained himself to the congressman, and
Washburne got his hands on the entire post-Donelson correspondence concerning Grant. The letters and telegrams proved
Grant's innocence, and they were valuable pieces of evidence
should future problems arise.

But Grant's victory had been costly. He had been so shocked
at Halleck's removing him from command that tears had filled his
eyes. "I don't know what they mean to do with me," he wailed
to a friend. "What command have I now?" He experienced the
whole affair as a disgrace, and felt for the rest of his life that he
had been placed "under arrest." It was as if those fearsome West
Point authorities with their bags of black marks had suddenly
materialized in the midst of his personal field of laurels. In the
excitement and joy of his recent busy life, he had forgotten that
"They" existed. Halleck's reminding him struck a tender mark.

"I say I don't care for what the papers say but I do," he admitted. He never recovered the delight he felt in himself in 1861, and he retreated from the confident assertions of superiority over Jesse. He even felt compelled to write a reassuring letter to Julia. "Your husband will never disgrace you nor leave a defeated field." And he added a deflated note. "We all volunteered to be killed if needs be, and whilst any of us are living there should be no feeling *other* than we are so far successful." Even given Grant's conventionally odd syntax, his statement reveals how deadly a wound he had taken to his pride. It would have deadly results a few weeks later.[9]

When Grant arrived in Savannah, Tennessee, to launch his attack against Corinth, Mississippi, he was not in good shape. The "little spat"—as he termed it—had made him physically ill. Though his "Diaoreah" had left him and he no longer felt "an inclination to Chills & Fever," he was still weak. Savannah was on the Tennessee River, due south of Donelson, but on the southern edge of the state, twenty miles north of the Alabama line and just thirty miles north of Corinth, Mississippi. Albert Sidney Johnston and Beauregard were at Corinth with 30,000 Confederates, and Grant meant to get them. William Tecumseh Sherman, who had taken over at Cairo when Grant left for Belmont, had picked a site just south of Savannah as camp for the Union army.[10]

Intense, perceptive, and sensitive, Sherman was one of the most brilliant men to wear an Army uniform. He lived on nerves pulled taut by an inability not to feel strongly about everything, and that caused people to think him a little odd. His appearance didn't help. Sherman always looked as if he was just in from pulling children from a burning building. Red hair poked at odd angles from his smallish, round head, and pale eyes started and flashed from his pinched and crumpled face. He was too thin. His clothing—of good quality—was badly kept, and he seldom buttoned his blouse correctly. He talked incessantly, a disadvantage in the laconic Midwest. Everything about him seemed disrupted. When his father died in 1829, Sherman was taken to live as one of the family in the Ohio home of John Ewing—a powerful man in the state. When he was United States senator, Ewing, who adopted the boy, saw to Sherman's appointment to the Military Academy. He graduated in 1840, sixth in his class, and served six peacetime years in various southern posts. He liked his assignments in Mobile and Charleston Harbor, and learned to enjoy not only Southerners but southern ways. He sat out the Mexican War in California and then served for two years as a courier for Winfield Scott. In 1850 he married his foster sister, Ellen Ewing. Sherman worked in the commissary department in St. Louis until 1852, then went to New Orleans, where he grew tired of the bureaucracy and quit the Army. He tried the banking business, first in California, then in New York, but proved inadequate to the financial panic of 1857 and failed. Law practice in Leavenworth, Kansas, with two of his foster brothers—Hugh and Thomas Ewing—came next. But Sherman hated civilian life. When the opportunity arose in the autumn of 1859 to be headmaster of the Seminary of Learning and Military Academy at Alexandria, Louisiana, he went south.

His brother, John Sherman, was then competing for the speakership of the House of Representatives, and William Sherman feared he would be branded an abolitionist. He soon put himself right with the "extreme southerns" by clarifying his anti-slavery and anti-black attitudes, and settled into a happy routine of preparing their undisciplined sons to be soldiers. He told his wife after three months at the academy that he finally was beginning to feel his footing after years of oppression, and promised he'd soon be strong enough to "get saucy." But by January 1861 Sherman was in an equivocal position. Louisiana Secessionists had taken the Federal arsenal in Baton Rouge and sent to Sherman all the stolen weapons. He had to move out of his bedroom to make space for the stacks of wooden crates marked "U.S." At the end of February he went north, where his reception was cooler than his southern send-off. Six months later, in command at Louisville, Sherman wildly said that 200,000 Federal troops would be necessary to put down Kentucky's Confederate foe. Under severe emotional strain from taking up the sword against his former friends, Sherman was hounded out of Kentucky for being "insane." But Henry Halleck sent him south to join in the taking of Corinth.[11]

Commanding a brigade of new volunteers, Sherman arrived at Pittsburg Landing, Tennessee, set up camp on a plain well suited for drilling, and waited for Grant. The two men knew one another only slightly, but they seemed to get along immediately. Grant saw Sherman the day he arrived in Savannah, approved the placement of troops, and agreed with Sherman that there was no reason to put up any kind of breastworks. The 40,000 men would only be there until 30,000 reinforcements arrived, and then it was straight to Corinth. Sherman was slightly less confident than his chief. He told a newsman that the Army was "in great danger" at Pittsburg Landing, but he wouldn't sound an alarm because "they'd call me crazy again."

Even if he sensed danger, Grant had his own reasons to appear unshaken after his recent trouble with Halleck. He told Julia that he only wanted to do his duty and carry on his "part of the war successfully." He wrote Halleck that he believed the rebellion was on its last legs. "The temper of the rebel troops is such that there is little doubt but that Corinth will fall much more easily than Donelson did when we move. All accounts agree in saying that the great mass of the rank and file are heartily tired." To Julia, on April 3, he wrote that he expected to fight the "greatest battle of the war. . . . However, I do not feel that there is the slightest doubt about the result and therefore individually feel as unconcerned about it as if nothing more than a review was to take place." Two days later, on April 5, he told Halleck, "I have scarsely the faintest idea of an attack, (general one,) being made upon us but will be prepared should such a thing take place."[12]

Grant went every day to Pittsburg Landing and watched over drills and chatted with division commanders. Sherman's green Midwesterners were on the southernmost edge of the camp. The other divisions were spread over the roughly triangular area bounded on one side by the Tennessee River, on another by two creeks, and on the third—south-facing—by a thicket of greening woods. The men were in good spirits, played cards, cooked suppers, picked lice from their uniforms, and tried their luck at fishing. Like all camps, the one at Pittsburg Landing was cordoned by a picket line—a rope fence strung through trees and bushes a hundred yards or so from the camp itself. Artillery caissons, wagons, ambulances, and the mules and horses which pulled them were parked at the line, which was guarded by pickets. Guard duty was dangerous and tended to make men skittish. The pickets were easy targets for enemy skirmishers—the first wave of advancing troops and the only ones allowed the luxury of covering a field on the broken run. One of Sherman's colonels lost seven pickets on Friday night, April 4. The next day the uneasy officer told Sherman of a gathering host of Rebel forces. Irritated, and determined not to be alarmed, Sherman finally rode out to look for himself. When he got back he told the frightened colonel to take his "damned regiment back to Ohio. Beauregard is not such a fool as to leave his base of operations and attack us in ours. There is no enemy nearer than Corinth." But Confederate cavalry had been seen off and on for two days, and on Saturday, nine or ten Rebels had been caught and sent to Grant at Savannah for questioning. Grant didn't think to interrogate them. He wrote his letter to Halleck about no attack, and went to bed early. He was in excruciating pain. During his drill-ground reconnaissance on Thursday, his horse had slipped in the mud and fallen, pinning his leg. He hadn't taken off his boot for two days and had to have it cut away on Saturday, his leg was so badly swollen.

Dawn was just breaking on Sunday when Grant hobbled into his headquarters office. Rawlins was already awake and sorting through the mail. Grant talked to an Illinois officer just returned from leave, and glanced through the correspondence. At six, breakfast was announced, and Grant put crutches under his arms and sawed his way into the dining room. The steward poured coffee for Grant and Rawlins and for W. S. Hillyer, the lawyer who had shared offices with the Boggs and Grant real estate firm in St. Louis. The men exchanged a few pleasantries. Grant reached for his coffee cup. Then a dull, jarring boom echoed around the dining room, shaking windows and rattling spoons against saucers. Grant knew the sound was artillery. He put down his cup, quickly pushed away from the table, and stood up. "Gentlemen," he announced, "the ball is in motion, Let's be off."

Grant's army was interrupted in its Sunday breakfast too. Men stumbled out of their beds, relieved themselves behind their tents, and filled cans with water for coffee. They lit their campfires and poked bayonets around them to hang up pots. The soldiers were too sleepy or hungry to pay any attention to the birds which started out of the woods to the south. They were only lightly interested when a noise like tearing canvas rattled up and chased a flock of squirrels and rabbits across the field. But when some of Sherman's pickets dashed into camp shouting, "Get in line! the rebels are coming!" the men moved. An officer ran to the edge of the camp, peered south, and returned with the news that the "rebs are out there thicker than the fleas on a dog's back!" A courier mounted his horse and took the news to Sherman's headquarters. "You must be badly scared over there," Sherman answered, and settled back to his coffee. In a few minutes, it was Sherman who was scared. A line of Confederates emerged from the woods just yards from his tent. "My God, we're attacked!" he shouted as shots ripped across his headquarters, instantly killing his orderly. Sherman leaped on his horse and started to the rear to rally the army. The nervous Ohio colonel, seeing Sherman go, collapsed. "This is no place for us," he yelled as he ran for a tree, from where he issued his final order of the day: "Retreat! Save yourselves." Most of the regiment did, but enough stayed to form a line, and when Sherman returned, his novices were giving as good as they got. The brambly ground over which the Confederates were advancing looked like "a pavement of dead men" to one of the ones who stayed.

By that time southern heavy artillery had been brought up. Beauregard had settled his staff inside a little rural church called Shiloh Meetinghouse. He leaned against the doorway and watched his soldiers disappear through the woods on their way toward Grant's Army of the Tennessee.

———

Within minutes, Grant was out of his Savannah mansion. He took time to write a note to Don Carlos Buell informing him that the army's advance was attacked, mounted his horse, and rode aboard his headquarters boat to Pittsburg Landing. When he arrived, he could see that something more than an assault on his forward positions was under way. The roar coming down from the plateau to the southwest sounded like a major battle. Directly ahead, at the steamboat landing, tucked under the bluff, thousands of his soldiers huddled in panic. Grant made his way through the streams of men pouring down the cliffs to safety and shouted orders to establish a battery of guns aimed squarely at the escape route of his own army. He left no confusion in the minds of his subordinates that they were to shoot any Federals who came their way. Then he lashed his crutches to his saddle and rode off to see Sherman. The men with Grant watched him carefully. They found him looking "anxious," but "giving no evidence of excitement or trepidation." One of them thought he seemed as unconcerned as if he were conducting a review in his buff-colored satin sash and sword. Though his crutches spoiled a strictly military look, the unlit cigar he held clenched in his teeth gave him a doggedness which his men liked. He didn't talk at all.

By the time Grant got to Sherman, the Union army was routed. Defenders collected here and there, stood their positions, fired on the advancing Confederates, and ran backward until their hard-pressed commanders could line them up again. There was no battle going on, but a maelstrom. Dozens of separate fights were taking place and there was no direction to anything. Artillery horses, pulled loose from their traces, trampled down tents, which caught fire on still-cooking breakfasts. Mules bouncing empty wagons behind them tangled together against nets of harness caught on trees and bushes. The eerie waver of the Rebel yell— which stood northern boys' hair on end—played havoc with Federal orders, which went unheard in the din of muskets and cannon. A riverboat captain stoked the boiler of his three-story packet and steamed up his calliope for blasts of "Hail, Columbia" and "John Brown's Body."

Grant was rigid as stone. Some of his subordinates found him torpid and thought him unequal to the occasion. But controlled calm was the only way he knew how to handle an emergency. He sat his horse or stood his ground and muttered quiet commands around an unlit cigar. A bullet ricocheted off his sword scabbard once, but he didn't seem to notice. He only nodded slightly when a courier ran up with news of yet another disaster. And when the courier stepped back into a canister shot which tore off his head, Grant silently wiped the blood and brains from his new satin sash and gave another order. Few of his orders were or could be obeyed that day in the Army of the Tennessee, but things were just as bad in the Confederate Army of the Mississippi.

The Rebel boys were unhinged by their own success. The smell of all that cooking breakfast was too much for men who hadn't eaten anything but cornmeal for two days, and they squatted around Union campfires while the sun climbed overhead and a tenacious band of Yankees gathered into what became known as the Hornets' Nest. Albert Sidney Johnston led his troops right into the nest, through an orchard of pink blooming peach trees, into a solid sheet of artillery fire. He caught a minié ball in the thigh and died a few minutes later.

By midafternoon, when Beauregard had taken over field command, more than two hundred pieces of heavy artillery were trained on the field at Shiloh. Federal gunboats, armed with siege mortar, joined the fray. The chaos of the morning became something like hysteria. None of the officers or men on either side had ever experienced anything like Shiloh. When sixty-two Confederate guns opened fire on the Hornets' Nest and literally blew the land and everything on it to pieces, the Rebel soldiers who stormed into the void were too numbed to take much advantage. They were too numbed to do anything but walk forward, fire, stop to reload, and fire again. A Federal officer tried to intervene. He rode toward the Confederates shouting, "Boys, for God's sake stop firing, you are killing your friends!" He was shot dead and the boys went walking on, still firing. Union soldiers were killing their friends too. Young northern companies came to war in the hometown gray suits their mayors had chosen and were cut to pieces by blue-clad comrades. It was impossible for artillerists to avoid launching shots into their own men—even if they had the skill to find their marks. And the mob of Federal soldiers that began to collect under the lee of the bluff early in the morning kept growing. By late afternoon, a conservative estimate put the number of panicked troops at more than 10,000. They refused to budge. Officers waved flags as they rode back and forth shouting exhortations at the skulkers, and earned for their efforts nothing but scorn. A chaplain got no better treatment. Praying over the miscreant flock gathered on the shores of the river, the preacher shouted, "Rally men, rally and we may yet be saved! O rally, for God and your country's sake, rally. . . ." Rally they would not, and an officer coming ashore with the long-delayed blessing of Buell's reinforcements made his first advance on the parson. "Shut up, you Goddamned old fool, or I'll break your head. Get out of the way."

The reinforcements arrived too late to do Grant any good on Sunday, but he didn't worry. Even at midday when the tide of the battle was driving the Union army into the Tennessee River, Grant said things didn't look "so very bad. We've got to fight against time now." Time had gone against him early in the day, but as the sun set he could contradict an aide who mourned how poorly the battle was going. Clamping his cigar tighter in his teeth, Grant said calmly, "They can't break our lines tonight—it is too late. Tomorrow we shall attack with fresh troops and drive them, of course." Rawlins, who had been overwrought since his interrupted breakfast, blurted out a need for reassurance. "Do you think they are pressing us, General?" Grant turned his blue eyes on Rawlins and quietly said they "have been pressing us all day, John, but I think we will stop them right here."

The Confederates were stopped, but so were the Union soldiers. Officers on both sides gave meaningless orders to cease fire as night and rain began to fall. The men were too exhausted to go on. Most lay where they dropped on their muskets, careless that their mate might be a dead man. The artillerists didn't rest. The guns on both sides kept firing with no purpose other than fear. Soldiers lying close to the guns noticed that their noses were bleeding and that blood trickled from their ears. They didn't know why. And they were mystified to discover that the sound of the night softened and soon they couldn't hear anything at all. It was a "weird, wearisome and wrathful" landscape through which a newspaper correspondent walked that night. The rains, he said, "quenched the fires raging in the woods, which had already burned many wounded men to death."

Grant didn't sleep. James McPherson, an Ohio colonel who was not yet as close to the general as he would be in the future, rode into Grant's encampment and was greeted with a cheery "Well, Mac, how is it?" It was decidedly bad, McPherson told Grant. A third of the army was out of action. He asked if Grant was contemplating a retreat. "Retreat? No. I propose to attack at daylight and whip them." But he was physically and emotionally beaten himself by that time. He hobbled wearily into the log house Rawlins had chosen for his headquarters, only to find it had been impressed as a hospital. The pile of sawed-off arms and legs outside was bad enough. The interior was worse. Mangled men who had been boys that morning were stuffed in until there was no room for even one more body, living or dead. Grant turned around and went back outside, curled up under a tree, and tried to get some rest. Sherman came to see him sometime after midnight, and the two lay together in the rain, smoking and silent.

Grant did attack at daybreak the following day. He did whip Beauregard's Army of the Mississippi. With half again as many men as the Rebels, Grant's army pushed their adversaries back to a point where there was nothing left to gain. The Confederates retreated to Corinth. Sherman made a halfhearted try at following them, but there was not enough left in any of the Union soldiers to make a meaningful pursuit. "We chased them one-quarter mile," wrote a Federal soldier, then we "threw ourselves on the ground and rested. Oh, mother, how tired I was, now the excitement of action was over." Another said he'd never seen "so many broken down and exhausted men in all my life. I was sick as a horse, and as wet with blood and sweat as could be, and many of our men were vomiting with excessive fatigue."

Casualties in all prior American wars—the Revolution, the War of 1812, and the Mexican War—came to about 23,000. Close to 20,000 were killed or wounded at Shiloh, and most of the casualties were Grant's.[13]

He wrote Julia on April 8 that the "terrible battle" he had just won "has no equal on this continent," and he was apparently proud of the work. "The best troops of the rebels were engaged to the number of 162 regiments as stated by a deserter from their camp, and their ablest generals. . . . I got through all safe having but one shot which struck my sword but did not touch me. I am detaining a steamer to carry this and must cut short. Give my love to all at home. Kiss the children for me. The same for yourself."

A celebratory mood infused headquarters, and the staff joined in expansive good times. Grant had a good laugh over a letter brought under a flag of truce from Beauregard. The Confederate commander wrote a lengthy explanation of his retreat, including a defensive apology for having withdrawn. Grant thought the missive hilarious—and very much in keeping with the temperament of the South. But he was not so jovial about Beauregard's request to allow a burial party—including kin of the Confederate dead—inside Yankee lines. Grant replied that Federal details had already been sent "for this purpose and it is now accomplished." He apparently was not being candid. Sherman was still anguished over the condition of the field several days after that, and more than one soldier sent letters home describing week-old unburied dead. The diggers worked as fast as they could. Mass graves were the order of the day, with one shallow ditch widened to make room for more than seven hundred Confederate bodies.

Perhaps Grant was simply ignoring the flotsam left behind by the fight. Though he still sickened at meat if a cook served his dinner underdone, the stench of a week-old battlefield was far worse than anything he'd smelled in the tanyard at Georgetown. But it was war, and in war it was necessary to keep going to get ahead. He wrote Julia on April 15 that he was "looking for a speedy move" against the Confederates who were once more established in Corinth. There would be only "one more fight," he said, "and then easy sailing to the close of the war." But associates found him somewhat "wearied and depressed," and Grant hinted to Julia that it was so. "I really will feel glad when this thing is over." His laurels were already being tarnished. "I suppose you have read a greatdeel about the battle in the papers and some quite contradictory? I will come in again for heaps of abuse from persons who were not here."

First reports about Shiloh gloated over a great Union victory, and the North celebrated. "Unconditional Surrender" Grant had done it again. But subsequent stories recounted a hideous slaughter foisted on an unready army. Grant was pilloried. Charges of cowardice and drunkenness filled newspapers. There had to be some explanation for the bloodbath, and Grant was the easiest answer. He responded privately with questionable defenses of his army and himself. On April 26, he wrote Jesse that he intended to pay no attention to the criticism. "There is one thing I feel well assured of; that is, that I have the confidence of every brave man in my command. Those who showed the white feather will do all in their power to attract attention from themselves. I had perhaps a dozen officers arrested for cowardice in the first day's fight at this place. These men are necessarily my enemies."

He was able to rationalize the intensity of the outrage over Shiloh by again summoning up "enemies." His staff kept him from questioning himself, and kept his eyes focused forward. If they said he was blameless for the poor preparations at Shiloh, he would believe them. But the matter was not clear in his own mind. "As to the talk about a surprise here," he wrote Jesse, "nothing could be more false. If the enemy had sent word when and where they would attack us, we could not have been better prepared. Skirmishing had been going on for two days between our reconnoitering parties and the enemy's advance. I did not believe, however, that they intended to make a determined attack, but simply that they were making a reconnaissance in force." Grant was unwilling or unable to admit he could not have it both ways—that he had been perfectly prepared for the enemy while expecting only a reconnaissance. Though his logic was so tangled it took him a year and a half to prepare an official report on Shiloh, he always believed he had won a great and necessary victory there.[14]

Grant's letter to Jesse was published in a Cincinnati newspaper, but understandably did little to quiet the controversy. Many of the stories were written by journalists attached to the headquarters of various Grant subordinates. Some were critical in the extreme; most were inaccurate. Grant was accused of being drunk on the field, of not being on the field at all, and of running away. These tales were written as a matter of fact, and were given currency in the Army of the Tennessee. They were also being read in Washington. On April 23, Secretary of War Stanton sent a telegram to Henry Halleck. "The President desires to know [w]hy you have made no official report to this department respecting the late battles at Pittsburg landing. An[d] whether any neglect or misconduct of General Grant or any other officer contributed to the sad casu[a]lties that befell our forces on Sunday." Halleck told Stanton he was reserving judgment on Grant—he was not about to take a position which might prove untenable—but did say that a "Great Battle cannot [b]e fought or a victory gained without many casualties."

Halleck's ambiguous support did not mean he had found no immediate cause for concern with the commander of the Army of the Tennessee. The aftermath of Shiloh was not only a sickening physical debacle but also a replay of the Fort Donelson fiasco. Roving bands of authorized marauders—legitimized by the Federal government's dictate that "commerce follow the flag"—descended on Pittsburg Landing to see what could be bought or sold. This far south, cotton might be purchased from Confederate agents, and was. Liquor could be sold, with the result that the camp became a carnival of gun-shooting rowdies. Pickets joined the parties, and guards fell asleep. Sutlers, whores, families of the wounded, clergy for the dead, itinerant peddlers, embalmers, coffin salesmen offering zinc-lined specials, and politicians crowded onto the field. Slaves wandered into camp looking for freedom and found unpaid work digging ditches if they could prove they had belonged to Confederates. Blacks owned by known Union sympathizers were returned at once to their owners. The rain which had started falling the night of April 6 continued and turned the earth into a morass of mud and human waste. Hospitals swelled with sufferers of diarrhea—the "Tennessee quickstep," it was called—and with ominously increasing numbers of typhoid victims. Henry Halleck sent a telegram to Grant saying the army was in no condition to defend itself, and set off for Tennessee to assume personal command of the forces in the field.

Grant never thought about his army defending itself. The purpose of his troops was to give battle, not get it. He wanted to head south, and found instead that he'd been effectively kicked upstairs with a meaningless title of second-in-command of the armies in the West. He wrote Julia the news April 25 that he was "no longer boss. Gen. Halleck is here and I am truly glad of it. I hope the papers will let me alone in the future." He was deeply hurt, and was sincerely happy to have Halleck on the field. In the presence of higher authority, Grant could relinquish responsibility and make himself comfortable within the fraternity of his staff. On orders, he turned command over to George Thomas, a big, quiet Virginian who had ridden the Texas court-martial circuit with Robert Lee. Lodged in a headquarters compound pitched far away from the main body of the army, Grant spent his evenings with his friends around the campfire, smoking and talking about the Mexican War. When he did mention Shiloh, he began to invent a different battle. He wrote a friend that with fewer than 35,000 men he had withstood an attack of 80,000 Confederates. Doubling his adversity while halving his resources was a fair reflection of his emotional state. He said he would like to go "to New Mexico, or some other remote place, and have a small command out of the reach of the newspapers," and nostalgically described Galena as a safe haven at war's end. "I am saving money from my pay now," he told a visiting newsman, "and shall be able to educate my children." If nothing else, he would not come out of the war as badly worn as he had in California. But within days, he began to talk about going home immediately. "I feel that the time cannot be long before I see you," he wrote Julia.[15]

Apparently the time Grant was spending on the sidelines had

become insupportable in all ways. It is "generally understood through this army," he wrote Halleck, "that my position differs but little from that of one in arrest." Then he asked to be "relieved entirely from further duty. I cannot, do not, believe that there is any disposition on the part of yourself to do me any injustice, but my suspicions have been aroused that you may be acting under instructions, from higher authority, that I know nothing of."

Heavy correspondence was going on between Grant's aides and Elihu Washburne, and Halleck knew it. The Galena gang's position was not yet inviolable, but it was strong. Grant took advantage of it by hinting to Halleck that he would keep his request private for the time being. The hand of Rawlins was apparent in the new difficulty with Halleck, and Rawlins was prompting Grant to make a trip to Washington in his own defense. Grant told Julia he might go. He also told her he could be transferred to the East Coast, a move William Rowley was promoting in a series of letters to Washburne.

Insiders said the army was suspicious of Grant. The men watched the little general pass without greeting him. Grant had gone from attracting no attention at all as a civilian to attracting the worst kind of hypercritical scrutiny. Everyone seemed to have an opinion about him. Sherman, who had opinions about everything, couldn't keep quiet. Luckily, he came in on Grant's side. "We all knew," Sherman wrote his father-in-law/stepfather, "we were assembling a vast army for an aggressive purpose. The President knew it. Halleck knew it, and the whole country knew it, and the attempt to throw blame on Grant is villanous." Grant, Sherman said, was as "brave as any man should be" and was entitled to praise. But the press was pulling him down, "and many thousands of families will be taught to look to him as the cause of the death of their fathers, husbands and brothers. The very object of war is to produce results by death and slaughter, but the moment a battle occurs the newspapers make the leader responsible for the death and misery, whether victory or defeat." Grant, he said, "is not a brilliant man and has, himself, thoughtlessly used the press to give him *éclat* in Illinois, but he is a good and brave soldier, tried for years; is sober, very industrious and as kind as a child." When Sherman learned from Halleck that Grant was planning to go home, he rode over to Grant's camp and found the general tying bundles of letters together with red tape. He asked Grant why he was going.

"Sherman," Grant replied, "you know. You know that I am in the way here. I have stood it as long as I can, and can endure it no longer."

Where would he go?

"St. Louis."

Did he have any business in St. Louis?

"Not a bit."

Sherman begged him to stay, saying if Grant went away the war would go right along, and Grant would be left out. If he remained with the army, some "happy accident" might restore him to "favor and his true place."

Sherman's pep talk apparently worked, but to stay at his post Grant needed Julia. "You must join me as soon as possible," he wrote. Julia was delighted to get the invitation and intelligent enough to respond immediately. She had been sequestered in miserable silence in Covington with Grant's parents, and had been "shocked and almost stunned" by what she called the "ribald abuse" of Grant in the newspapers. "I felt too deeply wounded to weep," she wrote. "I felt hard and revengeful." She also felt bold enough to write a letter of thanks to Elihu Washburne, who had delivered to his House colleagues an impassioned defense of Grant.

By the time Julia and the children arrived in Memphis, Grant had been restored to his command and his power had been enhanced. It had taken Halleck more than a month to move the twenty miles from Shiloh to Corinth, Mississippi. When the army finally got to its destination, the Confederates had moved farther south, leaving behind welcome signs painted on buildings. Lincoln and Stanton were chagrined at the ponderous progress Halleck made when no victory—not even a battle—resulted. Grant's three stars were looking good to official Washington.

Julia traveled eastward from Memphis to Corinth as if she were making a state visit. The children were ecstatic. Young Fred was a veteran camp follower by the summer of 1862, but Buck, Nellie, and Jesse were having their first look at the war zone. Julia had outfitted herself with a new wardrobe chosen to reflect the image of a major general's wife. Luckily, a Dent cousin who had shopped with her in Cincinnati had suggested that Julia remove the jaunty red-and-white cockade which trimmed her new butter-nut-brown velvet bonnet. Julia had unwittingly bought a feminine version of Confederate headgear. "I thought you knew our colors," demurred the cousin whom Julia described as an "outrageous little rebel." But Julia experienced no qualms about other southern trappings. She was accompanied to Corinth by the slaves she had to do without in Galena and Cairo. Mississippi was not a free state like Illinois, so the wife of the Union Army general was quite within her legal rights carrying her slaves with her. If the presence of Black Julia and the others caused pain to any of Grant's abolitionist Republican subordinates, they were gentlemanly enough—and politic enough—not to mention it to Washburne.

When Julia's train pulled into Corinth, Grant was waiting with an ambulance wagon to drive the family to the sumptuous house he had occupied. "The General and two or three of his staff officers accompanied us on horseback to headquarters," Julia wrote. "The General was so glad to see us and rode close beside the ambulance, stooping near and asking me if I was as glad to see him as he was to see me." Grant reached inside the wagon and took Julia's hand. They rode together—she perched demurely on the seat, he firmly astride his big bay horse—holding hands, smiling, and whispering to one another.

The family settled into the affectionate, homely routine which so endeared Grant to his staff. Julia was a great favorite of the officers, who found her sprightly and lovable. The cause she was so reluctant to claim had proved as beneficial to her as it had to Grant. And they celebrated their good fortune by turning the torpor of Mississippi midsummer into a romance of moonlight and magnolias. In the early evening the children would dash barefoot into the garden and pad along the carefully raked dirt walks to cool themselves before bed. As dusk shadowed the mansion's portico into drowsy reverie and whippoorwills called in the deepening blue, Julia and Grant sat together and held hands. They seldom spoke. They didn't need to. They were together and the future looked good.

When Julia left Corinth at the end of August, Grant was making plans for a direct assault southward aimed at Vicksburg and the tidying up of the last vestiges of the Confederacy west of the Alleghenies. His position in the Army had never been more secure. A disastrous series of battles in the East had focused national hopes on the West, and brought Grant the government's approbation for being the sole successful Union general. "I can't spare this man," President Lincoln told Grant detractors, "he fights."[16]

CHAPTER

16

LEE ARRIVED in Richmond two weeks after Jefferson Davis was inaugurated on February 22, 1862, under the equestrian statue of George Washington in Richmond's Capitol Square. Abraham Lincoln's symbolic claim on the anniversary of Washington's birthday—he had declared it a national holiday and issued General War Order No. 1—was a good deal stronger than Davis's that year. The war situation for the Confederacy was bleak.

Grant had taken away Kentucky by his victory at Fort Donelson, the state of Tennessee was sure to go, western Virginia was already gone, the Union Army was sopping up all the southern Atlantic coastal islands, and the Union Navy was threatening Mobile and New Orleans. There were just over 210,000 Confederate soldiers to stand against more than 525,000 Federals. The dark military scene only mirrored the political and economic picture.

With the Unionization of southern sea islands, the blockade of Confederate ports Lincoln ordered after Sumter became increasingly effective, and enhanced the already superior war-making power of the North. At the outset, the North had almost 90 percent of the nation's industrial capacity—11 times as many ships as the South, 15 times as much iron, 32 times as many firearms, 17 times the amount of textiles, 24 times as many locomotives, and twice the production of foodstuffs. Though an occasional Federal campaign might lack provisions, the Union Army was superbly mounted. One frugal Union officer somewhat embarrassedly admitted that a "French army of half the size of ours could be supplied with what we waste." Yet that army was not doing well.[1]

"Young Napoleon" George McClellan possessed all the ambition of his namesake, but had none of his impetuous, aggressive drive. His Army of the Potomac was a dazzling drill-ground performer, but McClellan apparently had no desire to soil their uniforms in the mud of Virginia. Mercurial of mood and torpid of military spirit, he was a great favorite with his troops, and a painful thorn to Abraham Lincoln. McClellan put Allan Pinkerton on the Army payroll and the private investigator turned loose dozens of mysteriosos who roamed the South gathering false information. By the spring of 1862 McClellan believed there were more than 100,000 well-armed Confederates arrayed against him in Virginia and refused to attack until he had sufficient men to overcome the numerical superiority.

Jefferson Davis would have been delighted to share McClellan's head count. Davis knew he had fewer than 60,000 soldiers in the entire state of Virginia. And he had been no luckier than Lincoln in getting his sparse force on the field. P. G. T. Beauregard had stemmed the Federal advance into Virginia during the summer of 1861, but he sought personal glory and thus had been banished to the West. Joe Johnston, a bitter enemy of Davis, moved his army to the Peninsula, east of Richmond, and proved no more willing to stick than he had in the mountains. Few Army men could work easily with Davis, who thought himself the most astute military mind in the country, and he was equally unpopular with the politicians. By the time he took office, two Secretaries of State had resigned, the first Secretary of War had stalked out of office in a rage and the second had been hounded out by public clamor.

Part of Davis's difficulty with his Cabinet and with the Congress arose from the reluctance of the best southern men to enter Confederate politics—it was considered far better to serve in the

Army. But other difficulties arose from the caliber of men Davis appointed to serve him. The President's best quality—unswerving loyalty—was also his worst. He tended to pick advisers and cabinet members on the basis of ancient ties or outmoded analyses. The results were often dire. Commissary General Lucius Northrop—corrupt, inept, or both—set up a system of supply which left half the Army starving half the time while dumps of stores rotted on waysides. Grant's soldiers had been sickened by the stench of improperly salted pork turning to gelatin outside Fort Donelson, while Buckner's defenders inside the fort had empty stomachs. But supplying various fronts was a problem that would have stymied a better man than Northrop. Southern railroads—where they existed—had no common gauge. Rail lines ended abruptly at one spot, and began at another, and goods had to be portaged over the interval. The lack of known iron deposits put an end to repairs other than those made by cannibalizing existing routes.

But money was the big problem in the Confederacy. Many Southerners rested on the comfortable assumption that they held the world's economy in a cotton bale. Refuse to ship cotton, they said, and England would beg for relief by recognizing the Confederate nation or join the war on the southern side. Committees of public safety imposed an embargo on cotton, and most of the 1861 crop was either hidden or destroyed. Lee had watched South Carolina cotton being burned in order to keep it out of Federal hands. Less than half the normal amount of seed was sown in 1862—the rest of the farmland was turned to food production. But the primacy of cotton was not secure. English textile mills were glutted in 1861 with unused fibers from a bumper 1860 crop, and by 1862 England had planted cotton in India. The Confederacy had to create money to make up for the collapse of cotton revenues. Levying national taxes was anathema to states' rights' ideology, so Congress floated bonds instead. More than $15 million was raised during the patriotic fervor of the country's early days, but the amount scarcely met military needs. Various loans proved no more reliable at supplying a steady income. As a last effort, the

Congress accelerated the printing press. More than $500 million in treasury notes had been turned out by 1862, and the resulting inflation emptied cupboards across the South.[2]

"I hope you girls are learning to be useful & have entered into domestic manufactures," Lee wrote his daughter. "Take separate departments & prepare fabric, or it will end in destitution." The tease was not a joke. Destitution was becoming a reality in the Confederacy, and nowhere was it worse than in Richmond. Prices had doubled, and refugees had absorbed all available housing. Luxuries like coffee and corsets had disappeared from retail stores, and fashionable women had to trim up fading silks to keep up appearances. Anxiety over domestic privations worsened the mounting fear in Richmond that the city would fall to the Federals.[3]

Davis knew that McClellan would start a spring 1862 drive to Richmond. The thrust would come by water. Virginia was roughly triangular in shape, its flat southern edge resting on the North Carolina state line. The new western boundary, created when West Virginia declared a separate peace with the Federal government, followed the Blue Ridge escarpment northward, easing east as it went. From there, Virginia's border followed the Potomac River to the Atlantic. The interior of the state was laced with rivers that ran southeast to the sea. Directly below the Potomac, the Rapidan flowed into the Rappahannock at Fredericksburg, fifty miles south of Washington. Some twenty-five miles south of the Rappahannock, the Mattaponi and the Pamunkey formed the York. Another twenty-five miles south, the Appomattox and the Chickahominy flowed into the James around Richmond. The James and York outlined the Peninsula, anchored on the west by Richmond and spreading seaward across thickly wooded and rolling land. Navigable inland almost fifty miles, Virginia's tidal rivers were almost indefensible. But bluff-top forts could reduce flotillas and the land itself was good defense should an enemy leave the rivers for overland westward marches. George McClellan was thinking of just such a march. The defenses at the mouth of the James which Lee had helped build in the 1830s proved inadequate to Union assaults, and Fortress Monroe was firmly within Federal grasp. By mid-March, McClellan began to land at Fortress Monroe 120,000 troops for an assault against Richmond, fifty miles to the west.

In what would become a habit of turning military liabilities into assets, Lee took advantage of McClellan's gathering forces and wrote to the commander of the Shenandoah Valley district. Since the Federals' attention was focused eastward, could Thomas Jackson combine with Dick Ewell and strike a blow against the small force McClellan had left behind? "The troops used," said Lee, "must be efficient and light." He assured Jackson this was not a command—"I cannot pretend at this distance to direct operations"—and said he was only making "suggestions" for Jackson's "consideration."[4]

He could not have asked a better man. Since his West Point days Jackson had created a reputation for single-mindedness unsurpassed in all the Army. His display at the academy's blackboard—sweating, shaking, and tenacious—was a kind of calling card for his early career, which saw him breveted for rigid obedience at the Chapultepec gates in Mexico. Born in Clarksburg in 1828, near Mary Lee's Annefield birthplace, Jackson had grown up in the poverty of upland Puritan Virginia. His father died when he was small, and when his mother died a few years later, he was left to care for his ailing stepfather, a man who apparently hated the boy. When he was big enough to hold a hoe, Jackson was farmed out to relatives who used him as a field hand on their small, unrewarding places, and he learned early to produce or die. He never forgot the lesson.

After Mexico, he applied for a job at Lexington's Virginia Military Institute and with Lee's recommendation got it. He successfully courted the daughter of Washington College's president in Lexington, and after he married her, moved into the red brick president's house on campus. It was there he began his earnest efforts to unravel the mystery of God. Like most Lexingtonians, Jackson was a Presbyterian, but more than most he obsessively held to the Blue Light covenanter faith. That was the look of his eyes, clear blue under a high and smoothly rounded forehead. Those steady eyes dominated an oval face, not unhandsome,

with a long narrow nose. The full brown beard hid a slack mouth
that was tightened into a grim slit by the time he was an adult.
Jackson was middling tall, but he stooped, and that narrowed his
shoulders and focused attention at his feet, which were huge and
badly shod. He cared little for clothes but was fascinated by his
body, which he believed had somehow turned against him. With
great seriousness he told his students at VMI that his entire left
side was withering because it failed to get proper nourishment. To
counteract this difficulty, he avoided pepper, which he said worsened the condition, and constantly sucked lemons, which he said
helped.

When war came, he took his cadets to Richmond to aid Lee
in training volunteers, then went to Manassas, where he earned
the name "Stonewall" for truculence or bravery. After that, he
faded into glorified guard duty in the Alleghenies and displayed
his irritation by offering to resign.

Jackson seized Lee's suggestion and went to work in the Shenandoah Valley with the same zeal he brought to the practice of
religion. His men seldom carried more than their muskets, and
moved so fast they came to be known as Jackson's "foot cavalry."
He asked the impossible and usually got it. Richard Ewell joined
him in May 1862, and learned to admire Jackson's genius, but said
he was "certain of his lunacy," and never saw one of Stonewall's
couriers approach "without expecting an order to assault the north
pole." When Zachary Taylor's son Dick rode into the Valley
with his Creole band playing a waltz, Jackson took a pull on a
lemon, nodded toward the musicians, and said, "Thoughtless
fellows for serious work." Jackson's work was killing the enemy,
and he was deadly serious. When one of his officers explained that
the men had so admired an opponent's bravery they spared his life,
Jackson said he especially wanted the brave ones dead. Praying
and fighting seemed his idea of the whole man, said one of his
subordinates, and Taylor believed Jackson was absorbed by "an
ambition boundless as Cromwell's and as merciless." He "loathed
it," Taylor said, "perhaps feared it; but he could not escape it—it
was himself—nor rend it—it was his own flesh. He fought it with

prayer, constant and earnest—Apollyon and Christian in ceaseless combat."[5]

Lee knew he had a fighter in Jackson. He was less certain about his old friend Joe Johnston on the Peninsula. "Prince" John Magruder was still holding down the York River with little more than the flair for theatrics which had him directing Grant in *Othello* fifteen years earlier in Mexico. Magruder circled his handful of men on stage and off twice or three times daily for demonstrations which convinced Federals they faced a mighty foe. He protected empty "forts" with "Quaker guns"—skinned trees painted black and placed like artillery cannon. But the drama, which had been running almost a year, was wearing him and his men out. By mid-April, McClellan had landed his army and started toward Richmond. The going was slow but steady, and that was what bothered Lee. The weather was about the only effective defense Virginia had. Spring rains filled the already oozy bottomlands east of Richmond with water, creeks became freshets, and the Chickahominy and Pamunkey rivers were fast-flowing lakes. A disconcerted Federal soldier swore that the sludge was so bad he had seen a mule, ears and all, sink out of sight. And a Union private said the mud—which "took the military valor all out of a man"—equaled reinforcements of 20,000.

Something seemed to take the military valor out of Johnston. He fell back so close to Richmond that townsfolk looking eastward from Church Hill could see Federal observation balloons bobbing up and down a few miles away. The sight was frightening, yet excited envy. Richmond's ladies offered their ball gowns for the sake of a patchwork silk balloon which was tethered to a locomotive and pulled eastward for duty, filled with laughing officers. But train stations were packed with seriously frightened families, and carriages heading for safety crowded the roads westward. Davis sent his wife, Varina, and their children to North Carolina, and the Confederate Cabinet left town. The atmosphere turned to panic when word arrived that McClellan was sending gunboats up the James. The sole governing body left in the capital was the city council, and the mayor said he would burn

Richmond to the ground rather than let it fall into vandal hands.[6]

Mary had continued to live with Charlotte at the White House until early May, when Magruder's show at Yorktown closed and the Union Army was on its way. She saw to getting Chass, who was pregnant again, off to the Wickhams' Hanover County home, Hickory Hill, and wrote a note to the enemy: "Northern soldiers who profess to reverance Washington, forbear to desecrate the home of his first married life, the property of his wife, now owned by her descendents." She signed it "A Granddaughter of Mrs. Washington," nailed it to the door, and left. Several days later, the house in which she was staying was searched by Union soldiers. While the men were about their business, Mary communicated to the "General in Command." "Sir," she wrote, "I have patiently & humbly submitted to the search of my house by men under your command, who are satisfied that there is nothing here which they would want; all the plate & other valuables have long since been removed to Richmond & are now beyond the reach of Northern marauders who may wish for their possession." This letter she signed "Wife of Robert Lee, General C.S.A." The commanding general was Fitz-John Porter, who sent a pair of messengers to Mary offering a guard around the residence. She refused so haughtily that the surprised young officers said it was not safe for her to remain unprotected. Mary then left for Malbourne, the plantation of Edmund Ruffin. After firing the first shot at Sumter, Ruffin stood his post as a full-fledged member of Charleston's Palmetto Guard, then manned a cannon at Manassas, where he pridefully claimed to have bagged at least three Yankees. He had left his slaves in charge of Malbourne, and they looked after Mary Lee for the few days she was there.

"It is true your Mother, Annie & Mildred are in the hands of the enemy," Lee wrote Agnes at the end of May. "The house was surrounded by a body of the enemy's Cav & the farm I understand taken possession of." The situation was awkward. Word was sent to George McClellan that he had a special prisoner within his lines who needed safe-conduct. Then Lee sent Roy Mason to collect some "property in the hands of the enemy" which McClellan had agreed to deliver.

McClellan had been a West Point roommate of Mason's brother-in-law, and he invited the Confederate to dine. In time, a carriage approached. "The curtains were cut off," Mason remembered, "and it was drawn by a mule and a dilapitated old horse, driven by a negro of about ten or twelve years, and followed by a cavalry escort." McClellan jumped up and warmly greeted the wife of his former Mexican War superior. He introduced Mason to Mary Lee and offered to ride with the party as far as the river. Mary declined. When Mason drove her into the Confederate camp, "cheer after cheer went down the long line of soldiers."[7]

Lee was on the field when he got his wife back from the Federals—and in command. Joe Johnston had been wounded on May 30, and somewhat reluctantly, Davis gave Lee Virginia's army on June 1. Lee named his troops the Army of Northern Virginia and immediately got to work defending Richmond. "McClellan will make this a battle of posts," he wrote Davis. "He will take position from position, under cover of his heavy guns, & we cannot get at him without storming his works, which with our new troops is extremely hazardous." Getting at the enemy was a novelty in Virginia, and there were other changes too. Lee complained that our "people are opposed to work. Our troops, officers, community & press. All ridicule & resist it. It is the very means by which McClellan has & is advancing." He ordered the troops to entrench and start building a massive system of earthworks around Richmond, and earned for his efforts a new title in the press—"King of Spades." Though Lee had told his daughter-in-law he wished command had "fallen upon an abler man," and was well aware that his field experience was limited to acting under orders in the Mexican War, he was accustomed to wielding considerable military power. And he meant to be obeyed.[8] Aboard his new gray horse, he rode the lines daily, sometimes alone and sometimes with staff, often out of uniform and always quietly. "We thought at first he was a jolly easy going miller or distiller on a visit as a civilian to the front," an officer remembered. Though they grumbled about the digging, the soldiers began to feel more secure as the solid wall of works rose in a semicircle around the capital.[9]

More secure did not mean safe or comfortable. It rained nearly every day and the hot summer sun turned standing water inside the trenches to steam. Frogs, rats, lice, and no quiet were hard on nerves. The finished lines were often as close as a mile from Union works and terrified soldiers on round-the-clock duty sometimes unraveled, "sobbing in their broken sleep, like a child crying just before it sinks to rest." Sharpshooters—lone gunmen who ranged the woods looking for lone targets—made rest impossible, and units stampeded in the middle of the night for no reason other than contagious fear. But when tensions were unbearable, often as not the men declared truces. As soon as night fell and their commanders were safely gone, opposing armies would holler out to stop firing, then creep out of the trenches for trading and talk. Northern men usually had newspapers and hardtack. Southerners had tobacco. Sometimes they argued politics, and at least once passions became heated and a fistfight ensued. Not satisfied with battering one another, the antagonists took to their trenches and started to fire—ineffectually—until angry officers put an end to the private war.

Soon it was time to war in earnest. On the night of June 24, Lee told his aides he wanted to be alone. No one knew if he slept. The following day he issued his orders, and on June 25 there began the series of battles that came to be known as the Seven Days.

Six separate fights, starting northeast of Richmond and occurring in a south-moving crescent, took place between June 25 and July 1. The critical day was June 30. McClellan was inching backward to safety on the James River. It was possible, thought Lee, if the corps acted quickly and in concert, to head off the Federals and capture the entire army. But nothing went right. To the bafflement of historians ever since, Jackson simply sat out most of the Seven Days. He arrived late, was slow, and spent part of June 30 sitting on a log. Lee's other division commanders were almost as ineffectual. Regiments got lost, orders went undelivered or arrived late, divisions clogged into massive traffic jams as petulant generals argued over who got to go first.

The strain on Lee was obvious. He just managed to be civil to Jefferson Davis, whose ubiquitous presence he found irritating, and he complained of being unable to obtain any kind of information. He rode back and forth behind his lines trying to find subordinates or get to ground high enough see how things were going. At dusk, he knew the day had gone against him. That evening, Jackson's brother-in-law, D. H. Hill, voiced foreboding about the day ahead. The Federals occupied a small plateau once owned by Lee's mother and now growing in wheat and topped by a heavily timbered and cut-up piece of land. "If General McClellan is there in strength, we better let him alone," Hill cautioned. Hill was a thorough Calvinist, like his brother-in-law, and like Jackson, he was described as a "born fighter—as aggressive, pugnacious and tenacious as a bulldog." If Hill was worried, there was something to worry about. But Pete Longstreet laughed. "Don't get scared now that we have got him whipped," he poked at Hill. And when Jubal Early, a Unionist mountain man who went with Virginia into the Confederacy, made a remark about the enemy getting away, Lee lost his composure. "Yes," Lee shot back, "he will get away because I cannot have my orders carried out!" Early slunk off to bed, and Lee tried to calm himself for the next day's work.[10]

The morning sun filtered through splendid old trees on Malvern Hill and picked out more than a hundred Federal cannon parked hub to hub. The sight seemed not to deter Lee. He ordered an artillery barrage to be followed by a general assault. But as on the day before, his orders got confused and brigades were bottlenecked in the woods. When Confederate guns finally began to fire, there were fewer than twenty of them—the rest were mired in Peninsula mud or tangled in tight-knit undergrowth. It was midafternoon before the infantry got in place. The attack command came above the noise of Yankee guns, and 10,000 boys clambered to their feet, and started to walk up the hill. Wave after wave swept upward, and ebbed, blocked by a solid wall of shot.

It was over by dark. The wind came up at midnight and the rain began to fall.

"Such rain, and such howling set up by the wounded," a young Rebel remembered, "such ugly wounds, sickening to the sight even of the most hardened as the rain beat upon them, washing them to a pale purple; such long-fingered corpses, and in piles too, like cordwood." Lee sat silently at headquarters. Pete Longstreet offered commiseration. "I think you hurt them as much as they hurt you." Lee was not consoled. During the night when he rode about his camps trying to discover what had gone wrong, he came upon John Magruder sitting by his campfire. Lee stopped his horse and asked Magruder why he had gone ahead with the assault. "In response to your orders, twice repeated," Magruder snapped. Lee rode on without answering. He had ordered Magruder to attack—twice—but that was earlier in the day when the plan called for a hundred cannon to clear the way for an assault. Magruder's orders had been delayed into absurdity, but he had obeyed, and Lee insisted on obedience.[11]

That night McClellan began a retreat to the James, a move which earned from a subordinate the opinion that "such an order can only be prompted by cowardice or treason." The Confederates were dispirited too. Moxley Sorrell, a Georgian who served as aide to Longstreet, carried a message to Dick Ewell the following morning and found him doubled up in grief on the floor of a little shanty with his head under a cover. Jackson had taken one look at the base of Malvern Hill and put his soldiers to work neatly stacking their dead in piles. D. H. Hill, whom Lee appointed caretaker to the dead and wounded, had the final say on Malvern Hill. The battle, he wrote, "was not war, it was murder."[12]

After July 1, field hospitals with waving flags—red for the Federals, orange for the Confederates—filled up on the Peninsula. Men from both sides spent days burying the dead. "The sights and smells that assailed us were simply indescribable—corpses swollen to twice their original size, some of them actually burst asunder with the pressure of foul gases and vapors. The odors were so nauseating . . . that in a short time we all sickened and were lying with our mouths close to the ground, most of us vomiting profusely."

More than 36,000 Americans ended the Seven Days as casualties. Like Shiloh, the Peninsula battles east of Richmond were proving grounds for what had been and what was to come and men learned to harden themselves to war. "We don't mind the sight of dead men no more than if they was Hogs," a Yankee defensively wrote home. A southern counterpart noted that he could not describe the change in himself, or say when it took place, "yet I know that there is a change for I look on the carcass of a man now with pretty much the same feeling as I would were it a horse or hog." There was much bitterness on both sides— bitterness like that growing in the West—and it became something like hate. "Teach my children to hate them," a Confederate wrote about the Yankees, while Federal troops passed stories of Rebel atrocities. A New York regiment, enraged at what they thought had been done to one of theirs captured by the Rebs, seized a Confederate picket in retaliation. They "put a rope around his neck," a horrified Union observer noted, "and hoisted him on a tree, made a target of his suspended body, then cut him down, bayoneted him in a dozen places, then dragged him to the road where they watched till long trains of wagons made a jelly of his remains." A Louisianan answered a call for help by stepping to the side of a wounded Federal and bashing out his brains. But veterans got together between their picket lines and had a July 4 celebration. "Our boys and the Yanks made a bargain not to fire at each other, and went out in the field leaving one man on each post with the arms, and gathered berries together and talked over the fight, traded tobacco and coffee and exchanged newspapers as peacefully and kindly as if they had not been engaged for the last seven days in butchering each other."[13]

Lee returned to his farmhouse headquarters on the Nine Mile Road, and wrote Mary that his military "success has not been as great or complete as I could have desired, but God knows what is best for us." Neither after the Seven Days nor later when he had juster cause did Lee criticize the officers under him. He had assumed responsibility when he assumed command, and he ab-

sorbed his losses with equanimity. Subordinates found him magnificent in his disappointment, and learned to love him for it. Men
in the ranks, rather than blaming Lee for their losses, passed
stories about his kindness and cheered him wildly whenever he
rode by. He was hailed in the press as Richmond's savior.

Salvation was costly. Lee had lost 20,000 irreplaceable men.
The city of Richmond became a hospital. Hollywood Cemetery,
west of the Capitol, opened its gates daily to dozens of funeral
processions. Two of Lee's daughters helped care for the sick and
wounded. Mary Lee was there too, and on July 5 she wrote Eliza
Mackay Stiles what life was like at the front:

> I was much gratified to hear from you that you were all well, &
> enjoying your grandchildren at your own sweet home, ours at the
> White House is in ashes—unfortunately we left all the furniture
> there, not supposing such an act of vandalism could be committed
> on a place sacred as having been the early home of Washington
> in wedded life with my Grandmother—The theavish villains,
> although they had military stores there to the value of millions,
> employed their time & transports in robbing the house of every
> article it contained, even to some old dresses, & then forced off all
> our negroes, in spite of their tears and supplications, and not only
> those but a thousand they had enticed there from all neighboring
> plantations they had not even the pretext of freeing ours as by my
> father's will they would have been free this winter, all done, no
> doubt for individual emolument—& ere this I believe many of the
> poor wretches are safely lodged in Cuba. They also burned a large
> barn containing 8000 bushels of wheat, & have destroyed all the
> fences & every crop on the place—I trust I may live to see the day
> of retribution. As soon as I can get all the particulars I shall have
> them published to the world.

Mary was obviously overwrought. Everything she possessed
was disappearing. The Carters' Shirley was not immune, and
Rooney's son had died of pneumonia in the North Carolina mountains. Mary's only hope—her sole revenge—was her husband.
That Lee "has been made the honored instrument of baffling our

vainglorious foe, is a pride & joy to me," she wrote. "I pray that God may strengthen him for the contest."[14]

Something was strengthening Lee. Richmonders watched him as he rode up Broad Street to the Confederate Executive Mansion on Cary, his body held stiffly in the saddle. They watched him at church as he strode down the aisle, slightly inclining his head to greetings from new admirers. They asked if anyone really knew him. "I doubt it," said that most insightful of South Carolinians, Mary Chesnut. "He looks so cold and quiet and grand." His staff, who knew him as well as anyone else, said he complained about spending his time in "fruitless talk" in Richmond but never criticized President Davis. "Of all the men in the Confederate Army," said an aide, "none had a greater deference for authority" than Lee. And they knew the cold grandeur and self-conscious deference were hard-won. "No man could see the flush come over that grand forehead and the temple veins swell on occasions of great trial of patience and doubt that Lee had the high strong temper of a Washington, and habitually under the same control," said an aide. Except for chuckling at his own teasing, Lee seldom laughed anymore. He wrote Mary as soon as he heard that his grandson, the namesake he had hoped would resuscitate family fame, was dead. "I cannot help grieving at his loss & know what a void it will occasion in the hearts of his parents. But when I reflect upon his great gain by his merciful transition from earth to Heaven, I think we ought to rejoice." Some Lee watchers were struck that summer by something other than his reserve. One noted that his eyes were "the saddest it seemed to me of all men's."[15]

Lee was looking northward. In July, he pulled his army close to Richmond, where, he told Jefferson Davis, "it can be better refreshed and strengthened, and be prepared for a renewal of the contest, which must take place at some quarter soon." He had already proposed some kind of campaign into Maryland and Pennsylvania. After the Seven Days, he took up the idea again, and discussed it at length with members of his staff. He knew there was little chance of actually capturing Washington, but it was possible to threaten it, and that might be enough to throw Abraham Lincoln off balance. Lee wanted to "frustrate the enemy's design," his secretary said, "to break up campaigns undertaken with vast expense and with confident assurance of success, to impress upon the minds of the Northern people the conviction that they must prepare for a protracted struggle, great sacrifice of life and treasure, with the possibility that all might at last be of no avail." By using his army politically—or symbolically—Lee could give the Confederacy a power far beyond its martial capacity. If he could demonstrate that the Lincoln administration could not defend its capital, then the "disappointment of the promises so often repeated, of a speedy 'suppression of the rebellion' would have been overwhelming, and the party headed by Mr. Lincoln would have been driven from office by an indignant and deceived people." Lee knew that Lincoln had refused to thin the ranks of the capital's defenders to reinforce McClellan and that he had been alarmed by Jackson's success in the Shenandoah Valley. He believed that Lincoln would draw the Union Army northward to protect Washington, and that would relieve the pressure on Richmond. Moreover, there was a slim chance that if he won, he might just force the war to the bargaining tables.[16]

In July, Lee sent Jackson to the Fredericksburg area and a month later joined him. Union General John Pope, a much-despised martinet who aroused the enmity not only of Virginians but of his own army, was already on the scene and irritating Lee, whose nephew served on Pope's staff. Louis Marshall—Ann's son—had "asked very kindly after his old uncle," Lee wrote. "I am sorry he is in such bad company. But I suppose he could not help it." Less generously, Lee also said he could forgive his nephew's "fighting against us, but not his joining Pope," and bitingly attributed it to his brother-in-law's "B[lack] republican principles." He termed Pope's army "barbarians" who were "capable of any enormity that meanness, pusilanimity & malice could invent."[17]

Lee's men were keen to defeat Pope, but they were mystified about how they would be used to do it. They watched their commander, camped close to Jackson, for signs, and wrote home about him. Charles Minor Blackford, of Jackson's staff, said he felt himself "in the presence of a great man" when he met Lee, "for surely there never was a man upon whom greatness is more stamped. He is the handsomest person I ever saw; every motion is instinct with natural grace, and yet there is a dignity which, while awe-inspiring, makes one feel a sense of confidence and trust that is delightful when it is remembered that there are at present so many contingencies dependent upon his single will." Like many officers in the Army of Northern Virginia, Blackford was slightly undone by the anxiety of facing the much larger Federal army. And like most of Lee's soldiers, he was suffering from exhaustion and dysentery. But Lee's good manners were enough to lighten a courier's head. Blackford said Lee always made him "feel of some consequence."

"This is not the case with General Jackson," Blackford wrote.

He is ever monosyllabic and receives and delivers a message as if the bearer was a conduit pipe from one ear to another. There is a magnetism in Jackson, but it is not personal. All admire his genius and great deeds; no one could love the man for himself. He seems to be cut off from his fellow men and to communicate with his own spirit only, or with spirits of which we know not. . . . The men, in addition to the confidence they have in the genius of Jackson, have for Lee a proud admiration and personal devotion "passing the love of woman." He is called "Marse Robert" and "Uncle Bob" and whenever seen the men shout and rally around him as their darling chief for whom they would willingly die. He receives the adulation of the men with the most graceful courtesy and acknowledges their shouts with uncovered head and a bow Louis XIV might have envied.

I often think how these two men, so utterly different in their characteristics and style should not only be such friends and have such confidence in each other, but should each seem to be the perfect military leader. Another very remarkable fact is that they are types respectively of the two classes of civilization which have marked and classified the Anglo-Saxon world for more than two centuries. Jackson is as distinct a Roundhead covenanter as Crom-

well or Ireton. A Presbyterian by faith, a predestinarian by conviction to the extent of fatalism, and with every practice, habit and
style of life which marked the leaders of the Commonwealth. He
is not wanting in that forbidding manner and costume which
robbed their virtues of so much that was attractive, yet he has all
the fiery zeal which makes them successful and formidable.

Lee, on the other hand has all the characteristics of the Cavalier
except their vices. Their virtues come to him through a long line
of distinguished ancestry from the original Lee who came over
with the conqueror and whose descendants fought under the banner of Charles I and secured to Virginia the legend: "En Vat
Virginia Quintam." In appearance, bearing and manner he is a
perfect type of all that is admirable in that class, and yet he arouses
in others that enthusiasm that is as effective as the zeal of the
puritan as a motive of action.

Blackford's garbled version of the Lee genealogy was current
in the Army. Perhaps it helped him and others explain what was
beginning to seem like Lee's invincibility.[18]

Around midnight on August 30, Jefferson Davis received a telegram from General Lee: "This army achieved today on the plains
of Manassas a signal victory over combined forces of Genls
McClellan and Pope." The nation was jubilant. Lee had separated his much smaller army into two wings in the face of overwhelming numbers, and had managed to bring off a stunning
victory. Jackson's exploits were wondered over and cheered. Stories were told of how he had issued his men three days' rations,
awakened them in the middle of the night with orders to abandon
the rations and everything but their weapons, and set them off at
double march around Pope's flank. Jackson's foot cavalry had
captured the largest dump of Union Army supplies ever gathered,
filled themselves with meat and cheese and soft white bread and
vegetables, dressed themselves in Army blue, and shod themselves
in U.S. leather. Then they burned the remainder. Jackson was
said to have ridden up and down his lines under heavy fire on
August 30 waiting for Longstreet—who was late—saying, "Two
hours men, only two hours; in two hours you will have help. You

must stand it two hours." Then back again, back and forth: "Half an hour men, only half an hour; can you stand it for half an hour?" And again: "They are coming once more men; you must stand it once more." And the men stood it, and afterward, sobbing in love for Old Jack, they rang the hills with cheers for the crazy Puritan who made them win. A captured Federal officer was transfixed by the sight of Jackson, battle flag in hand, leading his men in an assault. "What officer is that, Captain?" inquired the Yankee of his Confederate captor. When told it was Stonewall Jackson, the hatless Federal flourished his broken sword and rushed at the Confederate line, shouting, "Hurrah for General Jackson! Follow your General, Boys!" The sight brought tears to the eyes of his equally young guard, who said that proved the officer was too good a fellow to be made prisoner. The Confederate showed the Yankee officer a path to freedom. "He saluted me with his broken sword and disappeared in an instant. I hope he escaped."

But there were other stories about the battles in northern Virginia. Longstreet, it was said, was slow, and had almost convinced Lee not to fight at all. Only when circumstances overruled his opinion did he put his corps to work. Lee had met Grant's old friend Pete Longstreet before, but had not known him well. At forty, Longstreet was filled out into the portly masculine look admired in the nineteenth century, and was considered handsome. Tall, sandy-haired, and red-faced, he was thought by his staff to possess "unsurpassed soldierly bearing." He had been something of a rounder, and had disgraced himself with more than one drinking and gambling spree in the early months of the war. But when three of his children—come with their mother from Georgia to be near their father—died during a weeklong scarlet fever epidemic in Richmond earlier in 1862, Longstreet became serious and reserved, took up the Episcopalian faith, and seemed to rigidify in his opinions. Like Sherman, Longstreet met the onset of the war with a deep hurt. He never thought of the Union Army as anything but his former home and the current residence of close and valued friends. When he learned that one of his brigadiers before the Seven Days had ordered the retreat toward Richmond mined, he threatened to cashier the man on the spot and said that such practices were "not considered in the limits of legitimate warfare." The men of his corps loved him and he was a great favorite with the public.

Longstreet was difficult, tended to be pompous, and was slightly truculent. He didn't seem to share with Lee—as did Jackson—a common point of view. Lee could tell Jackson what he thought should be done, and Jackson understood, told Lee he would do it, and did. Longstreet had his own ideas, and he didn't hesitate to express them. Observers thought it strange that Lee seemed to grow hesitant in the face of Old Pete's objections. During the battle of Second Manassas on August 30, when Lee seemed to defer to Longstreet, there were no dire results. But like Lee's mishandling of the outrageous Henry Wise in the Virginia mountains, it set a dangerous precedent.[19]

DANGERS OF A different kind loomed for the Lincoln administration after the telegraph brought news of the Union Army's slaughter and rout. Citizens wondered how it was possible, with more than 100,000 expensively maintained soldiers in the field, to be so soundly drubbed in what should have been an easy shot at suppressing the rebellion. Moreover, Second Manassas had occurred in a military atmosphere that had become total war against the South. Lincoln had at last lost patience with McClellan and called Henry Halleck east to become general-in-chief. Halleck was a less than perfect solution to Lincoln's military problems, but he did offer hope. After Second Manassas, it was anyone's guess what might cure the political ills which swirled around the White House.

Lincoln had met with border state representatives in the hopes of getting them to back gradual emancipation which would be financially underwritten by the Federal government. When they refused, Lincoln admonished them that they were "blind to the signs of the times," and started work on a proclamation of emancipation. But there were conflicting signs that summer. Lincoln had to find some position that satisfied radical abolitionists without angering anti-black Democrats.

On August 14, the day Lee left Richmond for Manassas, Lincoln told a deputation of black leaders that "slavery was the greatest wrong inflicted on any people." But abolition would not alter the prejudices of the American people. "Your race suffer very greatly, many of them, by living among us," he said, "while ours suffer by your presence." He then proposed that the delegation act as promoters of a pilot plan for colonization. The move was denounced by some blacks and was excoriated by some radicals, but others saw it as clever maneuvering. Colonization, said one abolitionist, "is a damn humbug, but it will take with the people." On August 22, Lincoln replied in print to New York *Tribune* editor Horace Greeley's call for abolition. "My paramount object in this struggle *is* to save the Union," Lincoln wrote, "and is *not* either to save or to destroy slavery. If I could save the Union without freeing *any* slave I would do it, and if I could save it by freeing *all* slaves I would do it; and if I could save it by freeing some and leaving others alone, I would also do that." He closed by carefully pointing out that the letter represented his "view of official duty; and I intend no modification of my oft-expressed personal wish that all men everywhere could be free." The disclaimer reflected Lincoln's masterful handling of language. He spoke to abolitionists by saying he did not *intend* his letter to be taken as a reflection of his personal feelings. He could not, after all, be responsible for the assumptions of others.

It was widely assumed in Washington that slavery freed many southern whites for military duty and also provided a military labor force available to the North only in the form of recruits. If the Federal government could strip the South of its slaves, complete suppression of the rebellion would soon follow. But the timing was critical. When Lincoln showed a draft of his proclamation to his Cabinet on August 22, Seward suggested waiting until the Army had won a major battle. Because of the "depression of the public mind, consequent upon our [military] reverses," the proclamation might seem like "the last measure of an exhausted Government, a cry for help." In effect, that was just what the Emancipation Proclamation was, but Lincoln knew Seward was right. Anti-war sentiment had swelled after the Seven Days and Lincoln's call for new enlistments had fallen on deaf ears. When word of the debacle at Manassas reached Washington, Lincoln told a delegation of Chicago clergymen calling for the immediate publication of the proclamation that such an act would have all the force of the "Pope's bull against the comet!"[20]

"THE PRESENT SEEMS to be the most propitious time since the commencement of the war for the Confederate Army to enter Maryland," Lee wrote Jefferson Davis on September 3.

> The purpose, if discovered, will have the effect of carrying the enemy north of the Potomac, and if prevented, will not result in much evil. The army is not properly equipped for an invasion of an enemy's territory. it lacks much of the material of war, is feeble in transportation, the animals being much reduced, and the men are poorly provided with clothes, and in thousands of instances are destitute of shoes. Still we cannot afford to be idle, and though weaker than our opponents in men and military equipments, must endeavor to harass, if we cannot destroy them. I am aware that the movement is attended with much risk, yet I do not consider success impossible, and shall endeavor to guard it from loss. . . . What occasions me most concern is the fear of getting out of ammunition.

The following day, from Leesburg, Lee wrote that he was more than ever convinced of the wisdom of crossing the Potomac, and would "proceed to make the movement at once, unless you should signify your disapprobation." With the advance of his army already rolling up its trouser legs to ford the river, he didn't give Davis much time to express his disapproval.[21]

Just north of Leesburg, a Confederate Army ambulance jolted to a halt. Hundreds of men squatted or lay on the dirt road. General A. P. Hill, called Powell by his friends, leaned out of the wagon and began to shout. "Move out of the road, men."

Hill's fellow passenger countermanded the order. "Never

mind, General," Lee told Hill, "we will ride around them." Then Lee told the boys on the path to lie still. He was nursing a painful injury. His big gray horse, Traveller, had shied several days earlier during a thunderstorm. Lee reached for the bridle and tumbled forward as leather straps fouled in his heavy rubber rain gear. The fall had broken a bone in his right hand and sprained the left, and both were swathed in bandages. He couldn't even feed himself, and was touchy as a bear. The superstitious might have found an omen in Lee's injury, especially since Jackson was also dismounted from a fall and Longstreet was hobbling around in carpet slippers because of an infected foot. The Army was as crippled as its commanders. The men had been without provisions for days, and filled themselves on raw corn from farmers' fields or gnawed on hard little green apples from roadside trees. The diet made them sick, and only worsened the malnutrition and diarrhea which sidelined thousands of them on their march north. Even the healthy ones were having trouble keeping up. Fully one-quarter of the 50,000 men were without shoes. Most hadn't minded bare feet when they were padding along the soft dust trails of Virginia, but up near the Potomac, the orange clay turned to gray rocks, which cut their feet to ribbons.

But they were a game bunch—"None but heroes are left" shouted veterans from the Peninsula and Manassas—and their regimental bands struck up "Maryland, My Maryland" for the crossing, which began September 6. The day had been hot and clear, and a cavalryman thought it "a magnificent sight as the long column . . . stretched across this beautiful Potomac. The evening sun slanted upon its clear placid waters and burnished them with gold, while the arms of the soldiers glittered and blazed in its radiance." A less romantic young Marylander got a closer look at the soldiers bearing those arms across the waters and branded them "the dirtiest men I ever saw, a most ragged, lean and hungry set of wolves. Yet there was a dash about them that the Northern men lacked. They rode like circus riders. Many of them were from the far South and spoke a dialect I could scarcely understand. They were profane beyond belief and talked incessantly."

A northern reporter saw Stonewall Jackson for the first time and noted that he "was dressed in the coarsest kind of homespun, seedy and dirty at that; wore an old hat which any northern beggar would consider an insult to have offered him and in general appearance was in no respect to be distinguished from the mongrel, bare-footed crew who follow his fortunes. I had heard much of the decayed appearance of the rebel soldiers, but such a looking crowd! Ireland in her worst straits could present no parallel, and yet they glory in their shame."

On September 8 Lee sat in his tent in an oak grove near Frederick and wrote a proclamation to the "People of Maryland," promising "no intimidation will be allowed. Within the limits of this army at least, Marylanders shall once more enjoy their ancient freedom of thought, and speech. We know no enemies among you, and will protect all of every opinion. It is for you to decide your destiny, freely and without constraint."

Maryland was unimpressed. Though Barbara Frietchie never offered her old gray head to Stonewall Jackson as the poet suggested, thousands waved the Stars and Stripes whenever a Confederate appeared. Merchants closed their shops. Farmers locked their barns. In part, the appearance of Lee's "famished Rebel horde" prompted such plucky Union sentiment. "Seeing and *smelling*" the Confederate Army did not inspire confidence, said one would-be recruit. But Lee made good his promise to protect the citizens. Maryland citizens remembered the invasion as being as disciplined as it was unwelcome. Forage and farm animals were paid for—often in greenbacks—and no destruction of private property occurred. Even fence rails stood.

Though he said he was disappointed at the poor show of support, Lee's confidence in his mission was not flagging. The same day he wrote his proclamation, he tried to push President Davis one step closer to peace. "The present posture of affairs, in my opinion, places it in the power of the Government of the Confederate States to propose with propriety to that of the United States the recognition of our independence," Lee wrote. Issuing such a proposal with the Army of Northern Virginia camped near Washington's doorstep, Lee said, would be taken as an act of strength, not weakness. "The rejection of this offer would prove to the country that the responsibility of the continuance of the war does not rest upon us, but that the party in power in the United States elect to prosecute it for purposes of their own. The proposal of peace would enable the people of the United States to determine at the coming elections whether they will support those who favor a prolongation of the war, or those who wish to bring it to a termination. . . ." Lee had no wish to prolong the war himself, and had no illusions about the ultimate outcome of a long-term military conflict. But like Lincoln, he knew he had to have a military victory to set his plan in motion.[22]

Lee wrote Special Orders No. 191, detailing his plan of attack, on September 9. Confident that McClellan—reinstated after Second Manassas as commander of the Army of the Potomac—would be slow to respond to the Maryland emergency, Lee again decided to divide his army. Jackson would go to Harpers Ferry while Longstreet would march across the South Mountain range west of Frederick toward Hagerstown. Lee had his adjutant, R. H. Chilton, send copies of the orders to Longstreet, Jackson, and D. H. Hill, who was commanding in place of Ewell. Since Hill had been part of Jackson's corps, Stonewall had an additional copy of Special Orders No. 191 sent to Hill. Hill gave the extra one to one of his aides, who stuffed it in his pocket. The following day the army was on the march out of Frederick. Hill's aide, readying for the move, apparently fumbled around for a wrapper for three cigars he'd taken for the trip. He found a piece of paper in his pocket, wrapped the cigars, and tucked the packet into his vest. He was unaware that it fell out.

McClellan was slow. It was not until September 13 that the Union Army moved into the empty Confederate camps at Frederick. As the men settled in for the night, a pair of men enlisted in an Indiana regiment found a package of three cigars. When they unwrapped their find, they saw that the paper was official and gave it to their captain. An adjutant to one of McClellan's subordinates read Special Orders No. 191 with skepticism until he saw the signature. He was a close friend of Chilton's, recognized the writing, and swore to McClellan that the order was genuine. "Here is a paper with which if I cannot whip Bobbie Lee I will be willing to go home," said McClellan. By the next evening, he was finally ready to go, and at sunrise the Union army moved west after Lee. Three columns—88,000 men—marched, wrote an observer, like a "monstrous, crawling, blue-black snake, miles long, quilled with the silver slant of muskets . . ." Hill was watching them from his aerie in a South Mountain gap. What he saw made him think that "the Hebrew poet whose idea of the awe-inspiring is expressed by the phrase, 'terrible as an army with banners,' had his view from the top of a mountain." Hill found McClellan's army "a grand and glorious spectacle" which was impossible to look at "without admiration." But he had never "experienced a feeling of greater *loneliness*. It seemed as though we were deserted by 'all the world and the rest of mankind.' " Indeed, it was almost so.

Hill and Longstreet were heading a forlorn hope of 18,000 men against the 28,000 McClellan peeled off to throw at them. By nightfall, 2,700 Confederates were casualties and the rest were vanquished. A Union soldier, on the trail of the retreating Confederates, visited the scene of battle at South Mountain and got a first-time close look at his enemies. He thought the Southerners were "undersized men mostly . . . with sallow hatchet faces, and clad in 'butternut,' a color running all the way from a deep, coffee brown up to the whitish brown of ordinary dust." Such dust-to-dust brought pity to the heart of the New York volunteer. "As I looked down on the poor, pinched faces, worn with marching and scant fare, all enmity died out. There was no 'secession' in those rigid forms, nor in those eyes staring blankly at the sky."

"The day has gone against us, and this army will go by Sharpsburg and cross the river," Lee wrote to a subordinate. All his grand plans seemed to have come to ruin with those poor butternut boys scattered in the grass at South Mountain. Perhaps God had not favored his northern undertaking after all.

But around noon September 15, a courier delivered a message from Stonewall Jackson: "Through God's blessing, Harpers

Ferry and its garrison are to be surrendered." Lee was transfixed. Jackson's news changed everything. Now Lee would stay where he was and fight.

McClellan did not expect such tenacity. He wrote Halleck in Washington that he had "perfectly reliable" information that the Confederate army was crossing the Potomac, and that Lee had "stated publicly that he must admit they had been shockingly whipped." There was much of the boy in McClellan, and he could not help crowing a bit to his former mentor, Winfield Scott. Scott was in retirement at West Point, corpulent and dying, when he got McClellan's wire. "R. E. Lee in command. The rebels routed, and retreating in disorder." Scott manfully wired his congratulations: "Bravo, my dear general! Twice more and it's done." The cryptic qualifier was not what McClellan had been looking for, and neither was he expecting the news he got the afternoon of September 15. The Confederate army seemed to be investing ground around Sharpsburg, Maryland. It was not retreating.[23]

Sharpsburg was a tiny town of neat houses and little churches surrounded by neat, squared cornfields that had ripened in the warm September days. The land was limestone tough and pushed upward toward the right-angling Potomac River on its west and south and downward toward Antietam Creek on its east. Armed with what he called the "victory of the indomitable Jackson," and very little else, Lee arranged his 20,000 men on the eastern edge of Sharpsburg, and sent word to Harpers Ferry for Stonewall to come at once. Lee's position was as strong as nature could make it, and about as militarily weak as was possible. His line looked right into the marching advance of 88,000 Union soldiers. On September 16, Longstreet took his field glasses and peered at the valley ahead. It was a sea of blue-clad soldiers. The "spectacle" was "awe-inspiring," Longstreet said, and it strengthened his conviction that he and every other Confederate soldier should be back in Virginia. Lee was not at all of the same mind.

By noon, Jackson had arrived from Harpers Ferry. His corps pushed the Confederate count to 30,000 and he shared Lee's optimism. The two generals were puzzled by McClellan's uncharacteristic alacrity, but they weren't afraid of him. Jackson had left Powell Hill with a division to guard Harpers Ferry, assuring a safe retreat southward if necessary. Lee sent Jackson to the north end of the Confederate line, Longstreet was on the south, and D. H. Hill occupied the center.

McClellan had been watching Lee's preparations all day, and as the sun set he ordered two divisions on his northern end to cross Antietam Creek. John Hood, the burly Texan who rode with Lee around the hills of Camp Cooper twelve years earlier, met the Federal advance with a stiff show of strength. The skirmish was over in minutes, but it had lasted long enough to convince Lee that McClellan would attack him from the north.

The next morning Lee was on the lines before first light. He had learned during the Seven Days not to depend on his division commanders, and he had personally directed the placement of all the batteries and all the men. On September 17 he would personally direct the battle. Apparently sensing success, he sent word for A. P. Hill to come from Harpers Ferry and then went to work. He rode north and circled quietly through his troops, bending over a commander for words of encouragement, then riding on to the next brigade.

John Gordon had come to war from the mountainous triangle where Alabama, Tennessee, and Georgia met. He was elected captain of the "Raccoon Roughs" in 1861 and his first military experience was suppressing the rebellion of his men when they were told their services were not needed. Coonskin caps bouncing on their backs, the Roughs unhitched their troop train from its engine and forced Gordon to march them through Atlanta to camp. Finally mustered in as part of the 6th Alabama in Montgomery, the Roughs and Gordon were part of Dick Ewell's corps, but Ewell had lost a leg at Second Manassas and Gordon was now under the command of D. H. Hill in the middle of Lee's line. He could see the entire field, an "open plain," with no "breastworks, no abatis, no intervening woodlands."

Just after dawn Federal batteries erupted in strangely silent white clouds of smoke trailed by ear-shattering roars. Lee's artillery responded. Then the Federal right, in disciplined straight rows, trotted through the cornfield and threw itself against Lee's left. In a moment the Confederates recovered, and answered with musket fire "like a scythe," which cut the Union advance into near shocks of dead who lay as they fell, in disciplined straight rows. What followed was called a "fighting madness" by some who swore that it was soon impossible to take a step without treading on a dead or wounded man. The two lines hurled themselves at one another for six hours. When the far northern attack was over—at noon—13,000 Americans were dead or wounded. But Jackson's corps had held off McClellan's initial thrust. Elated and chewing on a peach, Stonewall heard the news that 5,000 of his men were gone and said, "God has been very kind to us this day." He confidently told his surgeon that the Federals had done him their worst.

John Gordon surmised that the battle on the north edge was finished when "an ominous silence" settled over the field. It was, and as he waited, his commander rode up. Lee told Gordon that his Alabamans would get it next, and he added that the spot Gordon was in—far in front with no support—must be held at any sacrifice. Then Lee rode off to stiffen others' resolve. Gordon turned toward Lee and shouted at his back: "These men are going to stay here, General, till the sun goes down or victory is won."

"The day was clear and beautiful with scarcely a cloud in the sky," Gordon remembered. "The men in blue filed down the opposite slope, crossed the little stream (Antietam), and formed in my front, an assaulting column four lines deep. The front line came to a 'charge bayonets,' the other lines to a 'right shoulder shift.' The brave Union commander, superbly mounted, placed himself in front, while his band in rear cheered them with martial music. It was a thrilling spectacle. The entire force, I concluded, was composed of fresh troops from Washington or some camp of instruction. So far as I could see, every soldier wore white gaiters around his ankles. The banners above them had apparently never been discolored by the smoke and dust of battle. Their gleaming bayonets flashed like burnished silver in the sunlight. With the precision of step and perfect alignment of a holiday parade, this magnificent array moved to the charge, every step keeping time to the tap of the deep-sounding drum. As we stood looking upon that brilliant pageant, I thought, if I did not say, 'What a pity to spoil with bullets such a scene of martial beauty!' But there was nothing else to do. Mars is not an aesthetic god." The Federals walked right into Gordon's line, were decimated, regrouped, and walked in again. Gordon was shot four times during the day. "I remembered the pledge to the commander that we would stay there till the battle ended or night came. I looked at the sun. It moved very slowly; in fact, it seemed to stand still." His last effort on the field at Antietam Creek was reminding his men of the promise he had given Lee. As he began to walk down his line, the fifth shot got him squarely in the face. He pitched forward unconscious and was carried to the rear.

Lee was in the saddle all day long, rallying the dispirited. A singularly unlucky private, hightailing it to safer ground, ran right into the commander of the Army of Northern Virginia. In answer to Lee's stern questions about his destination, the rattled soldier explained that he had been "stung by a bung, and I'm what they call demoralized." Lee smiled after him as the ragged man scampered on. Though he didn't share Jackson's euphoria, he remained calm and seemingly collected as he moved his men like chess pieces across the field. In the morning, he stripped his right of all available men and cannon to aid Jackson's fight on the left. By midday, he was sending the exhausted remnants of the north end battle back to the front to help glue the thin center line that Gordon and D. H. Hill's men were trying to hold. As part of Jackson's artillery came stumbling southward, Lee urged the crew forward. A young private approached Lee and asked, "General, are you going to send us in again?" Lee looked kindly on the lad and answered, "Yes, my son, you all must do what you can to help drive these people back." It was Rob. Lee's youngest son had gone to war a private gunner and had been with Stonewall Jackson for five months.

"These people," Lee's favorite euphemism for his opponents, were not exactly driven back in the center, they had come to a standstill through exhaustion. No sooner did that fight drift to a close than it began in earnest on Lee's right. Longstreet, an unsmoked cigar clenched in his teeth, had been hobbling around in his carpet slippers all day, barking orders at his men to hurry toward weak spots along the line. Now it was his turn, and he hadn't anything to hold off the attack which came his way in force at 1 p.m. All day, too, Lee had been looking for some sign of A. P. Hill. With ammunition almost gone, and men to use it exhausted or wounded or dead, Lee's army was about finished. Federal soldiers could be seen on the streets of Sharpsburg, and blue flags were as common as red ones along the undulating Confederate line. Around 3 p.m. Lee finally saw a column of soldiers approaching from the southeast. Excited, he called out to an artillery lieutenant, "What troops are those?" The officer trained his glass on the road and sadly announced the troops were flying the United States flag. But another column, farther off, could just be seen raising up a dust cloud in the southwest. The artillerist looked, and gleefully told Lee they were flying the Virginia and Confederate flags. With no visible sign of emotion, Lee quietly said, "It is A. P. Hill from Harpers Ferry."

It was Hill and it was deliverance. Wearing the red shirt he thought was lucky, Hill had put his men on a near-run and made the distance from Harpers Ferry in about eight hours. Two thousand soldiers were too tired to keep up, but the 3,000 who made it just kept rushing forward. They didn't stop at all, but looked sidelong at their commanders for instructions, and giving the Rebel yell, hit the Federals on Lee's right side and exploded them backward in panic. The men in blue recoiled in a fright which made their last stands, huddled together in the corn, weak echoes of the work they had done that day.

Twinkling lights of the medical corps began to show on the banks of the creek and the pigeons were settling back onto shell-pocked houses as Lee's generals gathered for an early-evening meeting with their chief. Jackson, D. H. Hill, Hood, Early, Powell Hill—all of them had bad news. More than one-fourth of the army was gone. Most of the generals had one thing in mind—retreat. But Lee's response was to ask where Longstreet was. When a red-faced and winded Longstreet rolled in on his clumsy carpet slippers, the unlit and worn cigar still between his teeth,

Lee jumped to his feet. "Here comes my war horse," he exclaimed as he slid his arm around Longstreet's shoulders. The war horse had no better news than the others. There were just over 26,000 spent men left. Lee was silent for a moment; then he announced to the startled assemblage that he would give McClellan battle again in the morning.

The men who served Robert Lee learned something about him that night. As his boyhood teacher had asserted, his specialty was finishing up and he meant to finish up his work in Maryland. It was not suicidal, this desire to take on three times his number. His lines that night were close to where they had been twenty-four hours earlier. His men had held. McClellan had proved himself as timid as he expected. Even though little Mac had thwarted a major Confederate offensive, he had treated the Army of Northern Virginia as if it were a natural disaster that had to be contained piece by piece. At no one time did McClellan use more than 20,000 of his 88,000 men. Lee believed if McClellan would repeat those tactics the next day, the Confederates had a chance of winning the peace he so badly wanted.

So it was that on the morning of September 18 Lee's men were waiting behind their bayonets, staring toward the blue soldiers behind Antietam Creek. But McClellan did not move. As the sun climbed overhead, the guns were still silent, but wounded men writhing between the lines cried for water. Thousands of dead horses swelled in the heat, their legs poking skyward like sticks on a balloon.

By two in the afternoon, Lee knew there would be no attack. He rode to Longstreet's position and gave the order to withdraw. That night, the Confederates built campfires, and left them burning unattended as they stole off toward the Potomac. Lee was with the advance, and left first, but when the tag end of the army got to the river the following morning, he was sitting astride his horse in the water. He asked the final division commander for news of the army, and heard that everyone was safe. "Thank God," he said, and turned southward himself.[24]

———

That day after the great battle of Sharpsburg, Lee made his men lie on their lines and prove to McClellan and themselves that they could take anything the Federals threw their way. They might be hungry or wearing rags, but they had met Lee's test and he admired them. A determinedly jaunty mood filled the camp near Winchester for the two months the Army of Northern Virginia rested. After refusing lodging in a comfortable farmhouse, Lee had his tents pitched in a field and opened social shop. Neighboring civilians arrived with gossip, food, and offers of party invitations. The provisions were sent on to hospitals, but the ladies, much to his young officers' delight, were welcomed with unflagging charm. Other visitors, including an Englishman surprised that Lee never "evinced any bitterness of feeling" for the North, added to festivities. A wave of revivals swept through the Confederate camps, and by mid-October, prayer meetings and church services were more common among the tents than were theatricals and drinking sessions. Lee approved of this unforeseen turn of military events, but churchgoing and entertaining offered him little relief from wresting enough supplies from Richmond to feed and clothe his men. It was trying, and, as usual, dealing with bureaucracy made him irritable. But Lee seldom lost control of himself. Walter Taylor said that Lee "the man" always gave way "to Lee the patriot and soldier." This discipline was remarkable, Taylor said, because "General Lee was naturally of a positive temperament, and of strong passions; and it is a mistake to suppose him otherwise; but he held these in complete subjection to his will and conscience. He was not one of those invariably amiable men whose temper is never ruffled."

The "habitual self-command" Taylor admired in Lee was sorely tried in the autumn of 1862. His expectations for the Maryland campaign had grown from his understanding of the symbolic results of a Confederate victory north of the Potomac. Though his army had held its line against McClellan, it had not won. It had not pushed close enough to Washington to shake northern confidence in the Lincoln administration. And on that single day in the valley of the Antietam, more than 23,000 Americans had fallen. Lee's losses for the entire campaign had been more than 13,000, and those 13,000 were the best he would ever have. Conscription might fill the ranks, but it could never replace the volunteers he left on the field near Sharpsburg.

It had also turned out that Lee was not the comet the North had imagined. McClellan had defended the capital against the Confederate offensive—and that was all he really wanted to do. Though Lincoln was exasperated by Little Mac's refusal to push on and gather up the Army of Northern Virginia, he was enough satisfied with Antietam to issue the Emancipation Proclamation.

Lincoln's edict, dated September 22, 1862, declared that slaves in states still in rebellion against the United States on January 1, 1863, "shall be then, thenceforward, and forever free." The relish of salvation had been added to the war for Union. "Fellow citizens, *we* cannot escape history," Lincoln said in his 1862 State of the Union address. "The fiery trial through which we pass, will light us down, in honor or dishonor, to the latest generation. . . . The dogmas of the quiet past, are inadequate to the stormy present. . . . As our case is new, so we must think anew, and act anew. . . . In *giving* freedom to the *slave,* we *assure* freedom to the *free.* . . . We must disenthrall ourselves, and then we shall save our country."

Few could find more personal ironies in Lincoln's speech than Robert Lee. As it happened, Lee was giving freedom to the Custis slaves on the exact date the proclamation was to take effect. And his labors in behalf of liberating Virginia slaves were made more arduous because half of them had run off with the Union Army. But the real significance for Lee of Lincoln's message rested on the President's interpretation of history. Lee would agree with Lincoln that the American experience was a religious one— dogma meant something very different from constitutional law. But Lee's Civil War action was exactly the opposite of Lincoln's. He may well have wanted to save the past founded by Washington, but he sincerely believed that that was the only way to save the country. He understood when he went South that his work was a defensive posture against a stormy future. He did not believe that the country's case was new. Nor did he believe it necessary to think anew. Only by acting anew could Lee safe-guard the dogma of the past, and even so acting, could summon the ancient precedent of George Washington. He had followed Washington's example, but after Antietam he began to feel he had failed to meet Washington's mythical mark.[25]

Lee told Mary to settle herself permanently away from Rich-mond. He could never see her, he said, because he could never leave his men. If he lived, he hoped to be with her "for the few remnant years of my life," but until the war was over, everyone must make up his mind to forsake home and family. Three weeks later, he learned that it was he who was forsaken. Precious Annie, the gentle daughter who was the closest to him of all his children, had died of diphtheria in the mountains of North Carolina. The news was "agonizing" to Lee. But God, he said, "has mingled mercy with the blow in selecting that one best prepared to leave us. He has taken the purest & best." When he thought about "all she will escape in life" and all she will enjoy with her "sainted" grandmother, he could not "wish her back." But he felt aban-doned and alone, and was depressed when he left Mary after a short visit to Richmond in early November. Every time now, he said, "the feeling increases. The probability of return grows dim-mer. The prospect of the future grows shorter." And the probabil-ity of death was no longer cause for celebration as it had been in the past. As those "dear to me are diminished," he wrote to his daughter Milly, "I cling more anxiously to those who remain." He prayed, he said, that God "grant that we may one day be all again united in this world, when we must the more love each other & remember affectionately the dead." In the past when someone Lee loved died, he had yearned to be united with them in the hereafter. Earthly bonds were loosened, he had said, as one by one were taken from him. But the deadly business of war was teaching him to love the living more.[26]

CHAPTER
17

DURING THE AUTUMN of 1862, Grant was headquartered at Holly Springs, Mississippi, a railroad crossing just south of Corinth. When he moved farther south to Oxford, he left behind not only Julia but also the largest military supply dump west of the Allegheny Mountains. On December 20, he nearly lost both.

Julia was assigned quarters in a Holly Springs mansion being kept by Mrs. Pugh Govan, the wife of a Confederate officer. Julia remembered being warmly received the night of her arrival and thought Mrs. Govan a "fine, noble woman." At breakfast the following morning, she was treated so cordially she forgot, she said, that she was "actually in the enemy's camp." But when her hostess indicated that she was to use a separate drawing room, Julia was filled, she said, with "chagrin and mortification." In time, her fellow lodgers began inviting Julia into their private quarters for socializing and listening to Confederate war songs, performed "grandly, with power, pathos and enthusiasm." Apparently too moved, Julia declined to attend repeat performances on the grounds she would "be a traitor to listen again to such songs."

Julia's Holly Springs visit ended with a December 20 note from Grant saying the route to Oxford was finished. She must join him there at once. By afternoon, she was on the road, and so was Confederate general Earl Van Dorn. Julia and the Rebel commander apparently crossed paths, and she arrived in Oxford about the same time Van Dorn swept into Holly Springs and captured the supply depot. Van Dorn knew Julia had been there, and was disgruntled at not bagging such a prize. The Grant family returned at once in what Julia defended as a "retrograde movement, which was in no sense a retreat." They settled themselves in a "beautiful Italian villa" and accepted, at Christmas, a fat turkey from her former hostess. The dinner, and the information that Mrs. Govan had refused Van Dorn's demand to surrender her baggage, did much to warm Julia's holiday. Grant, however, was silent over the embarrassment of once again leaving himself open to an unexpected Confederate offensive, which was cited in the press as further evidence of his ineptitude.[1]

LEE WAS BEING lauded that Christmas as the savior of the South. Ambrose Burnside, chosen as a potentially more aggressive commander to replace George McClellan, had massed the Army of the Potomac on the north bank of the Rappahannock River for an assault on Fredericksburg. The ancient little town, final resting place of George Washington's mother, had long since passed its prime. But its location was squarely on the Richmond, Fredericksburg & Potomac railway line, halfway between Washington and Richmond. Lee camped on the south side of the Rappahannock, quietly watched Burnside gather his troops, and just as quietly scattered Confederate defenders along high ground south and west of town. On December 13, the Union army crossed the river and, in a series of assaults masterminded by Burnside, threw itself across an open field and up Marye's Heights into Confederate guns. That night what remained of the Army of the Potomac slept in place and tried not to notice the Rebel soldiers who crept out of their defense works to strip Union dead of shoes and coats. The following day Federal burial parties scooped up the fallen and dispensed with their remains as best they could—sometimes stuffing dozens of bodies into single icehouses. Then Burnside withdrew his men, leaving Lee disappointed. "Yesterday evening I had my suspicions that they might retire during the night, but could not believe they would relinquish their purpose after all their boasting & preparations, & when I say the latter is equal to the former, you will have some idea of its magnitude. This morning they were all safe on the north side of the Rappahannock." His sarcasm grew from increasing bitterness toward the Army of the Potomac. "Those people delight to destroy the weak & those who can make no defense," he said of Burnside's army, "it just suits them." Many Union soldiers agreed, and wrote home outraged accounts of looting at Fredericksburg. When the Federals recrossed the river, they left behind a ruin so desolate that Confederate officers created a relief fund and shared with displaced townsfolk what little food and clothing they could muster.

Enmity, however, faded when both sides declared a kind of Christmas peace on the banks of the river. When Federal bands clustered on the northern shoreline to lift Yankee spirits with rousing renditions of "Hail, Columbia" and "The Star-Spangled Banner," Rebels yelled over from the south side for them to play some Confederate songs. Soon both sides of the river were crowded with men singing "Dixie" and "The Bonny Blue Flag." Then they turned to "The Girl I Left Behind Me"—a favorite with all troops—and a slow, shared version of "Home, Sweet Home." Finally the armies of Northern Virginia and the Potomac fell silent. The experience opened a surprising kind of commerce. Men clever with their hands fashioned little sailboats to carry cargoes of northern newspapers and food or southern tobacco back and forth. Regiments vied for honors in creating the spiffiest boats, and soon the Rappahannock was speckled with merry reminders of the season. Officers on both sides were under orders to stop the prank. None did.[2]

Lee was invited by Stonewall Jackson to share in what turned out to be a lavish Christmas feast, but he declined, and gave himself over to morose musings, which were voiced in a letter he wrote to War Secretary Seddon. "In view of the vast increase of the forces of the enemy, of the savage and brutal policy he has proclaimed, which leaves us no alternative but success or degradation worse than death, if we would save the honor of our families from pollution, our social system from destruction, let every effort be made, every means be employed, to fill and maintain the ranks of our armies, until God, in His mercy, shall bless us with the establishment of our independence." Lee's using fundamentalist Confederate rhetoric on Seddon was not simply politic. He had expressed similar feelings to his brother Carter earlier. "We must endure to the end," he wrote, "and if our people are true to themselves and our soldiers continue to discard all thoughts of self and to press nobly forward in defence alone of their country and their rights, I have no fear of the result. We may be annihilated, but we cannot be conquered." There was nothing to do but press on. "Yet what have we to live for if not victorious?"[3]

As Lee suffered with his army through one of the most severe winters in Virginia's history, his sense of isolation increased. He never believed the Confederacy could depend on European aid, and by the winter of 1863 most other Southerners agreed with him. What substance there was in the notion that England and France would be forced by economic need to support the South was swept away by the Emancipation Proclamation. His sole hope—stirring up the already restive anti-war Northerners—seemed to be buried on the field at Antietam. Yet he was charged with the maintenance of Confederate troops, and had sworn to defend Virginia with his life. In February he wrote Custis that he had seen in the newspapers that the "Federal Congress has put the whole power of their country into the hands of their President. Nine hundred millions of dollars & three millions of men. Nothing now can arrest during the present administration the most desolating war that was ever practiced except a revolution among their people. Nothing can produce a revolution except systematic success on our part. What has our Congress done to meet the exigency? I may say extremity, in which we are placed?" Nothing, he said.

His army was starving and freezing. Mules and horses lacked forage, and men dipped into reserves of corn feed for their own provisions. Headquarters fare was so meager that an invitation for a visitor to dine sent Lee's cook on a mission to borrow a piece of bacon—which was faithfully returned after being boiled with dried peas. Soldiers were taught to sleep on spots recently raked clean of campfires. A third of the army was shoeless and the men tried Longstreet slippers—pieces of rawhide folded and tied over the feet—but ice formed on the cow hair and turned the slippers into skates. Federal couriers found the Rebels "ragged, slovenly, sleeveless, without a superfluous ounce of flesh upon their bones, with wild matted hair, in mendicants' rags." And Union prisoners wrote shocked descriptions of Confederate camps at Fredericksburg. "Their artillery horses are poor, starved frames of beasts, tied to their carriages and caissons with odds and ends of rope and strips of raw hide; their supply and ammunition trains look like a congregation of all the crippled California emigrant trains that ever escaped off the desert out of the clutches of the rampaging Comanche Indians. The men are ill-dressed, ill-equipped, and ill-provided, a set of ragamuffins that a man is ashamed to be seen among, even when he is a prisoner and can't help it. And yet they have beaten us all to pieces, beaten us so easily that we are objects of contempt even to their commonest private soldiers. With no shirts to hang out the holes of their pantaloons and cartridge boxes tied around their waists with strands of rope."[4]

The ease with which the Rebels scorned their glossier Federal foes did not arise only from besting them in battle. Nor did the embarrassment of Union soldiers grow only from being beaten by a half-starved enemy. It was the mystical but very real presence of the American Revolution which informed emotional responses to the war. Every soldier in America had been reared on stirring stories of the underdog Continental Army's endurance and final victory over the well-dressed, well-equipped, and well-provided British. The thrilling nobility of Valley Forge—blood-soaked rags on freezing feet—stiffened Americans' pride in themselves as a people. It was impossible for soldiers in the Civil War to ignore the correlation between the Revolutionary troops and the Army of Northern Virginia. The shame of the Union prisoner arose as much from playing the part of the British as it did from mingling with Lee's wretched men. And those ragged soldiers took enormous and sustaining pride in emulating their Revolutionary forefathers. So did their commander.

But Lee had little more than abstract hope in divine mercy as spring broke on the Rappahannock. With 62,000 men, he sat on the south side of the river vigilantly watching Burnside's replacement, Joseph Hooker, and his 130,000. "He runs out his guns, starts his wagons & troops up & down the river, & creates an excitement generally," Lee wrote about Hooker. "Our men look on in wonder, give a cheer, & all again subsides 'in statu quo ante bellum.'" Lee hated being passive in the face of the enemy, and he hated not knowing where the Federal push would come. "I owe Mr. F. J. Hooker no thanks for keeping me here in this state of expectancy," he wrote Mary. "He ought to have made up his mind long ago what to do." But he admitted he didn't know how to cope with the three-to-one odds against him should Hooker make a move.

Rations at Fredericksburg were about a pound of flour and four ounces of fat meat each day. "Symptoms of scurvey are appearing" among the men, he complained to the Secretary of War, "and to supply the place of vegetables each regiment is directed to send a daily detail to gather sassafras buds, wild onions, lamb's quarter, & poke sprouts." In such a state, his army would not be able to endure the coming campaign. Lee had to send Longstreet's corps a hundred miles away, to the Southside below Richmond, to feed itself and find forage. "We are in a liquid state at present," he wrote Mary. "Up to our knees in mud & what is worse on short rations for men & beasts. This keeps me miserable."

"Old age & sorrow is wearing me away, & constant anxiety & labour, day & night, leaves me but little repose," he wrote. An unsuccessful trip to Richmond to procure aid for the army seemed the final blow. On March 30, working in his tent in Fredericksburg, he had a heart attack.[5]

ULYSSES GRANT was only slightly better off. He was much perplexed, he told Julia on March 27. "Heretofore I have had nothing to do but fight the enemy. This time I have to overcome obsticles to reach him."[6]

The particular obstacle was the Mississippi River. In January, acting on rumors that Lincoln's friend John McClernand had gotten a go-ahead for a private campaign against Vicksburg, Grant decided to lead the Army of the Tennessee against the last Confederate stronghold on the river. Since an overland thrust by Sherman had resulted in a bloody stalemate, there seemed to be no alternative but an attempt on Vicksburg from the water. And that seemed impossible. Below Memphis, the Mississippi coiled like a piece of loose string into what navigators called "bends." The riverbed looped north, south, east, and west across pine-studded land which one day would be the richly productive Delta but in 1863 was a mass of buckled ground veined with rivers and bayous and tangled with swampland brush. Vicksburg sat secure on a high riverfront bluff, defended on the east by the wilderness and on the west by batteries which were the most effective in the Confederacy.

Grant approached the problem with Yankee ingenuity and the kind of serviceable nineteenth-century technology common on Ohio farms. If one of the bends below Vicksburg could be cut, the flow of the river might forge a new channel and leave the fortress high and dry. The idea sounded good to Army engineers who had studied Robert Lee's work at St. Louis. But the canal was cut the wrong way, and instead of drying out Vicksburg, it flooded out the Union army. "Grant's ditch" was the source of much hilarity for Mississippians, and northern newspapermen eagerly filed stories about the failure. Grant was furious, but undeterred. His next plan called for a series of dams and dikes to be built on Lake Providence, Louisiana, which would flood enough bayous to float troopships south to a point below Vicksburg. The dams broke. The levees cracked. Grant's mood fell, and Vicksburg was not his only vexation.

Grant commanded most of the western theater, and had to juggle military campaigns with a difficult and confusing peace in Tennessee. Committed to the Federal government's notion that commerce should follow the flag, eager patriots swarmed to Memphis to do their duty by getting rich in the cotton boom which followed Union victories in Tennessee and Mississippi. Grant was bedeviled by soldiers who claimed discharges on the basis of illness, then stayed in the department to trade bales. In early February, he wryly noted that some of the certificates of disability seemed "to indicate a disease that might be called *Cotton on the brain.*" He issued an order requiring resigned soldiers to leave in order "to remove as far as practicable all contagious tendencies of the disease." But it was impossible to remove well-connected citizens. Charles Dana, an emissary from Secretary of War Stanton, came south to trade, but instead wrote Stanton that every "colonel, captain or quartermaster is in secret partnership with some operator in cotton; every soldier dreams of adding a bale of cotton to his monthly pay." Dana didn't mention his own dreams, which were thwarted anyway.

Grant thought the vice was less widespread, but did admit that "no honest man has made money in West Tennessee in the last year, whilst many fortunes have been made there during that time." He would have to include the money made by J. Russell Jones, an entrepreneur who happened to be a close friend of Elihu Washburne. Though Jones's sole purpose for visiting Tennessee was to engage in some seemly cotton trading, he succumbed to avarice and excitedly wrote Washburne that he "could have made an eternal, hell-roaring fortune" if he had only been better-heeled. As it was, he had to content himself with a mere $25,000 gain. Grant was never one to turn a back on a friend of a friend, and Jones traveled with the general and messed at headquarters. Old Jesse Grant was not so lucky. His desire to emulate Jones apparently was the cause of his son's issuing an order which proved highly embarrassing to the Lincoln administration. General Orders No. 11 read as follows:

I. The Jews, as a class, violating every regulation of trade established by the Treasury Department, and also Department orders, are hereby expelled from the Department.
II. Within twenty-four hours from the receipt of this order by Post Commanders, they will see that all this class of people are furnished with passes and required to leave, and any one returning

after such notification, will be arrested and held in confinement until an opportunity occurs of sending them out as prisoners unless furnished with permits from these Head Quarters.

Though anti-Semitism was common in Civil War America, Ulysses Grant was the only U.S. Army officer who codified it. Apologists claimed Grant meant all merchants, and not merely Jews. But Jewish involvement in the illicit cotton trade was the focus of widespread Army discontent, and Grant himself had often singled out Jews as offenders in the unsavory business. The immediate spur to his order was probably the arrival in Memphis of Jesse with the Mack brothers, two Jewish merchants from Cincinnati who agreed to cut Jesse into one-quarter of their profits if he would use his influence with his son. Following publication of the directive, Elihu Washburne wrote Grant that his "order touching Jews has kicked up quite a dust among the Israelites. They came here in crowds and gave an entirely false construction to the order and Halleck revoked it. . . . You will see by the paper I send you they moved in regard to it in our House yesterday, but they did not make anything by it. All the democrats were fierce to censure your action."[7]

Washburne's casual bigotry would have interested Grant less than the congressman's pointed reference to party politics. Despite cheerful assertions by the truly committed such as Rawlins that the war for Union was a nonpartisan national endeavor, the conflict had a decidedly Republican official flavor. James Wilson, a young Republican cavalry officer who had watched what he considered McClellan's pro-Confederate showing at Antietam, arrived at Grant's headquarters with much news from Washington. Rawlins briefed him on Army politics. Wilson, in turn, fueled Rawlins's already incendiary suspicions about the workings of the War Department. The two formed an alliance to protect Grant. Rawlins stepped up headquarters housekeeping, and without Grant's knowledge, successfully got rid of a trio of scoundrels. Wilson promised to help Rawlins keep Grant sober forever, and agreed to aid in the handling of Charles Dana.

The two decided that the best way to treat the War Department spy was to welcome Dana as a member of the headquarters family, materially assist him in gathering carefully controlled information, and put on a show of camaraderie under fire. The plan was enhanced by Wilson's serving the myopic Dana as secretary and helping him "edit" his correspondence. It worked to a point. Dana started writing glowing reports on Grant to Stanton, but proved himself more adept at investigation than Rawlins and Wilson thought. They were unaware that Dana's real job was not just to collect information about Grant but to send to the War Department precise readings on Grant's staff and subordinate officers. These analyses were not—and apparently not intended to be—limited to assessments of military skill. They were character studies that focused most acutely on the politics of the men in question. Stanton had himself been a Democrat, and was converted before the war to radical abolitionism. Like many converts, he was zealous and single-minded. Dana needed no such change of heart. A New Englander, he had spent time at Brook Farm before joining the New York *Tribune* as an editor. He was either fired or quit when publisher Horace Greeley—an early supporter of abolition and the war—began to fold in the face of mounting casualties. Dana leapt at the chance of getting to the front and doing what he could to ensure that none but the politically sound were promoted. This duty was especially important and sensitive in the West, where Copperhead sentiments might be found in any number of powerful military men. Dana's correspondence with Stanton contained hints about certain generals' former Democratic ties, attitudes toward emancipation, or support of Lincoln.[8]

By early spring the Federal war for Union had changed in both cause and effect. The Emancipation Proclamation was not popular in the Army, but it did serve crucial political purposes, not the least of which was a test of absolute loyalty. Abolitionists, antislavers, and Republicans could easily pass by a process of political osmosis through the ideological barrier thrown up by Lincoln's manipulating the war into a struggle against slavery. Hard-line constitutionalists, Democrats, and anti-blacks were clumped together in a mass of political have-nots who were easily identified and often branded as traitors. Though Lincoln still tried to mollify his political opponents, his Cabinet was sorting out the Republican saved from the non-Republican damned. No one was better at this or more committed to the cause than Edwin Stanton. And no one was more eager to please Edwin Stanton than Ulysses Grant.

Grant was no ideologue. Beyond a kind of inchoate desire to punish Virginia, his only purpose in entering the war was to flex his military talents. Since the time in 1861 when he told his father that slaves were incidental to his wartime mission, Grant had quietly—with the aid of Rawlins and Galena Republicans—done what the powers in Washington expected of him. His orders about slaves in his department folded back upon each other in a dizzy system of rescinding which mirrored the vagaries of the Lincoln administration. Only one constant anchored the Army's policy: Slaves which belonged to Union supporters must not be tampered with. This imperative added a touch of the inquisition to the actual process of accepting or turning away blacks who sought refuge within Union Army lines, and the problem got worse after January 1, 1863.

Under the provisions of the Emancipation Proclamation, only those slaves owned by individual citizens of the states or portions of states in rebellion against the United States were set free. Because of Lincoln's desire to attract support from border state Unionists, Tennessee and Kentucky were excluded from the emancipation process. Grant was forced to consider individual cases on a piecemeal basis in Tennessee, and worse waited in Mississippi. He had been shipping "contrabands" to Cairo, but was told by the War Department to stop. Being a practical man, Grant then stopped accepting blacks into Army lines—there was no way to care for the thousands who petitioned the soldiers for safety. "Humanity dictates this policy," he wrote Henry Halleck.

But administration humanity in early 1863 was an abstraction that had little to do with practicality. Grant knew he'd made a mistake. His old West Point roommate, Fred Steele, failed of promotion because he returned a fugitive slave to its owner. Steele came to Grant carrying a letter of explanation from none other than Abraham Lincoln. Grant wrote Washburne assuring the Republican representative that Steele was faithfully obedient to "the orders of his superiors. No matter how far any policy of the Government might vary from his individual views he would conform to it in good faith. Besides I have never heard him express an opinion against any policy of the Administration and know he would do nothing to weaken the power of the President or any officer serving under him. Gen. Steele is a Northern man, never gave a vote in his life and I presume never influanced one. He has, I think, four brothers, all but one Republicans, and that one, as you know, a conservative Democratic Member of Congress." Grant, it seemed, knew the rules of the war, but he had misplayed his hand. Within weeks, his order denying harbor to freed slaves was canceled.[9]

In the deep South Grant's army encountered the kind of slavery which horrified the civilized world. The huge plantations of southern Louisiana and Mississippi operated like smooth-running machines, with slaves the necessary cogs in the wheels of sugar and cotton production. Few masters were stupid enough to use field hands like Simon Legree did—Mrs. Stowe's fictional plantation was set near Grant's Louisiana works—but only because it didn't pay. There were exceptions, such as the benevolent community at Davis Bend, but the dehumanized factories were repugnant even to apologists. Perhaps it was the search for any kind of vitality that brought thousands of blacks—"like oncoming cities"—into Union lines. They crowded together along roads and begged for work or safety. "There was no plan in this exodus, no Moses to lead it," remembered Chaplain John Eaton of the 27th Ohio Regiment. "Unlettered reason or the more inarticulate decision of instinct brought them to us. Often the slaves met prejudices against their own color more bitter than any they had left behind." But there was no way to care for them. "There were men, women, and children in every stage of disease or decrepitude, often nearly naked, with flesh torn by the terrible experiences of their escapes. Sometimes they were intelligent and eager to help themselves; often they were bewildered or stupid or possessed by the wildest notions of what liberty might mean—expecting to exchange labor, and obedience to the will of another, for idleness and freedom from restraint. Such ignorance and perverted notions produced a veritable moral chaos. Cringing deceit, theft, licentiousness—all the vices which slavery inevitably fosters—were the hideous companions of nakedness, famine and disease. A few had profited by the misfortunes of the master and were jubilant in their unwonted ease and luxury, but these stood in lurid contrast to the grimmer aspects of the tragedy—the women in travail, the helplessness of childhood and old age, the horrors of sickness and of frequent death. Small wonder that men paused in bewilderment and panic, foreseeing the demoralization and infection of the Union soldier and the downfall of the Union cause."

Grant assigned the blacks to Chaplain Eaton, promised the minister he would do all he could to help, and pretty much forgot about the problem. Policy was being dictated by Washington, and Washington—as Henry Halleck wrote confidentially—wanted the Army to strip plantations of all able-bodied blacks. "You may rely on my carrying out any policy ordered by proper authority to the best of my ability," Grant replied.[10]

He was feeling a little testy just then about his ability to further either the Union's or his own cause. The press was hounding him again for wasting lives in unproductive sallies at the Mississippi mud. Soldiers were sending home graphic accounts of comrades collapsing into swamplands. Cholera was only one of the diseases mentioned, and tales of no land dry enough even to dig graves made front-page news. Grant wrote letters to Halleck and Washburne denying the reports. And he tried to sweeten the press's attitude toward him by revoking a subordinate's order outlawing distribution of the anti-war, Democratic Chicago *Times*. He should have saved himself the effort. "Your man Grant has shown his cloven foot and proves himself to be little better than a secesh," Joseph Medill, editor of the rival Chicago *Tribune,* wrote Elihu Washburne after learning about Grant's order. Grant, he said, had lost all support from *"loyal*—that is Republican—officers and men. . . . He stands confessed as a copperhead and openly encourages the dessemination of secession and treason in his army. . . . I write to you because it is through your influence mainly that he holds the trust which he thus betrays. . . . We have kept off of him on your account. We could have made him stink in the nostrils of the public like an old fish had we properly criticized his military blunders. Look at that miserable and costly campaign into northern Miss. when he sent crazy Sherman to Vicksburg and agreed to meet him there by land. Was there ever a more weak and imbecile campaign? But we forbore exposing him to the excrutiation of the people. But I assure that if he has become the patron saint and protector of the secession again we shall not be so tender on him in the future." Washburne apparently passed the word to Grant that he need not be so easy on the opposition press. Grant, who kept two journalists at headquarters, was free to act upon his own instincts. As he told Julia in mid-February, he wanted to see the Lincoln administration "commence a war" against all outspoken critics. "They should suppress the disloyal press and confine during the war the noisy and most influential of the advocates."

He never had any deeply felt notions about civil liberty, nor did he care much about political principles. Grant believed that the best way of handling vexatious demonstrations of pluralism was straightforward power. He began to come down harder on suspected Army malcontents—dispatching them out of the department under threat of imprisonment—he ordered a Memphis newspaper editor arrested, and he unhesitatingly agreed to the banishment and seizure of property of pro-Confederate civilians in Memphis. He was acting with the tacit approval of the Lincoln administration—approval Henry Halleck hinted at in a March 20 letter. "The character of the war has very much changed with in the last year," Halleck wrote. "There is now no possible hope of a reconciliation with the rebels. The union party in the south is virtually destroyed. There can be no peace but that which is enforced with the sword. We must conquer the rebels, or be conquered by them. The north must either destroy the slave-oligarchy, or become slaves themselves—the manufacturers—mere hewers of wood and drawers of water to southern aristocrats.

This is the phase which the rebellion has now assumed. We must take things as they are."[11]

Two weeks after reading Halleck's letter, Grant wrote to a subordinate saying that the rebellion "has assumed that shape now that it can only terminate by the complete subjugation of the South or the overthrow of the Government it is our duty therefore to use every means to weaken the enemy by destroying their means of cultivating their fields, and in every other way possible." Grant was calling for a scorched-earth policy, and he got it. The Army of the Tennessee succeeded in restoring much of northern Louisiana and Mississippi to a wilderness. "Our men have treated these people too roughly to suit my taste," William Sherman wrote headquarters, "and they are encouraged in it by many officers. There are some widows who have large families of young children or girls, and no sons who have been stript of nearly every thing they had to eat and of all means of making crops. In such cases, it is my intention to give up teams & sufficient to prevent distress. Am I right?"

He was wrong.[12]

Grant had no special affection for administering even a belligerent peace. What he wanted to do, as he said to Julia, was to get at the enemy and fight. And he couldn't seem to do that. The management of slaves and widows and politicians only dragged at his heels and added to his frustration. He fell back on the kind of hearty optimism he'd summoned up earlier in his life for probable failures. "We are going through a campaign here such as has not been heard of on this continant before," he told Elihu Washburne in mid-March. That was true, but Grant wasn't talking about the engineering failures. His command was in such good shape, he said, that Vicksburg would be reduced in a month. Why didn't the congressman come down to Louisiana and get in on the fun? The strained politicking was mostly bravado. He was dangerously close to depression. Grant was drinking again, a dissatisfied subordinate said, and Grant's friends had had to call in Julia more than once to look after her husband. Though the officer's story was taken as sour grapes, Grant's staff knew their chief needed watching. Rawlins stepped up his vigilance.

Though he claimed his health was excellent, Grant suffered from indigestion and a painful case of boils. His mouth was sore, and to make matters worse, his servant threw out his false teeth— the only set he had. Grant mumbling and gumming his food seemed an appropriate corollary to all his other ills. And he was also having recurrent sick headaches. Julia was the only person who could relieve the excruciating pain with her cure of vinegar water and mustard plasters. But it was her presence which helped most.[13]

Julia had left Holly Springs and gone to Memphis when Grant went to Louisiana. On April 6 Grant ordered her to come down to Milliken's Bend and she obediently bundled their children aboard the *Tigress* and got under way.[14] Grant also wanted his family to watch his final effort at reaching the enemy. He had decided to give up engineering in favor of an all-or-nothing run down the Mississippi right under Vicksburg's nose. Sherman was convinced it wouldn't work. The War Department took an equally dim view of the new plan, but Lincoln gave the go-ahead. Though another disaster would inspire the peace movement, a try at running Vicksburg's batteries was better than stalling. Weeks earlier Rawlins, Wilson, Sherman, and a handful of other Grant subordinates talked about Vicksburg on the headquarters boat. Sherman was still convinced it could be captured by land from the north. Others were uncertain how it could be taken. Rawlins said there was only one possibility left, to run the batteries with a fleet of ironclads. Others said it couldn't be done without terrible loss of life and prestige. Grant remained silent.[15]

April 16 was clear and warm. Eleven boats were strung up along the Mississippi's shore. With coal barges lashed to gunwales and decks piled with water-soaked cotton bales, the ironclads were ready to go. Grant came out on the upper deck of his headquarters boat with Julia at dusk, and they sat together while Rawlins, Dana, and various clerks and aides quietly joined them. Wilson took a chair near the Grants, and little Jesse crawled into his lap. The boat got under way.

Grant's skipper anchored near the Louisiana shore and killed the engines. The general stuck a cigar in his mouth and reached for Julia's hand. Just before ten o'clock, Dana took out his notebook. "It was a strange scene," he wrote. "First a mass of black things detached itself from the shore, and we saw it float out toward the middle of the stream. There was nothing to see but this big mass, which dropped slowly down the river. Soon another black mass detached itself, and another, then another. It was Admiral Porter's fleet of ironclad turtles, steamboats, and barges. They floated down the Mississippi darkly and silently, showing neither steam nor light, save occasionally a signal astern, where the enemy could not see it." But the enemy knew they were coming. Just before the flotilla moved under Vicksburg's guns, Confederates on the opposite shore torched a frame house, flooding the river with light. The batteries—four miles of artillery, stacked in layers up the Vicksburg bluffs—opened fire. Porter's ironclads answered. Little Jesse Grant threw his arms around Wilson's neck and the headquarters boat tensed into anxious silence. Grant would later say the cannonade was "magnificent, but terrible." At the time, he just chewed on his cigar and held Julia's hand. For two hours and more the blasts went on. Then, around one o'clock, the noise died out and once again the river was dark. No one spoke as the pilot started the engines of the headquarters boat, but the same question was on everyone's mind. Had the boats gotten through?

Before dawn, Grant rode seventeen swampland miles from Milliken's Bend to New Carthage to see the result. Excepting some burned boats and a scuttled transport, everything was safe. Not one life was lost.[16]

Grant knew what had to be done could be done. Now he wanted to do it quickly. He issued orders for transports and barges filled with medical supplies, provisions, and equipment to make a southward run past Vicksburg on April 22. He sent Julia back north. He called James McPherson, who had been in Louisiana, to join

McClernand's corps at New Carthage. He was in the saddle most of the day, in his chair most of the night dashing off quick notes and orders. All the elements of mounting a campaign with 100,000 soldiers had to run smoothly. Troops were to march south along a route which skirted swampland west of the river. They were to assemble on the Louisiana shore opposite Grand Gulf, Mississippi, wait for Admiral Porter's gunboats to reduce the Confederate fortress there, then cross. This would put the army well south of Vicksburg—a site Confederate defenders hadn't thought about, which was just the point. Grant needed speed if he were to outwit the Mississippians. On April 24 he left Milliken's Bend for his own ride south. Weaving in and out between marching soldiers, he often as not called to them to hurry, and got a nod in return. The men never cheered him.

The army—or at least a portion of it—seemed incapable of the kind of quickness demanded by its commander. This jeopardized the plan for coordinating the crossing with a feint Sherman was to make north of Vicksburg. McClernand held a review to introduce his new bride to the joys of campaigning, when he should have been collecting his men on the shores of the Mississippi. And those shores were proving problematic. When Porter took on the batteries of Grand Gulf, he nearly lost his entire river fleet. After seven hours of shelling, Grand Gulf's Confederate guns were not reduced. It was obvious to his staff that Grant was pressed, and they admired the way he handled it. Dana said he never even heard Grant curse.[17]

But Grant did give signs of impatience to his family. He wrote a curt note to Julia ordering her to go to St. Louis and handle the technicalities of what should have been a jolly stroke of revenge—paying cash for Lewis Dent's Wish-ton-Wish and reclaiming Hardscrabble. And he wrote an even more sour letter to his father. Alluding to Jesse's failed cotton venture, he said Army followers who speculated "off the misfortunes of their country" were "aiding the enemy more than they possibly could do by open treason," and should be "drafted at once and put in the first forlorn hope." But he defensively told his father he was doing his "best" and was "full of hope for complete success. Time has been consumed but it was absolutely impossible to avoid it. An attack upon the rebel works at any time since I arrived here must have inevitably resulted in the loss of a large portion of my Army if not in an entire defeat. . . . I never expected to have an army under my command whipped unless it is very badly whipped and *cant help it* but I have no idea of being driven to do a desperate or foolish act by the howlings of the press. . . . I have never saught a large command and have no ambitious ends to accomplish. Was it not for the very natural desire of proving myself equal to anything expected of me, and the evidence of my removal would afford that I was not thought equal to it, I would gladly accept a less responsible position."[18]

The letter was written when Grant was just shy of his forty-first birthday—and in command of an entire army. He might have written similarly to Jesse from West Point or Oregon or St. Louis, or expressed the same feelings hauling wood in Ohio, so little had his need to measure up changed. It was understandable he would tell his father about his "natural desire" to prove himself equal to superiors' expectations. Jesse was the author of that nature. But the twinge of self-justification—he was doing his best; the delays were not his fault—was troubling just then. At the end of April he controlled 100,000 men—an army he swore would never be beaten except by being "very badly whipped." Even then it wouldn't be his fault.

Grant knew he was expected to cross the river, and on April 29, stymied by the guns at Grand Gulf, he tried another tack. With the aid of a black Mississippian who knew the area, he chose a spot farther south than Grand Gulf, and headed down to Bruinsburg. On April 30—set aside by President Lincoln "as a day of national humiliation, fasting and prayer" to aid a nation which had "forgotten God"—Grant left the cabin of his headquarters boat and stepped onto the shore in Mississippi. "When this was effected I felt a degree of relief scarcely ever equalled since," he wrote. "Vicksburg was not yet taken it is true, nor were its defenders demoralized by any of our previous moves. I was now in the enemy's country, with a vast river and the stronghold of Vicksburg between me and my base of supplies. But I was on dry ground on the same side of the river with the enemy."[19]

LEE ON APRIL 30 knew that his four months of waiting and watching were over. "Fighting Joe" Hooker had crossed the Rapidan River west of Fredericksburg and was heading south. Lee issued orders for a contingent of his army to stay in Fredericksburg and keep an eye on a corps of Federals still in place across the Rappahannock. Then he rode west on the plank road toward a wide spot in the woods known as Chancellorsville.

He had spent the first two weeks of April more or less confined to bed in a neighboring farmhouse. Though he confessed to being weak on his "pins," and told Mary he was "feeble and worthless," he said his doctors thought he was threatened "with some malady which must be dreadful if it resembles its name, but which I have forgotten." He said he hadn't been "so very sick though have suffered a good deal of pain in my chest, back, & arms. It came on in paroxysms, and was quite sharp & seemed to me to be a mixture of your's and Agnes' diseases." The doctors were treating him with quinine, and "have been tapping me all over like an old steam boiler before condemning it." Neither Lee nor his doctors knew what troubled him. It took later, more sophisticated diagnosticians to arrive at the conclusion that he suffered from angina. The high color which associates always complimented in Lee's face and the increasing girth—he ordered a new jacket and instructed the tailor to add several inches to the "horizontal" measurement—were not the signs of good health and strength they were thought. Lee did not rest easy in his sickbed and he actively disliked intrusions on his privacy. He agitated to get back to his tent and insisted that Perry—an ex-slave from Arlington now a paid employee of Lee's—cook for him and bring him camp fare.[20]

He was happier back at headquarters, where his staff welcomed him warmly. Lee was a great favorite with the young men who served him. His constant teasing was accepted with only occasional irritation, and his self-conscious frugality was understood as noble self-denial. He passed up the sole slice of beef at dinner and seemed to relish hard and moldy biscuits. His one luxury was a daily egg, deposited on his camp bed by his pet hen. His illness seemed to have dissipated his early-winter snappishness, but it did not cool his ardor for getting at the enemy. He was following Grant's Mississippi campaign closely, and wrote the Secretary of War that he thought the best way to relieve pressure in the West—for he seemed to think that Grant would be successful—would be for the Army of Northern Virginia to cross the Potomac again and make a feint against Maryland. But that was not possible, he said, because of the condition of his men. "We are scattered, without forage & provisions, & could not remain long together if united for want of food." Still, it was all-important, he said, to go on the offensive after the first of May.

He didn't say how he planned to do so with fewer than 50,000 troops, but he seemed hopeful. "The war will terminate some of these days & we shall all then be at peace," he wrote Mary, who had left Richmond for what she hoped would be a rest in Shirley. "I do not think our enemies are so confident of success as they used to be. If we can baffle them in their various designs this year & our people are true to our cause & not so devoted to themselves & their own aggrandisement, I think our success will be certain. We have to suffer & must suffer to the end. But it will all come right. . . . If successful this year, next fall there will be a great change in public opinion at the North. The Republicans will be destroyed & I think the friends of peace will become so strong as that the next administration will go in on that basis. We have only to resist manfully." It was in this frame of mind that Lee heard the news that Hooker had moved at last.[21]

Federal balloons were overhead as Lee rode the lines with Stonewall Jackson the morning of April 30. Hooker's troops were clearly visible north of the Rapidan. Jackson wanted to attack then, but Lee said to wait. It would not do to throw a force against three times its number. But when Hooker sent his army across the fords of the Rapidan, Lee was ready for him. He knew he had a powerful ally in Virginia's geography, and never did his native land support him so well. Hooker was advancing straight into what was known as the Wilderness, a rolling, densely wooded tract of land bordered on the north by the Rapidan River and on the south by Spotsylvania County. What made the Wilderness such a fine place to defend was its brush-covered terrain. The large hardwoods and pines that originally had forested the region were long since gone to feed the fires at Catherine's Furnace, a relic of the state's colonial iron-smelting centers. By 1863, the Wilderness was the mournful abode of owls and small game, dense and dim, a nearly impenetrable thicket knit together by brush, saplings, woodbine, and creeper. The sole hostelry in the area—the old foursquare red brick Chancellor's House—had seen many years pass since it had welcomed an overnight visitor.

Perhaps it was the look of the Wilderness, or it may have been some character fault in Fighting Joe, but the Union army seemed spooked on May 1. It moved east toward Fredericksburg and made a few tentative thrusts at the Confederate advance, then moved back. Assuming that Hooker had lost his nerve, Lee told Jackson that Confederate cavalry had discovered that Hooker's right flank was "in the air." That meant the Union army—strung along a roughly north-south line—had its left or northern side secured by the Rapidan, while its right or southern end simply petered out in the woods. Jackson would take 28,000 men, move southwest—around Hooker's right—and come up on the weak flank. The two sat together over their maps, heads bent in earnest whispers while the orange light of the fire flickered on their profiles and whippoorwills called through the woods. It was after midnight when Jackson rose and left Lee staring at his fire. Only 18,000 men would face Hooker while Jackson was off on his hunt. Only 10,000 were left at Fredericksburg. Lee wrapped his old blue Army coat around him and lay down on the ground to sleep.

Before first light, Jackson was off. He had only fourteen miles to go, but the route was narrow, rough, and difficult to follow. By the time the advance was in place, the rear was just getting started. The damp orange clay quieted the movement, but by midmorning the officer commanding the Federal right had been told the Rebels were up to something in the woods. The officer—Oliver O. Howard, the cadet Custis Lee outdistanced at West Point—sent out a reconnaissance mission. Everything was better than fine, Howard told Hooker. The Confederate army was retreating. So it was when Jackson's 28,000 came screaming out of the woods and hit Howard's corps, surprise alone helped crumple the Federal right. By dusk, Jackson had pushed the Federals back more than two miles. By dark, fighting stopped. Jackson was eager to press his advantage and took a few aides for a ride toward the Rapidan—he wanted to see how easily he could cut off retreat should Hooker make a run for the river in the morning. Satisfied that it was possible to take the entire army, Jackson turned back toward his lines. In the anxious dark, his own men thought he was a Union officer and opened fire. Jackson caught at his left arm, reeled, and began to topple forward. An aide hurried to his side and propped him upright, grabbed for the reins of the horse, and struck for the woods. They hit a small copse of trees, and Jackson was swept to the ground by a low branch. He was bleeding heavily by the time the surgeons got to him.

Lee was sleeping soundly at two-thirty in the morning when a courier from Jackson arrived. The young officer told the general the great news of Stonewall's success, and recounted the hours-long battle. Finally, quietly, he said that Jackson had been wounded. Lee started, moaned, and jumped to his feet. "Ah," he cried, "don't talk about it; thank God it is no worse," and tears welled in his eyes. In time, composed, he questioned the officer about the placement of Jackson's men. When he heard that Hooker had his back to the Rapidan, he pulled on his boots. "Those people must be pressed today," he said.

Jackson's command had fallen to A. P. Hill—the red-shirted general who had saved the day at Sharpsburg—but Hill had been wounded in the salvo that took out Stonewall. Cavalry leader J. E. B. Stuart was the next ranking officer on the field, and he eagerly accepted command. If the Confederacy was enthralled with Stonewall Jackson, it was enamored of Jeb Stuart. Tall, auburn-haired, and broad of chest, Stuart satisfied Southerners' romantic yearnings for a cavalier. Dressed in a gold-laced uniform trimmed in golden satin and topped by a soft felt hat which anchored a long plume, he seemed the very flower of the Old South. Stuart was a superb horseman, and was adept at playing war as a kind of game—a talent which not only endeared him to his men but also captivated the hearts of the population. He kept a band of minstrels on his staff which entertained nightly at his headquarters. Parties, balls, reviews, and theatricals livened up Stuart's command. Given an assignment from Lee, he was sure to complete it in ways that dazzled both friend and enemy. Just before the battles on the Peninsula, he had led his cavalry on a ride around the entire Union army—a feat that exceedingly embarrassed McClellan. It was Stuart who penetrated General Pope's headquarters prior to Second Manassas. He made off not only with important documents but also with a suit of Pope's clothes and left behind a bottle of champagne and a clever note. And it was Stuart who probed farther north than any other Confederate during the Antietam campaign, singing "J'in the Cavalry" while a banjo-playing sidekick tried to keep up the pace.

Stuart was in the saddle on the morning of May 3. If the Stonewall Brigade had doubts about following Stuart, they soon got over them. Waving a sword and urging the troops forward, Stuart rode up and down his lines, pausing now and then to point his body Union-ward and break into a taunting song—"Old Joe Hooker, Won't You Come Out and Fight?" The refrain was beat out by two dozen Confederate guns which raked the retreating Yankees. By midmorning, Stuart had pushed Jackson's troops into a solid phalanx which drove the Federals into a confused mass. A well-placed Confederate shot landed squarely on the porch of Mr. Chancellor's house, splintering the white wooden columns and startling Hooker, who had sought refuge there. The shock seemed to scramble his thinking, for he lurched off northward on foot, followed by subordinates who kept asking him to turn over command.

Not far away, Lee sat impassively in the burning woods while his men flung themselves at the Federals and the Federals fell back. Around ten o'clock he rode slowly west on the Orange plank road, and turned north to see for himself how bad were

Hooker's fortunes. The field was littered with abandoned caissons, dying artillery horses, discarded muskets and haversacks— the detritus of a routed army. He knew then that he had won. His aide Charles Marshall went with him and never forgot the scene.

"The fierce soldiers with their faces blackened with the smoke of battle, the wounded crawling with feeble limbs from the fury of the devouring flames, all seemed possessed with a common impulse. One long, unbroken cheer, in which the feeble cry of those who lay helpless on the earth blended with the strong voices of those who still fought, rose high above the roar of battle, and hailed the presence of the victorious chief. He sat in the full realization of all that soldiers dream of—triumph; and as I looked upon him in the complete fruition of the success which his genius, courage, and confidence in his army had won, I thought that it must have been from such a scene that men in ancient days rose to the dignity of gods."

Like all epic moments, Lee's glory at Chancellorsville was marred. As he sat his horse, viewing the scene of his victory, a note arrived from Stonewall Jackson, congratulating his commander on the battle. Lee's voice broke as he directed Marshall to write a reply. Tell Jackson the victory is his, Lee said. Tell him that for the good of the country I wish I had been wounded in his stead.

Lee sent other messages to Jackson during the next five days— as he directed the Confederate attempt to regain land lost to the Federals at Fredericksburg while his back was turned; as Hooker's army once again slipped away under cover of darkness; as he worried and prayed for Jackson. "Surely, General Jackson must recover," Lee said when he heard that Stonewall's strength was ebbing away after the amputation of his arm—his left arm, ironically, the one he always believed was bad. "God will not take him from us, now that we need him so much. Surely he will be spared to us, in answer to the many prayers which are offered for him!" On Sunday, May 10, he sent a message to Jackson by an Army chaplain. "Give him my love," Lee said, "and tell him that I wrestled in prayer for him last night, as I never prayed, I believe, for myself." But Jackson was drifting away. He requested his favorite hymn—"Shew pity, Lord; O Lord, Forgive; Let a Repenting Rebel Live"—and muttered under his breath, ordering assaults. "A. P. Hill," he commanded, "prepare for action." At midafternoon, he rallied himself, tried to sit, and in that oddly sweet, soft voice, invited his army to peace. "Let us pass over the river, and rest under the shade of the trees."[22]

There was no way to replace the man Lee called "great and good" and no time to mourn him—Lee even had to refuse a request to allow veterans of the Stonewall Brigade to accompany the dead general's body to Richmond. The government, it seemed, was trying to take away a portion of Lee's army, and he found himself struggling—at a distance—with Ulysses Grant. On the day Jackson died, Lee wrote Seddon arguing against sending part of Longstreet's corps to Vicksburg. It would weaken the Army of Northern Virginia, he told the Secretary of War. Hooker's army was getting reinforcements—his aggregate strength, Lee thought, was over 159,000. "You can therefore see the odds against us and decide whether the line of Virginia is more in danger than the line of the Mississippi." As a final argument, Lee said that his Virginians "would be greatly endangered by the climate" around Vicksburg. And even if Virginia troops were sent, they would not arrive until the end of May. "If anything is done in that quarter, it will be over by that time as the climate in June will force the enemy to retire."[23]

Grant had no intention of retiring, but Lee didn't know that. Lee knew the name, not the man. And U. S. Grant, who smarted under the ongoing implied censure of the northern public, found himself not only unredeemed by his Mississippi pluck but largely ignored as the press published more and more stories about the invincible Robert Lee. Grant knew the name.

ON THE DAY Lee officially announced the death of Stonewall Jackson, May 11, Grant was proclaiming news of a very different nature.

"My forces will be this evening as far advanced towards Fourteen Mile Creek—the left near Black River and extending in a line nearly east and west—as they can get without bringing on a general engagement. I shall communicate with Grand Gulf no more except it becomes necessary to send a train with heavy escort. You may not hear from me again for several days." The note was addressed to Henry Halleck in Washington, and was written from Cayuga, Mississippi. The final sentence was a good indication of Grant's mood. His telling Halleck he would be incommunicado was less an explanation than it was a command. He was saying I am too busy for such foolishness as reporting to Army headquarters.

One week earlier he had gotten the last of his 23,000 soldiers across the Mississippi River and had turned north to transform the fort at Grand Gulf from a Confederate stronghold to a Union base. He was in the saddle from dawn until past midnight every day, and the little time he spent resting was used for cranking out no-nonsense directives to subordinates. He was urging speed and boldness and he was usually on hand to see that he got it. "Push right along, men," he said quietly around the cigar he chewed. "Close up fast and hurry." The men nodded, sometimes doffed their hats and gave him a "Good morning, General," or "Pleasant day, General," and walked on. Grant never aroused the kind of misty-eyed cheering Lee did, but he attracted what one of his subordinates thought a "certain sort of familiar reverence." They said they admired "his energy and his disposition to do something," and they also liked his simplicity. The midwestern boys who had sloughed around in the mud of the Mississippi for three months liked him because of his lack of "superfluous flummery," the absence of which had nearly cost him a commission at the outset of the war. "Everything Grant directs is right," enthused one of the men. "His soldiers believe in him." He was described as a "man who could be silent in several languages," and when he did talk on the march was as likely to discuss "Illinois horses, hogs, cattle, and farming" as he was "the business actually at hand." And the business at hand was handled "with so little friction and noise that it required a second look to be sure that he was doing anything at all." Grant, said a campaigning journalist, "has none of the soldier's bearing about him, but is a man whom one would take for a country merchant or a village lawyer. He had no distinctive feature; there are a thousand like him in personal appearance in the ranks. A plain, unpretending face, with a comely, brownish-red beard and a square forehead, of short stature and thick-set. He is we would say a good liver, and altogether an unpronounceable man." There was no nonsense about Grant, one of the officers noted, "no sentiment; only a plain business man of the republic, there for the one single purpose of getting that command across the river in the shortest time possible." Once he had the campaign moving forward Grant was infused with new energy and purpose. "None who had known him the previous years could recognize him as being the same man. . . . From this time his genius and his energies seemed to burst forth with new life." The usually torpid commander "seemed wrought up to the last pitch of determination and energy."[24]

The determination arose from Grant's freedom to move. The very thing he was accomplishing was an expression of that unnamable power which others had sensed in him over the years. Grant saw the Civil War—had seen all wars, actually—as inchoate energy and empty space. The energy could be formed into armies. The space could be tamed—or "annihilated" as he liked to say— by disciplining it the way a painter divides an empty canvas. He moved his army in his mind, blocking in first one area, then another as he filled the space with strokes of conquered armies and fallen cities. He had given signs of this talent before. Ohio representative Tom Hamer was the first to recognize the way in which young Lieutenant Grant clarified the mysteries of battles for him in Mexico. There were others—Rawlins, Julia, Julia's mother, cohorts in Michigan and New York, and drinking buddies in St. Louis—who knew Grant had an uncommon ability to reduce military matters to simple geometry. Sherman said that he had "a much quicker perception of things" than Grant, but Grant balanced "the present and remote so evenly that results follow in natural course." Sherman was only slightly wide of the mark. Results seemed to follow in "natural course" only because Grant, beginning with nothing, directed what followed. But he wasn't always successful at keeping control. War as empty space was what got him in trouble at Shiloh—he ignored the possibility that anyone else might be dabbling on his canvas. But Mississippi was in fact nearly empty.

The Confederate army was more or less useless. Many able-bodied white Mississippians were with Robert Lee in Virginia. Most able-bodied black men were either serving Grant's army as ditch diggers and janitors or sequestered from the advancing Federals. Jefferson Davis had made a trip to his home state the previous December and had promised legislators that Vicksburg would be defended. Davis somewhat reluctantly gave command of the western theater to Joe Johnston and charged him with the safekeeping of Mississippi. Unfortunately, safekeeping meant different things to the two men. Davis wanted to defend land. Johnston wanted to defend armies. Vicksburg commander John Pemberton was accused by some Mississippians of not wanting to defend either, and found himself sitting on a fence erected by his superiors. Defend Vicksburg at all costs, Davis said. Abandon Vicksburg and save your army, Johnston said. Pemberton tried to do a little of both, and accomplished neither. But his greatest failing was his inability to understand Grant. The Confederate general entertained the ladies of Vicksburg with reassuring propositions about meeting Grant's army on its northward march. He had indeed defended the southern approaches to Vicksburg, but Grant wasn't going there.

While Pemberton rested certain, Grant was uncharacteristically zigzagging his course toward the enemy. He decided to head due east and take care of Jackson, the state capital, before turning westward against Vicksburg. Sherman told Grant he was crazy to set off inland with no certain route of supply. But Grant believed that the army could live very nicely on the countryside, and ordered up most of the troops who guarded Grand Gulf. He knew his plan was much less risky than it seemed. In the Mexican War he had provided his regiment with food and transportation from the land over which Winfield Scott's army marched. Compared with Mexico, Mississippi was a breadbasket, and Grant knew it could supply his army. Issuing commands to take whatever was needed and destroy the rest, Grant set off eastward heeled by an increasingly zany batch of invaders leaving an increasingly devastated wake. With few wagons to run food and ammunition back and forth, the Army of the Tennessee impressed from local plantations whatever vehicles it could commandeer—stylish carriages, buckboards, hay wagons, surreys, sleds, coaches, and ambulances. The troops quick-stepped through the countryside, which Grant said "stood on end," tearing down houses for bridge building and gathering furnishings to outfit themselves with camp necessities. Virtually alone among Union commanders, Sherman balked at what he thought was the unnecessary ruin of Mississippi, but Grant had implicitly okayed scorched Confederate earth. The rebellion had taken a hard turn, he had said, it must be ended in hard ways.

His troops had no difficulty adjusting to a policy of ruin. Louisiana, and Mississippi were the Deep South of magnolias and moonlight and unrivaled luxury. Broad, tree-lined avenues led to mansions surrounded by wide verandas. Huge gardens burst with May's bloom of roses, osage oranges, and exotic subtropicals, while fish caught in the Mississippi for absent masters' dinner tables circled slowly in pools sunk by kitchen walls. Storehouses bulged with corn and hams. After house slaves were run off and stores were transported to campsites, more often than not the boys had some fun in the form of slashing portraits, hacking moldings, burning furniture, and ripping curtains. Not a few venerable and symbolic southern silver teapots could be found wedged into Illinois haversacks. Orders were strict about protecting the property of known Union supporters, but everything else was overlooked by officers as high-spirited animosity.

Grant had no time to concern himself with the extracurricular activities of his army, but he shared his men's good spirits. "Two days more, or Tuesday next, must bring on the fight which will settle the fate of Vicksburg," he wrote Julia before setting off inland. "No Army ever felt better than this one does nore more confidant of sucsess. Before they are beaten they will be very badly beaten. They look for nothing of the kind and could not be brought to a realizing sense of such a possibility before the fact. Important news will no doubt follow close upon this. I am very well camping in the forests of Mississippi. People all seem to stay at home and show less signs of fear than one would suppose. These people talk a great deel about the barbarities of the Yankees."[25]

A couple of hard-fought battles with troops Pemberton sent from Vicksburg brought Grant to the outskirts of Jackson, and the town surrendered. He was welcomed to the capital by his son Fred, who had set off with Charles Dana from the headquarters boat on the river. Young Grant and Dana rode into Jackson just as the Rebels left. So precipitate was the Confederate flight that when Grant and his aides walked into the local hotel, the flustered innkeeper showed him into a room he said Joe Johnston had occupied the night before. Grant had Sherman accompany him on what must have been an exceedingly satisfying tour of the town. The two poked into the railway terminal and post office, and found a fabric mill where female workers were still turning out gray cloth marked "CSA." Grant said he thought the women had done enough. Sherman told them to gather up all the material they could carry and get out. Moments later the factory was burned to the ground.

That night, most of Jackson burned. Smarting under censure from old southern friends, Sherman years later insisted he had ordered only the firing of strategically important buildings. Another, equally defensive Union man blamed the fire on the citizens of Jackson as well as "some stragglers and bummers from the ranks of the Union army. . . . The streets were filled with people, white and black, who were carrying away all the stollen goods they could stagger under, without the slightest attempt at concealment and without let or hindrance from citizens or soldiers." Townsfolk applied to Grant's headquarters for protection. None got it. Grant was thinking ahead. He'd just read a letter from Secretary of War Stanton which made his way all that clearer.

"General Grant," Stanton wrote to Charles Dana, "has full and absolute authority to enforce his own commands, to remove any person who, by ignorance, inaction, or any cause, interferes with or delays his operations. He has the full confidence of the

Government, is expected to enforce his authority, and will be firmly and heartily supported; but he will be responsible for any failure to exert his powers." The story of Stanton's letter to Dana had its beginnings in Dana's complaints to the War Department about Lincoln's Illinois pet and Grant's nemesis, John McClernand. Stanton was saying that Grant could shelve McClernand anytime he wanted. But he was also communicating something far more significant. Grant, Stanton wrote, "has the full confidence of the Government." He had the unequivocal support of Lincoln, and Lincoln was commander-in-chief.[26]

Grant's route from Jackson was almost due west, straight to Vicksburg. Pemberton was still attempting to sit on the defensive fence. The day Grant rode into Jackson, the retreating Johnston ordered Pemberton to bring out the Vicksburg troops and join with his army for a last stand. Pemberton refused. But on May 16, Pemberton and 20,000 men set off—too late to join Johnston— to keep Grant out of Vicksburg. The Confederates stopped at a place called Champion's Hill, which was more of a deep-fissured rise than anything else, only 140 feet high and wooded. They waited and looked east for Grant, who soon arrived with his 29,000. What ensued was a five-hour battle described by a Union officer as "one of the most obstinate and murderous conflicts of the war."

By May 17, Grant was on the Big Black, the final river between him and Vicksburg. Headed by James Wilson, a quasi corps of engineers—farm boys mainly, accustomed to fencing and improvising on western plains—were throwing up cotton bales, cannibalized farmhouses, and everything else they could get their hands on to use as bridging materials. The next day, Grant kept going until he got to the base of the bluffs. After four grueling months the army was at Vicksburg.

The prize Grant wanted was within his grasp. The next day, he ordered a "general charge of all the corps along the whole line." He expected his men to keep right on charging through Vicksburg's defenses. It came as something of an unpleasant surprise to everyone when those hills erupted in musket and artillery fire. The repulse was unimaginable to Grant. His army, he had boasted only recently, would never be whipped unless it was badly whipped. So he instructed Rawlins to write another general order for another try. In what would be the first clock-timed battle in history, the assault of May 22 began precisely at 10 A.M.[27]

Union soldiers broke out of their positions at the base of Vicksburg's backside, pressed their muskets to their chests, and trotted up the hill in double time carrying ladders to scale the parapets. They were met with murderous musket fire, broken at intervals by cannonballs lighted by hand and rolled down the hill. By noon, Grant's men knew they had been whipped. Several hours later the general reluctantly agreed. They hadn't been badly beaten—just over 3,000 of them had been killed and wounded—but they had been beaten.

"Today an attempt was made to carry the City by assault," Grant telegraphed Henry Halleck in Washington, "but was not entirely sucsessful. We hold possession however of some of the enemy's forts and have skirmishers close under all of them. Our loss was not severe." Two days later he was a little more candid but no less defensive. "I attempted to carry the place by storm on the 22d but was unsuccessful," he admitted. "Our troops were not repulsed from any point but simply failed to enter the works of the enemy. . . . The whole loss for the day will probably reach 1500 killed & wounded." The actual count was double, but even that hadn't been his fault, he claimed. "Gen. McClernands dispatches misled me as to the real state of facts and caused much of this loss." He had gotten one of McClernand's boastful messages during the battle and decided to press what he thought was the Illinois general's advantage. Sherman advised against it, saying he didn't believe McClernand. Grant went ahead because McClernand's message underwrote—flimsily—his own desires. When the assault failed, Grant was free to point the finger at McClernand, a man who had lost the protection of their mutual friend in Washington.

The contested land was in such intolerable condition by May 25 that John Pemberton wrote Grant a letter from Vicksburg asking "in the name of humanity" for "a cessation of hostilities for 2½ hours, that you may be enabled to remove your dead and dying men. If you can not do this, on notification from you that hostilities will be suspended on your part for the time specified, I will endeavor to have the dead buried and the wounded cared for." At six o'clock that evening, Federal burial parties, nervously waving white flags, crept out of their trenches and began the nasty job of picking up corpses. That done, there was nothing to do but hunker down and wait out a siege.[28]

Grant's men were determined to make the best of it. When the burial crews went out to clean up after the May 22 assault, most of the army followed. Confederates hopped over their defense works and welcomed their visitors. It happened that Federals from Missouri, cresting the Union assault three days earlier, discovered former neighbors manning Confederate outposts. Now, relatives found one another, introduced new friends and enemies all around, and commenced trading stories, newspapers, tobacco, and food.[29]

Vicksburg had been staunchly Unionist at Mississippi's Secession Convention, but with the vote to go out, supported the war, which seemed far away for two years. Handsome homes, built high above flower-filled gardens to catch breezes, continued to house dinner parties, musicales, amateur theatricals, and poetry readings. The clock on the courthouse square chimed lazy hours while townsfolk strolled up streets shaded with old hardwoods to pay afternoon calls. But by mid May 1863, Emma Balfour, wife of a Vicksburg physician, wrote in her diary: "Oh, will God forsake us now?" The following day she wondered what "is to become of all living things in this place when the boats commence shelling—God only knows—shut up as in a trap—no ingress or egress—and thousands of women and children. . . ."

Siege guns on both sides of town—mounted on boats on the river and settled on semi-permanent housings on the invested eastern slopes—shelled the town twenty-four hours a day. With houses tumbling around them and no safe place to hide, people cut warrens for themselves in the smooth gray clay. Being a necessary adaptation of the southern house, the Vicksburg caves were uncommonly civilized. Often of more than one room, connected by narrow corridors and curtained off for privacy, the caves were furnished with chairs and tables, bedsteads and drapes. Housekeepers hung family portraits on the walls and covered the damp earth with oriental carpets. Vicksburg's Sky Parlor, a fanciful pavilion built on one of the highest hills, was crowded with the sleepless who watched the shells crisscrossing overhead in the night. Mortars were the worst, "for if they explode before reaching the ground which they generally do, the pieces fly in all directions—the very *least* of which will kill one and most of them of sufficient weight to tear through a house from top to bottom! The parrot shells come *directly* so one can feel somewhat protected from them by getting under a wall, but when both come at once and so fast that one has not time to see where one shell is going before another comes—it wears one out."[30]

On May 26, Grant sent a letter to his brigadier on the Big Black ordering him to destroy everything he could lay his hands on, and heard several days later that the valley of the Yazoo River also had been laid waste. Such work made Sherman uneasy. Ordered to move slightly east and keep watch over ground Johnston might try to pass, Sherman wrote Grant that he found Confederate cavalry thickly posted on river approaches to plantation houses and moved the women and children behind Union lines, leaving fine houses "filled with elegant furniture & costly paintings to the chances of war." He feared the families "may appeal to the tender heart of our Commanding General." Grant quickly set him straight: "You need not fear General, my tender heart getting the better of me, so far as to send the secession ladies back to your front. On the contrary I rather think it advisable to send out every living being from your lines, and arrest all persons found within, and who are not connected with the army[.]"[31]

Though he knew the capitulation of the town was inevitable, Grant didn't want to wait. As June days lengthened into oppressively hot exercises in endurance, Grant found himself with very little to do. Sherman reported his "complaining of illness," and a few days later Charles Dana noted that Grant was "ill." The indispositions may well have been the same. In what became one of the most celebrated Grant scandals of the war, he apparently got roaring drunk on June 6 and set in motion a series of charges and countercharges that continued for more than twenty-five years. According to the best sources, Rawlins became apprehensive about Grant around the first of June. On the morning of June 6, he strode up to Grant and handed him a letter. Grant put the letter in his pocket as he boarded a steamer bound for Sartoria, Mississippi. No one ever knew when Grant read Rawlins's letter, dated 1:00 A.M., June 6.

The great solicitude I feel for the safety of this army leads me to mention what I had hoped never again to do—the subject of your drinking. This may surprise you, for I may be (and I trust am) doing you an injustice by unfounded suspicions, but if an error it better be on the side of this country's safety than in fear of offending a friend. I have heard that Dr. McMillan, at Gen. Sherman's a few days ago, induced you, notwithstanding your pledge to me, to take a glass of wine, and to-day, when I found wine in front of your tent and proposed to move it, which I did, I was told you had forbid its being taken away, for you intended to keep it until you entered Vicksburg, that you might have it for your friends; and to-night, when you should, because of the condition of your health if nothing else, have been in bed, I find you where the wine bottle has just been emptied, in the company with those who drink and urge you to do likewise, and the lack of your usual promptness of decision and clearness in expressing yourself in writing tended to confirm my suspicions. You have the *full* control of your appetite and can let drinking alone. Had you not pledged me the sincerity of your honor early last March that you would drink no more during the war, and kept that pledge during your recent campaign, you would not to-day have stood first in the world's history as a successful military leader. Your only salvation depends upon your strict adherence to that pledge. You cannot succeed in any other way. . . . If my suspicions are unfounded, let my friendship for you and my zeal for my country be my excuse for this letter; and if they are correctly founded, and you determine not to heed the admonitions and the prayers of this hasty note by immediately ceasing to touch a single drop of any kind of liquor,

no matter by whom asked or under what circumstances, let my
immediate relief from duty in this department be the result.

Nothing Rawlins ever wrote to Grant better reflected the relationship of the two men. His near-hysteria over Grant's alleged
bender had the shrill ring of a frightened dependent. He felt
himself partially—perhaps wholly—responsible for having
steered Grant into what he saw as his premier standing in "the
world's history as a successful military leader." The ambition
which had gnawed at Rawlins in Galena was in grave peril if
Grant's drinking should get out of hand. But it was also true—as
the letter clearly demonstrated—that Grant was at least open to
the kind of chiding Rawlins was giving him. When things were
going poorly for Grant—and he certainly thought they were
going poorly after the failed assault of May 22—he had a tendency
to turn from annihilating the space of his military compositions
to obliterating the space in his head. Everything was fine if he
could reach out and blend himself into Julia. But in her absence
he was vulnerable to fogging off into drink.

Rawlins's fears were well-founded. Charles Dana, who accompanied Grant on June 6, said the story of the episode was true.
Sherman, who liked to have the last—and first—word on everything, may well have had it after Rawlins's letter, following
Grant's death, appeared in an article written by a New York *Sun*
journalist. "We all knew at the time that Genl Grant would
occasionally drink too much," Sherman wrote. "He always encouraged me to talk to him frankly of this & other things and I
always noticed that he could with an hours sleep wake up perfectly sober & bright—and when anything was pending he was
invariably abstinent of drink." Sherman insisted that Lincoln also
knew about Grant's drinking habits, and didn't care. The story,
Sherman wrote, was as old "as that most wonderful series of
events which began with the Mexican War, 1846. Grants whole
character was a mystery even to himself—a combination of
strength and weakness not paralleled by any of whom I have read
in Ancient or Modern history."

Charles Dana agreed with Sherman. In an editorial in the *Sun*—presumably written by Dana and appearing under the headline "General Grant's Occasional Intoxication"—the assertion was made that Grant's "seasons" of drunkenness occurred only "once in three or four months" and never at critical moments. Grant, said Dana, "always chose a time when the gratification of his appetite for drink would not interfere with any important movement that had to be directed or attended to by him." In short, Grant had neither more nor less trouble with alcohol than half the Army. Given the universality of friends' claims that he was always willing to "own up" to his drinking or urge others, like Sherman, to "talk to him frankly" about it, he apparently wanted someone else to assume responsibility for him when his own sense of authority wavered.

The combination of strengths and weaknesses which Sherman thought made Grant a mystery even to himself was really not so complex as some observers believed. They were simply misled by Grant's quiet reserve and seeming self-confidence. The men around Grant needed him to be strong and dependable—he was commander of a large army engaged in a life-and-death struggle—so they read those qualities into him. All Grant wanted to do, as he told his father in April, was to prove himself "equal to anything" expected of him. He knew he was expected to take Vicksburg—especially since he had sworn to take it easily within a matter of days—and he experienced the failure of the May 22 assault as proof that he was not equal to the expectations of authorities. Since he had failed, he would fail completely, just as he would see that his army, if beaten, would be completely beaten. Life as an absolute contest in winning or losing was a game he had learned from his father. He played it well, but at terrible cost to himself.

Two days after his upriver trip, Grant summoned his nurse: "Having written to you to start for Vicksburg as soon as you heard the place was taken, and thinking that would be before another letter would reach you, I wrote no more," Grant told Julia. But he needed her now, not to help him celebrate the capture of the city, but to bring calm—or, as he called it, "sunshine"—to his life. "You may start down as soon as you receive this letter," he said. "If Vicksburg is not in our hands then you can remain on board the steamer at the landing with the prospect of my calling to see you occasionally. . . . I want to see you very much dear Julia and also our dear little children." He signed the letter "Ulys."[32]

The parents of Vicksburg's children would have been surprised to discover such tender need on the part of the man they considered their tormentor. Diaries were filled with notations about the strains of looking after young ones in the midst of the shelling. Emma Balfour was horrified to learn that a "child was *buried in the wall* by a piece of shell, *pinned* to it." Mary Loughbourough spent a sleepless June night in her cave listening to the moans of a mother whose child was killed in bed. "How very sad this life in Vicksburg!" As the siege continued and temperatures rose, malaria, dysentery, and malnutrition began to take their toll on the Confederate soldiers, who moved back, closer to town, and struck up friendships with Vicksburg's children. Gifts of dollhouse furniture carved by soldiers out of minié-ball lead delighted the youngsters. One girl was presented with a tiny set of cutlery made from the shell fragment dug out of her arm; another got a little bed.

All excess horses and mules were driven out of the city the first week of June; there was not enough fodder to feed the animals. By the middle of the month, there was little enough to feed anyone, and the very mules discharged two weeks earlier had become a mourned-over food loss. Eating mule meat was at first only a rumor, but it soon became real enough, and was followed by dressed rat hanging in butcher-shop windows. "Tom-cat wienerwurst" was the staple of local jokers, who slyly added, "What's become of Fido?" A local wag wrote up the "Bill of Fare" from the "Hotel de Vicksburg," offering, among other comestibles, "Mule Rump Stuffed with Rice," "Mule Tongue Cold a la Bray," "White Oak Acorns," and "Mississippi Water Vintage 1492 Superior." Jeff Davis was given as the proprietor.[33]

Union soldiers could joke that General Pemberton was being replaced by "general starvation" as head of Confederate defenses, but they were almost as miserable as their adversaries. Rebel artillery was no worry—it was seldom fired—but the haphazard nature of southern sharpshooting wrenched Union nerves. The weather was awful. When Robert Lee airily told Secretary of War Seddon that no campaign was possible at Vicksburg during June, he knew his climatology—he just hadn't reckoned with Grant's determination. The humidity had men soaked with sweat, which only made lice bites worse. Rainstorms coming up from the south were more in the nature of hurricanes than anything else, and even boys who knew midsummer lightning on the prairies quaked in trenches chest-high in water, dodging uprooted trees. There was no leaving the trenches. Nothing could live in the open, and the constant strain made men "tired, tired, tired," said one. Grant's siege had the men constantly extending and enlarging the trenches. Foot by foot, the labyrinth of redans, embrasures, and chevaux-de-frise grew upward toward the Confederate works. At one time the lines were only a hundred yards apart, and soon they were down to eighty yards. The soldiers couldn't resist the proximity and took to tossing hardtack into Confederate trenches. Sometimes they threw hand grenades, which were usually thrown back. In time the trench system was so massive that a column of men could march four abreast and unseen from one spot to another.

Grant made tours of the trenches almost every day and he hunkered down next to his soldiers to offer encouragement. "We have got them right where we want them," he'd say, adding that it was only a matter of time before Vicksburg "surrendered or starved." It was impossible for them to get supplies, Grant assured his troops. "The time must come when the last meal" would be eaten.

Charles Dana lived at Grant's headquarters—just north and to the rear of the trench lines. During the day he rode with Grant; during the night he wrote to Secretary Stanton. In time, he would say that "Grant was an uncommon fellow—the most modest, the most disinterested, and the most honest man I ever knew, with a temper that nothing could disturb, and judgment that was judicial in its comprehensiveness and wisdom. Not a great man, except morally; not an original or brilliant man, but sincere, thoughtful, deep, and gifted with courage which never faltered; when the time came to risk all, he went in like a simple-hearted, unaffected, unpretending hero, whom no ill omens could deject and no triumph unduly exalt. A social, friendly man too, fond of a pleasant joke and also ready with one; but liking above all a long chat of an evening, and ready to sit up with you all night, talking in the cool breeze in front of his tent. Not a man of sentimentality, not demonstrative in friendship, but always holding to his friends, and just even to the enemies he hated."

No sooner did the Union Army secure the northern Mississippi river approach to town than steamers arrived, loaded with well-wishers, anxious relatives, ministers and nurses, junketing politicians, sutlers and performers. It seemed impossible to keep down a circus wherever Grant's army went. Sanitary commission representatives—the Civil War version of Red Cross volunteers—arrived to dispense succor and salvation but more often than not earned raucous insults for their efforts. Grant thought the trouble was the chickens they brought. He wryly noted that the boys had eaten no meat other than "foraged" fowl for months. Radical Republicans, abolitionist clergymen, and liberal intellectuals came to check up on the army's handling of ex-slaves.

By June 1863, blacks were being actively recruited for Army duty—a policy which was strongly criticized. Especially in the West, snide jokes were common about the motives of whites trying to stay out of front lines, along with caustic comments about the inability of black men to carry guns. Grant did as he was told, making certain his subordinates worked within administration policy, all the while mollifying the sensibilities of anti-black officers. Lincoln approved Grant's handling of black recruits, and the War Department was also pleased with him. In mid-June he clamped down on all trading in Mississippi and put into effect a strict license system which made cotton trafficking and liquor smuggling much less rewarding. But none of the praise brought relief from the irritation of untangling bureaucratic snarls and waiting out a siege he didn't want. His mood was grim and he was worried about his son. His game little Fred, a headquarters favorite, was breaking down in the Mississippi heat. Julia's brother Lewis took Fred to the government-commandeered Louisiana plantation he'd been given, and that made Grant's need for Julia all the stronger.[34]

The siege was becoming routine and Union soldiers went about business as usual as if they were shooting small game. Letters home made more references to the tedium of shelling and the tiresome noise than to Vicksburg's suffering inhabitants. Even the commanders seemed to be lulled into numbness, and Admiral Porter, directing mortar fire from his gunboats on the river, could tell Grant that there was calm all around despite adding incendiary shells to his quiver and burning "a house now and then." In the city, "danger had long since ceased to cause fear," a Rebel soldier noted, "and fighting was a recreation and pastime with the majority of the men. Exploding shells and whistling bullets attracted but little notice. Even death had become so familiar that the fall of a comrade was looked upon with almost stoical indifference; eliciting, perhaps, a monosyllabic expression of pity, and most generally the remark, 'I wonder who will be the next one.' "

The heat killed a number of the wounded and sick. But hospital attendants thought the shelling was worse. The relentless noise seemed to throw patients into anxiety, and mending—always problematical during the war—was prolonged. Most of Vicksburg's hospitals lay under the flight of Union shells and mortars. Many Rebels, pulled half dead from their ditches, were finally done in by cannonballs in their beds. Northern medical units were only slightly more comfortable, but they were well staffed. Southern wards went untended as all available manpower was pressed to the front.

The streets of Vicksburg were barricaded with earthworks, a Rebel remembered, and almost deserted, save for "starving and wounded soldiers, or guards lying on the banquettes, indifferent to the screaming and exploding shells. The stores, the few that were open, looked like the ghost of more prosperous times, with their empty shelves and scant stock of goods, held at ruinous prices. . . . Palatial residences were crumbling into ruins, the walks torn up by mortar shells, the flower beds, once blooming in all the regal beauty of spring loveliness, trodden down, the shrubbery neglected. . . . Fences were torn down, and houses pulled to pieces for firewood. Even the enclosures around the remains of the revered dead were destroyed, while wagons were parked around the graveyard, horses tramping down the graves and men using the tombstones as convenient tables for their scanty meals, or a couch for uncertain slumber. Dogs howled through the streets at night; cats screamed forth their hideous cries; an army of rats, seeking food, would scamper around your very feet, across the streets and over the pavements. Lice and filth covered the bodies of the soldiers. Delicate women and little children, with pale careworn and hunger-pinched features, peered at the passerby with wistful eyes, from the caves in their hillsides."

A Vicksburg woman noted that June 25, the day Grant detonated a large mine under a Confederate outpost, was "the most horrible yet to me, because I've lost my nerve."

On the morning of July 3, 1863, a Federal officer saw white flags appear above the parapets. He signaled a cease-fire and watched as two horsemen rode toward Union lines. They carried a letter from Vicksburg commander John C. Pemberton. Dated the same day, the letter was addressed to Ulysses S. Grant:

"I have the honor to propose to you an armistice for — hours, with a view to arranging terms for the capitulation of Vicksburg—[.]"

Grant responded:

"Your note of this date is just received, proposing an armistice for several hours for the purpose of arranging terms of capitulation through commissioners to be appointed, & c.

"The useless effusion of blood you propose stopping by this course can be ended any time you may choose, by an unconditional surrender of the city and garrison. Men who have shown so much endurance and courage as those now in Vicksburg, will always challenge the respect of an adversary, and I can assure you will be treated with all the respect due to prisoners of war."

At three that afternoon, accompanied by a handful of aides, Grant sat waiting near the Jackson road for Pemberton. When the Pennsylvania native, who had gotten himself into "bad company," according to Grant, appeared over the top of the Confederate works, Grant rode out to meet him. The two generals— Grant, dressed in rumpled blue, round-shouldered, short, and scruffy; Pemberton, tall, slender, well tailored, but clearly under strain—dismounted and, leaning into one another, began to walk slowly under a live oak. Pemberton balked over the demand for unconditional surrender, but Grant refused to withdraw it. Irritably, the two turned away from one another, and the conference seemed at an end. But aides intervened, and when Grant rode back to his headquarters, it was with the promise that he would send Pemberton his final terms by ten o'clock that night.

"In conformity with agreement of this afternoon, I will submit the following proposition for the surrender of the city of Vicksburg, public stores & c. On your accepting the terms propo[sed] I will march in one Division as a guard and take possession at 8 A.M. to-morrow. As soon as rolls can be made out and paroles signed by officers and men you will be allowed to march out of our lines the officers taking with them their side arms and clothing, and the Field, Staff & Cavalry officers one horse each. The rank & file will be allowed all their clothing but no other property."

Grant had gotten at the enemy. Now they were his—30,000 of them.[35]

CHAPTER

18

WHILE GRANT WROTE the terms of Vicksburg's surrender during the night of July 3, five hundred miles to the north, Lee was bent over a table in A. P. Hill's headquarters, studying a map.

He had been eager to take on the Federal army in Pennsylvania for one last try at toppling the Lincoln administration. But now he slumped on a campstool, his eyes sunk into the fatigue which had begun building three days earlier, pondering over getting the remnants of his army safely home. It would be said that the very stars fought against Lee at Gettysburg.

The failure of the Maryland campaign had not convinced Lee that his aims of disturbing Washington were wrong. He only knew he failed. He also believed "Richmond is never so safe as when its defenders are absent." Given the "arithmetic"—as Lincoln said—of Union army numbers, defending Richmond in any face-on military way was sure to end in defeat. He had to coax the Federals away. Moreover, Lee's victory at Chancellorsville ignited the anti-war anger which had been feeding on reports of Grant's fumbling on the Mississippi—reports Lee read in northern papers. Even when Grant was safely on "dry ground on the same side of the river with the enemy," the public mood remained sullen. No one was more sensitive to the disaffection with the war than Abraham Lincoln. "My God! My God!" he moaned when news of Chancellorsville reached Washington. "What will the country say?" He knew too well.

Lincoln understood he was taking a political risk with the Emancipation Proclamation. Many midwestern Democrats called for a counterrevolution to stave off what they saw as the President's dictatorial policies. The South "cannot and ought not be subdued" on the basis of emancipation, a former governor of Illinois claimed. County Democratic conventions issued statements calling for "cessation of hostilities," stating that "we will not render support to the present Administration in carrying on its wicked abolition crusade against the South." So openly did many anti-war newspapers demand peace at any price that readers began to urge their boys in uniform to desert: "I am sorry you are engaged in this . . . unholy, unconstitutional, and hellish war . . . which has no other purpose but to free the negroes and enslave the whites. . . . Come home, if you have to desert, you will be protected." Almost an entire regiment from Illinois heeded the advice, claiming they would "lie in the woods until moss grew on their backs rather than help free the slaves." Grant had to disband another regiment when half its members deserted, leaving the other half to agitate for desertion.

Both Indiana and Illinois elected Democratic legislatures in 1862, offsetting Republican governors chosen in 1860. To counter the effect, Governor Richard Yates of Illinois adjourned his legislature, citing an obscure provision of the state constitution. Governor Oliver Perry Morton of Indiana colluded with Republicans to assure that no quorum was assembled. Morton ran Indiana for two years with no legislature and no money. "If the Cause fails," he told Edwin Stanton, "you and I will be covered with prosecutions, imprisoned, driven from the country." Stanton, undeterred by dangers in following the faith, told Morton that "if the Cause fails, I do not care to live."

No political conflict was more dramatic in the spring of 1863 than the arrest for treason of Ohio gubernatorial candidate Clement Vallandigham. After the Union debacle at Fredericksburg, Stanton sent the unsuccessful general Ambrose Burnside to Cincinnati to keep him out of trouble. But the general was apparently determined to procure some kind of political victory. On April 19—as Joe Hooker made ready to cross the Rapidan into Lee's Wilderness—Burnside issued a general order aimed at scotching Copperhead "treason" in Ohio. Vallandigham, campaigning on the Democratic ticket, made a speech which tested Burnside's order. "King Lincoln" should be dethroned, Vallandigham said. The Emancipation Proclamation should be repudiated and the North should invite Confederates to a peace conference and reestablish the old Union—without New England, if necessary. Burnside sent a company of soldiers to Vallandigham's Dayton home, where they arrested him at 2 A.M. on May 5. His trial—a military tribunal—was short. By the evening of May 6, Vallandigham had been sentenced to imprisonment for the duration of the war.

The outcry was immediate and passionate. Democrats and some Republicans denounced military meddling in a civil case and wondered "whether this war is waged to put down rebellion at the South or destroy free institutions at the North." When the court's action was upheld, mass meetings were called all over the North. "It is not merely a step toward revolution," New York's Governor Horatio Seymour declared. "It *is* revolution. . . . It establishes military despotism." By mid-May, Lincoln realized that he might have a rebellion within a rebellion on his hands. He commuted Vallandigham's sentence, ordering him sent south instead. On May 25 he was rowed across the Ohio River and pressed into the surprised and unwilling hands of the Confederate Army in Tennessee.

There was no question that Vallandigham's treatment was illegal. Nor was there much question that various war measures— suppression of newspapers, the suspension of habeas corpus, Grant's stripping suspected southern sympathizers of their property—were also extralegal. Lincoln attempted to cut through constitutional arguments and present the situation in terms of moral logic. "Must I shoot a simple-minded soldier boy who deserts," Lincoln asked a visitor, "while I must not touch a hair of a wily agitator who induces him to desert?"

Hard questions were being asked in the North in 1863, while in the South a few men with some easy answers were gaining the ear of President Davis. Alexander Stephens, the former Whig friend of Lincoln's and the current—if often absent—Vice-President of the Confederacy, believed Lee's military successes had created an opportunity to sue for peace. He wanted Davis to open negotiations. Stephens, banking on his past relationship with Lincoln, would deliver the message. Davis agreed, and even went so far as to sign himself, not as the President of the Confederate States of America (the North did not recognize any such nation), but as the commander-in-chief of the various Army and Navy forces at war with the United States. Lincoln refused to see Stephens. Perhaps if the Confederacy could win one more stunning battle, the peace that both sides said they wanted might be more easily discussed.[1]

On May 15, Lee met with Davis and Secretary of War Seddon in Richmond and pleaded his case for an invasion of the North. He had already told Seddon that the Confederate government must decide between Mississippi and Virginia, and he intended to influence the decision. The following day, he spoke before the Confederate Cabinet. A thrust against Pennsylvania would accomplish the same ends he sought in Maryland nine months earlier, he said. The threat against Washington would frighten Lincoln and surely result in his withdrawing the Army of the Potomac from Virginia. It might even result in Lincoln's calling some of Grant's troops east. At the very least, Pennsylvania's rich, unharvested fields would feed and fodder the army. And there was even the chance that the Army of Northern Virginia might win.

The argument was appealing, but didn't convince all the secretaries. Postmaster General John Reagan, for one, backed the plan presented earlier by Pete Longstreet, who wanted to detach himself from Lee and lead a campaign into Tennessee for the purpose of diverting the Federal buildup at Vicksburg. Reagan, a Texan, told the Cabinet that the real threat to the Confederacy was not coming from the North, but was pushing from the West. The

Army of the Tennessee, not the Army of the Potomac, was the danger and Grant was the man to stop. Lee didn't think so, and Lee had the final word. In his mind, the future of the Confederate nation rested on the safety of Viriginia—indeed, Virginia was the nation. That being so, there were only two choices: "either to retire to Richmond and stand a siege, which must ultimately have ended in surrender, or invade Pennsylvania." The Cabinet voted to invade Pennsylvania.

Lee had won his point, in part because his confidence in his army had never been higher. After Chancellorsville, he believed the Army of Northern Virginia was "invincible." "There never were such men in any army before," he wrote John Hood. "They will go any where and do anything if properly led." The qualifier was important. Jackson was gone, but he had supported the northern invasion; in fact, he had ordered a detailed map of western Virginia, Maryland, and Pennsylvania drawn during the first months of 1863. Lee had studied that map with Jackson, and he had it in his possession. Moreover, he believed—perhaps needed to believe—that Jackson's spirit was "diffused over the whole Confederacy." He himself felt infused by Stonewall's Cromwellian presence. "We must endeavor to follow the unselfish, devoted and intrepid course he pursued, and we shall be strengthened rather than weakened by his loss." The intrepid course Jackson apparently wanted led straight to the heart of Pennsylvania.[2]

Lee was right about Jackson's spirit. The funeral in Richmond was a two-day extravaganza of grief during which most of the city and a good part of the state filed by his coffin in the Capitol. After it was over, and his remains were returned to the Shenandoah Valley for the last time, Confederate mourning became something very like celebration. "He is not dead," young matrons assured one another. Such a spirit could never be killed. Jackson would live forever. And, as Lee predicted, the transmogrification of Jackson the folk hero into Jackson the heroic divine did strengthen Southerners' ideas of themselves as a people. He was the first national Confederate martyr, and he was killed at a time when southern life, honing against daily deprivation and death, was sharpening into a sense of American community not felt since the Revolutionary War. Just as the Army of Northern Virginia came to see itself and be seen as the legitimate heir of the Continental Army, so too did Confederate civilians experience themselves repeating the suffering and virtue of the Revolution. Southern living conditions—in Richmond in particular—were dreadful as the war entered its third year. The meanest staples were beyond the reach of most inhabitants and inflation created real want. Soldiers' families were made destitute by the vagaries of a pay system that functioned sporadically if at all. The few available jobs—usually clerical and often for the government— were taken by well-connected ladies with names never before seen on work applications. Salaries barely covered rents for portions of rooms in Richmond's houses, and never amounted to enough to feed or clothe a family.

Richmond had its first bread riot in early 1863, and many of its inhabitants feared they had seen the last of butter, eggs, and meat. Families that managed to maintain some kind of income from farms, northern investments, or various war-related enterprises managed better, but even those with money to spend found little to buy. The South had always depended on imports, and by 1863 the Union blockade was so effective that medicines, paper, leather goods, ink, cloth, and toiletries were unavailable. One blockade runner risked Federal gunboats at Wilmington to land a cargo of corsets. The whalebone wasp-waisters sold out in one day to women who, often as not, patched and mended, dyed and trimmed, tore and turned their dresses until the fabric was rotting away. Hats were homemade, usually woven from straw, and trimmed up with ribbons saved from better days. Like the army that defended them, southern women suffered from want of leather, and eventually cut up carpets to cover their feet. Poverty became a badge of virtue. It was a widely held maxim that no one could "honestly and conscientiously amass wealth." But there were some Richmonders who profited from the war and inflated with the economy. A young Virginia patrician recorded with contempt that "there were those who were before poor, now purchasing fine estates, driving fine horses, rolling in the finest coaches they could procure, and faring as sumptuously as our market would allow. While others were growing poorer and poorer, retrenching in expenditures, doing all they could, and giving all they had to spare for the support of the cause in which the interests of the South were so fully involved." Like their northern counterparts, southern speculators took advantage of a system well oiled by bureaucratic graft. But Southerners set on doing well in wartime could not claim that they were also doing good. Stores of food, odd lots of blockade-run merchandise, and various and sundry necessities were bought up, held until inflation doubled their paper value, then offered for public sale. Like gambling-hall owners, barkeeps, and streetwalkers who openly plied their trades, speculators seemed untouched by remorse.

Though long-standing social resentment may well have generated the glee with which the nouveaux flaunted their riches, the cutting edge between the haves and the have-nots was the ideology of the Cause. As families of distinction placed their household furnishings on sale in one of the growing number of auction houses, they looked to future rewards. Fortunes had been destroyed by the Revolution too, the sacrifice was not too great. "We were carried back to the days of our grandmothers," a young woman claimed. It was not just the weaving and dyeing and the coping that bore Virginia women back to their pasts, it was the sense of shared privation and suffering that was ennobling. It bound them together in the service of their cause, and it gave them hope, courage, and a fierce kind of joy. Amidst the overcrowding, the scant food, and the deaths, they were happy. One diarist who married well, only to end up delivering her second child alone in an unheated cabin outside the city on Christmas night, declared she had never been so happy in her life. The total commitment to war was an unintended effect of the North's total war. Suffering made a people good, and goodness made a people great. Few societies are able to actually live out their foundation myths. That Confederates were able to, and did, made them feel invincible. As Lee had told his brother, "they may annihilate us, but they can never conquer us."

No Virginia woman felt more unconquerable than Mary Custis Lee. The war had swept away Arlington, it had killed her daughter and grandchild, but it restored the era she had been reared to love. Those long hours spent with her father sifting through the artifacts and the fantasies of the Revolutionary War were the perfect prologue for Mary Lee's Civil War life. Her very personality—industrious, thrifty, mindless of social niceties, careless of convention and dress—was right for the time, and her reputation flourished. "Mrs. Lee is never seen at receptions," a young Richmond woman wrote a friend. "She and her daughters spend their time knitting and sewing for the soldiers, just as her great-grandmother, Martha Washington, did in '76." "Her room was like an industrial school—everybody so busy," a chagrined South Carolinian noted. "Did you see how the Lees spend their time! What a rebuke to the taffy parties!" In fact, Mary Lee had found her time—or rather the time had found her.

By 1863, Mary was confined to a "rolling chair," unable even to hobble across a room. She kept up various treatments—medicines when they were available, visits to mountain baths in the summer—but she was in constant pain. Travel was difficult, but the government allotted her a railroad freight car—the Lees' sole wartime perquisite—which was fitted out as a bedroom. She apparently didn't mind her novel conveyance but chose not to comment on how the child of Arlington felt being wheeled aboard a baggage car for visits to friends. She seldom made visits, however. She wanted to stay close to Richmond, she said, in case her husband or sons were injured and needed her help. And she knit. Day and night, month in and month out, Mary knit socks and gloves and mufflers and sent them to Lee for distribution. So zealous was her commitment that Lee had to tell her to stem the tide of woolen goods which flooded his headquarters even in the summer.

Like Lee, Mary found in the war a duty worth doing, and that discovery drew her closer to her husband than she had ever been. She did not so much glow in Lee's reflected light—as Julia did with Grant—as she warmed to him like other Southerners who found in Lee the secure reincarnation of George Washington. She apparently wrote him nearly every day. And though he expressed irritation at her demands for constant correspondence, his letters confided to her the secrets of his heart and the plans of his military campaigns. They seldom saw one another. Lee was usually with his army and, unlike other Confederate officers, he never had Mary in camp. Perhaps it was the self-conscious abstraction of their wartime roles—Lee as George Washington, Mary as his Martha—that each of them found so appealing, but their marriage had never been better.[3]

Lee's army welcomed him with cheers when he arrived in camp west of Fredericksburg on May 20. The men sensed something big was in the making, and they were eager to see what Uncle Robert had in mind. Hooker was north of the Rappahannock at Fredericksburg, and Lee thought the Federals meant to attack. He knew another battle at Fredericksburg—even a successful one—would do the South no good, and the idea of being trapped into fighting there, or, worse, falling back toward Richmond, agitated him. His mood tightened into irritable anxiety as he tried to cut his army loose from Virginia and get it on the road north. The immediate problem was replacing the irreplaceable Jackson. He reorganized the army into three corps: Longstreet would still head the First Corps, A. P. Hill would command the Third Corps, and Dick Ewell, minus a leg he left at Second Manassas, plus a new bride—a widow whom he always introduced as "my wife, Mrs. Brown"—would take over Stonewall Jackson's Second Corps.

A cavalryman, Ewell had spent a decade on the western plains and he swore he'd learned everything about commanding fifty soldiers and "forgotten everything else." A Louisianan who served with Ewell said his lisp, his "bomb-shaped" head, and his beaked nose "gave him a striking resemblance to a woodcock; and this was increased by a bird-like habit of putting his head on one side to utter his quaint speeches. He fancied that he had some mysterious internal malady, and would eat nothing but frumenty, a preparation of wheat." Ewell talked about himself "as if he were some one else," and had no faith in his opinions or decisions. He had groveled on the floor and hid his head after Malvern Hill, and he didn't like command. He preferred riding to the front and fighting with his men, and was so nervous he seldom slept. Curled around a campstool all night, Ewell would startle his companions by suddenly asking out loud, "What do you suppose President Davis made me a major general for?" He honestly didn't know.

Lee left Fredericksburg on June 6 for a nighttime ride northwest to Culpeper. Jeb Stuart had been at Culpeper for two weeks, and on the morning of June 8 sent his commander an invitation to review the cavalry. Spurred on by roars of approval from the troops, Lee put his gray horse to a gallop and raced down the three-mile line, wheeled at the turn, and raced back without stopping or breaking his pace. Red-faced and winded but smiling, he pulled to a stop at the reviewing stand and acknowledged the applause of spectators. Flags snapping in the hot, dry air, spurs jingling, sabers at present arms, Stuart's cavalry then rode past Lee, who sat chatting with the ladies crowded around the parade ground. The day's events were brought to a thrilling close by Stuart's igniting blank-loaded cannon while yelling cavalry members charged with brandished swords. Several of the ladies fainted in appreciation.

But the following day Union cavalry surprised Stuart at Brandy Station. Lee arrived on the scene just in time to watch his son Rooney being carried off the field with a shattered leg.[4]

It seemed an ill omen. Lee didn't know if Hooker would follow him north. Fighting Joe might just as easily make an overland thrust against Richmond now that he knew the Rebels were no longer blocking his way. But there seemed to be something more than outguessing the Federals bothering Lee. Though he had gotten a formal go-ahead from Davis and the Cabinet, he was still trying to convince Seddon of the wisdom of his move. "I am aware," he wrote, "that there is difficulty & hazard in taking the aggressive with so large an army in its front, entrenched behind a river where it cannot be advantageously attacked. Unless it can be drawn out in a position to be assailed, it will take its own time to prepare and strengthen itself to renew its advance upon Richmond, and force this army back within the intrenchments of that city. This may be the result in any event, still I think it is worth a trial to prevent such a catastrophe." Since the "trial" was under way at the time he wrote Seddon, Lee may well have been calling for reassurance. He may even have been trying to convince himself. A few days later, after Brandy Station, he told Seddon he had only half as much cavalry as he needed. "If I weaken it I fear a heavier calamity may befall us than that we wish to avoid." He seldom used words like "catastrophe" and "calamity." You "must all remember me in your prayers," he wrote Mary, "& implore the Lord of Hosts for the removal of the terrible scourge with which he has thought best to afflict our bleeding country."[5]

Several days before Lee ordered Jackson's old Second Corps to start its northern march, he also took the unprecedented step of addressing President Davis on political issues. The purpose of the letter, he told Davis, was to bring to the President's attention "the manner in which the demonstration of a desire for peace at the North has been received in our country.

"I think there can be no doubt that journalists and others at the South, to whom the Northern people naturally look for a reflection of our opinions, have met these indications in such wise as to weaken the hands of the advocates of a pacific policy on the part of the Federal Government, and give much encouragement to those who urge a continuance of the war." Lee was opposing those who crowed over Chancellorsville, claiming the Confederate army would exterminate its Union foe. Not so, Lee told Davis, and the reason was Lincoln's "arithmetic." Confederate "resources in men are constantly diminishing, and the disproportion in this respect between us and our enemies, if they continue united in their efforts to subjugate us, is steadily augmenting." Only God's mercy had sustained the army thus far.

"Under these circumstances we should neglect no honorable means of dividing and weakening our enemies. . . . It seems to me that the most effectual mode of accomplishing this object, now within our reach, is to give all the encouragement we can, consistently with truth, to the rising peace party of the North." The encouragement, Lee said, should make no distinction between northern Unionists and those who wished for unconditional peace. "We should bear in mind that the friends of peace at the North must make concessions to the earnest desire that exists in the minds of their countrymen for a restoration of the Union, and that to hold out such a result as an inducement is essential to the success of their party.

"Should the belief that peace will bring back the Union become general, the war would no longer be supported, and that after all is what we are interested in bringing about. When peace is proposed to us it will be time enough to discuss its terms, and it is not the part of prudence to spurn the proposition in advance, merely because those who wish to make it believe, or affect to believe, that it will result in bringing us back to the Union." The wording was complex enough to prompt a suspicion that Lee himself may have wished to "bring back the Union." His bitter denunciations of the total war—"unworthy of a civilized nation"—desolating Virginia focused on the armies of Abraham Lincoln. If Lincoln and his administration were overturned, then Lee's only objection to reunion would be swept away. Perhaps fearing he had revealed too much, he went on to assure Davis that we "entertain no desire for union, nor doubt that the desire of our people for a distinct and independent national existence will prove as steadfast under the influence of peaceful measures as it has shown itself in the midst of war."

The role of statesman playing political manipulator was foreign to Lee, but Davis had drawn him into Confederate councils and clearly implied that the future of the country in large part rested on his command. Lee knew it was so. But in June 1863, the responsibility, rich with hope and fear, was a burden he could barely support.[6]

Lee said goodbye to Ewell on June 13 and pointed the Second Corps toward Jackson's old stamping grounds in the Shenandoah Valley. Longstreet left Culpeper on June 15, and A. P. Hill, after reporting that the Federals at Fredericksburg had hauled down their balloons and gone, started marching north the following day. Lee rode out of Culpeper on the sixteenth, packing along his sagging tent and his headquarters menagerie. The march went well enough, but Lee was uneasy. He didn't hear from Stuart, whose cavalry was to keep him abreast of Hooker's movements, until June 22. "I judge the efforts of the enemy yesterday were to arrest our progress and ascertain our whereabouts," Lee responded to the long-awaited cavalry report. "Perhaps he is satisfied. Do you know where he is and what he is doing? I fear he will steal a march on us and get across the Potomac before we are aware." It was unlike Lee not to pinpoint his adversary. He told Stuart to find out if the enemy was moving north, and if so—provided that two cavalry brigades could guard the rear—to head north himself on Ewell's eastern flank. You can best judge how to proceed, Lee said, but added that the cavalry "must move on & feel the right of Ewell's troops, collecting information, provisions, &c."[7]

The route from Culpeper had taken the army through what used to be one of the richest areas in Virginia. The land was still green and lush, but it was no longer used for farming. Only grass covered fields gone fallow from two years of war. Shells of houses, empty barns, and the hungry people angered the soldiers. "I find it hard to control a burning desire for revenge when I hear the piteous tale of wrongs which these people of Clarke have suffered at the hands of yankee soldiers," an aide to Longstreet wrote home. But Lee had "given orders there is to be no pillaging," a Virginian told his wife. "All supplies to be taken that way are to be paid for in Confederate money. Does that not seem strange? Especially when we consider how this country we are now in has been treated." Lee was acutely sensitive to the mood of his men. He issued orders congratulating them on their march and reminding them of their obligation. "There have however been instances of forgetfulness on the part of some, that they have in keeping the yet unsullied reputation of the army, and that the duties exacted of us by civilization and christianity are no less obligatory in the country of the enemy than in our own. The commanding general considers no greater disgrace could befall the army, and through it our whole people, than the perpetration of the barbarous outrages upon the unarmed, and defenceless and the wanton destruction of private property that marked the course of the enemy in our own country. . . .

"It must be remembered that we make war only upon armed men, and that we cannot take vengeance for the wrongs our people have suffered without lowering ourselves in the eyes of all whose abhorrence has been excited by the atrocities of our enemies, and offending against Him to whom vengeance belongeth, without whose favor and support our efforts must all prove in vain." Lee armed his men with such a noble vision of themselves that they obeyed. They grumbled but obeyed, and it made them even stronger as they reached the Potomac.[8]

A little boy who had watched the Army of Northern Virginia on its way to Sharpsburg posted himself on the banks of the river for the excitement. "I had never supposed so many horses were to be found in the world," he remembered. "It was not only the multitude that impressed those who saw that march; it was also the splendid discipline of the army. They were different from the corps we had seen the year before. These men were well clad and shod, and they came through the town with flags flying and bands playing 'Dixie,' 'Dixie,' all day long. . . . Day after day an unbroken line passed on due north, and at night the rumble of the wagons made sleep impossible for nervous people."

Lee crossed on June 25 and sat his horse on the Maryland side watching Longstreet's First Corps. William Blackford, serving as judge advocate in the First Corps, told his wife that it was hard to leave Virginia. "As I crossed the Potomac today I felt a great gulf was fixed between us, and the thought saddened me. The head of our corps struck the Potomac about noon today, Pickett in front. . . . I have never seen the army in such fine condition. We marched from Berryville here with scarcely a straggler and the report from every division is the same. Of course I feel anxious about the result but I never have been so confident of success before. . . . The crossing of the river by our troops was very picturesque. General Lee was on the bank of the Maryland side surrounded by ladies who came down to see the sight and to admire him. The soldiers waded into the water without stopping to roll up their pantaloons and came over in good order as if on review, cheering at every step. One fellow, as he stepped on the Maryland shore, exclaimed: 'Well boys I've been seceding for two years and now I've got back into the Union again!' Another said to the crowd of ladies he thought were Union in their sentiments; 'Here we are ladies, as rough and ragged as ever but back again to bother you.' "9

Ewell's Second Corps, after proving itself still worthy of Stonewall Jackson by clearing the Union Army out of the northern Shenandoah Valley, had crossed the Potomac days earlier. The advance was headed by a former governor of Virginia, General "Extra Billy" Smith, who decided to march on York, Pennsylvania, in a rather singular fashion. "Go back and look up those tooting fellows," Smith ordered an aide, "and tell them first to be sure their drums and horns are all right, and then to come up here to the front and march into town tooting 'Yankee Doodle' in their very best style." The band arranged itself at the head of the column, and Smith, bowing and saluting to the citizenry—"and especially every pretty girl he saw"—led the march forward. The Yorkers, said an artillerist with Smith, "seemed at first astounded, then pleased, and finally, by the time we reached the public square, they had reached the point of ebullition, and broken into enthusiastic cheers as they crowded about the head of the column." Smith's progress impeded by the jolly burghers, he ordered his brigade to stack arms. "It was a rare scene—the vanguard of an invading army and the invaded and hostile population hobnobbing on the public green in an enthusiastic public gathering."

Turning in his saddle and smiling, Smith said their intentions were honorable. "You see, it was getting a little warm down our way. We needed a summer outing and thought we would take it at the North, instead of patronizing the Virginia springs, as we generally do." Laughter and applause. "We are sorry, and apologize that we are not in better guise for a visit of courtesy, but we regret to say our trunks haven't gotten up yet; we were in such a hurry to see you that we could not wait for them." More laughter, more applause. Smith drawled on until the ceremonies were interrupted by shouts of profanity coming from the rear. It was Jubal Early, the nastiest-tongued man in the Confederate Army, slashing at the Rebel soldiers and pushing his way to Smith's side. Arrested in midsentence by Early's demanding to know "what the devil" he was doing "stopping the head of this column in this cursed town," Smith answered that he was having fun. Early—whom Lee called "my bad old man"—erupted in a stream of curses, which had little effect on the impervious traffic jam. In time, Smith and his brigade rode on, leaving the Yorkers, thought the artillerist, "wondering what manner of men we were."

There was no doubt on the part of the Confederates about what manner of men they were—they were invincible, and they marched into their northward lark with good-humored confidence. The army loped along roads cordoned by civilians waving Union flags and shouting taunts at the invaders—who occasionally shouted back. A girl—"very bold looking," according to the southern gentleman who reported the tale—was standing on a porch swathed in a giant American flag which was pinned to her chest.

"Look here, Miss, you'd better take that flag off," shouted a soldier.

"I won't do it. Why should I?" retorted the female patriot.

"Because, Miss, these old rebs are hell on breastworks."

Not unexpectedly, the storied General Lee came in for the closest scrutiny. Crowds waited for hours to catch sight of him riding by. "What a large neck he has," one bystander commented, apparently disappointed. While another, a young lady who daintily lofted an American banner, let her national duty flag when she caught sight of Lee. "Oh," she sighed, "I wish he was ours." Confederate sympathizers poured into Lee's headquarters compound in Maryland. Women brought cakes and flowers and buttermilk. The men brought information. Carrying his map of Maryland and Pennsylvania, Lee asked questions of a visiting physician: What roads ran into the Lightersburg pike? Did the Cavetown pike cross the mountain? What sort of crossing was it? Could cannon be easily brought over it? His right flank would then be protected by the Blue Ridge until he reached Gettysburg?

And on his return should he come that way? Were there good roads running to the river west of the one on which he now stood? Could artillery be moved over them? Was the valley well wooded and watered all the way to Gettysburg? His callers were surprised to find that his hair—only last September still dark—had turned completely white.[10]

"The feeling of the men for him is that of blind devotion," said a soldier as Lee led the army into entirely hostile Pennsylvania. And the look of the land only made the triumphal march better. "It's like a hole full of blubber to a Greenlander!" exclaimed a general, eyeing well-stocked farmyards and fields burgeoning with wheat. Pennsylvania's richness was one of the reasons the Army of Northern Virginia was there, and commissaries and quartermasters, their pockets stuffed with Confederate money, fanned out from each regiment to harvest the wealth. Native farmers were none too happy about exchanging grain, animals, meat, and vegetables for cash they knew was worthless. But the Confederates drove irresistible bargains, and made off with their purchases, some of which turned out to their disadvantage. Pennsylvania horses—Percherons and Clydesdales—required twice the feed and could do only half the military work of "our compact hard-muscled little horses," an artillerist said. "It was pitiful later to see these great brutes suffer when compelled to dash off at full gallop with a gun, after pasturing on dry broom sedge and eating a quarter of feed of weevil-eaten corn." Even on the march, the horses pulled up lame on the macadamized roads.

The rain which started to fall the day Lee crossed the Potomac seemed a fitting reflection of his mood. He didn't share the optimism of his men. He was worried. He hadn't heard from Stuart for five days. "Can you tell me where General Stuart is?" Lee asked a startled courier. No, the courier didn't know. "Where on earth is my cavalry?" he asked of no one in particular. Even worse were his anxious inquiries about the Federals. He confided to his secretary that he feared he had not drawn the Union army north with him. He began to think the Federals might be marching south against Richmond. The idea grated him into restless agitation. "Have you any news of the enemy's movements? What is the enemy going to do?"[11]

Had Lee known that Stuart was nowhere near Ewell's eastern flank, but instead was riding around the District of Columbia, he would have been even more anxious. Eager to reestablish the reputation he had tarnished at Brandy Station, Stuart set out after getting Lee's letter on June 23 to repeat his Pennsylvania feat of riding around the Union army. But his plan soured, and as his commander tensed in wait for him at Chambersburg, Stuart found himself separated from Lee by the whole Army of the Potomac.

Lee went to bed early the night of June 28, but was awakened by one of Longstreet's aides. A "scout"—spy—named Harrison had just arrived with information. Would Lee see him? "I do not know what to do," Lee confessed. He had no confidence in such unsavory business, but he nevertheless agreed to the interview. When the scout was ushered into Lee's tent, he had some startling news. The Army of the Potomac was north of the river—had been for two days. At least two corps were assembled at Frederick, Maryland, and more were on the march west. Joe Hooker was gone—fired—and a Pennsylvanian named George Gordon Meade was in charge of the rapidly advancing enemy army. Lee sent orders to his corps commanders: Ewell, still roving around the Susquehanna River at York, was to turn south immediately and march toward either Cashtown or Gettysburg, whichever was easier. Hill, camped near Longstreet around Chambersburg, was to start east. Longstreet would hold the rear and follow the next day.

On June 29, when he broke headquarters at Chambersburg and started east himself, there were two things Lee knew: Richmond was safe; the Army of Northern Virginia wasn't. He still wasn't sure exactly where his opponents were or how numerous they were. He pitched camp at Greenwood, about ten miles west of Gettysburg, and tried to walk off some of the tension. A visitor was astonished to find him pacing back and forth, alternately clutching at his head and recovering himself, apparently reminded that he was not alone. Lee never had publicly demonstrated such anxiety, and he didn't do it for long at Greenwood. John Hood sought out the commander for reassurance. Smiling, Lee told Hood that "the enemy is a long time finding us; if he does not succeed soon, we must go in search of him." Indeed, like most of Lee's teases, that one covered a hard core of uncomfortable truth. As the rain poured down on those ragged Pennsylvania hills, Lee was groping blindly toward an unseen foe. He was quick to counter one of his aides' easy brags. "General Meade will commit no blunder in my front," Lee corrected the officer, "and if I make one he will make haste to take advantage of it."[12]

As it turned out, Lee and Meade more or less blundered into one another. A courier from A. P. Hill arrived at headquarters the night of June 30 with the news that one of Hill's divisions walked into Gettysburg looking for shoes, and found instead at least one division of Union soldiers. Lee couldn't believe it. His best information—secondhand and from an untrustworthy spy—put the Federals south of him. What were they doing in Gettysburg?

The troops had literally stumbled into each other on the streets of the tiny college town. Each side recoiled in shock and ran for safety. The Union brigadier disabused his nervous soldiers of their halfhearted hope that nothing would come of it. Oh no, he said. "They will attack you in the morning and they will come booming—skirmishers three-deep. You will have to fight like the devil."

The morning dawned clear over Lee's campsite on the Chambersburg Road, which cut upward toward Gettysburg through rockbound gorges. Lee stood outside his tent watching the First Corps go eastward, the rhythmic thud of their marching syncopating with the ticks of bayonets on water canteens. He hailed Longstreet, swung aboard his horse, and sauntered alongside. The men who saw him thought he was in grand spirits. He shifted in his saddle to keep pace with the artillery limbers creaking and banging into the climb. He cocked his head to one side and slowed his horse. He thought he heard something ahead. Spurring forward, he stopped on high ground to listen. It was artillery. But whose? Then, as if to explain his confusion, he said aloud that he'd been in the dark since he'd crossed the Potomac. His staff knew he was angry.

When Lee topped the crest of the last ridge west of Gettysburg, he said goodbye to Longstreet and rode ahead toward A. P. Hill at Cashtown. Hill was sick in bed and could only tell Lee that one division had orders not to give battle until the rest of the army was up. Lee rode on eastward. When he found a division commander, he asked the officer what was happening. The man couldn't say. "I cannot think of what has become of Stuart," Lee said. "I ought to have heard from him long before now." Without the cavalry, he didn't know what his army was facing. "It may be the whole Federal army, it may be only a detachment."

It was something of both. When Meade replaced Hooker the first thing he did was scrap his predecessor's plan for moving west against Lee's supply lines. He would strike out for the north—York actually, where Ewell's army was delighting the populace—and use his troops as a buffer against Washington and Baltimore. That decision was what bottled up Jeb Stuart's cavalry. At the same time it gave Lincoln some reassurance that he'd chosen the right man to stop Robert Lee. Meade's troops were less certain. Forty-eight years old and looking sixty, Meade, according to a journalist, had more of "a learned pundit than a soldier" about him. The balding head fringed with wisps of wiry grizzle, the dark eyes sunk into pouches lying on either side of the bony hooked nose, and the thin mouth pursed into a sharply whiskered chin gave him a curmudgeon quality reflected by his personality. "I know they call me a damned old snapping turtle," Meade said of his men. From the time when he wrote home letters criticizing Zachary Taylor's handling of the morals of his army in Mexico, he had maintained himself as a fault-finding naysayer in the Regular Army. The irascible new commander was given a wide berth even by his staff.

Though most of Meade's 90,000 men were disappointed with their unglamorous commander, they were relieved to be going home. "It is refreshing to get out of the barren desert of Virginia and into this land of thrift and plenty," an officer wrote about Pennsylvania. Cheers rather than insults greeted the Army of the

Potomac, which found itself welcomed as salvation on the march. "We felt some doubt about whether it was ever going to be our fortune to win a victory in Virginia," a Union soldier explained, "but no one admitted the possibility of a defeat north of the Potomac." No one but George Meade. By the time he actually got his men close enough to sense the ominous presence of Robert Lee's army, Meade notified his division commanders that it was no longer his intention "to assume the offensive." He would "wait until the enemy's movements or position should render such an operation certain of success." Then he instructed them to fall back within the defense lines his engineers were building should the enemy's movements render failure a certainty. Meade's advance, under the brigadier who warned his boys the Rebels would come on them "three-deep" and "booming," was arranged along a little north-south-running creek on the western edge of Gettysburg called Willoughby Run.[13]

When Lee on July 1 sifted through the noise of his First Corps's march and picked out the sound of artillery, his advance was locked into a conflict with those soldiers Meade had told to retreat if necessary. But Meade's Federals didn't think it was necessary. They stood their lines bracing against the Confederate onslaught while cannon from each side lobbed shells overhead. One entire Confederate brigade was captured and its Maryland-born commander, James Archer, was caught and taken to Union general Abner Doubleday. "Archer!" shouted Doubleday, striding toward his old friend, hand outstretched. "I'm glad to see you."

"Well," growled Archer, keeping his hand at his side, "I'm not glad to see you by a damn sight." The degree of Archer's chagrin was unprecedented. He was the first of Lee's generals ever to be taken.

By the time Lee was close enough to see the action, it looked as if Archer would not be the last. It was almost two o'clock when Lee turned into a grassy field several miles west of Gettysburg and rode up a rise which gave him a view to the east. Pulling out his binoculars, he peered through the artillery smoke which clouded the misty air. The greensward on which he stood sloped downward toward Willoughby Run, then rose again into another north-south-running ridge. Beyond that, and parallel, was a third ridge, this last one topped by a seminary which gave the hill its name. Gettysburg lay at the foot of Seminary Ridge. Past the town, to the southeast, an ugly-looking stretch of rock outcroppings, aptly called Cemetery Ridge, was strung along the Emmitsburg Road, which ran through low-lying ridges and entered Gettysburg from the south. From his vantage point Lee could sweep the entire field with his glasses. What he saw would make any commander nervous. His own men were held tight west of Seminary Ridge. The Federals had the high ground in back of the Confederates, and, worse, there was a seemingly endless range of more high ground behind them. A Confederate brigadier, just back from the heaviest fighting, stood at Lee's elbow. "Had I better not attack?" Lee hesitated. "N-no," he said indecisively, still raking the field with his binoculars. Then, with more certainty: "I am not prepared to bring on a general engagement today. Longstreet is not up."

Lee was fairly certain what he had in front of him—the whole Federal army. Longstreet was not far away, but his First Corps was strung out for almost ten miles along the Chambersburg Road. Lee thought he would make a mistake by taking on the Federals without the powerhouse punch Longstreet provided. But just then, Lee saw the Federal line begin to bend. Within minutes Union soldiers were running eastward, heeled by screaming Rebs. Lee quickened. Send in two divisions, he commanded A. P. Hill, who had just ridden up. Sweep the field.

A young Union cannoneer watched them: "First we could see the tips of their colorstaffs coming up over the little ridge, then the points of their bayonets, and then the Johnnies themselves, coming on with a steady tramp, tramp, and loud yells." The Federal artillerists stood at attention. "Load—Cannister—Double!" Then: "Ready!—By pieces!—At will!—Fire!!" But the Rebels kept coming, muskets blazing. "Up and down the line men reeling and falling; splinters flying from wheels and axles where bullets hit; in rear, horses tearing and plunging, mad with wounds or terror; drivers yelling, shells bursting, shot shrieking overhead, howling about our ears or throwing up great clouds of dust where they struck; and musketry crashing on three sides of us; bullets hissing, humming, and whistling everywhere; cannon roaring; all crash on crash and peal on peal, smoke, dust, splinters, blood, wreck and carnage indescribable." The field was swept, but only in a manner of speaking. The 24th Michigan met the Confederate assault with 496 officers and men. Only 97 lived. The North Carolinians fared worse. One company took the field with 83 soldiers and came off with two, while a second went in with 91 and lost them all. A Confederate officer insisted it was the deadliest fight he had ever seen—or heard. In the woods wounded from both sides writhed on the ground, some foaming at the mouth, others screaming, unaware, it seemed, that they were making any noise. The sight appalled the officer, who explained the bizarre scene to himself as arising from the men's having met "quick, frightful conflict following several hours of suspense."

Lee had ridden slowly eastward on the edge of the attack and sat astride his horse on the crest of Seminary Ridge. The Federals had been driven back of Gettysburg, and those who stayed on the western part of the town did so as prisoners of war. Hundreds more bluecoats huddled in misery on Gettysburg's streets and made no attempt to follow the Union companies which ran eastward, trying to find protection on the rocky slopes of Cemetery Ridge. Lee knew an opportunity when he saw one. He called for Hill's advice. Absolutely, Hill replied, attack right now and all the high ground around Gettysburg is ours. But Hill hadn't the force to do it. After eight hours' fighting, his veterans were in no condition to make the final assault. Ewell's II Corps had arrived earlier in the day from York. Though they'd experienced some hot fighting—Ewell himself had taken a hit and amused a subordinate by waggling aloft his wooden leg, showing the bullet lodged in the pine—the corps was pretty well intact. Lee told his adjutant, Walter Taylor, to ride to Ewell and tell him to "push those people" off Cemetery Hill and try to do it without committing the entire army.

As Taylor sped northward with the orders, Longstreet rode to Lee's side. Lee excitedly pointed to the hill on the north edge of

Cemetery Ridge. Longstreet took out his binoculars and looked, but he seemed less interested in what he saw than in what he did not see on the two highest peaks of the ridgeline. Gesturing to the pair of knobby hills—called Round Top and Little Round Top— poking up a mile or so south of town, Longstreet told Lee the army should move in that direction. If the Confederates came around the south edge of their opponents, they could place themselves between the Union Army and Washington. Once established, they could await the attack Meade would surely launch at them. Lee seemed puzzled by Old Pete's ignorance of the present opportunity. "If the enemy is there," Lee answered, once again pointing to the north edge of Cemetery Ridge, "we must attack him."

"If he is there," Longstreet replied, "it will be because he is anxious that we should attack him—a good reason, in my judgment, for not doing so."

Lee said nothing. When Longstreet's dander was up, it was better to ignore him. He just kept staring at the hill. He expected Ewell to be hotly engaged, but the field was quiet. When a message arrived from a commander urging reinforcements to move on the hill, Lee said that he had "no troops to occupy" the higher ground. Impatiently, he asked Longstreet where the First Corps was. One of the divisions was six miles away, Longstreet said coldly. He had no idea where the rest might be. Lee let that pass. He knew Longstreet tended to pout when he didn't get his way, and Longstreet hadn't gotten his way about any aspect of the Pennsylvania campaign. Once the Cabinet had committed him to invasion, Longstreet tried to talk Lee into a defensive position north of the Potomac. That was what he was suggesting late in the afternoon of July 1, and Lee was ignoring his advice.

Stonewall Jackson, who seldom thought of defense, was sorely missed on July 1 by the Second Corps. The order Ewell received from Lee directing him to advance on either Cashtown or Gettysburg made him nervous. In the past, he had simply done what Jackson told him to do. He pointed his army toward Gettysburg and hoped for the best. When Lee's adjutant arrived with directions to take Cemetery Hill if he could, Ewell was incapable of deciding anything. Jubal Early, his second-in-command, had already convinced Ewell that it was impractical to continue the advance that day. When Lee galloped up with irritated questions about the Second Corps's failure to push on, Ewell kept his mouth shut and deferred to Early. The three men sat under an arbor behind a little house on the north edge of Gettysburg as dusk gathered around them. Lee fell as silent as the Confederate guns. He wanted that hill, and he wanted Ewell to take it. But Early insisted it was too dangerous. Lee was still without his cavalry and didn't know what the Federals might have in back of them on Cemetery Hill. Perhaps it was just as well to wait.

Ewell's men didn't think so. An artillerist with Early exulted that afternoon to see the Federals so badly beaten that a sixteen-year-old rounded up a batch of fifty bluecoats and singlehandedly herded them into captivity. "I am aware this statement sounds incredible," the soldier later admitted, "but the men had thrown away their arms and were cowering in abject terror in the streets and alleys. Upon no other occasion did I see any large body of troops, on either side, so completely routed and demoralized as were the two Federal corps who were beaten at Gettysburg the evening of July 1st." Itching to go ahead, the men in the Second Corps—accustomed to Jackson's intrepid lurch for victory—were mystified, then stymied, and finally outraged by the halt.

Young Robert Stiles, a northern-born Yale graduate come South to fight beside his father's Georgia kin, led a battery during that first day's fight, and strained to hear the order shouted at him from his passing commander.

"Lieutenant, limber to the rear!"

"To the front, you mean, Major!"

"No, *to the rear!"*

"All right, boys," Stiles told his men, "I reckon the town's barricaded, and we'll just pass round it to the front."

But Stiles discovered he was involved in a retreat. "It is my nature to be reverential toward rightful authority and not to question the wisdom of its decisions; but on this occasion I chafed and rebelled until it almost made me ill. I was well nigh frenzied by what appeared to me to be the folly, the absolute fatuity of delay."

John Gordon, the brigadier who had led his men at Sharpsburg until he took his fifth shot of the day full in the face, was at least as upset as Stiles. "As far down the lines as my eye could reach, the Union troops were in retreat. . . . In less than half an hour my troops would have swept up and over those hills." Gordon ignored the first order to retreat. He disobeyed the second. Only when his superior told him for a third time to fall back could the Georgian bring himself to obey. "No soldier in a great crisis ever wished more ardently for a deliverer's hand than I wished for one hour of Jackson when I was ordered to halt." Arriving at the rear, Gordon paced back and forth until darkness covered the field. Ahead, toward his front, he could hear Union artillery being dragged into position and listened to the sound of Union spades digging into the rocky soil of Cemetery Hill. When his frustration became unbearable, he rode to Ewell's headquarters. Let me attack now, Gordon pleaded. If we wait until morning the Federals will be entrenched and the battle will be lost. But Ewell said no.

By that time it was nearly midnight, and the armies rested uneasily under the full July moon which glowed faintly orange from smoke. Some, like Gordon, didn't rest at all. Lee was still awake, though the fatigue of the day slowed his writing as he sat in the candlelight preparing another order for Ewell. Ewell, through Early, had told Lee during their meeting that the best way to come at Cemetery Hill was a double punch from both the north and the south. Lee demurred, saying if they did it that way, then Longstreet would have to bear the brunt on the south. Longstreet wanted to go farther south, all the way around the Round Tops, and he was none too dependable when his heart wasn't in a fight. "Longstreet is a very good fighter when he gets into position and gets everything ready," Lee told Ewell, "but he is so slow." Such candor—coming as it did like public criticism— was rare in Lee. But the whole day had been unusual. Strangest of all, perhaps, was Lee's agreement with Ewell on his plan. But by midnight, Lee was having second thoughts, and ordered Ewell to join Longstreet. Ewell soon arrived at Lee's headquarters and told him the idea was impossible. Lee changed his mind again. Ewell could stay where he was. Around one o'clock, with his staff asleep outside, Lee lay down on his cot. It had been a long day and he was very tired.[14]

At three, campfires were lit and Lee was sitting on the edge of his cot pulling on the black cavalry boots he liked. They were too big for his small feet, but they were comfortable. He always washed his hands and face and changed his shirt if he could, and carefully brushed the thinning white hair which receded from his reddened face. He buckled a sword around his waist, then joined his staff at the campfire for breakfast. As soon as the sky lightened, Lee was on the ridge, staring at the hill in front of him. He couldn't have spotted George Meade, who arrived on that hill around the same time. Meade just then was staring toward Lee. If the Union commander had known where to look, he could have seen a small knot of officers collected around the white-haired man on the ridge. One of them was Longstreet—still pouting, still pushing for his own plan, and still, as Lee knew he would be, very slow. Impatiently, Lee interrupted Longstreet's argument with a fist shaken in the direction of George Meade. "The enemy is here," Lee insisted; if we don't beat him, he will beat us.

Longstreet turned away and whispered to a subordinate: "The general is a little nervous this morning; he wishes me to attack." Longstreet didn't want to attack, he said, because he was missing at least one of his divisions. "I never like to go into battle with one boot off." Some of those present believed the only battle Longstreet wanted that morning was one with Robert Lee.

At nine, Lee got the first good news he'd had in days. The engineer he sent on a southward reconnaissance returned with the information that not only was the southern end of Cemetery Ridge empty but the two hills which anchored the ridge were also clear of Federal soldiers. He had received word the day before that the long-lost Stuart was alive and well in Carlisle, north of Gettysburg, and would be arriving in midafternoon. Lee directed Longstreet to march down Seminary Ridge, come about, and then launch an attack northward up the Emmitsburg Road toward Gettysburg. A. P. Hill's Third Corps would join Longstreet from the west while Ewell would bang away on the northern end. If the timing was right, they would succeed in gaining all of Cemetery Ridge. Then, armed with information from the cavalry about Union strength and positions, Lee could aim the army at Washington. He mounted his horse and went quickly to find Ewell. His usual "quiet self-possessed calmness was wanting," said an officer who rode with Lee, noting that the general "was not at his ease, but was riding to and fro, frequently changing his position, making anxious inquiries here and there, and looking careworn."

When Lee arrived at Ewell's headquarters and climbed to the top of the Gettysburg almshouse for a look at the field, he had even less reason for calm. John Gordon's sense of what would occur overnight had been correct. The north end of Cemetery Ridge was full of Union soldiers. Heavy artillery was in place. Lowering his binoculars, Lee sighed. "The enemy have the advantage of us," he said, "and we are too much extended. We did not or could not pursue our advantage of yesterday and now the enemy are in good position." His disappointment was obvious. So was his irritation. Two hours had passed since he'd told Longstreet to get moving. "What *can* detain Longstreet? He ought to be in position now," Lee said as he swung back in the saddle for a ride to Seminary Ridge. Coming on an artillerist, Lee chastised him for not moving out quickly enough, then had to apologize when the officer said he was not part of Longstreet's corps. His mood "manifested more impatience than I ever saw him exhibit upon any other occasion," a subordinate said later. "Lee seemed very much disappointed and worried that the attack had not opened earlier, and very anxious for Longstreet to attack at the very earliest possible moment."

When Lee rode into his command post on Seminary Ridge, whom should he see but Longstreet. Pete was still waiting for one of his divisions while across the Emmitsburg Road from Seminary Ridge the Federals were massing infantry and pulling artillery into position. Lee's diplomacy was strained to the point of collapse, and he came as near to issuing a peremptory order as he had ever done in his life. Longstreet huffed off and finally put his men in motion. As the First Corps went southward, Lee paced back and forth, pausing only to peer across the valley at the army on Cemetery Ridge. Blue-coated soldiers were plainly visible all the way down to the Round Tops. It didn't look good. "Ah, well," he said, "that was to be expected. But General Meade might as well have saved himself the trouble, for we'll have it in our possession before night."

It was noon by then, and Longstreet's veterans were sweating and thirsty and covered with dust, but their spirits were good. "There was a kind of intuition, an apparent settled fact," wrote an officer later, "that after all the other troops had made their long marches, tugged at the flanks of the enemy, threatened his rear, and all the display of strategy and generalship had been exhausted in the dislodgement of the foe, and all these failed, then when the hard, stubborn, decisive blow was to be struck, the troops of the First Corps were called on to strike it." The claim was just, but on July 2 the need for a stubborn blow increased diametrically to the opportunity for a decisive one. It was close to four o'clock by the time Longstreet's men were in line, and by that time the Federals were not only cresting Cemetery Ridge, they were also collecting at the base of the Round Tops, clustered in a peach orchard. "The view presented astonished me," one of Longstreet's officers said, "as the enemy was massed in my front, and extended by my right and left as far as I could see."

The Federals on the Confederates' right had astonished even General Meade. They were two divisions which belonged to Dan Sickles, a hot-tempered—some said intemperate—politician who had aroused a good deal of attention and some sympathy by shooting his wife's lover dead on the streets of Washington. Edwin Stanton—then a practicing lawyer—successfully defended the cuckolded husband on the grounds of "temporary aberration of the mind." Impatient at following Meade's orders to wait out the Confederates, Sickles took his men into the orchard with such style that observers thought it looked like a dress parade. "How splendidly they march!" a Union officer declared of the advance. Winfield Scott Hancock, the now middle-aged Union general who graduated from West Point after being tested by Robert Lee, thought differently. "Wait a moment," Hancock cautioned his friend, "you'll see them tumbling back."

But an hour later they were still there, 10,000 of them watching Longstreet's corps get ready to attack. There were 70,000 more Federals along a three-mile line strung behind Sickles. Lee's 50,000 arched convexly around the Union front for five miles south to north. Longstreet had less than a third that number with him. By four, when the attack was ready, it was clear to division commanders that the attempt was absurd. Lafayette McLaws, inching out on the Emmitsburg Road, sent a verbal message to Longstreet saying his men would be cut to pieces if they went up the road. Longstreet was adamant about following Lee's orders to the letter. When young John Hood took to the road, he sent Longstreet a similar request for a change. The response was terse: "General Lee's orders are to attack up the Emmitsburg Road." Hood thought he hadn't made himself clear. He repeated his request. He got the same answer: "General Lee's orders are to attack up the Emmitsburg Road." Hood sent one last message. "General Lee's orders are to attack up the Emmitsburg Road," he got back. Thrice given, the order for what Hood and the others knew would be a woeful disaster could not be ignored. Lest he have any doubts, Hood got a brief visit from Longstreet, who said he "must obey the orders of General Lee."

With artillery booming and regimental bands playing hearty polkas, the Confederates moved out. From south to north, in echelon, lofting battle flags borne atop the wild Rebel yell, the First Corps threw itself into what one survivor declared "was more like Indian fighting" than a battle. "Every fellow was his own general," another said. "Private soldiers gave commands as loud as the officers; nobody paying any attention to either." Flanked by enfilading fire from Cemetery Ridge, the Confederates had to turn eastward and throw themselves against the Union high ground. A lieutenant from Wisconsin stood above and watched. "We see the long gray lines come sweeping down upon Sickles' front, and mix with the battle smoke; now the same colors emerge from the bushes and orchards upon his right and envelop his flank in the confusion of the conflict. O, the din and the roar, and these thirty thousand Rebel wolf cries! What a hell is down that valley!"

Indeed, the ground at the base of the Round Tops bore the name Devil's Den thereafter. An Alabama colonel who headed straight into that den with the cry of "Forward!" came out with an odd assortment of memories—moss growing in damp recesses between the boulders, a "cavernous coolness," almost welcome had it not been for the Federal sharpshooters, and his men toppling face down into their own blood. Beyond the Devil's Den was Round Top, and another Alabaman pushed his men up its craggy face. "The sharpshooters retreated up the south front of the mountain, pursued by my command," he wrote. "In places the men had to climb up, catching to the rocks and bushes and crawling over the boulders in the face of the fire of the enemy, who kept retreating, taking shelter and firing down on us from behind the rocks and crags which covered the side of the mountain thicker than gravestones in a city cemetery." Some of the men fainted, others were killed. But they made it to the top, where they dropped in exhaustion. There was no rest, however. Over the protest of their commander, who suspected lunacy or worse, the Alabamans were ordered to leave the trophy which was theirs and march down. They were to take Little Round Top instead. By the time the men reached the base of Little Round Top, the Federals were on its crest.

A captain in the 20th Maine, under former Bowdoin College professor Colonel Joshua Chamberlain, watched the Rebels coming. "Again and again was this mad rush repeated, each time beaten off by the ever-thinning line that desperately clung to its ledge of rock, refusing to yield. . . . The front surged backward and forward like a wave. At times our dead and wounded were in front of our line, and then by superhuman effort our gallant lads would carry the combat forward beyond their prostrate forms. Continually the gray lines crept up by squads under protecting trees and boulders, and the firing became at closer and closer range. . . . The dead and the wounded clog the footsteps of the living." But the Rebels still came, hand over hand, rock over rock, closing up ranks and stepping over the bodies of their dead. Chamberlain readied his regiment for the final wave, which burst over the ridge. "Fix bayonets!" he shouted at his decimated Federals. "Charge bayonets, charge!" But the boys were too frightened to move. A young lieutenant sprang onto the rocky ledge. "Come on! Come on! Come on, boys!" he shouted. And his friend remembered that with "one wild yell of anguish wrung from its tortured heart, the regiment charged."

The Confederates knew it was over on Little Round Top. "With a withering and deadly fire pouring in upon us from every direction, it seemed that the regiment was doomed to destruction. While one man was shot in the face, his right-hand or left-hand comrade was shot in the side or back. Some were struck simultaneously with two or three balls from different directions. . . . My dead and wounded were nearly as great in number as those still on duty. They literally covered the ground. The blood stood in puddles in some places on the rocks; the ground was soaked with the blood of as brave men as ever fell on the red field of battle." How could honor at least be saved? "It seemed impossible to retreat," a colonel wrote. He told his captains to return to their companies, for "we will sell out as dearly as possible." But when the 20th Maine charged over the ledge one more time the colonel felt that honor had satisfaction enough. He ordered his men back.

Union survivors, too shocked to walk, crawled around groping for something live and grabbed one another's hands. Those with energy enough pulled themselves to the ledge to watch the action below. "A great basin lay before us full of smoke and fire, and literally swarming with riderless horses and fighting, fleeing, and pursuing men." The air, he said, was "saturated with sulphurous fumes," the "wild cries of charging lines, the rattle of musketry, the booming of artillery and the shrieks of the wounded" accompanied "a scene very like hell itself."[15]

On Seminary Ridge, Lee sat watching through his binoculars. It was impossible for him to see the Round Tops—the air was so still that smoke hung on the field. But he could make out the wave of action that followed his loss on the south. Exactly below him, men milled around chafing to get in on the action. But orders were confused and timing went wrong. While thousands were being slaughtered, others stood by, waiting. An aide-de-camp to Lafayette McLaws wrote to a friend years later telling how he set those men loose: "You remember how anxious General Barksdale was to attack the enemy, and his eagerness was participated in by all his officers and men and when I carried him the order to advance his face was radiant with joy. He was in front of his brigade, hat off, and his long white hair reminded me of the 'white plume of Navarre.' I saw him as far as the eye could follow, still ahead of his men, and leading them on. Do you remember the picket fence in front of his brigade? I was anxious to see how they would get over it. When they reached it the fence disappeared as if by magic, and the slaughter of the 'red-breeched zouaves' on the other side was terrible!"

Fred Haskell, a young Wisconsin officer, wrote his family about the battle rolling northward up the Emmitsburg Road. "Such fighting as this cannot last long. It is now near sundown and the battle has gone on wonderfully long already." Long enough, it seemed. "The Rebel cry has ceased, and the men of the Union begin to shout there, under the smoke, and their lines to advance. See, the Rebs are breaking! They are in confusion in all our front! The wave has rolled upon the rock and the rock has smashed it." To Haskell, the entire Confederate line seemed to quiver, "and the pride of the chivalry, fled like chaff before the whirlwind, back down the slope, over the valley, across the Emmitsburg Road, shattered, without organization in utter confusion fugitive into the woods, and victory was with the arms of the Republic."

Lee continued to watch. Only occasionally talking quietly with his aide Armistead Long, he kept apart from the group of Confederate spectators gathered on the crest of Seminary Ridge. He sat on the stump of a tree, alone, training his binoculars over the carnage at his feet.

It was nearly seven o'clock before Ewell had his Second Corps's say in the second day's battle. The contest was ill-timed, ill-coordinated, ill-advised, and very brutal. An artillerist later said one Confederate battery "had been hurled backward, as it were, by the very weight and impact of metal from the position it had occupied on the crest of a little ridge, into a saucer-shaped depression behind it; and such a scene as it presented—guns dismounted and disabled, carriages splintered and crushed, ammunition chests exploded, limbers upset, wounded horses plunging and kicking, dashing out the brains of the men tangled in harness; while cannoneers with pistols were crawling around through the wreck shooting the struggling horses to save the lives of the wounded men."

In the afterglow of the setting sun of July 2, Fred Haskell looked at the now quiet fields beneath him, "plowed and scored by the shot and shell, the orchards splintered, the fences prostrate, and the harvest trodden in the mud." Knapsacks and haversacks were thickly strewn about and "canteens of cedar of the Rebel men of Jackson, and of cloth-covered tin of the men of the Union; blankets and trousers, and coats and caps, and some are blue and some are gray; muskets and ramrods, and bayonets, and swords, and scabbards and belts, some bent and cut by the shot or shell; broken wheels, exploded caissons, and limberboxes, and dismantled guns, and all these are sprinkled with blood . . . the men of South Carolina were quiet by the side of those of Massachusetts, some composed, with upturned faces, sleeping the last sleep, some mutilated and frightful, some wretched, fallen bathed in blood, survivors still and unwilling witnesses of the rage of Gettysburg.

"And yet with all this before them, as darkness came on, and the dispositions were made and the outposts thrown out for the night, the Army of the Potomac was quite mad with joy. No more light-hearted guests ever graced a banquet than were these men as they boiled their coffee and munched their soldiers' supper tonight. Is it strange?"

As lanterns of the medical corps twinkled over the field, Lee rode slowly back to his headquarters on the Chambersburg Road. He had lost 9,000 men that day and had seen his army come apart. None of the regiments which climbed Cemetery Ridge had been properly supported. None had been reinforced. The same had been true of Ewell's truncated sundown attempt at snatching a victory from the jaws of his own failure. And Lee had sat alone and silent and watched. He didn't issue one order that day.

At night, in the quiet of his campground, he continued to sit alone. Neither Ewell nor Hill paid a call, and Longstreet stayed away. There was nothing to say. But sitting there, Lee made the same kind of decision which so shocked his subordinates at Sharpsburg. A year earlier in Maryland, Lee ordered the apparently beaten troops to keep their line and accept a new fight. At Gettysburg, he decided to give battle once again after two defeating days. What had happened on July 2 was impossible to call a success, but with hope and trust that perhaps God would help, it might not be called a complete failure. The men who had been ordered to attack up the Emmitsburg Road were in fact sleeping on their muskets not far from that road. If the army could come together into one powerful fist, perhaps it could smash a single hole through the defenses on Cemetery Ridge and get at the Federals from the rear. If Ewell, still in place on the north edge of the ridge, could attack first and draw attention and defenders away from the assault, the plan might work. Lee wrote out orders to Hill and Ewell. He would see Longstreet in the morning. At one, he lay down to rest.

He was up again at three, but doubt now colored hope. He knew Pickett's division of the First Corps was only three miles away. It would get to the field in plenty of time, but Longstreet needed more than plenty of time. Lee sent Ewell another message. Delay your attack, he said. We won't be ready to go until ten o'clock or later.

Riding southeast, Lee heard the sound of artillery off to his left.

It had to be Ewell. His message had not arrived in time, and for once, ironically, Crazy Dick was displaying aggression. The chance for coordinating an attack was lost. Longstreet would have to do it alone.

While Ewell was getting pounded to pieces on the left, Lee found Longstreet camped just to the west of Round Top. Oddly, Old Pete was in excellent spirits. He started to his feet and strode toward Lee. "General," he said, "I have had my scouts out all night, and I find that you still have an excellent opportunity to move around to the right of Meade's army and maneuver him into attacking us." Lee quietly looked at Longstreet and pointed northward, toward the center of Cemetery Ridge. "The enemy is there, and I am going to strike him." Years later, Longstreet said of Lee that when "the hunt was up, his combativeness was overruling." It was an astute assessment, and one he may have made in the midst of the battle of Fredericksburg, when Lee turned from the field and told him that it was "well war was so terrible—we should grow too fond of it." This seemingly innate aggressiveness found so little reflection in his drawing-room self that many of Lee's associates were not even aware it existed. But it did exist and was perhaps even the essence of the man. Hampered by the self-imposed constrictions of lifelong duty to ailing women and of trying to divine God's purpose for him while devoting his professional life to the dreary details of military bureaucracy, Lee may well have welcomed the "hunt" which released him from his own exactions. Only once before—in Mexico—did he have an opportunity to exercise this combativeness, and it took him four years to get over losing it. Strange as it seemed, this apparently gentle man, who plucked violets for gifts and celebrated small children in lacy dresses, had the soul of a warrior. On the morning of July 3, 1863, the hunt was up.[16]

One of the few men who understood Lee in this respect was facing him from the heights of Cemetery Ridge. George Gordon Meade had been ready to withdraw the Union army. Only the passionate objections of his aides kept Meade in place. On July 3, the subordinates felt vindicated. The morning seemed peaceful. "The men roused early," a Federal lieutenant wrote. "Then ensued the hum of an army, not in ranks, chatting in low tones, and running out and jostling among each other, rolling and packing their blankets and tents . . . They packed their knapsacks, boiled their coffee and munched their hard bread just as usual." Meade stayed vigilant and rode the lines, looking across the valley. Someone suggested Lee would retreat. No, Meade said, Lee will attack.

Lee's orders were for Longstreet to take field command of the eleven brigades who would make the assault. Confederate batteries—140 guns massed along Seminary Ridge; the largest concentration of artillery ever assembled on the continent—would soften the enemy. Then two divisions—one under George Pickett, the other under James Pettigrew—would move out, align themselves, and direct their charge toward the little clump of trees just there, in the middle of the Federal position on Cemetery Ridge. Longstreet took the news quietly. Lee had a depressed Longstreet come along on a ride over the ground that would be covered. They were greeted by most of the officers. When one of the brigadiers who had reached the crest of Cemetery Ridge stopped to boast of his July 2 exploits, Lee asked if he could get there again.

"No, General, I think not," was the reply.

"Why not?"

"Because, General, the enemy have had all night to entrench and reinforce. I had been pushing a broken enemy, and the situation now is very different."

Lee made no comment, and rode on. A. P. Hill asked if he shouldn't send in his entire corps. No, Lee said, what remained of his corps would be the only reserve. It would be needed "If General Longstreet's attack should fail." At nine o'clock Longstreet left to have the cannon arranged, and Lee rode north alone to meet the head of Pickett's division as it came onto the field from the Chambersburg Road. A Pickett veteran remembered that Lee, "or better known as Uncle Robert," watched "anxiously" as the division arrived. "I must confess that the General's face does not look as bright as though he were certain of success. But yet it is impossible for us to be any otherwise than victorious and we press forward with beating hearts." The new recruits of Pickett's command dispelled tension by pelting one another with small green apples as soon as they reached a temporary halting place in an orchard. Less anxious soldiers drowsed in what one said was a perfect summer day. "Never was sky or earth more serene, more harmonious, more aglow with light and life."

George Pickett was as buoyant as his men. A West Point classmate of Stonewall Jackson's—Pickett graduated fifty-ninth out of a class of fifty-nine—he had gone to Mexico, where a disgruntled Grant watched him and Longstreet scale the walls at the Chapultepec gate. The taste for glory never left Pickett. He spent the next fifteen years courting disaster or fame. Vain, contentious, and convinced of his superiority, he wore his hair shoulder length and his beard in a natty triangle. On July 3, he was "entirely sanguine of success in the charge, and was congratulating himself on the opportunity," said an officer.

As Pickett's men filed into position behind Seminary Ridge, Lee rode north to check on the troops assembled under James Pettigrew. He came away visibly shaken. "Many of these poor boys should go to the rear; they are not able for duty," he exclaimed when he saw the ragged remnants of the division. He had perhaps not realized until then how thin were his ranks. The unfit boys, bandaged and lame from two days' fighting, stood gamely before their chief in regiments which had suffered devastating losses. Lee said softly that he missed "the faces of many dear friends." Shaking his head, he whispered to himself as he rode away. "The attack," he said, "must succeed." Solemn, almost leaden, he passed Pickett's division for the final time. As he rode, the soldiers stood in companies and silently removed their hats. Staring into their faces, Lee took off his own soft black felt.

There was nothing to do but wait. Two of Pickett's brigadiers crept to the top of Seminary Ridge and looked across the valley. Neither spoke. Finally the younger turned to his friend and broke the silence: "This is a desperate thing to attempt."

The men knew their commander spoke the truth. "No disguises were used, nor was there any underrating of the difficult work at hand," a veteran declared. A Tennessee sergeant, stricken by the sudden need to move, jumped to his feet and demanded of himself, "June Kimble, are you going to do your duty?" The answer, given immediately, was heard by June's friends. "I'll do it so help me God." Then June felt better, and lay down again. Orders were for the cannonade to begin with the firing of two shots around one o'clock.

Close to one o'clock, twenty-eight-year-old Porter Alexander, in command of the First Corps batteries, was startled by a message from Longstreet. Alexander was to decide if the cannonade was effective; if it was not, he should advise Pickett not to advance. Alexander immediately wrote back saying he would make no such decision. Longstreet insisted, and ordered Alexander to tell Pickett when to charge. The young man had never imagined such a momentous responsibility would be his. He rode to the front of his batteries and asked a friend what he thought. "Is it as hard to get there as it looks?"

"The trouble is not in going there. I went there with my brigade yesterday. There is a place where you can get breath and re-form. The trouble is to stay there after you get there, for the whole Yankee army is there."

Just then, the whole Yankee army was drowsing after lunch. The day was exceedingly hot. "We dozed in the heat and lolled upon the ground with half open eyes," wrote Fred Haskell. "Our horses were hitched to the trees munching some oats. A great lull rests upon all the field. Time was heavy, and for want of something better to do, I yawned and looked at my watch. It was five minutes before one o'clock."

Porter Alexander looked at his watch too. It was almost one. He quickly sent off a note to Longstreet: "General, When our fire is at its best, I will advise Gen. Pickett to advance."

Then there were five minutes of heavy, twitching silence.

Porter Alexander looked at his watch again. He nodded.

Eleven thousand Confederate soldiers and half that many Federals shook alert as a dull jarring boom broke the torpid quiet covering Gettysburg. For what seemed minutes but was not,

20,000 soldiers tensed and listened until a second shot echoed through the valley between Seminary and Cemetery ridges.

"Down! Down!" shouted the Union officers as their troops dove for cover. "The air was all murderous iron," said one terrified soldier. Shells plunged into Union lines, mangling horses, plowing trenches in the earth, and scattering batteries. "All in the rear of the crest for a thousand yards as well as among the batteries, was the field of blind fury," wrote a Federal officer. Federal guns opened up minutes after the Confederate barrage began. Flattened against the slope of Seminary Ridge, Pickett's men shouted at their commanders to get down, while men prayed— "loudly too." Stretcher bearers refused to answer the calls of "Wounded!" so heavy was the shot. Dozens joined in cheering a terrified rabbit on to safety. "Run, old hare, if I was an old hare I'd run too."

For what was either fifty minutes or two hours—each account-keeper had his own internal, nerve-wound clock—the cannonade continued, and Lee rode up and down his lines, hailing officers and reassuring cannoneers. His appearance in front of Pickett's men "both thrilled and horrified the line," a veteran remembered. They shouted at him to get back to safety. Lee doffed his black felt hat and left.

Alexander was riding his battery lines too, anxiously watching to see if the fire was softening Federal defenses. "It seemed madness," he wrote later, "to order a column in the middle of a hot July day to undertake an advance of three-fourths of a mile over open ground against the center of that line. But something had to be done." The little clump of trees which was the objective had disappeared into the smoke on Cemetery Ridge, but Alexander knew there was nothing to do but tell Pickett to send his men over. "General," he wrote, "If you are to advance at all, you must come at once or we will not be able to support you as we ought." No sooner did Alexander send the message than he noticed a decided reduction in Federal fire. Immediately he wrote again: "For God's sake come quick."

Pickett was next to Longstreet when Alexander's note arrived.

He read it, handed it to Longstreet, waited a minute, and asked Pete if he should go. Longstreet did not—or could not—respond. He turned away and nodded. Pickett saluted. "I am going to move forward, sir."

Only a few of his men could hear Pickett's exhortation: "Don't forget today that you are from old Virginia." Indeed they did not want to. The division took pride from the knowledge that one of their regiments was George Washington's original military unit. Pettigrew, commanding a division of North Carolinians, passed the word to his officers to advance. "Now, Colonel, for the honor of the good old North State, forward!" Chaplains hurried forward, blessing the men and praying aloud as colonels walked up and down the lines repeating their orders. "Advance slowly, with arms at will. No cheering, no firing, no breaking from common to quick-step. Dress on the center." The men stood in companies and joined in singing hymns as they began to walk forward. Lewis Armistead—who only two years earlier had said goodbye with tears in his eyes to his best friend, Winfield Scott Hancock, now waiting for him across the valley—rode up to his color bearer. "Sergeant," he demanded, "are you going to plant those colors on the enemy works today?" The man looked into his general's face and said he would try, "and if mortal men can do it, it shall be done." At that, Armistead removed his hat, stuck it on the end of the sword pointing into the red sky at Gettysburg, and rode to the front of his column. "Attention, 2d Battalion, the battalion of direction! Forward guide centerrr, *march!*"[17]

A Union commander got a whispered message: "General, they say the enemy's infantry is advancing." Federal defenders passed the word: "They are moving out to attack." The artillerists had stopped firing their overheated guns to give them a rest, and hoped the quiet might bring on the attack. "Thank God! Here comes the infantry!" one exclaimed. "Every eye could see his legions," an officer wrote. "More than half a mile their front extends; more than a thousand yards the dull gray masses deploy, man touching man, rank pressing rank, and line supporting line, the red flags wave, their horsemen gallop up and down . . . barrel and bayonet, gleam in the sun, a sloping forest of flashing steel." Some found the sight frightening, others magnificent. "Beautiful, gloriously beautiful, did that vast array appear in the lovely little valley." A noncombatant thought the Confederates seemed "impelled by some irresistible force." And in the quiet wait the "murmur and jingle" of equipment and the "rustle of thousands of feet amid the stubble" rose up strangely loud to the heights on Cemetery Ridge.

Silently watching the advance, Federal soldiers readied themselves. "The click of the locks as each man raised the hammer to feel with his fingers that the cap was on the nipple; the sharp jar as a musket touched a stone upon the wall then thrust in aiming over it, and the clicking of the iron axles as the guns were rolled up by hand a little further to the front, were quite all the sounds that could be heard. Cap-boxes were slid around to the front of the body; cartridge boxes opened, officers opened their pistol-holsters."

The last of Pickett's men cleared the crest of Seminary Ridge and started forward, waving back at their own cannoneers, who raised hats in greeting and goodbye. "Soon we were past the crest of the hill and out of sight of them. Before us stood Cemetery Heights, of which we could get glimpses through rifts in the clouds of powder-smoke which enveloped them. We could not see whether or not there were troops there to defend them against us." They moved on at a pace of about a hundred yards a minute, crossed over a five-foot post-and-rail fence, and paused to realign. Just then, the first shot fired since the charge began struck the ranks, rolling along the line picking up bodies as it went. "The smoke now lifted from our front and there, right before us stood Cemetery Heights in awful grandeur." No one in those lines wondered any longer if the heights were defended.

The entire Federal crest opened in a solid sheet of shot and the gray line which had seemed irresistible began to dissolve. "We had a splendid chance at them," a Union soldier said, "and we made the most of it." Elated, gunners shouted over their works: "Come on, Johnny! Keep on coming!"

And they did. In perfect formation. The lines re-formed and began to march forward again. Pickett, coming from the right, had his captains keep the troops moving with a "Left oblique!" to close up ranks with Pettigrew's men. A halt was called and each man looked right while feeling with his left hand for comrades who fell out of reach.

"My God," a Union infantryman shouted, more in disgust than in admiration, "they're dressing the line!"

Despite cannon shot which poured on them from the left, right, and center, they were indeed dressing the line even as the line melted into the dead. The far left buckled, then broke and bolted, but the rest went on. "Don't crowd, boys," an officer quietly admonished men from the two divisions when they came together just at the base of the hill. Then they started up into the musket fire which poured on their heads from above. "Everything was a wild kaleidoscopic whirl," a survivor remembered. An officer brandished his sword and urged his men to go on, victory was only five minutes away, then fell with a bullet in his thigh. "Home, boys, home!" a young lieutenant cried over his shoulder. "Remember, home is over beyond those hills." A brigadier told his boys to be calm and keep marching—"Make ready. Take good aim. Fire low. *Fire!*"—then reeled dead from the saddle. Another, turning and calling to Armistead to hurry and help him take the heights, was blasted away before his friend could get to him. Armistead, his hat still on his sword, shouted that his men "never looked better on dress parade." "Come on, boys! Give them the cold steel!" he yelled as he stepped onto the rock mass of Union defenses. "Follow me!" His hat rolled off his sword as he toppled onto the barrel of a Federal cannon, a bullet in his head. The rock defense line was littered with thirty of thirty-eight Confederate battle flags borne up Cemetery Hill. A Mississippi regiment jammed its colors between rocks, then, making its loss count perfect, had its last living man shot. A lone North Carolinian struggled uphill with his regimental flag and planted the red banner under the eyes of Union gunners who held their fire in admiration or pity.

The Confederates who scaled those rocky walls fell on the Federals in hand-to-hand combat while Union officers on horseback milled about, wildly emptying pistols into the crowds of butternuts. Screams from wounded, shouts from officers, curses from men blended into something "strange and terrible," a sound "like a vast, mournful roar."

A junior officer, wounded, lay at the bottom of the hill. "There—listen—we hear a new shout, and cheer after cheer rends the air. Are those fresh troops advancing to our support?" No. "Oh God! Virginia's bravest, noblest sons have perished here today and perished all in vain!"

It was over. A deflated young officer told his aide to order their men back. "Let them go," he said wearily. Going was not easy, and the men who tried to get back across that field struggled with honor and fear. "I looked to the right and left, and felt we were disgraced," a young lieutenant said. "We had for the first time, failed to do our duty." He forgave himself only when he saw his fellows were dead, not gone. June Kimble, the nervous Tennessee sergeant, survived and ran. But he stopped himself, turned around, and made the last yards walking backwards, ashamed that he might be found shot in the back. Some ran and stumbled, throwing away their muskets. Others came slowly, filled with grief and pride.

Lee was waiting for them. He had ridden up to Porter Alexander's artillery post just as one last brigade marched toward Cemetery Ridge for no purpose at all. He was alone. He dismounted and walked toward the running soldiers, reaching out with his arms. "Don't be discouraged," he said. "It was my fault this time." "Form your ranks again when you get under cover." "All good men must hold together now." Perhaps because they thought of him as Uncle Robert, the survivors tended to run in his direction. "All will come right in the end—we'll talk it over afterwards," he reassured them. And the ones who had voice enough raised their hats and gave him weak cheers.

When Pickett rode by, Lee called to him: "Place your division in rear of this hill, and be ready to repel the advance of the enemy. . . ." Lee feared that Meade would take advantage of the rout and send the whole Union army against Seminary Ridge.

Pickett whispered around his tears, "General Lee, I have no division now. . . ."

"Come, General Pickett," Lee said, "this has been my fight and upon my shoulders rests the blame. The men and officers of your command have written the name of Virginia as high today as it has ever been written before." More men clustered around. "Your men have done all that men could do; the fault is entirely my own." Just then, Lee saw a stretcher being dragged to safety. "Captain," he asked a Pickett staffer, "what officer is that they are bearing off?"

"General Kemper."

Lee went to Kemper's side and took his hand. He asked if he could do anything for the brigadier who had led George Washington's old regiment.

Kemper spoke softly and Lee leaned toward him. Yes, said Kemper, there was something Lee could do. He could "do full justice to this division for its work today."

Lee bowed his head. "I will," he quietly promised.

Lee knew what the day's work had cost as he sat late that night in the tent of A. P. Hill. He realized he would never get his invincible army to Washington. He wasn't certain he could even get them back to Virginia. Grant at that moment was readying for a triumphant entry into Vicksburg. Lee knew what that would mean. More than 50,000 Americans at Gettysburg were casualties of the three-day effort.

John Imboden, commander of an independent cavalry unit assigned to lead off the retreat with the wounded, waited at headquarters while the general conferred with Hill. Around one o'clock, Imboden saw Lee "riding alone, at a slow walk, and evidently wrapped in profound thought.

"When he arrived there was not even a sentinel on duty at his tent, and no one of his staff was awake. The moon was high in the clear sky and the silent scene was unusually vivid." Lee reined in his horse and tried to dismount. He was too exhausted to move. Imboden hurried toward Lee, "but before I reached his side he had succeeded in alighting, and threw his arm across the saddle to rest, and fixing his eyes upon the ground leaned in silence and almost motionless upon his equally weary horse. . . . The moon shone full upon his massive features and revealed an expression of sadness that I had never before seen upon his face. Awed by his appearance I waited for him to speak until the silence became embarrassing."

"General," Imboden said, "this has been a hard day on you."

Lee looked up. "Yes, it has been a sad, sad day to us." Then he fell silent.

"I said no more," Imboden wrote. "After perhaps a minute or two, he suddenly straightened up to his full height, and turning to me with more animation and excitement of manner than I had ever seen in him before, for he was a man of wonderful equanimity, he said in a voice tremulous with emotion: 'I never saw troops behave more magnificently than Pickett's division of Virginians did to-day in that grand charge upon the enemy. And if they had been supported as they were to have been . . . the day would have been ours.' "

Lee was silent again.

Finally his agonized voice rose and echoed through the camp-ground: "Too bad! *Too bad!* Oh! TOO BAD!"[18]

CHAPTER

19

TEN MONTHS AFTER he led his victorious army into
Vicksburg, Ulysses Grant received a letter from Abraham Lincoln: "Not expecting to see you again before the Spring campaign
opens, I wish to express, in this way, my entire satisfaction with
what you have done up to this time, so far as I understand it. The
particulars of your plans I neither know of, or seek to know. You
are vigilant and self-reliant; and pleased with this, I wish not to
obtrude any constraints or restraints upon you. While I am very
anxious that any great disaster or the capture of our men in great
numbers shall be avoided, I know these points are less likely to
escape your attention than they would be mine— If there is
anything wanting which is within my power to give, do not fail
to let me know it. And now with a brave Army, and a just cause,
may God sustain you."

That letter, which would have sustained any Army man,
capped a period of unadulterated personal success for Grant
which started when he received another letter from Lincoln in
mid-July 1863. The President confessed that his own ideas for the
Mississippi campaign had been completely at odds with Grant's.
"I now wish to make the personal acknowledgement that you
were right, and I was wrong," he said. Any doubts that lingered in Grant about how securely he held his position were dissipated.[1]

LEE HAD ALSO been affirmed as commander, but the knowledge only added to the despair he felt after Gettysburg. The retreat from Pennsylvania was already under way when he took one last ride to the crest of Seminary Ridge on Independence Day. He sat silently on his horse for a time, staring at the ruin beneath him. As he turned away, he quietly admitted again that it was "all my fault." Then: "I thought my men were invincible."

In rain so heavy commanders couldn't see more than two or three feet, the Army of Northern Virginia limped to the banks of the Potomac. It was flooded, impossible to ford. For more than a week Lee sat on the wrong side of the river, watching over his shoulder for the attack he felt was coming. But the threat of ruin did not daunt him, he wrote Jefferson Davis: "I hope Your Excellency will understand that I am not in the least discouraged, or that my faith in the protection of an all merciful Providence, or in the fortitude of this army, is at all shaken."

Two weeks later, with his army safely back on Virginia soil— and Meade under censure for not annihilating the vulnerable Confederates—Lee began to cope with the shaken faith of the southern people. Discontent over Gettysburg was widespread. Lee was criticized for what was seen as overnice concern with northern civilian property, and his army was charged with incompetence. He readily accepted personal barbs, but was outraged that his army was maligned. "The army has laboured hard, endured much & behaved nobly," he wrote Mary. "It ought not to have been expected to have performed impossibilities or to have fulfilled the anticipations of the thoughtless & unreasonable." He didn't hedge about being the author of those anticipations. "The army did all it could," he wrote. "I fear I required of it impossibilities. But it responded to the call nobly and cheerfully, and though it did not win a victory it conquered a success. We must now prepare for harder blows and harder work." It was wrong to criticize the army "for its failure to accomplish what was projected by me," he told Davis, "nor should it be censured for the unreasonable expectations of the public. I am alone to blame, in perhaps expecting too much of its prowess & valour." He had thought a victory at Gettysburg was possible, he said. "I still think if all things could have worked together it would have been accomplished. But with the knowledge I then had, & in the circumstances I was then placed, I do not know what better course I could have pursued. With my present knowledge, & could I have foreseen that the attack on the last day would have failed to drive the enemy from his position, I should certainly have tried some other course. What the ultimate result would have been is not so clear to me."

It was clear to Lee what his own course should be. A week later he again wrote to Davis, offering to resign. When Davis denied his request, Lee said he would command the army until the President gave him another job. "The lower the position, the more suitable to my ability, and the more agreeable to my feelings. Beyond such assistance as I can give an invalid wife and three houseless daughters I have no object in life but to devote myself to the defense of our violated country's rights."[2]

G R A N T ' S   N E W L Y elevated position was redounding to his benefit. Julia and the children joined him for a gala occupation of Vicksburg, which had his entire family—domestic and official—boarding in a twenty-six-room house which Julia breathlessly described as "not unlike the Executive Mansion in Washington." She received Unionist ladies in the parlor while Grant received the adulation of the country. Even Rawlins waxed lyrical during those midsummer Mississippi months. The Lums, who owned the house in which Grant lived, employed as governess a Connecticut beauty who soon melted John Rawlins into a husband-to-be.

Grant left Vicksburg at the behest of the Secretary of War. Edwin Stanton was taking the unprecedented step of visiting an Army officer instead of calling him into his august presence in Washington. But what could have been a triumph for Grant got off to a bad start. Accompanied by Julia, who was in a fit of nervous anxiety, Grant was to meet Stanton in Louisville. But Stanton caught up with them in Indianapolis and ordered their train held. Grant dutifully waited until Stanton climbed into the

car, and he watched dismayed as the Secretary charged down the
aisle heartily greeting the Army of the Tennessee's physician.
"General Grant," Stanton exclaimed, pumping the hand of Dr.
Kittoe, "I would have known you anywhere!" The meeting between the two men went better than it began. Earlier, in Vicksburg, Grant had been offered—and declined—command of the
Army of the Potomac. Virginia and Robert Lee were not much
on his mind; he wanted the West, and that was what he got. At
Louisville, Stanton gave Grant command of the Military Division of the Mississippi. He now controlled all the space west of
the Alleghenies.

On October 20, still suffering from the effects of a painful fall
from a horse during a celebration in New Orleans, Grant left for
Chattanooga, and a try at clearing the Confederates out of Tennessee. Longstreet, finally succeeding in detaching himself from
Lee, had come west and joined Braxton Bragg in the battle of
Chickamauga, which ended with the Federals besieged in Chat-
tanooga. With hard freezes gripping the mountainous region, the
army was in real danger of being starved out. Three days after
Grant arrived, he'd solved the problem of supplies with a "cracker
line" to Knoxville. A month later he'd solved the problem of
Chattanooga and added a new name to the list of his victories—
Missionary Ridge.

By mid-December 1863 he'd set up his headquarters in Nashville, ordered Julia to his side, and sat back and read accounts of
his progress in the newspapers. He was hailed as the salvation of
the Union, a second Washington, and his name was mentioned
by more than one editor as presidential material. Congress struck
a gold medal and passed a joint resolution thanking him for his
efforts. What was more, Elihu Washburne introduced a bill
reviving the rank of lieutenant general of the United States Army
that had been buried with George Washington at Mount Vernon.
Though a grateful nation had bestowed the brevet of lieutenant
general on Winfield Scott for Mexico, it never codified it. There
was only one reason for establishing the rank in 1863. "Grant's star
is still in the ascendant," Rawlins said after Chattanooga.

Men who met him for the first time in late 1863 got to know

a different Grant from the uncertain captain who left Galena. Adam Badeau, who joined Grant as secretary, said his new boss "had no fear of not doing all that he was put in his place to do. He did not know, he said, how long it might be before he accomplished his task, nor what interruptions or obstacles might intervene, but of its eventual accomplishment no shadow of a doubt ever seemed to cross his mind." Another subordinate said Grant was "very far from being a modest man, as the word modest is generally understood. . . . His absolute confidence in his own judgment upon any subject which he had mastered added to his accurate estimate of his own ability." That confidence—the same which had Julia quietly trotting at heel—now found expression in a decisiveness which could be brusque. An emissary from the Quartermaster General's office in Washington, arriving in Nashville, said Grant "knew exactly *what* he wanted, and *why,* and when he *wanted* it." The speed with which he roared through bureaucratic details prompted the officer to ask Grant if he was sure he was always right. "No," Grant answered, "I am not, but in war anything is better than indecision. *We must decide.* If I am wrong we shall soon find it out and can do the other thing. But *not to decide* wastes both time and money and may ruin everything." Grant as a coy political candidate was equally novel.

Pro-war Democratic newspapers in December began running editorials hailing Grant as a new Andrew Jackson. His very political ignorance, they said, was a prime quality for a presidential candidate. They had had enough politicians at the helm. "Your letter of the 8th inst. asking if you will be at liberty to use my name before the convention of the 'War Democracy' as a candidate for the office of the Presidency is just received," Grant wrote an Ohio committee member in mid-December. "The question astonished me. I do not know of anything I have ever done or said which would indicate that I could be a candidate for any office whatever within the gift of the people. I shall continue to do my duty, to the best of my ability, so long as permitted to remain in the army, supporting whatever administration may be in power in their endeavor to suppress the rebellion and maintain National unity, and never desert it because my vote, if I had one, might have been cast for a different candidate."

For a man with no vote, Grant could write a very politic letter. His hint that his heart was still with the Democrats was expressed so carefully that it would be hard for even a radical Republican to take exception to what he said. Predictably, the matter did not rest there. Grant had to write letters to congressmen, military politicians like Frank Blair, his father, and friends of Elihu Washburne insisting he was not interested in running for office. He did not, like Sherman would later, categorically rule out such a happenstance. But he scotched a present candidacy. Rawlins, discussing the happy turn of events with James Wilson, said Grant's handling of the issue was astute. "The nomination for the office has not been tendered him by the people; nor has it by either of the great political parties or any portion thereof, through delegates from the people and duly authorized to do so. To write a letter of declination now would place him much in the position of the old maid who had never had an offer declaring she would not marry . . ." Lincoln heard the talk and sought out Washburne for his opinion as to what Grant would do. Washburne said he actually didn't know Grant very well, and turned the President over to J. Russell Jones, the Chicago financier who had followed Grant around Memphis, making money in cotton. Jones, who by then was producing a lot of money for Grant, reassured Lincoln that Ulyss was happy in the field.[3]

L e e   w a s   a s happy in the field as he would have been anywhere else that winter. He pitched his headquarters tent south of the Rapidan, in Orange County, and tried to make do. He had been half sick since his illness a year earlier, and the cold weather bothered him more than ever. A recurrence of the angina—he thought he had rheumatism—kept him off a horse for a month. And he couldn't get Gettysburg out of his mind. The "loss of our gallant officers and men," he said, "causes me to weep tears of blood and to wish that I never could hear the sound of a gun again." His son Rooney, injured at Brandy Station and taken to his wife's home near Hanover Junction to recuperate, was captured while Lee was at Gettysburg. He called Rooney's imprisonment an "additional affliction" and prayed for the strength to bear it. But as the months wore on and Rooney remained incarcerated at Fortress Monroe, Lee began to mourn his lost son. Chass, Rooney's wife, fell into morbid grieving and died on Christmas night from what that romantic age would call a broken heart.

Not even the loss of his daughter Annie could better symbolize to Lee the devastation brought on his family by the war than did his daughter-in-law's death. Lee had intended Rooney and Chass to live out the life of old Virginia gentility which he himself had been unable to create. And Chass—that beautiful Carter woman Lee had worried would be too delicate for a soldier's wife—left nothing behind as a monument to her union with the Lees. Both of her children were dead too. The quickening toward a future that Lee felt during the first two years of the war was arrested by Gettysburg. It died with Chass. "Thus dear Mary is link by link of the strong chain broken that binds us to earth, & smooths our passage to another world," he wrote. When he revived the phrase he used when Mary's mother died, he was not so much abandoning his love for the still living as he was admitting the impossibility of a future earthly life. He thought there was no future—either for himself or for his country—and he believed the fault was his.[4]

GRANT WAS ASSUMING a different kind of responsibility in early 1864, and that caused some problems for his most loyal supporters. He was a malleable man, open to suggestion, and he was in for an all-out assault on his stability. The very self-effacement of his public personality lent itself to misinterpretation. Almost anything could be read into that expressionless face. Grant as hero filled a deep northern need. Two years of unaccountable military losses and constant reminders of the prowess of Robert Lee famished a nation reared under the shadow of Washington legends. Most of Grant's headquarters regulars were delighted that he was the toast of the nation, but his dependable friends worried. Sherman took the opportunity of responding to a genuinely graceful letter of thanks from Grant to issue a warning to his commander:

> Don't stay in Washington. Halleck is better qualified to stand the buffets of intrigue and policy. Come West; take to yourself the whole Mississippi Valley. Let us make it dead sure, and I tell you the Atlantic slopes and Pacific shores will follow its destiny as sure as the limbs of a tree live or die with the main trunk. We have done much, but much still remains. Time and time's influence are with us; we could almost afford to sit still and let these influences work. Even in the seceded states your word would go further than a President's proclamation or an act of Congress. For God's sake and your country's sake come out of Washington.

Sherman took a dimmer view than most of the machinations of politics, but he understood the prices to be paid for national glory. Grant would not be able to avoid profound pressures, and Sherman didn't think he could withstand them. Rawlins was even more worried, but his fear grew from a sensitivity to Grant's need for recognition. What Rawlins demanded of his chief was repudiation of all the ancillary rewards of success, and Grant wasn't ready to forgo such salves to his ego. After Chattanooga, he couldn't appear in public without attracting droves of well-wishers bent on telling friends they'd shaken hands with the famous General Grant. He was embarrassed by such demonstrations, but he enjoyed the flattery. No incident in that very eventful year offered more balm to his sensibilities than a triumphal visit to St. Louis. Julia had gone ahead to care for Fred, whose Vicksburg-contracted fever held him dangerously ill until January 1864. By the time Grant arrived, Fred was past his crisis, and Grant settled down to a round of parties, theatergoing, and testimonial dinners. Harry Boggs—his old real estate partner, now a penitent-in-waiting—and Louisa Boggs partied with the Grants and basked in the reflection of the dazzling hero. Grant was lofted from his seat by shouts to show himself at the theater, and was called upon to give speeches at the dinners. For a man who five years earlier was hounded out of a rented shack because he couldn't borrow money, the magnificent return to St. Louis must have been sweet indeed.

Rawlins thought "the eagerness, or willingness rather, of him we love to say is so modest and unassuming to acknowledge the notice people are taking of him" was reprehensible. But Rawlins's footing was none too sure. "Oh greatness," he exclaimed, "how dost thou lift up in themselves those whom thou favorest. I feel that to go with them is ascending heights too far above the level of my plebian birth; beyond the reach of any influence I can exert for my country's good."

Julia felt denuded by Grant's limelight too. At Nashville, she was mortified when wives of subordinates cattily suggested that Grant's frequent absences were caused by her presence. She defended herself by weakly saying her husband had sent for her, but when she informed Grant about the unpleasantness, he said she was to tell her tormentors that not only was she welcome but Grant moved his headquarters to Nashville "for the sole reason that I might have you with me." She had always thought herself ugly, and she was embarrassed by her crossed eye. She cringed at the attention of strangers because she felt they were staring at a spectacle, not admiring the wife of General Grant. When he left the celebration at St. Louis, Julia stayed behind. She said she had never before had "the courage to consent" to eye surgery, "but now that my husband had become so famous I really thought it behooved me to look as well as possible. So I consulted the doctor on this, to me, the most delicate subject, but alas! he told me it was too late, too late." Despondent, Julia timidly confessed to Grant that she had seen a doctor and nothing could be done. Grant responded by saying he liked her eyes "just as they are," and forbade her to "make any experiments, as I might not like you half so much with other eyes."

Julia savored the reassurance but continued cautious. When she went with Grant to Washington, where he would assume his duties as head of the Army, she was terrified. Sherman was with them and Julia nervously sought his social advice. He couldn't imagine a woman not knowing at least the rudiments of repaying calls, and his response did nothing to quiet her fears. A shopping trip in Philadelphia helped. She outfitted herself in style and then went on to Washington with a new wardrobe which "gave me both comfort and peace of mind."

Apparently nothing could comfort Rawlins. Grant put in his name for promotion to brigadier general, and he was irritated that confirmation was too slow in coming. His health was failing—the tuberculosis which had killed his first wife was eating out his lungs by early 1864—and he despised the medical treatments. Ironically, the zealous teetotaler was getting daily doses of the nineteenth century's only medication for lung disease—opium. But worse than anything was Rawlins's notion that he was losing Grant. Headquarters by that time was staffed with more than a dozen soldiers whose expertise and confidence made Rawlins feel all the more "plebian." The good times in the West, where Rawlins could shout around and rant at Grant, were over. The two men were "measurably drifting apart," a staffer noted. "There was no rupture, and no public withdrawal of confidence or respect, but Rawlins soon came to understand that there were influences at work which he could not always locate or counteract." Rawlins could only lament that his relationship with Grant "was not what it used to be."

The truth was that after the fall of Vicksburg the change had come not so much in Grant as in his circumstances. His natural desire to please authority was the same. By early 1864, however, the authority to which Grant answered—his only authority, for, as he told Edwin Stanton, he even outranked the Secretary of War—was the President of the United States. When he accepted the stars of a lieutenant general, he did not realize his lifelong dream of equaling Winfield Scott, he surpassed him. By the spring of 1864, Ulysses Grant didn't need Rawlins anymore because he was just what he had always wanted to be—"safe fer life."[5]

THOUGH LEE SAID he was "endeavoring to maintain a bold front," his circumstances kept worsening. As winter settled over northern Virginia and the few attempts he made to dislodge

Meade from north of the Rappahannock failed, maintaining a bold front got harder and harder. Thousands of men were without shoes, and most of them were without blankets or coats. When food was available at all, it never amounted to more than a few ounces of rancid fatback and a handful of meal. Desertions had never been higher. The cavalry was unhorsed as iron for shoes disappeared and forage more often than not was bark gnawed from trees. "Unless there is a change, I fear the army cannot be kept together," Lee wrote Secretary Seddon in late January. "I am granting furloughs at the rate of 16 for each company of one hundred men. . . . It is absolutely necessary that the army should be properly fed." Impressment of food was out of the question. Lee acidly told Commissary General Lucius Northrop that he was under the impression the law forbade such practices—he was right—and if it didn't, he would not do it anyway. Why not buy food from farmers rather than steal it? Or better yet, since many civilians refused Confederate money, why not barter Confederate cotton or tobacco for food? His suggestions were ignored.

Lee had no answer for his men who sent a polite and embarrassed committee to inquire if he knew they were starving. But on January 22, 1864, he issued General Order No. 7, which read, in part:

"Soldiers! You tread with no unequal step the road by which your fathers marched through suffering, privations, and blood, to independence. Continue to emulate in the future, as you have in the past, their valor in arms, their patient endurance of hardships, their high resolve to be free, which no trial could shake, no bribe seduce, no danger appal, and be assured that the just God who crowned their efforts with success will, in His own good time, send down his blessing upon yours."

He went to Richmond on Washington's birthday for a conference with Davis, and came close to being captured by Federal colonel Ulric Dahlgren. Dahlgren was leading an independent cavalry raid against Richmond with the apparent purpose of liberating Union soldiers from Belle Isle prison. The Union man was caught and killed, but he caused more furor dead than alive. A search of his pockets produced a document which prescribed the assassination of Jefferson Davis and members of the Confederate Cabinet. Southerners demanded blood, and Seddon wrote Lee asking if he would canvass the troops about executing the men captured with Dahlgren. He asked the wrong man. "Assuming that the address & special orders of Col Dahlgren correctly state his designs & intentions," Lee responded, "they were not executed, & I believe, even in a legal point of view, acts in addition to intentions are necessary to constitute a crime." With that cool admonition, Lee went on to mention activities of southern brigands who roved over the mountains holding up railroad cars and plundering northern civilians. He closed by saying he thought "it better to do right, even if we suffer in so doing, than to incur the reproach of our consciences & posterity."

He also adhered to his oath never to draw his sword save in defense of his native state. When Jefferson Davis wanted him to go to Tennessee—where he might have met Grant at Chattanooga—he said no. He explained to Leonidas Polk, who had faced Grant in Missiouri at the outset of the war, that he couldn't be of service in the West because he couldn't do much of anything anywhere. The disclaimer didn't keep him from giving advice. Lee was watching Grant closely. After Grant's Chattanooga victory, he wrote Davis urging him to act quickly "to insure the discomfiture of Grant's army." The problem was not Tennessee at all, he said, but rather the route Tennessee provided into the heart of the Confederacy. "Upon the defence of the country threatened by Genl Grant depends the safety of the points now held by us on the Atlantic, and they are in as great danger from his successful advance as by the attacks to which they are at present directly subjected."

Lee's reading of the situation was right, but it took Grant five months more to launch Sherman's march from Tennessee to the sea. Davis, apparently awakened to the danger for the first time, asked Lee to go to Georgia. The answer again was no. "My heart and thought," he wrote a subordinate in the Army of Northern Virginia, "will always be with this army."

Lee knew that Meade was still sitting across the Rapidan with 100,000 men frozen into winter quarters, but that army would not be quiet for long. In early March, he quietly made the first move of the 1864 campaign by sending a division into the Wilderness, around Chancellorsville. He was also worried about Ulysses Grant. Grant had published orders announcing that he would be in the field with the Army of the Potomac. Lee didn't believe it. Nor did he believe Grant's statement that Richmond would be the primary Union objective. "There is to my mind an appearance of design about the order," he wrote Davis, "which makes it of a piece with the publications in the papers, intended to mislead us as to the enemy's intention, and if possible, induce corresponding preparation on our part. You will remember that a like ruse was practised at Vicksburg." Grant would stay in the West, Lee thought, and make another jab at Joe Johnston.

Three days later, he knew he was wrong. "It looks as if Grant was really going to operate the Army of the Potomac," he wrote Longstreet, who was still in Tennessee. "One of our scouts even reports that he did come up in the train of the 24th, all the cross roads, stations, &c. having been strictly guarded to prevent the train being molested. If he is really going to operate here, we may expect a concentration of troops in this region." Lee knew how Grant liked to fight, but he still wasn't convinced that Grant was going to be fighting him. "It behooves us to be on the alert, or we will be deceived. You know that is part of Grant's tactics. He deceived Pemberton when he turned him, and in this last move of Sherman threw dust in Polk's eyes. If a good move could be made before they are ready to execute their plans, we would confound their schemes and break them up."[6]

GRANT WAS NOT trying to deceive Lee, he was merely attempting to establish himself as head of the United States Army and exert some kind of control over the Army of the Potomac. When he arrived in Washington in March, he was scrutinized and criticized. As a Westerner, he was immediately suspect. The men of the Army of the Potomac had had their share of western generals who injured their pride and then lost anyway, and they were irritated at the public acclaim won by the Army of the

Tennessee. The dismal record of the eastern troops had done nothing to shake their faith that they were superior to their western brethren. Officered and staffed by grandsons of New England founders, the Army of the Potomac regarded itself as the legitimate guardian of the Union. It might have felt uncomfortable about playing the British to Confederate Rebels, but its lineage traced as straight a line to the Continental Army as did that of Lee's Army of Northern Virginia. That proprietary arrogance disposed it to dismiss the West as readily as it sought to defeat the South. What was more, when Grant arrived to take the helm, the Army of the Potomac was still basking in the victory at Gettysburg.

Despite Grant's propulsion to national hero, Vicksburg never achieved the symbolic import of Gettysburg. Vicksburg changed the war, but Gettysburg changed the country. Though Meade was criticized for not following up his advantage, Gettysburg satisfied war supporters that the North could win. In late July, when draft rioters in New York attacked Negro orphanages, anti-black sentiment was humiliated by the quick military action which left more than two hundred demonstrators dead. Lincoln had always known he needed a great battlefield victory for the war and emancipation to win the hearts and minds of his people. He got it at Gettysburg. What he gave in response was a vision of the war which sanctified the North and ennobled the work of the Army of the Potomac. In November, standing on the hill on the north edge of Cemetery Ridge—the hill which Ewell did not take for Lee on July 1 and could not take for Lee on July 2 and 3—Lincoln delivered the Gettysburg Address, and focused the eyes of the world on the Civil War as fought in the East.

Grant had no intention of belittling the honor of the Army of the Potomac. He only wanted to use it as part of a combined effort of the kind Lee had foreseen would strangle the Confederacy. Sherman would move toward Atlanta, Ben Butler would go up the James River from his command post at Fortress Monroe, and Meade would cross the Rapidan and take on Lee. Grant would be with Meade for this final push on to Richmond.

On March 23, Grant sat for a photograph by Mathew Brady,

kissed Julia goodbye, and left Washington for Virginia. A journalist sat in the lobby of the Willard Hotel and watched Grant go. "He gets over the ground queerly," the newspaperman noted. "He does not march, nor quite walk, but pitches along as if the next step would bring him on his nose. But his face looks firm and hard, and his eye is clear and resolute, and he is certainly natural and clear of all appearance and self-consciousness." Eager for something quotable from the laconic Grant, the reporter charged after him: "I suppose, General, you don't mean to breakfast again until the war is over?"

Grant stopped, narrowed his eyes, and took his cigar out of his mouth. "Not here I don't."

Meade's army awaited Grant with suspicion. What they saw was an unimpressive "slim figure, slightly stooped, five feet eight inches in height, weighing only a hundred and thirty five pounds." He made a poor impression on the parade ground. No matter how vigorously the drummer beat the cadence, Grant couldn't, or wouldn't, march in time. No ear, he said, explaining that he knew but two songs. "One is Yankee Doodle, the other isn't." Men who knew Grant only from press reports were surprised to find him so small. They were further surprised by his voice, which was soft and musical and exceedingly clear. His manner—reserved, cordial, and shy—disarmed individuals prepared to dislike him.

Meade became a Grant fan immediately, and wrote his wife glowing accounts of the new lieutenant general. Meade's aide, Theodore Lyman—of the New England Puritan Lymans—carefully observed Meade's relationship with Grant, for he found the western general fascinating. Grant, he wrote, was a "man of natural, severe simplicity, in all things—the very way he wears his high-crowned felt hat shows this: he neither puts it on behind his ears, nor draws it over his eyes; much less does he cock it on one side, but sets it straight and very hard on his head. His riding is the same: without the slightest 'air,' and, *per contra,* without affectation of homeliness; he sits firmly in the saddle and looks straight ahead, as if only intent on getting to some particular point." Grant "talks bad grammar," said Lyman, "but he talks it naturally, as much as to say, 'I was so brought up and, if I try fine phrases, I shall only appear silly.' " He demonstrated only three emotions, Lyman thought—"deep thought; extreme determination; and great simplicity and calmness."

Some of Meade's subordinates were less enthusiastic. Grant fell so far short of their notions of a real general that his appearance at reviews failed to stir more than a casual shrug of here-we-go-again. The men in the ranks were somewhat warmer, and wrote home letters about finally getting a "real boss." Some officers noted that success in the West was all very good, but Grant had never faced Bobby Lee.

Lee, in fact, was as close a presence in the Army of the Potomac's Culpeper campground as was the new commander. Grant told Meade that Lee's army was the object of the campaign, and let it go at that. It was clear to his friends that he was chafing under constant allusions to the silent foe on the south side of the Rapidan. But he was too busy then to indulge any rivalry. The final plans for the massive spring 1864 campaign had to be completed, and that meant trips, conferences, and long hours working over specially prepared maps. Ben Butler needed close supervision on his contemplated push up the James. Sherman could pretty much make it alone—Grant merely had his aide and engineer, Cyrus Comstock, send Sherman a map of the Confederate States of America on which he had drawn heavy blue arrows. At the same time, Grant was breaking in a new cavalry commander, Phil Sheridan. Diminutive, dark-eyed, and black-haired, Sheridan struck some of the more polished members of the Army of the Potomac as diabolical. He shared with Comstock—quickly becoming Grant's new headquarters pet—a favorite maxim: "Smash 'em up! Smash 'em up!" and his air of grim, humorless determination seemed to suggest that he could do just that. Sheridan was not popular in the Army, but Grant trusted him to carry out the kind of war against Lee's horsemen that was necessary.

By the end of April, everything seemed ready. Grant celebrated his forty-second birthday, invited Elihu Washburne down to get in on the fun of the new campaign, and reviewed the army one last time.[7]

LEE SEEMED OBSESSED with Grant that spring. It was obvious that Grant was a different kind of commander from any he'd dealt with before, but Lee didn't understand him. He only knew that Grant won, and that bothered him. "Their plans are not sufficiently developed to discover them," he wrote about the Army of the Potomac, "but I think we can assume that if Genl Grant is to direct operations on this frontier he will concentrate a large force on one or more lines . . ." Lee told a relative that she must "sometimes cast your thoughts on the Army of Northern Virginia, and never forget it in your prayers. It is preparing for a great struggle." He wrote Davis that "all information that reaches me goes to strengthen the belief that Genl Grant is preparing to move against Richmond." Characteristically, that made Lee want to move against Grant. Walter Taylor remembered being surprised by Lee's turning to him and exclaiming, "Colonel, we have got to whip them; we must whip them, and it has already made me better to think of it!" Jefferson Davis got a somewhat more measured response: "If Richmond could be held secure against the attack from the east, I would propose that I draw Longstreet to me & move right against the enemy in Rappahannock. Should God give us a crowning victory there, all their plans would be dissipated, & their troops now collected on the waters of the Chesapeake will be recalled to the defence of Washington."

Lee got Longstreet, and at the end of April, rode over to Mechanicsville to welcome back the veterans of the First Corps. It was the first review in more than eighteen months, and both Lee and the men approached the ceremony as a solemn beginning of the "struggle to a finish." Longstreet's chief of artillery said participants "felt the bond which held them together. There was no speaking, but the effect was as of a military sacrament." After the review, the men crowded around Lee "and seemed satisfied to lay their hands on his gray horse or to touch the bridle, or the stirrup, or the old general's leg—anything that Lee had was sacred to us fellows who had just come back. And the General—he could not help from breaking down . . . tears traced down his cheeks, and he felt that we were again to do his bidding." A South

Carolinian asked one of Lee's aides if it didn't make "the General proud to see how these men loved him?"

"Not proud," was the answer. "It awes him."

Staring northward at the daily clouds of dust raised by more than 120,000 members of the Army of the Potomac, Lee, with less than 70,000 men, had reason for fear. "If victorious," he wrote Custis, "we have everything to hope for in the future. If defeated, nothing will be left for us to live for. . . ."[8]

ON THE NIGHT of May 3, Grant gathered his senior staff members around him in the red brick house he was using as headquarters at Culpepper. After dinner he lit a fresh cigar and then rose from his chair. He walked over to a map of Virginia which hung on the wall and told his men that Lee's army, not Richmond, would get his attention. Stroking his red-brown beard, he pulled the cigar out of his mouth and swept it around the area which showed Richmond and Petersburg on the map. "When my troops are there," he said, "Richmond is mine. Lee must retreat or surrender." Then Grant let his staff know it was time for them to go. The day had been long. Around noon, wagons had started bumping into lines which would stretch for more than sixty miles tongue to toe before they were completed. Tents were struck, rations issued. Close to midnight, Grant went outside and took one of the chairs near his tent and motioned Washburne and Rawlins into the other two. Rawlins was thrilled to be included in the intimacy of these final hours before starting off to catch Robert Lee. He became voluble again—as he always did when he was excited—and made an urgent counterpoint to Grant's slow conversation about politics and the Mexican War. Grant just wanted to turn things over in his mind as he used to do in the leather-goods store in Galena. Washburne said little. Clad in the black suit which had Army wags swearing that Grant had brought along his staff undertaker, Washburne knew he was in on the making of history and let Grant lead the conversation. Midnight came and they talked on. These three from Galena had come a long way since the night three years earlier when they had met at a recruitment rally.[9]

Close by, on Clark's Mountain, Lee's signalman, through the night, kept an eye on the Union campfires. He had been looking for hours, trying to see around the dust and discover a direction to the Federals' motion. Lee had come up to that mountain two days earlier, when it was still quiet across the way, and said he thought "those people over there" would make a move soon.

"Sergeant," Lee asked, "do you keep a guard watch at night?"
"No, sir."
"Well, you must put one on."

He came back again the next day, and stood staring at the white canvas tents that spread northward over the Federal horizon. Just below him, where the foot of the hill plunged into the Rapidan, were the two fords used by Hooker just one year earlier. Lee raised a gloved hand and pointed there. "Grant will cross by one of these fords," he said. No one who heard him believed Grant would do such a stupid thing.

By midnight the signalman was not at all certain who was going where, but he did know something important was going on. He flashed a signal to Lee's headquarters tent, which was pitched five miles to the west. The answer was not long in coming. Tell General Ewell, Lee signaled, to have his command ready to move at daylight.[10]

CHAPTER

20

GRANT WAS AWAKE earlier than usual, buoyed by the excitement which kept him sleepless half the night. He could hear the measured tread of his men, 120,000 strong, moving southeast to look for Robert Lee. He felt confident. As he told Julia, "I believe it has never been my misfortune to be placed where I lost my presence of mind." He dressed with unusual care that morning. He pulled polished black boots backed with gold spurs over his new blue pants, sashed his uniform coat with silk, and hung a new gold sword around his slim waist. His hat was new, too, black felt and corded with gold. Last, oddly—his staff had never seen him wear them before—Grant put on a pair of buff-colored gloves. After a quick breakfast, he swung aboard his favorite horse, Cincinnati. With Rawlins and Washburne, Grant steered his horse toward the Rapidan's Germanna Ford.[1]

Just as the sun was breaking over Fredericksburg, Lee got a message from his lookout on Clark's Mountain. All the southeast roads were filled with enemy troops, and the Germanna Ford seemed to be their objective. This was the news he wanted. His men were already striking tents to move east. The Richmond Howitzers, an elite artillery of Virginia's finest, gathered in the woods for Bible reading and hymn singing. The boys held hands and took a solemn oath to pray for the souls of Howitzers who weren't going to make it out alive. They seemed to share with Lee the feeling that meeting Grant was a do-or-die proposition. So did the ragtaggles who unbent themselves from sleep west of the Wilderness. They were done up in "campaign trim"—a standing joke—of well-worn shirts and jeans. Most were barefoot. Their haversacks, loose canvas slings, were looped across left shoulders, tobacco pouches were knotted to shirt buttons, and frying pans were tied around waists. A toothbrush might be pushed through the topmost buttonhole as a wry boutonniere.

Lee had wintered his Confederates in Orange County, named for William and Mary, but aptly so, because of the color of the soil. The best bricks in Virginia were made from the russet clay which supported fine stands of trees and equally fine plantations. James Madison's Montpelier was in Orange, and the father of the United States Constitution was buried there next to his Dolley in a tiny family graveyard. Thoughtful men might have wondered at the irony of that. Richard Ewell was the corps commander camped closest to Montpelier, and his wife, "Mrs. Brown," bore him a son there. Ewell had Lee come for the christening and stand as godfather to the little boy. Now, on the morning of May 4, Ewell was in the saddle early. Lee had told him to move at dawn, and Ewell meant to do what Lee wanted. Around noon Lee sent Ewell another message. Grant was crossing the Rapidan and heading into the Wilderness.[2]

It was noon when Grant and his staff crossed the river. Grant rode into the yard of an old farmhouse, dismounted, and walked onto the sagging front porch. He sat down gingerly on one of the rickety chairs and reached into his pocket for a cigar. Everything was going well. The army had seized the fords and the river crossing was easy. Lee must know the roads the troops were taking, but he might not understand that a full-scale movement was under way. It wouldn't be long, Grant said, before Lee gave them some hint about "what he intends to do." Then he watched the Sixth Corps—commanded by Lee's former subordinate from Fort Hamilton, John Sedgwick—roll southward. Lunch was spread on a large campaign table set under the trees, and men sorted themselves into unthinking but conscious ranks. Grant sat at the head of the table, quiet, abstracted, and picked at his food. He ate less, his new secretary, Horace Porter, thought, than any man in the Army, and his appetite, always finicky, was particularly so that day. He still wore his buff gloves.

Back on the porch after lunch Grant looked quizzically into the sudden question of a reporter. How long, the newspaperman asked, will it take you to get to Richmond? Grant took the cigar out of his mouth and paused. "I will agree to be there in about four days. That is, if General Lee becomes a party to the agreement. But if he objects, the trip will undoubtedly be prolonged." A ripple of relieved laughter played through the staff. But Grant was only half joking. He wanted to get through northern Virginia as quickly as possible. He knew Lee would try to block his path, but he thought it would be no very hard thing to knock off the Confederate advance. He didn't want to attack Lee in his formidable entrenchments. What he wanted was to lure the Rebels out of their defense works west of the Wilderness, and fight on open ground—to the south. A messenger arrived early in the afternoon with a copy of the ciphered message Lee had sent Ewell. This, said Grant, waving the paper, "gives just the information I wanted. It shows that Lee is drawing out from his position, and is pushing across to meet us." His plan was working. The staff was elated.

The mood at Grant's headquarters was a good deal brighter than the one settling over the soldiers. The day had started well— fresh and warm—and the troops swung south through blossoming orchards, shedding overcoats and keeping step to regimental bands. But as the sun moved overhead, and the men moved into the river, "a sense of ominous dread which many of us found impossible to shake off" stopped the jokes and stilled the singing. The Rapidan held bad memories for the Army of the Potomac. Almost a year ago to the day, veterans of that army had retreated wildly toward safety, leaving their dead and wounded comrades to roast in the burning Wilderness. They were retracing the same route, crossing at the same fords, and plunging into the same somber dimness on the south side of the river. Winter had washed thin layers of soil away from shallow graves and horses nervously pawed at bones stuck with shreds of Union army blue. Night came early, and even though it was warm, men lit fires to ward off chills. The talk was gloomy as the men fried bacon and broke hardtack into coffee. Stonewall Jackson's left arm was buried nearby, it was said. A sergeant tried a joke on messmates camped near the burned-out Chancellor's House. Kicking a skull away from the scorched brick foundation, he held it aloft. "This is what you are all coming to," he intoned, "and some of you will start toward it tomorrow." No one laughed. Nervous young recruits thought the woods would surely burn if they had to fight in there.

Grant's plan for the whole campaign was on schedule. Butler was moving up the James, and Sherman was on his way to Georgia. And Lee, it seemed, was too frightened to attack. With the cavalry under Phil Sheridan already reconnoitering south of the Wilderness, it looked as if the whole army could get across that space with no trouble at all. Around midnight, Grant said good night and went into his tent. He tied the flaps behind him. A narrow camp bed, made of canvas stretched over a wooden frame and mattressed with inflated India rubber, a washbasin on an iron tripod, two folding chairs, and a small collapsible pine table furnished the tent. Those and one small trunk were all he needed. He didn't plan to stay long.[3]

Lee was out of bed by three o'clock on May 5, barreling around his headquarters west of the Wilderness and exuding good humor. The night before, Jefferson Davis had reported that Butler was making an assault on Richmond. Equally bad news had come from the Shenandoah Valley, where Union general Franz Sigel was apparently in the process of sweeping away Confederates in order to join forces with Grant. Lee told Davis that P. G. T. Beauregard could nicely thwart Butler, and he wrote General John Breckinridge—former United States Vice-President and the candidate who opposed Abraham Lincoln in 1860—to stop Sigel. That order given, he had turned his attention to the work in front of him, and around midnight had sent a message to Ewell. He was to keep moving and "be prepared for action." He gathered his half-dozen staff members around him for a jocular breakfast of Confederate coffee and biscuits. Lee said Grant's charging into the Wilderness was a stroke of luck impossible to overestimate, and he was surprised that his adversary had placed himself in the same predicament as Joe Hooker. He had told an aide that he didn't really understand Grant beyond knowing that he possessed a certain canniness and had a ferocity which made him prefer all-out assaults. But with Ewell headed straight toward the Union army, and A. P. Hill paralleling Ewell in the east, Lee thought he just might have another Chancellorsville in the making. Longstreet's First Corps—as usual far behind the other two—was even now on its way to what Lee hoped would be a very active front.[4]

Just after sunrise Grant sat at his breakfast table sleepily drinking coffee, dressed in the same uniform he'd worn the day before— even the gloves. At eight-thirty, he sent off a message to Meade, who was farther on, close to Wilderness Tavern. "If any opportunity presents [it]self for pitching into a part of Lee's Army do so without giving time for [di]sposition." Then he took another drink of coffee, glanced briefly at a newsman who crashed the headquarters breakfast, and went back to his cigar. A few minutes later, he suddenly bolted from the table and called for his horse. He couldn't wait to see if any pitching was going on. The staff ran around the campsite, issuing orders for striking tents and packing gear, and chased after their chief.

Grant was intercepted a mile or so down the road by a courier from Sedgwick, who told him Lee's army was moving toward them fast. By the time Grant found Meade at Wilderness Tavern, excitable old George was near panic. Sedgwick's corps was going to be ambushed, he said, and Lee probably had sent off Longstreet to annihilate Winfield Hancock, who was trying to get back to the main army. "That's all right," Grant said in a quiet, reassuring way, then very deliberately ordered his camp set up close to Meade. Wilderness Tavern, halfway through the nasty area, was surrounded by rocky ravines choked with brush and cut with dozens of tiny streams. Second-growth pine trees poked skyward from the stump-riddled rolling ground. As an observation point, it could hardly be worse—it was impossible to see more than twenty feet in any direction. Grant didn't seem to mind, though, and Meade's staff looked on in amazement as their commander ambled over to a tree, crossed his legs on the ground, lit a cigar, and began whittling a stick with a pocketknife. As he sat, "looking sleepy and indifferent" with a soft smile, he prompted one of Meade's aides to observe that it was evident Grant "believes in his star and takes a bright view of things." It seemed he was right. The sound of musket fire—"like thousands of sheets of canvas being torn"—suddenly welled up all around Wilderness Tavern. Someone was pitching into something.[5]

Three miles away, Lee reined up his horse and strained to listen. It was musket fire, and it sounded as if it was coming from Ewell. Lee had told Ewell—as he had done at Gettysburg—to avoid a general engagement until Longstreet and the First Corps were up. But once again the Federals decided the issue. Ewell was attacked by General Gouverneur Warren—the man who had saved Little Round Top for the Union—and he waxed hysterical as his line was broken and scattered every which way in the woods. Screaming to John Gordon that the day depended on him, Ewell ordered the Georgian to attack at once. Gordon sent his division toward the oncoming Federals and watched his men neatly pierce Warren's line, stream through the break, and pull up almost shoulder to shoulder with the Federals. Commands got separated, troops shot at friends, and no one knew who—or where—the enemy was. By noon the pandemonium was general. Both armies were facing all points on the compass, and the compass was the only way commanders could locate their men. Dark worse than night—there were not even stars to steer by—turned the Wilderness into a "battle of invisibles with invisibles," said one veteran.

A Federal private remembered that no one "could see the fight fifty feet from him. The roll and crackle of the musketry was something terrible, even to the veterans of many battles. The lines were very near each other, and from the dense underbrush and the tops of the trees came puffs of smoke, the 'ping' of the bullets, and the yell of the enemy. It was a blind and bloody hunt to the death, in bewildering thickets, rather than a battle. . . . In advancing it was next to impossible to preserve a distinct line, and we were constantly broken into small groups. The underbrush and briars scratched our faces, tore our clothing, and tripped our feet from under us."

A newcomer to the Army of the Potomac thought the Wilderness sounded like "the noisy boiling of some hell-cauldron." "Artillery was wholly ruled out of use; the massive concentration of three hundred guns stood silent, and only an occasional piece or section could be brought into play in the roadsides. Cavalry was still more useless. But in that horrid thicket there lurked two hundred thousand men."[6]

Grant sat silent and noncommittal, trying to let Meade run the particular war that was going on on May 5. He seemed unconcerned about division commanders arriving with reports of new losses and new disasters, until a General Griffin arrived, cursing about the lack of support he was getting. Meade, unaccountably calm in the face of so much misery, quieted the frazzled officer and sent him away. But Grant's attention had been drawn. He never allowed so much as a hint of insubordination.

"Who is this General Gregg? You ought to put him under arrest," Grant called out to Meade.

Meade said the offender's name was Griffin, not Gregg, "and that's only his way of talking." Fully absorbed by his kindly paternalism, Meade reached out and patted Grant and buttoned up his coat for him.

Grant apparently was too interested in the sound of musket fire to feel patronized, but he was getting irritated. None of his battles had ever gone like this. Excited couriers kept wheeling into the compound, carrying news of fresh trouble, and Horace Porter told him General Hayes was dead. Grant paused in his whittling and looked at Porter. "Hayes and I were cadets together for three years," he said quietly. "We served for a time in the same regiment in the Mexican War." Then he went back to shaving sticks.

Nightfall made the fighting worse. "You see nothing," said an officer, "and the very mystery augments the horror; nothing was visible, and from out the depths came the ruin that had been wrought in the bleeding shapes borne in blankets or on stretchers." By eight, except for the cries of the wounded and occasional spurts of nervous gunfire, it was quiet. Men lay exhausted on their muskets, mindless that their near neighbor might be their enemy, too tired to eat but still able, if pushed, to defend honor. A Confederate private remembered that opponents were no more than a "biscuit's toss" away from one another. They began talking together, going over the fight, with each side claiming victory. Soon the talk grew into abuse, and a Federal snarled that his Rebel counterpart was a son of a bitch. "The reply to this was a shot, and the reply to that was a volley, which we answered in turn, and for a while we had a little battle all to ourselves."

Lee's headquarters that night were in the yard of the widow Tapp's farmhouse—not four miles south of Grant. Ewell, to his north, had more or less held his line, and though Hill's Corps—down to 15,000—was scattered around him like "a worm fence, at every angle," he expected Longstreet to arrive before daylight and fill the gaps. When Hill asked Lee if he should straighten his lines during the night, Lee said no, let the men sleep. At eleven, Lee telegraphed Seddon that both Ewell and Hill had "successfully resisted repeated & desperate assaults." All was well. "By the blessing of God we maintained our position against every effort until night, when the contest closed." He went to bed around midnight, filled with fight and hope. If this was Grant's worst, then Lee did have another Chancellorsville on his hands.

Talk was slow around Grant's campfire. The day's work, he said, "has not been much of a test of strength. I feel pretty well satisfied." Lee had failed to flank him. Tomorrow should go even better. Some of the officers were less certain. A regular leaned closer to his companion and quietly said, "When Lee takes command of both armies, as he had done several times before, we shall go rattling back to the Potomac." Grant told Meade to throw Hancock's corps against A. P. Hill and have Warren and Sedgwick attack Ewell in an all-out assault at four-thirty the next morning. Ambrose Burnside, having failed to restore his reputation by his disastrous creation of the Vallandigham incident in

Ohio, was commanding a separate force which had remained north of the Rapidan. Grant had ordered Burnside to come quickly, but he had gotten lost somewhere in the Wilderness. Those troops apparently would be of no service early on May 6, but they were undoubtedly not necessary. Meade demurred. And it was impossible, he said, for the men present to be trimmed up by four-thirty. How about six? Grant thought for a minute, then like a good Ohio haggler, settled on five. Done, said Meade, and left. The campfire was smoldering into embers, and Grant got up.[7]

At four o'clock, Grant was awakened by the sound of marching troops. It was Burnside's men, found at last and on their way to support the attack. Grant's staff was surprised to see him once again outfitted in his first day's garb. The worn gloves—plainly showing pink fingertips at all points—completed the uniform. He sat at the table, ordered a cup of coffee, and picked up a cucumber, which he sliced, doused with vinegar, and carefully ate, piece by piece. He seemed unusually quiet. The staff gave him a wide berth. He stuffed a cigar into his mouth as he walked over to yesterday's tree, but he didn't sit. Pacing back and forth, Grant seemed anything but calm. At five, a roar of artillery came from the south. The assault had begun right on time.

Lee had been up for two hours when he heard the attack. He knew immediately that Hill's Third Corps had been hit. He ran for his horse and rode toward the front, and found himself in the middle of a confused mass.

A sharpshooter, a private with one of Hill's brigadiers, was on the line when Hancock's Federals bashed through the defenses. He looked around him in "surprise and shame" to see remnants of yesterday's fight fall back without firing a shot. "It was perfectly disgraceful," he said. He had never seen troops "behave so badly." The men were jittery, and "ran like deer through the woods, leaving the enemy far behind. And the further they went, the greater seemed to grow their fright." They ran out of the woods, down a slope, and across a brook, never looking behind at their general, who raced along swinging his sword and shouting at them to stop. What stopped them was running right into General Lee.

"My God! General McGowan," shouted Lee, who sat his horse in the middle of the road, "is this splendid brigade of yours running like a flock of geese?"

No, no, not at all, McGowan stammered. "They only want a place to form, and they will fight as well as they ever did."

"No troops in the world could have stood *that*," the private reported, "the halt was immediate and decisive." McGowan's men came about, formed a line, and managed to wrestle a gun into position in time to lob a shell at the Federals who were pouring out of the woods. The men "at once began throwing up an earthwork, digging up the ground with bayonets, & tin cups and plates."

Lee stayed in the middle of the road, rigid with anxiety as both Federals and Confederates advanced on him.

"Longstreet must be here," he shouted at his aide. "Go bring him up!"

Longstreet was there. In a repetition of A. P. Hill's lifesaving dash at Sharpsburg, Longstreet and his advance rode into a company of soldiers marching in the opposite direction. They parted neatly to let the First Corps pass, and only when their red-faced and hoarse commander rode up shouting, "They are running, damn them!" did Old Pete understand the crisis. He spurred forward. Lee quickly explained to Longstreet what had happened, then rode back to his position in the middle of the road. He was facing the Federals as the first of Longstreet's men, commanded by General Gregg, started by him.

"General, what brigade is this?" Lee yelled.

"The Texas Brigade."

"I am glad to see it. When you go in there, I wish you to give those men the cold steel—they will stand and fire all day, and never move unless you charge them."

Gregg turned toward the troops. *"Attention, Texas Brigade, the eyes of General Lee are upon you, forward, march."*

One of Gregg's privates wrote later that "scarcely had we

moved a step, when Gen. Lee, in front of the whole command, raised himself in his stirrups, uncovered his grey hairs, and with an earnest, yet anxious voice, exclaimed above the din and confusion of the hour, *'Texans always move them.'*

"Reader," wrote the private, "for near four years I followed the fortunes of the Virginia army, heard, saw and experienced much that saddened the heart or appealed in one form or another to human passions, never before in my lifetime or since, did I ever witness such a scene as was enacted when Lee pronounced these words, with the appealing look that he gave. A yell rent the air that must have been heard for miles around, and but few eyes in that old brigade of veterans and heroes of many a bloody field was undimmed by honest, heartfelt tears. Leonard Gee, a courier to Gen. Gregg, and riding by my side, with tears coursing down his cheeks and yells issuing from his throat exclaimed, 'I would charge hell itself for that old man.'"

Lee seemed intent on charging with them. The horrified men watched as he urged Traveller through a break in the trenches and, still hatless, with eyes fixed on the Federal line ahead, moved through the troops to the head of the column. His aides rode beside him, grabbing at his arms, at the reins of his horse, trying to push their way in front of him, but he shook them off and kept on. Minié balls and bullets began to rake the brigade, and the frightened men shouted at Lee. "Go back, General Lee! Go back!" The brigade commander ordered a halt and rode to Lee's side. "We won't go in unless you go back!" the men yelled while Gregg tried to reason with Lee. Finally, one of Lee's staff physically turned him toward Longstreet, who sat on his horse nearby. You have wanted to see Longstreet, said the aide, "see there he is yonder." While the Texans shouted over and over, "Lee to the rear! Lee to the rear!" the flushed and excited commander was more or less pushed into Longstreet's presence. Old Pete pronounced Lee "off his balance," and gave him his choice of commanding the corps himself or using Longstreet—"If my services were not needed I would like to ride to some place of safety, as it was not quite comfortable where we were." That seemed to bring Lee to his senses, and he started rearward, pausing only once to point out a trouble spot. When he passed a new First Corps brigade advancing to help the Texans, Lee shouted, "What troops are these?"

"Law's Alabama Brigade," was the response.

Tearing his hat off his head one more time, Lee yelled, "God bless the Alabamians!" and watched them go whooping and crying toward the front.[8]

"General," a nervous aide said as he approached Grant, "wouldn't it be prudent to move headquarters to the other side of Germanna road till the result of the present attack is known?" Ewell's corps was by then throwing shells into Grant's compound.

Grant, puffing on a cigar, answered slowly: "It strikes me," he said, "it would be better to order up some artillery and defend the present location."

Burnside's presence was crucial after all, and Burnside, unfathomably, appeared to have gotten lost again between headquarters and Hancock's line four miles away. Horace Porter found the general resting under a tree, helping himself to a champagne picnic. Battle results coming into headquarters were not encouraging. A steady stream of wounded—from whom Grant flinched and turned away—kept pace with a flood of bad news. Burnside apparently could not—or would not—aid Hancock, and Hancock was being drubbed by Longstreet.

By noon, it was clear to Grant that the attacks were faring no better than those of the previous day. The morning's fight was petering out into a series of disconnected skirmishes, and Lee's entire army was now on the field. Grant suspended the battle, and ordered another two-pronged attack—a repeat of the early-morning assault—to begin at 6 P.M. Then he called for a map and sat under his tree studying the lay of Virginia land. He had to rethink his entire plan. His main problem was getting out of the Wilderness with as much of his army as he could save. He was sorely disappointed, and in one of the day's few understatements said he did "not hope to gain a very decided advantage from fighting in this forest." The best idea seemed a move southeast, to try to get around Lee's army. He sent orders to his rear guard to remove the pontoon bridges over the Rapidan. He obviously was not planning to fall back.

While Grant sat looking at his map, Lee was coping with the Federal advance. The lull which gave Grant time to issue new orders and make new plans was caused by Longstreet's being gunned down by his own men. Pete had routed Hancock, and as the Federals went running for cover, he rode forward to see how easily they might be flushed from their shallow trenches. On his way back he was mistaken for a Union officer. Rebels opened fire and a bullet caught him squarely in his ample throat as one of his companions screamed at the firing throng, "Friends! They are *friends!*" Longstreet was still alive—barely—but the battle against Hancock was not. Rumors coursed through the ranks that Longstreet was dead, and that deflated the men. Lee rushed to the scene, checked to see that Pete would be all right, then personally began the task of untangling commands from the underbrush. He had no way of knowing that Grant planned an attack at six, but Lee was not preparing to defend anything. He wanted to attack again as quickly as possible.

Grant was out for a short walk waiting for his six o'clock assault to begin when the sound of musket fire came up from the south like "the noise of a boy running with a stick pressed against a paling fence, faster and faster until it swelled into a continuous roar." It was only four-fifteen. Lee had beaten him to the punch.

The Rebels made a straight line for Hancock's breastworks. But worse than Confederate fire was one roaring through the woods from the north. "The men fought the enemy and the flames at the same time," a Union private remembered. "Their hair and beards were singed and their faces blistered. At last, blinded by the smoke and suffocated by the hot breath of the flames, the whole length of their intrenchments a crackling mass of fire, they gave way and fell back to the second line of intrenchments. With a shout the rebel column approached the road and attempted to seize the abandoned position. The impartial flames drove them back."

It was not war, a Confederate remembered, "science had as little to do with it as sight. Two wild animals were hunting each other; when they heard each other's steps they sprang and grappled. The conquerer advanced or went elsewhere. . . . Here, in blind wrestle as at midnight, did two hundred thousand men in blue and gray clutch each other—bloodiest and weirdest of encounters. . . . On the low line of the works, dimly seen in the thickets, rested the muzzles spouting flame; from the depths rose cheers; charges were made and repulsed, the lines scarcely seeing each other; men fell and writhed and died unseen, their bodies lost in the bushes, their death-groans drowned in the steady, continuous, never-ceasing crash."

Lee watched his men assault Hancock's burning breastworks, and he watched them being driven off, first by the fire, then by the realigned Federals. It was time for help, and he rode through the burning woods in search of Ewell. He found him with Early in the rear of the Second Corps. Without dismounting, Lee demanded to know if something could "be done on this flank to relieve the pressure on our right?" Ewell was as speechless as he had been at Gettysburg. Once again it was Jubal Early who explained why nothing could be done. Lee listened in "grim silence," and was turning away when John Gordon intercepted him. He had been out in front and believed he could easily turn Sedgwick's flank. Gordon had been trying unsuccessfully to get permission for such a move all day, and by six was nearly frantic from losing the opportunity. Lee listened, nodding, and when Gordon finished, told him to mount the attack immediately. Swinging into action, Gordon's men swept over the Union position with such ease that they pronounced it the "finest frolic" of the war. The party was too soon over. Night saved the Federals as Gordon's men crashed blindly through underbrush.

There was little talking between the lines that night, and little motion save that of an occasional Rebel who stole into dead-man's-land to loot a Union corpse. Lee rode the three miles back to his headquarters through a scene which an officer described as "unutterable horror." Wind howled through the tops of blazing pines, "ammunition-trains exploded; the dead were roasted in the conflagration; the wounded, roused by its hot breath, dragged themselves along with their torn and mangled limbs, in the mad energy of despair, to escape the ravages of the flames; and every bush seemed hung with shreds of blood-stained clothing. It was as though Christian men had turned to fiends, and hell itself had usurped the place of earth."

But Lee saw divinity at work there, and wrote a telegram to Seddon saying that every enemy advance, "thanks to a merciful God, has been repulsed." Then he went to bed. Longstreet was lost to him in the Wilderness, just a year after Jackson had been killed in the same way, in the same place. A. P. Hill had collapsed from nervous exhaustion, and spent the day propped up against the wheel of an artillery limber. If Grant attacked tomorrow, whom could he call upon?[9]

But Grant was not thinking about attacking anyone just then. When Gordon had hit Sedgwick, only a mile from Grant's headquarters, the Wilderness Tavern command post had gone to pieces. At Meade's tent Grant tried to make sense of conflicting reports. Commanders were dashing up—"talking wildly and giving the most exaggerated reports," Porter thought—asking what they should do. Everyone was talking about "Lee, Lee." Grant stood first on one foot, then on the other, and finally went back to his own tent and sat on a chair. A field commander ran toward Grant. "General Grant," he said, winded from excitement, "this is a crisis that cannot be looked upon too seriously. I know Lee's methods well by past experience; he will throw his whole army between us and the Rapidan, and cut us off completely from our communications."

That brought Grant to his feet. He yanked the cigar out of his mouth and angrily raised his voice. "Oh, I am heartily tired of hearing about what Lee is going to do. Some of you always seem to think he is suddenly going to turn a double somersault, and land in our rear and on both of our flanks at the same time. Go back to your command, and try to think what we are going to do ourselves, instead of what Lee is going to do."

But that was just the problem. Grant himself had characteristically not thought very much about what Lee was going to do. It was the old Shiloh problem again—Grant directing his troops through a vacuum. He had said Lee's army was his objective, but he had failed to flesh out that army into the tenacious rabble who fell on his flanks in the Wilderness. Lee the commander had been little more than a disembodied reputation to Grant. The surprise of confronting the reality, and two days of restraining his disappointment and disciplining his anxiety, finally claimed their toll. After writing orders for the following day—including one to the commander of his rear guard admitting the Confederates could easily cut off his supply line—he slumped into a chair and sat motionless in front of his tent. After some time, he remarked softly to Meade that Joe Johnston would have retreated "after two such days' punishment." One of Meade's aides added the period: "Lee won't retreat." At that, Grant bolted to his feet and ran to his tent. Rawlins followed him and watched Grant throw himself on his cot—face down. Rawlins said later that Grant "gave way to the greatest emotion" inside that tent, and Charles Francis Adams, Jr., a friend of Meade's aide, who was there, swore he had never seen "a man so agitated in my life." Grant, said Rawlins, "was stirred to the very depths of his soul."

Hours later, when the embarrassed observers had faded away, Grant came out of his tent. Silently smoking, crossing and recrossing his legs, one over the other, he stared into the campfire. The gold-corded felt hat, covered with dust and stained with woodsmoke, was pulled down over his brow, and he buried his chin in the turned-up collar of his Army coat. It was well past midnight when a reporter joined him there, and Grant didn't notice the man's arrival. Shortly, apparently aware for the first time that he was not alone, Grant straightened up and began to chat. "Neither of us," the journalist later said, "alluded to what was uppermost in our mind for more than a half hour. I then remarked that if we were to get any sleep that night, it was time we were in our tents; and that it was a duty in his case to get all the rest he could." Grant smiled, and only then mentioned "the sharp work" Lee had been giving him. He turned and walked into his tent, and tied the flaps behind him. He'd had 18,000 casualties in two days, and he hadn't expected that. If Lee attacked him in the morning, he'd be trapped.[10]

Fog and smoke blanketed the men, dead and alive, who lay under the charred mat of trees at dawn on May 7. Lee was riding through the woods to see John Gordon, whose frolic the night before had gone unsupported and had amounted to little more than the final blow to Grant's shaky control. Lee liked the man who'd come from Georgia in 1861 at the head of the Raccoon Roughs and stayed with the Army of Northern Virginia, and he talked to Gordon that morning about Ulysses Grant. He couldn't remember Grant, he said. He knew Grant had been in Mexico, and thought they might have met once, but even newspaper photographs had failed to jog his memory. But he had learned during the past two days that Grant was not like other Union generals. He had an indomitable will, and his "untiring persistency" was exactly what could bring the Confederacy to its knees. Moreover, said Lee, Grant "could command to any extent" the "limitless resources in men and materiels" of the Federal government. The Confederacy, he said, was out of both. He had lost only 8,000 men out of 65,000 during the fighting on May 5 and 6, but he couldn't replace those 8,000. What few men had come in as a result of the last Confederate conscription were, in fact, the final sweepings. But there was still hope. If he could keep Grant fighting for the rest of the summer, it was possible that public opinion in the North might "induce the authorities at Washington to let the Southern States go." This last hope was the first hope, unchanged, which had set Lee off for Maryland and Antietam Creek. He had kept the Federals at bay for almost two years and he thought he needed only a few more months—just until the November elections.

Gordon, an optimistic fellow whose belief in his cause often clouded his judgment, reassured Lee. Grant was retreating, Gordon said; hadn't Lee heard?

Yes, Lee answered, even the scouts said it.

Well, then?

"General Grant is not going to retreat," Lee said, turning in his saddle to face Gordon. "He will move his army to Spotsylvania."

At six-thirty that morning, Grant wrote an order to Meade: "Make all preparations during the day for a night march to take position at Spotsylvania C.H. . . ." That done, he seemed to rally, and joined his staff at the breakfast table. One of the officers said he'd seen a teamster, pressed into the ranks by Grant's ordering all able-bodied men to carry a gun, marching by his mule. The mule threw its head back and belted out a shattering bray. The teamster stopped, turned to the mule, and snarled: "Oh you better not laugh, old Simon Bolivar. Before this fight's through I bet they'll pick you up and put you into the ranks too!" Grant howled, and the relieved staff erupted in giggles. After breakfast, Grant settled into the chair in front of his tent. Horace Porter, apparently emboldened by Grant's show of good humor, inquired about the previous day's fight. Well, Grant said, in one sense it was a drawn battle. Neither position was much changed from when the fight began. But the Union army still held the field, and the Confederates had taken up a defensive position. In the main, he was satisfied, he said. "This will enable me to carry out my intention of moving to the left, and compelling the enemy to fight in a more open country and outside of their breastworks." This was his first idea, when he'd underestimated the potential of the enemy and decided to pitch into Lee regardless of the consequences. Later, sitting under his tree, he made a prediction about the Confederate commander: "Tonight," he said to members of Meade's staff, "Lee will be retreating south." An attaché somewhat caustically remarked that Lee was not Pemberton. If Lee were going to move south, it would be to place himself across the path of the Army of the Potomac. Grant smiled cryptically. Ah, he said, good old Pemberton was his "best friend."

In the early afternoon, Lee was sitting on the porch of A. P. Hill's headquarters when he got the news that Federal wagons were moving south. He ordered Dick Anderson, a division commander who took over for Longstreet, to pull the First Corps off the lines as soon as it was dark and head for Spotsylvania.

Grant's tent was struck after an early dinner, and headquarters gear was packed into wagons. The day had never cleared, and the night was hot. The wagon train had started moving at three that afternoon. By eight-thirty, Grant was ready to go. He swung aboard Cincinnati, eased his seat in the saddle, and set off toward Richmond.

The men on the lines had known all day that they were moving. Most of them assumed they were retreating. Grumbling that Grant was no better than the other generals, the exhausted soldiers had packed their rations and haversacks and gotten ready to go home. Around nine, they heard the clatter of the headquarters cavalcade and lined the road to get a better look. It was Grant, all right. But he was headed south, not north. They were not beaten. They were moving on. "Men swung their hats, tossed up their arms, and pressed forward to within touch of their chief, clapping their hands and speaking to him with the familiarity of comrades," Porter remembered. "Pineknots and leaves were set on fire, and lighted the scene with their weird, flickering glare. The night march had become a triumphal procession for the new commander." Grant had never been cheered like that, but he just grumped to his staff about the "most unfortunate" uproar, which would give away the move. Rawlins was not impressed by the disclaimer.

Grant's impatience got the best of him after a two-hour wait at Hancock's headquarters, and he insisted on pushing around the snarl of infantry jammed into the narrow Wilderness roads. Led by a guide whom Rawlins accused of treachery, the men headed down a dark side road, and before long were lost. Grant's aides were aware of his aversion to turning back, which "amounted almost to a superstition," one said, and they knew he would balk at the idea. That night, however, "a slight retrograde movement became absolutely necessary." Grant reluctantly yielded. They reached Todd's Tavern—about halfway between Wilderness Tavern and Spotsylvania Court House—near midnight, too late to set up camp. Grant turned his horse over to an orderly, curled up on the ground, and went to sleep.

Lee stayed in his headquarters near Hancock's Federals that night, but his First Corps under Anderson set out at dark and marched south until close to dawn. An hour after the men settled down for rest, a messenger arrived from the cavalry. Jeb Stuart had been engaged with Phil Sheridan at Spotsylvania the previous day, and the Confederates had barely held the field. Stuart thought Federal infantry was coming up. Anderson prodded the soldiers onto the road again and put them at a double-quick trot. A cavalryman was waiting: "Run for our rail piles!" he shouted. "The Federal infantry will reach them first if you don't run!" They raced into line just as Warren's corps came marching out of the woods. The Federals stopped stock-still. A solid wall of entrenched Rebels stretched across the route they'd been ordered to take.[11]

Grant's morning had started well enough. He was in such good spirits that he joined the joke on himself. He'd spent the night sleeping in a pigpen, and didn't know it. They laughed about it all morning. But by midafternoon, when it seemed that Lee had beaten him to Spotsylvania, Grant grew glum. Even the arrival of Charles Dana—whom he liked to have around—didn't cheer him. The day was hot and his men seemed to be slowing down. Some were breaking down under the pressure of a forced march coming on the heels of the Wilderness fights. For no particular reason, Grant rode into the woods alone, and stayed there, though he could see nothing but his own men pumping bullets into the trees. Theodore Lyman decided that "Grant felt mad that things did not move faster, and so thought he would go and sit in an uncomfortable place."

Losing the race to Spotsylvania was particularly onerous, because it brought Grant face to face once again with the man he had overlooked when planning his winning war. He had often seen Lee in Mexico, riding by in the midst of Winfield Scott's staff. Once, before Mexico City was taken, Grant had carried a message to Scott's headquarters and been gently turned away by Lee. Scott, Lee told Grant, had ordered that couriers come to headquarters fully uniformed, and Grant was wearing the rumpled garb of a quartermaster. He went back to his camp and changed. Later, after the capital fell and Grant was running his regimental bakery, Lee occasionally stopped by to visit Grant's commander. Grant had delivered wood to Jefferson Barracks in St. Louis during Lee's tenure as commander, but he hadn't seen him since Mexico. Grant knew—as did everyone connected to the United States Army—that Lee had been offered the job that Grant now held. But Grant now outranked Lee, Winfield Scott, and everyone but George Washington. The man he was thinking of now, however, was Zachary Taylor. His staff was used to Grant's talking about Mexico, and they were only mildly surprised when he said that afternoon that the battle of Palo Alto had been on his mind all day. He said he had been impressed by the first fight of the Mexican War. The battle "assumed a magnitude in my eyes which was positively startling. When the news of the victory reached the States, the windows in every household were illuminated, and it was largely instrumental in making General Taylor President of the United States." He paused. "Now," he said, "such an affair would scarcely be deemed important enough to report to headquarters." Was it pride or disappointment he was feeling?[12]

Lee arrived in Spotsylvania around three that afternoon. It was Sunday, and he liked to be by himself, so he rode in from the Wilderness alone. He felt weak and tired, but still had to arrange his 50,000 men to meet an attack by twice that number. The strain was telling on him. He rode slowly over the ground which Anderson's runners had claimed that morning, and looked at defenses. When Federal bullets brought with them the familiar shouts from his men to go to safety, Lee did not respond with gratitude. "I wish I knew where my place is on the battlefield," he snapped. "Wherever I go some one tells me it is not the place for me to be."

Spotsylvania County was not a very good place for anyone to be. The open, rolling, marshy ground was veined by streams which fed the Mattaponi River. The land was sour, known locally as the "poison fields." Scoured by the war, the county harbored abandoned farmsteads and fallow fields. "There was not a farm animal, not even a fowl," a private remembered. "How these people live in the track of two great armies" was a mystery to all the men. Wooded in spots, and cut by nasty ravines, the area was called "bewildering" by men who tried to align their troops just north of the jail where Light-Horse Harry Lee had once been held.

The next morning both generals rode out to inspect their troops. Lee had devised a breastwork entrenchment which was a variation on the pile of fence rails thrown up by Jeb Stuart's men. Formed along a natural rise and looking like the name the soldiers gave it—the "Mule Shoe" or "Horse Shoe"—the work arced into a long, open piece of ground which sloped downward toward a copse of Federal-held woods. Lee had his soldiers digging all day. By nightfall the six-foot-high solid wall of dirt-covered logs was backed by a long, deep trench, cut every ten feet or so by traverses. The Rebels thought they were safer than they'd been in days.

Grant rocked along half the day on the back of a pony-sized, black pacer liberated from the Davis plantation in Mississippi. He rode it that day because it had a soft gait—he was suffering intensely from boils on his backside. His reconnaissance only exacerbated his discomfort. The Army of Northern Virginia was digging in. Grant's chances of getting at Lee were apparently going to be no better at Spotsylvania than they would have been west of the Wilderness—in the winter quarters Meade had tried unsuccessfully to assault. Still, Grant had the men and he had the guns—artillery would be useful in the more open ground he wanted to claim.

Rain that had been threatening for three days broke on May 10, and that did nothing to help Federal soldiers staring up at Lee's three-mile defense work. None of them had ever seen anything like it. It was constructed, said an officer, "in a manner unknown to European warfare, and, indeed, in a manner new to warfare in this country." But Grant planned to assault it. In the morning, he had telegraphed Halleck: "Enemy hold our front in very strong force and evince strong determination to interpose between us and Richmond to the last. I shall take no backward step. . . ." That afternoon he sent a division forward, and it looked for a time as if his whole army could follow. Dodging Confederate artillery, the men leapt onto the embankment and broke through.

Surprised while cooking supper, the Confederates lost their balance and bolted. An old captain, who had been frying his bacon, "tore after them, showering them with hot grease and hotter profanity." He slapped the men into submission with the bottom of the sooty pan, and led the countercharge, "leaping upon the works, wielding and waving his frying pan." The bacon fryer was helped by General Lee, who ran to the front on foot when he heard the attack and was heading toward the hole the Federals had cut into his interior. The men were getting used to this kind of thing, and yelled at him again to go back. He would go, he shouted, only if the men reestablished the line—and at once. It "must be done!" he yelled. It was. But the Federals, who found themselves alone and unsupported behind Confederate lines, took with them on their retreat almost an entire brigade of Rebel prisoners.

The shock of the assault and repulse weakened already fragile Union nerves. A half dozen of Sedgwick's pickets were brought inside the line after dark, "crazy from want of sleep." A week of fighting, marching, digging, and thrusting and parrying was eroding a Union army diminished by 20,000 casualties. "Here it is, as I said: 'Left face—prime—forward!'—and the *wrang, wr-r-rang,* for three or four hours, or for all day, and the poor, bleeding wounded streaming to the rear," a newcomer wrote. "That is the great battle in America."

Officers were wearing out and growing bitter over glowing accounts of the battles they read in the northern press. Edwin Stanton was doctoring reports from the field and feeding editors a line of constant Union victory. Theodore Lyman was infuriated: "The newspapers would be comic in their comments, were not the whole thing so tragic. More absurd statements could not be. Lee is *not* retreating: he is a brave and skilful soldier and he will fight while he has a division or a day's rations left. These Rebels are not half-starved and ready to give up—a more sinewy, tawny, formidable looking set of men could not be. In education they are certainly inferior to our native-born people; but they are usually very quick-witted within their own sphere of comprehension; and they know enough to handle weapons with terrible effect. Their great characteristic is their stoical manliness; they never beg, or whimper, or complain."

The armies were quiet that night, and the Federal troops could hear a Confederate band playing "Nearer, My God, to Thee." A Union band answered with the "Dead March" from *Saul*. Grant ignored the gallows humor. He gave a promotion to the colonel who led the charge against Lee, smiled, and said that things were going splendidly. "A brigade today," he told Meade, "we'll try a corps tomorrow."[13]

By morning, Grant knew he would need at least another twenty-four hours. Elihu Washburne, for one, didn't have time to wait. He was disappointed that he'd been stringing along for ten days with little more than exhaustion and a dirty suit of clothes to show for the effort. He had business in Washington, and he wanted to leave. At breakfast, Washburne asked Grant to write a letter which he could take back with him.

"We have now ended the sixth day of very heavy fighting," Grant wrote Halleck. "The result to this time is much in our favor. But our losses have been heavy as well as those of the enemy. . . . I think the loss of the enemy must be greater we having taken over four thousand prisoners. . . . I am now sending back to Bell Plaines all my wagons for a fresh supply of provisions and Ammunition, and propose to fight it out on this line if it takes me all Summer. . . . I am satisfied the enemy are very shaky and are only kept up to the mark by the greatest exertion on the part of their officers, and by keeping them entrenched in every position they take."

Grant apparently was so pleased at the note he struck that he repeated his promise to "fight it out on this line" in a copy he sent to Stanton the same day. The letter was a hit in Washington. Within days, "I propose to fight it out on this line if it takes all summer" was in the headlines all across the country. This was the kind of talk the nation wanted from its generals.

Grant was even more optimistic with Julia. The fighting has been hard, he wrote, and he guessed he'd have to stay at it "at least a week more." But the "advantages have been on our side, & I feel no doubt about the result in the end." He ended cheerily: "I never felt better in my life."

Lee was particularly vigilant the afternoon of May 11. A lookout in the courthouse had sent information that a Federal movement was under way, and the news was corroborated by Rooney Lee, recently released from prison and once again on duty with Jeb Stuart. Lee got two messages from Rooney saying that Fredericksburg, which Grant had changed from a tiny bombed-out southern town into a Yankee supply dump and health-care center, was bustling with activity. That could mean Grant was moving. But perhaps it was only a sham. Lee still considered Grant the most duplicitous of Union generals; it would be just like him to try a night attack, or worse, to steal away under cover of darkness and get his army on the open road to Richmond. Lee disagreed with his subordinates' assessment of Grant as little better than a butcher. "I think General Grant has managed his affairs remarkably well up to the present time," he said. Then he told the group that he suspected Grant was retreating toward Fredericksburg. "I wish you to have everything in readiness to pull out at a moment's notice. . . . We must attack those people if they retreat."

A. P. Hill, still too weak to command, was appalled. Let them continue to attack our breastworks, he said. "We can stand that."

No, answered Lee. "The army cannot stand a siege, we must end this business on the battlefield, not in a fortified place." He had said from the war's beginning that it would "only be a matter of time" if the Federals pushed the Army of Northern Virginia into trenches around Richmond. But Grant was providing Lee with the greatest hunt of his life, and Lee was responding with the same kind of combativeness which Longstreet said sent Pettigrew and Pickett against Union guns at Gettysburg. "Let danger never turn you aside from the pursuit of honour or the Service of your Country," Lee wrote in the copybook he kept in his tent during the war. "Know that death is inevitable & the fame of virtue is immortal." Neither honor nor virtue was served by crouching in a trench. As he said during the Mexican War, standing over the grave of Markie Williams's father, there was no more noble end for a soldier than death on the battlefield.

After leaving Hill, Lee rode to the apex of his Mule Shoe breastworks and stared into the rain. Twenty-two guns pointing toward the Federals' woods backed him. With the ground turning to pudding underfoot, it would be impossible to get the artillery out of the salient in time if a Federal retreat was already under way. Better pull them back now, Lee told Ewell. Across the way the regimental bands of the Army of the Potomac began to play.[14]

The rain was battering against Lee's tent at four-thirty on May 12, but he could hear the sound of artillery. He had been up since three and had just returned from another ride to the Mule Shoe. The noise breaking around him cleared his confusion about Grant's plans. He had been attacked.

The men in the earthworks were not surprised. Surrounded by Federal guns, they were nervous when their artillery had been taken away. There was "a nameless something in the air," one soldier remembered. As the night wore on, the men got frightened. A rhythmic shudder which sounded to some like the muffled thunder of a waterfall was building out there in the rainstorm. Veterans knew the sound. It was troops moving into position. Word went out to bring back the artillery, but at four-thirty, when Hancock's entire corps came running and yelling up the slope toward the Mule Shoe, there were no guns. There were only men holding muskets to ward off thousands of soldiers bashing into the center of the line.

Some Rebels ran forward, not knowing what had happened, but shouting back and forth that Yankees had broken through their breastworks. The guns, all twenty-two of them, were being wrestled into position by terrified men who screamed "Where shall I point them?" at officers who couldn't tell them. Federals and Confederates mixed together in the maze of trenches and traverses, and Hancock's infantry just kept pouring through the hole in Lee's works. A fair number of Rebels started running rearward, but the hapless fugitives fell into new trouble.

Lee had ridden toward the center, and he rode right through the middle of the fleeing soldiers. "Hold on!" he shouted, snatching his hat off so the men would recognize him. "Your comrades need your services. Stop, men!" For the first time in the war, Lee was not obeyed instantly, and it infuriated him. "Shame on you, men; shame on you," he growled. "Go back to your regiments; go back to your regiments." Lee spurred anxiously forward, where he met a courier who said Johnson's entire brigade was gone—taken prisoner. Lee found Gordon aligning his men for a countercharge and very deliberately rode to a point near the center of the line. Gordon thought his general was resolved to lead the charge "or perish in the effort." He grabbed the horse's bridle and told Lee that the "men behind you are Georgians, Virginians and Carolinians. They have never failed you on any field. They will not fail you here." Then turning toward the men, Gordon shouted, "Will you, boys!" The answer welled around Lee and filled the woods with a roar. "No, no, no; we'll not fail him!" Gordon turned again toward Lee. "You must go to the rear," he shouted, and the echo which rolled across the field sounded like a "mighty anthem." "General Lee to the rear! General Lee to the rear!" the men repeated as they surged around Lee, turning his horse and shoving him back. Transported with the idea of saving the day for General Lee, Gordon's men stormed into the wall of Hancock's corps.

As Grant knew, Hancock's move toward the Confederate defense works had gone so smoothly there was even time for stringing telegraph wires between headquarters and the front. Grant settled down to wait in front of the campfire that sputtered and waned in the rain and wind. He heard the artillery open, and knew the fight was on, but it was nearly an hour before he had any news.

At five-thirty a courier reported that Hancock had captured the first line of the Confederate works. Fifteen minutes later another messenger announced that prisoners had been taken. There were more reports: two thousand prisoners, two general officers, the Confederate breastworks in Federal hands, and the Rebels driven back two and one-half miles. "That's the kind of news I like to

hear," Grant said. Aides came by with a string of "stirring bulle-
tins all bearing the glad tidings of overwhelming success."
Grant's men cheered and shouted, and yelled at one another that
"Lee was entirely beaten," while Meade's staff thought the Westerners absurd in their confidence. Meade sat down beside Grant
in the blowing rain to wait for more news. He was there at
six-thirty when a horseman accompanied by Union soldiers arrived and dismounted. The man's Confederate uniform was covered with mud, and a tuft of hair poked through a hole which
gaped in his hat. Coughing to hide his embarrassment, the disheveled rider strode forward. Meade stared at the newcomer for a
minute, then jumped to his feet and shook hands. He introduced
Edward Johnson, whose division had been rounded up an hour
earlier.

"How do you do?" Grant asked, shaking hands with Johnson.
"It is a long time since we last met." Johnson agreed that it had
been a long time indeed, and expressed some regret at meeting
under such circumstances. "It is one of the sad fortunes of war,"
Grant answered—not altogether candidly—offering Johnson a
cigar.

While the uncomfortable Confederate was being escorted rearward, Grant got more good news. The famous Stonewall Brigade
was in Federal hands. "Push your troops so as to keep up the
connection with Hancock," Grant wrote Burnside. He soon
learned the push was stalling. He kept his aides running hard,
carrying messages to funnel power to the weakening point, but the
Federals were slowly being driven back. Mounting his pacer,
Grant rode to the front. With his binoculars trained on the field,
he could easily have seen a silver-haired horseman behind the
Confederate trenches.[15]

"I was much impressed with the calmness and perfect poise of his
bearing," an artillerist said of Lee that day, "though his centre had
just been pierced by forty thousand men and the fate of his army
trembled in the balance." Lee was not calm. He barely managed
to control the impulse to dash into battle himself. He sat his horse,
glasses trained at the pressure point, and issued rapid orders for

passing troops forward. Feeding the fight, it was called, and he kept moving artillery, sending out desperation calls for crack battalions, including one for Longstreet's most dependable guns—McIntosh and his South Carolinians. They arrived just in time to bombard still another Federal assault.

All the attacks that day immediately became defenses. When the Federals exploded Lee's line, they rolled through the hole into the U-shaped salient while the Confederates fell back. But the bluecoats were not only confused by their success, they were strangled by it. Twenty thousand of them rushed forward in an elbow-to-elbow mass while thousands more kept pushing from behind. There was not room enough to fire a gun, or room enough to move. By eight, when Grant and Lee sat on opposite hills watching the fight, the battle line was bumping against the outer salient, and Federals fought with their backs to Lee's breastworks. By ten, the Federals jumped the works but stood their ground, and the two armies locked themselves in a fight which no one ever forgot.

"The fence rails and logs in the breastworks were shattered into splinters, and trees over a foot and a half in diameter were cut completely in two by incessant musketry fire. . . . We had not only shot down an army, but also a forest. The opposing flags were in places thrust against each other, and muskets were fired with muzzle against muzzle. Skulls were crushed with clubbed muskets, and men stabbed to death with swords and bayonets thrust between the logs in the parapet which separated the combatants. Wild cheers, savage yells, and frantic shrieks rose above the sighing of the wind and pattering of the rain, and formed a demonical accompaniment to the booming of the guns. . . ." During momentary lulls, each side screamed at the other to surrender. When a small group of Rebels held out a trembly white handkerchief, their comrades shouted, "Shoot them fellows! Shoot them fellows!" and brought them down along with the surrender flag. Crouching in the ditch, Confederates reached up and grabbed musket muzzles and held them aloft until they had been fired, then pushed their own weapons above the embankment and pressed triggers with their thumbs. Muskets fouled by rainwettened powder were fitted with bayonets and tossed as spears across the breastworks which ever after would be known as the "Bloody Angle." Men in the front ranks leapt onto the embankment and fired rifles in one another's faces, then reached backward for freshly loaded weapons. "As those in front fell, others quickly sprang forward to take their places." Confederate bodies rolled into the ditch and were pressed into the mud by soldiers who trampled to the front. "The bullets seemed to fly in sheets." Rank after rank of Federals was "riddled by shot and shell and bayonet thrusts, and finally sank, a mass of torn and mutilated corpses; then fresh troops rushed madly forward to replace the dead, and so the murderous work went on." It went on all afternoon. It was still going on as darkness gripped the Bloody Angle.

Lee divided his time between overseeing the construction of a new line of trenches and trying to get into the fight. Once, when he insisted on leading Billy Mahone's division into the center "of a fire from hell itself," he was again physically turned back and the Mississippians promised to "drive those people" from his works. Then he rode to the rear and urged the men to dig faster, faster.

Around nine that night, front-line officers started passing word to the rear. The men were used up. They couldn't take any more.

You must keep it up, they were told. Just a little longer.

At ten, they sent word again. The men were finished.

Not yet, they were told.

At eleven, the officers' cry was desperate. No one could stand it.

The answer was the same. Not yet.

But at midnight, relief—too late to make much impression—came. The new trenches were ready. And the men groped out of ditches shoulder deep in blood, rainwater, and bodies, and crawled to safety.

Federals and Confederates lay motionless as rain poured down on the Bloody Angle. Some of them were asleep. Eleven thousand of them were dead—or soon would be.[16]

May 13—a Friday—was a day of bookkeeping for the commands
of the two armies. Lee sent a short telegram to Seddon announcing the results of the battle, and he sent an even shorter note to
Davis: "If Genl Hoke with fresh troops can be spared from
Richmond it would be of great assistance. We are outnumbered
and constant labor is impairing the efficiency of the men." He
didn't mention the loss of one of his numbers which caused him
as much pain as anything that happened during the war. At
midnight, as he had returned to his tent, he got word that Jeb
Stuart was dead, killed by Phil Sheridan's men in a ruinous cavalry raid just north of Richmond. The Confederate's cavalier, the
man Union general John Sedgwick—also now dead—had called
"the best cavalry officer ever foaled in America," was gone. If any
such event can be appropriate, Stuart's being shot off his horse
during the middle of May 1864 was fitting. With his red-lined
cape and waving plume, his banjo picker, parties, and taunts, Jeb
as a symbol no longer made any sense. After giving Stuart his
highest compliment—the officer had never brought him a piece of
false information—Lee disappeared inside his tent. He could not
think of Stuart without crying, he said, and it wouldn't do for his
army to see him in tears that night.

Grant had troubles to clear up. His staff approached him early in
the day—too early, for Grant had been up past two o'clock the
night before—with a request: Dispense with Meade. The staff
was made up of many new men, but they shared with their Shiloh
predecessors the assumption that Grant could do no wrong. Since
there had to be some explanation for what was going on in Virginia, they settled on Meade's incompetence. But Grant resisted
this salve to his wounded ego. Meade would stay.

Then he turned his attention to ferrying Rebels north. The
thousands of prisoners taken during the Wilderness and Spotsylvania campaigns were penned into Belle Plain, just north of
Fredericksburg, on the Potomac, until transports could take them
to Union prisons. Grant had ordered all prisoner exchanges
stopped before the campaign began. Resting his argument on the

Confederacy's unwillingness to trade black soldiers captured during battles, he effectively drained off men who before could return to Lee's army. The dictum had some unpleasant consequences for the Union, however. The Confederacy, which left its own army half starving, was overwhelmed by the numbers of Federal soldiers it was required to keep. Converted tobacco warehouses in Richmond and Danville, and hastily constructed prisons—Andersonville in Georgia was built at that time—were soon crowded with men who sickened and died as the worst victims of the kind of neglect which had Lee's veterans buckling from hunger.

But Grant's provisions for his own prisoners and wounded were as well managed as his supply routes. Belle Plain and Fredericksburg were commercial centers where the products of battles crossed paths with the products of war. Houses were commandeered as hospitals and staffed by trained and adequately supplied medical personnel. The Belle Plain landing was busy with wagons ferrying ammunition and food to the front. Rebel prisoners experienced for the first time the largess of the Federal military enterprise and docilely lined up for their shares of the wealth.

Grant was puzzled about these prisoners and their comrades still in arms. In the midst of the Bloody Angle fighting, with six more impossible hours to go—he had telegraphed Halleck that the eighth day of battle was closing, "leaving between three and four thousand prisoners in our hands for the days work. . . . The enemy are obstinate and seem to have found the last ditch." Twenty-four hours later, Grant was not so sure the trench at Spotsylvania would be the last ditch. Despite receiving a letter of congratulations from Winfield Scott—an obviously desirable testimony for Grant—he was chastened. "The ninth day of battle is just closing with victory so far on our side," he wrote Julia. "But the enemy are fighting with great desperation entrenching themselves in every position they take up. We have lost many thousand men killed and wounded and the enemy have no doubt lost more." He was "very well" and "full of hope," he said, but the "world has never seen so bloody or so protracted a battle as the one being fought and I hope never will again. The enemy were really whipped yesterday but their situation is desperate beyond anything heretofore known. To loose this battle they loose their cause. As bad as it is they have fought for it with a gallantry worthy of a better."

Three years had passed since Grant told his father-in-law that Virginia should "be made to bear a heavy burden of the War for her guilt." Grant could not have excluded Robert Lee—a man who broke his oath to the United States government and took up Union-wrecking—from a major share of Virginia's guilt. But Grant was discovering Virginia and Robert Lee not only unrepentant but also willing to bear the heaviest burden he could inflict. He had not expected that. Nor had he expected to find himself admiring his "reprehensible" foe.[17]

There was rainfall the next few days. Some men were moved from one spot to another to strengthen defenses or launch feeble attacks, but nothing much happened. The lines were close, and belligerence was so far from the mood at Spotsylvania that a new officer found the pickets' behavior astonishing. "These men are incomprehensible," he wrote, "now standing from daylight to dark killing and wounding each other by the thousands, and now making jokes and exchanging newspapers! . . . The greatest staples of conversation are the size and quality and rations, the marches they have made, and the regiments they have fought against. All sense of personal spite is sunk in the immensity of the contest." It was with horrified sympathy that the men in the new Confederate trenches watched the solitary Union soldier left to die in no-man's-land each day raise himself to a sitting position, and weakly holding on to the barrel of his musket, tentatively try to bash his own head in. He always failed. Each day he made fewer attempts. Finally, he didn't try at all. An officer of the Army of Northern Virginia walked along the lines and stared into the powder-blackened faces of the men he'd sent to die. Something meaningful had to come of it, he thought, and decided "the blood of the martyrs is the seed of the church."[18]

The rain turned Spotsylvania County into a quagmire, slowing troop movements and irritating Grant. His army was sodden— water everywhere, no dry clothes, and wood so wet it wouldn't burn. "You can assure the President and Secretary of War that the elements alone have suspended hostilities and that it is no manner due to weakness or exhaustion on our part," he wrote Halleck. That note had the ring of Grant's old defensiveness in it. His frustrations were mounting. Each day since the battle of the Bloody Angle, he'd been shifting troops around, extending his line southward, all the while feeling out the defenses in his front. Lee had set his men to digging again and had soon constructed a new series of earthworks more formidable than the first. Grant ordered a major attack for May 18, the result of which was an exultant telegram from Lee to Secretary of War Seddon. "The enemy opened his batteries at sunrise on a portion of Ewell's line, attempted an assault, but failed. He was easily repulsed."

It was a difficult loss for Grant. A Confederate cannoneer said the entrenched Rebels "could not believe a serious attempt would be made to assail such a line." When they found the attack was real, the gunners, still smarting over losing so much artillery at the Bloody Angle, welcomed it as "a chance to pay off old scores." The Confederates waited as the Federals double-timed forward "in successive lines, apparently several brigades deep, well aligned and steady, without bands, but with flags flying, a most magnificent and thrilling sight, covering Ewell's whole front as far as could be seen." The thrilling sight was soon mangled by twenty-nine Rebel guns.

There was more bad news. Franz Sigel, sent to clear out the Shenandoah Valley, was instead demolished at New Market by a handful of defenders which included the cadet corps—average age: fifteen—from Lexington's Virginia Military Institute. And that was not all. Ben Butler had backed himself into Virginia's Bermuda Hundred, a tract of land on the south side of the James, and was being kept at bay so successfully by Beauregard that Grant said he "was as completely shut off from further operations directly against Richmond as if it had been in a bottle strongly corked." There was no hope for Sigel and Butler to join Grant as he had planned. The push to Richmond would have to come from the Army of the Potomac. Grant shared the day's disasters with his staff. "I thought the other day that they must feel pretty blue in Richmond over the reports of our victories." He had been mistaken, he said. The Confederates "probably did not feel as badly as we imagined." It was in this mood that he accepted the casualty report. Looking at the figures on the "butcher's bill," as it was called—more than 33,000 since May 5—Grant said to Charles Dana, "Well, General, we can't do these little tricks without losses."

The trouble was, the tricks were getting harder to play. "We fought here. We charged there. We accomplished nothing," a Union gunner said about the May 18 assault. An infantryman believed the troops had not been demoralized by the Wilderness, but Spotsylvania was different: "Here the Confederates are strongly intrenched, and it was the duty of our generals to know the strength of the works before they launched the army against them." On May 19, Meade wrote his wife that "even Grant thought it useless to knock our heads against a brick wall."

Wondering to himself how the Confederates held on, John Gordon explained that "these worn and battered soldiers of Lee seemed determined to compensate him for his paucity of numbers by a self-immolation. . . ." After Grant's failed assault, Walter Taylor wrote in his diary that the Army of Northern Virginia was in "excellent condition, its morale as good as when we met Grant—two weeks since—for the first time. He will feel us again before he reaches his prize." The prize—Richmond—would be Grant's at great cost, Taylor said, admitting ultimate Union success. "His losses have been already fearfully large . . . he does not pretend to bury his dead, leaves his wounded without proper attendance, and seems entirely reckless as regards the lives of his men. This, and his remarkable pertinacity, constitute his sole claim to superiority over his predecessors. He certainly holds on longer than any of them. He alone, of all, would have remained this side of the Rapidan after the battles of the Wilderness."[19]

By May 21, both armies were leaving Spotsylvania County and the men found the change was good. As they marched south, it seemed they even left the war behind. "Forests were standing untouched, farm lands were protected by fences, crops were green and untrampled, birds were singing, flowers blooming—Eden everywhere," wrote an artillerist. The Richmond Howitzers' glee club was so restored that they sang for the first time in three weeks, and Federal bands played brightly.

Lee was not as merry as his men. He knew that Grant had closed down Belle Plain, and was being supplied from Port Royal on the Rappahannock. This meant the Union army would move south. Therefore, Lee reasoned, he would probably head toward Hanover Junction, the crossroads of the Virginia Central and the Richmond, Fredericksburg & Potomac railways—a depressing twenty miles closer to Richmond than Spotsylvania. Issuing orders for his three corps commanders to move out, Lee left the "poison fields" the night of May 21. He had some twenty-five miles to go. But the Federals had at least thirty-five.

When Lee arrived on the banks of the North Anna River, just above Hanover Junction, two of his corps were already in position. Not a Federal was in sight. He was far from elated at outrunning the Union army. Quite the contrary—he felt as if he were retreating. Posting pickets to watch for Yankees, Lee wrote an apologetic letter to Jefferson Davis and ended by telling him he "should have preferred contesting the enemy's approach inch by inch; but my solicitude for Richmond caused me to abandon that plan." He said the same thing to Mary the next day, after he had set up headquarters at Hanover Junction. "Fearing he might unite with Sheridan & make a sudden & rapid move upon Richmond I determined to march to this point so as to be within striking distance. . . . Still I begrudge every step he makes toward Richmond." The grudge arose from Lee's natural distaste for the defensive. Moreover, the Army of Northern Virginia, not Richmond, was the object of his affections. It was no secret to his staff that he experienced the capital of the Confederacy as a millstone around his neck. He said so. He knew he would destroy his army and lose Richmond as well if he had to keep backing up.

Grant was no happier about approaching Richmond step by step. He learned during the day that Lee was moving too, but he still thought the Federals, broken into two bodies of troops, could beat the Rebels across the North Anna River. Hanover Junction was his objective, and he followed the telegraph road which skirted the RF&P railway in order to make haste. He was working through a Virginia which was new to him and his brushes with civilian gentry did nothing to sweeten his mood. A member of the headquarters group noted that most able-bodied men were gone, and those who remained were impoverished beyond imagination. "What is even more extraordinary than their extreme suffering, is the incomprehensible philosophy and endurance of these people. . . . Find a well-dressed lady, and you find one whose hatred will end only with death—it is unmistakable, though they treat you with more or less courtesy." Despite social strains, Grant continued to seek out plantation house porches for rest. At Guiney Station, he visited a farm and was entertained by a woman who shared an important piece of information. Did Grant know, she asked, that Stonewall Jackson had died in that very house? Grant sat through a lengthy description of mighty Stonewall's final days, final hours, final minutes, and final words. Shifting from one side to another in his chair—he still had the boils—he said something about Jackson's being a "sterling, manly cadet" and beat a retreat to his headquarters.[20]

Lee was waiting just above Hanover Junction, peering northward through field glasses, when the first Federal soldiers came into view up the telegraph road. Two of his corps were already in position on the south bank of the North Anna River, and had guns trained right at the advancing Northerners. When word came from A. P. Hill—back in command of the Third Corps but still weak—that another group of Federals had been spotted upstream to the west, Lee rode over for a look. Union soldiers were there, to be sure, but Lee told the courier to go back and notify Hill that it was "nothing but a feint. The enemy is preparing to cross below." By the time he returned to his command post to wait for Grant, he knew he had been wrong. The sound of artillery and musket came down from the west as Warren's corps bucked across the North Anna on hastily improvised pontoons. Lee was furious—though he himself had made the error in judgment—and stormed at Hill, "Why did you not do as Jackson would have done—thrown your force upon those people and driven them back?" The public outburst was so unusual that everyone who heard it lapsed into embarrassed silence. Lee returned to his tent, worked through the night to figure out how to keep his army from being crushed in a Union vise, then fell into bed, wracked with pain from a gastrointestinal seizure.

Grant was pleased with Warren's thrust, but disturbed at other news. The Confederate Army seemed to have disappeared. Urging caution, he himself uncharacteristically proceeded slowly. He was beginning to get a feel for the wiles of his enemy, and he was afraid Lee had an unpleasant surprise for him. Indeed, when Grant discovered how Lee was welcoming him to the North Anna, he ground to a halt. Lee had devised V-shaped earthworks, the apex of which neatly bisected Grant's army. Warren was off in the woods to the south of the river, with no way to join Hancock or Burnside without taking an impregnable fortress. Theodore Lyman was astonished at the device, and wrote home that the Rebels were wizards at building. "It is a rule that, when the Rebels halt, the first day gives them a good rifle pit; the second, a regular infantry parapet with artillery in position; and the third a parapet with an abattis in front and entrenched batteries behind. Sometimes they put this three days' work into the first twenty-four hours." Grant arrived at the North Anna twenty-four hours too late.

Except for a few minor probes at the works, he didn't even try to assault them. He candidly told one of Meade's staff that he had never imagined he would meet with so much resistance from Lee's army. He had never seen such fighting in his life, he said. He could not even conceive of such fighting. Then he dispiritedly ordered his armies to move on and leave Lee alone. Apparently still suffering from boils, Grant now got one of his unbearable migraine headaches. Nursing himself with chloroform, he followed his army southeast.

Lee lay in his bed, too sick to take advantage of the situation he had created and attack one wing of Grant's army. "We must strike them a blow—we must never let them pass us again—we must strike them a blow!" he repeated over and over. His mood, his staff thought, was like a caged lion's. One of his staunchest admirers stalked out of the general's tent after a particularly heated exchange. "I have just told the Old Man he is not fit to command this army and that he had better send for Beauregard!" Charles Venable shouted. But the aide was not as sensitive to the emotional realities of the army as was Lee. The general well knew—had said so, in fact—that it was imperative for him to personally lead his men. Jackson, Longstreet, Stuart were all gone. A. P. Hill in effect was gone—the Wilderness had undone him and he never commanded well again. Ewell had buckled and Lee was phasing him out. Only Lee and his men were left. On May 24, still too sick to sit a horse, Lee directed his men southward to intercept Ulysses Grant. A young artillerist watched as Uncle Robert went by, and said he would never forget "how shocked and alarmed we were at seeing him in an ambulance."[21]

Some of the Federal soldiers cheered Grant as they saw him start southward the same day. They were relieved at not being ordered to attack another Confederate earthwork. But others complained. "Now what is the reason that we cannot walk straight through them with our far superior numbers?" a Michigan soldier asked. "They must understand the country better, or there is a screw loose somewhere in the machinery of our army." Lyman wrote that his family should "not, for a moment, look for the 'annihilation,' and 'hiving,' or the total rout of Lee. Such things exist only in the New York *Herald.*" Moreover, Lyman was sympathizing with the deposed and perhaps traitorous original commander of the Army of the Potomac, George McClellan. We were all so quick to criticize McClellan's apparent fear of the Army of Northern Virginia, Lyman said. But "anyone that has seen that army fight and march would, were he wise, proceed therewith with caution and wariness, well knowing that defeat by such an enemy might mean destruction."

The army was not proceeding with particular caution the last week of May—only with wary exhaustion. At each stop they made on their southeast swing from Hanover Junction toward the Virginia Peninsula, Lee blocked their route. They were demoralized. Their losses were huge—more men than Lee had in his entire army—and they could barely tolerate it. Sick from poor provisions and no rest, the officers were flagging. Commanders, and even some of Grant's staff—notably Rawlins—began to whisper about the awful cost of this failed campaign.

But Grant pushed on, and by the first of June he was one of the few men in Federal uniform who tried to display a modicum of good cheer. After writing reassuring letters to Washington that Lee's army was finally whipped, he set himself up on the south side of the Pamunkey River and reopened Rooney Lee's White House as his transportation depot. Then he engaged in a little housekeeping and crouched on the riverbank to wash out his underwear. Meade's blue-bloods were surprised, but Grant's staff was merely bemused; they knew their chief's horror of dirt. He was so fastidious he carried along in his headquarters gear a collapsible rubber bathtub. Horace Porter at first found it odd that Grant retired to a closely tied tent whenever he changed clothes or bathed, and, asking veteran staff members about it, discovered that no one in the army—not even his black body servant—had ever seen Grant nude. It may have been his mother in him or the need to cleanse away and keep at bay the dirty work around him.

Tidying up made him happy, and more than his underwear was involved. He was privately formulating a bold move. On May 30, he wrote Henry Halleck and asked him to send to City Point every pontoon bridge that could be found. This was a big order, which portended big things. City Point was a Union-held supply depot. And it was on the south side of the James River.

Lee knew nothing about orders for pontoon bridges, but he did realize that the Army of the Potomac was being reinforced. Assuming that Grant would be interested in a strategically important crossroads nine miles east of Richmond, near Cold Harbor, he arranged his lines around the area and set off to find him. Though he was strong enough to ride, Lee was not well, and was still in a mood of desperate bellicosity. For no good reason, and plenty of bad ones, he sent a brigade after a group of Federals he spied coming up the road near Bethesda Church. The little group double-timed right into an entire division of the Union Army. Lee at least knew where Grant was—he was moving on to Cold Harbor. That was all right. What worried Lee was the possibility of Grant on the James River. He asked for reinforcements from Beauregard, who commanded the Army of the James, an attenuated group of 10,000 which had Butler bottled up south of Richmond. Beauregard refused. "General Beauregard says the Department must determine what troops to send," Lee wrote Davis. "The result of this delay will be disaster." The last time Lee used the word "disaster" was on the way to Gettysburg. Davis sent him reinforcements.

Both armies were drawn up on the west side of Cold Harbor by June 1. Too eager to wait for the corps due to arrive at the White House, Grant ordered an attack for that day which a subordinate described as "murderous." The Federals, said the outraged officer, were "recklessly ordered to assault the enemy's entrenchments, knowing neither their strength or position." The Confederate earthworks were actually sparse, and that was why Grant wanted to attack them before the Rebels had their three days or twenty-four hours to dig in. But elaborate entrenchments were unnecessary on the Peninsula. The maze of swamps, streams, hills, and woods served as adequate defense, which was lucky, because the Confederate repulse of the Federal assault was no gallant effort.

The Army of Northern Virginia was in bad shape. A handful of crackers and one or two pieces of moldy bacon were all the rations they had had since leaving the North Anna a week earlier. And Lee had emptied field hospitals, garrisons, and drawing rooms in order to field a force of 60,000. One newcomer was South Carolina's Lawrence Keitt—the former U.S. congressman who had burst into the December 1860 wedding reception with the news for President Buchanan that South Carolina had seceded. Keitt, convinced at last that the war effort could no longer continue without him, funded a private regiment, dressed it in handsomely tailored green uniforms, and set off to find General Lee. Though he had never been in battle, Keitt found himself leading a brigade to stem the June 1 attack. He drew taunts and sympathy for his daring dash to the front, saber drawn, beckoning to his men to follow. Predictably, he was shot dead. Understandably, his dandies disgraced themselves. A veteran said Keitt's troops "groveled upon the ground and attempted to burrow under each other in holes and depressions."

After the unsuccessful June 1 attack, Grant blew up at a man he found beating a team of horses. Trying to soothe him, his staff settled him into new headquarters at Bethesda Church and sent to the White House for barrels of fresh oysters, which he loved. The dinner seemed to do the trick, though his anxiety spun him off into a lengthy discourse on horse-training and descriptions of his future dotage on his farm in St. Louis, where he would spend his time "sitting in a big arm-chair in the center of a ring,—a sort of training course,—holding a colt's leading-line in my hand, and watching him run around the ring." It seemed like a pleasant alternative to the misery he was facing in Virginia.[22]

Corps commanders of the Army of the Potomac received instructions for an assault to be made at 4:30 A.M. on June 3. They were told to spend the afternoon of June 2 "making examinations of the ground on their front and perfecting the arrangements for the assault." There were no provisions for coordination, no details at all. It seemed to most of the officers that the plans were slipshod and overconfident and that a major attack of 60,000 men was being set in motion almost as if it were an afterthought. When Horace Porter walked along the lines near dinnertime, he thought the men were mending their clothes. Closer inspection revealed they were writing their names and addresses on slips of paper and sewing them inside their coats as identification tags. One blue-clad went a step further. Just after midnight, he noted in his diary: "June 3. Cold Harbor. I was killed."

At 4:30 A.M., just at dawn, and soon after the Confederates had finished putting the last log above their shallow trenches, Federal guns opened and 20,000 Union soldiers, arms at trail, charged, cheering on the run. Rebels were waiting. "Sergeant, give them double charges of canister; fire, men; fire!" Fire they did, all along the line, "at very short range, into a mass of men twenty-eight feet deep, who could neither advance nor retreat, and most of whom could not even discharge their muskets at us." An infantryman remembered that the "enemy were within thirty steps. They halted and began to dodge, lie down, and recoil. The fire was terrific . . . and made frightful gaps through the dense mass of men. They endured it but for one or two minutes, when they retreated, leaving the ground covered with their dead and dying." What was occurring was unfathomable to the Confederates, for within a few minutes another wave of men advanced at them. "The charging column, which aimed to strike the Fourth Alabama, received the most destructive fire I ever saw. I could see the dust fog out of a man's clothing in two or three places at once where as many balls would strike him at the same moment. In two minutes not a man of them was standing. All who were not shot down had lain down for protection. One little fellow raised his head to look, and I ordered him to come in. He came on a run, the Yankees over in the woods firing at him every step of the way. . . ."

Back toward Gaines's Mill, at Lee's headquarters, a civilian visitor was making an unwelcome reconnaissance. Postmaster General Reagan, out from Richmond on a holiday junket, came upon the Confederate commander standing alone in the woods while Federal shells bounced around him. Wasn't the artillery fire remarkably heavy? Reagan asked.

"Yes," Lee answered. "More than usual on both sides. That does not do much harm here." Motioning toward Cold Harbor, where the sound of musketry rose like a wall, Lee added: "It is that that kills men. Grant is hurling columns six to ten men deep against our lines at three places in order to break them."

What reserves had Lee in case Grant broke through?

Lee leveled his dark eyes on Reagan: "Not a regiment."

He didn't need reserves. Though later observers would swear that the Federal soldiers simply refused to obey orders for further assaults, they did obey—but in their own fashion. Learning from commanders that none of the three corps were, or could be, coordinated, line officers merely repeated instructions for renewed charges and looked the other way as some men balked, some ran ahead, and others crept forward on their bellies, firing muskets skyward. At one-thirty the words everyone knew were inevitable arrived from headquarters: "For the present all further offensive operations will be suspended." Suspended, not stopped. Late in the afternoon Grant told Porter that he hoped Lee would come out and take the offensive. He wanted a chance to "turn the tables." But it was clear that Lee would give Grant no opportunity for revenge. With his staff sitting silent at dinner, Grant picked at his food. Finally he lifted his head and said quietly, "I regret this assault more than any one I have ever ordered." Cold Harbor was never mentioned at his headquarters again.

Grant was not the only one who didn't want to talk about Cold Harbor. Called the "Golgotha of American history," it did not excite the participants' Victorian need to describe as did other major battles of the Civil War. A line here, a reference there, a paragraph tucked into voluminous reminscence were all the chroniclers could bring themselves to write. There was nothing romantic about the assault, nothing noble, no gallantry beyond the dutiful obedience of men who sewed name tags inside their jackets. But Cold Harbor was agonized over for years. At the time, it caused a terrible rift between Grant and Rawlins, which only widened the space which separated them. Rawlins didn't blame Grant for Cold Harbor. It was Cyrus Comstock, the special staff pet, whose "Smash 'em up! Smash 'em up!" attitude drove Grant to such excesses, Rawlins said. "I do think there has been too much assaulting, this campaign!" was the June 3 entry in Theodore Lyman's diary. Meade wrote his wife after the attack that "Grant has had his eyes opened and is willing to admit now that Virginia and Lee's army is not Tennessee and Bragg's army." "I am disgusted with the generalship displayed," a New Englander said in a letter dated June 4. "Our men have, in many cases, been foolishly and wantonly slaughtered." Corps commander Gouverneur Warren was unstrung by the event. "For thirty days now, it has been one funeral procession past me," he shouted at a friend of Meade's, "and it is too much!" Indeed, it did seem too much for the Army of the Potomac. Union losses at Cold Harbor were not much higher than those at the Bloody Angle—about 7,000.

But most of those 7,000 were brought down in less than ten minutes. The horror of the thing was its speed, and five acres of dead and wounded arranged in neat little triangles along the Confederate front. The flag bearers and the brave or foolhardy formed the apex of the sorry geometry. The boy who wrote that he had been killed, was. So was Fred Haskell, the Wisconsin youth whose fifty-page letter about Gettysburg would have to serve as his legacy.

Heavy but sporadic firing occurred between the lines during the night of June 3. Federals armed themselves with insults like "Come on! Come on! Bring up some more Johnnies! You haven't got enough!" But they were only saving face. Neither side was launching anything more. When the field fell quiet, Lyman stood at Meade's headquarters and looked over the opposing lines, close now since the Federals had entrenched during the evening. "And there the two armies slept, almost within an easy stone's throw of each other; and the separating space ploughed by cannon-shot and clotted with the dead bodies that neither side dared to bury! I think nothing can give a greater idea of deathless tenacity of purpose, than the picture of these two hosts, after a bloody and nearly continuous struggle of thirty days, thus lying down to sleep, with their heads almost on each other's throats! Possibly it has no parallel in history." Perhaps it did not. And perhaps the picture of men dressed in different uniforms curling up to sleep near one another gave an idea of trust and love as well as deathless tenacity—like brothers caught in witless and immutable conflict who crawl at night into a peacefully shared bed.[23]

The following day, Grant wrote a chatty letter to his daughter Nelly, telling her he would buy her a gold watch if she did well with her German. He asked her to send him a photograph of herself appearing at a local fair as the "Old Woman that Lived in a Shoe." He would be home, he said, when the army got to Richmond, then he would hitch Jess's pony, Little Rebel, to a buggy and take her for a ride. "Tell Ma to let Fred learn French as soon as she thinks he is able to study it. It will be a great help to him when he goes to West Point. . . . Be a good little girl as you have always been, study your lessons, and you will be contented and happy." It was like Grant to think of such things at a time of grim reality. But some of his subordinates thought a better use of his time would have been arranging for the care of his casualties. Just as he ignored his dead and wounded after the May 22, 1863, assault at Vicksburg, he overlooked the aftermath of Cold Harbor. The difference was that there were five times as many wounded and dead in Virginia, and—as Theodore Lyman had pointed out to him a month before in the Wilderness—Lee was not Pemberton. There would be no letter from the Confederate commander requesting a truce to care for Federal casualties. A Union officer explained Grant's reluctance by saying that it was commonly assumed that the commander who sent a flag of truce and requested permission to care for his wounded and bury his dead was tacitly admitting defeat. But as much as anything, Grant simply didn't want to admit that 7,000 men were on the ground because of his mistake.

On June 5, the day a Richmond diarist noted that deserters swore Grant intended "to *stink* Lee out of his position," George Meade begged Grant to write to Lee. Grant finally complied.

"It is reported to me that there are wounded men, probably of both armies, now lying exposed and suffering between the lines," Grant wrote. He suggested that unarmed litter bearers from both sides be allowed to collect casualties when no action was in progress. He closed saying, "Any other method equally fair to both parties you may propose for meeting the end desired will be accepted by me."

"I fear that such an arrangement will lead to misunderstanding and difficulty," Lee wrote back. "I propose, therefore, instead, that when either party desires to remove their dead or wounded a flag of truce be sent, as is customary. It will always afford me pleasure to comply with such a request as far as circumstances will permit."

Grant had not expected this, and took several hours to compose a response which had nothing to do with Lee's message. "Your communication of yesterday is received. I will send immediately, as you propose, to collect the dead and wounded between the lines of the two armies, and will also instruct that you be allowed to do the same."

Lee had proposed nothing of the sort, and he reminded Grant of that in his answer. I "regret to find," Lee wrote, "that I did not make myself understood in my communication." He had not proposed an informal collection of the dead and wounded, and he told Grant again that he would honor only a formal request of Grant's made "by flag of truce in the usual way."

Grant's second letter to Lee had a slightly Rawlinsesque play to it. The third, though chastened, was defensively Grant's. "The knowledge that wounded men are now suffering from want of attention compels me to ask a suspension of hostilities for sufficient time to collect them; say two hours."

Lee agreed. When Federal crews finally began probing through the festering mass on the field, they found only two men still alive.[24]

The men on the lines had no way of knowing that the niceties of military protocol were being honed into tests of will by the two adversaries. All they knew was that human beings cried for aid day after day, as the sun beat down and sharpshooters from both sides kept up deadly target practice. And they knew that each day the cries got weaker and fewer and the stench from the already quiet required makeshift masks over mouths and noses. Though the Confederates wondered what manner of men would leave their comrades to suffer so, they kept up a barrage of firing which effectively blocked Federals from retrieving their friends. Union men watched in horror while turkey vultures glided overhead and corpses exploded in the sun. But they showered Rebels with musket fire so accurate that no aid could come from that side. Those days on the lines at Cold Harbor were among the most arduous of the war. Neither army had water, and the soldiers lapped moisture which oozed from the clay walls of their embankments. No rain for weeks and suffocating heat made the filth and lice and red bugs harder to bear. The tents fashioned out of guns and blankets did nothing to brake the nauseating smell.

"This is likely to prove a very tedious job I have on hand but

I feel very confident of ultimate success," Grant wrote Julia on June 6. He was not referring to the job at hand. He was looking past Cold Harbor and seeing ahead of him the unpleasant prospect of a siege. The day before, he had explained his next move to Halleck. "I now find, after thirty days of trial, that the enemy deems it of the first importance to run no risks with the armies they now have. They act purely on the defensive, behind breast-works, or feebly on the offensive immediately in front of them and where in case of repulse they can instantly retire behind them. Without a greater sacrifice of human life than I am willing to make, all cannot be accomplished that I had designed outside of the city." He would, therefore, secure the area around the Virginia Central Railroad and then "move the army to the south side of James river. . . ."

Cold Harbor, for Grant, was in effect a non-event. He un-doubtedly hoped the assault would succeed, and he may even have planned it as a gift for Abraham Lincoln, who was standing for reelection that fall. There was no certainty Lincoln would even get his party's nomination when Republicans convened the first week of June. The nominations would be made on June 5—what better way to assure a shoo-in than the announcement that Grant had captured Robert Lee and Richmond? But Grant was looking beyond Cold Harbor before it even happened. He already had ordered pontoon bridges sent to the James, and on the afternoon of Cold Harbor told Meade he was closing down the White House as the Federal supply depot. City Point on the James would now take care of the Army of the Potomac.

"My idea from the start has been to beat Lee's army, if possible, north of Richmond," he told Halleck. He had failed to do that, and one of the reasons for the failure was his loss of focus. Grant's great gift as a militarist was his creative use of space, but from the time he crossed the Rapidan, the only space he concentrated on was the one occupied by Robert Lee. He had made the mistake of falling into a personal rivalry with Lee, and that caused him to direct the campaign in a cramped, pointed way. He had perhaps even imagined himself as a Lee-like general, a leader of mighty hosts who would sweep down on the foe and emerge victorious after an ennobling exercise in military gallantry. This was the stuff of his youth, the excitement of parades at West Point and the thrilling conquest of Mexico by Winfield Scott. He had even outfitted himself in gold sword, silk sash, and gloves for such an endeavor. But by the time he pulled into Virginia's Peninsula the gloves were gone and so were some 56,000 Union soldiers, casualties of the vaunted images of the new lieutenant general. Cold Harbor was merely an afterthought, a kind of last chance of the pomp and circumstance he never could march to anyway. After the first of June, he would create his kind of war.

Lee kept to his tent for a week after Cold Harbor, dispatching scouts for information about his opponent's next move. He knew Grant had sent Sheridan west, and he feared little Phil would swing into the Shenandoah Valley and cut Richmond off from its food supply before falling south and crossing the James above Danville. Lee sent away his own cavalry, now under the command of South Carolinian Wade Hampton, to block the Union horsemen. He also had a hunch that Grant wasn't going to attack him again. He wrote Jefferson Davis on June 11 saying the Federals were strengthening their trenches. Lee believed that meant Grant was pulling back a portion of his army for a move to the James. If he was right, there was little he could do about it. Lee had told Jubal Early that they "must destroy this army of Grant's" before he got to the James River. "If he gets there it will become a siege, and then it will be a mere question of time." Lee had finally ordered Ewell into face-saving retirement on Richmond's local defense, and he gave Early Jackson's old Second Corps and sent it back to the Shenandoah Valley. The Union commander who had been humiliated at New Market by VMI cadets had been replaced by the hard-eyed abolitionist David Hunter, who Lee said was now "infesting" the valley. Hunter was an officer struck in the mold of the much-hated John Pope, and he had headed straight for Lexington, where he visited the grave of the mighty Stonewall. Then he burned VMI to the ground, and gutted and fired the buildings at Washington College. Certain picked civilian homes—among them that of Governor Letcher—were also vandalized and torched. Hunter couldn't know he had missed the greatest symbolic booty of all. George Washington's silver, which Lee had sent to VMI for safekeeping, was buried under the very ground Hunter and his "marauders" were tearing up. Mary Lee was terrified that the relics would be found and desecrated. Lee sent her reassurances, and he sent Jubal Early to the Valley. That left Lee fewer than 28,000 men to turn back Grant's advance to the James.[25]

Cyrus Comstock and Horace Porter rode into Grant's camp on June 12. The two men had been poking around the James embankments for five days, looking for a suitable crossing site. They settled on Old Fort Powhatan—Carter country, just above Shirley—which lay opposite flatland ten miles below Federal-held City Point. Grant was tense with excitement and anxiety. The men could hardly get the words out of their mouths "fast enough to suit him. He kept repeating, 'Yes, yes,' in a manner which was equivalent to saying, 'Go on, go on'; and the numerous questions he asked were uttered with much greater rapidity than usual." Porter said it was obvious that Grant "was wrought up to an intensity of thought and action which he seldom displayed. At the close of the interview he informed us that he would begin the movement that night." Porter had joined Grant at Nashville. Had he been an older hand, he would have recognized his chief's mood. This was the Grant of the Vicksburg campaign. He was finally getting his footing in Virginia.

Grant mounted Cincinnati in the early evening and rode away from Robert Lee. It was dry in Virginia that June and the Peninsula mud had baked into hard clay which powdered under the hooves of horses and rose in clouds around the cavalcade. There was little talking. At dawn on June 13, Grant crossed pontoons which bridged the Chickahominy. At night he camped on the James.

Lee wrote to Secretary Seddon the same night: "At daybreak this morning it was discovered that the army of Genl Grant had left our front. Our skirmishers were advanced between one and two miles, but failing to discover the enemy[,] were withdrawn, and the army was moved to conform to the route taken by him."

Twelve nervous hours later, Lee wrote to Jefferson Davis: "I think the enemy must be preparing to move south of James River. Our scouts and pickets yesterday stated that Genl Grant's whole army was in motion for the fords of the Chickahominy from Long Bridge down. . . . It may be Genl Grant's intention to place his army within the fortifications around Harrison's landing, which I believe still stand, and where by the aid of his gunboats, he could offer a strong defense. I do not think it would be advantageous to attack him in that position. He could then either refresh it or transfer it to the other side of the river without our being able to molest it, unless our ironclads are stronger than his." This last was either ironic criticism or a joke. There were no usable Confederate ironclads.

Some three hours later, Lee told Davis that, as far as he could judge, "Genl Grant has moved his army to the James River in the vicinity of Westover. A portion of it I am told moved to Wilcox's Landing, a short distance below." Lee had sent a division to Drewry's Bluff in order to drop quickly to Petersburg if it was needed.

As Lee wrote to Davis on June 14, work was just beginning on the pontoon bridge Grant ordered built across the James River. One hundred boats were being lashed together, gunwale to gunwale, and the whole would be overlain with planks. By eleven o'clock that night, it was completed.

At six-thirty the next morning, the Army of the Potomac—thirty-five miles of wagons and artillery, 4,000 cavalry, 3,500 head of cattle, and 60,000 infantrymen, who were told not to march in step in order to keep down the waves—began crossing the 2,100-foot-wide river. Grant was up early, standing on a bluff looking southward. In his pocket was a telegram he had just received: "I begin to see it. You will succeed. God bless you. A. Lincoln." Porter watched Grant watching his army. "His cigar had been thrown aside, his hands were clasped behind him and he seemed lost in the contemplation of the spectacle . . . A fleet of transports covered the surface of the water below the bridge, and gunboats floated lazily upon the stream, guarding the river above. Drums were beating the march, bands were playing stirring quicksteps, the distant booming of cannon on Warren's front showed that he and the enemy were still exchanging compliments; and mingled with these sounds were the cheers of the sailors, the shouting of the troops, the rumbling of wheels, and the shrieks of steam whistles." Grant roused himself from his reverie, mounted his horse, and rode aboard the steamer which carried him across the James.[26]

On the morning of June 15 Lee got a visit from a courier who told him that if Beauregard didn't get reinforcements south of the James immediately, only God Almighty could save Petersburg. Lee's response to this was a quiet "I hope God Almighty will." Something saved Petersburg that day. Baldy Smith's Federal corps marched straight to the Petersburg defense works after crossing the river. Inside those works—commanded by old Henry Wise, the spirited ex-governor of Virginia who took to the field as Lee's nemesis in 1861 with his own private "legion"—were fewer than 1,500 able-bodied defenders. Smith, with recent memories of Cold Harbor, had no taste for another frontal assault and decided to wait. With the sun setting and no help in sight, Smith sent his 16,000 men against the outer works, which dropped so easily into his hands he may have expected a ruse. At any rate, he didn't press his luck. When night fell, Petersburg stood weak and open but still in Confederate hands. Grant was disappointed, but from his tent at City Point he took time to write to Julia. "I am in excellent health," he wrote, "and feel no doubt about holding the enemy in much greater alarm than I ever felt in my life." His confusion over who was feeling the alarm was clarified only by the final sentence. "They are now on a strain that no people ever endured for any great length of time."

Lee was sitting atop Drewry's Bluff, on the south side of the James, at ten o'clock the following morning when he replied to a telegram he just received from Beauregard: "Your dispatch of 9:45 received. It is the first that has come to hand. I do not know the position of Grant's army, and cannot strip the north bank of James River. Have you not force sufficient?" At three that afternoon, Lee again telegraphed Beauregard: "Am glad to hear you can hold Petersburg. Hope you will drive the enemy. Have not heard of Grant's crossing James River." An hour later another wire went out from Lee: "Has Grant been seen crossing James River?" At eight that night, though he knew the works at Petersburg had been attacked, he still did not know if the assailant was Grant or Butler—who had been let out of his Bermuda Hundred bottle by Beauregard's withdrawing the cork.

In the meantime, Grant was having his own troubles. The Army of the Potomac was "near the breaking point," an officer noted, and seemed unable to turn its early arrival at Petersburg into an advantage. Grant went to the front in the morning and looked over Smith's ten-to-one debacle, and rode back to City Point. On the way, he met Meade, and curtly ordered the general—who was savage of spirit himself—to get a move on and go attack Petersburg. Like all the others, the June 16 assault was desultory and failed. But it didn't seem to matter all that much. Grant went to bed early, and was happily awakened in the middle of the night by a courier from Meade. Dressed only in his underwear, and for once not bashful, he sat up to hear the news. Every last soldier, each gun and wagon, all the cattle—the entire Army of the Potomac—was now resting on the south side of the James. Smiling quietly to himself—"like one who has done a clever thing," thought the courier—Grant breathed deeply. "I think it is pretty well to get across a great river, and come up here and attack Lee in his rear before he is ready for us!"

"Can you ascertain anything of Grant's movements?" Lee telegraphed Beauregard at 6 A.M. on June 17. "I am cut off now from all information." At noon, he sent another wire. "Until I can get more definite information of Grant's movements I do not think it prudent to draw more troops to this side of the river." At three-thirty in the afternoon, Lee telegraphed Rooney, who with a handful of cavalry was combing the Peninsula, trying to pin down the whereabouts of the Union Army: "Push after enemy and endeavor to ascertain what has become of Grant's army," Lee wrote. An hour later, he sent another wire to Beauregard: "Have no information of Grant's crossing James River, but upon your report have ordered troops up to Chaffins Bluff."

Portions of the First Corps were already in Petersburg and they crept in the dark through the trenches, quietly placing artillery. One officer found the experience strange and unforgettable. "Of all the moonlight nights I can remember, I recall that Saturday night, as, perhaps, the most brilliant and beautiful. The weather was exceedingly dry, the air perfectly calm, with an exhilerating electrical quality in it. The dust rose with every movement and hung in the air. The whole landscape was bathed and saturated in silver, and sounds were unusually distinct and seemed to be alive and to travel everywhere. It was not a night for sleep in the trenches." Nerves were taut from lack of sleep and from the strain of locating the lost enemy. The click of limber wheels drew volleys of Federal artillery shot and random blasts of musketry. The Rebels responded, imagining themselves attacked. Gradually tension and noise subsided, and the trenches of Petersburg grew quiet.

By midafternoon on June 18, Grant knew he was in for a protracted siege. A final assault had resulted in the Army of the Potomac's merely lying in place, too exhausted to make a dent in the defenses, which now included the entire Army of Northern Virginia. At three-thirty that morning, Lee was finally convinced that Grant and his whole army were investing the tobacco town south of Richmond. By three in the afternoon, both armies had more or less assumed their places. Petersburg was vital to Richmond. The Weldon Railroad, which entered from the south, was the sole link to North Carolina and the rest of the Confederacy. The defense works, constructed more than a year earlier, were massive entrenchments curving around the east side of town, anchored on both ends by the winding Appomattox River. Federal approaches were from the east. There was no immediate chance of surrounding the city and forcing it into starvation. This siege would take time. At ten that night, Grant told Meade he would "rest the men, and use the spade for their protection until a new vein can be struck." His losses for the three days at Petersburg were more than 8,000—bringing his casualty list to 65,000 for the entire campaign. But he had been reinforced, and could string some 110,000 Federals along the lines facing the Rebels.

Lee's losses since May 4 were around 30,000. Now he could field fewer than 50,000 for the work ahead. Lee knew what that work was, but some of his men didn't immediately understand. It took them several weeks to conclude that however "bold we might be, however desperately we might fight, we were sure in the end to be worn out. It was only a question of a few months, more or less. We were unable to see it at once. But there soon began to spring up a chain of permanent works."[27]

CHAPTER

21

To General U. S. Grant
Commanding United States Army

              Headquarters, Confederate States Armies

                           March 2, 1865

General:

. . . Sincerely desiring to leave nothing untried which may put an end to the calamities of war, I propose to meet you at such convenient time and place as you may designate, with the hope that upon an interchange of views it may be found practicable to submit the subjects of controversy between the belligerents to a convention of the kind mentioned. In such event I am authorized to do whatever the result of the proposed interview may render necessary or advisable. Should you accede to this proposition I would suggest that, if agreeable to you, we meet at the place selected by Generals Ord and Longstreet for their interview at 11 A.M. on Monday next.

                        Very respectfully, your obedient servant

                                R. E. Lee

                                General

The letter was ferried under flag of truce to Grant's headquarters at City Point. He read it, promised to give an answer by noon the following day, and sent it on to Secretary of War Stanton in Washington.

A few hours later, Grant got his reply: "The president directs me to say to you that he wishes you to have no conference with General Lee unless it be for the capitulation of Lee's army, or on solely minor and purely military matters. He instructs me to say that you are not to decide, discuss or confer upon any political question: such questions the President holds in his own hands; and will submit them to no military conferences or conventions— mean time you are to press to the utmost your military advantages."

The next day Grant sent Lee his answer. As Abraham Lincoln took his oath for a second term, promising malice toward none, Grant told Lee he could not meet him to discuss ending the war.

There had been other peace proposals—Longstreet had been working for more than a year through channels created by friendships within the Army of the Potomac—but none had come from Lee. Lee alone could have directed any meaningful peace movement in the South, and, as he confessed to Jefferson Davis on March 2, he was not sure that even he could do it. Grant, he said, "will consent to no terms unless coupled with the condition of our return to the Union. Whether this will be acceptable to our people yet awhile I cannot say." Yet awhile. Lee had known since the previous June that it was only a matter of time until the Confederacy would disintegrate, and he had implied, as early as June 1863—on his way to Gettysburg—that the reunion with the Federals would be the obvious result of peace. Davis apparently vacillated between accepting the inevitable and adopting the "last man" stance. But Lee sincerely wanted to make an attempt to "put an end to the calamities of war." The spring campaign would open soon, and he knew it would be both bloody and hopeless. The eight months between the week in June 1864 when he ordered the Army of Northern Virginia into Petersburg's trenches, and his March 1865 letter to Grant, had been both bloody and hopeless.[1]

LEE WAS UNWILLING—perhaps even unable—to simply resign the army and himself to a conventional siege once he took the defensive. At the end of June, his spirits rose with each northward mile marched by Jubal Early and the Second Corps. Early had successfully cleaned Union general David Hunter out of the Shenandoah Valley and pushed on to Harpers Ferry. By the first of July, it seemed likely that Early could cross the Potomac and sweep eastward toward Washington. Lee was banking on Lincoln's once again getting agitated over a threat to the capital—especially during the politically delicate pre-election months of 1864. Lincoln's opponent for the presidency was the former commander of the Army of the Potomac, George McClellan. Many people, including Lincoln himself, thought McClellan would win. The anticipated victory of the Democrats could be made a virtual certainty by the embarrassment of fewer than 10,000 Confederates marching down Pennsylvania Avenue. Lee knew Lincoln would tell Grant to send troops to Washington, and he thought Grant would balk. "It is so repugnant to Grant's principles and practice to send troops from him that I had hoped before resorting to it he would have preferred attacking me." Grant did not attack. He shipped troops to Washington, and though Early's men got close enough for Confederate pickets to spot a tall, thin man dressed in a black stovepipe hat striding along the outer defense works, nothing more came of the raid than miles of hysterical northern newspaper copy and dashed hopes for Lee.

Throughout the late summer and fall, Lee responded to Grant's series of assaults by shuffling ever smaller numbers of men from one pressure point to another, all the while trying to maintain his hold on the railroads which entered Petersburg from the south. It was a desperate time, made worse by life in the trenches—sickness and starvation and constant stress. Siege warfare, as practiced by Grant, began with his army creating a line and digging itself in. Advances were made by creeping forward, establishing a new line, and entrenching. Month after month of gradually encroaching belligerence produced a calendar filled with round-the-clock sharpshooting, quick, surprising death, and sudden all-out attempts at breaking the Federal attacks. Lee mounted an occasional assault which more often than not he led himself. He was, it was whispered in the army, getting very reckless.

He responded to trench life at Petersburg with the kind of guilty anxiety he felt earlier in his life when he abandoned the duties of home for the pleasure of the Army. "Never forget me or our suffering country," he told Mary the day he arrived in Petersburg. A week later he said he was committing her and "my dear daughters to the hands of our Merciful Father in Heaven, with the firm belief that He will order all things for the best for us, both in this world & the next." He confessed that caring for Mary was "beyond my power," and said that "God has been very merciful & kind to us & how thankless & sinful I have been. I pray that He may continue His mercies & blessings to us & give us a little peace & rest together in this world & finally gather us & all He has given us around His throne in the world to come."

Though he raged throughout the war at the devastation wrought on an innocent citizenry by "the Republican" army, he never before expressed the kinds of feelings he passionately held in Petersburg. A visit by Mary to a plantation west of Richmond prompted Lee to decry the number of "happy homes" our enemies "destroyed, & turned the occupants adrift in the world with nothing. From how many hearts have they expelled all hopes of happiness forever." Writing Mary about the death of his uncle Williams Carter, the old man harassed and imprisoned when the Federals captured Rooney at Hickory Hill, Lee said it was "a great relief to think he was now beyond the reach of his cowardly persecutors the Yankees, & enjoying the mercy of an everloving God. . . . With the exception of Mrs. Fitzhugh he was the last connecting link to the persons whom I enjoyed in my boyhood & who made my days so happy."

With links to the past—albeit embroidered with a joy which hadn't existed—destroyed, hope for the future driven away, Lee endured, coped with starving horses, starving men, no supplies, and ongoing Federal attacks. "As usual," he wrote following a skirmish, "we have to mourn the loss of brave men & officers, worth more to me than the whole Federal nation. But we must bear all that an ever loving God inflicts upon us, until He is graciously pleased to pardon our sins & to relieve us from the heavy punishment they have brought upon us."

Lee at Petersburg seemed in many ways to be the Lee of old—a combination of Calvinist and cavalier. He attended dinner parties—such as they were, two boiled potatoes, a slice of bacon, and sweet-potato coffee—entertained scores of visitors at his headquarters, invited the children of Petersburg out to play, and polished up his correspondence with wry commentaries on belles, beaux, dances, and weddings. He encouraged the sweet young things who called at headquarters on trips from Richmond to give balls, dress beautifully, and entertain Army swains. Gone were the dour criticisms of the early war, when he accused even his own daughters of lacking serious commitment to the cause. It was as if he had joined his countrymen in a defiant decision to go down in style.

Style was about all the civilians had left. Petersburg came under a Vicksburg-type bombardment which had cannonballs and mortar shells firing through the streets day and night. The constant interruption of rail service from the south made food supplies haphazard, but small amounts of victuals from country estates to the west kept starvation away. Like the Mississippians before them, the townsfolk adapted themselves to the siege, tended their flower gardens, and resumed social life. It was soon considered no dangerous thing to stroll city streets dodging Federal missiles, but the ruin of ancient homes—built on tobacco fortunes by forebears who supplied the pipes of Georgian England from vast storehouses lining approaches to the Appomattox River—was heartbreaking. Petersburg approached its difficulties rather sedately. Richmond, on the other hand, was caught up in a kind of last-chance gaiety which earned it the condemnation of more sober citizens. The rich seemed bent on consuming everything they could lay hands on—food, wine, money, and life—while the genteel poor compensated themselves with musicales, poetry readings, starvation balls, and theatricals. Weddings were the rage. Church attendance rose. Believers flocked to St. Paul's daily services and struggled to understand God's motives for punishing them so severely. They sought guidance from Old Testament stories and sifted through legends of displaced Israel for a typological heritage for the Confederacy. And more than ever, the first families clung to Revolutionary War bearings as a way of strengthening themselves for the ordeal their lives had become.

The Lees were living in a red brick Federal row house not far from Capitol Square. The rented Franklin Street house, called the "Mess" from its early use as officers' lodgings, harbored Mary, her daughters, Custis—who was serving under Dick Ewell on the Richmond defenses—and as many relatives as its cramped rooms could accommodate. Lee had refused a house offered him by the Richmond city council, and he refused to let any member of his family draw rations from the Commissary Department, as was common with Confederate officers. Mary, completely crippled by then, and "the girls" continued to turn out mountains of socks, which Lee took with him back to Petersburg after his frequent short visits to the city.

He spent most of his time, as he had done since 1862, with his army. He lived four months at Violet Bank, a plantation just outside Petersburg. But in November he moved inside a house—a wartime first for him. His health, he told Mary, necessitated the novel living arrangements, which did not, it turned out, include weatherproof rooms. Lee's door wouldn't close and the usual assortment of puppies, kittens, and wilder creatures found their way to his fireside. So did the citizenry, with gifts of food and clothing, which he customarily sent on to the hospitals. One exception was a peach, the first, he said, that he had seen since 1862. He sent it to Mary. His cook was hard-pressed to keep up with the demands Lee's entertaining placed on the kitchen, but by 1864, no one expected more than a biscuit and some potatoes. Lee seemed to accept the inevitable—and could even joke about Grant enjoying Petersburg so much that he refused to move—but he had retrieved the costume of the cavalier only to cloak the pain of the coming destruction of the army he loved more than any nation—Federal or Confederate.[2]

For months Grant tried to avoid the tedium of a siege by a rhythmic swing of attacks on each of Lee's flanks. Now striking south, near the railroad lines, next hitting north of the James

River to force Lee to weaken his southern edge, Grant set in motion a pendulum of harassment which did little more than advance his lines closer to Petersburg. His one try at blasting into victory ended in the most dramatic failure of the siege. Just at daybreak on July 30, the fuse was lit on a dynamite-packed tunnel dug under a Confederate fort on the north end of the line. An observer noted a "slight tremor of the earth for a second, then the rocking as of an earthquake, and with a tremendous blast which rent the sleeping hills beyond, a vast column of earth and smoke shoots upward to a great height, its dark sides flashing out sparks of fire, hangs poised for a moment in mid-air, and then hurtling downward with a roaring sound showers of stones, broken timbers and blackened human limbs, subsides." The Federals, 10,000 of them, turned their backs to the morning sun and began shuffling forward by twos and threes through a narrow pass which led to the explosion site. What they saw before them stopped them short. A crater 175 feet long by 50 feet wide yawned 30 feet deep at their feet. Inside was a mass of red clay, half-buried weapons, and completely buried men. Schooled in the need to outdo Rebel trench-building, they immediately recognized in the crater a ready-made rifle pit which bested every other rifle pit of the war. They streamed into the hole—all 10,000 of them—and milled around in confusion which soon gave way to panic. The Confederates rallied, and little Billy Mahone arrived to set up his men for shooting the blue-clad fish in the barrel. Federal casualties numbered some 4,000 in what Grant told Halleck "was the saddest affair I have witnessed in this war."

There were equally dismal results from other attacks, and though Grant and Lee both knew it was only a matter of time before the Army of Northern Virginia was routed out of the Petersburg trenches, many men in the Army of the Potomac did not. Grant's star was on the wane again during the late summer and fall of 1864. "Grant the butcher" was a common epithet, and grumblings from officers over what they saw as the botched campaign which started with Grant's blundering into the Wilderness grew into passionate letters home decrying his generalship. A division commander said "the popular idea of Grant is, I believe, very wrong. . . . To sit unconcerned on a log, away from the battlefield whittling—to be a man on horseback or smoking a cigar—seems to exhaust the admiration of the country; if this is really just, then Nero fiddling over burning Rome is sublime." Old-guard New Englanders, convinced of his eastern failures, dismissed Grant's western victories as dumb luck. Grant's staff responded with complaints about the army. "His plans are good," an aide wrote of Grant, "but the great difficulty is that *our troops cannot be relied on.* The failure to take advantage of opportunities pains and chafes him beyond anything that I have ever before known him to manifest." About all headquarters could hope was that the Army of the Potomac "may yet actually *blunder* into Richmond."

There were other problems too. Grant was acutely sensitive to the possibility of Lincoln's not being reelected. Though it was rumored his concern arose from knowing Lincoln's defeat at the polls would cost him his job, Grant admired the President, and saw an established Republican administration as necessary for winning the war. Writing to Elihu Washburne, Grant said "a determined unity of sentiment" in the North was all that was necessary for success. "The rebels have now in their ranks their last man." Troops could not be replaced, he said. "They have robbed the Cradle and the grave equally to get their present force. . . . I have no doubt but the enemy are exceedingly anxious to hold out until after the Presidential election. They have many hopes from its effects. They hope for a counter revolution. They hope for the election of the peace candidate. In fact, like McCawber, they hope *something* to turn up."

Grant might have been reading Lee's mind, but when November rolled around, the election was not left to the hopes of the opposing generals or to the "sentiment" of the North. Charles Dana, by then Assistant Secretary of War, said all "the power and influence of the War Department, then something enormous from the vast expenditure and extensive relations of the war, was employed to secure the re-election of Mr. Lincoln." Republican soldiers were sent home to vote, and Republican officers were given leaves in order to campaign for Lincoln. Democrats who wanted to keep their commissions kept quiet. Expressing anti-Lincoln views was a sure way of losing stripes.

In the end, Lincoln won handily, Grant kept his job, and the war went on. Sherman captured Atlanta in September, and after ordering a 100-gun salute at Petersburg, Grant got busy neatening the noose he was trying to pull around the Confederacy. He set Sheridan loose on the Shenandoah Valley to "eat out Virginia clear and clean as far as they go, so that crows flying over it for the balance of the season will have to carry their provender with them." Underwriting Sherman's planned march to the sea from Atlanta, Grant told him to "clean the country where you go of railroad tracks and supplies. I would also move every wagon, horse, mule and hoof of stock as well as the Negroes. As far as arms can be supplied . . . I would put them in the hands of Negro men. Give them such organization as you can. They will be of some use." Organization did not mean induction into the United States Army. Grant was calling for arming the slaves as well as sweeping Georgia clean. Long before Sherman said it, Grant knew winning war was hell. In December, Sherman telegraphed Lincoln announcing Savannah as a Christmas present to the President. The swath from Atlanta was a smoldering ruin. Sheridan was victorious in the Valley. Grant ordered more 100-gun salutes at Petersburg.

Ironically, the successes on other fronts did little to lessen the criticism he was getting for the stalemate at Petersburg. Dissension continued to rip through the Army of the Potomac, and Republican newspaper editors, relieved of the need to stifle discontent in the service of Lincoln's reelection, let loose renewed salvos of criticism. George Meade was one of the few men outside Grant's immediate circle to defend him. Meade told his wife that Grant had indeed lost prestige, "but as I know it has not been in his power to do more I cannot approve of unmerited censure, any more than I approved of the fulsome praise showered on him before the campaign commenced." Meade by then had settled into an analysis of Grant which would keep until postwar bitterness changed his mind. "Grant is not a mighty genius," he wrote, "but he is a good soldier with great force of character, honest and upright, of pure purposes. . . . His prominent quality is unflinching tenacity of purpose, which blinds him to opposition and obstacles—certainly a great quality in a commander, when controlled by judgment, but a dangerous one otherwise. Grant is not without his faults and weaknesses. Among these is a want of sensibility, an almost too confident and sanguine disposition, which is apt to put him, unknown to himself, under the influence of those who should not influence him and desire to do so only for their own purposes. Take him all in all, he is in my judgment the best man the war has yet produced."3

Grant was not feeling overconfident just then. His assaults had failed, and winter froze any hopes of renewing an offensive before spring. Staff members noted ongoing—even mounting—anxiety on his part. Predictably, he fell off the wagon at least once and disgraced himself during a bibulous visit to Ben Butler at Norfolk. Equally predictably, he became ill again, and during December actually took to his bed. Clearly it was time for Julia.

After restoring White Haven to an elegance it had never before enjoyed, Julia had moved to Burlington, New Jersey, to be within several hours of Grant. She enrolled the children in schools, and began the life of an East Coast lady of leisure. Money was no problem, and Julia customarily had an allowance of $500 a month for running the house. Good fortune was augmented by good luck in January 1865, when the citizens of Philadelphia presented the general and his lady a handsome, completely furnished town-house. "It is with feelings of gratitude and pride that I accept this substantial testimonial of esteem," Grant replied. To Julia, he said he thought "you had as well arrange to move into your new house at once. . . . The house being furnished it is likely $1,000.00 will fit you up elegantly. I can get that for you easily." He told her to buy a carriage. But she didn't move into her new house. She went to City Point.

Julia had already visited Virginia for several stays which had Grant snugged into her steamer cabin and sleeping late. At Christmas she arrived with the children for a gala holiday which smacked of a royal excursion. Grant, of course, reigned supreme at the headquarters, which was more like a vast commercial metropolis than a military post. Little Jesse, wearing a kilt of questionable tartan based on an apocryphal Grant tie with ancient Highland clans, was allowed to march with the men. Fred sported about like the young lord, commanding duck-shooting excursions on the James, coming under Confederate fire for his cheek. Julia was not simply suffered like the children. Grant's men were delighted when she was around. She calmed her husband and quieted his staff's fears for him and looked after his health. An aide remembered he was a very "injudicious eater, and his stomach was his weak point. He ate very little—too little in fact—but he was quite as apt to eat pickles and cake, mingled with cream and vinegar and lettuce, as he was to take more wholesome food." Julia put an end to that nonsense and presided over balanced meals. She nursed his headaches, held his hand, and sat quietly with him as darkness and snow blanketed headquarters. When she wasn't with Grant she went calling in what by early 1865 had become the town of City Point. Tents had been replaced by wooden structures designed with more or less permanence depending upon the skill of the owners. There were hospitals with more than 4,000 beds, office buildings, warehouses, repair sheds, sanitary commission headquarters, and guest facilities. The wharf was stacked with supplies and provisions. Boatloads of gawkers arrived daily from Fortress Monroe to stand outside the military pale waiting for a glimpse of the cigar-smoking hero. Folks from Illinois, Missouri, and Ohio came for personal interviews and left disappointed that all those stars had not wrought more dramatic changes in old "Useless." Abraham Lincoln often visited, and in early February, so did peace commissioners from the Confederate government.

Francis Blair, the man who had offered command of the Union Army to Lee, had presented to Jefferson Davis in January 1865 an invitation to discuss peace with northern counterparts. Despite Blair's dictum from Lincoln that the purpose of the conference was to bring peace to "the people of our one common country," and Davis's assertion that it was "to secure peace for the two countries," on January 31 Alexander Stephens, John Campbell, and Robert M. T. Hunter showed up at Grant's headquarters. Grant housed them in a steamer and the following day wrote Stanton saying he was convinced the men were sincerely interested in ending the war. "I am sorry, however, that Mr. Lincoln cannot have an interview with . . . all three now within our lines." Lincoln immediately telegraphed Grant saying that he would arrive at Fortress Monroe as soon as possible. But the talk Lincoln had with his old friend Stephens did little more than convince both him and Davis that there could be no successful bargain just then.[4]

The troops were more disappointed than the politicians. As Stephens and the other commissioners were being escorted under flag of truce across Confederate breastworks at Petersburg, shouts of "Peace! Peace!" rolled up and down the lines. "Cheer upon cheer was given," a Federal artillerist remembered, "extending from some distance to the right and left of the lines, each side trying to cheer the loudest. . . . Officers of all grades, from lieutenants to major generals, were to be seen flying in all directions to catch a glimpse of the gentlemen who were apparently to bring peace so unexpectedly." The men had lived seven months in the trenches, and they had come to understand that further war had no purpose. "It is a common saying around here that the war could be settled in half an hour if they would leave it to the two armies," a Union officer wrote in a letter home. Action on the north end of the lines—adjacent to the crater—tended to be unremittingly hostile, but farther south, the activity was so pacific that opposing pickets walked about chatting with one another. If officers—either blue or gray—happened by, the boys warned one another and usually made some show of firing their weapons. Notes were passed back and forth, and warnings about impending action usually preceded hostilities. "Get into your holes, Yanks, we are ordered to fire," was a common call. And "Tell the fellow with the spy-glass to clear out, or we shall have to shoot him," was a message wrapped around a stone tossed into a Federal trench. When a greenhorn Rebel accidentally fired his musket at the Feds across the way, his comrades leapt out of the trenches and begged their antagonists not to retaliate. "You'll see how we'll fix him," they shouted. Sure enough, in five minutes the hapless lad was set to marching up and down on top of the breastworks with a fence rail lashed under his arms.

Some of the officers also began to draw the war to a close in their minds. "As we lay there watching the bright stars," wrote a Confederate, "many a soldier asked himself the question: What is all this about? Why is it that 200,000 men of one blood and one tongue, believing as one man in the fatherhood of God and the universal brotherhood of man, should in the nineteenth century of the Christian era thus be armed with all the improved appliances of modern warfare and seeking one another's lives?" Theodore Lyman discovered much to regret in his own army—no "caste" of command—and much to admire in the men who were his foes. Confessing in a letter home that it seemed "sort of lonely and hopeless" sitting in the trenches, he told his parents it was time to end the war. "Instead of being exasperated at the Southerners by fighting against them, I have a great deal more respect for them than ever I had in peace-times. They appear to much more advantage after the discipline of war than when they had no particular idea of law and order. . . . The great thing that troubles me is, that it is not a gain to kill off these people—now under a delusion that mounts to a national insanity. They are a valuable people, capable of a heroism that is too rare to be lost." Federal respect for the Army of Northern Virginia naturally extended to its chief. "There can be no doubt that Lee is a man of very high character," a Union officer wrote. "He carries on war in a merciful and civilized way."

The long, slow fever of the Petersburg winter allowed unwelcomed leisure to think and watch. Charles Blackford, the young Virginian who had gone to war as Stonewall Jackson's attaché, wrote his ten-year-old daughter, Nannie, that for some strange reason the worst thing he had seen in those two years of terrible sights was a blackened and dried-up corpse of a Union soldier resting inside a cabin which stood between the lines. At the corpse's side was the shriveled carcass of a dog. Blackford said local blacks had tried to lure away the dog and feed it, but it refused. "Master and dog lie there together," he wrote Nannie, "strangers in a strange land, unburied and unwept, and perhaps far away in the North, he has some little girl like you who is still hoping for her father's return and picturing the joy of having him back and romping with the faithful dog. War is a sad thing."

Indeed, war seemed saddest from the perspective of the Army of Northern Virginia. "Let us oppose constancy to adversity, fortitude to suffering, and courage to danger," Lee said in a statement issued around Washington's birthday in 1865, "with the firm assurance that He who gave freedom to our fathers will bless the efforts of their children to preserve it." Lee's recent appointment as commander-in-chief of the Confederate Army gave hope to the cause, but it seemed less portentous than mournful tales told. There was Hetty Cary, a bride of three weeks, attending her brigadier general husband's funeral. There was Leonidas Polk, the fighting bishop of New Orleans and early adversary of Grant's, who found final peace in Georgia after walking into Yankee guns near Kennesaw Mountain. There was old Edmund Ruffin, witness to John Brown's hanging and firer of Charleston cannon, who sold his last possessions and prepared to shoot himself in the head.[5]

There were stories told by wives, mothers, and kinswomen from Mississippi to North Carolina in letters which arrived daily for Lee's troops about starvation, disease, death, and loss. They urged their men to come home. Many did. Desertions reached 100 a day during the severe freeze of February. Those who stayed "felt sorry and ashamed" about the brethren who abandoned the cause, but they ignored orders to shoot runaways. Scurvy and night blindness blighted the Confederate trenches. Superficial wounds failed to heal. Despite Lee's ongoing efforts to secure food and clothing for his men, little was available. Nor was there any lead for percussion caps, and Federal pickets watching Rebels scamper out of trenches at night to glean spent bullets for remelting "could not help comparing them with so many women with cloaks, shawls, double-bustles, and hoops, as they had thrown over their shoulders blankets and tents which flapped in the wind." "Really, they looked like malevolent spirits," a Union officer wrote. Confederate prisoners stumbled into Union camps with ice on their beards and hair gone stiff with matted snarls. "We were shocked at the condition, the complexion, the expression of the men, and of the officers too, even the field officers; indeed we could scarcely be made to realize that the unwashed, uncombed, unfed, and almost unclad creatures we saw were officers of rank and reputation in the army."

Walter Taylor wrote in his diary toward the end of February that *"They"* were "trying to corner this old army, but like a brave lion brought to bay at last it is determined to resist to the death, and if die it must die game." Indeed, the men who remained, and knew there would be no immediate peace, did not give up. "We had early forbidden ourselves to think of any end to the struggle except a successful one," wrote a cavalryman, "and that being an impossibility, we avoided the subject altogether." The fervid religiosity which swept through the camps at Fredericksburg was replaced by a wild, occult mysticism. Omens were found in dried springs and hens' eggs and impending disaster seemed only to strengthen faith in some unnamable thing which would end the suffering. "I think hardly any man in that army entertained a thought of coming out of the struggle alive. The only question with each was when his time was to come, and a sort of gloomy fatalism took possession of many minds. Believing that they must be killed sooner or later, and that the hour and manner of their deaths were unalterably fixed, many became singularly reckless."

The day after Washington's birthday, 1865, Lee wrote to Mary. "No one can tell what will be the result of the approaching contest," he said of the impending spring campaign. "We can only toil & trust. I must commit you & my dear children to a merciful God, knowing he will do all things right." With his line composed of one man for every twenty feet of space, Lee knew what the result of the "approaching contest" would be; that was why he retrieved from the personal agony of his past the command to "toil & trust." The following week, he wrote his March 2 letter to Grant.[6]

The night Lee received Grant's answer, he retired to his room alone. He paced for hours, and at midnight he sent a message to

John Gordon ordering the Georgian to come to headquarters at once. It took Gordon two hours to travel the rutted road between his command on the far southern edge of the defense works and Lee's headquarters at Edge Hill. Lee was awake and fully dressed. His head rested on the arm he had flung across the mantel covering a tiny fire. He looked sick, or at least worn down and exhausted. Motioning to a long table covered with documents, Lee invited Gordon to sit down and read what various commands were reporting. Gordon was prepared, he said, to see how attenuated the ranks had become. What was startling to the thirty-three-year-old officer was the destitution of the army. No shoes, no overcoats or blankets, no food, men scrambling between the legs of horses for dung to sift for undigested corn. Insanity, exhaustion, wounds gone gangrenous. Gordon sat silent until Lee broke into his reverie with more information. At most, he had 50,000 men—fewer than 35,000 present for duty, he said. Grant had close to 150,000. Lee walked slowly back and forth across the room for what seemed an hour to Gordon, then turned abruptly and sat down at the table.

Well, asked Lee, what should I do?

Gordon, frightened, thought for a moment, cleared his throat, and said there were only three choices; make terms with the enemy, abandon Richmond and Petersburg and join Joe Johnston in his North Carolina stand against Sherman, or stay and immediately launch an attack. Gordon sat uncomfortable during the silence that followed.

Finally, somewhat caustically, Lee responded: "Is that your opinion?"

Gordon replied that it was, and if Lee had not wanted to hear it he should not have summoned him. What, Gordon asked, did Lee think?

"I agree with you fully."

Making terms with the Federals was no longer an option. As to the second of Gordon's suggestions—joining Johnston in North Carolina—Lee said the condition of the soldiers and the starving artillery and cavalry horses would make retreat difficult. Moreover, it was unlikely that Jefferson Davis would allow such a move. Even if he did, Grant undoubtedly would not. Lee interrupted his recitation of gloom and turned to Gordon with an unexpected twinkle in his deep black eyes. "By the way," he said, "I received a verbal message from General Grant today." A courier had told Lee that Grant had said to "give General Lee my personal compliments, and say to him that I keep in such close touch with him now that I know what he eats for breakfast every morning."

Lee told Gordon that he responded by saying to Grant that "there must be some mistake about the latter part of his message; for unless he had fallen from grace since I saw him last, he would not permit me to eat such breakfasts as mine without dividing his with me."

The momentary leavening failed to raise either man's spirits. Wearily unbending himself from his chair, Lee said he would leave immediately for a conference with Jefferson Davis.[7]

The talk with the President did not go well. Davis seemed to have hardened into intransigence after Lincoln dashed his expectations and hurt his pride by refusing to discuss peace on his terms. Lee would not be allowed to pull his men out of the Petersburg defenses. There was only one choice left—fighting. That night, paying a rare visit to his family on Franklin Street, Lee barely managed to keep the conversation going at dinner. After his daughters left the room, he went into the parlor, where his son Custis sat reading a newspaper. He began to pace the room, eyes fixed on the floor, silent. Suddenly, he stopped and wheeled on Custis.

"Well, Mr. Custis," he said, a hard edge to his voice, "I have been up to see the Congress and they don't seem to be able to do anything except eat peanuts and chew tobacco while my army is starving.

"I told them the condition we were in, and that something must be done at once, but I can't get them to do anything, or they are unable to do anything."

Custis made no response. It was better not to talk when Lee was in such a mood.

"Mr. Custis, when this war began I was opposed to it, bitterly opposed to it, and I told these people that unless every man should do his whole duty, they would repent it; and now . . ." Lee paused. "And now they will repent."[8]

LIFE AT UNION HEADQUARTERS gave no one reason to repent anything. Grant's mood rose with the promise of action. Elihu Washburne showed up for a lengthy visit, bringing with him a three-pound gold medal struck by Congress in honor of Grant's victory at Vicksburg. The night of March 11 was set aside for a formal presentation. Standing in the main cabin of the headquarters steamer, Grant—wearing "an expression as if about to courageously have a large tooth out," according to Lyman— accepted the medal with a mumbled one-sentence thank-you. That painful bit of oratory over, the military band struck up a series of tunes, assembled guests pawed at the medal, and Grant ignored or didn't get the barbed witticisms thrown his way by Meade's Brahmins. Julia, hostessing a contingent of ladies who arrived with Washburne, suggested a dance, and her Dudy uncharacteristically agreed to join in.

The party really got going after the following day, when a courier of Sheridan's arrived during dinner. Julia and Mrs. Rawlins found the "scout" exciting in his piratical garb, but not nearly as exciting as Grant found the message he brought from little Phil. Sheridan had not only reduced the Shenandoah Valley to such a wasteland that a year later it was still uninhabitable, but also captured most of Jubal Early's army. The cavalry leader arrived at City Point the following week. Grant wanted him in on what looked like the kill of the Army of Northern Virginia. He apparently also wanted Lincoln. On March 20, taking a hint from Washburne, he telegraphed the President: "Can you not visit City Point for a day or two? I would like very much to see you, and I think the rest would do you good." Lincoln accepted immediately and on March 24 arrived with his wife, Mary, and the youngest of his sons, Tad. His timing was perfect. He was on hand for the last assault of the Army of Northern Virginia.

THERE WAS SOMETHING in Lee's mood when he returned from his interview with Jefferson Davis which alarmed his staff. "I do not, cannot, yet despair," Taylor wrote, "but it is evident there has been a rapid, radical change in the tone of public sentiment . . . Some in high authority tell us that the people are tired. . . . I do not think our military situation is hopeless by any means; but I confess matters are far worse than I ever expected to see them."

Two weeks later, on March 23, Taylor made another entry in his diary. "The dread contingency of which some intimation has been given is at hand. No one can say what the *next week* may bring forth, although the calamity may be deferred a while longer. Now is the hour when we must show of what stuff we are made."

A few days later, in the still dark early morning, John Gordon prodded his men out of their trenches and sent them across the field toward Fort Stedman, a Federal-held breastwork on the north end of the line.

The rustle of troops brought the Federal pickets to their feet. "What are you doing over there, Johnny? What is that noise? Answer quick or I'll shoot."

"Never mind, Yank," the Rebel infantryman called back. "Lie down and go to sleep. We are just gathering a little corn. You know rations are mighty short over here."

"All right, Johnny; go ahead and get your corn, I'll not shoot at you while you are drawing your rations."

By then the Confederates were in line, ready to charge, and Gordon gave the order for them to move. The men started across the stubbled field and stopped, apparently arrested by their consciences. Drawing a deep breath, one yelled toward the Federal picket: "Hello, Yank! Wake up; we are going to shell the woods. Look out; we are coming!"

They did not go far. Too tired to do more than poke through the Union outpost, Lee's men were ground to a halt.

The Fort Stedman affair was so weak that Lincoln reported it to Stanton as "a little rumpus." Two days later Taylor noted in his diary that the "probable contingency is a foregone conclusion."9

As Walter Taylor tried to record the unspeakable, William Tecumseh Sherman was entertaining Grant with tales of his march to the sea. Sherman arrived at City Point on March 27 and was greeted by his chief with smiles and hugs. "Their encounter was more like that of two school-boys coming together after a vacation than the meeting of the chief actors in a great war tragedy," Horace Porter wrote. So engrossing was Sherman's story that Grant forgot all about Lincoln. After more than an hour, the two sheepishly went to pay their respects to the President, who was sequestered on the steamer *River Queen,* ministering to his overwrought wife. An ugly incident involving the wife of a subordinate, whom Mary Lincoln volubly accused of flirting with her husband, had cast an embarrassed barrier between the Lincolns and the Grants. Sherman broke Lincoln loose from Mary and brought him back to Grant's tent. Onlookers never forgot the scene. Lincoln—looking like a "highly intellectual and benevolent Satyr" to Lyman—Grant, Sherman, and Sheridan sat together like four Westerners huddled round a cracker barrel, talking about the future which quite clearly was theirs.[10]

ON MARCH 29, the day Mrs. Jefferson Davis and her children left Richmond for North Carolina and safety, Grant said goodbye to Julia. The Army of the Potomac was pulling out of winter quarters. Sherman had gone back south to put the finishing touches on Joe Johnston. Sheridan had set off with 10,000 cavalry to round Lee's right and smash through Rebel defenses south of Petersburg. Grant stood at the door to his little cabin, kissing Julia over and over, holding her close and whispering. He had ordered her to move onto the dispatch boat moored in the James in case the Rebs got to City Point. He turned and walked away as the headquarters horses were loaded onto the train which would carry him to Petersburg. Lincoln walked up the quay to say goodbye. The President seemed abstracted, almost depressed during the visit, and now, unaccountably, with Grant going off to finish Robert Lee, he looked even more serious. "The lines on his face seemed deeper," Porter thought, "and the rings under his eyes were of a darker hue." He cracked one feeble joke, then, his eyes filling with tears, said, "Good-by, gentlemen. God bless you all! Remember, your success is my success." Grant shook his hand, and stepped aboard the train. As the little engine jerked them westward, Grant told his staff that Lincoln was the most anxious man in the country. His heart was wrapped up in the army, Grant said. "I think we can send him some good news in a day or two." A few hours later, from his command post south of Petersburg, Grant telegraphed Sheridan: "I feel now like ending the matter . . ."

The "matter" was prolonged by a spring rain which turned clay roads into sheets of water and mired the Army of the Potomac in mud. Tempers flared, none worse than John Rawlins's. Lung disease had taken all the fight out of him, and on the morning of March 30 he intercepted Grant and began to rave about the impossibility of getting forage, the probability that Lee would cut them to pieces, and the necessity of going back to City Point. Grant ushered Rawlins into his tent, which hid the two but did not muffle the murmur of argument rising through the canvas walls. Rawlins and Grant were still inside the tent when Sheridan arrived. "Forage!" he snorted. "I'll get all the forage I want." Then he began to walk back and forth in the rain, repeating his readiness to "strike out to-morrow and go to smashing things." Sheridan soon replaced Rawlins as Grant's tent mate and by the time he emerged from his conference he had the O.K. to smash anything he could find. He would operate as a separate command, first striking Lee's defenses, then pushing on to cut off any possible retreat. Though Federal forces outnumbered Confederates three to one, Lee had demonstrated how well his few could maneuver themselves.

Confederate defense lines were substantially unchanged from where they were staked out the previous June. Beginning on the northeast edge of Petersburg, at the Appomattox River, they curved southward before pushing northwest and again picking up the river. On April 1, Sheridan, backed by a corps of infantry, hit the northwestern curve of the lines at a little place called Five

Forks. By seven o'clock that night, Confederates under Lee's nephew Fitz and George Pickett knew they were beaten, caught in cross fire which strewed the field with casualties. "They had no commanders, at least no orders, and looked in vain for some guiding hand," a northern reporter wrote. "A few more volleys, a new and irresistible charge . . . and with a sullen and tearful impulse, five thousand muskets are flung upon the ground."

When Grant got Sheridan's note announcing the victory, he sat for a moment, folded the paper, and put it in his pocket. "All right," he said. Then he ordered an attack all along the line for the following morning.[11]

Lee didn't sleep that night. At four in the morning, a tentative knock sounded on his door. It was A. P. Hill, who hadn't slept for days, not since he had alarmed Richmond kinsfolk by saying he hoped he wouldn't survive the fall of the city. He had no command by then, and there was no reason for him to be with Lee beyond a need for solace or hope from the equally exhausted man who lay half-dressed on the couch. Longstreet arrived an hour later, mended but still suffering from the bullet he'd taken in the Wilderness. He was easier since his return to the army the previous October, when he found Lee aged and worn. The three men sat in silence as dawn lightened the room—Lee and his lieutenants, remnants from the early glory days.

Lee stirred himself and began telling Longstreet to move the First Corps southward when the door burst open and an aide rushed in. The road outside was filled with wagons and teamsters, the officer yelled. Lee wrapped his dressing gown around him and walked to the front door. Peering through the dim light, he saw a line of skirmishers advancing on the house. It was impossible to tell whether the soldiers wore blue or gray. Lee ordered a courier out, but it was Hill who ran to his horse and rode away at a gallop. Lee hurried to dress himself. Oddly, for he seldom wore one, he buckled on his dress sword. Then he ordered that all the furniture which "kindly neighbors" had donated to winter headquarters be returned.

By the time he was in the saddle, Lee could hear the sound of firing rolling up toward the house from both the south and the east. He saw a small group of approaching horsemen. It was Hill's staff and one of them was riding Hill's horse. Lee waited until the men drew up in front of him. Hill, they said, had ridden straight into a bank of Federal stragglers and had been shot dead. Lee was not surprised. "He is at rest now," he said hoarsely, his eyes filled with tears, "and we who are left are the ones to suffer." The suffering began soon enough. There was no longer any question about which troops were advancing on Edge Hill. They were Federals and they were coming fast.

"As we advanced in a handsome line of battle over rolling and open country," a Union officer remembered, "our batteries galloped to the front and opened fire in a most spirited manner." Rebel guns fired on the Federal left, but kept changing position. Each time the battery moved the advancing soldiers saw "a fine looking old officer, on a gray horse, who seemed to be directing its movements."

As Federal shells came lobbing into the yard at Edge Hill, Lee dictated a hurried telegram to the Secretary of War: "I see no prospect of doing more than holding our position here till night. I am not certain I can do that. . . . I advise that all preparation be made for leaving Richmond tonight." Then the field telegraph was dismantled. Lee directed one last disposition as his headquarters took direct hits, and turned his horse's head eastward for the ride into Petersburg's interior fortifications. He kept Traveller to a walk and stared straight ahead until a shell struck close, disemboweling a horse. An aide noted his rage. The hunt was up, but for the first time in his life, Lee himself was the quarry. The old belligerent was at bay. "This is bad business," he said as he turned eastward again. He didn't speak during the mile-long ride to temporary headquarters close to Petersburg. But as he pulled to a stop, he turned to a staff member. "Well, Colonel," he said angrily, "it has happened just as I told them it would at Richmond. The line has been stretched until it has broken."

Lee spent the rest of the day writing orders to get his army away from Richmond and Petersburg. He had 15,000 with him in the immediate vicinity. Anderson on the far southern edge of town commanded the 3,500-man remainder of the Five Forks fiasco, Billy Mahone had close to 4,000 in the Bermuda Hundred area to the north, and Dick Ewell oversaw some 6,000 north of the James around Richmond. Federals now occupied the entire fishhook of Confederate outer defense works from Richmond all the way down and around Petersburg. The Army of Northern Virginia would have to cross to the north side of the Appomattox River if it was to get away. Lee's route then would curve west, just below the Richmond & Danville Railroad, to Amelia Court House, where all the troops would meet, feed, and rest, before continuing southward to Burkeville. From there, it was a relatively short march to Danville, just shy of the North Carolina state line—and Joe Johnston's army. The entire journey was something over 140 miles.

Shortly before noon, Lee wired Jefferson Davis: "I think it is absolutely necessary that we should abandon our position tonight. I have given all the necessary orders on the subject to the troops, and the operation, though difficult, I hope will be performed successfully. I have directed General Stevens to send an officer to your excellency to explain the routes to you by which the troops will be moved to Amelia Court House, and furnish you with a guide and any assistance you may require for yourself." Lee knew the telegram would cause trouble, but he was not prepared for the particular kind of difficulty it created. Later that afternoon he got Davis's reply saying that "to move tonight will involve the loss of many valuables, both for want of time to pack and of transportation." This cracked Lee's discipline. He tore the paper to shreds, saying hotly that he was sure he had given Davis "sufficient notice," and sent a testy response to Richmond. "Your telegram received. I think it will be necessary to move tonight. I shall camp the troops here north of the Appomattox. The enemy is so strong that they will cross above us & close us in between the James & Appomattox Rivers, if we remain."[12]

This was not what Grant had in mind. After skirting the Federal corps which made the advance against Lee's headquarters at Edge Hill, Grant sat down, and balancing a writing book on his knee, began issuing orders. He knew that Lee's men were broken at Petersburg, but he didn't want the shards of that army to get away from him. Confederate defense was particularly strong near the bridge across the Appomattox River. If Lee could escape the tightening circle of Union troops around Petersburg, then there was no telling what could happen. Grant had confessed just before leaving City Point that he was afraid the Army of Northern Virginia would make its way to the western mountains, from there to launch years of private war against the Union. After seeing what he could do to prevent such an end to the siege at Petersburg, Grant sent a message to Julia: "I am now writing from far inside what was the Rebel fortifications this morning but what are ours now. They are exceedingly strong and I wonder at the success of our troops carrying them by storm. But they did do it, and without any great loss. We have captured about 12,000 prisoners and 50 pieces of artillery. As I write this news comes of the capture of 1,000 more prisoners. Altogether this has been one of the greatest victories of the war. Greatest because it is over what the Rebels have always regarded as their most invincable army. . . ." In truth, the Confederate army—which Lee had already characterized as an "effigy"—couldn't put up enough fight to qualify the Federal work on April 2 as any kind of a victory. What Grant exulted in was his own gain over the invincible Robert Lee. This campaign would not be another Wilderness.

So certain was he by then of his own success that he wrote a short note to Abraham Lincoln, recapping the prisoner count and inviting Lincoln to join him in Petersburg the following day. He fully expected the Confederates to be gone by then, but he no longer worried that they would escape.[13]

Richmond's St. Paul's Episcopal Church was crowded with communicants the morning of April 2, 1865—a first Sunday. Jefferson Davis sat in the pew he had used since his baptism two years earlier. Just after the invocation an aide hurried up to Davis and handed him a telegram. Observers noted "a sort of gray pallor creep over his face" as he read the message from Lee. Then he rose and quickly walked down the aisle. A few staff members and couriers followed the President, but the rest of the congregation kept their seats. Later, thinking over the day, one of the worshippers thought Richmonders' manners too good to make much show of concern.

By noon, most of the citizens knew the city would be abandoned. Railroad cars on the Danville line were hastily packed with boxes of official papers and an estimated $528,000 in gold and silver, and government officials tried to secure household goods and get reservations on the James River Canal packet boats for their families. The better sort of residents quietly retired to their homes, where ladies sewed valuables into small cloth sacks which they strung under their hoop skirts. The city was relatively quiet until mid-afternoon, when fear overcame breeding and set the streets alive with terror. Excited families, hauling personal goods by their sides, ran into railway stations seeking passage westward. Depositors stormed closed banks. Soldiers trundled wheelbarrows of Confederate specie onto the lawn at Capitol Square and lit the first fires of the day. Artillerists jockeyed cannon into the James, to join the handful of Confederate naval vessels being scuttled. Prisoners emerged from their abandoned jails and began sacking food stores and dry-goods shops. The dispossessed joined the free-for-all of looting, and helped themselves to everything that was left of food for the army. The city council ordered all whiskey destroyed, and Richmond police bashed in barrel heads and poured thousands of gallons of liquor into gutters soon lined by looters who dipped up what they could and lapped up all they wanted. The scene, wrote a resident, was "the saddest of many of the sad sights of war—a city undergoing pillage at the hands of its own mob, while the standards of an empire were being taken from its capitol."

At eight that night, Jefferson Davis, after sending a favorite armchair to Mary Lee with a message saying he hoped it would help her arthritis, straightened the accessories on his desk—it wouldn't do for the Yankees to think him slovenly—mounted his horse, and rode to the railway station. At eleven, his train pulled out of Richmond, bound for Danville—the new capital of the Confederate States of America.

At the same time, citizens stood quietly on their sidewalks and watched the last of their military defenders swing southward over the James in the glow of fires from tobacco warehouses. A south wind soon swept the flames onto the great riverfront flour mills, and at two in the morning, a powder magazine at Rocketts Landing blew up. At three, the national arsenal went, and 750,000 loaded shells began arcing through the sky. "The earth seemed fairly to writhe as if in agony," a citizen wrote, "the house rocked like a ship at sea." This last blast shattered plate-glass windows blocks away, and was followed by explosions from three ironclads run aground on the James. The city was in flames, and the Mayo Bridge—the last one standing—was packed with tar-filled barrels. An officer posted himself near the abutments watching troops march south. Finally, he rode to the engineer who stood waiting, touched his hat, and reported: "All over. Goodbye. Blow her to hell."

Walter Taylor was one of the last soldiers out of the city. He had come to Lee at sundown with an unusual request—leave to go to Richmond and get married. Lee gave Taylor the go-ahead, and told the impetuous secretary where to meet him after the ceremony. Taylor found Lee exactly where he said he would be, standing on the north end of Petersburg's bridge over the Appomattox. Lee had been there for six hours, watching his men get under way for Amelia. When the last man was over, Lee swung aboard Traveller and followed his men. Behind him, Richmond burned.[14]

Grant rode into Petersburg at nine o'clock on the morning of April 3. The day was fine, bands were playing, and soldiers yelled for the simple pleasure of yelling. The city itself was eerily quiet, and Porter somewhat nervously explained to himself that many of the citizens had fled with the army. Those who stayed, stayed behind closed doors, except for a few groups of blacks who sent up a cheer or two. Grant rode up Market Street, stopped in front of No. 21, and walked onto the porch. A new aide, Robert Lincoln—eldest of the President's three sons—soon appeared in the street, directing his father and little brother Tad to Grant's temporary headquarters. Grant's aide watched the President dismount and come in through the front gate with "long and rapid strides, his face beaming with delight. He seized General Grant's hand as the general stepped forward to greet him, and stood shaking it for some time, and pouring out his thanks and congratulations with all the fervor of a heart which seemed overflowing with its fullness of joy." The two men sat together for more than an hour, until Grant could wait no longer for word of Richmond, which he had hoped would come while he was with the President. He needed to join the army on its westward race. Again shaking hands with Lincoln, Grant called to his staff, mounted his horse, and set off to join the Army of the Potomac.

A courier caught up to Grant's cavalcade nine miles west of Petersburg with a message he had been waiting for: Union troops had entered Richmond at eight-fifteen that morning. Regimental bands struck up "Hail, Columbia" and "The Star-Spangled Banner," and waves of cheering echoed off the newly greening Virginia hills. That night, after he made camp, Grant continued issuing orders for bagging Robert Lee. He believed Lee would do exactly what he was doing—follow the Danville railroad to Burkeville, then drop into North Carolina for a rendezvous with Johnston. He had no particular desire to hit the rear guard of the Army of Northern Virginia. What he wanted to do was beat it to Burkeville. It would be a repeat of Wilderness swings, but this time Grant not only had the inside line—the Union route to Burkeville was thirty miles shorter than that of the Rebels—he also seemed to have an inside track on Lee's mind.

George Meade was bouncing along in an ambulance, struck down by nervous exhaustion and an intestinal disorder. Meade's illness had cleared the stage of even protocol for the final thrust, and Grant turned that push over to Phil Sheridan, giving him control of an infantry corps. On the night of April 3, Sheridan was somewhere out in front, beating at the left flank of Lee's army, while an infantry corps jammed it from behind. When Grant finished his paperwork he dropped a note to Sherman.

"This army has now won a most decisive victory and followed the enemy. That is all it ever wanted to make it as good an army as ever fought a battle."[15]

Lee's veterans did not feel beaten on April 3, and their commander did not seem disheartened. "I have got my army safely out of its breastworks," he told an aide, "and in order to follow me, the enemy must abandon his lines and can derive no further benefit from his railroads or the James River." He was counting on his old ally—Virginia land—to help him escape. Each mile the army marched westward was a little rougher, a little steeper, a little more tangled, a little more hostile to an invading army. Lee believed that even though his men and horses were exhausted, they could make Amelia Court House the following day. There they could rest and eat before moving on. The men were no less hopeful. It may have been because every one of them laid eyes on reassuring Uncle Robert as they walked away from their trenches, but spirits were high.

The Rebels with Anderson—tag ends of the Five Forks fight—and Ewell's troops from Richmond were in much worse shape. Anderson's 3,500, stung hourly by Sheridan's cavalry raiders, were, in fact, completely demoralized. "The Confederacy was considered as 'gone up,' and every man felt it his duty, as well as his privilege, to save himself," an officer said. "I do not mean to say there was any insubordination whatever, but the whole left of the army was so crushed by the defeats of the past few days that it straggled along without strength and almost without thought. So we moved in disorder, keeping no regular column, no regular pace. When a soldier became weary he fell out, ate his scanty rations—if indeed, he had any to eat—rested, rose, and resumed the march when his inclination dictated. There were not many words spoken. An indescribable sadness weighed upon us. The men were very gentle toward each other." To another officer, the march seemed "like a troubled vision" until the morning of April 4, when Longstreet and his veterans came into view followed by John Gordon—"it would put fight in a whipped chicken just to look at him."

None of the army had slept or eaten much since leaving Petersburg, but they quickened their step toward the relief waiting for them in Confederate boxcars shunted to a siding on the Danville line at Amelia. Lee was with Longstreet's advance and arrived at the wayside around noon on the fourth. He found the boxcars and ordered them opened. Inside were 96 loaded caissons, 200 crates of ammunition, and 164 boxes of artillery harness. No food. The train from Lynchburg bearing provisions had been hurried to Richmond two days earlier to collect the Confederate government and the train from Richmond which Lee expected to carry rations to his men apparently was impressed for carrying the government to Danville. "No one who looked upon him then, as he stood there in full view of the disasterous end, can ever forget the intense agony written upon his features," an officer wrote of Lee.

Lee gave the bad news to his division commanders, then wrote an appeal to "the Citizens of Amelia County" asking them "to supply as far as each one is able the wants of the brave soldiers who have battled for your liberty for four years." He detached foraging expeditions and ordered his army to make camp. Precious time was being lost, but the men and animals were literally dropping in their tracks. Moreover—predictably—nothing had been heard from Dick Ewell. Lee knew he was on the road, but lagging far behind. It was impossible to move on without him. There was no choice but to wait out the hours lost to Grant.[16]

At dawn on April 5, Lee discovered the wait was in vain. The citizens of Amelia County had already been cleaned out by Confederate impressment crews. Those farmers who managed to secrete food for the winter apparently had had enough of struggling for liberty—theirs or anyone else's. Lee's forage wagons came back to camp empty. A hard, cold rain began to fall as he boarded Traveller early that morning. His order to move ahead was obeyed as fast as the men could pull themselves to their feet. It may have been exhaustion and hunger, or it may have been a certain sense that to be left behind was to die, but the soldiers setting out toward Burkeville didn't complain. They stumbled along, tearing branches off trees and gnawing buds, while artillery mules collapsed, unnoticed, in roads turned to mire by the rain.

Nervous jerks of halts and starts found men sinking to their knees or wandering off in search of rest or food. Many commands marched heedlessly on without orders. Wagons churned into mudded ruts and stopped, sunk axle-deep and too heavy for the horses, which stood weak-kneed and patient in the road as the army marched around them. Every man, said one, knew it "was now a race for life or death." But by two o'clock that afternoon Lee learned he had lost the race for Burkeville. Longstreet, still taking the lead, marched into a skirmish line of bluecoats and deployed his men to brush off what he thought was cavalry. It was, but Sheridan's horsemen were backed by an entire Federal corps strung out between Lee and his only chance to get to North Carolina.

By the time Lee came up, the Army of Northern Virginia was stopped. He took out his field glasses, trained them on the road ahead, and sighed. Lowering the glasses, he quietly ordered his army back in motion. The route now would be due west toward Lynchburg. Regimental commanders delivered what they thought was "the most cruel marching order" they had ever given the men in four years of fighting. It was almost sundown. It no longer mattered. "Night was day. Day was night. There was no stated time to sleep, eat, or rest, and the events of morning became strangely intermingled with the events of evening. Breakfast, dinner, and supper were merged into 'something to eat,' whenever and wherever it could be found." And all around them Federals were moving in. Every mudhole and "every rise in the road," was choked with blazing wagons, a marcher remembered. And the air was filled with "deafening reports of ammunition exploding, and shells bursting when touched by the flames—dense columns of smoke ascending to heaven from the burning and exploding vehicles. Dead "mules, dead horses, dead men everywhere." After each jerking halt in that long, black night, many men who sank down for a few minutes' rest failed to rise, and lay by the side of the road staring at the backs of their friends stumbling west. Lee's face, it was noted, was still calm, "but his carriage was no longer erect, as his soldiers had been used to see it. The troubles of those last days had already plowed great furrows in his forehead. His eyes were red as if with weeping; his cheeks sunken and haggard; his face colorless."[17]

The Federals felt they were on a holiday. "They began to see the end of what they had been fighting four years for," an officer remembered. "Nothing seemed to fatigue them. They were ready to move without rations and travel without rest. . . . Straggling had entirely ceased, and every man was now a rival for the front." When Grant stopped at sundown to make camp on the evening of April 5, he learned the front was near at hand and very active. He was sitting on the porch of the old town tavern at Nottoway Court House when a courier from Sheridan brought news that Lee had been stopped at Burkeville. But Sheridan had a complaint. Meade, still sick, had ordered the Army of the Potomac into what he thought was a much-needed night of rest. Rest was the furthest thing from Sheridan's mind. "I wish you were here yourself," little Phil fumed at Grant. "I feel confident of capturing the Army of Northern Virginia if we exert ourselves. I see no escape for Lee." Grant's answer was to select a handful of staff members and a small cavalry escort and set out through twenty miles of dense forest to find Phil Sheridan and capture Robert Lee. By ten-thirty that night, Grant rode into Phil Sheridan's camp.

"Why there's the old man," Sheridan's grimy horsemen called from their blanket-roll beds. "Boys, this means business." "Great Scott!" another shouted, "the old chief's out here himself. The rebs are going to get busted to-morrow certain." This was echoed by "Uncle Sam's joined the cavalry sure enough. You can bet there'll be lively times here in the morning."

There were not, unless the cavalry thought galloping twenty more miles overland lively times. At dawn, Grant discovered that Lee had prodded his men westward on that "most cruel" march. Grant sent Sheridan on a northwest swing aimed at coming up in Lee's face, and ordered another corps of infantry to join the push to his rear. Setting off after the Rebels, Federal soldiers started across the ground covered the night before by their quarry, and some grew quiet at what they saw. The road was strewn with wreckage, broken-down forage wagons, abandoned cannon and battery wagons, trembling mules, and horses starved to skin and bones, "so weak as scarcely to be able to lift their heads when some soldier would touch them with his foot to see if they really had life." Farm carts piled with household goods, driven by sullen or overexcited civilians, were stuck in the boulder-strewn roads and slowed Union going even further. So did prisoner collecting. Dead Confederate bodies were ignored in favor of those who were rounded up from aimless wandering in the woods but who still managed a try at American joking. "Yes, you've got me," drawled a North Carolinian as he dropped his musket, "and a hell of a git you got."

Sheridan's git that day was a good one. The marching order for the Army of Northern Virginia had been reversed by Lee for a push toward Farmville. Longstreet still led the way, and Gordon still protected the rear, but Ewell and Anderson had been wedged in the middle—apparently for safekeeping. Gordon was hit hard by the Union Sixth Corps, and sent word to Ewell to wait, but Ewell either didn't get the message or wasn't willing to respond. The gap that opened between the Rebel corps was quickly filled by Federal horsemen. A similar gap developed between Anderson—who was rumored to have taken to the bottle again—and Longstreet. Anderson and Ewell somehow sloughed down into a tiny valley created by an Appomattox River feeder stream called Sayler's Creek. Phil Sheridan summoned up a neat row of artillery batteries and began raking the 6,000 men who milled around in the moist green swale. "I had seldom seen a fire more accurate nor one that had been more deadly," a Confederate artillerist said, not without a note of approval for the enemy. "The expression of the men's faces indicated clearly enough its effect upon them. They did not appear to be hopelessly demoralized, but they did look blanched and haggard and awe-struck."

Sheridan recognized the look. "Never mind your flanks," he shouted at his men. "Go through them! They're demoralized as hell!"

They were not sufficiently gone to fail any kind of defense. Rebel batteries swung into position and pointed barrels upward at the slowly advancing Federals, while gray-backed infantry crouched holding muskets to their chests. At the order—"Fire!"—everyone did, and the advancing blue line recoiled. It was only then that the Confederates became demoralized. Off their balance from lack of food and sleep, they forgot four years of training, and every one of them jumped up and started toward the Federal line on the run. The ensuing debacle "degenerated into a butchery and a confused melee of personal conflicts," said a Confederate officer. "I saw numbers of men kill each other with bayonets and the butts of muskets, and even bite each other's throats and ears and noses, rolling on the ground like wild beasts. I saw one of my officers and a Federal officer fighting with swords over the battalion colors." The savagery was so general that men turned upon their friends. "I saw a young fellow of one of my companies jam the muzzle of his musket against the back of the head of his most intimate friend, clad in a Yankee overcoat, and blow his brains out. . . . I well remember the yell of demonical triumph with which that simple country lad of yesterday clubbed his musket and whirled savagely upon another victim." Officers and a handful of men escaped before the Federals swooped in and began rounding up the 6,000 prisoners, including Dick Ewell and Custis Lee—beaten on his first field foray of the Civil War.

Custis's father was watching. Riding with Longstreet that morning, but becoming increasingly alarmed about the absence of Ewell and Anderson, Lee had turned toward Sayler's Creek, where he rode into Rebel survivors—"hurrying teamsters without their teams and dangling traces, infantry without guns, many without hats, a harmless mob." "My God! Has the army been dissolved?" he shouted, spurring forward.

Billy Mahone was at his side in a minute. "No General, here are troops ready to do their duty."

But as soon as Mahone left to send his division against the Federals, Lee again spurred Traveller forward into a gallop. Leaning from his saddle, he snatched a Confederate battle flag from a skulker running rearward. He slowed his pace and rode through Mahone's assembling men, holding the flag staff high in one hand. The wind caught the flag and snapped and curled it around his silver head, brushing his shoulders and face and wrapping his body in red. Mahone's men fell silent as he rode on. Then they began to cry and shout for their Uncle Robert. And Lee stopped at the crest of the hill while Anderson's fugitives streamed past him. Grim and erect, still, he held the red silk flag flapping in the sun setting on Sayler's Creek and Robert Lee's last battle.[18]

CHAPTER

22

Near the Appomattox River, Virginia
Headquarters Armies of the United States
April 7, 1865—5 P.M.

General R. E. Lee,
Comd.g C.S.A.

General: The result of the last week must convince you of the hopelessness of further resistance on the part of the Army of Northern Va. in this struggle. I feel that it is so and regard it as my duty to shift from myself, the responsibility of any further effusion of blood, by asking of you the surrender of that portion of the C.S. Army known as the Army of Northern Va.

Very respectfully, your obt. svt,
U. S. Grant,
Lt. Gn
Commanding Armies of the United States

April 7, 1865
General,

I have recd your note of this date. Though not entertaining the opinion you express of the hopelessness of further resistance on the part of the Army of N.Va. I reciprocate your desire to avoid useless effusion of blood & therefore before Considering your

proposition ask the terms you will offer on condition of its surrender.

Very respectfully, your obedient servant

R. E. Lee, General

To Lieut.-Gen. U. S. Grant, Commanding Armies of the United
States.

April 8th, 1865

Gen. R. E. Lee, Comd.g C.S.A.

Your note of last evening, in reply to mine of the same date,
asking the conditions on which I will accept the surrender of the
Army of N.Va. is just received. In reply I would say that *peace*
being my great desire, there is but one condition I would insist
upon, namely: that the men and officers surrendered shall be disqualified from taking up arms again, against the Government of
the United States, until properly exchanged. I will meet you or
will designate Officers to meet any officers you may name for the
same purpose, at any point agreeable to you, for the purpose of
arranging definitely the terms upon which the surrender of the
Army of N. Va. will be received.

Very respectfully

your obt. svt.

U. S. Grant,

Lt. Gn

April 8th, 1865

To Lieutenant-General U. S. Grant, Commanding Armies of the
United States

General—

I recd at a late hour your note of to-day—In mine of yesterday
I did not intend to propose the Surrender of the Army of N.Va—
but to ask the terms of your proposition. To be frank, I do not
think the emergency has arisen to call for the Surrender of this
Army, but as the restoration of peace should be the Sole object of
all, I desired to know whether your proposals would lead to that
end. I cannot therefore meet you with a view to Surrender the
Army of N—Va—but as far as your proposal may affect the C.S.
forces under my Command & tend to the restoration of peace,

I should be pleased to meet you at 10 A m tomorrow on the old stage road to Richmond between the picket lines of the two armies.

Very respectfully, your obedient servant,
R. E. Lee, General

Apl. 9th 1865

Gn. R. E. Lee
Comd.g C,S,A,

General: Your note of yesterday is received. As I have no authority to treat on the subject of peace the meeting proposed for 10 to-day could lead to no good. I will state however General that I am equally anxious for peace with yourself and the whole North entertains the same feeling. The terms upon which peace can be had are well understood. By the South laying down their Arms they will hasten that most desirable event, save thousands of human lives and hundreds of Millions of property not yet destroyed. Sincerely hoping that all our difficulties may be settled without the loss of another live, I subscribe myself,

very respectfully
your obt. svt.
U. S. Grant
Lt.Gn

April 9th 1865

General,

I received your note of this morning on the picket line whither I had come to meet you and ascertain definitely what terms were embraced in your proposal of yesterday with reference to the surrender of this army. I now request an interview in accordance with the offer contained in your letter of yesterday for that pu[r]pose.

Very respectfully
Your obt. servt.
R. E. Lee

Lt. Gen U. S. Grant
Comdg U.S. Armies[1]

THE CONFEDERATE CAUSE was lost—"ended—just as I have expected it would end from the first," as Lee said after Sayler's Creek. But his verbal skirmishes with Grant during their exchange of letters were designed to ensure that neither he nor his army would be dishonored. Any hint that pride would be capitulated, and he would have listened more closely to a lieutenant's proposal to scatter "like rabbits and partridges" and fight on from the hills of Virginia.

Grant read Lee well. "There was no pause, no hesitancy, no doubt what to do," his secretary said. "He commanded Lee's army as much as he did ours."

On the afternoon of April 7, Grant entered Farmville and learned from Sheridan that they were certain to capture provision trains Lee had ordered to Appomattox station. When he went to his room in the local hotel—which the innkeeper falsely swore was occupied by Lee the night before—he had a short interview with a prisoner of war. The man told of seeing Dick Ewell crouched on the floor of his captors' headquarters cradling his head on his knees. "Our cause is lost," Ewell had whimpered. "Lee should surrender before more lives are wasted." That helped Grant decide to write to Lee. The dispatch was given to an aide, Seth Williams, Lee's adjutant at West Point. His men sensed a final victory and started lighting bonfires along Farmville's streets. They made torches of straw and pine knots and sent up a roar of cheers which echoed off the bluffs of the Appomattox. Bands played, "banners waved, and muskets were swung in the air," Porter remembered. "A regiment now broke forth with the song of 'John Brown's Body,' and soon a whole division was shouting the swelling chorus of that popular air, which had risen to the dignity of a national anthem. The night march had become a grand review, with Grant as the reviewing officer."

When Grant's letter arrived, Lee was in a farmhouse with Longstreet. He read the note and handed it, silently, to Pete. They had forced what troops were left on a quick march to Appomattox Station and a train of food from Lynchburg. They didn't know Grant had already beaten them to it.

Longstreet read the message of his old friend, handed it back to Lee, shaking his head. "Not yet," he said.

Lee rose, and without calling for his secretary as he usually would have done, composed his response to Grant.

Despite his bravado disclaiming the "hopelessness of further resistance," Lee most certainly was implying it by asking Grant for terms. He had lost 8,000 men at Sayler's Creek three days before, and thousands more had straggled off or dropped. What hope remained was forlorn, but it was still game. "Over, sir? Over? Why, sir, it has just begun," an exhausted officer had imperiously responded to a nervous civilian's query. The men, said a cavalry officer, were "only waiting for General Lee to say whether they were to face about and fight."[2]

But General Lee had just asked General Grant for terms. If there had been any doubt in Grant's mind about the need for delicacy in the correspondence, it had to be removed by the message from Lee. Curt, almost supercilious, the letter shifted responsibility for bloodshed back onto Grant while at the same time assuming a superior position of authority in the exchange. It was little wonder that Grant devoted more than six hours to his reply. When it was finished, the following morning, the letter was a combination of tact and restraint. The only terms to be demanded were that the men and officers be "disqualified from taking up arms" until they were properly exchanged. Grant's most sensitive touch was reserved for Lee himself. By suggesting that their respective officers might conduct the surrender, he was offering to spare the vanquished general the humiliation of appearing in person.

Lee refused to be vanquished. "I will strike that man a blow in the morning," he said of Grant on April 8. And during the day, when he was approached by one of his officers about surrender, his response was abrupt: Surrender? he thundered. "I trust it has not come to that! We certainly have too many brave men to think of laying down our arms. They still fight with great spirit whereas the enemy does not." Then he wavered. Besides, he said, "if I were to intimate to General Grant that I would listen to terms, he would at once regard it as such evidence of weakness that he would demand unconditional surrender—and sooner than that I am resolved to die. Indeed, we must all determine to die at our posts." He was quite sincere. Dying at his post was a far better thing than living out a life as a failed revolutionary. It was the end he had celebrated for twenty years. "The warmest instincts of every man's soul declare the glory of the soldier's death," he'd written in his journal. There "is true honor; the glory of duty done—the honor of the integrity of principle."

Lee received Grant's terms during the evening. "That man" was being kind. But he still could not bring himself to lay down the army he loved. Lee responded with a suggestion to Grant that they meet, not to discuss surrender, but to treat for general peace. That was what he had unsuccessfully tried to do in March. He must have known that Grant could not comply.[3]

The Federal aide arriving at midnight at Grant's new headquarters in a farmhouse near the rear of Lee's troops, hesitated delivering the message from Lee for fear of waking the general. "Come in," Grant called from the room he was sharing with Rawlins. "I am awake." He was in severe pain, suffering since morning, when he had collapsed with one of his headaches soon after sending his letter to Lee. Mustard plasters and foot baths failed to provide relief. Grant sat up on the sofa and handed Lee's dispatch to Rawlins, who read it in a voice so loud it could easily be heard by the excited staffers waiting below. Rawlins swore, but Grant just shook his head. "It looks as if Lee still means to fight," he said. "I will reply in the morning."

At 1 A.M. on April 9, Charles Marshall, Lee's aide-de-camp, was awakened by the sound of infantry marching. "We lay upon the ground near the road, with our saddles for pillows, our horses, picketed nearby, eating the bark of trees for want of better provender, our faces covered with the capes of our greatcoats to keep out the night air. . . . We were so completely surrounded by the swarming forces of General Grant that at first when I woke I thought the passing column might be Federal soldiers." They were Confederate, the last of the Texans whom Lee had cheered into the Wilderness. The brigade was on the march to carry out

Lee's desperation attempt to force through the Federals to the mountains and safety.

The headquarters camp stirred and the men put on their caps and saddled their horses. Lee, however, dressed himself carefully in a new uniform he had brought back from his most recent trip to Richmond. He tied a silk sash around his waist and buckled on a presentation sword sent him by a group of English admirers. "I have probably to be General Grant's prisoner today," he explained, "and thought I must make my best appearance." Lee's staff now made what Marshall called "last meal in the Confederacy." "Somebody had a little cornmeal, and somebody else had a tin can. . . . A fire was kindled, and each man in his turn, according to rank and seniority, made a can of cornmeal gruel." General Lee declined his share.

When Porter went to wake Grant at four o'clock, the room was empty. Grant was outdoors, pacing, clutching his head in both hands. Porter gently suggested a cup of coffee at Meade's nearby headquarters. The coffee helped, and now Grant answered Lee's letter. The ten o'clock meeting would "lead to no good," he wrote. "I have no authority to treat on the subject of peace . . ."

The Army of Northern Virginia's last skirmish began at five. By eight it was over. A courier brought the message from John Gordon: "I have fought my corps to a frazzle, and I fear I can do nothing." If Gordon couldn't do it, then it was over. Lee took the news without flinching, though the color in his face deepened. "Then there is nothing left me to do but go and see General Grant, and I would rather die a thousand deaths."

Gordon knew what his message meant. When a subordinate asked where he should form his line, Gordon replied in a monotone: "Anywhere you choose." To clarify this oddest of orders, he whispered that they were going to be surrendered. Though none of the officers or men had any confirmation of that, most of them suspected it. Most refused to believe it. "I did not think the word surrender was in General Lee's book. I felt sure we would

fight," a South Carolina corporal said. Loudly proclaiming a desire to take on any regiment in the Union Army as a way of
settling "the question," he was silenced by a quiet word from a
newspaper reporter: "I guess this question is already decided." An
advance man inched forward for a vantage point of what he
assumed would be a small tussle before gaining those rations
waiting at Appomattox Court House. He was shocked to find the
space filled with a huge train of parked wagons and "men dressed
in black (blue you know)." Returning to the road, he "found that
the regiment had not moved 100 yards from where we left it. And
here I saw a sight that I can never forget. Men, soldiers, looking—
well, I have no words to describe their appearance—worn out,
disappointed, hopes gone, and asking what they will do with us."
A North Carolina soldier heard the rumor and "hooted it." "It
was simply preposterous." But a less hearty private fell to his
knees shouting, "Blow, Gabriel, blow! My God! let him blow!
I am ready to die!" Some of Gordon's men cried, others broke
their guns against trees, muttering, "No Yankee will ever shoot
us with you."[4]

Union infantry attached to Sheridan were nearly as shocked as
their enemy. "It is the end!" a brigadier from Maine exclaimed
as he crested the hill. Below, around the edges of the river, he
could see "a swarming mass of chaotic confusion. . . . Had one
the heart to strike at beings so helpless, the Appomattox would
quickly become a surpassing Red Sea horror." The bluecoats
instinctively stopped. "We are lost," one said, "in a vision of
human tragedy."

Porter Alexander pleaded with Lee not to surrender. "You don't
care for military glory or fame," he told his chief, "but we are
proud of your name and the record of this army. We want to leave
it to our children . . . a little blood more or less now makes no
difference." Alexander urged Lee to disband the army and let it
scatter to the hills informally.

Lee heard him out, then quietly told the twenty-eight-year-old
artillery officer that generations of guerrilla warfare—bushwhack-
ing—would destroy Virginia and the rest of the country as well,

even if it worked. "Then, General, you and I as Christian men have no right to consider only how this would affect us." I expect to meet General Grant in the morning, he said, "and surrender the army."

Alexander's eyes filled with tears, and he turned away with a convulsive sob. But another aide remonstrated with Lee: "Oh, General, what will history say of the surrender of the army in the field?"

I know they will say hard things, said Lee. "But that is not the question, Colonel: The question is, is it right to surrender this army? If it is right, then I will take all the responsibility."

The responsibility for surrender was different from the responsibility for failed campaigns, and the burden was too much. Lee looked out at the battlefield taking shape under the lifting morning fog. "How easily I could be rid of this, and be at rest!" he cried. "I have only to ride along the line and all will be over!" The urgency of his desire held everyone speechless. But discipline won out. Finally, quietly, he denied himself this ultimate pleasure. To no one in particular he said, "it is our duty to live."

It was also Lee's duty to surrender his army, and he presented himself promptly for his ten o'clock appointment with Grant. He dismounted, and stood erect under a flag of truce, in full view of Grant's army. Intermittent firing was heard, and Lee's aide, with reason, feared an attack was in the offing. When Federal couriers arrived, they were not escorting Grant, as Lee anticipated, but rather were bringing Grant's letter saying the meeting "would lead to no good."

Lee read the message, reflected for a few moments, and said to Marshall, "Well, write a letter to General Grant and ask him to meet me to deal with the question of the surrender of my army, in reply to the letter he wrote me at Farmville."

He had accepted Grant's terms. Marshall handed the letter to a Federal officer and told him the message required a "suspension of hostilities." That could not be, was the answer. An attack had been ordered and the officer did not have authority to stop it.

Lee still stood under the flag of truce. The Federal soldiers asked him to withdraw. Instead, he wrote again to Grant:

9th April 1865

General,

I ask a suspension of hostilities pending the adjustment of the terms of the surrender of this army, in the interview requested in my former communication today.

Very respectfully, your obt. servt.

R. E. Lee Genl.

He was now directly in the path of the oncoming advance. He was warned again to leave immediately. His face set and eyes expressionless, he mounted his horse and road back through his own rear guard. Shortly after eleven o'clock, a Federal courier appeared requesting safe-conduct through Confederate lines. Meade had authorized a cease-fire. Lee once more rode to the front, where he wrote a third letter of the morning to Grant:

Hd Qrs A N Va

9th April 1865

General: I sent a communication to you today from the picket line whither I had gone in hopes of meeting you in pursuance of the request contained in my letter of yesterday. Maj Gen Meade informs me that it would probably expedite matters to send a duplicate through some other part of your lines. I therefore request an interview at such time and place as you may designate, to discuss the terms of the surrender of this army in accordance with your offer to have such an interview contained in your letter of yesterday.

Very respectfully,

Your obt. servt.

R. E. Lee

Genl

If pride was not capitulated, it came very close. Gone from this final field letter from the headquarters of the Army of Northern Virginia were peremptory orders for Grant to explain himself. The tone was nearly supplicatory.[5]

———

The first of Lee's April 9 letters reached Grant while he was riding along the river on his way to meet Sheridan at Appomattox. After reading it, he handed the note to Rawlins. "You had better read it aloud, General," Grant said. Rawlins did, in a voice dipping and rising over the lump in his throat. When he finished, Grant and his men were silent. "No one looked his comrade in the face," a reporter remembered. Grant immediately sat down on a grassy bank by the road and wrote his reply:

April 9, 1865

General R. E. Lee, Comd.g C.S.A.

General, Your note of this date is but this moment, 11:50 a.m. rec'd., in consequence of my having passed from the Richmond and Lynchburg road to the Farmersville & Lynchburg road. I am at this writing about four miles West of Walker's Church and will push forward to the front for the purpose of meeting you. Notice sent to me on this road where you wish the interview to take place will meet me.

Very respectfully, your obt. svt,
U. S. Grant,
Lt. Gn

No formal closure was ever more heartfelt. Grant later admitted that he was nervous about finally meeting Lee, and his anxious explanation of his whereabouts during the intervening two hours since Lee had first asked for a meeting seemed conciliatory. But he spurred forward, excited to get to Appomattox Court House and Robert Lee. Five miles from the little town, Grant was intercepted by an aide of Sheridan's who arrived bearing the last Lee letter. Porter asked him how he felt. A grin spread over his face. "The pain in my head seemed to leave me the moment I got Lee's letter."

Now the party was being slowed by the crowded road, and Grant and his men took a shortcut toward Gordon's corps. "It looked for a moment as if a very awkward condition of things might possibly arise," Porter said, "and Grant become a prisoner in Lee's lines instead of Lee in his. Such a circumstance would have given rise to an important cross-entry in the system of campaign bookkeeping." Despite Grant's aversion to retracing his steps, he turned around and went back the way he had come.[6]

A South Carolinian, incredulous at the rumor of surrender, sought out Gordon. He found his commander "in the woods, crying, half-dressed, taking off his old dirty uniform, and putting on a brighter, newer one, used on state occasions." By that time, most of the men knew Lee was going to surrender, and created what one private thought was "a lamentable spectacle." Some seemed to be glad that it was all over, he said, "but mostly they were sad and gloomy faces. For myself, I cried; I could not help it. And all about were men crying,—plenty of them." The private swore he would never be surrendered, and got ready to leave for North Carolina and a chance at joining Joe Johnston. Shouldering his knapsack, he took a last look and turned south. "I left the little tattered, weary, sad and weeping army—*our* army,—left them there on the hill with their arms stacked in the field, all in rows,— never to see it any more. And oh, it was my sweetheart who was dead that day in April." And as he rode away, he felt that "some great bundle of treasure-holding years have been torn out of my life,—some sweet thing slipped out of my grasp."

Awake since one in the morning, Lee now waited again for Grant, near Appomattox Court House. "We made a little couch for General Lee under an apple tree," an aide remembered. "We put some rails down there, spread some blankets over them, and General Lee . . . who was very much fatigued, lay down and went to sleep. We stayed about him for an hour perhaps." A Grant staff officer arrived with the letter his commander had written on the road at noon. Lee read the message, got up, and spoke briefly to the Federal officer, Orville Babcock, then ordered Marshall to get ready. The men rode into town.

"General Lee told me to go forward and find a house where he could meet General Grant," Marshall said, "and of all people, who should I meet but McLean." Marshall's surprise equaled McLean's bad luck. The landowner had retired to Appomattox

Court House after his original farm, which stood at Manassas Junction, was overrun at the first battle of Bull Run. Now, four years later, his property was once again full of soldiers. It seemed somehow fitting. Marshall asked McLean to show him a place where the two generals could meet, and, perhaps in response to his assessment of things military, McLean ushered Marshall into a "house that was all dilapitated and had no furniture in it." Told that would not do, McLean allowed that his own house might serve the generals. Marshall went in, followed soon by Lee and Babcock. The three conversed in the "most friendly and affable way," according to Marshall.[7]

"Is Lee over there?" Grant asked Sheridan as he rode up to the group of officers lolling about on the edge of town.

"Yes," said Sheridan, nodding toward one of the half-dozen houses lining the village's single street. "He is in that brick house, waiting to surrender to you."

"Well, then, we'll go over."

Colonel Babcock had sighted his commander approaching the McLean house and Lee rose with him as Grant entered the room. Grant extended his hand. "General Lee," he said. The two shook hands.

Grant summoned in his staff officers, then sat in an old office chair in the center of the room. Lee took a cane-seated armchair beside a square, marble-topped table. "We walked in softly," Porter said, "and ranged ourselves quietly about the sides of the room, very much as people enter a sick-chamber when they expect to find the patient dangerously ill." Porter's attention was drawn to the "contrast between the two commanders . . . as they sat, six or eight feet apart, facing each other." Grant was dressed in a muddy dark blue flannel blouse, "unbuttoned in front and showing a waistcoat underneath." Plain top boots, without spurs and spattered with mud, had trousers tucked inside. "He had no sword or sash, and a pair of shoulder straps was all there was about him to designate his rank. In fact, aside from these, his uniform was that of a private soldier." Lee, on the other hand, looked "as if he had turned out to go to church that Sunday afternoon, while with us our outward shabby garb scarcely rose to the dignity even of the 'shabby genteel.' "

Grant wanted to talk and began with a friendly overture: "I met you once before, General Lee, while we were serving in Mexico, when you came over from General Scott's headquarters to visit Garland's brigade, to which I then belonged. I have always remembered your appearance, and I think I should have recognized you anywhere."

"Yes," replied Lee, "I know I met you on that occasion, and I have often thought of it, and tried to recollect how you looked, but I have never been able to recall a single feature."

Undeterred by the cool reception of his camaraderie, Grant continued to chat. The weather was mentioned.

Lee interrupted him. "I suppose, General Grant, that the object of our present meeting is fully understood. I asked to see you to ascertain upon what terms you would receive the surrender of my army."

"The terms I propose are those stated substantially in my letter of yesterday," Grant replied; "that is, the officers and men surrendered to be paroled and disqualified from taking up arms again until properly exchanged, and all arms, ammunition, and supplies to be delivered up as captured property."

Lee nodded. "Those are about the conditions which I expected would be proposed."

"Yes," Grant said, "I think our correspondence indicated pretty clearly the action that would be taken at our meeting, and I hope it may lead to a general suspension of hostilities, and be the means of preventing any further loss of life." Grant later said that his objective during the Appomattox campaign had been to remove Lee and have him use his influence in inducing the surrender of the other Confederate armies. He now warmed to the idea, and spoke at length of the happy prospects for reunion.

Lee merely inclined his head at Grant's hopes. The time had passed for him to discuss peace. He was now with Grant to surrender, and once again interrupted. "I presume, General Grant, we have both carefully considered the proper steps to be taken, and I would suggest that you commit to writing the terms you have proposed, so that they may be formally acted upon."

Grant called for his order book, which he opened and laid on the table brought to him from the end of the room. He wrote rapidly, pausing only to glance at the sword on Lee's side. Then he added another line or two and called his secretary to read his message. The two went over the written terms. Grant directed his aide to underline a half dozen or so words and cross out a word. He handed the letter to Lee.

Lee "pushed aside some books and two brass candlesticks which were on the table," Porter remembered, "then took the book and laid it down before him while he drew from his pocket a pair of steel-rimmed spectacles, and wiped the glasses carefully with his handkerchief. He crossed his legs, adjusted the spectacles very slowly and deliberately, took up the draft of the terms, and proceeded to read them attentively."

> Appomattox C. H. Va.
> April 9th, 1865
>
> General R. E. Lee, Comd., C.S.A.
>
> Gen.: In accordance with the substance of my letter to you of the 8th inst. I propose to receive the surrender of the Army of N.Va. on the following terms: to wit:
>
> Rolls of all the officers and men to be made in duplicate. One copy to be given to an officer designated by me, the other to be retained by such an officer or officers as you may designate. The officers to give their individual paroles not to take up arms against the Government of the United States until properly . . .

Lee paused in his reading, looked up, and said to Grant, "After the words 'until properly' the word 'exchanged' seems to be omitted. You doubtless intended to use that word."

"Why, yes," Grant said, surprised, "I thought I had put in the word 'exchanged.'"

"I presumed it had been omitted inadvertently and, with your permission, I will mark where it should be inserted."

"Certainly," Grant replied.

Lee felt his pocket for a pencil. Porter supplied one, and noted that during the remainder of Lee's reading he "kept twirling this pencil in his fingers and occasionally tapping the top of the table with it." Lee read on:

> (exchanged) and each company or regimental commander to sign a like parole for the men of their commands. The Arms, Artillery, and public property to be parked and stacked and turned over to the officer appointed by me to receive them. This will not embrace the side arms of the officers, nor their private horses or baggage.— This done each officer and man will be allowed to return to their homes, not to be disturbed by the United States Authority so long as they observe their paroles and the laws in force where they may reside.
>
> Very respectfully,
> *U. S. Grant,*
> Lt. Gn.

Lee's face brightened toward the end of his reading time, and Grant's aides assumed it was in response to his exclusion of the officers' swords and horses from the provisions of surrender. But Lee's relief was for his men, who would not be penned like prisoners but allowed to go home. He looked toward Grant and said, somewhat warmly, "This will have a very happy effect upon my army."

Now it was Grant who changed the subject. "Unless you have some suggestions to make in regard to the form in which I have stated the terms, I will have a copy of the letter made in ink, and sign it."

Lee hesitated momentarily. "There is one thing I should like to mention. The cavalrymen and artillerists own their own horses in our army. Its organization in this respect differs from that of the United States. I should like to understand whether these men will be permitted to retain their horses."

Lee's reference to the armies of two countries startled the Federals, and Grant's response was immediate. "You will find that the terms as written do not allow this, only the officers are permitted to take their private property."

Lee read over the second page of the surrender again. "No, I see the terms do not allow it; that is clear." His face showed his disappointment.

It was an awkward moment. Grant rushed to fill it: "Well, the subject is quite new to me. Of course I did not know that any private soldiers owned their animals; but I think we have fought the last battle of the war." He presumed most of the men were small farmers, he said, and would need their horses to plant a crop. "I will arrange it this way," he went on—though he'd keep the terms as written, he would tell his officers "to let all the men who claim to own a horse or mule take the animals home with them to work their little farms."

"This will have the best possible effect upon the men," Lee answered. "It will be very gratifying and will do much toward conciliating our people."

The surrender was given to Grant's aide, who borrowed ink from Lee's secretary in order to copy it. Marshall then borrowed paper from Grant's staff to write Lee's reply.

> Headquarters, Army of Northern Virginia
> April 9, 1865
> General: I have received your letter of this date containing the terms of surrender of the army of northern Virginia as proposed by you—As they are substantially the same as those expressed in your letter of the 8th inst, they are accepted—I will proceed to designate the proper officers to carry the stipulations into effect—
>
> Very respectfully, your obedient servant,
> *R. E. Lee*
> General

Lieutenant-General U.S. Grant
Commanding Armies of U.S.

While the letters were being copied, Grant introduced his officers to Lee. With a few exceptions, Lee's response was a formal bow. He did extend his hand to Seth Williams, and he also thanked Williams for bringing him news of Custis's safety. But he subdued the familiarity of his old friend, and cut short Williams's reminiscences of their days together at West Point.

Once again Lee turned his attention to the business at hand and informed Grant that he had more than one thousand Federal prisoners whom he could not feed. "I have, indeed, nothing for my own men," said Lee. "They have been living for the last few days principally upon parched corn. . . . I telegraphed to Lynchburg, directing several train loads of rations to be sent by rail . . . and when they arrive I should be glad to have the present wants of my men supplied from them."

The Federal officers glanced at Sheridan. They knew his cavalry had captured the train the night before. Without telling Lee this, Grant inquired about the number of his troops.

"Indeed," Lee hesitantly responded, "I am unable to say. My losses in killed and wounded have been exceedingly heavy and besides, there have been many stragglers and some deserters. All my reports and public papers and indeed some of my own private letters had to be destroyed . . . to prevent them from falling into the hands of your people."

Grant proposed sending over rations for 25,000 and asked if the quantity was sufficient.

"Plenty, plenty. An abundance, I assure you."

Nothing remained but to wait for the secretaries to finish copying the letters. A silence fell on the group, which Grant, once again, sought to fill. "I started out from my camp several days ago without my sword," he said, "and as I have not seen my headquarters baggage since, I have been riding about without any sidearms. I have generally worn a sword, however, as little as possible— only during the active operations of a campaign."

Now the letters were ready. The terms, signed by Grant, were given to Lee's aide. The acceptance, signed by Lee, was given to Grant's secretary. Lee shook hands with Grant, bowed to the other officers in the room, and, accompanied by Marshall, left the room.[8]

A crowd of anxious sightseers clustered about the front porch of the house, waiting for a look at General Lee. A Federal officer noted his "clear, ruddy complexion—just then suffused by a crimson flush, that rising from his neck overspread his face and even tinged his broad forehead, which, bronzed where it had been exposed to the weather, was clear and beautifully white where it had been shielded by his hat."

Lee was carrying his hat and gloves as he walked onto the porch, where he paused, put on his hat, and slowly drew on his gloves, staring absently into the yard ahead. Twice, perhaps three times, he unconsciously fisted his left hand and struck the palm of his right. Still abstracted, he automatically returned the salute given him by officers crowding on the porch, then walked down the stairs. His scabbard banged against each sloping wooden step. He seemed, said an observer, "utterly oblivious to his surroundings. Then, apparently recalling his thoughts, he glanced deliberately right and left, and not seeing his horse, he called in a hoarse, half-choked voice: 'Orderly! Orderly!' " Lee smoothed Traveller's forelocks as the orderly fit the bridle into the horse's mouth, then with a slow, tired pull, mounted. "He settled into his seat," an officer said, "and as he did so there broke unguardedly from his lips a long, low deep sigh, almost a groan in its intensity, while the flush on his neck and face seemed, if possible, to take on a still deeper hue." Grant had walked out on the porch by then, and as Lee rode past him toward the little valley where the Army of Northern Virginia lay waiting, the two men's eyes met. Each silently lifted his hat to the other.

Lee went down a steep slope, across one of the few wooden structures spanning the Appomattox River left unburned, and into the orchard where he had rested early in the afternoon. As he rode, a few advance soldiers met him with the question: "General," they shouted, "are we surrendered?" He couldn't answer. His staff posted themselves around the orchard as pickets, and left him alone as he began to pace backwards and forwards. Union officers ambled over, and those who would not be turned away got cold greetings. Lee "shook hands with none of them," an aide noted. "When he would see Colonel Taylor coming with a party towards his tree he would halt in his pacing and stand 'at attention' and glare at them with a look which few men but he could assume." The interviews were short.

After an hour parrying friendly Federal thrusts, Lee was composed enough to undertake what for him was the greatest ordeal of all. Mounting Traveller, he put the horse at a walk and began the mile-long journey to his headquarters tent. Two solid walls of men lined his road, and as he came into view they began to cheer wildly. Tears started in his eyes and the cheers of his men turned to "choking sobs as with streaming eyes and many cries of affection they waved their hats. . . . Each group began in the same way with cheers and ended in the same way with sobs, all the way to his quarters.

"Grim-hearted men threw themselves on the ground, covered their faces with their hands and wept like children. Officers of all ranks made no attempt to hide their feelings, but sat on their horses and cried aloud."

"I love you just as well as ever, General Lee," shouted an emaciated Rebel as he made his way toward his commander.

"Those who could speak said goodbye, those who could not speak, and were near, passed their hands gently over the sides of Traveller."

Lee fixed his eyes on a line between his horse's ears, and with tears still trickling down his cheeks, stared straight ahead. When he got to his tent, he paused. "Men," he whispered, "we have fought through the war together; I have done my best for you; my heart is too full to say more." He silently mouthed a "goodbye," then disappeared inside his tent, alone.

The Federal camp was euphoric. A volunteer never forgot the sight: "out of the dark pine woods, down the rock-strewn road, like a regiment of whirlwinds they come: Meade, bareheaded, leading them, his grave, scholarly face flushed with radiance, both arms in the air and shouting with all his voice: 'It's all over, boys! Lee's surrendered! It's all over now. . . .' The men listen for a moment to the words of their leaders, and then up to the heavens goes such a shout as none of them will ever hear again. . . . The air is black with hats and boots, coats, knapsacks, shirts and cartridge-boxes, blankets and shelter tents, canteens and haver-sacks. They fall on each other's necks and laugh and cry by turns. Huge, lumbering bearded men embrace and kiss like schoolgirls, then dance and sing and shout, stand on their heads and play at leap frog. . . . The standard bearers bring their war-worn colors to the center of the mass and unfurl their tattered beauties amid the redoubled shouts of the crowd. The bands and drum corps seek the same center, and not a stone's throw apart, each for itself, a dozen bands and a hundred drums make discordant concert. . . . All the time from the hills around the deep-mouthed cannon give their harmless thunders, and at each hollow boom the vast concourse rings out its joy anew that murderous shot and shell no longer follow close the accustomed sound. But soon from the edges of the surging mass, here and there, with bowed heads and downcast eyes men walk slowly to the neighboring woods. Some sit down among the spreading roots and, with heads buried in their hands, drink in the full cup of joy. . . . Others in due and ancient form, on bended knees, breath forth their gratitude . . . while others still lie stretched among the little pines and cry and sob and moan. . . . For a brief moment, now and then, the clamor rounds itself into the grand swelling strains of 'Old Hundredth,' 'The Star-Spangled Banner' or 'Marching Along.' And the waving banners keep time to the solemn movement."

Union soldiers now drifted into the Confederate camp and soon knots of blue- and gray-clad men dotted the hills around Appomattox Court House.

A light rain began to fall.

As soon as Lee and Grant had left the McLean house, Federal officers began to buy all the furniture in the surrender room. Porter explained it as a desire for "relics." George Custer got the table Grant used. General Ord paid forty dollars for Lee's. Chairs went, couches went, even a doll—dubbed the "silent witness"— was purchased. While McLean was unwillingly being separated from his goods, Grant and his staff were making their way back to headquarters. Porter remembered that Grant had not notified the government of Lee's surrender, and Grant sat down on a stone and wrote a telegram: Dated 4:30 P.M., April 9, and addressed to Secretary of War Stanton, the message informed Washington that "Gen. Lee surrendered the Army of Northern Va this afternoon on terms proposed by myself."

Grant seated himself outside his tent while his excited staff assembled for a firsthand account of his feelings as conquering general. "Our expectations were doomed to disappointment," Porter, not without disapproval, wrote, "for he appeared to have already dismissed the whole subject from his mind." The aide was disgusted by Grant's incongruous conversation. For some odd reason, Grant chose to spend the remainder of their time together recounting the antics of a white Mexican mule.

The story was about a pack mule that Grant and other officers had taken with them on their April 1848 ascension of Mount Popocatepetl. Much to the consternation of the young climbers, the mule lost its footing and tumbled down the side of the mountain. The accident seemed portentous, Grant said, for that same day a blizzard arrested the men halfway up the slope. The next morning, Grant and a few others abandoned the climb and left their comrades—mainly Southerners, Beauregard among them— to go it alone to the top. On Grant's cross-country trek to easier hiking, what should appear on the path before the party but the white mule, battered, dirty, and scuffed, but nevertheless hale enough and determined to carry on. Grant howled as he told the story to his mystified staff. Perhaps only Rawlins might have understood. Years later, in response to a question about his first thoughts when he received Lee's offer to surrender, Grant said it was his "dirty boots and wearing no sword." He was embarrassed for Robert Lee to see him. Face to face for the first time in almost twenty years with the man who had sent him from Winfield Scott's headquarters to change his uniform, Grant may have found the mule a fitting symbol of himself—a scuffed and dirty survivor who won the race for victory. The only race that ever really mattered.

Late in the day, Grant said he'd leave for Washington in the morning. "We wished to see something of the opposing army, now that it had become civil enough for the first time in its existence, to let us get close up to it," Porter remembered. "The general, however, had no desire to look at the conquered—indeed, he had little curiosity in his nature." Porter's pique was only slightly lessened by Grant's agreeing to wait at least until noon, when the railroad tracks being laid by Federal engineers would be finished.[9]

Lee spent the morning of April 10 in his tent, receiving the goodbyes of his officers and urging them to go home, plant a crop, and obey the law. There was also hated paperwork to do, grimmer now that it was all over—collecting information from field officers for the preparation of his final report to Jefferson Davis. He also put the finishing touches on General Order No. 9, the last order from the Army of Northern Virginia. At ten, a courier arrived with a surprising piece of information: Ulysses Grant was waiting at Confederate picket lines. Lee immediately rode out alone to see him, and as the Federal headquarters staff melted into the background, the two walked their horses side by side, talking earnestly, their heads leaning together. Slightly different versions of that conversation came down through the years, but one thing was obvious: Grant was on what he believed to be a mission from Abraham Lincoln. As recently as a week earlier—on the porch at Petersburg—Lincoln had talked about his wish to let the South "down easy." What he wanted was a union, not a victorious North punishing a vanquished and treasonous foe. Grant asked Lee to use his influence to make peace throughout the South. Lee responded that peace was already a reality since there was virtually no Confederate military defense left, but that as a soldier, he could not supersede the civil authority of President Davis. Then Grant asked if Lee would go to Washington and meet Lincoln. Again, Lee said such a move was impossible. The talk apparently was cordial enough for Lee to confess that he had always supported the Union in his heart, and that he could find no justification for the politicians—"extremists on both sides"—who had brought on the war. What he would do, Lee told Grant, was devote his "whole efforts to pacifying the country and bringing the people back to the Union." Grant promised to carry Lee's message to Lincoln immediately.[10]

Union officers were riding into the Confederate camp as Lee

returned to his tent, and one called out a hello. It took Lee some time to recognize the engineer he had commanded in Mexico. "But what are you doing with all that gray in your beard?" he demanded of George Meade.

"You have to answer for most of it!" Meade retorted.

The two pulled chairs close together and talked of the final campaign while Theodore Lyman made mental notes about the Confederate commander. "In manner he is exceedingly grave and dignified—this, I believe, he always has; but there was evidently added an extreme depression, which gave him the air of a man who kept up his pride to the last, but who was entirely over-whelmed. From his speech I judge he was inclined to wander in his thoughts. You would not have recognized a Confederate of-ficer from his dress, which was a blue military overcoat, a high grey hat, and well-brushed riding boots." When Meade intro-duced Lyman and another aide, "Lee put out his hand and saluted us with all the air of the oldest blood in the world. I did not think . . . that I should ever shake the hand of Robert E. Lee, prisoner of war!" Meade was still with Lee when "a great oddity" ap-peared at the door of the tent. An old man—his thick white hair matted with red Virginia clay, his body shrouded in a wet parti-colored rug, his legs wrapped in torn shreds of gray wool blan-ket—greeted Lee, then shook hands with Meade. It was Virginia governor Henry Wise—the only man who kept his command at Sayler's Creek—from the first shot to the last ditch a soldier. Meade hugged Wise. The men were brothers-in-law.

It was raining that afternoon as Grant saddled up and rode out of Appomattox Court House. It was still raining the following day when Lee issued his final order to his troops:

> After four years of arduous service, marked by unsurpassed courage and fortitude, the Army of Northern Virginia has been compelled to yield to overwhelming numbers and resources.
>
> I need not tell the brave survivors of so many hard fought battles, who have remained steadfast to the last, that I have con-sented to the result from no distrust of them.

But feeling that valor and devotion could accomplish nothing that would compensate for the loss that must have attended the continuance of the contest, I determined to avoid the useless sacrifice of those whose past services have endeared them to their countrymen.

By the terms of the agreement officers and men can return to their homes and remain until exchanged. You will take with you the satisfaction that proceeds from the consciousness of duty faithfully performed, and I earnestly pray that a Merciful God will extend to you His blessing and protection.

With an increasing admiration of your constancy and devotion to your country, and a grateful remembrance of your kind and generous considerations for myself, I bid you all an affectionate farewell.[11]

Lee could have gone, but he stayed. He needed to finish the war up and wait until his army was a thing of the past. The men knew he waited in his tent during the last review.

Joshua Chamberlain conducted the formal stacking of arms and he never forgot it. "It was now the morning of the 12th of April," he wrote. "I had been ordered to have my lines formed for the ceremony at sunrise. It was a chill gray morning, depressing to the senses. But our hearts made warmth. Great memories uprose; great thoughts went forward. We formed along the principal street, from the bluff bank of the stream to near the Court House on the left,—to face the last line of battle, and receive the last remnant of the arms and colors of the great army which ours had been created to confront for all that death can do for life. We were remnants also: Massachusetts, Maine, Michigan, Maryland, Pennsylvania, New York; veterans, and replaced veterans; cut to pieces, cut down, consolidated, divisions into brigades, regiments into one . . . men of near blood born, made nearer by blood shed. Those facing us—now, thank God! the same. . . .

"Our earnest eyes scan the busy groups on the opposite slopes, breaking camp for the last time, taking down their little shelter-tents and folding them carefully as precious things, then slowly forming ranks as for unwelcome duty. And now they move. The dusky swarms forge forward into gray columns of march. On they

come, with the old winging route step and swaying battle flags
. . . crowded so thick, by thinning out of men, that the whole
column seemed crowned with red. . . .

"Before us in proud humiliation stood the embodiment of manhood: men whom neither toils and sufferings, nor the fact of death
nor disaster, nor hopelessness could bend from their resolve;
standing before us now, thin, worn, and famished, but erect, and
with eyes looking level into ours, waking memories that bound us
together as no other bond. . . ."

Without official sanction, and all unplanned, Chamberlain suddenly gave the order for the Union soldiers to "order arms" in that
deepest mark of military respect. "Gordon at the head of the
column, riding with heavy spirit and downcast face, catches the
sound of shifting arms, looks up, and, taking the meaning, wheels
superbly, making with himself and his horse one uplifted figure,
with profound salutation as he drops the point of his sword to the
boot toe." Gordon ordered his men to respond in kind—"honor
answering honor. On our part not a sound . . . but an awed
stillness rather, and breath-holding, as if it were the passing of the
dead!

"As each successive division masks our own, it halts, the men
face inward towards us across the road, twelve feet away; then
carefully 'dress' their line. . . . They fix bayonets, stack arms; then,
hesitatingly, remove cartridge-boxes and lay them down. Lastly—
reluctantly, with agony of expression—they tenderly fold their
flags, battle-worn and torn, blood-stained, heart-holding colors,
and lay them down. . . .

"What visions thronged as we looked into each other's eyes!
Here pass the men of Antietam, the Bloody Lane, the Sunken
Road, the Cornfield . . . The men who swept away the Eleventh
Corps at Chancellorsville; who left six thousand of their compan-
ions around the bases of Culp's and Cemetery Hills at Gettys-
burg; these survivors of the terrible Wilderness, the Bloody
Angle at Spotsylvania, the slaughter pen of Cold Harbor!

"Here comes Cobb's Georgia Legion. . . . Here too comes
Gordon's Georgians and Hoke's North Carolinians, who stood

before the terrific mine explosion at Petersburg, and advancing retook the smoking crater and the dismal heaps of dead—ours more than theirs—huddled in the ghastly chasm.

"Now makes its last front A. P. Hill's old Corps, Heth now at the head, since Hill had gone too far forward ever to return; the men who poured destruction into our division at Sherpardstown Ford, Antietam, in 1862 . . . the men who opened the desperate first day's fight at Gettysburg. . . .

"Now the sad great pageant—Longstreet and his men: What shall we give them for greeting that has not already been spoken in volleys of thunder and written in lines of fire on all the riverbanks of Virginia? . . . Now comes the sinewy remnant of fierce Hood's Division. . . .

"Ah, is this Pickett's Division?—this little group left of those who on the lurid last day of Gettysburg breasted level crossfire and thunderbolts of storm to be strewn back drifting wrecks, where after that awful, futile, pitiful charge we buried them in graves a furlong wide, with names unknown!

"Met again in the terrible cyclone-sweep over the breastworks of Five Forks; met now, so thin, so pale, purged of mortal,—as if knowing pain or joy no more.

"How could we help falling on our knees, all of us together, and praying God to pity and forgive us all!"[12]

EPILOGUE

"I T I S N O W nearly 11 O'Clock at night and I have received directions from the Sec. of War, and President, to start at once for Raleigh North Carolina," Grant wrote Julia on April 20, 1865.

I find my duties, anxieties, and the necessity for having all my wits about me, increasing instead of diminishing. I have a Herculean task to perform and shall endeavor to do it, not to please any one, but for the interests of our great country that is now begining to loom far above all other countries, modern and ancient. What a spectacle it will be to see a country able to put down a rebellion able to put half a Million of soldiers in the field, at one time, and maintain them! That will be done, and is almost done already. That Nation, united, will have a strength that will enable it to dictate to all others, *conform to justice and right*. Power I think can go no further. The moment conscience leaves, physical strength will avail nothing, in the long run.

No man in the United States mourned the death of Abraham Lincoln more than Ulysses Grant. Standing alone at the head of the casket during the funeral ceremonies, Grant attracted almost as much attention as the assassinated President. He seemed riven with anguish, as indeed he was. In his slow climb from Jesse's tanyards in Georgetown to that place at the head of Lincoln's coffin, Grant always followed a voice of authority. Except for the bad times—Oregon and then St. Louis and the first months in Galena—Grant had climbed toward ever higher authorities until at Vicksburg he understood he was finally "safe fer life" with the protection and support of Abraham Lincoln. Lincoln's death left Grant with only an inchoate and earnest desire to "perform" a Herculean task in the name of abstract national interest.

Unmoored from a lifetime of obeying, Grant bobbed along on the surface of political, financial, and emotional tides of which he wasn't even aware. Every politician attending Lincoln's funeral saw in the lonely little general a prime candidate for the 1868 presidency. His ignorance of statecraft and partisan play enhanced his attractiveness—already overwhelming because of his status as popular hero. The nation turned to the figure of the successful Union Army commander as a source of strength and safety after Lincoln's death. The Republican Party turned to him as an easily manipulated front man for a series of punitive Reconstruction measures and eventually, after he won the 1868 election, for a runaway attempt at controlling all three branches of the United States government. Though Grant joined Radical Republicans in their post-assassination lust for southern blood, he intervened in the matter of Lee's indictment for treason, claiming that his parole precluded civil action. The suit was dropped.

The three years intervening between war's end and Grant's occupying the White House had him running the Army, making gala tours of the country to accept the nation's gratitude, and settling himself into the bosoms of America's robber barons. The backwoods boy from Ohio was seized upon by the Rockefellers, Goulds, and Fisks in ways which compromised his political objectivity and made him very rich. A journalist noted during this period that Grant's life could be summed up by conjugating the verb "to receive." Receive he did—stock options, houses, lavish gifts—and he and Julia began a life as guests of the economic upper crust.

As President, Grant became embroiled in unprecedented scandals which involved Cabinet members and advisers. Predictably, he ran his administration as he had run the Department of the

Mississippi, with no mind for the subtleties of government, and completely willing to turn over to subordinates work which he felt could be done better by someone else—which was almost everything. Early on he astonished the Secretary of the Navy by saying he couldn't be bothered with the technicalities of legislation— experts had been elected to run the government. He saw his office as "a gift of the people" which had been given him as a reward for winning the Civil War. In turn, he handed out government jobs as gifts to former subordinates, and surrounded himself with the kind of men who had drawn critical comments from supporters as diverse as Rawlins, Charles Dana, and George Meade— "jolly dogs" who helped themselves to government largesse. Rawlins, in fact, was made Secretary of War. By 1868 Grant had broken completely with the consumptive lawyer from Galena, and only brought him into the Cabinet after Rawlins complained at being assigned a menial job in some military outpost. It was a short-lived position, because he died within the year. Though Grant was sent a telegram announcing the imminent demise of his old aide, he seemed to be in no hurry to say goodbye, and was not on hand at the end.

Julia moved through her days as First Lady with all the decorum her giddy joy would allow. She demonstrated a decided taste for the regal. Washington got a hint of what was to come by her fencing off for the first time in its existence the White House grounds so that her children could cavort in isolation. She remained loyal to old St. Louis friends, but preferred the company of such worthies as Mrs. Hamilton Fish. She married off Nellie to an English noble in a lavish White House ceremony. Nellie's marriage was less merry than the wedding—at which her father openly sobbed and presented her with a check for $20,000. The blue-blood husband proved a cad. Fred's marital connection was more stable but no less socially exalted, and he ensconced his new wife in his parents' home, where she gave birth to a little girl— Julia Dent Grant—who would ever after be known as the Child of the White House.

One of Grant's first acts as President was to invite Robert E. Lee to visit him. Lee had been collared by a committee bent on constructing a useful railroad line between Virginia's valley and Baltimore. Grant sent Lee word through various intermediaries that he would be happy if the general could pay him a call. The meeting, on May 1, 1869, did not go well. An embarrassed strain descended on the room when the two shook hands—observers thought each of them was suddenly struck by profound depression. As at Appomattox, Grant tried to fill the silence by making a joke or two. "You and I, General, have had more to do with destroying railroads than building them." Lee was not amused. After fifteen minutes, they shook hands again and parted forever. None of Grant's staff ever explained his invitation to Lee, but some thought it might have been based in politics. Lee's name had been bandied about in some die-hard northern papers as an 1868 Democratic candidate for the presidency. Grant was at first surprised by northern affection for Lee. As his presidency wore on, he became bitter about the growing national celebration of the Confederate leader. Most of the old-line Northerners whose antebellum historical and political ties were with the Revolutionary War South emotionally strengthened those bonds after 1865. But, surprisingly, New England abolitionist founding families created in Lee a symbol of all that they saw destroyed during Grant's administration. Grant was hurt and he tended to make critical comments about Lee and his generalship.

Though a third term for Grant was discussed, he decided not to run for reelection in 1876—thereby eliciting outraged tears from Julia over giving up her position, which she had assumed was for a lifetime. Soon after the Grants moved out of the White House they took to the road and spent almost three years traveling abroad, where they were received by the royalty of Europe and Asia. Bored and restless, Grant listened to entreaties about running for the presidency in 1880 and came home. He was disappointed to discover that former Republican friends—Elihu Washburne among them—were blocking his candidacy. Party stalwarts correctly decided that the country was sickened by Grant administration scandals and would never reelect him. "You know I can't afford to lose," Grant raged at a would-be campaign aide. Retiring to civilian life in New York, he turned his money over to his son Buck, who proved nearly as gullible a businessman as his father. Using Grant to draw investment funds from former military associates, Buck went into business with a rounder who absconded with every penny. Grant was left guilty, embarrassed, and destitute. The scandal, however, provided friends and future historians with ample proof that the financial mess arose from nothing more than his innocence, unchanged since his Georgetown horse-trading days. He swore to restitute all the money invested by former friends, and refused to accept offers of economic aid. He did agree to take money from Rockefeller—but only when the financier offered to buy his wartime memorabilia. Grant boxed up his gold medals, his swords, his trophies, and his flags and exchanged them for enough money to feed Julia. He also accepted an offer to write an article about one of his military campaigns and this brought him to the attention of Samuel Clemens.

Clemens—Mark Twain—approached Grant with the idea of writing his memoirs. Though Grant's health was none too good— predictably, he'd fallen sick from strain during the collapse of his investment house—he agreed. In what became the most hotly contested race of his life, he sped through days of writing, trying to beat the cancer of the throat which was gaining on him every day. Work on the second volume was dictated for a while, then went on through a series of penciled notes to his secretary. He could not talk nor eat. Wasted and bent, he worked on, and had the book in form enough to be completed by aides. He notified his son he wanted to be buried at West Point, where Winfield Scott had retired to die.

"I do not sleep though I sometimes doze a little," he wrote in response to his doctor's query. "If up I am talked to and in my effort to answer cause pain. The fact is I think I am a verb instead of a personal pronoun. A verb is anything that signifies to be; to do; or to suffer. I signify all three." His Ohio education carried him through to the end. At 8 A.M., July 23, 1885, silent, Ulysses S. Grant died.

June 13, 1865

To Lieutenant-General U. S. Grant, Commanding the Armies of United States.

General: Upon reading the President's proclamation . . . I came to Richmond to ascertain what was proper or required of me to do, when I learned that, with others, I was to be indicted for treason by the grand jury at Norfolk. I had supposed that the officers and men of the Army of Northern Virginia were, by the terms of their surrender, protected by the United States Government from molestation so long as they conformed to its conditions. I am ready to meet any charges that may be preferred against me, and do not wish to avoid trial; but, if I am correct as to the prosecution granted by my parole, and am not to be prosecuted, I desire to comply with the provisions of the President's proclamation, and, therefore, inclose the required application, which I request, in that event, may be acted on. I am, with great respect, Your obedient servant.

Enclosed in Lee's letter to Grant was a poignant request for pardon addressed to Andrew Johnson, the new President of the United States: "I graduated at the Military Academy at West Point in June, 1829," he wrote; "resigned from the United States Army, April, 1861; was a general in the Confederate Army, and included in the surrender of the Army of Northern Virginia, April 9, 1865." Lee asked for pardon as a way of demonstrating to his army that he himself wanted nothing more than to go home, plant a crop, and reunite with the Federal government. The request was never acted upon.

In the autumn of 1865 Lee accepted the presidency of Washington College in Lexington—a move which disgruntled some former subordinates, who knew just how lucrative a business proposition he was. Most schools in the South were closed—or soon would be—for lack of money and students. Washington College was on its last legs, and Lee, as president, was sure to attract donations. But more important to him was the forum the job provided for disseminating peace sentiments. Though he watched the Federal government's punishment of the South with growing dismay—and he was not a citizen, only a paroled prisoner of war—he continued to urge Southerners back into the Union.

He received hundreds of visitors and perhaps thousands of letters from civilians and former soldiers asking for advice. His response was always the same: Submit to the duly authorized government. He even told correspondents to take that most painful of steps and sign the loyalty oath required by the Federal government. When he took up his duties in Lexington, he said the same things to his students—not boys as in former times, but veterans for the most part, wild and heartbroken.

The family moved into Washington College's president's home, where Stonewall Jackson had lived as son-in-law of the school's former leader. Drapes and carpets from Arlington, sequestered for four years at Ravensworth, furnished the old Federal house. The Washington silver buried at nearby VMI was found to be tarnished but unharmed. The Arlington portraits fared less well; the packet boat bringing them to Lexington sank. The paintings were retrieved, restored, and hung in the dining room. Lee had a little room of his own which he furnished with an iron campaign bed. Oddments of a military lifetime were placed about, the pistol he kept on his saddle was slung over the bedstead, and his campaign chest was pushed into a corner. The Lee daughters were somewhat disdainful about Lexington social life—they found the mountain folk odd-mannered and lacking in Tidewater graces—but soon settled into a round of local calls and visits to flatland friends. Mary began painting again and kept up an active correspondence filled with anguished invective against the Yankees. Unable even to move from her wheelchair, she visited on American politics all the rage she felt at her helplessness. Rooney and Rob came for stays. Both of them had returned to their Peninsula land and planted corn. Custis taught at VMI.

In time, Lee settled into a routine so predictable that townsfolk could set their clocks by his activities. He worked in his office at the college, came home to dinner, and then mounted Traveller and rode off alone into the mountains. He was visibly depressed. He began to correspond with Markie Williams again, but the letters were flat-toned, like those from a man gravely weakened by fatal disease. His health, actually, was not bad. The quiet life at Lexington seemed to restore his strength. He turned his energies to accumulating data from subordinates in order to write a history of the Army of Northern Virginia. Despite repeated promises to set on record the accomplishments of his men—and numerous offers from publishers—he never wrote a book. Rendering the war was apparently too painful. It was easier to talk about it with journalists and foreign visitors who sought his fireside, and write about it in dozens of letters to officers—both Federal and Confederate—who fought on in their minds. He read accounts of campaigns and clipped them from journals, adding marginalia about the accuracy of the pieces. And he arbitrated ongoing charges and countercharges about various men's various failures during various battles. His sole literary effort was editing the memoirs of his father. Life itself, and the ambiguities of leading a generation of Southerners to their deaths in a cause he barely held, apparently brought Lee closer to Light-Horse Harry.

Ironically, Lee did assume the public place Mary had wanted for him when southern independence seemed possible. He became leader of his country. That country had no body politic, no elected officials, but it had a seat of government in Lexington. Knowing this, and understanding how the South looked to Lee as example and leader, the Thirty-ninth Congress of the United States called Lee to Washington during the winter of 1865–66 to testify. The House was packed as Lee, wearing a gray uniform from which all military insignia had been stripped, entered the room. It fell silent as he began to answer a series of questions aimed at airing Reconstruction grievances against the South. His responses were so measured, patient, and seemingly candid that the legislators abandoned their efforts to make of Lee a symbol of treasonable rebeldom. Herman Melville found in the Confederate general another kind of symbol, and wrote in his "Lee in the Capitol": *"Who looks at Lee must think of Washington; In pain must think, and hide the thought, So deep in grevious meaning is it fraught."* Except for heading the list of signatories of the "White Sulfur Letter"—written by former Confederates who wished to influence a softening of the harshest aspects of Reconstruction—Lee was never again directly involved in political processes. He refused to be considered for the governorship of Virginia—it

573

would be onerous for the state to have him, he said—and dismissed the call for his presidential candidacy in 1868 as journalistic lunacy.

With few exceptions—several trips to Richmond to testify at the aborted trial of Jefferson Davis, a restorative visit to Petersburg for the wedding of widower Rooney to Mary Tabb Bolling—Lee kept to Lexington. The college prospered under his aegis. He brought to his job the same benevolent discipline he had demonstrated as head of West Point, and attracted to the school a plethora of donations. Washington College finances were flush enough to allow the building of a new president's home, and Lee designed a house which echoed Stratford in four brick chimneys clustered over its center. He did not live there long.

Misguidedly, in 1870, he decided to follow a physician's recommendation and made a tour of the South for his health. The trip, which took him all the way to Florida, became a gala celebration which left Lee exhausted and weakened. His sole benefit seemed to be the emotional relief he got by visiting for the first time the North Carolina grave of his daughter Annie, who died after Sharpsburg, and paying another call at Dungeness, the Cumberland Island home where his father was buried.

That October, Lee took a chill while attending a vestrymen's meeting at Lexington's Episcopal church, and when he returned home he discovered he could not speak. Muttering incoherently and holding his body rigidly erect, Lee was helped to the cot which was brought into his dining room. For more than a week, his family attended him night and day. He watched them with "beautiful sad eyes." He rallied briefly, and at times seemed lucid, but otherwise "wandered to those dreadful battlefields," Mary said. Word was sent out that he was near death. During the afternoon of October 10, 1870, he took command once again. In a strong voice, Lee called out through the dining room: "Tell Hill he *must* come up!"

Then, later, "Strike that tent!"

In the mid-1970s a government clerk was riffling through old files in a Washington government bureau and discovered a yellowed piece of paper dated October 2, 1865. "I Robert E. Lee of Lexington, Virginia do solemnly swear, in the presence of Almighty God, that I will henceforth support, protect and defend the Constitution of the United States, and the Union of the States thereunder, and that I will, in like manner, abide by and faithfully support all laws and proclamations which have been made during the existing rebellion with reference to the emancipation of slaves, so help me God." No one knew how Lee's oath came to be forgotten in an old file drawer, but it was commonly believed the notarized document had been hidden in 1865 to suppress evidence that former Confederates were willing to restore the United States. More than a hundred years after his death, Robert E. Lee's oath was finally acted upon and his citizenship restored by the United States House of Representatives. The vote was not unanimous.

NOTES

These have been kept to a minimum. Sources are listed in the order in which they are used in the text. Names refer to authors listed alphabetically in the bibliography. For the full citation, refer to the bibliography. In the case of two authors sharing the same last name, first names are also used. In the case of one author writing several books used, the title of the specific book is cited. *The Papers of Ulysses S. Grant* are referred to in the notes as *Papers* with the appropriate volume number. *The Wartime Papers of Robert E. Lee* are referred to in the notes as *Wartime Papers*. A few sources have no author; these are referred to by title, listed alphabetically in the bibliography. Letters and unpublished manuscripts are denoted, with their sources listed. The vast majority of these are from the Ely-deButts Collection in the Virginia Historical Society in Richmond, Va. These are cited as V.H.S. Other manuscript sources include the William R. Perkins Library, Duke University, Durham, N.C.; the University of North Carolina Library, especially the Southern Historical Collection, Chapel Hill, N.C.; the Georgia Historical Society, and the Georgia Society of Colonial Dames of America, Savannah, Ga.; the Library of Congress, Washington, D.C.; the Washington and Lee University Library, Lexington, Va.; the Vicksburg Historical Society, Vicksburg, Miss.; and a small collection on file at the "Lee Boyhood Home," Alexandria, Va. ALS, "Autograph Letter Signed," is a library notation signifying an original letter.

CHAPTER I

1. Porter, 490–500—for further discussion of conversation, see Maurice, *Marshall*; Catton, *Grant Moves South,* 420; Garland, 313.
2. Grant, Julia, 150–53; Garland, 314.

3. Welles II, 278–83; Grant, Julia, 154–56.

4. Brooks, Noah, 229; Porter, 496–97; Young, John Russell, I, 356; Catton, *Grant Takes Command,* 475.

5. Lee, R. E., *Wartime Papers,* 935, 938.

6. Alexander, 603.

7. Longstreet, 375–76; Freeman IV, 158–61; for Richmond, see Putnam, 362–74; Stiles, 322; and McGuire, 344–53, 356–57.

CHAPTER 2

1. Henry Lee to Charles Lee, July 5, 1775, in Royster, 16; Charles Lee quoted in Royster, 14; Dowdey, 9; Royster, 37–38; Freeman IV, 66; Ichabod Burnett to Henry Lee, June 20, 1782, and Henry Lee to Nathanael Greene, Feb. 19, 1782, in Royster, 49.

2. Henry Lee to James Madison, April 4, 1792, in Freeman I, 7; Royster, 77.

3. Dowdey, 6–7; Freeman I, 27; Shirley is still owned by the Carter family, who live on and farm the old James plantation. It is open to the public.

4. Henry Lee to George Washington, Dec. 16, 1791, in Royster, 64; Henry Lee to George Washington, April 23, 1793, in Royster, 65; Henry Lee to Alexander Hamilton, May 6, 1793, in Royster, 66; Dowdey, 21, 14–15; Royster, 57.

5. George Washington to Henry Lee, July 21, 1793, in Freeman I, 22; Sanborn I, 12, 14–17; Samuel Storrow to "his sister," Sept. 6, 1821, in Sanborn I, 13.

6. Henry Lee to Patrick Henry, April 22, 1795, in Royster, 172–73; Henry Lee to George Washington, May 22, 1799, in Royster, 179; George Washington to Henry Lee, Jan. 25, 1798, in Royster, 177; Lee's funeral oration in Royster, 202.

7. John Maund to Robert Carter, Jan. 3, 1801, in Royster, 175; Will of Charles Carter in Dowdey, 24. There is no agreement on how R. E. Lee's mother spelled her name. Even she used Anne and Ann. Ann Lee quoted in Dowdey, 24; Ann Lee to Mrs. Richard Bland Lee, Feb. 18, 1799, quoted in Freeman I, 11; and Sanborn I, 18; Ann Carter Lee to Henry Lee, July 6, 1806, in Sanborn I, 22.

8. Ann Lee to Mrs. Richard Bland Lee, Jan. 11, 1807, in Freeman I, 12.

9. Ann C. Lee to Carter Berkeley, Nov. 1809, in Royster, 82–83; Sanborn I, 26; Royster, 156–67 and n. 134, 274, 232–33.

10. Ann Lee to "relative," from "Eastern View," Sept. 21, 1811, on file at "Lee Boyhood Home" in Alexandria, Va. The house is open to the public and is furnished as it was during the Lees' residence there. Mason, 24, 22; Sanborn I, 12; Ann C. Lee to Charles Carter Lee, Feb. 2, 1817, in Sanborn I, 44–45.

11. Henry Lee to Ann C. Lee, May 6, 1817, ALS, V.H.S. Henry Lee's letters to Charles Carter Lee are in R. E. Lee's biography of his father, "Life of Henry Lee," in the 1869 edition of Henry Lee's memoirs, 63–74; Henry Lee to [Henry Lee IV] Sept. 3, 1813, in Royster, 245; Royster, 5–7, 252.

12. Freeman I, 40; Sanborn I, 48; Henry Lee to Ann C. Lee, May 6, 1817, ALS, V.H.S.; Cassius Francis Lee to Mary Custis Lee, Nov. 8, 1870, ALS, V.H.S.;

Sarah Lee to Mary Custis Lee, Nov. 10, 1870, ALS, V.H.S.; reminiscences by Edmund Lee in Sanborn I, 46; Mason, 22–23, 25.

13. Freeman I, 45; Sanborn I, 51.

14. William Fitzhugh to John C. Calhoun in Sanborn I, 49–50; Henry Lee IV to John C. Calhoun in Freeman I, 43; Sarah Lee to Mary C. Lee, Nov. 10, 1870, ALS, V.H.S.

CHAPTER 3

1. Grant, Jesse R., *Ledger,* Jan. 17, 1868; Grant, U. S., *Memoirs* I, 63, 19–20; McFeely, 4–5; Richardson, Albert, 43, 45–47.

2. Grant, Jesse R., *Ledger,* Jan. 18, 1868; Lewis, 14.

3. Grant, Jesse R., *Ledger,* Jan. 18 and 21, 1868.

4. *History of Brown County,* 241–79, 343–44, 351, 389, 393, 395, 260–73; Richardson, Albert, 51.

5. Garland, 20, 5, 3, 6–7; Grant, Jesse R., *Ledger,* Jan. 20, 1868; Woodward, William, 17, 13; Richardson, Albert, 52.

6. Grant, U. S., *Memoirs* I, 29–30.

7. Grant, Jesse R., *Ledger,* Jan. 18 and 20, 1868; Richardson, Albert, 67.

8. Richardson, Albert, 69, 56; Lewis, 24, 33, 44; *History of Clermont County,* 186; Grant, Jesse R., *Ledger,* Jan. 18, 1868; Garland, 15; Grant, U. S., *Memoirs* I, 25.

9. Grant, Jesse R., *Ledger,* Jan. 21, 1868; Grant, U. S., *Memoirs* I, 26, 25; Lewis, 20–21, 46–47; Porter, 97.

10. Grant, U. S., *Memoirs* I, 20, 23, 33–34; Grant, Jesse R., *Ledger,* Jan. 17, 1868; Cramer, intro.; *History of Brown County,* 403; Nevins, *Ordeal of the Union* I, 139–45; Wilson, Edmund, 11–17.

11. Grant, U. S., *Memoirs* I, 25, 32; Grant, Jesse R., *Ledger,* Jan. 17, 1868; Lewis, 56–57; see Grant's *Papers* I, 3–4 n.

12. Richardson, Albert, 76; Grant, U. S., *Memoirs* I, 32, 24, 35; Lewis, 55–56, 60–61.

CHAPTER 4

1. R. E. Lee to Mary C. Lee, June 5, 1839, ALS, V.H.S.; R. E. Lee described in Freeman I, 68.

2. Freeman I, 51–53, 55, 56–58, 61–62, 64, 68; Long, 71.

3. R. E. Lee to G. W. Custis Lee, Jan. 12, 1852, ALS, Library of Congress (Middleton Collection).

4. Freeman I, 72–73; *Hamilton's Works,* edited by Grammont, a New York 1820 reprint of an 1810 edition, are the ones Lee read. Robert Schnare, librarian at the United States Military Academy, supplied this information.

5. Freeman I, 82–83; Ann Carter Lee to Smith Lee, April 10, 1827, in Freeman I, 88–90; Sarah Lee to Mary C. Lee, Nov. 10, 1870, ALS, V.H.S.; Ann Lee's will in Freeman I, 92.

6. R. E. Lee to [cadet at West Point] Nov. 13 and 15, 1852, Lee Letterbook, V.H.S.

7. MacDonald, 3–23.

8. George Washington to [Parke Custis's teacher], May 24, 1797, ALS, V.H.S.; George Washington to John McD-, Sept. 1798, ALS, V.H.S.; MacDonald, 3–23; Sanborn I, 77–78; deButts, intro., and 71–72, 116–20; Edward Everett quoted in Nevins, *Ordeal of the Union* I, 462; Arlington house has been restored to its condition during the Lee-Custis residence and is open to the public; Freeman I, 129–31.

9. Virginia houses: Brodie, Fawn, 468–70; *The Virginia Landmarks Register,* 99; interview with Margaret Peters, staff historian for the Virginia Historic Landmarks Commission, Richmond; interview with members of Mount Vernon Ladies Association; Leech, 17.

10. Nevins, *Ordeal of the Union* I, 462–97; Woodward, C. Vann, *Mary Chesnut's Civil War,* intro. and 29, 84, 113–14, 168, 227, 238, 246, 298, 729–30; Woodward, C. Vann, *The Private Mary Chesnut,* 42, 203, 211, 214; George Washington to G. W. Parke Custis, Nov. 28, 1796, ALS, V.H.S.; Sanborn I, 78; Cash, 84–85; Genovese; Freeman I, 392.

11. William Meade to Mary F. Custis, April 9, 1823, ALS, V.H.S.; William Meade to Mary F. Custis, April 16, 1826, ALS, V.H.S.; MacDonald, 19–20; for general discussion of wives of slave owners, see Clinton.

12. Long, 31; Sanborn I, 74–77; MacDonald, 30.

13. Harrison, 33; Long, 30; Freeman I, 110; MacDonald, 37–38; Sanborn I, 78; G. W. Parke Custis address defending Light-Horse Harry Lee delivered Sept. 1, 1812, Library of Congress; Sarah Lee to Mary C. Lee, Nov. 10, 1870, ALS, V.H.S.; Custis, 354–63.

14. Sanborn I, 72; R. E. Lee to "Miss E." [1829–30], ALS, Georgia Historical Society (Colonial Dames Collection); Sanborn I, 70.

15. MacDonald, 33–34; Sanborn I, 83–86; R. E. Lee to Andrew Talcott, July 13, 1831, ALS, V.H.S.

16. R. E. Lee to Andrew Talcott, July 13, 1831, ALS, V.H.S.; Freeman I, 119–21.

17. Mary C. Lee and R. E. Lee to Mary F. Custis, [1831], from Fortress Monroe, ALS, V.H.S.

18. Mary F. Custis to Mary C. Lee, Oct. 8, 1831, ALS, V.H.S.; R. E. Lee to Mary C. Lee, April 24, 1832, ALS, V.H.S.; R. E. Lee and Mary C. Lee to Mrs. E. A. Stiles, Jan. 4, 1832, ALS, Georgia Historical Society (Colonial Dames Collection).

19. R. E. Lee to Mary C. Lee, April 24, 1832, ALS, V.H.S.; R. E. Lee to Mary C. Lee, June 6, 1832, in Cuthbert (Lee), 264; R. E. Lee to Mary C. Lee, May 19, 1832, ALS, V.H.S.; R. E. Lee to [?], Feb. 24, 1833, ALS, Library of Congress (John Floyd Papers).

20. R. E. Lee to Mary C. Lee, June 6, 1832, in Cuthbert (Lee), 264; MacDonald, 42–48; R. E. Lee to Andrew Talcott, June 29, 1837, ALS, V.H.S.; R. E. Lee

to Jack Mackay, Feb. 27, 1834, ALS, Library of Congress (Middleton Collection).

21. Long, 44, 35; R. E. Lee to Jack Mackay, Feb. 3, 1834, in Freeman I, 124; R. E. Lee to Jack Mackay, June 26, 1834, ALS, Georgia Historical Society (Colonial Dames Collection); R. E. Lee to Jack Mackay, Feb. 27, 1834, ALS, Library of Congress (Middleton Collection).

22. R. E. Lee to Mary C. Lee, Nov. 27, 1833, in Cuthbert (Lee), 267–70; Mary C. Lee to Mary F. Custis, April 11, [1834], ALS, V.H.S.

23. R. E. Lee to Mary C. Lee, Nov. 27, 1833, in Cuthbert (Lee), 269; Mary C. Lee quoted in MacDonald, 48.

24. R. E. Lee to Andrew Talcott, Feb. 10, 1835, ALS, V.H.S.; R. E. Lee to Jack Mackay, Feb. 27, 1834, ALS, Library of Congress (Middleton Collection).

25. Freeman I, 133; Sanborn I, 105; R. E. Lee to Jack Mackay, Feb. 18, 1835, ALS, Library of Congress (Middleton Collection); Sanborn I, 106–8; Freeman I, 134; Dowdey, 62.

26. R. E. Lee to Mary C. Lee, Aug. 21, 1835, in Cuthbert (Lee), 271–73.

27. Lee to Talcott quoted in Dowdey, 62; Mary C. Lee to Mrs. Talcott quoted in MacDonald, 59–60.

28. Long, 31; Mary C. Lee to Eliza Mackay Stiles, Jan. 23, 1836, true copy of Stratford Association original on file in Georgia Historical Society; R. E. Lee to Andrew Talcott, May 5, 1836, ALS, V.H.S.; R. E. Lee to Andrew Talcott, June 9, 1836, and June 22, 1836, ALS, V.H.S.; R. E. Lee to Jack Mackay, June 22, 1836, ALS, Library of Congress (Middleton Collection).

29. R. E. Lee to Andrew Talcott, Feb. 2, 1837, ALS, V.H.S.; R. E. Lee to Jack Mackay, Oct. 22, 1837, ALS, Georgia Historical Society (Colonial Dames Collection); R. E. Lee to Mary C. Lee, Aug. 5. 1837, ALS, V.H.S.; R. E. Lee to Mary F. Custis Lee, Nov. 7, 1839, ALS, V.H.S.; R. E. Lee letters on his St. Louis investments in John Floyd Papers in Library of Congress; R. E. Lee to Mary C. Lee, Sept. 10, 1837, ALS, V.H.S.; R. E. Lee to Jack Mackay, Oct. 22, 1837, and Oct. 19, 1838, ALS, Georgia Historical Society (Colonial Dames Collection); R. E. Lee to Jack Mackay, June 6, 1838, ALS, Library of Congress (Middleton Collection).

30. R. E. Lee to Mary C. Lee, Oct. 16, 1837, ALS, V.H.S.

31. MacDonald, 67–71.

32. Bailyn et al., 554, 559; Nevins, *Ordeal of the Union* I, 138 ff.; Anderson, 68–72.

33. Mary C. Lee to Mary F. Custis, [1831], ALS, V.H.S.; Dowdey, 56–59; Mary F. Custis to Mary C. Lee, Oct. 8, 1831, ALS, V.H.S.; Bailyn et al., 549.

34. Sanborn I, 124–25; R. E. Lee to Jack Mackay, Oct. 19, 1838, ALS, Georgia Historical Society (Colonial Dames Collection); R. E. Lee to Jack Mackay, June 27, 1838, ALS, Library of Congress (Middleton Collection); R. E. Lee to Andrew Talcott, Aug. 7, 1838, ALS, V.H.S.; Mary Lee quoted in MacDonald, 75–76; R. E. Lee to Andrew Talcott, Aug. 15, 1837, Oct. 3, 1838,

and May 18, 1839, ALS, V.H.S.; R. E. Lee to Mary F. Custis, March 20, 1839, ALS, V.H.S.; R. E. Lee and Mary C. Lee to Mary F. Custis, May 24, 1838, ALS, V.H.S.

35. R. E. Lee to Mary F. Custis, Nov. 7, 1839, ALS, V.H.S.

CHAPTER 5

1. Lewis, 61–62; Garland, 42; Richardson, Albert, 75.
2. U. S. Grant to McKinstry Griffin, Sept. 22, 1839, *Papers* I, 5–7; Grant, U. S., *Memoirs* I, 26, 39; U. S. Grant to Col. Joseph Totten, March 20, 1840, *Papers* I, 8–9.
3. Lewis, 342; Porter, 342; Grant, U. S., *Memoirs* I, 38–39, 41; Woodward, William, 43–44.
4. Garland, 45, 49; Lewis, 80, 82, 93, 84, 85; Richardson, Albert, 90, 91; Grant, U. S., *Memoirs* I, 40; Church, 20.
5. Lewis, 65–67, 86–89; McFeely, 15; Young II, 289.
6. Grant, U. S., *Memoirs* I, 41; McFeely, 16; boycott notice in *Papers* I, 12.
7. Lewis, 64, 91, 93–94; Richardson, Albert, 92–93; Garland, 46; Grant, U. S., *Memoirs* I, 40, 42.
8. Lewis, 95; U. S. Grant to Julia Dent, Aug. 31, 1844, *Papers* I, 33–36; Grant, U. S., *Memoirs* I, 42–44; U. S. Grant to McKinstry Griffin, Sept. 22, 1839, *Papers* I, 7.
9. Grant, U. S., *Memoirs* I, 42, 51–52; Lewis, 100–2; U. S. Grant to Bvt. Brig. Gen. Roger Jones, Nov. 17, 1843, *Papers* I, 23.
10. Garland, 58–60; Lewis, 104–5, 112; Grant, Julia, 40–42; McFeely, 20–23.
11. Grant, Julia, 43, 30, 34, 41; Lewis, 103, 110, 105.
12. Grant, Julia, 46, 33–48; Lewis, 105.
13. Grant, Julia, 48–49; Grant, U. S., *Memoirs* I, 49–50.
14. Grant, Julia, 49–50.
15. U. S. Grant to Julia Dent, June 4, 1844, *Papers* I, 23–25; U. S. Grant to Julia Dent, Aug. 31, 1844, *Papers* I, 33–34; Grant, U. S., *Memoirs* I, 56–58; U. S. Grant to Mrs. Bailey, June 6, 1844, *Papers* I, 27.
16. U. S. Grant to Julia Dent, June 4, 1844, *Papers* I, 23–26; U. S. Grant to Julia Dent, July 28, 1844, *Papers* I, 29–32.
17. U. S. Grant to Julia Dent, Aug. 31, 1844, *Papers* I, 33–36.
18. U. S. Grant to Julia Dent, Sept. 7, 1844, *Papers* I, 37; U. S. Grant to Julia Dent, Jan. 12, 1845, *Papers* I, 40.
19. Grant, Julia, 51–52; Lewis, 121–22.
20. Bailyn et al., 608.
21. Grant, U. S., *Memoirs* I, 53; see U. S. Grant to Julia Dent, July 11, July 17, and Sept. 14, 1845, in *Papers* I; Lewis, 125–30.
22. U. S. Grant to Julia Dent, Sept. 14, Oct. 10, [Oct.], Nov. 11, and [Nov.–Dec.], 1845, and Jan. 2, Jan. 12, and Feb. 5, 1846, *Papers* I, 53–72; Lewis, 131.

CHAPTER 6

1. R. E. Lee to Mary C. Lee, May 12, 1846, ALS, V.H.S.

2. Freeman I, 182–83.

3. R. E. Lee to Jack Mackay, Nov. 7, 1839, ALS, Library of Congress (Middleton Collection); Long, 45–46.

4. Lee quoted in Freeman I, 177.

5. R. E. Lee to Jack Mackay, June 27, 1838, and Nov. 7, 1839, ALS, Library of Congress (Middleton Collection).

6. R. E. Lee to Jack Mackay, March 18, 1841, ALS, Library of Congress (Middleton Collection); R. E. Lee to Charles Carter Lee, Feb. 14, 1843, and Aug. 17, 1843, ALS, V.H.S.

7. R. E. Lee to Richard Stuart, Jan. 26, 1840, and R. E. Lee to Charles Carter Lee, Jan. 30, 1840, April 2, 1843, Feb. 14, 1843, and R. E. Lee to Bernard Carter, Oct. 25, 1852, all Lee Letterbook, V.H.S.

8. R. E. Lee will, dated Aug. 31, 1846, and correspondence about error in Lee Letterbook No. 1, V.H.S.; R. E. Lee to Mary F. Custis, Dec. 19, 1842, ALS, V.H.S.; various Lee holdings are listed in his Memorandum Book No. 5, V.H.S.

9. Mary C. Lee to Mary F. Custis, Oct. 27, 1844, ALS, V.H.S.; MacDonald, 83.

10. Interview with Cyrus L. Gray, M.D., Tampa, Fla., board-certified specialist in obstetrics and gynecology, about Mary Lee's health; MacDonald, 83–98.

11. Mary C. Lee to Mary F. Custis, Oct. 27, 1844, ALS, V.II.S.

12. Long, 66–67; R. E. Lee to Henry Kayser, June 16, 1845, and July 4, 1846, in *Letters of Robert E. Lee to Henry Kayser,* 38, 42–43.

13. Mary Lee quoted in Sanborn I, 139.

14. Craven, *"To Markie,"* for a general view.

15. R. E. Lee to Martha Custis Williams, Dec. 14, 1844, May 26, 1845, Sept. 17, 1845, June 7, 1846, in Craven, *"To Markie,"* 4–17.

16. R. E. Lee to Fred Smith, Aug. 12, 1839, Lee Letterbook, V.H.S.

17. Sanborn I, 147; R. E. Lee to Mary C. Lee, April 13, 1844, ALS, V.H.S.

18. R. E. Lee to Mary F. Custis, Nov. 22, 1842, ALS, V.H.S.; R. E. Lee to G. W. Custis Lee, Nov. 30, 1843, ALS, V.H.S.; R. E. Lee and W. H. Fitzhugh (Rooney) Lee to G. W. P. Custis Lee, Dec. 18, 1845, Lee Letterbook, V.H.S.; R. E. Lee to W. H. Fitzhugh (Rooney) Lee, March 1, 1846, ALS, V.H.S.

19. R. E. Lee to Col. Joseph Totten, June 17, 1845, Lee Letterbook, V.H.S.

20. U. S. Grant to Julia Dent, May 11, 1846, *Papers* I, 84–86.

21. R. E. Lee to Henry Kayser, July 4, 1846, *Letters of Robert E. Lee to Henry Kayser,* 43; R. E. Lee to Jack Mackay, June 21, 1846, ALS, Georgia Historical Society (Colonial Dames Collection); see R. E. Lee to Mary C. Lee, Dec. 25, 1846, ALS, V.H.S.

22. R. E. Lee to Mary C. Lee, Sept. 4, 1846, and Aug. [Sept.] 13, 1846, ALS, V.H.S.

23. Grant, U. S., *Memoirs* I, 102; Lewis, 138, 155.

24. U. S. Grant to Julia Dent, July 2, 1846, *Papers* I, 99; U. S. Grant to Julia Dent, July 25, 1846, *Papers* I, 101–2; Lewis, 159–60; U. S. Grant to Julia Dent, Aug. 4, 1846, *Papers* I, 103–4; U. S. Grant to Julia Dent, Aug. 14, 1846, *Papers* I, 104–5.

25. Grant, U. S., *Memoirs* I, 105–6; U. S. Grant to Julia Dent, Sept. 6, 1846, *Papers* I, 108–9.

26. Grant, U. S., *Memoirs* I, 110–11, 115–18; U. S. Grant to Julia Dent, Sept. 23, 1846, *Papers* I, 110–11; U. S. Grant to Julia Dent, Oct. 3, 1846, *Papers* I, 112–13.

27. R. E. Lee to Mary C. Lee, Oct. 19, 1846, and Feb. 13, 1847, ALS, V.H.S.

28. R. E. Lee to Mary C. Lee, Nov. 11, Nov. 4, Sept. 25, and Oct. 19, 1846, ALS, V.H.S.; R. E. Lee to Mary C. Lee, Dec. 25, 1846, ALS, V.H.S.

29. U. S. Grant to Julia Dent, Nov. 7, 1846, *Papers* I, 117; U. S. Grant to Julia Dent, Oct. 20, 1846, *Papers* I, 114–15; Lewis, 183; Thomas L. Hamer to a friend, quoted in *Papers* I, 121 n.; U. S. Grant to Mrs. Thomas L. Hamer [Dec. 1846], *Papers* I, 121; U. S. Grant to Julia Dent, Dec. 27, 1846, *Papers* I, 118–19.

30. U. S. Grant to Julia Dent, Feb. 1, 1846 [1847], *Papers* I, 123–24; Grant, U. S., *Memoirs* I, 99–102, 138–39; Lewis, 191, 117, Scott quoted 192; U. S. Grant to Julia Dent, Feb. 25, 1847, and Feb. 27, 1847, *Papers* I, 125–28.

31. R. E. Lee to G. W. Custis Lee and W. H. Fitzhugh (Rooney) Lee, Feb. 27, 1847, ALS, V.H.S.; R. E. Lee to Mary C. Lee, Nov. 26, 1846, and Feb. 22, 1847, ALS, V.H.S.

32. See R. E. Lee to Mary C. Lee, Feb. [March] 6, 1847, ALS, V.H.S.; Grant, U. S., *Memoirs* I, 125–26; U. S. Grant to Julia Dent, April 3, 1847, *Papers* I, 129; Lewis, 195–201; R. E. Lee to Mary C. Lee, March 27, 1847, ALS, V.H.S.

33. Scott quoted in Lewis, 203; Long, 69–70.

CHAPTER 7

1. R. E. Lee to Mary C. Lee, April 12, 1847, ALS, V.H.S.

2. U. S. Grant to [?], April 24, 1847, *Papers* I, 134; U. S. Grant to John W. Lowe, May 3, 1847, *Papers* I, 136; Sanborn I, 176.

3. R. E. Lee to Mary C. Lee, April 18, 1847, ALS, V.H.S.; Lewis, 208, 209; U. S. Grant to John W. Lowe, May 3, 1847, *Papers* I, 135–37; U. S. Grant to Julia Dent, May 17, 1847, *Papers* I, 138–40.

4. R. E. Lee to Mary C. Lee, April 25, 1847, ALS, V.H.S.; R. E. Lee to Mary C. Lee, May [8], 1847, ALS, V.H.S.

5. *Papers* I, 134–35; U. S. Grant to Julia Dent, May 17 and 18, 1847, *Papers* I, 138–40; U. S. Grant to Julia Dent, Aug. 4, 1847, *Papers* I, 142–43.

6. Lewis, 218–19; Grant, U. S., *Memoirs* I, 138–39.

7. Lewis, 224–25; Sanborn I, 181; Winfield Scott on Lee quoted in Sanborn I, 182, 183.

8. Grant, U. S., *Memoirs* I, 143; Joe Johnston on Lee in Sanborn I, 183; Dick Ewell in Lewis, 233; Francis Lee on Grant in Lewis, 236.

9. Gore quoted in Lewis, 251; Grant, U. S., *Memoirs* I, 158–59.

10. Lewis, 254–55, 247, 242–43.

11. U. S. Grant to Julia Dent, Sept. 1847, *Papers* I, 146–48; Grant, U. S., *Memoirs* I, 163.

12. R. E. Lee to Jack Mackay, Oct. 2, 1847, ALS, U.S. Army Military History Institute, Carlisle Barracks, Pa.

13. Nevins, *Ordeal of the Union* I, 3–33; Anderson, 99–102; Bailyn et al., 608–14 and Appendix for U.S. Constitution.

14. Lee's letter to wife of Col. Totten from Sanborn I, 193; Lewis, 160–61.

15. R. E. Lee to G. W. P. Custis, April 8, 1848, ALS, V.H.S.; see also R. E. Lee to Mary C. Lee, May 20, 1848, ALS, V.H.S.

16. R. E. Lee to Mary C. Lee, Feb. 13, 1848, ALS, V.H.S.

17. R. E. Lee to Mary C. Lee, Dec. 3, 1847, ALS, V.H.S.; R. E. Lee to Jack Mackay, Oct. 2, 1847, ALS, Library of Congress (Middleton Collection); R. E. Lee to G. W. Custis Lee, April 11, 1847, ALS, V.H.S.; R. E. Lee to Mary C. Lee, Dec. 23, 1847, ALS, V.H.S.

18. R. E. Lee to G. W. Parke Custis, April 8, 1848, ALS, V.H.S.; R. E. Lee to Mary C. Lee, March 24, 1848, ALS, V.H.S.

19. U. S. Grant to Julia Dent, Feb. 4, 1848, *Papers* I, 150–52.

20. R. E. Lee to "Mr. Bonaparte," Feb. 28, 1855, ALS, Bonaparte Papers, Maryland Historical Society; R. E. Lee to Mary C. Lee, Dec. 23, 1847, ALS, V.H.S.

21. Grant, U. S., *Memoirs* I, 180, 191–92.

CHAPTER 8

1. Garland, 104, 110; Grant, Julia, 53–55; Lewis, 283–84.

2. Grant, Julia, 55–56.

3. Grant, Julia, 57–59.

4. Grant, Julia, 59–62; Ross, Ishbel, 60–61.

5. U. S. Grant to Julia Grant, April 27, 1849, *Papers* I, 184–85; also see sworn statement dated June 27, 1848, and notes in *Papers* I, 162–63, and U. S. Grant to Bvt. Maj. Gen. Roger Jones, March 30, 1849, and notes, *Papers* I, 183.

6. U. S. Grant to Julia Grant, April 27, 1849, *Papers* I, 184–85; Grant, Julia, 65–66.

7. Lewis, 289–93; Grant, Julia, 67–69; Richardson, Albert, 138, 131; Garland, 111.

8. Grant, Julia, 67–69; Ross, 64–65; Lewis, 290.

9. U. S. Grant to Julia Grant, May 21, [1851], *Papers* I, 200–2; U. S. Grant to Julia Grant, May 28, 1851, *Papers* I, 202–3; U. S. Grant to Julia Grant,

June 4, 1851, *Papers* I, 204–5; also see U. S. Grant to Julia Grant, June 7 to July 13, 1851, *Papers* I, 207–20.

10. Grant, Julia, 70; Grant's pledge in Lewis, 293; Lewis, 294; U. S. Grant to J. B. Grayson, Nov. 12, 1851, *Papers* I, 231–32.

11. Grant, Julia, 71.

12. Lewis, 296–97; Grant, U. S., *Memoirs* I, 194; U. S. Grant to Julia Grant, June 20, June 24, and June 28, 1852, *Papers* I, 235–41; U. S. Grant to Julia Grant, July 1, 1852, *Papers* I, 242–45.

13. U. S. Grant to Julia Grant, [July 5, 1852], *Papers* I, 247.

14. See *Papers* I, 247–51, and Lewis, 298–303.

15. U. S. Grant to Julia Grant, Aug. 9, 1852, *Papers* I, 251–53.

16. R. E. Lee to Col. Joseph Totten, July 25, 1852, Lee Letterbook, V.H.S.

17. R. E. Lee to Smith Lee, June 30, 1848, quoted in Lee, R. E. (Jr.), 3–4.

18. R. E. Lee to Martha Custis Williams, Dec. 14, 1844, in Craven, *"To Markie,"* 7.

19. R. E. Lee to Mary C. Lee, May 2, 1849, ALS, V.H.S.

20. R. E. Lee to Mary C. Lee, July 8, [1849], ALS, V.H.S.; R. E. Lee to Mary C. Lee, July [1849], ALS, V.H.S.; R. E. Lee to Mary C. Lee, Aug. 15, 1849, ALS, V.H.S.

21. McPherson, 72–73; Freeman I, 307–8.

22. Lee, R. E. (Jr.), 6, 10–11; Sanborn I, 204; R. E. Lee to Martha Custis Williams, May 10, 1851, in Craven, *"To Markie,"* 24.

23. Mary C. Lee to Anna Maria Fitzhugh, March [?], 1850, ALS, V.H.S.; Mary F. Custis quoted in MacDonald, 106; Mary C. Lee quoted in MacDonald, 107; see R. E. Lee to Mary C. Lee, March 20 and July 25, 1857, ALS, V.H.S.; R. E. Lee to Mary C. Lee, Feb. 4, 1849, ALS, V.H.S.

24. R. E. Lee to Martha Custis Williams, Sept. 16, 1853, in Craven, *"To Markie,"* 37; R. E. Lee to Mary C. Lee, Aug. 13, 1849, ALS, V.H.S.; R. E. Lee to Adj. Gen. R. Jones, Jan. 7, 1850, Lee Letterbook I, V.H.S.; R. E. Lee to G. W. Custis Lee, April 13, 1851, ALS, V.H.S.

25. R. E. Lee to G. W. Custis Lee quoted in Freeman I, 311–12; R. E. Lee to G. W. Custis Lee, Feb. 1, 1852, ALS, V.H.S.

26. R. E. Lee to G. W. Custis Lee, March 28, 1852, V.H.S., true copy of original owned by Mrs. Ronald W. Jensen, Milton, Mass.

27. R. E. Lee to Mary F. Custis, March 17, 1852, ALS and Lee Letterbook I, V.H.S.

28. R. E. Lee to Martha Custis Williams, Oct. 8, 1852, in Craven, *"To Markie,"* 29; R. E. Lee to Martha Custis Williams, May 10, 1851, in Craven, *"To Markie,"* 27; MacDonald, 109–11; Sanborn I, 214; deButts, 25–28.

29. deButts, 27–31; Sanborn I, 217–19; MacDonald, 110; Lee, R. E. (Jr.), 11, 13; R. E. Lee to Mary F. Custis, March 17, 1852, ALS, V.H.S.; R. E. Lee to Annie Lee, Feb. 25, 1853, ALS, V.H.S.

30. R. E. Lee to Annie Lee, Feb. 25, 1853, ALS, V.H.S.

31. Sanborn I, 225; Freeman I, 319–49; Lee quoted in Freeman I, 341, 343; Lee, R. E. (Jr.), 18; Davis quoted in Freeman I, 339.

585

32. R. E. Lee to Martha Custis Williams, June 23, 1853, in Craven, *"To Markie,"* 30–31; R. E. Lee to Mary C. Lee, May 2, 1853, ALS, V.H.S.; R. E. Lee to Mary C. Lee, April 27, 1853, ALS, V.H.S.

33. R. E. Lee to Vernon Childe, Oct. 31, 1853, V.H.S. microfilm of Stratford Association original; R. E. Lee to Martha Custis Williams, May 26, 1854, in Craven, *"To Markie,"* 46, 48; R. E. Lee to Anna Maria Fitzhugh, April 3, 1854, ALS, V.H.S.

34. R. E. Lee to Martha Custis Williams, March 14, 1855, in Craven, *"To Markie,"* 52–53; deButts, 52–59; Sanborn I, 232–33.

CHAPTER 9

1. U. S. Grant to Julia Grant, Aug. 20, 1852, *Papers* I, 257–58; see also U. S. Grant to Julia Grant, Aug. 30, Sept. 14, Sept. 19, Oct. 7, Oct. 26, 1852, *Papers* I, 258–71; U. S. Grant to Julia Grant, Aug. 30, 1852, *Papers* I, 259; Grant, Julia, 72.

2. Lewis, 319–20.

3. Lewis, 315; Garland, 122.

4. U. S. Grant to Julia Grant, Feb. 2, 1853 [1854], *Papers* I, 316–18; U. S. Grant to Julia Grant, Feb. 6, 1854, *Papers* I, 320–22.

5. Richardson, Albert, 149; Lewis, 313.

6. U. S. Grant to Julia Grant, March 6, 1854, *Papers* I, 322–24; U. S. Grant to Julia Grant, March 25, 1854, *Papers* I, 326–28.

7. U. S. Grant to S. Cooper, April 11, 1854, *Papers* I, 328; U. S. Grant to S. Cooper, April 11, 1854, *Papers* I, 329.

8. Lewis, 330–31.

9. See Grant's letters to Julia, *Papers* I, 258–326; Grant, U. S., *Memoirs* I, 203; Garland, 123–24.

10. Lewis, 332, 336–38.

11. U. S. Grant to Julia Grant, May 2, 1854, *Papers* I, 333; for Jesse Grant–Jefferson Davis correspondence, see *Papers* I, 330–31 n.

12. Grant, Julia, 72, 73–75, 76, 80.

13. U. S. Grant to Julia Grant, Feb. 15, 1853, *Papers* I, 228; U. S. Grant to Julia Grant, March 31, 1853, *Papers* I, 296–97; Lewis, 313.

14. Grant, Julia, 75–76; see *Papers* I, 301; Garland, 129.

15. Lewis, 340–41; Grant, Julia, 76.

16. Grant, Julia, 78–79.

17. Hardscrabble was moved to Washington, D.C., as a tourist attraction. It was subsequently bought by the August Busch family and moved back to White Haven land (now in St. Louis). It can be seen on tours of the Busch-owned amusement park "Grant's Farm." U. S. would have liked that.

18. U. S. Grant to Jesse R. Grant, Dec. 28, 1856, *Papers* I, 334–35.

19. U. S. Grant to Jesse R. Grant, Feb. 7, 1857, *Papers* I, 336–37.

20. Grant, Jesse R., *Ledger*, Jan. 22, 1868; U. S. Grant to Mary Grant, Aug. 22, 1857, *Papers* I, 338–39; Grant, Julia, 77.

21. Richardson, Albert, 156; Garland, 136; Lewis, 356–57.

22. Lewis, 346–47, 357–58; Garland, 138.

23. Grant, Julia, 78.

24. U. S. Grant to Mary Grant, March 21, 1858, *Papers* I, 340–41; U. S. Grant to Mary Grant, Sept. 7, 1858, *Papers* I, 343; U. S. Grant to Jesse R. Grant, Oct. 1, 1858, *Papers* I, 344.

25. Grant, Julia, 80.

26. McPherson, 79–80, 77, 87, 89, 91; Kansas-Nebraska from Nevins, *Ordeal of the Union* II, 138–45.

27. Anderson, 100; *Collected Works of Lincoln* VII, 247–83; Sumner quoted in Nevins, *Ordeal of the Union* II, 438–41; Nevins, *Ordeal of the Union* II, 443–46 and 445 n.

28. Brown in Nevins, *Ordeal of the Union* II, 448; McPherson, 96; R. E. Lee to Mary C. Lee, Oct. [?], 1856, and R. E. Lee to Mary C. Lee, Dec. 13, 1856, ALS, V.H.S.; U. S. Grant to Jesse R. Grant, Sept. 23, 1859, *Papers* I, 352.

29. McPherson, 98–102; *Collected Works of Lincoln* III, 95; Cash, 83–4, 89–90.

CHAPTER 10

1. Lee quoted in Sanborn I, 242–43; Mrs. Johnston on Lee in Sanborn I, 244.

2. R. E. Lee to Agnes Lee, Aug. 4, 1856, ALS, V.H.S.

3. R. E. Lee to Mildred Lee, March 22, 1857, ALS, V.H.S.; Sanborn I, 258–59; Lee quoted in Sanborn I, 245; R. E. Lee to Mary C. Lee, April 12, 1856, ALS, V.H.S.; R. E. Lee to Eliza Mackay Stiles, May 24, 1856, and Aug. 14, 1856, ALS, Georgia Historical Society (Colonial Dames Collection); Rister, 40–54.

4. R. E. Lee to Eliza Mackay Stiles, May 24, 1856, ALS, Georgia Historical Society (Colonial Dames Collection); Hood, 8.

5. R. E. Lee to Mary C. Lee, Nov. 5, 1855, ALS, V.H.S.; R. E. Lee to Mary C. Lee, July 9, 1855, Nov. 19, 1856, Dec. 13, 1856, March 13, 1857, March 20, 1857, ALS, V.H.S.; R. E. Lee to Mary C. Lee, Jan. 17, 1857, ALS, Duke University Library.

6. R. E. Lee to Capt. N. G. Evans, Dec. 15, 1856, Aug. 3, 1857, Aug. 28, 1857, ALS, V.H.S.

7. R. E. Lee to Mary C. Lee, Aug. 8, 1856, ALS, V.H.S.; R. E. Lee to Andrew Talcott quoted in Sanborn I, 110; R. E. Lee to Henry Kayser, Oct. 15, 1845, *Letters of Robert E. Lee to Henry Kayser*, 30; R. E. Lee to Martha Custis Williams, Sept. 16, 1853, in Craven, *"To Markie,"* 37; Lee quoted in Sanborn I, 209; Adams, Henry, 57–58.

8. R. E. Lee to W. H. Fitzhugh (Rooney) Lee, Nov. 1, 1856, Lee Letterbook I, V.H.S.; R. E. Lee to Eliza Mackay Stiles, Aug. 14, 1856, ALS, Georgia Historical Society (Colonial Dames Collection).

9. R. E. Lee to Mary C. Lee, March 13, 1857, and [?] May 1857, ALS, V.H.S.; R. E. Lee to Mildred Lee, Jan. 9, 1857, ALS, V.H.S.; R. E. Lee to Mary

C. Lee, Nov. 5, 1855, and Aug. 8, 1856, ALS, V.H.S.; R. E. Lee to Mary C. Lee, Aug. 26, 1855, ALS, V.H.S.

10. Lee quoted in Sanborn I, 242; R. E. Lee to Mary C. Lee, Aug. 26, 1855, ALS, V.H.S.

11. R. E. Lee to Eliza Mackay Stiles, May 24, 1856, ALS, Georgia Historical Society (Colonial Dames Collection); R. E. Lee to Mary C. Lee, July 27, 1857, ALS, V.H.S.; R. E. Lee to Edward Vernon Childe, Jan. 9, 1857, V.H.S. microfilm of Stratford Association original; R. E. Lee to Mary C. Lee, Aug. 26, 1855, ALS, V.H.S.; R. E. Lee to Anna Maria Fitzhugh, Sept. 8, 1857, ALS, Duke University Library.

12. Custis will in Sanborn I, 270–71.

13. Edward Everett on Arlington in Nevins, *Ordeal of the Union* I, 462; R. E. Lee to Mary C. Lee, July 9, 1855, ALS, V.H.S.; Arlington house has been restored to its condition following the Lee remodeling by the National Park Service. It is open to the public. For description, see deButts, 71–72; Agnes Lee to W. H. Fitzhugh Lee, Oct. 2, 1858, ALS, V.H.S.

14. R. E. Lee to G. W. Custis Lee quoted in Sanborn I, 272; Pryor, 30; MacDonald, 125–26.

15. Leech, 9–20; Pryor, 35–40; and see Davis, Varina Howell, I.

16. R. E. Lee to Mary C. Lee, Sept. 20, 1857, ALS, V.H.S.

17. Lee to A. S. Johnston quoted in Sanborn I, 266; R. E. Lee to Anna Maria Fitzhugh, Nov. 22, 1857, and Nov. 26, 1857, ALS, Duke University Library; MacDonald, 125–26.

18. R. E. Lee to G. W. Custis Lee, March 17, 1858, ALS, Duke University Library; quoted in Sanborn I, 276–83.

19. R. E. Lee to Edward Vernon Childe, Sept. 6, 1858, V.H.S. microfilm of Stratford Association original; R. E. Lee to "Col. Thomas," June 16, 1859, ALS, Washington and Lee University Library; Mary Lee quoted in Mac-Donald, 131; R. E. Lee to G. W. Custis Lee, Aug. 17, 1859, ALS, Duke University Library.

20. R. E. Lee to W. H. Fitzhugh (Rooney) Lee, May [?], 1858, ALS, V.H.S.; R. E. Lee to [Mr.] Winston, June [?], 1858, ALS, V.H.S.; Custis will in Freeman I, 380; letters to New York *Tribune* quoted in Freeman I, 390–92.

CHAPTER 11

1. R. E. Lee to Mary C. Lee, Dec. 27, 1856, ALS, V.H.S.

2. McPherson, 80–81; *Collected Works of Lincoln* II, 255.

3. Mary C. Lee to Annie Lee, Aug. [?] 1860, ALS, V.H.S.

4. *Collected Works of Lincoln* II, 256.

5. Freeman I, 396–402.

6. Brown quoted in Nevins, *The Emergence of Lincoln* I, 77.

7. Brown's courtroom statement in McPherson, 116; Nevins, *The Emergence of Lincoln* I, 91.

8. Nevins, *The Emergence of Lincoln* I, 91–92.

9. Wise, 1–150.

10. Lee, R. E. (Jr.), 22–23; Lee quoted in Freeman I, 403.

11. Nevins, *The Emergence of Lincoln* I, 97; Craven, *Edmund Ruffin*, 175–77; Brown's note in McPherson, 116.

12. R. E. Lee to Henry Carter Lee, Dec. 6, 1859, ALS, V.H.S.

13. Nevins, *The Emergence of Lincoln* I, 98–112.

14. R. E. Lee to Edward Vernon Childe, Jan. 21, 1857, V.H.S. microfilm of Stratford Association original.

CHAPTER 12

1. Grant quoted in Lewis, 359–60; business card in Grant's *Papers* I, 346–47; U. S. Grant to Jesse R. Grant, March 12, 1859, *Papers* I, 345–47.

2. Grant, Julia, 81; Garland, 139; Lewis, 363.

3. Richardson, Albert, 159–62; Church, 58; U. S. Grant to Simpson Grant, Oct. 24, 1859, *Papers* I, 353.

4. U. S. Grant to Jesse R. Grant, Aug. 20, 1859, *Papers* I, 350–51; U. S. Grant to "Hon. County Commissioners," Aug. 15, 1859, *Papers* I, 348; Lewis, 367–68.

5. U. S. Grant to Jesse R. Grant, Sept. 23, 1859, *Papers* I, 351–53; manumission of slave in Grant's *Papers* I, 347.

6. Grant, Julia, 82.

7. U. S. Grant to Julia Grant, March 14, 1860, *Papers* I, 355–56.

8. R. E. Lee to Anna Maria Fitzhugh, Feb. 5, 1860, ALS, Duke University Library; Rister, 106–13, 102–5; R. E. Lee to Annie Lee, June 16, 1860, ALS, V.H.S.; R. E. Lee to Annie Lee, Aug. 27, 1860, ALS, V.H.S.

9. R. E. Lee to W. H. Fitzhugh (Rooney) Lee, March 12 and April 2, 1860, ALS, V.H.S.; R. E. Lee to Mary C. Lee, April 17, 1860, ALS, V.H.S.

10. R. E. Lee to W. H. Fitzhugh (Rooney) Lee, Sept. 7, 1860, ALS, V.H.S.; R. E. Lee to G. W. Custis Lee, Dec. 5, 1860, and March 13, 1860, ALS, Duke University Library; R. E. Lee to Anna Maria Fitzhugh, June 6, 1860, ALS, Duke University Library; Lee daughter in Freeman I, 442.

11. Ross, Ishbel, 81.

12. Lewis, 373–77.

13. Richardson, Albert, 169; Lewis, 391; Ross, 93; Church, 53.

14. Wilson, *The Life of John A. Rawlins*, 20–36; Rawlins quoted in Lewis, 379.

15. Nevins, *The Emergence of Lincoln* II, 118, 121–22, 125, 130, 180–81.

16. Nevins, *The Emergence of Lincoln* II, 217, 221, 224, 227.

17. Orvil Grant quoted in Lewis, 383; Garland, 153.

18. Garland, 153; Nevins, *The Emergence of Lincoln* II, 321.

19. Nevins, *The Emergence of Lincoln* II, 334–35.

20. Pryor, 111–15.

21. Buchanan's address in McPherson, 133.

22. Thomas, Emory, 57, 63; Vandiver, 19; Grant quoted in Lewis, 392–93.

23. Quoted in Freeman, 425.

24. R. E. Lee to G. W. Custis Lee, Nov. 24, 1860, ALS, Duke University Library; R. E. Lee to W. H. Fitzhugh (Rooney) Lee, Dec. 3, 1860, ALS, V.H.S.; Buchanan's address in Richardson, James D., VII, 3169; R. E. Lee to G. W. Custis Lee, Dec. 4–5, 1860, ALS, Duke University Library.

25. R. E. Lee to Mary C. Lee, Jan. 23, 1861, ALS, V.H.S.; R. E. Lee to Agnes Lee, Jan. 29, 1861, ALS, V.H.S.

26. R. E. Lee to Agnes Lee, Jan. 29, 1861, ALS, V.H.S.; R. E. Lee to W. H. Fitzhugh (Rooney) Lee, Jan. 29, 1861, ALS, V.H.S.

27. Rister, 158.

28. Caroline Darrow's recollections of Lee in *Battles and Leaders* I, 36; Rister, 161; Anderson quoted in Freeman I, 428–29.

29. R. E. Lee Memoranda Book No. 5, V.H.S.

30. Toombs quoted in McPherson, 145; Craven, *Edmund Ruffin*, 216; *Collected Works of Lincoln* IV, 332.

31. John Nicolay quoted in Freeman I, 436; R. E. Lee to Reverdy Johnson, Feb. 25, 1868, *Wartime Papers*, 4; Scott quoted in Freeman I, 437; R. E. Lee to Wade Hampton, 1868, quoted in Freeman I, 447.

32. R. E. Lee to Winfield Scott and Simon Cameron, April 20, 1861, *Wartime Papers*, 8–9.

33. Wilson, *The Life of John A. Rawlins*, 47–48; Grant quoted in Lewis, 400.

34. U. S. Grant to Frederick Dent, April 19, 1861, *Papers* II, 3–4.

35. U. S. Grant to Mary Grant, April 29, 1861, *Papers* II, 13–14; U. S. Grant to Jesse R. Grant, April 21, 1861, *Papers* II, 6–7.

36. Freeman, 445–46; see letters of R. E. Lee to Mary C. Lee, April–May 1861, *Wartime Papers*, 15–40.

37. R. E. Lee to Mary C. Lee, March 3, 1860, ALS, V.H.S.; R. E. Lee to Mary Custis, March 17, 1852, ALS, V.H.S.

38. Bill, 39–44.

39. Lee quoted in Freeman I, 465–67, 526.

CHAPTER 13

1. U. S. Grant to Julia Grant, May 1, 1861, *Papers* II, 16; U. S. Grant to Julia Grant, May 3, 1861, *Papers* II, 19; U. S. Grant to Julia Grant, May 21, 1861, *Papers* II, 33; U. S. Grant to Col. L. Thomas, May 24, 1861, *Papers* II, 35.

2. Chetlain quoted in Lewis, 423; Grant quoted in Young II, 214–15.

3. Grant quoted in Garland, 167; U. S. Grant to Julia Grant, May 15, 1861, *Papers* II, 30–31; Grant to Chetlain quoted in McFeely, 74; Lewis, 415.

4. Lewis, 427–28; Garland, 173.

5. U. S. Grant to Julia Grant, June 26, 1861, *Papers* II, 50; U. S. Grant to Jesse R. Grant, July 13, 1861, *Papers* II, 66–67; U. S. Grant to Julia Grant, July 13, 1861, *Papers* II, 69.

6. U. S. Grant to Jesse R. Grant, Aug. 3, 1861, *Papers* II, 80; U. S. Grant to Jesse R. Grant, May 6, 1861, *Papers* II, 22.

7. U. S. Grant to Mary Grant, Aug. 21, 1861, *Papers* II, 105.

8. Grant, U. S., *Memoirs* I, 249–50.

9. U. S. Grant to Jesse R. Grant, *Papers* II, 105; U. S. Grant to Julia Grant, Aug. 10, 1861, *Papers* II, 96–97.

10. U. S. Grant to Julia Grant, Aug. 26, 1861, *Papers* II, 140–41.

11. Grant, Julia, 89, 92; U. S. Grant to Julia Grant, Aug. 26, 1861, *Papers* II, 140–41; U. S. Grant to Julia Grant, Aug. 29, 1861, *Papers* II, 149.

12. U. S. Grant to Elihu Washburne, Sept. 3, 1861, *Papers* II, 183.

13. Stephens quoted in Davis, Burke, 22.

14. Long, 112–13; Taylor, Walter, 11–14; Taylor on Lee's appearance in Sanborn II, 11.

15. R. E. Lee to Gen. Daniel Ruggles, April 24, 1861, *Wartime Papers*, 11; R. E. Lee to Mary C. Lee, June 9, 1861, *Wartime Papers*, 45–46.

16. Eggleston, 70–75.

17. Bill, 45–52; Dowdey, 143–45.

18. R. E. Lee to Anne Lee Marshall, April 20, 1861, *Wartime Papers*, 9–10; Mary C. Lee to Winfield Scott, May 5, 1861, quoted in Lee, Fitzhugh, 93.

19. Mary C. Lee to Mildred Lee, April 30, [1861], ALS, V.H.S.

20. R. E. Lee to Mary C. Lee, May 11, 1861, *Wartime Papers*, 25–26; Mary C. Lee to Mildred Lee, May 11, 1861, ALS, V.H.S.

21. R. E. Lee to Mary C. Lee, May 2, 1861, *Wartime Papers*, 18.

22. McGuire, 26, 66–67; Cooke, *A Life of General Robert E. Lee*, 14–15; Eggleston, 28–31.

23. R. E. Lee to Mary C. Lee, May 25, 1861, *Wartime Papers*, 36; R. E. Lee's May–June 1861 correspondence in *Wartime Papers*, 34–55.

CHAPTER 14

1. Catton, *Grant Moves South*, 44–47.

2. Wilson, *The Life of John A. Rawlins*, 60–61; Catton, *Grant Moves South*, 69.

3. Wilson, *The Life of John A. Rawlins*, 61–63, 68–71.

4. See Grant correspondence, Oct. 28, 1861, *Papers* III, 82–83; Nov. 24, 1861, *Papers* III, 101–11; and Aug. 25, 1861, *Papers* II, 136.

5. U. S. Grant to John Cook, Dec. 25, 1861, *Papers* III, 343; U. S. Grant to Jesse R. Grant, Nov. 27, 1861, *Papers* III, 226–28.

6. See *Collected Works of Lincoln* V, 48–49; McPherson, 269–74.

7. Grant proclamation, Sept. 6, 1861, *Papers* II, 194.

8. Grant correspondence and notes on battle of Belmont, *Papers* III, 130–53; Catton, *Grant Moves South*, 74–80; Grant, U. S., *Memoirs* I, 272–81.

9. Richardson, Albert, 203; Catton, *Grant Moves South,* 83–84.

10. Official report of Belmont: Grant's *Papers* III, 141–43; see *Papers* III, 143 n. for rewrite and 152–53 n. for controversy; proclamation to troops, Nov. 8, 1861, *Papers* III, 130; Grant, U. S., *Memoirs* I, 280–81; Grant, Julia, 93.

11. Grant, Julia, 92–94; Catton, *Grant Moves South,* 105.

12. U. S. Grant to Mary Grant, Jan. 23, 1862, *Papers* IV, 96.

13. Grant quoted in Catton, *Grant Moves South,* 121; Grant, U. S., *Memoirs* I, 287; Lincoln to Simon Cameron, Jan. 10, 1862, *Collected Works of Lincoln* V, 95.

14. Taylor, Walter H., 16–17; R. E. Lee to Mary C. Lee, Aug. 4, 1861, *Wartime Papers,* 61–62.

15. Fuller, 47; R. E. Lee to Henry Wise, Sept. 21 and Sept. 25, 1861, *Wartime Papers,* 76–77.

16. R. E. Lee to Mary C. Lee, Aug. 4, 1861, *Wartime Papers,* 61–62; Freeman I, 554–68.

17. Taylor, Walter H., 19; Sanborn, 23, 27; R. E. Lee to Mary C. Lee, Sept. 9, 1861, *Wartime Papers,* 70–72; R. E. Lee to Mary C. Lee, Oct. 7, 1861, *Wartime Papers,* 80.

18. Long, 142; Sanborn II, 35.

19. R. E. Lee to Mary C. Lee, Jan. 18, 1862, *Wartime Papers,* 103–4; Sanborn II, 41; R. E. Lee to Annie and Agnes Lee, Nov. 22, 1861, *Wartime Papers,* 88–89; R. E. Lee to Mary C. Lee, Dec. 25, 1861, *Wartime Papers,* 96.

20. R. E. Lee to Judah Benjamin, Feb. 6, 1862, *Wartime Papers,* 110; R. E. Lee to Annie Lee, Dec. 8, 1861, *Wartime Papers,* 91.

21. R. E. Lee to Annie Lee, March 2, 1862, *Wartime Papers,* 121–22; R. E. Lee to Judah Benjamin, Dec. 20, 1861, *Wartime Papers,* 92–93; R. E. Lee to G. W. Custis Lee, Dec. 29, 1861, *Wartime Papers,* 97–98.

22. For Lee's Christmas letters, see *Wartime Papers,* 95–97; Sanborn II, 40; R. E. Lee to Mary C. Lee, March 14, 1862, *Wartime Papers,* 127.

CHAPTER 15

1. Catton, *Grant Moves South,* 134; Foote I, 183–84.

2. Grant, Julia, 96–97; Catton, *Grant Moves South,* 138.

3. Catton, *Grant Moves South,* 140–41; Foote I, 187–91; U. S. Grant to John Kelton, Feb. 6, 1862, *Papers* IV, 155–60; Richardson, Albert, 217.

4. U. S. Grant to Mary Grant, Feb. 9, 1862, *Papers* IV, 180.

5. Foote I, 192–215; Catton, *Grant Moves South,* 149–78; Richardson, Albert, 218–19, 226–27; U. S. Grant to Henry Halleck, Feb. 13, 1862, *Papers* IV, 207; U. S. Grant to George Cullum, Feb. 15, 1862, *Papers* IV, 212–13; U. S. Grant to Commanding Officer, Gunboat Flotilla, Feb. 15, 1862, *Papers* IV, 214; U. S. Grant to Simon Bolivar Buckner, *Papers* IV, 218.

6. Richardson, Albert, 227–33; Catton, *Grant Moves South,* 179–81; U. S. Grant to Julia Grant, Feb. 22, 1862, *Papers* IV, 271; U. S. Grant to Julia Grant, Feb. 24, 1862, *Papers* IV, 292.

7. Grant, Julia, 98; U. S. Grant to Julia Grant, Feb. 22, 1862, *Papers* IV, 271; U. S. Grant to Julia Grant, Feb. 26, 1862, *Papers* IV, 292; U. S. Grant to Julia Grant, March 23, 1862, *Papers* IV, 412–13; U. S. Grant to Julia Grant, March 5, 1862, *Papers* IV, 326.

8. Halleck-McClellan correspondence in Grant's *Papers* IV, 319–21 n.; U.S. Grant to Henry Halleck, March 5, 1862, *Papers* IV, 318.

9. Henry Halleck to U. S. Grant in Grant's *Papers* IV, 353 n.; U. S. Grant to Henry Halleck, March 7, 1862, *Papers* IV, 331; Catton, *Grant Moves South,* 209; Woodward, William E., 226; U. S. Grant to Henry Halleck, March 9, 1862, *Papers* IV, 334; U. S. Grant to Henry Halleck, March 13, 1862, *Papers* IV, 353; Halleck correspondence in Catton, *Grant Moves South,* 207–9; See citations in Grant's *Papers* IV, 318–31 for Halleck-McClellan-Grant controversy; Washburne in McFeely, 108; U. S. Grant to Elihu Washburne, March 22, 1862, *Papers* IV, 409; Grant quoted in Catton, *Grant Moves South,* 207; U. S. Grant to Julia Grant, March 23, 1862, *Papers* IV, 413; U. S. Grant to Julia Grant, March 11, 1862, *Papers* IV, 348.

10. U. S. Grant to Julia Grant, March 29, 1862, *Papers* IV, 443.

11. Howe, *Home Letters of General Sherman,* 12–33, 160–95 especially 162–63, 167–72, 177, 215–22.

12. Foote I, 323; U. S. Grant to Julia Grant, March 29, 1862, *Papers* IV, 443; U. S. Grant to Henry Halleck, March 21, 1862, *Papers* IV, 400–1; U. S. Grant to Henry Halleck, April 3, 1862, *Papers* V, 7; U. S. Grant to Henry Halleck, April 5, 1862, *Papers* V, 14.

13. See *Battles and Leaders* I, 465–609, for Shiloh; Foote I, 322–51; Woodward, William E., 352–54; Richardson, Albert, 348–54; Catton, *Grant Moves South,* 222–45; Garland, 202–5; McPherson, 225–29; Grant, U. S., *Memoirs* I, 335–70.

14. U. S. Grant to Julia Grant, April 8, 1862, *Papers* V, 27; Richardson, Albert, 254–55; U. S. Grant to P. G. T. Beauregard, April 9, 1862, *Papers* V, 30; U. S. Grant to Julia Grant, April 15, 1862, *Papers* V, 47; Woodward, William E., 255–56; U. S. Grant to Jesse R. Grant, April 26, 1862, *Papers* V, 78; Grant, U. S., *Memoirs* I, 368.

15. Stanton to Halleck quoted in Grant's *Papers* V, 50–51 n.; see Grant's *Papers* V, 48–51 n., on condition of army; Halleck to Stanton in Grant's *Papers* V, 51 n.; Halleck to Grant, April 14, 1862, in Grant's *Papers* V, 48–49 n.; U. S. Grant to Julia Grant, April 25, 1862, *Papers* V, 72–73; Richardson, Albert, 257–58, 260; U. S. Grant to George Ihrie, April 25, 1862, *Papers* V, 73; U. S. Grant to Julia Grant, May 11, 1862, *Papers* V, 115–16.

16. U. S. Grant to Henry Halleck, May 11, 1862, *Papers* V, 114–15; U. S. Grant to Julia Grant, May 11, 1862, *Papers* V, 115–16; Howe, *Home Letters of General Sherman,* 227–28; Sherman, 283–84. U. S. Grant to Julia Grant,

May 24, 1862, *Papers* V, 130; Grant, Julia, 99, 102–3; Julia to Washburne in Catton, *Grant Moves South*, 260–61; Lincoln quoted in Catton, *Grant Moves South*, 371.

CHAPTER 16

1. Foote I, 217–19; Putnam, 106–7; Thomas, Emory, 155; McPherson, 183, 198.
2. McPherson, 197–200, 217.
3. R. E. Lee to Annie Lee, March 2, 1862, *Wartime Papers,* 121–23; for Richmond during the war's early days, see Bill, 45–80; Harrison, 94 ff. and 130–36 ff.; Putnam, especially 188–96 ff.
4. R. E. Lee to Mary C. Lee, March 14, 1862, *Wartime Papers,* 127–28; see Lee's March–April 1862 correspondence in *Wartime Papers,* 127–61; R. E. Lee to John Pemberton, April 10, 1862, *Wartime Papers,* 145; R. E. Lee to Thomas J. Jackson, April 25, 1862, *Wartime Papers,* 156–57.
5. Taylor, Richard, 52, 37, 89–91.
6. Warren Goss quoted in *Battles and Leaders* II, 157–58; Sorrel, 88–89.
7. Mary C. Lee to "Northern Soldiers" quoted in MacDonald, 161–62; R. E. Lee to Agnes Lee, May 29, 1862, ALS, V.H.S.; Mary's exchange in *Battles and Leaders* II, 277.
8. R. E. Lee to Jefferson Davis, June 5, 1862, *Wartime Papers,* 183–84; R. E. Lee to Charlotte Lee, June 2, 1862, ALS, V.H.S.
9. Stiles, 77; Davis, Burke, 79.
10. Stiles, 65–66; Maurice, *Marshall,* 85–86; Foote I, 509; Freeman II, 202.
11. Stiles, 97, 116–17; Nevins, *The War for the Union* II, 137; Sanborn II, 67.
12. McPherson, 248; Sorrel, 47; Foote I, 515.
13. Wiley, *The Life of Billy Yank,* 144; Stiles, 95, 80–81; McPherson, 249–50; Seven Days in *Battles and Leaders* II, 313–439; Foote I, 479–519; McPherson, 244–53; Freeman II, 122–244.
14. R. E. Lee to Mary C. Lee, July 9, 1862, *Wartime Papers,* 229–30; Mary C. Lee to Eliza Mackay Stiles, July 5, 1862, ALS, Georgia Historical Society (Colonial Dames Collection).
15. Woodward, C. Vann, *Mary Chesnut's Civil War,* 116; Maurice, *Marshall,* intro. and 6–7; R. E. Lee to Mary C. Lee, [July] 10, 1862, *Wartime Papers,* 189; R. E. Lee to Annie Lee et al., [July 1862], ALS, V.H.S.; Sorrel, 67.
16. R. E. Lee to Jefferson Davis, July 6, 1862, *Wartime Papers,* 209; Maurice, *Marshall,* 74–75, 62–65.
17. Blackford, 84–87; R. E. Lee to Mary C. Lee, Aug. 17, 1862, *Wartime Papers,* 257–58; R. E. Lee to Mildred Lee, July 28, 1862, *Wartime Papers,* 240; Lee quoted in Sanborn II, 70–71.
18. Blackford, 114–16.
19. R. E. Lee to Jefferson Davis, Aug. 30, 1862, *Wartime Papers,* 268; Stiles, 123–24; Blackford, 105; Sorrel, 17, 31, 60.

20. McClellan quoted in McPherson, 254; McPherson, 270–79; A. Lincoln to Horace Greeley, Aug. 22, 1862, *Collected Works of Lincoln* V, 388–89 and 389 n.
21. R. E. Lee to Jefferson Davis, Sept. 3, 1862, *Wartime Papers,* 292–94; R. E. Lee to Jefferson Davis, Sept. 4, 1862, *Wartime Papers,* 294–95.
22. Freeman II, 355; Foote I, 663; Parks, 259; Foote I, 680; R. E. Lee to "The People of Maryland," *Wartime Papers,* 299–30; Nevins, *The War for the Union* II, 218; Long, 222; R. E. Lee to Jefferson Davis, Sept. 8, 1862, *Wartime Papers,* 301.
23. Special Orders No. 191, *Wartime Papers,* 191; McClellan quoted in McPherson, 281; Foote I, 674–75, 684, 681; R. E. Lee to Lafayette McLaws via R. H. Chilton, Sept. 14, 1862, *Wartime Papers,* 307–8; McClellan-Scott correspondence in Foote I, 682.
24. Antietam in *Battles and Leaders* II, 545–698; R. E. Lee to Jefferson Davis, Sept. 16, 1862, *Wartime Papers,* 309–10; Gordon, 82–90; Foote I, 675–700; McPherson, 280–88; Nevins, *The War for the Union* II, 222–28; Freeman II, 378–403 and 404 n.; Benson, 118–22; Sorrel, 108.
25. R. E. Lee to Gen. Samuel Cooper, Aug. 19, 1862, *Wartime Papers,* 312–24; Long, 227–29; Taylor, Walter H., 77, 76; McPherson, 293; Emancipation Proclamation in *Collected Works of Lincoln* V, 433–36, and Lincoln's State of the Union Address in V, 517–37, quote on 537.
26. R. E. Lee to Annie and Agnes Lee, Sept. 30, 1862, ALS, V.H.S.; R. E. Lee to Mildred Lee, Nov. 3, 1862, ALS, V.H.S.; R. E. Lee to Mary C. Lee, Dec. 2, 1862, Sept. 29, 1862, Oct. 26, 1862, Nov. 3, 1862, and Nov. 10, 1862, all ALS, V.H.S.

CHAPTER 17

1. Grant, Julia, 105–8.
2. R. E. Lee to Mary C. Lee, Dec. 16, 1862, ALS, V.H.S. For Fredericksburg, see *Battles and Leaders* III, 70–148; Foote II, 20–45; Nevins, *The War for the Union;* McPherson, 303–5; Blackford, 137–53; Alexander, 291, 308–9; Long, 237–40; Sorrel, 126–36; Stiles, 128–31, 134–35, 157–58.
3. R. E. Lee to Mildred Lee, Dec. 25, 1862, ALS, V.H.S.; R. E. Lee to Agnes Lee, Dec. 26, 1862, ALS, V.H.S.; R. E. Lee to Mary C. Lee, Dec. 26, 1862, ALS, V.H.S.; R. E. Lee to James Seddon, Jan. 10, 1863, *Wartime Papers,* 388–90; R. E. Lee to Charles Carter Lee, Oct. 26, 1862, in *Confederate Veteran,* XXXI, 287.
4. R. E. Lee to G. W. Custis Lee, Feb. 26, 1863, ALS, Duke University Library; Foote II, 238.
5. Thomas, Emory, 221–24; R. E. Lee to Agnes Lee, Feb. 6, 1863, ALS, V.H.S.; R. E. Lee to Mary C. Lee, Feb. 23, 1863, ALS, V.H.S.; R. E. Lee to James Seddon, March 27, 1863, *Wartime Papers,* 418; R. E. Lee to Mary C. Lee, Feb. 8, 1863, ALS, V.H.S.; R. E. Lee to Mary C. Lee, March 9, 1863, ALS, V.H.S.

6. U. S. Grant to Julia Grant, March 27, 1863, *Papers* VII, 479–80.

7. U. S. Grant to William Hillyer, Feb. 27, 1863, *Papers* VII, 367–68; Dana quoted in Catton, *Grant Moves South,* 352; Jones quoted in Catton, *Grant Moves South,* 351; General Orders No. 11 in *Papers* VII, 50; for Washburne, see Grant's *Papers* VII, note, 50–56 n.

8. See Grant's *Papers* VIII, 32 n.; Wilson, *The Life of John A. Rawlins,* 100, 121–23; Dana, especially 75–86.

9. See Grant's correspondence, Dec. 1862 to March 1863 in *Papers* VII; U. S. Grant to Henry Halleck, Feb. 18, 1863, *Papers* VII, 338 and 339 n.; U. S. Grant to Elihu Washburne, Feb. 15, 1863, *Papers* VII, 332–33.

10. Catton, *Grant Moves South,* 357–58; U. S. Grant to Henry Halleck, April 19, 1863, *Papers* VIII, 91–92; Halleck quoted in Grant's *Papers* VIII, 93–94 n.

11. U. S. Grant to Stephen Hurlbut, Feb. 13, 1863, *Papers* VII, 316–17; Medill to Washburne in Grant's *Papers* VII, 317–18 n.; U. S. Grant to Julia Grant, Feb. 14, 1863, *Papers* VII, 324–25; Halleck quoted in Grant's *Papers* VIII, 93–94 n.

12. U. S. Grant to Frederick Steele, April 11, 1863, *Papers* VIII, 49; Sherman quoted in Grant's *Papers* VIII, 50–51 n.

13. U. S. Grant to Elihu Washburne, March 10, 1863, *Papers* VII, 409–10; for Julia, and Grant's drinking, see Grant's *Papers* VII, 308 n.; U. S. Grant to Julia Grant, April 6, 1863, *Papers* VIII, 29–30; U. S. Grant to Julia Grant, Feb. 11, 1863, *Papers* VII, 311.

14. U. S. Grant to Julia Grant, March 6, 1863, *Papers* VII, 396–97; U. S. Grant to Julia Grant, April 6, 1863, *Papers* VIII, 29–30.

15. Wilson, James H., *Under the Old Flag,* 155–59.

16. Wilson, James H., *Under the Old Flag,* 162–64; Dana, 54–55; Grant, U. S., *Memoirs* I, 465.

17. Foote II, 331–43; Garland, 227; Catton, *Grant Moves South,* 419–25.

18. U. S. Grant to Julia Grant, April 20, 1863, *Papers* VIII, 100–1; U. S. Grant to Jesse R. Grant, April 21, 1863, *Papers* VIII, 109–10.

19. Foote II, 332; Grant, U. S., *Memoirs* I, 80–81.

20. R. E. Lee to Mary C. Lee, April 5, 1863, *Wartime Papers,* 427–28; Lee's angina discussed by John C. Krantz, Ph.D., Feb. 10, 1959, in "The Walter Reed Lecture" delivered before the Richmond Academy of Medicine, photocopy, V.H.S.

21. R. E. Lee to James Seddon, April 9, 1863, *Wartime Papers,* 429–30; R. E. Lee to James Seddon, April 16, 1863, *Wartime Papers,* 434–35; R. E. Lee to Mary C. Lee, April 19, 1863, ALS, V.H.S.

22. Chancellorsville: *Battles and Leaders* III, 152–240; Foote II, 272–313; McPherson, 319–22; Freeman II, 508–56; Maurice, *Marshall,* 172–73.

23. R. E. Lee to James Seddon, May 10, 1863, *Wartime Papers,* 482.

24. U. S. Grant to Henry Halleck, May 11, 1863, *Papers* VIII, 196; Foote II, 342, 218–19; Catton, *Grant Moves South,* 420.

25. Howe, *Home Letters of General Sherman*, 272–73; Foote II, 345–47; Nevins, *The War for the Union* II, 421–22; see Grant's correspondence, May 11–May 14, 1863, *Papers* VIII, 183–213; Dana, 47–49, 63–65; U. S. Grant to Julia Grant, May 9, 1863, *Papers* VIII, 189; Jones, Jenkin, 42–53.

26. Dana, 60, and 66 for Stanton letter.

27. Foote II, 372–75; Wilson, James H., *Under the Old Flag*, 204–7; Special Field Orders No. 134, *Papers* VIII, 237; General Field Order, *Papers* VIII, 245–46.

28. U. S. Grant to Henry Halleck, May 22, 1863, *Papers* VIII, 249; U. S. Grant to Henry Halleck, May 24, 1863, *Papers* VIII, 260–63; Pemberton to Grant in Grant's *Papers* VIII, 266–67 n.

29. Jones, Jenkin, 64–71; information concerning the siege from June 1, 1981, interview with Albert Schiller, park historian, Vicksburg National Military Park, Vicksburg, Miss.

30. Vicksburg siege: Swaney; Urquhart; Wheeler, 164–225; Hoehling, 170–84.

31. U. S. Grant to Peter Osterhaus, May 26, 1863, *Papers* VIII, 278; Sherman to Grant in Grant's *Papers* VIII, 443 n.; U. S. Grant to William T. Sherman, June 29, 1863, *Papers* VIII, 442–43.

32. Rawlins letter and postbellum war over Grant's drunk in Grant's *Papers* VIII, 322–25 n.; Dana, 90–91; Wilson, James H., *The Life of John A. Rawlins*, 128–29; U. S. Grant to Julia Grant, June 9, 1863, *Papers* VIII, 332.

33. See note 30 above and Hoehling, 136–37, 159; Twain; interview June 2, 1981, with Gordon Cotton, director of the Vicksburg Historical Society, Vicksburg, Miss.; Richardson, Albert, 334–35.

34. Hoehling, 119; Foote II, 407; Dana, 66–68; Wilson, James H., *Under the Old Flag*, 185; Sherman, 358; Grant, U. S., *Memoirs* I, 541.

35. Porter in Grant's *Papers* VIII, 384 n.; Hoehling, 125, 234–35, 229; Urquhart, 16–19; Pemberton to Grant in Grant's *Papers* VIII, 455 n.; U. S. Grant to Pemberton, July 3, 1863, *Papers* VIII, 455; U. S. Grant to Pemberton, July 3, 1863, *Papers* VIII, 457–58.

CHAPTER 18

1. Lee on Richmond in Maurice, *Marshall*, 73; Lincoln quoted in McPherson, 323; McPherson, 345–48; Catton, *Never Call Retreat*, 166.

2. Foote II, 431–34; R. E. Lee to John B. Hood, May 21, 1863, *Wartime Papers*, 490; Alexander, 322 n.; Lee to Hood, *Wartime Papers*, 490.

3. Putnam, 222–24, also 188–96; McGuire, 173, 188–201; Harrison, 94–98, 135–42, 127; Pryor, 235; Woodward, 573–74.

4. See Lee's *Wartime Papers*, 487–89, 495–97, 504–5; Taylor, Walter H., 36–37; R. E. Lee to Mary C. Lee, June 9, 1863, ALS, V.H.S.

5. R. E. Lee to James Seddon, June 8, 1863, *Wartime Papers*, 504–5; R. E. Lee to James Seddon, June 13, 1863, *Wartime Papers*, 513–14; R. E. Lee to Mary C. Lee, June 9, 1863, ALS, V.H.S.

6. R. E. Lee to Jefferson Davis, June 10, 1863, *Wartime Papers,* 507–9; R. E. Lee to James Seddon, June 13, 1863, *Wartime Papers,* 513–14.

7. R. E. Lee to J. E. B. Stuart, June 22, 1863, *Wartime Papers,* 523–24; R. E. Lee to J. E. B. Stuart, June 23, 1863, *Wartime Papers,* 526–27.

8. Blackford, 180–81; General Orders No. 73, June 27, 1863, *Wartime Papers,* 533–34.

9. Parks, 258 ff.; Blackford, 181–82.

10. Stiles, 202–4; Blackford, 185, 183, 184; Freeman III, 54; Parks, 261.

11. Foote II, 443, 456; Blackford, 184–87; Maurice, *Marshall,* 201–18; Taylor, Walter H., 92.

12. Freeman III, 60–64, Meade quoted on 63; Hood, 55.

13. Foote II, 467, 453–55, 466; Lee quoted in Freeman III, 67.

14. Foote II, 470, 474–76, 488; Commager, 6–22; Sorrel, 156–58; Alexander, 384–86; Long, 275–78; Taylor, Walter H., 94–97; Freeman III, 65–85; Stiles, 211–15; Gordon, 153–56.

15. Hood, 56–57, 58–59; Foote II, 491–92, 498, 496, 501; Long, 281; Haskell, 41; Miers, 140, 144–46, 150–52; Commager, 27, 34–35; Nevins, *The War for the Union* III, 103.

16. Freemantle, *Diary,* 208; Stiles, 218; Freeman III, 86–106; Lee-Longstreet from Foote II, 480; Freeman II, 462.

17. Haskell, 69–70, 81; Foote II, 524–25, 530–31, 534–35, 538–39, 547–48, 555; Miers, 211–12, 229–30; Alexander, 420–22, 423.

18. Foote II, 548, 553, 555–64; Haskell, 234–36; Miers, 232, 246; Commager II, 45; Alexander, 425–26; Freeman III, 128–31; Lee to Imboden in *Battles and Leaders* III, 420–21, see also 244–438.

CHAPTER 19

1. A. Lincoln to Grant, April 30, 1864, *Collected Works of Lincoln* VII, 324; A. Lincoln to Grant, July 13, 1863, *Collected Works of Lincoln* VI, 326.

2. Freeman III, 137; R. E. Lee to Jefferson Davis, July 8, 1863, *Wartime Papers,* 543–44; R. E. Lee to Mary C. Lee, July 26, 1863, ALS, V.H.S.; R. E. Lee to Margaret Stuart, July 26, 1863, *Wartime Papers,* 561; R. E. Lee to Jefferson Davis, July 31, 1863, *Wartime Papers,* 565; R. E. Lee to Jefferson Davis, Aug. 3, 1863, *Wartime Papers,* 589–90; R. E. Lee to Jefferson Davis, Aug. 22, 1863, *Wartime Papers,* 593.

3. Grant, Julia, 19–22; Wilson, James H., *Under the Old Flag,* 260; Catton, *Grant Takes Command,* 134–35, 90, 111, Grant quoted 107; Rawlins to Wilson, March 3, 1864, Wilson, James H., *The Life of John A. Rawlins,* 184–87.

4. Lee quoted in Freeman III, 154; R. E. Lee to Mary C. Lee, July 12, 1863, ALS, V.H.S.; R. E. Lee to Mary C. Lee, July 26, 1863, ALS, V.H.S.; R. E. Lee to Mary C. Lee, Dec. 25, 1863, ALS, V.H.S.; R. E. Lee to Mary C. Lee, Dec. 27, 1863, ALS, V.H.S.

5. Sherman to Grant in Catton, *Grant Takes Command,* 134; Rawlins in Catton, *Grant Takes Command,* 116, 117; Grant, Julia, 125–29; Wilson, James H., *The Life of John A. Rawlins,* 194.

6. R. E. Lee to Longstreet, Sept. 25, 1863, *Wartime Papers,* 604–5; R. E. Lee to James Seddon, Jan. 22, 1864, *Wartime Papers,* 659–60; R. E. Lee to Lucius Northrop, Jan. 5, 1864, *Wartime Papers,* 647–48; R. E. Lee to Alexander Lawton, Jan. 30, 1864, *Wartime Papers,* 664–65; General Orders No. 7, *Wartime Papers,* 659; R. E. Lee to James Seddon, March 6, 1864, *Wartime Papers,* 678–79; R. E. Lee to Leonidas Polk, Oct. 26, 1863, *Wartime Papers,* 614–15; R. E. Lee to Jefferson Davis, Dec. 3 and Dec. 7, 1863, *Wartime Papers,* 641–42; R. E. Lee to J. E. B. Stuart, Dec. 9, 1863, *Wartime Papers,* 642; R. E. Lee to Jefferson Davis, March 25, 1864, *Wartime Papers,* 682–84; R. E. Lee to Longstreet, March 28, 1864, *Wartime Papers,* 684–85.

7. McPherson, 342–43, 360–63; Anderson, 176–92; Foote III, 137; Porter, 83, 14–15; Agassiz (Lyman), 83.

8. R. E. Lee to G. W. Custis Lee, March 29, 1864, *Wartime Papers,* 685–87; R. E. Lee to Margaret Stuart, March 29, 1864, in Lee, R. E. (Jr.), 123; Taylor quoted in Freeman III, 264; R. E. Lee to Jefferson Davis, April 15, 1864, *Wartime Papers,* 700; Alexander, 493–94; R. E. Lee to G. W. Custis Lee in Freeman III, 268; R. E. Lee to Jefferson Davis, March 30, 1864, *Wartime Papers,* 687–88.

9. Porter, 37; Wilson, James H., *The Life of John A. Rawlins,* 212.

10. Davis, Burke, 280.

CHAPTER 20

1. U. S. Grant to Julia Grant, May 2, 1864, *Papers* X, 394; Porter, 41–42.

2. Davis, Burke, 281; Long, 326; Stiles, 243–44.

3. Grant quoted in Porter, 43–44; Foote III, 148, 150; Porter, 45.

4. R. E. Lee to Jefferson Davis, May 4, 1864, *Wartime Papers,* 719–20; R. E. Lee to John Breckenridge, May 4, 1864, *Wartime Papers,* 718–19; R. E. Lee to Richard Ewell, May 5, 1864, *Wartime Papers,* 720; Long, 327.

5. U. S. Grant to George Meade, May 5, 1864, *Papers* X, 399; Agassiz (Lyman), 91; Hyde, 183.

6. Gordon, 239; Foote III, 155; Warren Goss quoted in Commager II, 373–74; Long, 332–33.

7. Grant quoted in Porter, 50–54; Lee, Fitzhugh, 332; Benson, 256; Dowdey, 433; R. E. Lee to James Seddon, May 5, 1864, *Wartime Papers,* 721–22; Wilson, James H., *Under the Old Flag,* 403.

8. Grant quoted in Porter, 59; Benson, 258; Alexander, 503; Davis, Burke, 288; Commager II, 378–79; Long, 330; Foote III, 170.

9. Porter, 62–63, 66, 73; Foote III, 178, 167; Commager II, 376–77; Long, 333; Alexander, 508; Gordon, 250; Benson, 261; R. E. Lee to James Seddon, May 5, 1864, *Wartime Papers,* 722.

10. Porter, 69–70; Agassiz (Lyman), 102; Wilson, James H., *Under the Old Flag*, 390–91; Cadwallader, 181–82.

11. Gordon, 268; U. S. Grant to George Meade, May 6, 1864, *Papers* X, 408; Porter, 76, 79–81; Agassiz (Lyman), 102; Dowdey, 446; Foote III, 197.

12. Porter, 82–85; Agassiz (Lyman), 104–5; Maurice, *Robert E. Lee*, 288–89.

13. Lee quoted in Long, 387; Stiles, 229, 230, 255; Porter, 88; Foote III, 204; U. S. Grant to Henry Halleck, May 10, 1864, *Papers* X, 418; Sorrel, 240; Taylor, Walter H., 130; Hyde, 197; Agassiz (Lyman), 100–2.

14. U. S. Grant to Edwin Stanton, May 10, 1864, *Papers* X, 423; U. S. Grant to Julia Grant, May 11, 1864, *Papers* X, 444; Lee quoted in Foote III, 214–15; Lee Letterbook, "Headquarters File," V.H.S.

15. Benson, 283; Stiles, 259; Sorrel, 241; Gordon, 278–79; Porter, 101–5; Agassiz (Lyman), 110–11; U. S. Grant to Hancock, May 12, 1864, *Papers* X, 428–34.

16. Stiles, 259; Long, 340; Benson, 284–85; Gordon, 284–85; Sorrel, 241; Lee quoted in Dowdey, 454.

17. R. E. Lee to James Seddon, May 13, 1864, *Wartime Papers*, 728; Sedgwick and Lee quoted in Lee, Fitzhugh, 337; Grant quoted in Catton, *Grant Takes Command*, 235; Foote III, 240; U. S. Grant to Henry Halleck, May 12, 1864, *Papers* X, 428; Grant's letter from Scott in Grant's *Papers* X, 435 n.; U. S. Grant to Julia Grant, May 13, 1864, *Papers* X, 443–44.

18. Agassiz (Lyman), 106; Porter, 112; Alexander, 526; Hyde, 200–2; Lee, Fitzhugh, 335; Benson, 286–88; Gordon, 286.

19. U. S. Grant to Henry Halleck, May 17, 1864, *Papers* X, 451–52; R. E. Lee to James Seddon, May 18, 1864, *Wartime Papers*, 734; Foote III, 237, 238; Porter, 125; Dana, 179; Catton, *Grant Takes Command*, 242; Gordon, 293; Taylor, Walter H., 133.

20. Stiles, 268; Dowdey, 461; R. E. Lee to Jefferson Davis, May 22, 1864, *Wartime Papers*, 745–46; R. E. Lee to Mary C. Lee, May 23, 1864, ALS, V.H.S.; Lee on Richmond in Maurice, *Marshall*, 64–76, 182–85; Agassiz (Lyman), 132–33; Porter, 132–33.

21. Foote III, 267; Davis, Burke, 314–15; Agassiz (Lyman), 100, 126, 130; Stiles, 267.

22. Foote III, 268; Agassiz (Lyman), 124, 141; Wilson, James H., *Under the Old Flag*, 428, 448; Porter, 119–20; U. S. Grant to Henry Halleck, May 30, 1864, *Papers* X, 495–96; Alexander, 534; Lee quoted in Foote III, 280; Stiles, 274; Porter, 166–67.

23. Porter, 174, 178–79; Commager II, 393–94; Stiles, 288–301; Davis, Burke, 322; Foote III, 292, 294–95; Wilson, James H., *Under the Old Flag*, 443, 445; Agassiz (Lyman), 148, Warren quoted on 147; Hyde, 214.

24. U. S. Grant to Nellie Grant, June 4, 1864, *Papers* XI, 16; Foote III, 295; for Grant-Lee correspondence, June 5–June 7, 1864, see Grant's *Papers* XI, 17–27, including notes.

25. Alexander, 542–43; U. S. Grant to Julia Grant, June 6, 1864, *Papers* XI, 25–26; U. S. Grant to Henry Halleck, June 5, 1864, *Papers* XI, 19–20; R. E. Lee to Jefferson Davis, June 11, 1864, *Wartime Papers*, 774–75; Lee

to Early in Catton, *Grant Takes Command,* 301; R. E. Lee to Mary C. Lee, June 8, 1864, ALS, V.H.S.

26. Porter, 189–93, 199–200; Agassiz (Lyman), 156–57; R. E. Lee to James Seddon, June 13, 1864, *Wartime Papers,* 776–77; R. E. Lee to Jefferson Davis, June 14, 1864 (two letters), *Wartime Papers,* 777–79; A. Lincoln to Grant, June 15, 1864, in Grant's *Papers* XI, 45 n.; Porter, 199–200.

27. Lee quoted in Davis, Burke, 331; U. S. Grant to Julia Grant, June 15, 1864, *Papers* XI, 55; R. E. Lee to P. G. T. Beauregard, June 16, 1864, *Wartime Papers,* 784–85; Agassiz (Lyman), 166; R. E. Lee to P. G. T. Beauregard, June 17, 1864, *Wartime Papers,* 787–89; R. E. Lee to W. H. Fitzhugh (Rooney) Lee, June 17, 1864, *Wartime Papers,* 789; Alexander, 556–57; Porter, 210.

CHAPTER 21

1. R. E. Lee to U. S. Grant, March 2, 1865, *Wartime Papers,* 911–12; Stanton to Grant, in Grant's *Papers* XIV, 91 n.; R. E. Lee to Jefferson Davis, March 2, 1865, *Wartime Papers,* 911.

2. R. E. Lee to Jefferson Davis quoted in Freeman III, 459; R. E. Lee to Mary C. Lee, June 26, June 28, and June 30, 1864, ALS, V.H.S.; R. E. Lee to Mary C. Lee, July 31, Aug. 7, and Aug. 28, 1864, ALS, V.H.S.; Lee to Richmond city council quoted in Long, 321.

3. Catton, *Grant Takes Command,* 322, 341, 365; U. S. Grant to Henry Halleck, Aug. 1, 1864, *Papers* XI, 361–63; Garland, 284; U. S. Grant to Elihu Washburne, Aug. 16, 1864, *Papers* XII, 16–17; Dana, 227; U. S. Grant to Henry Halleck, July 14, 1864, *Papers* XI, 242–43; U. S. Grant to William T. Sherman, Oct. 12, 1864, *Papers* XII, 298; Meade quoted in Catton, *Grant Takes Command,* 408, 409–10.

4. U. S. Grant to Julia Grant, Jan. 4, 1865, and to benefactors, Jan. 3, 1865, quoted in Catton, *Grant Takes Command,* 413–14; Garland, 307; Cadwallader, 230–32; Catton, *Grant Takes Command,* 420–21.

5. Foote, III, 774; Agassiz (Lyman), 187, 181–82, 186–87, 125; Alexander, 558–59; Chamberlain, 2–5; Blackford, 270; Lee's address in Maurice, *Robert E. Lee,* 57; Putnam, 343; Harrison, 204–5; Sorrel, 188–89; Craven, *Edmund Ruffin,* 257.

6. Benson, 580; Foote III, 756; Agassiz (Lyman), 203; Stiles, 310–11; Taylor, Walter H., 143; Eggleston, 104, 177–78; R. E. Lee to Mary C. Lee, Feb. 23, 1865, ALS, V.H.S.

7. Gordon, 385–94.

8. Lee, George Taylor, 236–37.

9. Agassiz (Lyman), 318–19; Porter, 393–94, Grant quoted on 402; Taylor, Walter H., 144–46; R. E. Lee to Mary C. Lee, March 19, 1865, ALS, V.H.S.; Gordon, 408–9; Lincoln quoted in Catton, *Grant Takes Command,* 435.

10. Porter, 417–18, 414–15; Catton, *Grant Takes Command,* 436; Agassiz (Lyman), 325.

11. Porter, 413, 425–26, 428–29, 443–44; Grant quoted in Catton, *Grant Takes Command*, 440–41; R. E. Lee to Agnes Lee, March 29, 1865, ALS, V.H.S.; Davis, *Burke*, 369–70.

12. Dowdey, 540–41; Davis, *Burke*, 370–71; Hyde, 256–57; R. E. Lee to James Seddon, April 2, 1865, *Wartime Papers*, 924–25; Long, 410; R. E. Lee to Jefferson Davis, April 2, 1865 (two telegrams and one letter), *Wartime Papers*, 925–28.

13. Grant, Julia, 149; U. S. Grant to Julia Grant, April 2, 1865, quoted in Catton, *Grant Takes Command*, 447–48.

14. McGuire, 344–45; Putnam, 364–69; *Battles and Leaders* IV, 725–26; Foote III, 887–89; Stiles, 322.

15. Porter, 450; Agassiz (Lyman), 343; Grant to Sherman, April 3, 1865, quoted in Catton, *Grant Takes Command*, 450.

16. Lee quoted in Cooke, *A Life of General Robert E. Lee*, 451; Lee, Fitzhugh, 380–81; Long, 412–13; Foote III, 909; Sanborn II, 214; Lee to the citizens of Amelia County quoted in Freeman IV, 67.

17. Eggleston, 178–80, 130; Long, 412–13; Mason, 302–3; Alexander, 595; Stiles, 326–27.

18. Foote III, 915, 917–20; Porter, 454–56; Stiles, 330–34; Long, 414–16; Dowdey, 556–57.

CHAPTER 22

1. Correspondence between Grant and Lee, April 7–April 9, 1865, in *The War of the Rebellion*, 46, part 3, 619, 664; Grant's *Papers* XIV, 361–74; and Maurice, *Marshall*, 261–64; *Wartime Papers*, 931–34.

2. Lee quoted in Wise, 429; Alexander, 604–5; Nevins, *The War for the Union* IV, 307; Porter, 459; Freeman IV, 104, 109–10; Stiles, 318.

3. Lee's journal in the "Headquarters File," Virginia Historical Society. Wilson, James H., *The Life of John A. Rawlins*, 319–21; Porter, 463; Cadwallader, 317–20.

4. Maurice, *Marshall*, 259–60; Lee quoted in Freeman IV, 118; Porter, 463–64; Gordon, 438; *History of Company G.;* Benson, 663; Davis, *Burke*, 400.

5. Chamberlain, 235–38; Alexander, 605; Lee quoted in Freeman IV, 120–21; Maurice, *Marshall*, 263–65; R. E. Lee to U. S. Grant, April 9, 1865, *Wartime Papers*, 933.

6. Cadwallader, 322–23; U. S. Grant to R. E. Lee, April 9, 1865, *Papers* XIV, 372–73; Porter, 466–68.

7. Benson, 663–67, 662; Maurice, *Marshall*, 267–69.

8. Porter, 469–85, for the signing of the surrender except Lee's direct quotes; these were taken from Maurice, *Marshall*, 271–73, on the basis that Lee's secretary would better remember what he said; surrender in Grant's *Papers* XIV, 373–74 and n.

9. Davis, *Burke*, 422–25; Freeman IV, 144, 149; Nevins, *The War for the Union* IV, 313; Porter, 486–87, 488–89; Grant told Julia the story of the mule

in a letter from Mexico dated May 7, 1848, in his *Papers* I, 155–56; Young I, 455–56; Ross, Ishbel, 58.

10. The most dependable sources for the Lee-Grant conversation are Dana, 235; Maurice, *Marshall,* 235; and Young I, 458.

11. Agassiz (Lyman), 360–62; General Order No. 9, *Wartime Papers,* 934–35.

12. Chamberlain, 258–65.

EPILOGUE

U. S. Grant to Julia Grant, April 24, 1865, *Papers* XIV, 428–29. For Grant postwar, see McFeely, William Woodward, Albert Richardson, Julia Grant, and James H. Wilson's *Life of John A. Rawlins,* as well as Young, Hesseltine (especially 62–63), and Church. Grant's death is taken from McFeely, 516. The Lee-Grant White House meeting is from Flood, 208–10. Lee's June 13, 1865, letter to Grant and Andrew Johnson is in Lee, R. E. (Jr.), 164–66. For Lee postwar, see Flood, Freeman IV, Sanborn II, and Connelly. J. William Jones has reminiscences, as does Long. Lee's oath is on file at the Virginia Historical Society and at Duke University.

BIBLIOGRAPHY

Adams, Charles Francis, *Lee at Appomattox and Other Places*, Boston, 1902.

Adams, Henry, *The Education of Henry Adams*, Ernest Samuels, ed., Boston, 1973.

Agassiz, George R., ed., *Meade's Headquarters 1863–1865: Letters of Colonel Theodore Lyman from The Wilderness to Appomattox*, Boston, 1922.

Ahlstrom, Sydney, *A Religious History of the American People*, 2 vols., Garden City, N.Y., 1975.

Alexander, E. P., *Military Memoirs of a Confederate*, New York, 1918.

Anderson, Dwight G., *Abraham Lincoln: The Quest for Immortality*, New York, 1982.

Badeau, Adam, *Military History of Ulysses S. Grant*, 3 vols., New York, 1868.

Bailyn, Bernard, David Brion Davis, David Herbert Donald, John L. Thomas, Robert H. Wiebe, and Gordon S. Wood, *The Great Republic*, Boston, 1977.

Battles and Leaders of the Civil War, R. U. Johnson and C. C. Buel, eds., 4 vols., New York, 1884–88.

Benson, Berry Greenwood, Unpublished wartime reminiscences, University of North Carolina Library, Chapel Hill.

Bill, Alfred Hoyt, *The Beleaguered City: Richmond, 1861–1865*, New York, 1946.

Blackford, Susan Leigh, *Letters from Lee's Army*, New York, 1947.

Boatner, Mark Mayo, III, *The Civil War Dictionary*, New York, 1959.

Brinton, John H., *Personal Memoirs of John H. Brinton, Major and Surgeon, U.S.V.*, New York, 1914.

Brock, Sally, *Richmond During the War*, New York, 1867.

Brodie, Fawn, *Thomas Jefferson: An Intimate History*, New York, 1974.

Brooks, Noah, *Washington in Lincoln's Time*, New York, 1896.

Buell, Augustus, *The Cannoneer: Recollection of Service in the Army of the Potomac*, Washington, D.C., 1890.

Cadwallader, Sylvanus, *Three Years with Grant*, Benjamin Thomas, ed., New York, 1955.

Cash, W. J., *The Mind of the South*, New York, 1970.

Catton, Bruce, *Grant Moves South*, Boston, 1960.

———, *Grant Takes Command*, Boston, 1969.

———, *Never Call Retreat*, New York, 1967.

Chamberlain, Joshua, *The Passing of the Armies*, New York, 1915.

Church, William Conant, *Ulysses S. Grant and the Period of National Preservation and Reconstruction*, New York, 1897.

Clinton, Catherine, *The Plantation Mistress, Woman's World in the Old South*, New York, 1982.

The Collected Works of Abraham Lincoln, Roy P. Basler, ed., 8 vols., New Brunswick, N.J., 1953.

Commager, Henry Steele, *The Blue and the Gray*, 2 vols., New York, 1973.

Connelly, Thomas L., *The Marble Man: Robert E. Lee and His Image in American Society*, New York, 1977.

Cooke, John Esten, *A Life of General Robert E. Lee*, New York, 1871.

———, *Wearing of the Gray*, New York, 1867.

Cramer, Jesse Grant, ed., *Letters of Ulysses S. Grant to His Father and Youngest Sister, 1857–78*, New York, 1912.

Craven, Avery, *Edmund Ruffin Southerner: A Study in Secession*, Hamden, Conn., 1964.

———, ed., *"To Markie": The Letters of Robert E. Lee to Martha Custis Williams*, Cambridge, 1933.

Custis, George Washington Parke, *Recollections and Private Memoirs of Washington, by His Adopted Son, with a Memoir of the Author by His Daughter*, New York, 1860.

Cuthbert, Norma B., *"To Molly: Five Early Letters from Robert E. Lee to His Wife, 1832–1835," Huntington Library Quarterly*, May 1952.

Dana, Charles A., *Recollections of the Civil War*, New York, 1963 (reprint of 1898 original).

Dana, Charles A., and J. H. Wilson, *The Life of Ulysses S. Grant*, Springfield, Mass., 1868.

Davis, Burke, *Gray Fox: Robert E. Lee and the Civil War*, New York, 1956.

Davis, Jefferson, *The Rise and Fall of the Confederate Government*, New York, 1881.

———, *"Robert E. Lee," North American Review*, January 1890.

Davis, Varina Howell, *Jefferson Davis: A Memoir by His Wife*, 2 vols., New York, 1890.

deButts, Mary Custis Lee, *Growing Up in the 1850s; The Journal of Agnes Lee*, Chapel Hill, 1984.

De Leon, T. C. *Four Years in Rebel Capitals*, Mobile, Ala., 1890.

Dowdey, Clifford, *Lee*, Boston, 1965.

Eggleston, George Cary, *A Rebel's Recollections*, New York, 1875.

Flood, Charles Bracelen, *Lee: The Last Years*, Boston, 1981.

Foote, Shelby, *The Civil War: A Narrative,* 3 vols., New York, 1958–74.

Freeman, Douglas Southall, *R. E. Lee: A Biography,* 4 vols., New York, 1934–35.

Freemantle, Arthur James Lyon, *The Freemantle Diary,* Walter Lord, ed., New York, 1960.

———, *Three Months in the Southern States,* New York, 1864.

Fuller, Major General J. F. S. C., *Grant and Lee: A Study in Personality and Generalship,* Indianapolis, 1957.

Garland, Hamlin, *Ulysses S. Grant: His Life and Character,* New York, 1898.

Genovese, Eugene D., *Roll, Jordan, Roll,* New York, 1974.

Gordon, John B., *Reminiscences of the Civil War,* New York, 1903.

Goss, Warren, *Recollections,* New York, 1890.

Grant, Jesse, "The Early Life of Gen. Grant" by "His Father," New York *Ledger,* January 17, 18, 20, and 21, 1868.

Grant, Julia, *The Personal Memoirs of Julia Dent Grant (Mrs. Ulysses S. Grant),* John Y. Simon, ed., New York, 1975.

Grant, Ulysses S., *Personal Memoirs,* 2 vols., New York, 1885–86.

Harrison, Mrs. Burton (Constance Cary), *Recollections Grave and Gay,* New York, 1911.

Haskell, Frank A., *The Battle of Gettysburg,* Bruce Catton, ed., Boston, 1958 (reprint of 1908 original, published by the Wisconsin History Commission).

Hesseltine, William B., *Ulysses S. Grant, Politician,* New York, 1935.

The History of Brown County, Ohio, Chicago, 1883.

The History of Clermont County, Ohio, Philadelphia, 1880.

The History of Company G., Ninth S. C. Regiment, Infantry, S. C. Army, and of Company E., Sixth S. C. Regiment, Infantry, S. C. Army, Charleston, 1899.

Hoehling, A. A., *Vicksburg: 47 Days of Siege,* Englewood Cliffs, N.J., 1969.

Hood, John Bell, *Advance and Retreat,* New York, 1880.

Howe, Mark DeWolfe, ed., *Home Letters of General Sherman,* New York, 1909.

———, *Touched with Fire: Civil War Letters and Diary of Oliver Wendell Holmes, Jr.,* Cambridge, 1946.

Hyde, Thomas W., *Following the Greek Cross; or, Memories of the Sixth Army Corps,* Cambridge, 1894.

Jones, J. B., *Diary of a Rebel War Clerk,* Philadelphia, 1866.

Jones, J. William, *Personal Reminiscences, Anecdotes and Letters of Gen. Robert E. Lee,* New York, 1875.

Jones, Jenkin L., *An Artilleryman's Diary,* Wisconsin History Commission, 1914.

Lee, Fitzhugh, *General Lee,* New York, 1907.

Lee, George Taylor, "Reminiscences of General Robert E. Lee," *South Atlantic Quarterly,* July 1927.

Lee, Henry, *The American Revolution in the South,* with "Life of Henry Lee" by R. E. Lee, New York, 1869.

Lee, R. E. [Jr.], *Recollections and Letters of General Robert E. Lee: by His Son,* Garden City, N.Y., 1904.

Lee, Robert E., *Letters of Robert E. Lee to Henry Kayser, 1838–1846,* in "Glimpses of the Past," supplement of the Missouri Historical Society, January–February 1936.

Leech, Margaret, *Reveille in Washington 1860–1865,* New York, 1941.

Lewis, Lloyd, *Captain Sam Grant,* Boston, 1950.

Long, A. L., *Memoirs of Robert E. Lee,* New York, 1886.

Longstreet, James, *From Manassas to Appomattox,* Bloomington, Ind., 1961 (reprint of 1898 original).

MacDonald, Rose Mortimer Ellzey, *Mrs. Robert E. Lee,* Pikesville, Md., 1973 (reprint of 1939 original).

Mason, Emily V., *Popular Life of Gen. Robert Edward Lee,* Baltimore, 1872.

Massey, Mary Elizabeth, *Refugee Life in the Confederacy,* New York, 1964.

Maurice, Major General Sir Frederick, ed., *An Aide-de-Camp of Lee: Being the Papers of Colonel Charles Marshall,* Boston, 1927.

———, *Robert E. Lee the Soldier,* Boston, 1925.

McCarthy, Carlton, *Detailed Minutiae of Soldier Life in the Army of Northern Virginia,* Richmond, 1882.

McFeely, William S., *Grant: A Biography,* New York, 1981.

McGuire, Judith W., *Diary of a Southern Refugee During the War,* New York, 1972 (reprint of 1867 original).

McPherson, James M., *Ordeal by Fire: The Civil War and Reconstruction,* New York, 1982.

Melville, Herman, *Battle-Pieces and Aspects of the War,* Sidney Kaplan, ed., Amherst, Mass., 1972.

Miers, Earl Schenck, and Richard A. Brown, *Gettysburg,* New Brunswick, N.J., 1948.

Nevins, Allan, *Ordeal of the Union,* 2 vols., New York, 1947.

———, *The Emergence of Lincoln,* 2 vols., New York, 1950.

———, *The War for the Union,* 4 vols., New York, 1959.

Olmsted, Frederick Law, *Journey in the Back Country,* New York, 1860.

———, *Journey in the Seaboard Slave States,* New York, 1858.

The Papers of Ulysses S. Grant, John Y. Simon, ed., 14 vols., Carbondale, Ill., 1967–84.

Parks, Leighton, "What a Boy Saw of the Civil War," *Century Magazine* LXX, No. 2.

Porter, General Horace, *Campaigning with Grant,* New York, 1981 (reprint of 1897 original).

Pryor, Mrs. Roger A. [Sarah], *Reminiscences of Peace and War,* New York, 1904.

[Putnam, Sallie], "A Lady of Richmond," *In Richmond During the Confederacy,* New York, 1867.

Richardson, Albert D., *A Personal History of Ulysses S. Grant,* Hartford, 1868.

Richardson, James D., *Messages and Papers of the Presidents*, Vol. 7, New York, 1897.

Rister, Carl Coke, *Robert E. Lee in Texas*, Norman, Okla., 1946.

Ross, Fitzgerald, *Cities and Camps of the Confederate States*, Urbana, Ill., 1958.

Ross, Ishbel, *The General's Wife: The Life of Mrs. Ulysses S. Grant*, New York, 1959.

Royster, Charles, *Light Horse Harry Lee and the Legacy of the American Revolution*, New York, 1981.

Russell, William H., *My Diary North and South*, New York, 1954.

Sanborn, Margaret, *Robert E. Lee*, 2 vols.: *A Portrait*, New York, 1966, and *The Complete Man*, New York, 1967.

Schaff, Philip, "The Gettysburg Week," *Scribner's Magazine* XVI (July 1894).

Sherman, General W. T., *The Memoirs of Gen. William T. Sherman*, 2 vols., New York, 1891–93.

Smith, Justin H., *The War with Mexico*, Vol. I, Gloucester, Mass., 1963.

Sorrel, Moxley, *Recollections of a Confederate Staff Officer*, Jackson, Tenn., 1958.

Stiles, Robert, *Four Years under Marse Robert*, New York, 1903.

Swaney, Fred, ed., *Diary of Emma Balfour*, Vicksburg, Miss., n.d.

Taylor, Richard, *Destruction and Reconstruction*, R. Harwell, ed., New York, 1955.

Taylor, Walter H., *Four Years with General Lee*, New York, 1878.

Thomas, Emory, *The Confederate Nation: 1861–1865*, New York, 1979.

Twain, Mark, "Cave Life During the Siege of Vicksburg," reprint by the Vicksburg Historical Society from *Life on the Mississippi*, n.d.

Urquhart, Kenneth Trist, *Vicksburg: Southern City under Siege (The Letters of William Lovelace Foster)*, New Orleans, 1980.

Vandiver, Frank, *Their Tattered Flags: The Epic of the Confederacy*, New York, 1970.

The Virginia Landmarks Register: A Profile of the Life and Times of Virginians, Richmond, 1976.

Wainwright, Colonel Charles S., *A Diary of Battle*, Allan Nevins, ed., New York, 1962.

Walker, Peter, *Vicksburg: A People at War*, 1860–1865, Chapel Hill, 1960.

The War of the Rebellion: A Compilation of the Official Records of the Union and Confederate Armies, U.S. War Department, Washington, D.C., 1902.

The Wartime Papers of R. E. Lee, Clifford Dowdey and Louis Mannarin, eds., Boston, 1961.

Welles, Gideon, *Diary*, Howard K. Beale, ed., 3 vols., New York, 1960.

Wheeler, Richard, *The Siege of Vicksburg*, New York, 1978.

Wiley, Bell Irvin, *The Life of Billy Yank*, Baton Rouge, 1952, 1971.

———, *The Life of Johnny Reb*, Baton Rouge, 1970, 1978.

Wilson, Charles Reagan, *Baptized in Blood*, Athens, Ga., 1980.

Wilson, Edmund, *Patriotic Gore: Studies in the Literature of the American Civil War,* New York, 1966.

Wilson, James H., *The Life of John A. Rawlins,* New York, 1916.

———, *Under the Old Flag,* New York, 1912.

Wise, John S., *The End of an Era,* Boston, 1899.

Woodward, C. Vann, ed., *Mary Chesnut's Civil War,* New Haven, 1981.

Woodward, C. Vann, and Elizabeth Muhlenfeld, eds., *The Private Mary Chesnut: The Unpublished Civil War Diaries,* New York, 1984.

Woodward, William E., *Meet General Grant,* New York, 1928.

Young, John Russell, *Around the World with General Grant,* 2 vols., New York, 1879.

INDEX

ABOUT THE AUTHORS

Nancy Scott Anderson is a reporter for the San Diego *Tribune*.
Dwight Anderson is Professor of Political Science
at San Diego State University.